Madhur Jaffrey's World Vegetarian

Robi Dobi: The Marvelous Adventures of an Indian Elephant, illustrated by Amanda Hall

Madhur Jaffrey's Quick and Easy Indian Cooking

Madhur Jaffrey's Indian Cooking

Madhur Jaffrey's World of East Vegetarian Cooking

A Taste of India

Madhur Jaffrey's Cooking for Friends

A Taste of the Far East

Madhur Jaffrey's Spice Kitchen

Madhur Jaffrey's Flavors of India

An Invitation to Indian Cooking

Seasons of Splendour

Market Days

Far Eastern Cooking

Madhur Jaffrey's
World Vegetarian

Clarkson Potter/Publishers New York

Insert photography by Zubin Shroff
Food Styling by Roscoe Betsill
Prop Styling by Philippa Brathwaite

The following companies generously
loaned us their wares:
Sarajo
130 Greene Street, New York, NY
212-966-6156
Platter, pages 10–11. Turkish towel, page
8. Teak table, pages 6–7. Shawl, page 2,
bottom. Moroccan tea glass, page 9, top.

Jameson Whyte
46 Wooster Street, New York, NY
212-965-9407
Teak table pages 4, 8, 10–11, and 14–15.
Reed mat, page 4.

Joan Platt
1261 Madison Avenue, New York, NY
212-876-9228
Ceramic pedestal, page 3.

AERO Ltd
132 Spring Street, New York, NY
Homespun linen, page 1 and 9, bottom.
Small oval platter, page 6. Black glazed
sake cup, pages 14–15.

Published by Clarkson Potter/Publishers, 201 East 50th Street, New York, New York 10022. Member
of the Crown Publishing Group.

Random House, Inc. New York, Toronto, London, Sydney, Auckland
www.randomhouse.com

CLARKSON N. POTTER, POTTER, and colophon are registered trademarks of Clarkson N. Potter,
Inc.

Printed in the United States of America

Design by Memo Productions

Library of Congress Cataloging-in-Publication Data
Jaffrey, Madhur.
[World vegetarian]
Madhur Jaffrey's world vegetarian / by Madhur Jaffrey.—1st ed.
p.   cm.
Includes index.
1. Vegetarian cookery. 2. Cookery, International. I. Title.
TX837.J15   1999
641.5'636—dc21   98-30318
                                                                              CIP

ISBN 0-517-59632-6

10 9 8 7 6 5 4 3 2 1

First Edition

This book is dedicated to

Sanford

and our little big ones

Sakina, Meera, and Zia

with Craig and Frank

and their little ones

Jamila, Cassius, and Rohan

Acknowledgments

I would like to gratefully acknowledge the help given to me by Sara Abufares; Adela, Anjana, and Raju Advani; Amina Al Albani; Khadija Ali; Pia Alisjahbana; Aleene Allen; Frederick Allen; Sanford Allen; Allegra Antinori; Lorenzo Argenti; Margaret Arnold; Elena Averoff; Teresa Ayuso; Niki Bahariou; Ada Bassey; Albertina Brenes de Estrada; Shiu-Min Block; Bob's Red Mill in Portland; Catherine Brandel; Guiliano Bugialli; Mirta Carbonell; Lydia and Costas Carras; Ricki Carroll at the New England Cheesemaking Supply Co.; Casa Ruiz in Triana, Seville; Melissa Cheek; Sharda Chenoy; Tassoula David; Shamsi Davis; Danielle Delon; Sakina El Alaoui; Zeynep and Metin Fadilligolu; Amina de Freitas; Betty Fussell; Rosa Gran; Rosario Guillermo; Niloofar Haeri; Anita Harrell; Diane Holuigue; Jack Hurley; Meera Jaffrey; Sakina Jaffrey; Zia Jaffrey; Lalit Jaggi; Durupadi Jagtiani; Juanita Jarillo; Newell Jenkins; Mrs. Chanchal Kapoor; Promila Kapoor; Kassiani; Niru Row Kavi; Benita Kern; Pamela Krauss; Robert Krauss; Aglaia Kremezi; M. L. Taw Kritakara; Chris LaBrusciano; L. D. Lawrence; Kwei-Min Lei; Marina Liveriadou; Lola; Adela Lorenzo; Vali Manuelides; Presilla Maricel; Androche Markidis; Anna Elena Martinez; Zarela Martinez; Victor Matiya; Maya Bahadur; Amaral Milbredt; Mitthan Bhabi; Anna Montes; Marios Mourtezis; my mother; Aimilia Oikonomou; Felix Oksengorn; Gisella Orjeda; Helen Philon; Pinocho Restaurant in Barcelona; David Pring; Santha Ramanujam; Cheryl Rathkopf; Nasreen Rehman; Margarita Salinas; Victoria Salvy; Melle Derko Samira; Anand Sarabhai; Rakhi Sarkar; Savas; Elizabeth Schneider; Billur Selvi; Claire Seraphim; Pallavi Shah; Mohammad Sharif; Mimi Sheraton; Michele Sigler; Gwen Silva; Mrs. Keshar Singh; Carol Southern; Heawan Stuckenbruck; Azat Tasci; Kamal Tayebbhai; Panna Thakrar; The Çiragan Hotel in Istanbul; The Ormylia Monastery in Macedonia; The Raja of Mahmudabad in Lucknow; The Rasa Restaurant in London; The Spring Deer Restaurant in Hong Kong; The Ta Nissia Restaurant in Salonika; The Tiffin Restaurant in Port of Spain; Nora Vezirolou; and Marjorie Williams.

Contents

Introduction   viii

Dried Beans, Dried Peas, Lentils, and Nuts   2

Vegetables   124

Grains   324

Dairy   510

Soups, Salads, and Drinks   574

Sauces and Added Flavorings   656

Equipment, Glossary, and Resources   709

Index   741

INTRODUCTION

This book is written for everyone — for vegetarians, for partial vegetarians (like me), and for all those who are non-vegetarians but wish to add exciting new dishes to their daily repertoire.

As I travel around the world, I see that we seem to be heading toward a softening of boundaries between all cuisines. In a way, this has always happened. There is no nation that has not absorbed, sometimes with ease and sometimes with great disquiet and fulmination, new produce and new cooking techniques from other worlds. Mixing and matching, borrowing and lending, we are constantly enriching our cuisines. Today, this is happening at a faster pace than it did 500 years ago. We live in a new world where each of us not only knows at least a dozen other food traditions—other than the one we were born with—but are on close and easy terms with them. London, for example, now has a very large, superb, refectorylike restaurant that serves only Asian noodles. The line of waiting diners, sophisticated food enthusiasts, and impoverished students snakes through Soho's narrow lanes. In Portland, Oregon, you can sit at a simple, coffee-shoplike counter and eat a Japanese soup cheaply. Indian hotels, on the other hand, serve Italian and Chinese foods with great pride, spicing up the dishes slightly to serve local tastes.

My own family, like so many others, is mixed. I, of course, am Indian. I am married to an American. My children, through their marriages, have brought in Italian, Irish, English, and French blood to those nearest to me, my grandchildren. Two of my daughters studied in China and Taiwan and are complete Sinophiles, at least as far as food is concerned. I, myself, have traveled the world constantly since the sixties, moving from East Asia to North Africa to Australia to southern Europe to Central American and the Caribbean. It is impossible not to pick up good ideas, good recipes and new ingredients as one travels; it is so easy and natural to turn into a seasoned culinary "collector" as one learns more and more about the craft.

This book, then, is my handpicked collection of the world's best vegetarian recipes for you to cook at home, both for everyday meals and for entertaining. Of course, the recipes are chosen from my point of view and reflect my taste. I love well-seasoned foods, whether they come from Mexico, Indonesia, or India. I also have a passion for foods that can be cooked quickly and are imbued with a classic simplicity, such as Italian pasta with a plain tomato sauce, pasta with olive oil and garlic, or pasta with zucchini (courgettes) and onion. Give me a dish of Indian split mung beans and basmati rice and I am as happy as a lark. Give me a well-made Mexican chile and I am just as happy. All these are well-known, classic dishes. I have just tried to give you the very best versions of them.

On the other hand, when I came across the Trinidadian soup-stew, Kallaloo, in Port-of-Spain, I was excited beyond all measure. Where had this inspired gumbolike creation been all my life? I felt I had been deprived. Who had thought of putting colocasia (dasheen) leaves, okra, green beans, hot chilies, and coconut milk together? This soup, quite new to me, just had to be in my book. (Do not worry. If you cannot get colocasia leaves, you may use the green sections of chard leaves! Yes, I have suggested substitutes for all hard-to-get ingredients.)

I felt exactly the same way when I was offered Spinach with Rice (Spanakorizo) in Metsovo, Greece. Just think of it. Young, cooked spinach leaves, glistening with olive oil and tangy with lemon juice and bound together with a light rice sauce made rather simply by just letting a tablespoon or so of rice cook with the dressing. And the whole thing garnished with a little fresh dill cut in with a pair of scissors. Wonderful! Of course, this recipe is in the book, too.

Sometimes I am intrigued by an ingredient. Take the very nutritious and easy-to-use chickpea flour. It is known in limited parts of the East and West and totally unknown in others. It deserves better. So I have collected what I believe to be some excellent recipes for it—for pizzas, pancakes, chips, and stews—and included them here. The chips (or fries) come from southern France; one of our best friends grew up on them in Marseilles and this is her recipe. The pizza is from southern France and the Genoa region of Italy. It is slithery and gorgeous. I first had it in a market in Nice and loved it with the very first bite. The pancakes and stews are from India. I know them well.

Beans and split peas intrigue me too. In just how many ways can they be cooked? I have enjoyed counting the myriad ways. Starting with a 6000-year-old dish, the famous khichri of India, that combines split peas and rice in a stew and seasons it with cumin seeds and ginger, and going on to an unusual and elegant black bean soup from Costa Rica flavored with green coriander and green peppers, there is a whole world that remains unexplored. I have devoted a great deal of space to this exploration as I love beans and feel they are needlessly dismissed in much of Western cooking. I have given detailed descriptions of all the legumes so readers unfamiliar with them can identify them and use them with ease.

There are almost 200 vegetable recipes in the book. I suppose a part of me is still answering the question posed to me by a woman in Springfield, Illinois, a few decades ago, "What do vegetarians eat? Lots of boiled broccoli, I suppose!" I have looked at vegetables in a global manner, drawing recipes from Morocco and Trinidad, India and Mexico, Italy and Cyprus alike. (I loved being in Cyprus, as so many cuisines seem to merge there. African ingredients, Arab techniques, Asian spices and Greek tastes all seemed to have coalesced, many tributaries making a strangely wonderful, technicolored river.) You will find at least a dozen recipes for eggplant alone. Almost every nation in the world cooks it. How they cook it is what makes the dish regional or national. If there are mustard and fennel seeds in it, it must be Bengali. If it is creamed with olive oil and lemon, it has to have a Middle Eastern or a Greek/Turkish bias. If it is cooked with honey, it could be Moroccan. After working on the book for 10 years, I had a hard time choosing which recipes to leave out.

In the Grains chapter, I have included many grains that are now suddenly available to us in our local health food stores such as millet and quinoa. While providing some traditional recipes for them—the buckwheat section has buckwheat noodles and buckwheat pancakes—I have created others where there seemed to be a dearth, such as a recipe for whole, browned buckwheat groats. I have always provided basic techniques so you can improvise recipes yourself.

Vegetarian traditions have existed in China and India for thousands of years, and like the dietary rules and restrictions of Islam and Judaism, have been prompted by the strong religious beliefs of large numbers of people. There is, thus, a deep core to them that explains their endurance. The great variety in Eastern vegetarian dishes can be explained by their slow evolution as they were tested and added to over time.

Vegetarianism has come to the West in a series of somewhat unnatural heaves, prompted not by a general belief of the masses but by individual conclusions, often reached independently. Recipe and menu development has gone on in the same ad hoc fashion. Now there are actually magazines devoted to the subject and many of the best chefs offer vegetarian alternatives in their restaurants. Pickles, chutneys, salsas, and sauces, important flavorings for vegetarian meals, are flooding our supermarkets.

I hope my book will open up an international world of new and exciting foods for you to cook and eat. As you turn the pages, you will find old traditional recipes and newly created ones, recipes where new and old ingredients are combined and recipes from one nation that may be made with ingredients from another. That seems to be the kind of world we are living in today.

With every major dish, I have given serving suggestions to help you make up nutritious menus. A word about weights and measurements. While I have been very exact in some recipes, in others I have used looser weights (such as "1 medium onion" instead of an exact weight). This just means that a little more or a little less will not make a great difference in that particular recipe.

Dried Beans, Dried Peas, Lentils, and Nuts

Azuki (Aduki/Adzuki) Beans 8

Black Beans 11

Black-Eyed Peas 15

Chickpeas (Garbanzos), Chana Dal, *and Chickpea Flour* 25

Fava Beans, Dried 43

Kidney Beans (Red, Large) 46

Kidney Beans, White, and Other White Beans (Including Lima Beans) 52

Lentils, Green, Brown, and Red 58

Mung Beans 72

Pigeon Peas (Toovar Dal, Arhar Dal) 85

Pinto Beans 88

Soybeans 90

Split Peas 109

Urad Beans (Ma, Urad Dal) 112

Cashew Nuts 116

Peanuts 120

Dried beans, dried peas, and lentils, also known as legumes or pulses, are among the earliest of cultivated crops. These little nutritional powerhouses, bursting with protein, vitamins, minerals, fiber, and complex carbohydrates, are mere seeds that grow in large and small pods. Valued as nuggets of gold, they sustained ancient Vedic India, the biblical Middle East, the pharaohs of Egypt, and the royals who strolled in the gardens of Babylon.

What our ancestors did to plow the earth and wrest from it foods to nourish us is something we of the supermarket culture have quite forgotten. As a child, I remember sitting with my mother and all the other women of our large Indian household, perpetuating my little place in a family ritual.

The oldest woman of the house—generally my grandmother—would place a few handfuls of lentils, split peas, or beans into the big metal plates we each held. Quite automatically, we drew the legumes to the edge nearest our bodies. Then, in an ancient ritual, enacted as if in a half-remembered dance, we began pushing the lentils toward the far side one by one, plucking up and discarding all sticks and stones as we did so. Sometimes we sang, sometimes we gossiped, sometimes we were lost in our own silences.

As we were doing this in India, Chinese, Syrians, Mexicans, and Peruvians were doing the same in their own courtyards, gardens, and kitchens. The following poem, "A Woman Cleaning Lentils," comes from Turkey, written by the Armenian poet Zahrad. It unites us all.

> A lentil, a lentil, a lentil, a stone.
> A lentil, a lentil a lentil, a stone.
> A green one, a black one, a green one, a black. A stone.
> A lentil, a lentil, a stone, a lentil, a lentil, a word.
> Suddenly a word. A lentil.
> A lentil, a word, a word next to another word. A sentence.
> A word, a word, a word, a nonsense speech.
> Then an old song.
> Then an old dream.
> A life, another life, a hard life. A lentil. A life.
> An easy life. A hard life, Why easy? Why hard?
> Lives next to each other. A life. A word. A lentil.
> A green one, a black one, a green one, a black one, pain.
> A green song, a green lentil, a black one, a stone.
> A lentil, a stone, a stone, a lentil.

In this chapter, I tackle legumes alphabetically, starting with azuki beans. (You will also find a photograph of all the beans used in this book in the color section.)

In each area of the world different legumes are cherished. Whether these were native to the soil or were transported there centuries ago by travelers has been recorded, if only to show that some recipes have remained unchanged for two thousand years while others kept absorbing outside influences. Most of my recipes are traditional; I like the clarifications that time and custom bring. Sometimes the period of time does not have to be long. But local traditions need to be strong and overpowering, not the daily buffeting of rootless fads.

I was raised in a nation where legumes and legume flours are eaten daily. In India lightly sprouted beans may appear in a salad with tomatoes and cucumbers, chickpea flour may be made into fritters or pancakes, and mung beans may appear as a halvah for dessert.

For this chapter, I began by looking for similar dishes from around the world. The Riviera yielded Italian and French pancakes as well as great "fries" made from chickpea flour; Mali had the best black-eyed pea dumplings and Trinidad some of the most mouthwatering soups. In Cyprus, I found excellent black-eyed peas cooked with chard and chickpeas with spinach. Nuns in Macedonia baked delicious large white kidney beans. Legumes were transformed into sweet coconut-flavored porridges in Indonesia and into fermented bean paste soups in Korea and Japan. Some of these recipes appear in this chapter. Others are scattered throughout the book.

It is believed that the more legumes you eat the more you can eat them. In other words, while they may be hard to digest for those unused to their consumption, slowly increasing the daily quantity ingested greatly helps the body to adjust to them. In order to make the most of a protein-rich food filled with the B-complex vitamins (thiamine, pyridoxine, niacin, and folic acid), as well as dietary fiber that is thought to prevent some types of cancer and heart disease, and help with weight control and complex carbohydrates that provide long-term energy, this is a step worth taking. One-half cup of cooked lentils, for example, has only 115 calories and provides 20 percent of our daily protein requirement. It is also cheap. As legumes do not generally provide a complete protein, however, they need to be supplemented. This can be done easily by adding a grain (corn, rice, or wheat), nuts or seeds (cashews, sesame), or dairy (eggs, milk, yogurt, or cheese) to the meal.

I find it utterly charming that the two regions of the world known for their daily consumption of legumes, India and Latin America, have very similar sayings *"dey dal may pani"* and *"ponle mas agua a los frijoles,"* which translate to mean that when guests exceed the quantity of food, just "add water to the beans"! It represents conviviality, sharing, and never saying no to the hungry.

The Indian word *dal,* which will appear frequently in this chapter, actually means a bean or pea (or any seed) that has been split. The verb *dalna* means "to split." The word still retains its correct usage, but at times it is used generally in India to stand for the whole family of legumes.

While legumes may be bunched together for their general nutritional value, they all have their own very individual textures and tastes. Some feel "powdery," others are viscous, and a few can turn deliciously creamy. There are beans with dark bitter flavor, others that are earthy, and a few that are light, delicate, and downright "aristocratic." Legumes can also be manipulated to have different textures and tastes. For example, they can be cooked until soupy or so that they retain their shape and crispness. And combining several legumes creates new flavors and textures.

Canned beans: Canned beans, sold by all supermarkets, may be used instead of the dried ones, though their taste is never quite as clean as the taste of beans that you have soaked and cooked yourself. Also, the tinny liquid from the cans is unusable, whereas the liquid from home-cooked beans is naturally sweet and perfect for soups and stews.

Buying legumes: The world of dried legumes is very large and includes whole beans, whole lentils, and whole peas and chickpeas. But most peas, beans, and lentils have skins or hulls that can be removed, thus hastening the cooking, and making hulled legumes yet another category. Beans and peas may also be split, with or without having their hulls removed first. So the permutations become quite endless. In a good legume shop you will find hulled split beans and hulled split peas as well as unhulled split beans and peas, hulled split lentils, large pale chickpeas and small yellow chickpeas as well as hulled and split chickpeas. In addition there may be dozens of bean flours. There should not be too many broken pieces or any signs of infestation.

Storing legumes: While legumes lend themselves well to long storage, ideally they should be kept no longer than a year. Keep them in tightly closed jars in a cool, dark cupboard. Remember that the fresher the legume, the faster it will cook.

Picking over and washing legumes: These days most legumes we buy in supermarkets are fairly free of debris. However, it is still a good idea to pick over them in case there is a lurking stone that could ruin your teeth. Measure out the legumes you intend to cook and spread them on one side of a large white plate. Move the legumes a few at a time to the opposite side, discarding any sticks, stones, or deformed or worm-eaten seeds.

Next, transfer the picked-over legumes to a bowl and cover with water. Swish the legumes around quickly, then pour out the water. Be speedy here, as you do not want the legumes to soak up any of the dirty water. Husks and sticks will float away. Do this 4 or 5 times, or until the water runs clear. Drain.

Soaking beans: Whole dried beans often require an overnight soak to help them cook evenly—and relatively quickly—the following day. This does not generally apply to split peas and lentils. Another reason for soaking whole beans—and for discarding the soaking water—is to get rid of some of the oligosaccharides that cause flatulence. It is interesting to note that many of the Latin American nations that have been cooking whole red kidney beans, pinto beans, black beans, lima beans, and navy beans for thousands of years do not soak them overnight. They just add water to the dry beans and set them to cook slowly, adding extra boiling water whenever it is needed. I can only assume that over the millennia, their bodies have adjusted to the oligosaccharides and that the effect now is minimal. But for most of us, it is still wisest to soak. Put the picked-over and washed beans in a large bowl, cover with water by about 5 inches, and leave overnight or at least 8 hours. Drain thoroughly the next morning, discarding the soaking water, and then proceed with the recipe. Generally, the beans will expand to three times their original volume.

The Quick-Soak Method We cannot always plan ahead and sometimes we need to hurry up our bean cookery. This is where the Quick-Soak Method comes in handy. Pick over the beans and wash them as above. Now put them in a saucepan and cover with water by 5 inches. Bring to a boil and boil rapidly for 2 minutes, then cover the pan and turn off the heat. Let the beans soak in the hot water for 1 hour (longer, if you can spare the time). Drain thoroughly and proceed with the recipe.

Cooking legumes: Generally, legumes are boiled in 3 to 4 times as much water by volume, then seasoned when they are tender. Many believe that adding salt or sour too early inhibits the tenderizing process. Older beans can take much longer to cook, sometimes as much as an hour longer. Just keep testing them.

Do you have hard water? If you do, add ⅛ teaspoon bicarbonate of soda for every pound of legumes or use bottled water.

The pressure cooker method This is another way to speed the cooking of all legumes. As they tend to froth up a bit, adding 1½ teaspoons of peanut or corn oil to the water helps prevent the pressure cooker vent from clogging up. Salt is best added afterward. Look for specific pressure cooker directions for individual legumes in the alphabetical listing.

Seasoning legumes: Once you have cooked your legumes until they are tender, draw a teaspoon out to taste. They are bland and boring. You add some salt, but that does little. Fortunately, legumes transform easily. How you transform them depends upon your culinary background.

The most important item, common to all culinary traditions, is lubrication in the form of oil, butter, or coconut milk. The "dryness" associated with legumes vanishes with a dollop of good virgin olive oil, *ghee* (clarified butter), or creamy coconut milk. But so much more can be done to perk up legumes.

Look at three very different traditions, the *tarka* of India, the *tiganissi* of Cyprus, and the *sofrito* of the Latin world, that are used to finish off legumes and many other foods.

Tarka This Indian technique (also called *chhownk* and *bhagaar*) is used for vegetables, rice dishes, and snacks as well. Once the legumes are cooked, salt them and leave them in a warm place. Then heat oil or *ghee* in a small pan until it is very hot. To the oil add either a single spice or any combination of spices or seasonings that you like. When the spices begin to sizzle, quickly pour the oil and seasonings into the pot of legumes and put on the lid to trap all the hissing flavors.

In India literally hundreds of combinations of seasonings are used to give endless variety. Among the most ancient is whole cumin seeds, a common flavoring for beans and split peas in Vedic India. In Bengal, you might do a *tarka* of nigella, mustard seeds, and fennel seeds in mustard oil or bay leaves, cloves, and cardamom in *ghee*. In Tamil Nadu, it could be fresh curry leaves, mustard seeds, red chiles, and *chana dal* (the last being a split chickpea used rather unusually as a spice), all sizzled in sesame oil. In the Punjab, it could be ginger, garlic, and tomatoes in white butter.

Tiganissi Very similar to the *tarka* of India, this Cypriot technique involves heating oil—peanut or olive—in a small pan, then perhaps adding a dried red chile and garlic. When the garlic begins to color, the oil and seasonings are poured over the cooked legumes. Lots of lemon juice is squeezed over the top and the legumes are eaten with crusty local bread. Sometimes tomatoes, added to the pan just after the garlic, and cooked briefly, replace the lemon juice.

Sofrito Again, this technique is very similar to the *tarka* and *tiganissi*. Once the beans (probably black, lima, or navy beans) are cooked and salted, olive oil is heated in a pan. Chopped garlic, onion, tomato, fresh green chiles, and green herbs such as epazote or culantro are added and the mixture is lightly sautéed. Once softened, the mixture is emptied into the pot of beans and the flavors are allowed to meld together briefly before serving.

Cooked legumes may be eaten with rice or breads. They may be wrapped in tortillas and other flatbreads. Leftovers should be stored in the refrigerator in a covered container.

Cooked legumes, especially those that have been stewed, tend to thicken and jell as they sit. To reheat them, first stir them with a light hand to break up the jelled mass, adding a little water as you do so. Then reheat gently in a pan, stirring frequently, or in the microwave.

I have included cashews and peanuts in this chapter as well. Peanuts are technically a legume. But the cashew is a nut (or fruit). However, in India and Sri Lanka, where it grows with abandon near the sea, it is cooked like a legume. You will find recipes for both "nuts" at the end of this chapter.

Azuki (Aduki/Adzuki) Beans

These small red beans are very popular throughout East Asia. However, when I began searching for traditional recipes for savory main dishes in China, Korea, and Japan, I was hard put to find any. I knew of course that once cooked, pureed, and mixed with sugar, azuki beans (this is their Japanese name) become the chocolate of Eastern Asia and are used, among other things, as a stuffing in all manner of pastries. I have also had them in sweet soups and desserts in China, Korea, Japan, the Philippines, Thailand, Malaysia, and Indonesia. In both Korea and Japan there are also several festive dishes, this time savory ones, in which azuki beans are combined with glutinous rice or rice flour (page 374). But savory dishes that featured the beans alone?

I finally found two, both from southern China, in Yunnan. These recipes follow.

Cooking azuki beans (and whole unhulled mung beans, black beans, and whole unhulled *urad* beans): Pick over and wash the beans. Put them in a bowl with water to cover by about 5 inches and soak overnight. You may also Quick-Soak them according to directions on page 6.

Now, for every cup of dried beans add 3 cups of water. Bring to a boil, then reduce the heat to a simmer, partially cover, and cook 1½ to 1¾ hours, or until the beans are tender. About 1 teaspoon of salt should be added about 10 minutes before the cooking is finished, as should most other seasonings. A cup of dried beans will yield about 2½ to 3 cups of cooked beans.

Pressure cooker method for 1 cup of dried azuki beans (and for 1 cup whole unhulled mung beans, black beans, and whole unhulled urad *beans)* Put the picked-over, soaked, and drained beans into a pressure cooker with enough water to just cover them (about 1¾ cups) and 1½ teaspoons vegetable oil, preferably peanut or corn oil. Cover, bring up to pressure (15 pounds), then lower the heat while maintaining the pressure and cook 10 to 12 minutes. Allow the pressure to drop by itself. Remember that young beans may require a little less time and older ones a minute or two more. You will be left with very little liquid; if you need more, add a little water or stock. About 1 teaspoon of salt should be added at the end and the beans cooked without pressure over low heat for 2 to 3 minutes more.

Kwei-Min Lei's

Stir-Fried Azuki Beans with Green Pepper from Yunnan

CHINA

Hungdo Chow Ching Jiao

*This recipe calls for dried Chinese black mushrooms, which are really dried shiitake mushrooms.
Serve this with plain rice and vegetables. The beans are also very good when served over noodles, with a green salad on the side.*

When reheating the beans, you will probably need to add a little water; use the mushroom-soaking liquid, if you like.

1 cup red azuki beans, picked over, washed, and drained

6 dried Chinese black mushrooms

2 tablespoons peanut or canola oil

3 scallions, sliced into very fine rings (use all of the white and half of the green section)

3 garlic cloves, peeled and finely chopped

½ large green pepper, seeded and cored, cut into ⅛-inch dice

1 fresh hot green chile or to taste, finely chopped (optional)

2½ tablespoons soy sauce

¼ teaspoon salt (use if needed)

1 teaspoon sugar

2 teaspoons oriental sesame oil

Soak the beans overnight in 3 cups of water or use the Quick-Soak Method (page 6), using the same amount of water. Drain, discarding the soaking liquid.

Combine the beans with 3 cups of fresh water in a heavy pan and bring to a boil. Cover partially, turn the heat down to a low simmer, and cook gently for 1½ to 1¾ hours, or until the beans are tender. (If you wish to use a pressure cooker, see page 8.) Crush some of the beans lightly against the side of the pan with the back of a spoon.

While the beans are cooking, soak the mushrooms in 1 cup of hot water for 30 minutes. Lift them out of the soaking liquid and cut off the stems. (Strain the soaking liquid and save for stock or for thinning out the beans.) Cut the caps into ⅛-inch dice.

Put the oil in a wok or large frying pan and set over high heat. When hot, add the scallions and stir-fry rapidly for 30 seconds. Add the garlic, green pepper, chile, and mushrooms and stir-fry for 1 minute. Add the cooked beans and stir to mix. Turn the heat to low and add the soy sauce, salt, if needed, and sugar. Simmer gently for 2 minutes, stirring occasionally. Add the sesame oil and stir to mix.

SERVES 3 TO 4

Kwei-Min Lei's

Azuki and Whole Mung Beans, Crushed and Sautéed

CHINA

Chow Ar Ni

In an unusual dish from Yunnan in southern China, red and green beans are served side by side on the same plate, sometimes arranged in the yin and yang pattern. This may be eaten Chinese style with plain rice and other stir-fried vegetables or it may be eaten with bread, either flatbreads (pitas, tortillas) or crusty European-style loaves cut into thick slices. The texture of the beans is that of a coarse puree, so it is easily spooned or spread on bread. With some cheeses, cornichons, or pickles on the side, this can make a perfect light lunch or first course. You could also stuff the puree into pita bread, adding some chopped, seasoned tomatoes and some lettuce for a perfect "pocket" sandwich!

The red and green beans not only provide different colors on the same plate but are also seasoned differently to give diners a bit of variation. The mung beans are kept quite plain and seasoned with just oil, garlic, and a little sesame oil. The red beans, however, have scallions and either cayenne or a good dollop of garlic-flavored chili paste.

Soak and cook the two beans at the same time in different utensils. The beans can be cooked ahead and reheated separately before serving.

1 cup red azuki beans, picked over, washed, and drained

1 cup whole unhulled mung beans, picked over, washed, and drained

For the azuki beans

2 tablespoons vegetable oil, preferably peanut oil

3 garlic cloves, peeled and finely chopped

3 scallions, white parts and half the tender green part, cut into very, very thin rounds

1 teaspoon chili paste with garlic or
½ teaspoon cayenne (use more or less as desired)

Salt

Freshly ground black pepper

2 teaspoons oriental sesame oil

For the mung beans

2 tablespoons peanut oil

3 garlic cloves, peeled and finely chopped

¾ teaspoon salt

Freshly ground white or black pepper

2 teaspoons oriental sesame oil

For the final garnish

1 tablespoon oriental sesame oil

3 tablespoons finely chopped fresh cilantro

Soak the azuki beans and mung beans separately overnight in 3 cups of water each or use the Quick-Soak Method (page 6), using the same amount of water. Drain the beans and keep them separated, discarding the soaking liquid.

Combine the azuki beans with 3 cups of fresh water in a heavy pan and bring to a boil. Cover partially, turn the heat down to a low simmer, and cook gently for 1½ to 1¾ hours, or until the beans are tender. (If you wish to use a pressure cooker, see page 8.) At the same time, cook the mung beans in a separate pan in exactly the same way.

Put the oil in a wok or large frying pan and set over high heat. When hot, add the garlic and scallions and stir-fry rapidly for 30 seconds. Add the azuki beans and stir for 30 seconds, crushing the beans against the sides of the pan with the back of a spoon. Turn the heat to low. Add the chili paste, stir to taste, and then add salt to taste (about ½ teaspoon) and the pepper. Stir to mix. Pour in the sesame oil and give a final stir. Turn off the heat and keep warm.

In a second wok or large frying pan, combine the oil and garlic and set over high heat. As soon as the garlic starts to sizzle and turn golden, add the mung beans. Stir for 30 seconds to mix. Turn the heat to low, then add the ¾ teaspoon salt and pepper and stir to mix. Add the sesame oil, stir once, and turn off the heat.

To serve, ladle the beans side by side onto a large, preferably oval or round, platter. Drizzle the sesame oil over the top and sprinkle the chopped cilantro evenly over the central section of each of the beans.

SERVES 6 TO 8

Black Beans

We know that these small black beans of Central American origin have existed in Mexico for at least 5,000 years. Even after Spanish culture introduced the region to a whole new diet that included beef, rice, cheese, and chickpeas, black beans more than held their own and are still consumed daily as Refried Beans (page 12) and Black Beans with Rice (page 14) for breakfast, and Costa Rican Black Bean Soup (page 597) or Black Beans "Charros" (page 13) for dinner. The beans can also be used in stews.

Cooking black beans: Pick over and wash the beans and then add water to cover by about 5 inches. Leave to soak overnight or use the Quick-Soak Method (page 6). Drain and discard the soaking liquid. Now, for every 1 cup of dried beans add 3 cups of water and cook 1½ to 1¾ hours, or until the beans are tender. About 1 teaspoon of salt should be added about 10 minutes before the cooking is finished, as should most other seasonings. A cup of dried beans will yield about 2½ to 3 cups of cooked beans. For 4 cups of cooked beans, which one of the recipes requires, cook 1½ cups of dried beans; the cooking times will not change.

Pressure cooker method for 1 cup dried black beans Follow the instructions for azuki beans (page 8).

Rosario Guillermo's

Refried Beans

MEXICO

Frijoles Refritos

I find that these beans, although typically Mexican, go well with all meals, especially those that lend themselves to being eaten with breads. In Mexico, they are served with almost everything: I have been offered them on a plate with fried eggs, as a kind of dip with crisp tortilla chips stuck in them (to be had with beer, the kind where the rim of the can is first rubbed with a cut lemon and then with salt), and with heated soft corn tortillas to be rolled together with some spicy salsa and a little grated Parmesan or Monterey Jack cheese.

Rosario Guillermo, whose recipe this is, forms the beans into a cake and serves it beautifully on a bed of lettuce leaves. Tortilla chips are artistically arranged on the top to look like sails—or is it the Sydney Opera House that she is thinking of? (Rosario is a sculptress from the Yucatán.)

Parmesan cheese can be sprinkled over the refried bean cake.

It is best to use nonstick pans for the last stages of cooking.

1¼ cups dried black beans, picked over, washed, and drained

4 tablespoons canola oil

5 tablespoons finely chopped onion (½ medium)

2 garlic cloves, peeled and finely chopped

6 canned plum tomatoes, finely chopped

1 jalapeño or any other fresh hot green chile, finely chopped

1¼ to 1½ teaspoons salt

To serve

6 to 8 soft lettuce leaves

Tortilla chips

Soak the beans overnight in water to cover by 5 inches. Alternatively, you may Quick-Soak the beans (page 6) using the same amount of water. Drain thoroughly and discard the soaking liquid.

Combine the beans and 4 cups of water in a medium pan. Bring to a boil. Cover partially, turn the heat to low, and simmer gently for 1½ hours, or until the beans are tender. (Alternatively, you may pressure-cook the beans, page 8.)

Put 3 tablespoons of oil in a medium nonstick pan and place over medium-high heat. When hot, add the onion and garlic. Stir and cook for about 4 minutes, or until the onion is golden. Add the tomatoes, chile, and salt and stir and cook for 1 minute. Add the beans and their cooking liquid and continue to cook over medium-high heat, mashing the beans with a potato masher or a wooden spoon as you do. Cook for 15 to 20 minutes, or until the beans come off the sides of the pan easily. Remove from the heat.

Just before serving, put the remaining 1 tablespoon oil in a medium nonstick frying pan and place over medium-high heat. When hot, add in the beans and stir them around for about 2 minutes. Using a rubber spatula or the back of a wooden spoon, press the beans onto the bottom of the pan, flattening the top and forming a cake. Let it brown lightly on the bottom for about 5 minutes. Remove from the heat.

Arrange the lettuce leaves over the top of the bean cake in such a way that they extend a little around the edges. Now put a large plate over the frying pan and invert the cake onto the plate. The lettuce leaves should land at the bottom. Stick some tortilla chips into the cake and serve the rest on the side.

SERVES 6

Rosario Guillermo's

Black Beans "Charros"

MEXICO

Frijoles Charros

This stew, spicy and tart, may be served with heated corn or wheat tortillas, or with plain rice.

1¼ cups dried black beans, picked over, washed, and drained

1½ teaspoons salt

3 tablespoons canola or olive oil

5 tablespoons very finely chopped onion

4 garlic cloves, peeled and finely chopped

6 canned plum tomatoes, finely chopped, plus ¼ cup of their liquid

½ to 1 jalapeño chile or any other fresh hot green chile, very finely chopped

2 tablespoons finely chopped cilantro leaves

Soak the beans overnight in water to cover by 5 inches. Alternatively, you may Quick-Soak the beans (page 6) using the same amount of water. Drain thoroughly and discard the soaking liquid.

Add 4 cups of fresh water to the beans and bring to a boil in a heavy medium pan. Cover partially, turn heat to low, and simmer gently for 1½ hours, or until the beans are tender. (Alternatively, you may pressure-cook the beans, page 8.) Transfer half of the beans and their cooking liquid to a blender or food processor, add the salt, and puree. Return the pureed mixture to the pot with the whole beans and combine well.

Put the oil in a large frying pan and place over medium-high heat. When hot, add the onion and garlic, stirring and sautéing until they are golden. Add the chopped

(recipe continues)

13

tomatoes and their liquid and the jalapeño, and bring to a simmer. Cover and cook gently for 10 minutes. Stir the tomato mixture and the chopped cilantro into the beans, and bring to a simmer over low heat. Simmer gently for 5 minutes and serve hot.

SERVES 6

Albertina Brenes de Estrada and Ada Bassey's

Black Beans with Rice or "Spotted Rooster"

COSTA RICA

Gallo Pinto

So pervasive is Costa Rica's national breakfast dish, even the local McDonald'ses and Burger Kings feel the need to have it on their menus. Nourishing and hearty, it is often served with eggs (generally scrambled) and fine corn tortillas. A hot sauce, such as the tamarind-based Salsa Lizano, is always on the table. If you can't find it, Tabasco sauce will do. I like to put Simple Red Salsa (page 683) or Guacamole (page 613) on the table as well.

In Costa Rica, this is generally made from beans leftover after making Costa Rican Black Bean Soup (page 597), so the beans are both flavored and lightly salted. If you don't have any extra beans on hand, follow the general directions for cooking black beans (page 11) or use canned drained black beans.

¼ cup olive oil

1 medium onion, peeled and finely chopped

1 medium green or red bell pepper, cored and seeded, cut into ¼-inch dice

8 tablespoons chopped cilantro

4 cups cooked and drained black beans (1½ cups dried)

4 cups cooked plain long-grain rice (1⅓ cups raw)

Salt

Freshly ground black pepper

Put the oil in a large nonstick frying pan or nonstick wok and set over medium-high heat. When hot, add the onion and bell pepper. Stir and fry until the onion is translucent, turning the heat down if it begins to brown. Add the cilantro and stir for a minute, then add the beans. Stir for 2 minutes, breaking up any clumps, then add the rice. Stir as you break up clumps of rice with the back of a slotted spoon. Add salt and pepper to taste (this will depend upon how salted the beans were) and continue to stir and fry until the rice and beans are heated through.

SERVES 4

Black-Eyed Peas

Also known as cowpea (*lobhia* and *chowli* in India), this pea probably originated in western and central Africa, though its mention in Buddhist Indian literature of 2300 years ago has convinced some that at least one variety may be native to India.

These versatile peas may be stewed plain or with herbs, nuts, or other vegetables. I have eaten them mixed with roasted coconut in western India and with chard in Cyprus. They may also be made into fritters and pancakes, the former being very popular in central and western Africa, the latter in India. African slaves brought black-eyed peas with them to the Caribbean, where they are combined beautifully with rice and pumpkin; to South America, where they are made into fritters; and to the United States, where Southerners love to pile them on plain rice and scatter finely chopped or grated raw onions over the top. This dish, "Hoppin' John," is eaten year-round, but especially at New Year to ensure good fortune. Indeed, Athens, Texas, which calls itself the black-eyed pea capital of America, celebrates its "Texas caviar" with an annual July jamboree that takes the form of a cooking competition.

Cooking dried black-eyed peas: Pick over and wash the peas and then soak them overnight in water to cover by 5 inches. You may also Quick-Soak them according to directions on page 6. After that, the beans should be drained and cooked in roughly three times as much water or stock for about 40 minutes. (The exact amount of liquid will vary with the recipe.) At this stage, the peas are generally quite firm and separate. Further cooking for about 20 minutes softens them some more, if that is what is desired.

Pressure cooker method for black-eyed peas This is a surprisingly quick method that is ideal if you are really pressed for time. Quite magically, *no soaking is required.* For every cup of dried peas add 3 cups of liquid (water or stock) to *unsoaked* peas plus 1½ teaspoons peanut or corn oil to keep the froth from blocking the valve and 1 teaspoon salt (if needed). Bring up to pressure and cook for 8 to 10 minutes, allowing the pressure to drop by itself. Each bean will be soft and separate. It is worth noting that the texture will be somewhat softer than that of peas that have been soaked and boiled on top of the stove. It is a good idea, therefore, to cut down on the subsequent cooking times that follow the initial boiling in my recipes. Also, most of the water will be absorbed as the beans cool off; you might need to add a bit more if further cooking is called for.

Frozen black-eyed peas: In America, black-eyed peas are available frozen, which is a great convenience. Frozen peas may be cooked straight from the box, according to package instructions. You may also defrost them in hot water, drain them, and then cook them like soaked peas. Just note that for any recipe requiring 1½ cups of dried peas, you will need about 4 cups of defrosted frozen peas, as that is the volume they swell to after soaking overnight. Four cups of soaked peas should be the equivalent of two 10-ounces package of frozen peas, though I have noticed that the actual yield from these frozen packages is a bit less.

Sprouting black-eyed peas: Black-eyed peas are quite wonderful when sprouted and become very easy to digest. Soak ½ cup (3¼ ounces) peas in water that covers them generously for 12 hours, changing the water once (this can be after 8 hours). Drain. Line a tray with several thicknesses of dampened paper towels. Spread the soaked drained peas on top. Cover with another two layers of dampened paper towels and set aside in a dark place (I use the oven). Sprinkle with water every 8 hours or so to make sure the paper is damp. After 36 hours you should have about 3 cups of small sprouts, about 1 inch long. (If you do not, leave a little longer.) Wash the sprouts gently in a large bowl of water, discarding the skins that float to the top. Drain and store in a plastic bag or sealed container for up to a week. Sprinkle with water if the sprouts appear dry. You can also keep the sprouts in a bowl of water for 24 hours in the refrigerator. Change the water every 8 hours.

Cooking black-eyed pea sprouts: Sprouts cook in less than 10 minutes and, because of this, as well as their protein value and digestibility, they are a very popular breakfast food in India. The most common cooking method is to stir-fry them first in a little oil and then let them cook gently, covered, with a little salt and a little water (about 4 tablespoons for the amount sprouted above) for 7 to 8 minutes, until they are just tender. Almost any seasonings may be added.

Anita Harrell's
Black-Eyed Pea Fritters NIGERIA, MALI
Akara

Different versions of akara *can be found in nearly all of western and central Africa. The dish traveled to most places the slaves went and is eaten today in the Caribbean and in South America as well. (In Brazil, it is called* acarajé, *a word not too far from the original.)*

These delicious fritters are not very different from the North African/Middle Eastern falafel, except that instead of chickpeas or fava beans they are made with black-eyed peas. They are generally eaten as a snack or as part of a meal in Africa, but you may also serve them with drinks, offering a spicy dipping sauce (such as the Moroccan Chile-Garlic Paste, page 772; Trinidadian Pepper Sauce, page 771; Delhi-Style Cilantro and Mint Chutney, page 660; Kashmiri Sour Cherry and Walnut Chutney, page 659; or even store-bought ketchup or salsa) on the side. Of course, you may eat them just like falafel, stuffed into pita breads along with shredded lettuce, sliced tomatoes, and tahini sauce.

For those who do not have a food processor, which aerates as it grinds, the African method of making the batter is to put the soaked peas through a meat grinder and then to beat in the hot water in order to make a mixture that is light and airy with a drop-easily-from-the-spoon consistency.

1½ cups dried black-eyed peas, picked over
   and washed

1 small onion, peeled and coarsely chopped

1¼ teaspoons salt

Freshly ground black pepper

¼ to ½ teaspoon cayenne

Peanut or canola oil for deep-frying

Soak the black-eyed peas in water to cover by 5 inches for about 16 hours, changing the water once in the middle only if it is a very hot day. *Do not use the Quick-Soak Method here* as you need raw peas. Drain the peas and put them in a large bowl. Cover them well with fresh water. Dip both hands into the bowl and rub the peas between your palms. You will loosen many (though not all) of the skins, which will start to float in the water like jellyfish in the sea. Skim off the free skins, with a sieve or slotted spoon; leave the stubborn skins alone.

Drain the peas thoroughly and put them into the container of a food processor along with the onion, salt, pepper, and cayenne. Turn the machine on (medium speed, if you can control it) and process, pushing down with a rubber spatula again and again until you have a grainy paste. Slowly add about 5 tablespoons of hot water, processing all the while, until the paste has a dropable consistency. It should also look light and airy but remain very slightly grainy.

Put 1 inch of oil in a frying pan and set it over medium heat. Allow it to get very hot. Now work fast: Stir the batter gently and remove a very heaped teaspoon. Using a second teaspoon, drop the batter into the oil. (The fritters will be about 1½ inches in diameter.) Repeat until the frying pan is full. Fry the fritters for about 1 minute at medium heat, turning them over as they darken, and then turn the heat down to low. Continue to fry for another 6 minutes or so, turning the fritters now and then. You should end up with fritters that have an even, rich, reddish-brown color and are cooked through. Remove them with a slotted spoon and drain on paper towels. Make all the fritters this way, remembering at the start of each batch to *(a)* turn the heat back to medium and get the oil very hot again and *(b)* stir the batter once very gently from the bottom up. The fritters should ideally be served as soon as they are made.

(Leftover fritters may be stored in a closed container in the refrigerator and used to make the recipe that follows.)

MAKES ABOUT 40 FRITTERS; SERVES 6

Black-Eyed Peas with Herbs   MOROCCO/SYRIA

This is an absolutely delicious dish that you will surely want to make part of your repertoire. Variations of this can be found over much of the Mediterranean. We often eat it with greens and rice, but you may also serve it in a soup plate like a stew, garnished with lots of finely chopped parsley. Crusty whole wheat breads and perhaps a tomato and mozzarella salad are all that would be needed on the side.

1½ cups dried black-eyed peas

2 tablespoons olive oil

1 whole dried hot red chile

3 garlic cloves, peeled and finely chopped

2 to 3 bay leaves

1 teaspoon dried oregano or 1 tablespoon finely chopped fresh oregano

½ teaspoon dried thyme or 1½ teaspoons finely chopped fresh thyme

1 teaspoon paprika

1½ teaspoons salt

Pick over the black-eyed peas, wash, and drain. Soak the black-eyed peas overnight in water that covers them by 5 inches or use the Quick-Soak Method (page 6). Drain, discarding the soaking liquid.

In a large pot, bring the peas and 4½ cups of water to a boil. Cover, turn the heat to low, and simmer gently for 40 minutes, or until the peas are tender. Set aside without draining.

Put the oil in a frying pan and place over medium-high heat. When the oil is hot, add the chile and stir once; it should darken and puff up immediately. Quickly add the garlic and stir once. Add the black-eyed peas with all their cooking liquid, the bay leaves, oregano, thyme, paprika, and salt. Stir to mix and bring to a simmer. Simmer gently, uncovered, on low heat for 20 minutes. Serve hot.

SERVES 4 TO 6

Variation

Black-Eyed Peas in a Walnut Sauce

When the preceding recipe is fully cooked add Walnut Sauce (page 684) and combine thoroughly. This may be served at room temperature or hot. With a salad, some cheese, and bread, it makes for a very nutritious meal.

Black-Eyed Peas with Corn and Dill

Black-eyed peas are combined with corn in both West Africa and North India. We serve this particular version at our restaurant, Dawat, in New York, and it has been a big hit since the day it was introduced. It may be eaten with breads—Indian, Middle Eastern, North African, or European—or with rice. Some good pickles and chutneys and perhaps an Indian fresh cheese (paneer) dish or a yogurt dish is all that would be needed to complete the meal.

You may make this dish up to 24 hours ahead of time and reheat it. It should be stored in the refrigerator.

1½ cups dried black-eyed peas

3 tablespoons canola oil

½ teaspoon cumin seeds

½ teaspoon brown mustard seeds

1 to 2 whole, hot dried red chiles

15 to 20 fresh curry leaves (optional)

1 medium onion, finely chopped

3 to 4 garlic cloves, peeled and finely chopped

4 medium tomatoes or 2 cups canned plum tomatoes, finely chopped

4 to 5 tablespoons chopped fresh dill

2 cups fresh corn kernels (about 4 ears), defrosted frozen corn, or good-quality canned corn

1½ teaspoons salt

Pick over the black-eyed peas, wash, and drain. Put in a bowl with water to cover by about 5 inches and soak overnight. Alternatively, you may use the Quick-Soak Method (page 6). Drain and discard the soaking liquid.

Put the oil in a large, preferably nonstick pan and place over medium-high heat. When very hot, add the cumin and mustard seeds. As soon as the mustard seeds begin to pop (a matter of seconds), add the chiles. Stir once and add the curry leaves, if using. Stir once and add the onion and garlic. Stir and fry until the onion pieces begin to brown at the edges. Add the tomatoes and stir for a minute, then add the drained peas and the dill. Add 4½ cups of water, stir, and bring to a boil. Cover, turn the heat to low, and cook for about 40 minutes, or until the peas are tender. Remove the cover, turn the heat to high, and boil rapidly for 5 minutes. Stir in the corn and salt, and boil rapidly for another 10 minutes, or until the mixture is thick and all the flavors have melded.

SERVES 6

Marios Mourtezis'

Black-Eyed Peas with Swiss Chard   CYPRUS
Louvi

In Cyprus, black-eyed peas are eaten in many forms. When they are green and still in their pods, they are boiled up and served with a dressing of oil and lemon juice. Once the legumes are dried, they are cooked with whatever greens happen to be in season. Wild greens, often quite bitter, are exceedingly popular, but so is chard.

There are two ways of serving this dish. After the black-eyed peas and chard are tender, Greek Cypriots dress the mixture with good olive oil and lemon juice. That is the simple way of eating it. But there is another. The next day (or even the same day) they might dress it up by doing a tiganissi, *which means "to fry." This little step is exactly the same as an Indian* tarka: *oil is heated, seasoned with garlic, onion, and red chile, then poured over the warmed peas.*

In Cyprus, this dish, hot or cold, is served with crusty bread, black olives, tomatoes, cucumber, and some sheep cheese like haloumi. *You may also serve it with rice, perhaps the Soft Yogurt Cheese with Feta (page 559), Oven-Dried Tomatoes (page 304), and Crisp Zucchini Fritters (page 298).*

1 cup dried black-eyed peas

1 pound Swiss chard

1 teaspoon salt

2 tablespoons extra-virgin olive oil

1 tablespoon fresh lemon juice

For the **tiganissi** *(optional)*

3 tablespoons olive oil

1 dried hot red chile

1 smallish onion, peeled and finely chopped

3 garlic cloves, peeled and finely chopped

Pick over the black-eyed peas, wash, and drain. Cover with water by about 5 inches and leave to soak overnight. Alternatively, you may use the Quick-Soak Method (page 6).

Drain the peas and place in a heavy, medium pan. Add 3¼ cups of water and bring to a boil. Partially cover, leaving the lid very slightly ajar, turn the heat to low, and simmer gently for 40 minutes, or until the peas are tender.

While the peas are cooking, wash the chard and separate the dark green leafy sections from the pale stem and central vein areas. Cut the leafy section crosswise into ¼-inch-wide strips. Cut the tougher pale section into ¼-inch dice. When the peas have cooked for 40 minutes, add the chard and the salt. Stir to mix thoroughly and return to a boil over medium-high heat. Turn the heat to low, cover, and cook for another 30 minutes. Stir in the oil and lemon juice. Black-eyed peas are ready to serve as is or with the optional *tiganissi* below.

For the *tiganissi*, heat the oil in a small frying pan over medium-high heat. When hot, add the red chile and stir for 5 seconds. As soon as the chile darkens, add the onion and garlic. Stir and fry until the pieces of onion and garlic start to turn brown at the edges. Immediately pour the oil and seasonings over the cooked peas and chard. Stir to mix and serve hot, at room temperature, or chilled.

SERVES 4 TO 6

Black-Eyed Peas with Trinidadian Seasonings

TRINIDAD

Serve this over rice with fried plantains or greens on the side.

1½ cups dried black-eyed peas

3 tablespoons olive oil

2 scallions, cut into fine rounds (both green and white parts)

1 celery stalk, cut into small dice

1 carrot, peeled and cut into small dice

½ green pepper, cored and seeded, cut into small dice

½ teaspoon dried thyme or 1½ teaspoons finely chopped fresh thyme

1 teaspoon paprika

¼ to ½ teaspoon crushed dried red chiles or cayenne

½ teaspoon ground allspice

½ teaspoon ground mustard powder

1½ teaspoons salt

Pick over the black-eyed peas, wash, and drain. Soak the black-eyed peas overnight in water to cover by 5 inches or use the Quick-Soak Method (page 6). Drain, discarding the soaking liquid.

Put the oil into a large pot and place over medium-high heat. When hot, add the scallions, celery, carrot, and green pepper. Stir and sauté for about 5 minutes, or until the vegetables just start to brown. Add the drained peas, 4½ cups of water, thyme, paprika, chiles, allspice, and mustard and bring to a boil. Cover, turn the heat to low, and simmer gently for 40 minutes, or until the peas are tender. Add the salt, stir, and cook another 20 minutes on low heat.

SERVES 4 TO 6

Black-Eyed Peas with Watercress   INDIA

In India, different greens, varying with the seasons and the location, are added to black-eyed peas. Anything from radish greens, mustard greens, turnip greens, fenugreek greens, cilantro, mint, spinach, and of course watercress in the north can be used to make this vegetarian dish as nutritious as possible and to vary its flavor, adding slight bitterness, pungency, or freshness as the cook's palate dictates. Here I have used watercress, which, like spinach, cooks rather quickly. If sturdier greens are used, they may need to be cooked gently, covered with the addition of some water, for at least an hour.

Serve with rice or a crusty bread, a yogurt relish or cheese. For more sumptuous fare, add cauliflower or carrots dishes as well as salads from the Mediterranean, India, or the Far East.

2 cups dried black-eyed peas

1½ teaspoons salt

3 tablespoons canola or olive oil

1 bay leaf

1 small onion, finely chopped

1 (1-inch) piece of fresh ginger, peeled and
    cut into minute dice

3 tablespoons very finely chopped cilantro

1 smallish tomato (4 ounces), finely chopped,
    or 3 canned plum tomatoes

Large bunch of watercress (about 6 ounces),
    tough stalks discarded, leaves chopped

½ to 2 fresh hot green chiles, finely chopped
    (remove seeds for a milder heat)

¼ teaspoon cayenne (optional)

Pick over the black-eyed peas, wash, and drain. Cover with water by about 5 inches and soak overnight. Alternatively, you may use the Quick-Soak Method (page 6). Drain and discard the soaking liquid.

Put the peas in a heavy, medium saucepan. Add 4 cups of water and bring to a boil. Partially cover, leaving the lid very slightly ajar, turn the heat to low, and simmer gently for 40 minutes, or until the peas are tender. Add the salt and stir to mix.

While the black-eyed peas cook, heat the oil in a medium frying pan over medium-high heat. When hot, add the bay leaf. As soon as the bay leaf turns a shade darker, add the onion and ginger. Stir and fry for about 5 minutes, or until the onion pieces start to turn brown at the edges. Add the cilantro, tomato, watercress, and chile. Stir and cook over medium heat until the tomato pieces are soft, 3 to 4 minutes. Set aside.

When the black-eyed peas are tender, add the tomato-watercress mixture, turn the heat to medium-high, and cook, stirring now and then, for 5 minutes, or until all the flavors have mingled and the mixture is thick. Taste and add cayenne if more heat is needed.

SERVES 4 TO 6

Black-Eyed Pea Pancakes

Lobhia Ka Cheela

These may be eaten as flatbreads with a spicy dip or you may use them like crepes to wrap around a dish of spicy potatoes or cauliflower.

The batter can be made up to a day in advance and refrigeratored. Stir well before using.

To facilitate the pancake making, measure out 1/3 cup of water in a ladle or deep spoon so that you know exactly how much batter you will need for each pancake. You will also need a rounded soup spoon (or another metal ladle) to spread out the batter, which does not flow, and a rubber spatula to flip the pancakes.

1 1/2 cups dried black-eyed peas

1 (1-inch) piece of fresh ginger, peeled and cut into very fine dice

1/4 teaspoon cayenne

1/4 teaspoon ground turmeric

1 1/4 teaspoons salt

2 tablespoons finely chopped fresh cilantro

1 small onion, peeled and finely chopped

1/2 teaspoon cumin seeds

About 6 tablespoons peanut or canola oil

Soak the black-eyed peas in water to cover by 5 inches for 16 hours, changing the water once in the middle only if it is a very hot day. *Do not use the Quick-Soak Method here* as you need raw peas. Drain the peas and put them in a large bowl. Cover them well with fresh water. Dip both hands into the bowl and rub the peas between your palms. You will loosen many (though not all) of the skins, which will start to float to the surface. Skim off the free skins with a sieve or slotted spoon; leave the stubborn skins alone.

Drain the peas thoroughly and put them into the container of a food processor along with the ginger, cayenne, turmeric, and salt. Turn the machine on (medium speed, if you can control it) and process, stopping occasionally to push down on the peas with a rubber spatula until you have a grainy paste. Slowly add about 1 1/3 cups of water and process the puree for another minute. Add the cilantro, onion, and cumin. Process for 5 seconds. You should have a thickish batter with small flecks of onion, cilantro, and cumin visible.

Put 1 teaspoon of oil in an 8-inch nonstick frying pan and spread it around by tilting the pan. Set the pan over medium-low heat, and wait for the pan and the oil to get hot; this will take a little while. Stir the batter now with a ladle and measure out about 1/3 cup. Drop the batter in the center of the frying pan. Quickly put the rounded bottom of a soup spoon or a second ladle very lightly on the mound of batter and, using a gentle but continuous spiral motion, spread the batter outward

(recipe continues)

until you have a pancake that is about 7 inches in diameter. Dribble ½ teaspoon oil on top of the pancake and another ½ teaspoon around its edges. Spread the oil on top of the pancake gently with a rubber spatula and smooth out the ridges. Let the pancake cook for 2 minutes on its first side, or until it is reddish brown. (This first-cooked side is the "right" side.) Now flip the pancake over and cook the second side for another 2 minutes, or until it has a few reddish-brown spots. Remove the pancake to a plate and keep covered. Stir the batter each time and make the remaining pancakes in the same way.

MAKES 12 TO 14 PANCAKES

Black-Eyed Pea Sprouts with Garlic and Thyme INDIA
Chhoonki Lobhia

Once sprouted, black-eyed peas may be cooked with almost any seasonings and served hot, at room temperature, or even chilled. This particular dish may be served three different ways: exactly the way it is with rice and greens on the side; topped with a dollop of Simple Tomato Sauce (page 779), and with a green salad and crusty brown bread on the side; or topped with a "salad" made with 3 tablespoons of finely chopped onions, 4 tablespoons peeled, seeded, and diced tomatoes, 2 tablespoons lemon juice, and a little salt and pepper. Toss the black-eyed peas and "salad" just before eating and serve at room temperature with flatbreads or crusty loaves.

Thyme is not normally used in India, but I have substituted it for the tiny ajwain *seeds, which have a similar flavor and are rich in thyme.*

2 tablespoons peanut or canola oil

1 garlic clove, peeled and finely chopped

3 cups black-eyed pea sprouts (page 16)

½ teaspoon dried thyme

½ teaspoon salt

Freshly ground black pepper

¼ teaspoon cayenne (optional)

Put the oil and garlic in a large wok or frying pan and set over medium-high heat. The garlic will soon start to sizzle. As soon as the garlic is golden, add the sprouts. Stir once and add the thyme, salt, pepper, and cayenne, if using. Stir a few times, add 4 tablespoons of water, and bring to a boil. Cover, turn the heat down to low, and cook for about 6 minutes. Uncover, turn the heat up to medium-high again, and cook, tossing the sprouts, for 3 to 4 minutes, or until most of the liquid is absorbed. Taste for the balance of seasonings and make adjustments, if needed.

SERVES 3 TO 4

Chickpeas (Garbanzos), *Chana Dal,* and Chickpea Flour

There is a saying in India that if you eat ten chickpeas a day, you will never have a heart attack! I sincerely hope this is true, as I eat rather a lot of this ancient food through the course of a year. Sometimes I cook chickpeas in an Indian style—and there must be at least a few hundred recipes for them in that subcontinent alone—and sometimes I use a recipe from one of the Mediterranean or Middle Eastern countries, all of which seem to share my passion for this legume.

Chickpeas originated in ancient times, probably in the southern Caucasus region, helping to feed Turkey, Syria, Iran, and Armenia. The earliest mention of them in the Middle East dates back to 5400 B.C. They quickly spread through all of Afghanistan and then on to India, where the first mention we know dates back to 2500 B.C. They also traveled west, capturing the hearts of the entire Mediterranean, where they have remained a staple, especially in Spain, Sicily, Turkey, and Cyprus. In Southeast Asia, they are used, quite intriguingly, in sweet snacks.

The early chickpea was probably small and dark (this variety is still found in India) and was eventually bred to be large and pale. Most American chickpeas are grown in the fertile Northwest, the vast lentil and pea-growing Palouse region so named for its resemblance to a green lawn in spring.

It is interesting too that in the United States, where vast quantities of chickpeas are grown for home use and export, they are hardly ever sold when they are tender, green, and as delicious as fresh peas. Nor do we often see the feathery shoots of the plant, which are excellent in salads and may be cooked like snow pea shoots. For those nations that have been eating chickpeas for thousands of years, these are annual treats, not to be missed. I have been making a small noise about green chickpeas for a few years now. Perhaps all the dynamic and influential chefs who control the restaurant business will help rectify this culinary oversight.

The two types of chickpeas most readily available for use in recipes are the canned and the dried. Canned chickpeas have the advantage of convenience. They are fully cooked and you do not have to go through the time-consuming process of soaking and boiling them. However, they often have a metallic taste and their tinny-tasting liquid can never be used when recipes require it. Dried chickpeas, on the other hand, take time (but almost no effort) to prepare and they not only have better flavor, but their slightly sweet cooking liquid is a great bonus, being an almost perfect natural stock for soups and stews.

Here is something to keep in mind: 1 cup of dried chickpeas will yield 3 cups of cooked drained chickpeas; 1½ cups of dried chickpeas will yield 4½ cups of cooked drained chickpeas.

If you have to substitute canned chickpeas for the home-cooked ones, a 20-ounce can generally yields about 2¼ cups of drained cooked chickpeas. A 15½-ounce can will yield about 1¾ cups of drained cooked chickpeas. After draining, rinse the chickpeas well before using them. If the liquid from cooking chickpeas is required, use a vegetable stock.

Many of the following recipes call for 1½ cups dried chickpeas. Here is how you would prepare this amount:

Soaking chickpeas: Pick over the chickpeas and wash them in several changes of water. Drain. Cover with 5 cups of water and leave overnight. Drain. Alternatively, you could use the Quick-Soak Method (page 6). Drain.

Cooking chickpeas: In a medium pot, add 6 cups of water to the soaked and drained chickpeas and bring to a boil. Turn the heat down to low, cover, and cook gently for 1 to 3 hours, or until the chickpeas are very tender. About 1½ teaspoons of salt may be added in the last half hour of cooking only if the recipe does not require you to add it later.

Pressure cooker method for chickpeas Put the drained soaked chickpeas, 4 cups of water, and 1½ teaspoons peanut or corn oil into a pressure cooker. Cover, bring up to pressure, and cook for 20 minutes. Allow the pressure to drop by itself. Loosen the lid and let the chickpeas cool in their liquid. (If you wish to add salt, put in 1½ teaspoons and let the chickpeas simmer gently in the salted water, uncovered, for 5 minutes. Then let them cool in their liquid. If the chickpeas require further cooking, salt may be added later.)

Removing chickpea skins: The next thing to do is to remove the skins of the chickpeas, if you want to. (In India, we generally do not do this as the skins are considered to be excellent roughage. However, dishes do look neater without them.) To do this, drain the cooked chickpeas but save the cooking liquid to use in soups and stews. Put the chickpeas in a bowl and cover them with cold water. Rub the chickpeas lightly between the palms of your hands to loosen the skins.

Chana Dal: So far, I have only dealt with the large, pale chickpeas most easily found in much of the Western world and the Mediterranean region. At Indian grocers, however, you will see split chickpeas that look very much like yellow split peas but which are marked *chana dal*. These have a gentler, sweeter, and nuttier taste and a firmer texture than yellow split peas, and I much prefer their flavor. These are small chickpeas that have a brown skin and very yellow interior, which have been hulled and split. As a *dal* (and I have only used them as a *dal* in this book, though Indian shops also sell them whole), they generally cook in about 1½ hours and are wonderful combined with vegetables. Look for them in Chickpeas and *Chana Dal* Cooked Together in a Mint Sauce (page 34), where they are combined with the larger chickpeas and end up forming part of the sauce.

There is also another interesting use of *chana dal*. In south India they are fried until reddish-brown and used as a seasoning!

In India *chana dal* is used to make chickpea flour. Indians insist that Indian chickpea flour is much easier to digest than the versions sold in the Mediterranean, which are made with the larger chickpeas.

Chickpea flour: This nutrient-rich flour is used commonly throughout India and in parts of the Mediterranean as well. Also called *besan* or gram flour in Indian shops and by its French name, *farine de pois chiches,* in specialty stores, it may be made into pancakes, pizzas, dumplings, soups, stews, quiches, rolled "pasta," sweet halvahs, and even into *panisses,* which are rather like delicate French fries and found in the south of France.

A few tablespoons of roasted chickpea flour are sometimes added to seasoned stir-fried vegetables (such as green beans, bell peppers, or okra) in western India, a really delicious embellishment that increases their nutritional value and adds a nutty flavor and extra texture. Chickpea flour can be roasted by stirring it around in a cast-iron frying pan for a few minutes over medium heat. When it turns a medium brown color and no longer tastes raw, it is done. Add it to the stir-fried vegetables when they are almost cooked. It will mix with the oil, absorb all the moisture in the pan, and then cling to the vegetables almost like little bits of stuffing. Stir-fry the vegetables for another minute in order to complete the cooking.

Chickpea flour is also used in India as a thickener for soupy stews containing vegetables or dumplings or sometimes nothing more than a mix of seasonings. The chickpea flour here may be used raw but sometimes it is sautéed in oil first, rather like the making of a roux. It then acquires a wonderful, nutty aroma, very similar to the one it gets when it is roasted. Once browned lightly in oil, you may add boiling water to the flour as you stir briskly with a whisk to prevent lumps.

Making lump-free chickpea flour batter Before it can be cooked, chickpea flour is sometimes diluted with liquid. In India, this liquid is often thinned-out yogurt. As dairy products help to complete the natural protein in dried legumes, this is nutritional expediency. Of course the liquid can also be plain water.

As with most flours, chickpea flour has a tendency to lump when liquids are added. To avoid lumping, follow this procedure: Sift the chickpea flour into a bowl. Pour the liquid suggested in the recipe into the bowl very slowly as you stir briskly with a wooden spoon. While the mixture is still very thick and pastelike, stop adding liquid and stir the batter briskly. Try to remove all lumps at this stage as it becomes much harder when the batter is thinner. You may even press lumps against the sides of the bowl. Now add the remaining liquid a little faster, stirring as you go. If you let the batter sit for 30 minutes, any final lumps tend to vanish, but the batter can also be strained through a sieve before being used. Always stir the batter before using it as it tends to settle at the bottom. If you are making pancakes, stir well before you pour the batter out for every single pancake or the texture of your pancakes will vary considerably, with the last one being quite leaden!

Sara Abufares'

Whole Grain or "Bead" Hummus   SYRIA

Hummus

Most of us in the West think of hummus as a chickpea puree seasoned with lemon juice and olive oil and eaten with pita bread. There are actually many versions of hummus, which, after all, just means "chickpeas." Here is one where the chickpeas are not pureed at all, but left whole, like beads. It is a kind of salad that may be served as a light lunch with yogurt cheese (or any goat or sheep cheese), pita bread, olives, and perhaps a green salad.

8 garlic cloves, peeled

1¾ teaspoons salt

2½ cups cooked drained chickpeas (page 26)

6 tablespoons fresh lemon juice

2 medium tomatoes, chopped

5 to 6 tablespoons chopped fresh parsley

¼ teaspoon cayenne

5 tablespoons olive oil, preferably a good
    extra-virgin

In a mortar, crush the garlic and salt together. Transfer to a medium mixing bowl and add the chickpeas, lemon juice, tomatoes, parsley, and cayenne. Toss well to mix. Taste for the balance of flavors, adding more lemon juice, parsley, or cayenne to taste. Put the salad in a serving bowl and drizzle with the olive oil. Serve at room temperature or chilled.

SERVES 4

Middle Eastern Stew of Chickpeas, Potatoes, and Carrots

I like to serve this hearty stew in big soup plates with parsley sprinkled over the top. It is well suited to family meals as children love it. Breads, salads, and cheeses can be served on the side. You may also stuff some of this stew, along with some shredded lettuce, into a pita bread and eat it like a sandwich. Middle Eastern or North African salads would complement this dish perfectly.

¾ cup dried chickpeas, picked over, washed, and drained

2 to 3 tablespoons olive oil

3 tablespoons finely chopped onions

2 garlic cloves, peeled and finely chopped

¾ pound potatoes, cut into ½ × 1-inch chunks

1 medium carrot, cut into ¼-inch slices

4 canned plum tomatoes plus 1 cup liquid from the can

1½ teaspoons salt

½ teaspoon dried thyme

¼ to ½ teaspoon sugar as needed

3 tablespoons finely chopped parsley

Soak the chickpeas overnight in cold water to cover by about 3 inches. Alternatively, you could Quick-Soak the chickpeas in the same amount of water according to the directions on page 6. Drain and discard the soaking liquid.

In a medium pot, bring the chickpeas and 2½ cups of water to a boil. Cover, lower the heat, and simmer for 2½ to 3 hours, or until the chickpeas are very tender. (For the pressure cooker method, see page 6. Use about 2 cups of water.) You may, at this stage, remove the skins if you wish, following the directions on page 26, and then combine the cleaned chickpeas and their cooking liquid once again.

Heat the oil in a medium pan over medium-high heat. Add the onions and stir and fry until the onions are brown around the edges. Add the garlic and stir for 30 seconds. Put in the potatoes, carrot, chickpeas with their cooking liquid, tomatoes, tomato liquid, salt, thyme, and ½ cup water. If the tomatoes are very tart, add the sugar to taste. Bring to a boil. Turn the heat down to low, cover, and cook gently for 45 minutes. Sprinkle parsley over the top before serving. Serve hot.

SERVES 4 TO 6

Chickpea Stew with Six Vegetables   MOROCCO

This hearty stew is best served with a big platter of couscous. You may also serve it with Moroccan bread or with a crusty French or Italian loaf and Moroccan salads or any green salad.

In Morocco a very hot sauce known as harissa, made up of Moroccan Chile-Garlic Paste (page 674) and some liquid from the stew, is passed around in a bowl.

5 tablespoons olive oil

1 large onion, peeled and finely chopped

4 garlic cloves, peeled and finely chopped

1½ cups dried chickpeas, soaked and cooked according to the directions on page 26, with skins removed, if you wish, and the cooking liquid drained and reserved

1 (28-ounce) can plum tomatoes, finely chopped, liquid reserved or 2 cups peeled and chopped fresh tomato

2 medium waxy potatoes, peeled and cut into 1-inch pieces

5 to 6 tablespoons finely chopped fresh parsley

5 to 6 tablespoons finely chopped fresh cilantro leaves

2½ to 3 teaspoons salt

2 teaspoons ground cumin

½ teaspoon ground turmeric

1 teaspoon ginger powder

A few saffron threads or a pinch of saffron powder (optional)

¼ teaspoon cayenne (optional)

1 medium sweet potato, peeled and halved lengthwise, then cut crosswise into 1-inch pieces

3 small carrots, peeled and cut into 1-inch pieces

1 large zucchini, halved lengthwise, then cut crosswise into 1-inch pieces

Harissa Sauce

5 teaspoons Moroccan Chile-Garlic Paste (page 674)

½ teaspoon salt

Put the oil in a large (12-inch) pot and place over medium-high heat. Add the onion and stir and fry for 5 minutes, or until it begins to brown around the edges. Add in the garlic and stir for about 1 minute, or until it turns golden. Now add the chickpeas, 1¼ cups reserved cooking liquid, the tomatoes, potatoes, parsley, cilantro, salt, cumin, turmeric, ginger, saffron, and cayenne. Measure the reserved tomato liquid and add enough water to make 2½ cups of liquid in total. Add to the pot and bring to a boil. Cover, turn the heat to low, and cook for 20 minutes. Add the sweet potato and carrots. Bring to a boil, cover, reduce the heat again, and continue to cook for 10 minutes. Add the zucchini, bring to a boil once again, and cook, covered on low heat, for 7 to 8 minutes, or until the zucchini is tender.

Measure out ½ cup of the cooking liquid and place in a small bowl. Add the harissa ingredients and combine well.

Serve the stew hot with the harissa on the side.

SERVES 6 TO 8

Marios Mourtezis'

Cypriot Chickpea Stew with Spinach   CYPRUS
Revithia Yakhni

A simple chickpea stew is perked up very interestingly with a tiganissi—something between an Indian tarka and a Spanish sofrito—of red chiles, garlic, onion, and tomato. Serve with a crusty bread, feta cheese, or a yogurt dish and a salad.

1½ cups dried chickpeas, soaked and cooked according to the directions on page 26, with skins removed, if you wish, and the cooking liquid drained and reserved
2 celery stalks, cut into ¼-inch dice
1 pound spinach, trimmed, washed, and cut crosswise into very fine ribbons
1½ to 2 teaspoons salt

¼ cup olive oil
1 to 3 whole dried hot red chiles
1 medium onion, peeled and finely chopped
4 to 5 garlic cloves, peeled and very finely chopped
3 medium tomatoes, peeled and very finely chopped

Put the chickpeas in a large pot together with their reserved cooking liquid, celery, spinach, and 1½ teaspoons salt. Bring to a boil. Cover, turn the heat down to low, and simmer for 20 minutes, or until the greens are tender.

Meanwhile, put the oil in a large frying pan and set over medium-high heat. When hot, put in the chile(s). Stir for a few seconds, or until they turn dark. Quickly add the onion and garlic and reduce the heat to medium. Stir and fry until the onion has just begun to pick up a little bit of brown color. Now put in the tomatoes. Stir and cook for 3 to 4 minutes, or until the tomatoes have softened. Transfer the contents of the frying pan to the pot with the chickpeas, stir to mix, and continue to cook the chickpeas gently, stirring now and then, for another 5 to 10 minutes. Check the seasonings, adding more salt if needed.

SERVES 6

Chickpeas Cooked in a Moghlai-Style   INDIA

Moghlai Chanay

Served with pita breads or Indian naans along with other vegetables and salads, this is perfect party fare, and it may be made a day in advance.

If using the canned variety, you will need 7½ cups (2¾ pounds) of drained chickpeas; use vegetable stock or water for the chickpea cooking liquid.

2½ cups dried chickpeas, picked over, washed, and drained

5 tablespoons peanut or canola oil

2 bay leaves

2 small cinnamon sticks

6 whole cardamom pods

2 medium onions, peeled and finely chopped

1 (2-inch) piece of fresh ginger, peeled and grated to a pulp

3 to 4 garlic cloves, peeled and mashed to a pulp

1 tablespoon ground cumin

1 tablespoon ground coriander

½ cup plain yogurt

5 tablespoons pureed tomatoes (not paste)

2½ teaspoons salt

2 teaspoons garam masala (page 723)

1½ teaspoons ground *amchoor* (page 711)

1 tablespoon ground roasted cumin seeds (page 724)

¼ teaspoon cayenne, or to taste

½ cup finely chopped fresh cilantro, packed

Soak the chickpeas overnight in water that covers them by several inches or use the Quick-Soak Method (page 6), using 8 cups of water. Drain, discarding the soaking liquid.

Put the chickpeas in a pressure cooker with 5 cups of water. Cover and bring up to pressure. Cook 20 minutes. Allow the pressure to drop by itself, uncover, and set aside. (Alternatively, you could cook the soaked drained chickpeas with 8 cups of water for 1½ to 3 hours until tender.) Allow to cool in the cooking liquid.

In a large pot, heat the oil over medium-high heat. When hot, put in the bay leaves, cinnamon sticks, and cardamom. Stir a few times and add the onions. Stir and fry for 8 to 9 minutes, or until they turn brown around the edges. Put in the ginger and garlic and stir for about 1 minute. Add the cumin and coriander, stir for a few seconds, then stir in 1 tablespoon of the yogurt. Stir and fry until it becomes one with the onions. Add a second tablespoon of yogurt and stir until it, too, incorporates with the sauce. Continue adding yogurt a tablespoon at a time until the full ½ cup has been incorporated.

Stir in the tomatoes and cook for 2 minutes. Now add the chickpeas with their cooking liquid, 2 cups of water, the salt, garam masala, *amchoor,* cumin, and cayenne. Stir to mix and bring to a boil. Reduce the heat to low and simmer gently, uncovered, for 15 minutes. Add most of the cilantro and stir it in, leaving just a little for a final garnish.

SERVES 8

From Khadija Ali of Tiffin's, Port of Spain

Chickpea and Potato Curry, Caribbean Style

TRINIDAD

Potato Chana Curry

The foods of Trinidad are such an amalgam, not only of the produce and cooking styles of Africans, Amer-Indians, Indians, Syrians, Chinese, Spanish, Portuguese, and French but also of different periods in the food histories of all those involved.

The Indians of Trinidad, for example, came all the way from the villages and towns of India, starting in the early nineteenth century, mostly to work in the sugar plantations as indentured farmhands. Despite back-breaking working and living conditions akin to slavery, they managed to preserve their local food traditions. Over time, however, names of spices and dishes were half-forgotten or misremembered. New dishes, brought by Indians migrating from other regions of India, were incorporated into what was evolving into a separate Trinidadian Indian cuisine, sometimes disparagingly called "coolie food." Substitutions were made for original ingredients and new seasonings, either indigenous to the Americas or brought by Europeans, were added freely.

This chickpea dish is such an amalgam, and a glorious one at that. It has chives, thyme, and parsley (sold in fresh bundles in the markets as "seasoning"), which hint of the Mediterranean, it has culantro and hot habanero-type Scotch bonnets, which must have come from the original Amer-Indians, as well as a curry powder made with curry leaves (most unusual for a North Indian–style dish) and yet another *Indianish spice mixture known locally as* amchar masala, *whose name and makeup I find most intriguing. (More on that spice mixture on page 711.)*

The first time I had this dish was in a friend's office in Port of Spain. It was lunchtime and doubles *were sent for. Doubles, it turned out, consisted of two Fry Bakes (fried bread, page 756) and these chickpeas, all packed up together for us in greaseproof paper. We devoured it with generous dollops of Trinidadian Pepper Sauce (page 771) and Mango Chutney (page 695).*

If you cannot find culantro (sold as shadow beni *or* chadon bené *in Trinidad), use fresh cilantro. Serve this dish with Fry Bakes, as suggested above, or any flatbread. At a sit-down meal, serve a green vegetable and a yogurt relish as well and perhaps the Tomato "Choka" (page 300).*

(recipe continues)

1½ cups dried chickpeas, soaked and cooked according to the directions on page 26, with skins removed, if you wish, and the cooking liquid drained and reserved

2 tablespoons finely chopped culantro or cilantro

1½ tablespoons finely chopped fresh chives

2 scallions, white parts only, cut into very fine rounds

1 tablespoon finely chopped parsley

2 teaspoons fresh thyme leaves or ½ teaspoon dried

¼ finely chopped Scotch bonnet or other fresh hot chile

2 teaspoons salt

¼ cup peanut or canola oil

1 good-sized onion (6 ounces), peeled and finely chopped

2 garlic cloves, peeled and mashed to a pulp

4 teaspoons hot curry powder, such as Madras or use My Curry Powder (page 707)

2 medium potatoes, peeled and cut into 1 × ¾-inch chunks

2 teaspoons *amchar masala* (page 711)

Put the drained chickpeas (not their cooking liquid) in a bowl. Add the culantro, chives, scallions, parsley, thyme, Scotch bonnet, and 1 teaspoon of the salt. Mix gently and set aside.

In a large, wide pot or deep frying pan, heat the oil over medium-high heat. When hot, add the onion and stir and fry for about 4 minutes, or until the onion pieces turn brown at the edges. Put in the garlic; stir and fry for another minute. Now add the curry powder and stir once or twice. Quickly add the potatoes, the chickpeas, their reserved cooking liquid, the remaining teaspoon salt, and enough water to barely cover the potatoes and chickpeas, about 1¼ cups. Bring to a boil. Turn the heat to low, cover, and simmer gently for 30 minutes. Stir in the *amchar masala* and cook another 5 minutes. Serve hot.

SERVES 4 TO 6

Chickpeas and *Chana Dal* Cooked Together in a Mint Sauce

INDIA

Paraati Chana

Here is a perfect stewlike dish for large gatherings or a family get-together. This Punjabi specialty is sold in the streets of North India and people stop to buy a plate as Americans might stop for a hot dog. It is served from a large round, high-sided tray known as a paraat—*hence it is known as* paraati chana. *Decorating the edges are whole green chiles and wedges of limes and onions. The* chana dal *in the dish melts, providing the larger chickpeas with a lovely, spicy sauce that is best sopped up with Indian breads or Middle Eastern flatbreads such as pita. If you cannot easily get the exquisitely flavored Indian yellow split chickpea known as* chana dal, *use ordinary yellow split peas.*

This is generally eaten as a snack but it could easily be served at a meal with breads, vegetables, and a yogurt dish.

1½ cups dried chickpeas, picked over, washed, and drained

¾ cup *chana dal* or yellow split peas, picked over, washed, and drained

1 tablespoon peeled and finely chopped garlic

1 tablespoon finely chopped ginger

3 fresh hot green chiles, finely chopped

1 cup mint leaves, packed, washed, and coarsely chopped

¼ cup peanut or canola oil

2 medium onions, finely chopped

½ pound very ripe tomatoes, peeled and chopped

2½ teaspoons salt

1½ teaspoons ground coriander

1½ teaspoons ground cumin

½ teaspoon garam masala (page 723)

3 tablespoons thick tamarind paste (page 737) or fresh lemon juice to taste

Soak the chickpeas overnight in cold water to cover by about 5 inches. Alternatively, you may use the Quick-Soak Method (page 6). Drain, discarding the soaking liquid.

In a large pot, bring the chickpeas and 7 cups of water to a boil. Cover, lower the heat, and simmer for 1 hour. Skim off any chickpea skins that may be floating on the top. Add the *chana dal* or split peas to the pot, cover, and continue simmering for 1½ to 2 hours, or until the chickpeas and *chana dal* are tender. Set aside.

Meanwhile, combine the garlic, ginger, green chiles, and mint leaves in the container of a blender. Add 6 to 8 tablespoons of water as needed and blend, pushing down the mixture with a rubber spatula several times, until pureed. Set the minty mixture aside.

Heat the oil in a wide, medium pot over medium-high heat. Add the onions and stir and fry until they are a rich, reddish brown. Add the tomatoes. Stir and cook until the tomatoes reduce and darken and the oil begins to show at the sides of the pan. Add the green spice paste and stir over medium-high heat for 5 minutes. Add the chickpeas and their cooking liquid, then stir in the salt, coriander, cumin, garam masala, and tamarind paste, mixing thoroughly. Cover, lower the heat, and simmer gently for ½ hour. Serve hot.

SERVES 6 TO 8

Draupadiji's

Vegetable Stew with Chickpea Flour Sauce

INDIA

Karhi

This karhi *is a soupy stew made with a chickpea flour base that comes from India's western region of Sindh. It is nearly always served with plain basmati rice and requires nothing more than perhaps some pickles and chutneys.*

Other vegetables may be used either in place of or in addition to those suggested below, such as diced potatoes and small okra pods that have been fried first.

If curry leaves are unavailable, substitute fresh basil. The flavors are totally different, but have a similar freshness and intensity.

¼ cup peanut or canola oil

¼ teaspoon fenugreek seeds

20 fresh curry leaves

¾ cup chickpea flour

1 large tomato, finely chopped

1 (1½-inch) piece of fresh ginger, peeled and grated to a pulp

½ to 1 fresh hot green chile, finely chopped

½ teaspoon ground turmeric

¼ to ½ teaspoon cayenne

1¾ teaspoons salt

1½ to 2 tablespoons thick tamarind paste (page 737)

1 medium carrot, cut into 1½-inch-long sticks

1 scant cup fresh green beans, cut into 1-inch pieces

2 loosely packed cups medium cauliflower florets

Put a kettle of water on to boil. You will need 5 cups of boiling water.

Put the oil in a large pot and place over medium-high heat. When hot, add the fenugreek seeds and a second later the curry leaves. Stir once and quickly put in the chickpea flour. Turn the heat down to low and stir and fry for 2 to 3 minutes, or until the chickpea flour is a shade darker. Add the boiling water, a little at a time, while you stir vigorously with a whisk. When all the water has been added and the sauce looks smooth, stir in the tomato, ginger, chile, turmeric, cayenne, salt, and tamarind paste and bring to a simmer. Cover, reduce the heat to low, and cook gently for 15 minutes. Uncover and add all the vegetables. Stir to mix and bring to a simmer again. Cover, turn the heat down to low, and cook very gently for 12 to 15 minutes, or until the vegetables are tender.

SERVES 4

Basic Recipe for Plain Chickpea Flour Pancakes

Poora/Pudla

These are best made in a 5½- to 6-inch nonstick frying pan. While they should really be eaten as soon as they are made for optimal flavor and texture, you may wrap them up in a foil bundle and reheat the whole bundle in a medium oven for 15 minutes. You may also reheat them, one at a time for 1 minute, in a microwave oven.

In the West Indian state of Gujarat, where chickpea pancakes are very popular, they are served rather as the West serves omelets, either plain, as in this recipe, or mixed with flavorings, as in the variations that follow. The flavorings do not, of course, have to be Indian. You might want to use fresh herbs or a mixture of chopped bell peppers or grated cauliflower or even leftover lightly crushed green peas.

Serve these at breakfast or as a snack with yogurt relishes, sweet or savory chutneys, and pickles. You may also serve them with a meal in place of bread. Almost anything may be wrapped inside them, such as potato or cauliflower stews, beans, even grated cheese and salsas.

2 cups chickpea flour

1 teaspoon ground cumin seeds

¼ teaspoon ground turmeric

¼ to ½ teaspoon cayenne

1 teaspoon salt

6 to 7 tablespoons peanut or canola oil for cooking the pancakes

Sift the chickpea flour, cumin, turmeric, cayenne, and salt into a medium mixing bowl. Very slowly, stir in 2 cups of water with a wooden spoon, stopping while the batter is still pastelike to get rid of all lumps, then slowly adding the rest of the water. (For more on adding liquid to chickpea flour, see page 27.) Set the batter aside for 30 minutes. Strain it through a sieve if it is still lumpy.

Put 1 teaspoon oil in a 5½- to 6-inch nonstick frying pan and place over medium-high heat. When hot, stir the batter from the bottom and ladle about ¼ cup into the frying pan. Tilt the frying pan around to spread out the batter. Dribble another teaspoon of oil over the top. Cook the pancake for about 2 minutes, or until the bottom has golden-red spots. Turn the pancake over and cook the second side for a minute, or until it too has golden-red spots. Remove to a plate and keep covered with an overturned plate. Continue making pancakes until all the batter is used. Serve immediately.

MAKES ABOUT 10 PANCAKES

(recipe continues)

Variation I
Chickpea Flour Pancakes with Sesame Seeds

Follow the preceding master recipe for Plain Chickpea Flour Pancakes but with this difference: As soon as you pour the batter into the frying pan, sprinkle the top with about ½ teaspoon of sesame seeds. When you turn the pancake over, the seeds will toast slightly. (Use either beige or black sesame seeds.)

Variation II
Chickpea Flour Pancakes with Crushed Green Peas and Cilantro

Make the batter as in the master recipe, adding 1 teaspoon very finely grated fresh peeled ginger, 1 teaspoon very finely chopped fresh green chile, 1 tablespoon finely chopped fresh cilantro, and 1 cup fresh or frozen green peas that have been cooked, drained, and then lightly mashed. Mix well and set the batter aside for 30 minutes. Do not strain before making the pancakes. Remember to stir well before ladling out the batter for every single pancake.

Variation III
Chickpea Flour Pancakes with Fresh Green Herbs

Follow the master recipe but leave out the cumin, turmeric, and cayenne. Set it aside for 30 minutes. Strain, if necessary. Just before making the pancakes, stir in 1 tablespoon finely chopped fresh chives, 1 teaspoon finely chopped fresh thyme, 1 teaspoon finely chopped fresh tarragon, and 1 tablespoon finely chopped fresh parsley. Do not forget to stir well before making each pancake.

Pallavi Shah's
Chickpea Flour Pancakes with Tomato and Onion   INDIA
Tameta Kanda Na Poora

A few of these pancakes served with a green salad make a wonderful light meal. Because the tomato and onion release juices of their own, this recipe uses a little less liquid than the preceding ones.

2 cups chickpea flour

1 teaspoon salt

¼ to ½ teaspoon cayenne

1 teaspoon whole cumin seeds

¼ cup peeled, seeded, and finely diced tomato (see page 300 for instructions, if needed)

¼ cup finely chopped onion or finely sliced scallions

6 to 7 tablespoons peanut or canola oil, for cooking the pancakes

Sift the chickpea flour, salt, and cayenne into a mixing bowl. Very slowly stir in 1¼ cups of water with a wooden spoon, stopping while the batter is still pastelike to get rid of all lumps, then slowly adding the rest of the water. (For more on adding liquid to chickpea flour, see page 27.) Add the cumin seeds, tomato, and onion. Mix well. Set the batter aside for 30 minutes.

Put 1 teaspoon oil in a 5½- to 6-inch nonstick frying pan and set over medium-high heat. When hot, stir the batter from the bottom and ladle about ¼ cup into the frying pan. Tilt the frying pan around to spread out the batter. Dribble another teaspoon of oil over the top. Cook the pancake for about 2 minutes, or until the bottom has golden-red spots. Turn the pancake over and cook the second side for a minute, or until it too has golden-red spots. Remove to a plate and keep covered with an overturned plate. Repeat with the remaining batter. Serve immediately.

MAKES 9 TO 10 PANCAKES; SERVES 3 TO 4

Basic Recipe for Plain Chickpea Flour Pizza

FRANCE/ITALY

Socca/Farinata

This traditional morning snack for workmen in both Nice and Genoa is baked in brick ovens in large, round trays similar to those used for pizzas. The hot pizza is generally torn into strips with the fingers, but you may, if you wish, cut the pizza into wedges with a knife.

Since most of us do not have brick ovens at home, I have developed an alternate method that uses both the top of the stove and the broiler. The best utensil for this method is a sturdy, nonstick, 12-inch sauté pan or frying pan with a metal handle that can stand the heat of a broiler. If your pan is just a bit smaller or bigger, it should not matter much.

As with the chickpea flour pancakes, the pizza may be made plain or you may add herbs and olives. I also make one with herbs and grated Parmesan cheese, which is quite spectacular.

(recipe continues)

⅔ cup chickpea flour

⅓ teaspoon salt

3 tablespoons olive oil

Freshly ground black pepper

Sift the chickpea flour and salt into a bowl. Very slowly, stir in 1 cup of water with a wooden spoon, stopping while the batter is still pastelike to beat out all lumps, then slowly adding the rest of the water. (For more on adding liquid to chickpea flour, see page 27.) Set the batter aside for 30 minutes. Strain it through a sieve if it is still lumpy.

Preheat the broiler.

Put 1 tablespoon of oil in a 12-inch nonstick frying pan and set it over medium-high heat. When hot, stir the batter from the bottom and pour it into the frying pan. Pour 2 tablespoons of oil over the top of the pizza, sprinkle lightly with black pepper, and cook on top of the stove for about 4 minutes. During this time, big bubbles will rise from the bottom; you may burst them with the tip of a knife. When the pizza batter looks as if it has set, put the frying pan under the broiler about 5 inches from the source of heat for 4 to 5 minutes, or until it is golden all over and has some nicely browned patches. You may need to turn the pan around to achieve evenness. Serve hot.

MAKES 1 PIZZA; SERVES 2 TO 4

Variation I
Chickpea Flour Pizza with Thyme and Sage

Make the batter as in the master recipe for Plain Chickpea Flour Pizza but with this difference: When the batter has sat for 30 minutes, add to it 1 teaspoon chopped fresh thyme or ½ teaspoon dried thyme. Stir and pour the batter into the pan as in the master recipe and arrange 5 to 6 fresh sage leaves over the top. Proceed to cook as in the master recipe.

Variation II
Chickpea Flour Pizza with Rosemary, Tomato, and Parmesan Cheese

Make the pizza as in the master recipe for Plain Chickpea Flour Pizza but with this difference: When the batter has sat for 30 minutes, add ½ teaspoon finely chopped fresh rosemary or ¼ teaspoon dried crumbled rosemary. Stir and pour the batter into the pan and cook as in the master recipe. After 2 to 3 minutes, when the batter has just barely set, sprinkle 2 tablespoons peeled, seeded, and chopped tomatoes, 1 tablespoon finely chopped onion, 3 tablespoons coarsely grated Parmigiano-Reggiano cheese, and lots of black pepper over the top. Proceed to put the pizza under the broiler as in the master recipe.

Victoria Salvy's
Chickpea Flour "French Fries"   FRANCE
Panisses

If you have never had this polenta-like specialty from the south of France, I urge you to try it immediately. To make it, the chickpea flour batter is first cooked until thick and then allowed to set in shallow plates. When firm, it is cut into "fries," dipped in flour, and shallow-fried. These crisp "fries," or panisses, *may be eaten plain with a sprinkling of salt and pepper or served with a tomato-enriched vegetable, such as Stuffed Baby Eggplants (page 184) or Stir-Fried Eggplants with Tomato and Parmesan Cheese (page 185). You may also serve them with Simple Tomato Sauce (page 779) on the side and a green salad.*

The panisses *may also be served sweet with a generous dusting of confectioners' sugar.*

To set the batter: *You need old-fashioned dinner plates or side plates with a wide rim for this recipe. The batter is poured into the center section and quickly spread to a depth of about 1/8 inch. I use 2 medium dinner plates that have a diameter of 6 1/2 to 7 inches in the central section. If you use smaller side plates, you will need 3 of them with a diameter of about 4 1/2 inches in the central section. Remember that this chickpea flour batter, once cooked, sets in seconds, so work with great speed to get the batter from the pan into the plates and spread to the rim.*

For the shallow-frying, you may use a combination of peanut and olive oil or just olive oil.

Olive oil for oiling the plates plus 1 teaspoon for the batter

1¼ cups chickpea flour

Salt

½ cup unbleached all-purpose white flour

An equal combination of olive and peanut oil for shallow-frying

Freshly ground black pepper

Oil the plates you will be using to set the batter. Place a bowl of cold water nearby.

Sift the chickpea flour onto a sheet of wax paper or into a small bowl.

In a heavy saucepan, bring 2 cups of water to a boil. Add ½ teaspoon salt and 1 teaspoon olive oil and turn the heat to medium. Pour in the sifted chickpea flour in a steady stream, stirring all the while with a wooden spoon. Keep stirring vigorously with the wooden spoon for 10 minutes, or until the batter is thick and begins to come off the sides of the pan. Working very quickly now, divide the batter between the plates. Quickly wet your hands in the bowl of cold water and spread the batter evenly on each plate so it goes out to the rim and forms a thick pancake. It will begin to firm up in seconds and set completely within minutes.

(recipe continues)

The set "pancakes" may be held for several hours, covered with overturned plates of the same size, but don't fry the *panisses* until just before serving.

When ready to eat, spread the flour on a board. Lay the "pancakes" on the floured board and cut them into ¾-inch-wide strips. Cut the strips in half crosswise. Roll each piece in the all-purpose flour until it is well coated.

Pour the oil into a large frying pan to a depth of ⅛ inch and set on medium-high heat. When hot, put in the *panisses* and fry them for about 5 minutes on each side, or until golden-red. Use a slotted spatula to transfer the *panisses* to a plate lined with paper towels. Sprinkle with salt and pepper and serve immediately.

SERVES 2 TO 4

Chickpea Flour "French Fries," the Indian Way

INDIA

Saank

My mother made a dish very similar to the panisses *of southern France, only she mixed the chickpea flour batter first, adding to it ginger, green chiles, and fresh cilantro before cooking it in a pan. This was generally eaten as a snack with tea or served for Sunday breakfasts. Chutneys were served on the side.*

Follow the general directions for setting the batter in the preceding recipe.

Peanut or canola oil, enough for oiling the
    plates and shallow-frying

1¼ cups chickpea flour

Salt

¼ teaspoon ground turmeric

½ teaspoon ground cumin

1 teaspoon very finely grated peeled fresh
    ginger

1 to 2 teaspoons finely chopped fresh hot
    green chile

2 tablespoons chopped fresh cilantro

½ teaspoon whole cumin seeds

½ cup unbleached all-purpose white flour

Freshly ground black pepper

Oil the plates you will be using to set the batter (see page 41). Place a bowl of cold water nearby.

Sift the chickpea flour, ½ teaspoon salt, turmeric, and ground cumin into a bowl. Slowly add 2 cups of water (see page 27 if you need directions on how to add water to chickpea flour). If there are still any lumps, strain the batter through a sieve.

Now add the ginger, chile, and cilantro. Stir to mix and set aside for 10 minutes.

Heat 2 teaspoons oil in a medium saucepan over medium heat. When hot, add the whole cumin seeds. Ten seconds later, pour in the batter in a steady stream, stirring all the while with a wooden spoon. Keep stirring vigorously until the batter comes to a boil. Stir vigorously for another 10 minutes, or until the batter is thick and begins to come off the sides of the pan. Working very quickly now, divide the batter between the plates. Quickly wet your hands in the bowl of cold water and spread the batter evenly over each plate so it extends to the rim and forms a thick pancake. It will begin to firm up in seconds and set completely within minutes.

The set "pancakes" may be held for several hours, covered with inverted plates of the same size, but the "fries" should be prepared just before you are ready to eat them.

Just before serving, spread the all-purpose flour on a board. Lift the "pancakes" off the plates gently and lay them on the floured board. Cut them into ¾-inch-wide strips. Cut the strips in half, crosswise. Roll each piece in the flour until it is well coated.

Pour oil into a large frying pan to a depth of ⅛ inch and set over medium-high heat. When hot, put in the strips and fry them for about 5 minutes on each side, or until golden-red. Use a slotted spatula to transfer the "fries" to a plate lined with paper towels to drain. Sprinkle with salt and pepper and serve immediately.

SERVES 2 TO 4

Fava Beans, Dried

Fresh fava beans have been appearing more and more often in a scattered fashion on the well-designed plates of American master chefs, but the general public, on the whole, is still quite unfamiliar with them (see page 198 for fresh fava beans).

Americans seem to have even less knowledge of the dried bean, which, when cooked, has a delicious chestnutlike texture and a dark, earthy taste. This old bean, which was known in ancient Persia, in prehistoric Switzerland, all around the early Mediterranean sea routes, and has even been found in the tombs of Egyptian pharaohs, has yet to gain a foothold in America.

Of course, it could be that the Americas offered incoming Europeans such a kaleidoscopic plethora of new, mild-flavored beans, such as the haricot, that the large, slightly bitter, dried fava retreated into the background. Strangely enough, fava beans did travel to China sometime in antiquity and took root in the western part of that country. Today, not only are they stir-fried in their fresh form but most of the bean pastes in Sichuan are made, not with dried soybeans as might be expected, but with dried and fermented fava beans. They are also sprouted, with superb results.

Two types of dried fava beans are available in the market: those that have been skinned and split, and those that are whole with their leathery, inedible skins still on them. For making the kind of purees that are very popular in the Middle East and North Africa, it is easier to use the skinned and split fava beans. However, if you wish to sprout them or cook them whole, you will need the beans with skins.

Cooking skinned and split fava beans: Pick over and wash the beans following the procedure on page 5. Drain them. Now put them in a pan with roughly double the amount of water and cook gently for 40 to 60 minutes. The beans can now be mashed and seasoned to get a thick puree.

This puree forms an excellent bed for sautéed green vegetables, such as broccoli rabe or even stir-fried broccoli.

Cooking dried fava beans with skins: Pick over and wash the beans; drain. Soak them overnight in water to cover by 5 inches or use the Quick-Soak Method (page 6). Drain. Place the soaked beans in a pot with 4 cups of water for every cup of soaked beans and bring to a boil. Cover partially, turn the heat down to low, and cook gently for 30 to 50 minutes, or until the beans are just tender. Drain. Cool slightly and peel.

Sprouting fava beans: Pick over and wash 1 pound of whole, unskinned, dried fava beans. Spread them on a large rimmed platter or metal tray in a single layer and cover them with 1 inch of water. Soak for 24 hours. Drain, rinse gently, cover with water again, and leave for another 24 hours. The third day, tiny sprouts should begin to appear. Leave a little water in the bottom of the pan and cover the beans with a double thickness of wet paper towels. Put the platter or tray in a dark place, such as an unused oven. Keep the towels lightly dampened. By the fourth day, the shoots will be about ½ inch long. Rinse gently and drain. You can keep these sprouts for a week in a plastic bag in the refrigerator; sprinkle them now and then with a little water. One pound of beans yields about 6 cups of sprouts.

Unlike some sprouted beans, these sprouts need to be cooked and the skins are inedible. You almost have to suck the meat out of the skin as you eat.

Melle Derko Samira's

Fava Bean Puree

Bissara

In Morocco, bissara *or bean purees are made from different beans, including fava beans, chick-peas, and split peas (see page 109 for the split pea* bissara*). They are served in shallow soup plates or shallow bowls sprinkled liberally with cumin and paprika and with a thin layer of good olive oil floating at the top. The film of oil provides lubrication, flavor, and also prevents a skin from forming. To eat, diners break off thick chunks of Everyday Moroccan Bread (page 460) and dip it into the puree. Lemon juice may be squeezed on top of the puree if one so wishes.*

With the bissara, *you may serve Red Peppers Stuffed with Feta Cheese (page 265) and a selection of Moroccan salads.*

2 cups dried, split, and skinned fava beans

4 garlic cloves, peeled and left whole

9 tablespoons extra-virgin olive oil

¾ to 1 teaspoon salt

1¼ teaspoons ground cumin

1¼ teaspoons paprika

¾ teaspoon cayenne (optional)

Lemon wedges (optional)

Wash the fava beans in several changes of water. Drain.

Combine the fava beans, garlic, 1 tablespoon olive oil, and 4 cups of water in a medium pot and bring to a boil over medium heat. Cover the pot, turn the heat down to low, and cook gently for 50 minutes, or until the beans are very tender.

Add the salt. Mash the beans and garlic with a potato masher until you have a coarse puree. Add ¼ teaspoon of the cumin, ¼ teaspoon of the paprika, and ⅛ teaspoon of the cayenne, if using. Stir to mix. The puree should be thick enough to pick up with a piece of bread but not so thick that it feels solid. If it is too thick, the puree can be thinned with a few tablespoons of water.

To serve, heat the fava beans over medium-low heat, stirring as you do so. Ladle the fava beans into 4 old-fashioned soup plates. Sprinkle each serving with ¼ teaspoon cumin, ¼ teaspoon paprika, and ⅛ teaspoon cayenne, if desired. Drizzle enough olive oil to form a film over each serving. Garnish with lemon wedges and serve hot or warm. (Diners should squeeze as much lemon juice over the puree as they like.)

Note: The puree will get fairly solid when refrigerated. Add a little water to it slowly and stir as you reheat gently.

SERVES 4

Stir-Fried Fava Bean Sprouts

CHINA

Ching Chow Tsan Do Meow

Serve these as a snack or as a nibble with beer, or even as a first course. Just suck the meat out of the skins when eating. The Chinese would pick these up with chopsticks but you can use your fingers.

2 tablespoons peanut oil

2 thin slices of ginger

1 garlic clove, lightly crushed and peeled but
    left whole

2 cups fava bean sprouts

¾ teaspoon salt

1 teaspoon sugar

2 tablespoons Chinese Shao Hsing wine or
    dry sherry

2 teaspoons oriental sesame oil

Put the oil in a wok or large frying pan and set over medium-high heat. When hot, add the ginger and garlic. Stir and fry for 20 seconds, pressing down on the seasonings. Put in the sprouts. Stir for 10 seconds. Now add the salt, sugar, wine, and 1¼ cups of water and bring to a boil. Cover, turn the heat to medium-low, and simmer 30 minutes. Remove the lid, add the sesame oil, and cook until all the liquid has boiled away, stirring gently as you do so. Remove the ginger and garlic and serve hot or chilled.

SERVES 2

Kidney Beans (Red, Large)

These originated in Central and South America in ancient times and belong to the large family of common American beans *(Phaseolus vulgaris)* that includes the haricot. While they remain very popular in the lands of their origin, today they are grown and eaten around the world, sometimes in salads, sometimes in the Tex-Mex and now international favorite, chili, and sometimes in stews and soups.

In India, kidney beans seem to have found a permanent niche in the northwest region of Punjab, where they are a staple. In this region they, as well as flat corn breads, are a staple food. In the cold winter months both are lubricated with mounds of homemade white butter and consumed with great relish. Punjabis call the small, indigenous Indian black bean *"ma"* (see *urad,* page 112). They call the large red kidney bean *"rajma,"* or the "royal *ma,*" perhaps because of its size and startling color. Often, the larger beans are combined with smaller red or black beans.

Actually, "red kidney bean" is rather a loose name for a bean that can be small or large and ranges in color from pinkish-red to a dark, winy maroon. Any of these beans may be used in the recipes that follow, though small beans take less time (and less water) to cook, so you will need to make adjustments accordingly. The recipes that follow were all made using the large bean. Pinto beans, which cook exactly like red kidney beans, can be substituted.

Even though these beans are not soaked overnight in the lands of their origin, I find it advisable to do so.

Cooking large red kidney beans or pinto beans: Pick over and wash the beans (page 5). Drain. Soak overnight in water to cover by 5 inches or use the Quick-Soak Method (page 6). Drain and discard the soaking liquid.

Now, for each 1½ cups of beans (the quantity called for in most of my recipes), add 6 cups of water and bring to a boil. Cover partially, turn the heat down to low, and cook gently for 2 to 2½ hours, or until the beans are tender.

About 1½ teaspoons of salt may be added during the last 10 minutes unless further cooking is called for, in which case it can be added later, as directed.

Substituting canned beans: If you wish to use canned beans, note that 1½ cups of dried red kidney beans yield 4 cups of cooked drained beans. The liquid from canned beans should be discarded.

Pressure cooker method for large red kidney beans or pinto beans Soak the beans as suggested above. Drain.

Put the beans, 4 cups of water, and 1½ teaspoons peanut or corn oil into a pressure cooker and bring up to pressure. Cook 10 to 12 minutes and let the pressure drop by itself. Uncover and add 1½ teaspoons salt if no more salt is called for in the recipe, and cook gently, uncovered, for 5 minutes.

Spicy Punjabi Red Kidney Bean Stew   INDIA
Rajma

My family likes to eat this bean stew at least once a week. If I am serving it for lunch, it is often the main dish, offered in old-fashioned soup plates with a dollop of thick creamy yogurt in the center. Sometimes I sprinkle a little finely chopped cilantro or parsley over the yogurt.

In the Punjab, where this dish is a staple, two types of kidney beans, a very dark red one and a lighter red one, are often combined in equal proportions. You may do the same if you can find the lighter beans, often available at Indian groceries.

I like to serve thick, crusty whole wheat bread on the side but you may, if you prefer, eat the beans with rice or a bulgur pilaf. A salad and/or vegetable dish, such as the Homemade Indian Cheese with Spinach (page 570), may also be served on the side.

(recipe continues)

1½ cups dried red kidney beans, preferably a mix of light and dark

2 teaspoons salt, or to taste

3 tablespoons peanut or canola oil

1 cup finely chopped onions

1 tablespoon peeled and finely chopped garlic

1 tablespoon finely chopped fresh ginger

1¼ cups peeled and chopped ripe tomatoes

2 teaspoons ground coriander

¼ teaspoon cayenne

2 teaspoons ground cumin

1 fresh hot green chile, finely chopped

1 tablespoon *amchoor* (page 711) or 2 teaspoons fresh lemon juice

Soak and cook the beans according to general directions on page 47. Add the salt to the beans and stir to mix.

Put the oil in a wide, medium pot and set over medium-high heat. Add the onions. Stir and fry until the onions are a rich, reddish-brown color. Add the garlic and stir a few times, then add the ginger and stir once or twice. Add the tomatoes, coriander, cayenne, cumin, and chile. Stir and cook over medium heat for 5 to 6 minutes, or until the tomatoes are slightly reduced. Stir in the cooked beans and their liquid as well as the *amchoor*. Turn the heat to low and simmer gently for 10 minutes to marry all the flavors. Serve hot.

SERVES 4 TO 6

Red Kidney Beans for Jamaican "Peas and Rice"

JAMAICA

In Jamaica, the red kidney beans and rice are cooked together. I prefer to cook the beans separately and then serve them over plain rice. The Scotch bonnet chile gives its own very tropically citric aroma to the dish, but make sure that you do not allow the chile to puncture during cooking, as it is very fiery, and remove it before serving.

For this recipe you may use small, large, or a combination of small and large red kidney beans.

1½ cups dried red kidney beans

2 cups canned coconut milk, well-stirred

1 Scotch bonnet or other habanero-type chile

4 tablespoons finely chopped chives or 6 tablespoons finely sliced scallions, both green and white sections

3 to 4 fresh thyme sprigs or ¾ teaspoon dried thyme

2 garlic cloves, peeled and finely chopped

1 small onion, peeled and finely chopped

¾ teaspoon ground allspice

1½ to 2 teaspoons salt, or to taste

Freshly ground black pepper

Soak and cook the beans overnight in water to cover by at least 5 inches. Alternatively, you may use the Quick-Soak Method (page 6). Drain, discarding the soaking liquid.

In a large pot, bring the beans and 4 cups of water to a boil. Cover, turn the heat down to low, and simmer gently for 1 hour. Add the coconut milk, habanero, chives, thyme, garlic, onion, and allspice. Stir and simmer for 30 minutes. Add the salt and pepper, stir, and simmer another 30 minutes, or until the beans are tender. Taste for the balance of seasonings. Remove the habanero and the thyme sprigs before serving.

SERVES 4 TO 6

Anita Harrell's
Nigerian Red Kidney Bean Stew with a Peanut Sauce   NIGERIA
Itiakiet Stew

This is an absolutely wonderful and easy-to-make stew that our family loves. The peanut butter flavor just seems to melt away, leaving only an unctuous sense of creaminess. If you like, you may add 1 cup of fresh or frozen corn kernels when you add the cooked tomato mixture.

    I serve this stew with rice, though my youngest daughter eats it out of a bowl with crusty bread. I like to serve greens or green beans on the side.

1½ cups dried red kidney beans or pinto beans

2 teaspoons salt, or to taste

3 tablespoons peanut or canola oil

1 medium onion, peeled and finely chopped

2 garlic cloves, peeled and finely chopped

½ large green pepper, seeds removed and cut into small dice

1 teaspoon ground cumin

1 cup canned tomato sauce

¼ teaspoon cayenne

1 tablespoon fresh lemon juice

1½ tablespoons smooth peanut butter

Soak and cook the beans according to general directions on page 47; do not drain. Add the salt to the beans, stir to mix, and leave the beans in their cooking liquid.

Put the oil in a wide, medium pot and set over medium heat. Add the onion, garlic, and pepper. Stir and fry just until the onion has turned translucent, turning

(recipe continues)

the heat down as needed. Add the cumin and stir once. Put in the tomato sauce, cayenne, lemon juice, and ½ cup of water. Stir and bring to a simmer. Turn the heat down to low and simmer gently, stirring now and then, for 15 minutes.

Meanwhile, put the peanut butter in a small bowl. Slowly add about 6 tablespoons of cooking liquid from the beans, mixing as you go. Stir this mixture back into the pot of beans.

When the tomato mixture has finished cooking, pour it into the pot of beans as well. Stir and bring to a simmer. Cover, turn the heat down to low, and simmer gently for 10 minutes, stirring occasionally. Serve hot.

SERVES 4 TO 6

Red Kidney Bean Casserole
Chilaquiles

MEXICO

Mexican chilaquiles *is really a meat dish, often made with leftover meat that is layered between crisp pieces of day-old tortillas, doused in a sauce of ancho chiles and tomatoes, and then baked. Here, I have used red kidney beans in place of the meat. You could add corn or other vegetables to the casserole if you like.*

If you wish to use canned beans here, you will need about 4 well-drained cups. If you do not have the time to make an ancho chile sauce or cannot find ancho chiles, use 2 cups of store-bought hot salsa.

Serve with a crisp green salad.

1½ cups dried red kidney beans or pinto
    beans

3 tablespoons canola or olive oil

1 medium onion, peeled and finely chopped

2 garlic cloves, peeled and finely chopped

2 tablespoons golden raisins

12 pimiento-stuffed olives

1¼ cups peeled and chopped ripe tomatoes

1 tablespoon fresh lime juice

1 teaspoon sugar

2 teaspoons salt

Freshly ground black pepper

For the sauce

4 large ancho chiles

3 tablespoons peanut or canola oil

1 medium onion, peeled and finely chopped

2 garlic cloves, peeled and finely chopped

½ teaspoon ground allspice

1 teaspoon sugar

1 cup canned tomato sauce

¼ teaspoon salt, or to taste

2½ cups crushed tortilla chips, preferably
    baked (see Note)

5 ounces grated sharp Cheddar cheese

Soak and cook the beans according to the general directions on page 47 reserving the cooking liquid.

Put the oil in a large frying pan and set over medium heat. Add the onion and garlic. Stir and fry until the onion turns translucent, reducing the heat as needed. Now add the golden raisins and olives. Stir once and add the tomatoes. Stir and cook on medium heat for 5 to 6 minutes, or until the tomatoes are slightly reduced. Add the cooked beans and their liquid, the lime juice, sugar, salt, and pepper to taste. Stir and bring to a simmer and cook gently for 10 minutes. Taste for the balance of seasonings and adjust, if needed.

Meanwhile, make the sauce. Combine the ancho chiles and 1½ cups of water in a small pot and bring to a boil. Cover, turn the heat down to low, and simmer gently for 5 minutes. Turn off the heat and let the pot sit, covered, until the anchos are cool enough to handle. Lift them out of the liquid; save the liquid. Remove the stems and seeds. Put the anchos in a coarse sieve set over a bowl and press to push out as much pulp as you can. Stir the reserved cooking liquid into the pulp and set aside.

Put the oil for the sauce in a frying pan and set over medium heat. When hot, add the onion and garlic and stir and sauté until the onion is soft and translucent, turning the heat down as needed. Add the allspice, sugar, tomato sauce, salt, and 1 cup of water. Bring to a simmer, cover, and simmer gently for 10 minutes, stirring now and then.

Combine the tomato mixture and the ancho paste and blend until you have a coarse puree. Taste for the balance of flavors.

Preheat the oven to 350°F.

Lightly oil a 9×9-inch casserole dish and scatter half the crushed tortillas on the bottom. Top with the beans. Scatter the remaining tortillas over the beans. Pour the ancho sauce over all, then top it all with the grated cheese. Bake for 35 minutes, or until the cheese is lightly browned. Serve hot.

Note: If you have day-old tortillas lying around, use them for the tortilla-chip topping; crisp them in a low oven and then break them up. Otherwise, use purchased tortilla chips, preferably the baked variety. If baked chips are unavailable, use low-salt fried ones. You'll need only part of a 7-ounce bag.

SERVES 4 TO 6

Kidney Beans, White, and Other White Beans (Including Lima Beans)

I have, rather loosely, combined several varieties of white and semiwhite beans into this section, from the large "giant" white kidney beans and the smaller cannellini, navy, and Great Northern beans of the common American variety *(Phaseolus vulgaris)* to the lima beans of Central American origin *(Phaseolus lunatus),* which are distinguished by the fine ridges that radiate from their central "eye."

The sizes and shapes of these "white" beans go from very large and kidney-shaped to small and spherical or elongated specimens. They are cooked in more or less the same way, with the larger ones taking a bit longer than the smaller ones.

All these beans turn buttery when cooked until just done and then baked gently in a slow oven. You will find exquisite "casseroles" from areas as disparate as Greece and Cuba in this section.

Cooking white beans: Pick over the beans and wash them (page 5). Drain. Cover with 5 inches of water and leave to soak overnight. Alternatively, use the Quick-Soak Method (page 6). Drain, discarding the soaking liquid.

Cover the beans with about 3 times their volume of water (this varies a bit according to the recipe) and bring to a boil. Remove the scum that rises to the top. Cover partially, turn the heat down to low, and cook anywhere from 40 minutes to 2 hours, or until the beans are tender, adding 1 teaspoon salt for every cup of dried beans in the last 10 minutes of cooking.

More specifically, allow 1 to 1½ hours for cannellini beans, navy beans, Great Northern beans, and large limas; 40 minutes to 1 hour for small limas; and 1½ to 2 hours for large white kidney beans.

One cup of dried beans should yield about 3 cups of cooked drained beans.

Substituting canned beans: If you wish to use canned beans, note that 1½ cups of dried white kidney beans yield 4 cups of cooked drained beans. If the liquid from cooking the beans is required in the recipe, you will have to use water or a light stock, as the liquid from canned beans should be discarded.

Pressure cooker method for white beans Follow the soaking instructions given on page 6. Drain.

Put the beans in a pressure cooker. Add enough water to cover them by an inch. Cover and bring up to pressure. Cook cannellini, navy, Great Northern, and large lima beans for 8 minutes, smaller limas for 4 minutes, and large white kidney beans for 10 minutes, allowing the pressure to drop by itself. Salt should ideally be added in the next stage of cooking.

From the nuns at the Ormylia Monastery in Macedonia

Baked Lima Beans or Large White Beans

GREECE

Fassoulia Fourno

You may make this dish with large white beans or large lima beans. The nuns serve it as a main course, with bread, salad, fruit, and olives—a simple repast that is both nourishing and healthy.

1 cup dried lima beans or any large white beans, picked over and washed

¼ cup olive oil

1 medium onion, peeled, halved lengthwise, and cut into thin half moons

1 medium carrot, peeled and cut into ⅓-inch-thick slices

2 good-sized (6–7 ounce) tomatoes, finely chopped

1¼ teaspoons salt

Freshly ground black pepper

2 to 3 tablespoons finely chopped fresh parsley

3 tablespoons fresh oregano or 1 teaspoon dried oregano

Soak the beans overnight in water to cover by 5 inches or use the Quick-Soak Method (page 6). Drain, discarding the soaking liquid.

Put the beans in a pot with 3 cups of fresh water and bring to a boil. Remove the scum that rises to the top. Cover, turn the heat down to low, and simmer gently for 40 to 60 minutes, or until the beans are just tender.

Meanwhile, put the oil in a flame- and ovenproof casserole-type dish and set over medium-high heat. When hot, add the onion. Stir and cook for 1 to 2 minutes, or until the onion has just wilted. Put in the carrot and cook another minute, stirring now and then. Now put in the tomatoes and cook 7 to 10 minutes, or until the tomatoes have softened. Turn off the heat.

Preheat the oven to 325°F.

When the beans have finished cooking, add them and their cooking liquid to the dish with the onion, carrot, and tomatoes. Add the salt, lots of black pepper, the parsley, and oregano. Stir to mix. Put the casserole dish into the oven and bake, uncovered, for 2 hours. Serve hot.

SERVES 4

White Beans with Rosemary

I adapted this dish from a fashionable Paris bistro, making it completely vegetarian. You can make it with large white beans or large lima beans.

Here is my favorite way of serving it: I put it in the center of a large plate, grate some Parmesan cheese over it, and then top it all with some garlicky greens such as broccoli rabe, spinach, or Stir-Fried Beet Greens with Ginger and Green Chiles (page 215). All you need then is some crusty bread on the side.

1½ cups dried lima beans or any large white beans, picked over and washed

¼ cup olive oil

1 teaspoon finely chopped fresh rosemary or ½ teaspoon very finely crushed dried rosemary

1 medium onion, peeled and finely chopped

2 garlic cloves, peeled and finely chopped

1 medium tomato, finely chopped

1 bay leaf

1¼ teaspoons salt

Freshly ground black pepper

Soak the beans overnight in water to cover by 5 inches or use the Quick-Soak Method (page 6). Drain, discarding the soaking liquid.

Put the oil in a wide, medium pot and set over medium-high heat. When hot, put in the rosemary, onion, and garlic. Stir and fry for 3 to 4 minutes, or until the onion just starts to brown. Add the tomato and bay leaf and stir for a minute, then add the drained beans, 3½ cups of water, salt, and pepper to taste. Stir and bring to a boil. Cover, turn the heat down to low, and simmer gently for 1½ hours, or until the beans are quite tender.

SERVES 4

Mirta Carbonell's

Aromatic Cuban White Bean and Pumpkin Stew

CUBA

Potaje de Freijoles Blanco

Here is a wonderful stew for a crowd. You may easily halve the recipe if you like, but remember that it lasts well in the refrigerator for 2 to 3 days and may also be frozen. I sometimes serve it with rice or crusty French or Italian bread, vegetables, salads, and cheeses but often, for an informal buffet, I pile a stack of freshly steamed corn tortillas or heated pita breads on the side in a large napkin and also put out lots of grated cheese (Monterey Jack or Cheddar), some hot sauces (such as Trinidadian Pepper Sauce, page 771), some roasted and lightly dressed red peppers (page 262), and a green salad. People can then roll some of the food—such as the beans, pepper sauce, and cheese—in the tortillas or stuff pita pockets with it and have the rest on the side. It is not very Cuban but it is very good.

You may use any dried white beans, from the larger kidney beans to the smaller cannellini, navy, or Great Northern beans. The cooking times will vary slightly according to the size and age of the beans.

The two Cuban seasonings used here, culantro leaves and cachucha *chiles, are both highly aromatic and, alas, not so easy to find. The long serrated leaves of the former are similar in taste to fresh cilantro and are sold in Caribbean and some Thai markets. (It is called* shadow beni *in Trinidad,* pak chee farang *or "foreign cilantro" in Thai shops, and* recao *in some Hispanic shops.) If you cannot get them, fresh cilantro makes a reasonable substitute.*

Cachucha chiles are another matter. Of the Scotch bonnet family, they are small, green, and squat, with an amazing, tropical citrus perfume. What is more, they are not in the least bit hot so the somewhat similar habanero chiles—which have the perfume but a lot of heat—cannot be substituted. Cachucha chiles are sold only in Cuban shops. My suggestion would be to use a mild green pepper, such as the light green Italian or Greek pepper or even a green bell pepper when you are preparing the sofrito, *or sautéed mixture, and then throw in some lemongrass or grated lemon rind as well as some grated orange rind when you add the cooked beans to it.*

1 pound white kidney beans, cannellini beans, navy beans, or Great Northern beans, picked over and washed

12 ounces pumpkin or butternut squash, peeled, seeded, and cut into ¾-inch dice (about 2 cups)

Sofrito

5 tablespoons olive oil

1 medium onion, peeled and finely chopped

4 garlic cloves, peeled and finely chopped

8 to 10 *cachucha* chiles, seeds removed and finely chopped (or 3 tablespoons any other mild green pepper, seeded and finely chopped—see Note)

¼ cup finely chopped culantro leaves or fresh cilantro, packed

½ teaspoon ground cumin

1 cup canned tomato sauce

1¾ teaspoons salt, or to taste

Soak the beans overnight in water to cover by 5 inches or use the Quick-Soak Method (page 6). Drain, discarding the soaking liquid.

In a large pot, bring the beans, pumpkin, and 5 cups of water to a boil. Partially cover the pot, leaving it just slightly ajar, turn the heat down to low, and simmer gently for 40 to 80 minutes, or until the beans are tender. Older and larger beans will take longer to cook.

(recipe continues)

While the beans are cooking, prepare the *sofrito*. Put the oil in a large frying pan and set it on medium-high heat. When hot, put in the onion and garlic and stir and fry for a minute. Now put in the chiles and the culantro or fresh cilantro leaves, turn the heat to medium, and stir for a minute. Put in the cumin and stir once, then add the tomato sauce and bring to a simmer. Turn the heat to low and simmer very gently, stirring now and then, for 10 minutes.

When the beans are tender, add the salt and the *sofrito* to the pot. (If you used plain peppers, this would be the time to add the lemongrass, etc.) Stir and bring to a simmer. Simmer very gently for 10 to 15 minutes, or until all the flavors are blended, stirring now and then.

Note: If using green peppers, add the bottom 6 inches of a lemongrass stalk, with the bulbous end lightly mashed or 1 teaspoon grated lemon rind as well as 2 teaspoons grated orange rind. Remove the lemongrass before serving.

SERVES 8

Marios Mourtezis'

Cypriot Lima Bean Stew

CYPRUS

Fassoulia Yakhni

This is a simple everyday stew eaten in Cyprus with crusty bread, olives, cucumbers, grapes, and cheese. After all the stew ingredients have boiled, a traditional tiganissi *or final flavoring of red chile, onion, garlic, and tomatoes, all sautéed quickly in olive oil, is added to the mixture.*

1 cup dried lima beans or any medium white beans, picked over and washed (page 5)

1 large celery stalk, cut into ½-inch dice

1 medium carrot, peeled and cut into ½-inch rounds or dice

1 smallish potato, peeled and cut into ½-inch dice

1 teaspoon salt, or to taste

Freshly ground black pepper

For the tiganissi

3 tablespoons olive oil

1 whole dried hot red chile

1 smallish onion, peeled and finely chopped

2 garlic cloves, peeled and finely chopped

3 fresh or canned plum tomatoes, chopped

1 teaspoon tomato paste

Soak the beans overnight in water to cover by 5 inches or use the Quick-Soak Method (page 6). Drain, discarding the soaking liquid.

Put the drained beans and 3¼ cups of water in a heavy, medium saucepan. Bring to a boil. Partially cover, leaving the lid very slightly ajar, turn the heat down to low, and simmer gently until the beans are tender, anywhere from 40 to 80 minutes. Add the celery, carrot, potato, and salt and bring to a boil again. Cover, turn the heat down to low, and simmer gently for 30 minutes. Add pepper to taste and stir to mix. Set aside while you make the *tiganissi*.

Put the oil in a medium frying pan and set over medium-high heat. When hot, put in the red chile and stir for 5 seconds; the chile should darken. Now add the onion and garlic. Stir and fry for 3 to 4 minutes, or until the onion browns a little. Put in the tomatoes and stir for 2 minutes, or until the tomatoes soften. Add the tomato paste and stir for another 30 seconds. Empty the contents of the frying pan into the pan with the beans. Stir to mix. Check for seasonings, adding a bit more salt if needed.

SERVES 3 TO 4

Baked Beans with Nigerian Seasonings

NIGERIA

In this Nigerian recipe, the beans are baked with the addition of peanut butter and curry powder. It is exceptionally good. Serve this with a crusty bread and a salad or a selection of vegetables. Cheese may also be served on the side.

1 cup dried cannellini beans or other medium white beans

¼ cup peanut or canola oil

1 medium onion (4 ounces), peeled, halved, and thinly sliced

4 garlic cloves, peeled and finely chopped

1 tablespoon curry powder (hot or mild, as preferred—you may use My Curry Powder, page 707)

2 good-sized (12 to 13 ounces) tomatoes, peeled and finely chopped

1½ tablespoons smooth peanut butter

1¼ teaspoons salt

Freshly ground black pepper

Soak the beans overnight in water to cover by 5 inches or use the Quick-Soak Method (page 6). Drain, discarding the soaking liquid.

(recipe continues)

Put the beans in a pot with 3½ cups of water and bring to a boil, skimming off the scum that rises to the top. Cover partially, turn the heat down to low, and simmer gently for 40 to 60 minutes, or until the beans are just tender.

Meanwhile, heat the oil in a flame- and ovenproof, casserole-type dish over medium-high heat. Add the onion and stir and cook for 1 to 2 minutes, or until the onion has just wilted. Put in the garlic and cook another 2 minutes, stirring now and then. Add the curry powder and stir once or twice, then stir in the tomatoes. Cook 7 to 10 minutes, or until the tomatoes have softened. Turn off the heat.

Preheat the oven to 325°F.

Put the peanut butter in a small bowl or cup. When the beans have finished cooking, remove about 6 tablespoons of their liquid from the pot and slowly add it to the peanut butter, stirring as you go. Empty the beans with their remaining liquid into the casserole with the onion, garlic, and tomatoes. Stir in the peanut butter mixture, the salt, and lots of black pepper. Bake, uncovered, for 2 hours, until very tender. Serve hot.

SERVES 4

Lentils, Green, Brown, and Red

Archaeologists seem to think that lentils may well have been the first cultivated crop, probably in the same Tigris-Euphrates valley where civilization was dawning. The earliest lentils, dating back almost nine thousand years, have been found in Qalat Jarmo, Iraq. Ancient containers for lentils have been unearthed in Turkey; we know that traveling seeds made their way to an island in a Swiss lake when the region was still in the Bronze Age; and a pharaoh's tomb in Thebes has yielded a lentil puree, delighting us with the thought that not only were lentils enjoyed by the royals of the time (four thousand years ago) but that they were considered ideal food for otherworldly journeys.

The popularity of lentils has now spread to much of the world, although the United States, which began to cultivate them earnestly in this century and does a booming export business, has yet to integrate this protein-rich food into its daily diet. In much of the Middle East, Southern Asia, and the Mediterranean, they are combined with pasta, rice, herbs, and almost every conceivable vegetable to produce hundreds of exquisite dishes.

The lentils available to us today may be divided into three categories: ordinary lentils (either brown or green), small French lentils, and red lentils.

Ordinary lentils: These are the brownish or greenish lentils sold by supermarkets and health food shops. I will, from now on, just call them "lentils," as that is how they are labeled most of the time. Sometimes, I do see the "green lentils" or "brown lentils" label, but the two are interchangeable. On the whole, they cook in exactly the same way, though their final color might be slightly different. These lentils are whole, with their skins or "coats" still on. These are the lentils you need if you are going to sprout them. I find that as new varieties are cultivated, lentils are taking less and less time to cook.

Basic method for cooking lentils Pick over and wash the lentils. Drain. Combine 1 cup of lentils with 2½ cups of water and bring to a boil. Cover partially, turn the heat down to low, and cook for about 20 minutes for salads (drain the lentils and use), 30 to 35 minutes for main dishes, and 40 minutes for soups and purees. About 1 teaspoon of salt may be added toward the end of the cooking time.

How to sprout lentils: Lentil sprouts taste wonderful, and are fast cooking and easy to digest. To make them, soak ½ cup whole lentils in lukewarm water for 12 hours, changing the water once (this can be after 8 hours). Drain. Line a tray with several thicknesses of dampened paper towels. Spread the soaked lentils over the top. Cover with another 2 layers of dampened paper towels and set aside in a dark place (I use the oven). Sprinkle with water every 8 hours or so to make sure that the paper remains damp. After 36 hours, you should have small sprouts about ½ inch long. Wash gently, removing the skins that float to the top. Store in a plastic bag or sealed container for up to a week. Sprinkle with water if the sprouts appear dry. One-half cup of lentils will yield 2½ cups of sprouts.

Cooking lentil sprouts: Sprouts cook fast. To stir-fry them, put a little oil in a wok or frying pan set on medium-high heat and when hot, put in the sprouts. Stir-fry for 3 to 4 minutes. Add about ½ teaspoon salt, if you want, and toss. Almost any other seasonings may be added, even a salad dressing. If you wish to avoid the oil, cook the sprouts, covered, in 4 to 5 tablespoons of water for 3 to 4 minutes or steam them for 6 to 8 minutes and then dress them as you like.

French and Italian lentils: French lentils, called *lentilles à la reine* when Queen Marie Leszcznska, wife of France's Louis XV, decided to dine on them, and now known more simply as *lentilles le Puy* or *lentilles verte du Puy,* are smaller in size, take a bit longer to cook, and hold their shape better. In America's top restaurants, it is these that have the cachet that counts. There is another lentil from Castelluccio in Umbria, which is similar but harder to find. Cook either of these two varieties in 3 times as much water for 40 to 60 minutes, or until tender.

Red lentils: Even though Indian shops sell whole, unhulled red lentils *(sabut masoor)* and split but unhulled red lentils *(chilke wali masoor),* it is the hulled and split red lentils (sold in health food shops, specialty shops, Middle Eastern shops, and South Asian shops) that I have used in all the recipes in this book. Known as masoor dal in India and Pakistan and as Egyptian lentils or red lentils in the West, these are eaten throughout South Asia, the Middle East, and North Africa. In their raw state, they have a beautiful salmon color. Unfortunately, the color vanishes in the cooking and the lentils turn a dull yellow. Their taste is earthy and their texture slightly grainy.

They are excellent for both soups and stews and may be combined with other grains, lentils, and vegetables to add their own special "meaty" taste. I have known them to be used to great effect as a base for a Turkish stew, Anatolian Red Lentil Stew with Wheat Berries and Chickpeas (page 71). They can also be cooked very simply, with just a tarka of different spice combinations.

I find it very interesting that in India on holy days and fast days red lentils are never eaten by Hindus. It could be that because they came from the Middle East, even now, more than a thousand years later, they have not lost their foreignness in the we-never-forget eyes of Hindus or it could be that they are slightly "heavier" and therefore not considered ideal for times of cleansing and fasting. They are, however, very popular among the Muslims of the subcontinent.

To cook red lentils, see the basic technique in the recipe that follows.

Basic Red Lentils

Red lentils (also known as masoor dal) are cooked almost exactly like hulled and split mung beans (moong dal). Once cooked, they can be finished off in any of the ways suggested on pages 6 to 7. (Do not serve this basic recipe—it still needs finishing off with a tarka or with the addition of other ingredients or both.)

Turmeric should be added only for Indian dishes. Leave it out for all others.

1 cup red lentils (masoor dal), picked over, washed in several changes of water, and drained

¼ teaspoon ground turmeric

1 to 1¼ teaspoons salt

Put the red lentils and 4 cups of water in a heavy-bottomed pot and bring to a boil. Watch carefully to ensure that the contents of the pot do not boil over. Skim off the froth that rises to the top. Add the turmeric and stir once. Partially cover, leaving the lid very slightly ajar, turn the heat down to low, and cook very gently for 40 to 50 minutes, or until the lentils are tender. Add the salt and stir to mix.

You may finish off the dish right away or refrigerate the lentils for up to 3 to 4 days and reheat them. To reheat the lentils, stir well and add just enough water to prevent them from sticking at the bottom of the pot, usually just a few tablespoons. Set over low heat and stir now and then until just bubbling. You may now proceed with your chosen recipe.

SERVES 4 TO 6

Lentils with Onion and Garlic MIDDLE EAST

A simple dish to be eaten with Moroccan breads, pita bread, or any crusty European loaf. I just love to serve it with a Palestinian dish, Sliced Tomatoes in a Tomato Sauce (page 303). Salads and yogurt relishes may be offered on the side.

1 cup dried green lentils

3 tablespoons olive oil

1 medium onion (5 ounces), peeled, halved, and finely sliced

1 whole dried hot red chile

3 garlic cloves, peeled and chopped

1 teaspoon salt, or to taste

Freshly ground black pepper

Lemon wedges

Pick over the lentils and wash them in several changes of water. Drain.

Put the oil into a medium sauté pan and set over medium-high heat. When hot, add the onion. Stir and fry, turning the heat down as needed, until the onion is reddish-brown and crisp. Remove the onion with a slotted spoon and spread out on a paper towel. Put the red chile and garlic into the oil remaining in the pan. Stir for 10 seconds and put in the lentils and 2½ cups of water. Bring to a boil. Turn the heat down to low and partially cover the pan. Cook gently for 30 to 35 minutes, or until the lentils are tender. Remove the red chile, if desired. Add the salt and pepper and stir to mix.

To serve, sprinkle crisp onion slices over the top and offer lemon wedges on the side.

SERVES 4

Lentils Topped with Gingery Spinach and Yogurt

An elaboration on the preceding recipe, Lentils with Onion and Garlic, this is really a meal in itself. Prepare the lentils and crispy onions just as for that recipe, keeping the lentils warm in their own pan and reserving the fried onions to one side. (Lemon wedges are not needed.) Then proceed with the recipe below.

For serving, I find old-fashioned soup plates to be ideal. Spread the lentils at the bottom of each soup plate. Spread the spinach over the top of the lentils, bunched up a bit toward the center. Now put a generous dollop of creamy yogurt on top of the spinach. Scatter the browned onions over the top of the yogurt and the spinach. Serve while the lentils and spinach are still hot.

As a variation, you could substitute chard or any other greens of your choice for the spinach. The yogurt may be replaced with sour cream or a generous slice of grilled goat cheese.

3 tablespoons olive oil

1 (¾-inch) piece of fresh ginger, peeled and cut into very thin slices, then into very fine strips

20 ounces fresh spinach, trimmed and washed

½ teaspoon salt

⅛ teaspoon cayenne (optional)

1 recipe Lentils with Onion and Garlic (page 61)

4 generous dollops of creamy plain yogurt (Greek yogurt may be used, if available)

Put the oil in a large wok or sauté pan and set over high heat. When hot, add the ginger slices and stir for 20 to 30 seconds, or until the ginger just starts to brown. Put in the spinach, salt, and cayenne. Stir and cook until the spinach has wilted completely, 4 to 5 minutes. Turn off the heat. Serve as suggested above, with the lentils forming the bottom layer, the spinach next, and a final dollop of yogurt. Scatter the fried onions over the top. Serve hot.

SERVES 4

Androche Markidis'

Lentils with Rice

Moudjendra

This is a hearty, risotto-like dish which, with its tiganissi *or final flavoring of browned onions and its lemony aftertaste, has a distinct Cypriot feel to it—part Greek and part Arab. It is perfect for parties. Leftovers, if there are any, may be used as stuffing for tomatoes (page 303) and peppers or may be formed into patties and browned in a lightly oiled, nonstick frying pan.*

As a variation, this dish may be made with what Greek Cypriots call "fava," which is really yellow split peas. Instead of water, vegetable stock may be used. Rather than mix the lemon juice with the lentils and rice, Syrians, who have a similar dish, offer lemon wedges on the side. Sometimes I stir grated Parmesan cheese into the lentils before serving.

I love to serve this with Sliced Tomatoes in a Tomato Sauce (page 303), Soft Yogurt Cheese with Feta (page 559), and a crisp green salad.

2 cups lentils

1 cup long-grain rice (I use Thai jasmine rice but any long-grain rice will do)

1½ teaspoons salt

¼ cup fresh lemon juice

For the tiganissi

7 tablespoons olive oil

3 garlic cloves, peeled and finely sliced

1 medium onion, peeled, cut in half lengthwise, and then cut into fine half rings

Combine the lentils and 7 cups of water in a wide, nonstick pan. Bring to a boil. Cover, turn the heat down to low, and cook 25 minutes. Add the rice and salt. Stir to mix and bring to a boil again. Cover, turn the heat down to very low, and cook gently for another 25 minutes. Turn off the heat. The lentils and rice should have the slightly loose consistency of a risotto. Add the lemon juice and mix gently. Cover again and keep warm.

Put the oil in a medium frying pan and set over medium-high heat. When hot, put in the garlic and onion. Stir and fry, turning the heat down as needed, until the onion and garlic are medium brown and crisp. Quickly remove some of the onions and garlic with a slotted spoon and spread out on paper towels. Pour the remaining contents of the pan, oil and seasonings, over the lentils. Gently mix them in. Garnish with the reserved onions when serving.

SERVES 6 TO 8

Lentils in a Sauce

MOROCCO

Lentilles en Sauce

If you have access to French lentils, by all means use them because they do have a wonderfully firm texture. However, you may use ordinary supermarket lentils. Keep in mind that the cooking time may be shorter by a good 15 to 20 minutes.

Serve with bread (a Moroccan bread would be ideal but any crusty bread will do) and some vegetables, perhaps in the form of Moroccan, Greek, or Turkish salads. I happen to love it with two Palestinian dishes, Buttery-Soft Slices of Deep-Fried Eggplant with Garlic (page 191) and Sliced Tomatoes in a Tomato Sauce (page 303).

Grating tomatoes is a wonderful way to get a coarse puree and leave the skin behind!

1 cup dried lentils or French lentils (*lentilles le Puy,* also called *lentilles verte du Puy*)

1 medium onion, finely chopped or grated

1 medium, very ripe tomato, grated

2 garlic cloves, peeled and finely chopped

4 tablespoons finely chopped fresh parsley

2 tablespoons finely chopped fresh cilantro leaves

1½ teaspoons paprika

1 teaspoon ground cumin

Freshly ground black pepper

1¼ to 1½ teaspoons salt

1 tablespoon olive oil

Pick over the lentils and wash them in several changes of cold water.

Put the lentils, onion, tomato, garlic, parsley, cilantro, paprika, cumin, black pepper to taste, and 3 cups of water in a medium pot and set on medium-high heat. Bring to a boil without allowing it to boil over. Turn the heat down to low and cover partially. Cook gently for 30 minutes. Add the salt and stir well. Cook, partially covered, another 30 to 40 minutes, or until the lentils are tender. Stir in the oil. Serve hot.

SERVES 6

Tex-Mex Vegetarian Chili

UNITED STATES

I love chili and this is about as good as it gets. I do not use any commercially mixed chili powders as they tend to contain too much salt. It is much easier to put in all the spices that go into the making of a chili powder, which is what I have done here.

There are many ways to serve this. My favorite is to ladle the chili into individual bowls and offer baskets of fresh, hot tortillas and some Guacamole (page 613) on the side. If you are not up to all that, you may put a dollop of sour cream over each bowl and serve some tortilla chips and a green salad on the side. Another way is to put all the heated chili into a baking dish, cover the entire top with grated sharp Cheddar or Monterey Jack cheese, and then put the dish briefly under the broiler until the cheese melts and browns in spots. Pita breads or tortillas may be offered on the side as well as a green salad.

This is a great dish for parties, as it can easily be doubled or tripled. If you use a larger pot, all cooking times will remain the same. You may easily make it 24 hours ahead of time and then refrigerate it. If the chili thickens too much as it cools, thin it out with a little water when you reheat it.

I have suggested using anywhere from ¼ to 1 jalapeño pepper. A whole one will make the chili quite hot while ¼ will keep the heat at medium.

For the red kidney beans needed here, you may cook them yourself according to directions on page 47 or use canned ones.

Even though there are many ingredients here, the chili is very easy to make.

3 tablespoons canola or olive oil

1 medium onion, peeled and finely chopped

3 garlic cloves, peeled and finely chopped

½ large green pepper, seeds removed and finely chopped

¼ to 1 jalapeño pepper (or ½ to 2 any other fresh hot green chile), finely chopped

1½ teaspoons ground cumin seeds

2 teaspoons paprika

½ teaspoon dried thyme

½ teaspoon dried crumbled sage

1 teaspoon dried oregano

¼ teaspoon cayenne

1 cup lentils, picked over and washed

1 cup cooked drained red kidney beans

2 to 3 canned plum tomatoes, drained and finely chopped

3 tablespoons chopped fresh cilantro leaves

1½ teaspoons salt

1 tablespoon yellow cornmeal

Put the oil in a medium pan and set over medium-high heat. When hot, put in the onion, garlic, green pepper, and jalapeño. Stir and fry for about 3 minutes, or until the seasonings just start to brown. Turn down the heat to medium-low and continue to sauté for another 3 minutes. Now put in the cumin, paprika, thyme, sage, oregano, and cayenne. Stir briskly once or twice and put in the lentils, 4½ cups of water, the red kidney beans, plum tomatoes, cilantro leaves, and salt. Bring to a boil. Cover, turn the heat down to low, and cook gently for 50 minutes.

Mix the cornmeal with 3 tablespoons water and then pour the mixture into the chili pot. Stir to mix and bring to a simmer. Cover and simmer gently for 10 minutes, stirring now and then.

SERVES 4

Lentils Topped with Garlic Mushrooms

This is a meal in itself. Serve it with a nice crusty bread.

To make it, you need to cook lentils according to the recipe for Lentils with Onion and Garlic. Just keep the lentils warm in their own pan and keep the fried onions to one side. Make the mushrooms at the last minute. They take less than 5 minutes to prepare.

1 pound medium white mushrooms

¼ cup olive oil

3 garlic cloves, peeled and very finely chopped

1 to 1¼ teaspoons salt

Freshly ground black pepper

⅛ teaspoon cayenne (optional)

5 tablespoons finely chopped fresh parsley

1 recipe Lentils with Onion and Garlic
   (page 61)

4 large dollops of creamy plain yogurt (Greek
   yogurt may be used, if available)

Wipe the mushrooms off with a damp cloth and cut lengthwise, thinly and evenly, into slices that include the stem.

Put the oil into a large frying pan or wok and set over high heat. When hot, put in the garlic. Stir once and put in the mushrooms. Stir and fry until the mushrooms have wilted. Put in the salt, pepper, and cayenne, if using. Stir to mix. Put in 4 tablespoons of the parsley. Stir again and turn off the heat.

Serve hot in old-fashioned soup plates, with the lentils forming the bottom layer, the mushrooms heaped on top of the lentils, and a final dollop of yogurt. Sprinkle the browned onions over the yogurt and the remaining parsley over the very top. Offer lemon wedges on the side.

SERVES 4

Stir-Fried Lentil Sprouts with Ginger

This is light and simple.

2 tablespoons peanut or canola oil

1 garlic clove, peeled and lightly crushed

2 slices of fresh ginger

½ teaspoon salt

Lentil sprouts, made with ½ cup (3 ounces) lentils according to the directions on page 59

1 teaspoon oriental sesame oil

Put the peanut oil into a large wok or frying pan and set over medium-high heat. When hot, put in the garlic and ginger. Stir and fry, pressing down on the seasonings, for 15 seconds. Put in the salt and lentil sprouts. Stir and fry for 3 to 4 minutes, or until the sprouts are just cooked through. Add the sesame oil and toss again. Serve hot, at room temperature, or chilled.

SERVES 3 TO 4

Stir-Fried Lentil Sprouts with Mustard Seeds and Chiles   INDIA
Phuti Sabut Masoor

This can be made as spicy as you like.

2 tablespoons peanut or canola oil

1 teaspoon whole brown mustard seeds

1 scallion, cut crosswise into very thin rounds (green and white sections)

½ to 1 fresh hot green chile, finely chopped

Lentil sprouts, made with ½ cup (3 ounces) lentils according to the directions on page 59

½ teaspoon salt

1 tablespoon fresh lemon juice, or to taste

Freshly ground black pepper

Put the peanut oil into a large wok or frying pan and set over medium-high heat. When hot, put in the mustard seeds. As soon as they pop, a matter of seconds, put in the scallion. Stir and fry for 15 seconds. Put in the chile, lentil sprouts, and salt. Stir and fry for 3 to 4 minutes, or until the sprouts are just cooked through. Add the lemon juice and pepper to taste. Toss to mix and taste for the balance of flavors, adding more as needed. Serve hot, at room temperature, or chilled.

SERVES 3 TO 4

Red Lentils with Cumin and Scallion   INDIA
Tarka Masoor Dal

Here's a North Indian way to prepare this lentil.

1 cup red lentils *(masoor dal)*, cooked according
    to the basic recipe with ground turmeric
    on page 60

2 tablespoons *ghee* (page 723)

½ teaspoon whole cumin seeds

1 scallion, cut into fine slivers all the way up
    its green section

¼ teaspoon cayenne, or to taste

Heat the red lentils and keep over a low flame.

Put the oil in a small frying pan and set over medium-high heat. When very hot, put in the cumin seeds. Let the cumin seeds sizzle for 10 seconds. Now put in the scallion. Stir and fry until the scallion pieces turn brown at the edges. Now put in the cayenne, take the frying pan off the fire, and pour its contents into the pot with the lentils. Stir to mix.

SERVES 4 TO 6

"Dry" Red Lentils   MIDDLE EAST

When the lentils finish cooking in this recipe, they are not soupy and wet but almost dry. You may eat them just the way they are with a flatbread, a salad, and a yogurt relish, or else make a quick "sandwich" by stuffing them into pita bread halves, together with a yogurt relish, some chopped tomatoes (or a simple tomato-cucumber salad), and some shredded lettuce.

You may, if you like, add a mixture of chopped celery and carrot (about 2 tablespoons each) to the onion and garlic during the initial sautéing and, if you like, a selection of chopped fresh herbs, such as parsley, thyme, and oregano.

1 cup red lentils *(masoor dal)*

3 tablespoons olive oil

½ medium onion, cut into fine half rings

2 garlic cloves, lightly crushed and peeled but
    left whole

¾ teaspoon salt

Pick over the lentils and wash in several changes of water. Drain. Put in a bowl and cover well with water. Leave to soak for 3 hours. Drain.

Put the oil in a medium pot and set over medium-high heat. When hot, put in the onion and garlic. Stir and fry for about 4 minutes, or until the onion is medium brown. Add the drained lentils. Stir and sauté for a minute. Now add 1 cup of water and the salt. Stir and bring to a boil. Cover, turn the heat down to very low, and cook for 20 minutes.

SERVES 4

Red Lentils Hyderabadi

INDIA

Masoor Dal Hyderabadi

Here's a very simple way to finish off red lentils in the style of the southern Indian city of Hyderabad. If you cannot get fresh curry leaves, use 2 bay leaves or 4 to 5 fresh basil leaves. Each will give a different flavor.

This dish may be served with any flatbread or rice. Indian vegetables, yogurt relishes and pickles, or else a plain green salad should be served on the side.

1 cup red lentils *(masoor dal),* cooked according to the basic recipe with ground turmeric on page 60

2 tablespoons peanut or canola oil

½ teaspoon whole brown mustard seeds

1 to 2 whole dried hot red chiles

8 to 10 fresh curry leaves (see above for substitutes)

3 garlic cloves, peeled

A few squeezes of fresh lime juice

Heat the red lentils and keep over a low flame.

Put the oil in a small frying pan and set over medium-high heat. When hot, put in the mustard seeds. As soon as they pop, a matter of seconds, put in the red chiles. Stir them once and quickly put in the curry leaves. Stir once and put in the garlic cloves. Turn the heat to medium and lightly brown the garlic on all sides. Now pour the contents of the pot, oil and seasonings, over the cooked lentils. Squeeze lime juice over the top, stir, and serve.

Note: The red chiles should only be eaten by those who know what they are doing.

SERVES 4

Red Lentils with Zucchini

INDIA

Vegetarian Dalcha

The vegetable in this dish is usually the bowling pin–shaped, pale green bottle gourd. I have worked out a version using the faster-cooking zucchini. This is a specialty from the South Indian city of Hyderabad. Rice and a yogurt relish, such as Carrot "Raita" (page 547), should be served on the side.

1 cup red lentils *(masoor dal)*, picked over, washed in several changes of water, and drained

¼ teaspoon ground turmeric

Salt

¼ cup peanut or canola oil

4 whole cardamom pods

1 (1½-inch) cinnamon stick

2 bay leaves

½ teaspoon whole cumin seeds

1 medium onion, very finely chopped

2 teaspoons peeled fresh ginger grated to a pulp

3 garlic cloves, peeled and mashed

1 medium zucchini, cut into 1-inch rounds and then halved crosswise

Freshly ground black pepper

¼ to ½ teaspoon cayenne

A few squeezes of fresh lime juice

Put the red lentils and 4 cups of water in a heavy-bottomed pot and bring to a boil. Watch carefully so that the contents of the pot do not boil over. Remove the froth that rises to the top. Add the turmeric and stir once. Cover, leaving the lid very slightly ajar. Turn the heat down to low and cook very gently for 40 to 50 minutes, or until the lentils are tender. Add 1 to 1¼ teaspoons salt, just enough for the lentils, and stir to mix.

Put the oil in a nonstick frying pan and set over medium-high heat. When very hot, put in the cardamom pods, cinnamon, bay leaves, and whole cumin seeds. Stir for a few seconds and put in the onion. Stir and fry until the onion pieces turn medium brown. Put in the ginger and garlic. Continue to stir and fry for another minute. Now put in the zucchini, black pepper to taste, cayenne, and another ¼ teaspoon salt. Stir for a minute. Add ½ cup of water, cover, turn the heat down to low, and cook for 2 minutes. Uncover, stir gently again, and then empty the contents of the frying pan into the pot with the lentils. Stir gently to mix and cook on low heat for a minute. Squeeze lime juice over the top before serving.

SERVES 4

Anatolian Red Lentil Stew with Wheat Berries and Chickpeas

TURKEY

Eksili Çorba

This thick stew, containing lentils, wheat, chickpeas, eggplant, tomato, and mint, is a meal in itself. A thinned-out version was served as a soup when we visited this hotel, but in most homes a big bowlful would be the core of a meal, served with bread and a yogurt salad on the side.

If you like, put a dollop of plain yogurt on top of a serving and offer a green salad on the side. Alternatively, you could put a scoop of Turkish Vegetable Salad with Red Pepper Dressing (page 641) on top.

I generally make this stew in large amounts and keep it in the refrigerator. It tends to thicken even more as it sits, so I thin it out with some vegetable stock. It makes for a perfect lunch or light supper.

If you wish to substitute canned chickpeas for the dried ones, you will need about 1½ cups of drained and washed chickpeas. (Do not use the liquid in the can.) Add the canned chickpeas to the stew just when you would have put in the boiled ones.

I used 2 small eggplants for this dish, each about 2 ounces. You may use a 4-ounce portion from a larger one, about 1 cup when diced small.

¼ cup wheat berries

½ cup dried chickpeas

¼ cup olive oil

1 medium onion (4 ounces), peeled and finely chopped

2 small eggplants (about 4 ounces total), peeled and diced into ¼-inch pieces

2½ tablespoons tomato paste

1 cup dried red lentils *(masoor dal)*

5 cups vegetable stock or water (you may need more)

2 tablespoons dried mint

About 1½ teaspoons salt

1 tablespoon fresh lemon juice

2 tablespoons finely chopped fresh parsley

Put the wheat berries in a bowl with 4 cups of water and leave to soak in a cool spot for 12 hours.

Put the chickpeas in a bowl with 4 cups of water and leave to soak in a cool spot for 12 hours.

Drain the wheat berries. Put in a pot with 2¼ cups of water and bring to a boil. Cover, turn the heat down to low, and cook very gently for 1½ hours. Most of the water should be absorbed.

(recipe continues)

Drain the chickpeas. Put in a pot with 4 cups of water and bring to a boil. Cover, turn the heat down to low, and cook gently for 1 hour, or until the chickpeas are tender. Drain, but reserve the liquid. Put the chickpeas in a bowl of cold water and gently rub off the skins, which will float to the top. Discard the skins and the water.

Put the oil in a large, heavy pot and set over medium-high heat. When hot, put in the onion. Stir and fry for 4 minutes. Add the eggplants and stir and fry for 2 minutes. Turn the heat to medium-low and stir in the tomato paste, cooking for 30 seconds, then add the lentils. Stir and fry for 30 seconds, then add 4 cups of the stock or water (you may use the liquid from cooking the chickpeas as part of the stock) and the mint. Stir and bring to a boil. Cover partially, turn the heat down to low, and simmer for 40 minutes, or until the lentils are tender.

Empty the contents of the pot into an electric blender or food processor and blend. You may need to do this in more than one batch. Pour the puree back into the pot. Pour the remaining cup of stock or water into the blender container, swish it around, and pour that into the pot as well. Taste and add as much salt as you need (seasoned stock will require less salt). Put in the wheat berries and chickpeas. Stir and bring to a simmer. Simmer very gently for 15 minutes, stirring now and then. Check for salt again, add the lemon juice, and stir to mix. Sprinkle the parsley over the top when serving.

SERVES 4 TO 6

Mung Beans

This is the first legume that a North Indian child eats and probably the last one that is eaten through old age. It is easy to digest, cooks relatively quickly, and is imbued, so Indians believe, with spiritual qualities—perhaps just a Zen-like simplicity—that help in the upward journey of the soul. The bean originated in India in antiquity and is mentioned in Vedic texts dating back more than five thousand years. Early travelers carried mung beans to China and other eastern destinations. Of all the beans, it is the one that causes the least flatulence and this may well account for its popularity in India, where foods and their effects on the body have been carefully calibrated and documented since ancient times. Mung beans find their way into everything from porridges, stews, pancakes, fritters, noodles, crisp snacks, and salads to desserts.

In most North Indian homes, mung beans are served several times a week. They are sold in the market in many different forms.

Unhulled whole mung beans: These are fairly small, similar in size to green lentils except that they are cylindrical in shape and have lovely, shiny green skins. It is these whole beans that are used to make mung bean sprouts. They may also be cooked whole, as they are throughout East and Southern Asia. In Indonesia they are made into a morning porridge with coconut milk; in China, they are transformed into a sweet soup that is served cold in the summer; in the Philippines, they are cooked with bitter leaves and served with a drizzle of olive oil; and in India, they are cooked with a dizzying variety of spices. Unhulled whole mung beans are sold by most East Asian and South Asian grocers. They are generally labeled "mung beans."

For *cooking unhulled mung beans,* see page 8.

Unhulled split mung beans: These whole beans have been split in half but have not been skinned. As a result, their outsides are green and their insides pale yellow. While they have a coarser texture and more fiber than hulled and split mung beans, they are cooked in exactly the same way. As far as I know, they are only sold by Indian grocers under the name *chhilke-wali moong dal,* "*dal*" being the North Indian word for a split bean or pea.

Hulled and split mung beans: These beans have been hulled *and* split. The split beans, or *dal,* are pale yellow in color. While they are used for some recipes in East Asian nations like Korea and Vietnam, it is the Indians who use them in hundreds of daily and specialty dishes. The simplest of these dishes is known rather humbly as *moong dal,* the name of its major ingredient. For this, the split beans are just boiled with a dash of turmeric—turmeric is the rhizome that is believed to act like an antiseptic both inside the body and out and is therefore used routinely in Indian cookery. When the split beans are soft, salt is added, it being the opinion of many Indians that beans and split peas tend to toughen if salt is added in the beginning.

This is the basic *moong dal,* a kind of thick (or thin, according to your preference) soup or sauce that is eaten with rice or Indian breads. But it is rarely served in this basic way except to the sick, to infants, to those on special fasts, and to the elderly. It is almost always "perked up" with oil or ghee (clarified butter)—which cuts through the dryness of the beans—and with different spice and seasoning combinations that provide flavor and variety. The technique of heating oil, popping or frying spices and seasonings in it, and then pouring this flavoring agent into the cooked beans is known variously in North India as *tarka, baghaar,* or *chhownk.* For the purposes of this book, I have used the term *tarka.*

Because *moong dal* is required in many of the recipes that follow, I have provided a basic recipe on page 75.

"Dry" mung dal: These unhulled and split mung beans are cooked so they are not soupy but rather ricelike. To achieve this, the split beans are soaked for several hours and then cooked in just enough water to steam them through. The grains stay quite separate this way and the cooking time is shorter. See specific recipes for details.

Making fritters and pancakes out of hulled and split mung beans All manner of fritters and pancakes may be made out of the split beans. Some of the recipes follow. The fritters are utterly delicious and may be seasoned as you choose. It is useful to note that the beans need to be soaked first and then ground into a thick or medium batter.

Mung bean sprouts: Many beans and lentils are sprouted, but the bean that is sprouted most is the mung bean.

There are two varieties of mung bean sprouts, the long-tailed one used in Eastern Asia (with "tails" that are about 3 inches long) and the short-tailed one (with a ¼-inch sprout) used only in South Asia. The best place to buy the more common long-tailed sprouts are Chinese or Korean markets, as they tend to be very fresh, white, and crisp. Once you bring these sprouts home, they should be washed, drained, and then put in a bowl of water, covered, and refrigerated until use. It is best to change the water after 12 hours and to use them up within 24 hours. The Chinese, when they are being very proper, like to pinch off and remove the very thin, threadlike tip as well as the very top, which is the original mung bean itself. They are then left with just the very white, noodlelike body of the sprout. This is laborious work and best done by many hands working together. As it is not entirely necessary, I often leave out that step.

As these bean sprouts release a lot of liquid when cooked, they are sometimes blanched for a second before they are stir-fried.

It is hard to quantify long-tailed mung bean sprouts for the purposes of accurate recipe writing. One pound of very fresh, crunchy sprouts fit into a 4-cup measure. However, 1 pound of dark, dull, water-logged sprouts might well fit into a 2-cup measure. And, of course, there is every stage in between. Choose the brightest, crispest sprouts you can find.

Short-tailed bean sprouts, wonderful for both salads and stir-fries, are not sold in any market and must be made at home.

Making long-tailed or "regular" bean sprouts Pick over and wash ½ cup whole unhulled mung beans, discarding any that are broken. Soak in water to cover generously for 8 hours. Drain. Rinse gently and drain again. Put the beans in a plastic bag that has been punched with holes and then put the bag in a colander, making sure to leave the mouth open. Cover the mouth of the bag with a triple layer of paper towels that have been well dampened. Now place the colander in a large bowl to catch drippings and put the bowl in a dark, warm, and humid spot, which could be under the sink. Every 4 hours or so, remove the bowl and place the colander in the sink. Let lukewarm water pour over the paper towels, then over the beans and go out through the holes of the colander. Drain briefly and put the colander back in the bowl and the bowl back in its warm spot. Continue to do this for 3 to 4 days, or until the sprouts are 2 to 3 inches long.

Now put the sprouts in a large bowl, fill the bowl with water, and very gently rub the sprouts to loosen the green skins on the beans. The skins should float to the top. Pour the water with the skins away. Do this a few times. One-half cup of beans should yield about 6 cups of sprouts.

Store the sprouts in a water-filled container, uncovered, in the refrigerator. Change the water every day. The sprouts should last at least 3 days.

Making short-tailed sprouts These are a common breakfast food in India, especially among vegetarians. As the sprout barely emerges, they are much more substantial than their long-tailed relatives.

Soak 2 cups of whole unhulled mung beans in water to cover by 5 inches and leave for 12 hours. Drain. Line a large bowl with a triple layer of dampened paper towels. Put in the beans and cover with more dampened paper towels. Put the bowl in a warm, dark place, such as the oven, and leave for about 12 hours, or until the beans have ¼-inch sprouts. Two cups of beans should yield 6 cups of sprouts.

Cellophane noodles or transparent noodles: Also called bean thread vermicelli and mung bean vermicelli, these are fine, whitish translucent noodles made from mung bean starch. They are used throughout Eastern Asia. The noodles should be soaked in boiling water until softened (about a minute), drained, and rinsed in cold water before being used in salads and stir-fries. They may also be quickly dipped in water, shaken, and then deep-fried as a crisp topping for Chinese and Thai dishes. They can also be softened in hot water and then added to stews, but do not stew them longer than 10 minutes or they will become too gelatinous.

Basic Recipe for Cooked Hulled and Split Mung Beans

INDIA

Basic Moong Dal

Unadorned moong dal *can be served to little children just as is with some plain rice.*

1 cup hulled and split mung beans, picked over, washed in several changes of water, and drained

¼ teaspoon ground turmeric

1 to 1¼ teaspoons salt

Put the split beans and 4 cups of water in a heavy-bottomed pot and bring to a boil. Watch carefully to prevent the contents of the pot from boiling over. Skim off

(recipe continues)

the froth that rises to the top. Add the turmeric and stir once. Cover partially, turn the heat down to low, and cook very gently for 40 to 50 minutes, or until the beans are tender. Stir in the salt.

You may prepare and add the *tarka* right away, or reheat the beans and season later. To reheat beans that have been refrigerated, stir well and add just enough water to prevent them from sticking, usually just a few tablespoons.

SERVES 4 TO 6

Hulled and Split Mung Beans
with Browned Onion   INDIA

Pyaz Ke Tarkay Vali Moong Dal

The rich taste of crisply browned onions flavors the beans in this dish. The tarka *should ideally be done just before serving. Put the heated beans into a serving dish, prepare the* tarka, *and pour it over the top so it floats on the surface; the crisp onion, browned red chiles, and cumin seeds act as a garnish as well as a flavoring.*

1 cup hulled and split mung beans, cooked according to the basic recipe on page 75 and reheated if necessary

3 tablespoons peanut or canola oil

½ teaspoon whole cumin seeds

Generous pinch of ground asafetida

3 whole dried hot red chiles (a medium cayenne type is ideal)

1 small onion (2 ounces), peeled, halved lengthwise, and very thinly sliced

Put the cooked mung beans into a serving dish and keep warm.

Put the oil into a small frying pan and set over medium-high heat. When hot, put in the cumin seeds and let them sizzle for 10 seconds. Put in the asafetida and, a second later, the red chiles. Stir for 5 seconds, or until the chiles darken. Put in the onion and stir and fry for 2 minutes. Turn the heat down to medium-low and cook, stirring, another 2 minutes, or until the onion turns brown and crisp. Pour the contents of the pan evenly over the surface of the beans and serve immediately. (The whole red chiles add flavor and are decorative but should be nibbled at only by those who know what they are doing!)

SERVES 4 TO 6

Hulled and Split Mung Beans with Cumin and Asafetida

Heeng Zeeray Ke Tarkay Vali Moong Dal

This is perhaps the most common way of serving these beans in my family. The asafetida acts as a digestive and adds a trufflelike flavor.

3 tablespoons peanut or canola oil

¾ teaspoon whole cumin seeds

Generous pinch of ground asafetida

3 whole dried hot red chiles (a medium cayenne type is ideal)

1 cup hulled and split mung beans, cooked according to the basic recipe on page 75 and reheated if necessary

In a small frying pan, heat the oil over medium-high heat. When hot, put in the cumin seeds and let them sizzle for 10 seconds. Put in the asafetida and, a second later, the red chiles. Stir for 5 seconds, or until the chiles darken. Quickly pour the oil and spices over the heated beans. Cover the pot immediately to trap the aromas and set aside for 5 minutes. Stir and serve hot. (The whole red chiles should be eaten only by those who know what they are doing!)

SERVES 4 TO 6

Hulled and Split Mung Beans with Spinach

Saag Vali Moong Dal

It is always best to use fresh spinach but frozen chopped spinach, cooked according to instructions and drained, is an acceptable substitute. Serve with rice or an Indian or Middle Eastern bread and a yogurt salad or any dish with cheese.

3 tablespoons peanut or canola oil

½ teaspoon whole cumin seeds

2 garlic cloves, peeled and finely chopped

½ to 1 fresh hot green chile, finely chopped

1¼ pounds fresh spinach, cleaned, trimmed, and coarsely chopped

Scant ½ teaspoon salt

1 cup hulled and split mung beans, cooked according to the basic recipe on page 75 and reheated if necessary

(recipe continues)

Put the oil in a wok or a large pot and set over high heat. When hot, add the cumin seeds and let them sizzle for 5 seconds. Now put in the garlic and green chile. Stir and cook for 5 seconds. Add the spinach. Stir and fry for 5 to 7 minutes, or until the spinach has wilted completely. Add the salt and stir for another minute. Empty the contents of the wok (or pot) into the pot with the beans. Stir to mix. Taste for salt, adding more if needed. Cook gently for 5 minutes to allow all the flavors to blend. Serve hot.

SERVES 6

"Dry" Hulled and Split Mung Beans with Browned Garlic and Onions   INDIA

Lehson Aur Pyaz Ke Tarkay Vali Sookhi Mung Dal

In this preparation, the beans are not at all soupy. They are soaked and then cooked in very little water, which gets absorbed, producing separate kernels rather like rice.

This is best eaten with Indian breads or with any flatbreads from the Middle East. Indian, Middle Eastern, or North African vegetables and yogurt dishes may be served on the side.

1 cup hulled and split mung beans *(moong dal)*, picked over, washed in several changes of water, and drained

¼ teaspoon ground turmeric

½ teaspoon salt

2 tablespoons oil, or *ghee* (page 723)

½ teaspoon whole cumin seeds

1 to 2 whole dried hot red chiles

1 garlic clove, peeled and split in half lengthwise

½ medium onion, peeled, halved, and very thinly sliced

Put the hulled and split mung beans in a bowl. Add 4 cups of water and set aside to soak for 3 hours. Drain, discarding the soaking liquid.

Combine the beans, turmeric, salt, and 2 cups of water in a small, heavy pot. Stir and set over medium-high heat. Bring to a boil. Cover tightly, turn the heat down to very low, and cook for 15 minutes. Turn off the heat and leave the pot covered.

Put the oil or *ghee* in a small frying pan over medium-high heat. When very hot, put in the cumin seeds and red chiles. Stir once and quickly put in the garlic and onion. Stir and fry until the onion is brown and crisp. Pour the contents of the frying pan over the hot beans. (You may put the beans in a serving dish first and pour the oil and seasonings over the top.) Remove the garlic before serving. The hot chiles should be eaten only by those who know what they are doing.

SERVES 4

My sister, Kamal's
Unhulled and Split Mung Beans with Greens

Alan Ka Saag

Unhulled and split mung beans, which still have their green skins on them, are sold only by Indian grocers, as far as I know. You may substitute hulled and split mung beans if the unhulled beans are hard to come by.

Normally, this would be made with a combination of spinach and fresh fenugreek greens (green methi*). Methi* leaves are small and need to be picked off the stems before they are washed. To end up with the amount needed for this recipe, you should buy 4 pounds or more; most Indian stores sell the greens in season. In India, the season is winter but here it varies according to where the greens are grown. As they have a slightly bitter taste, you might use arugula as a substitute. Many Indians use all spinach and crumble in a handful of dried* methi *leaves just to get a hint of the proper flavor, which is a decent compromise. All Indian stores sell dried fenugreek.*

This particular dish is a specialty of my clan and is of ancient heritage. It features two tarkas, *one added at the beginning and one at the end.*

5 tablespoons peanut or canola oil

½ teaspoon whole cumin seeds

Generous pinch of ground asafetida

¼ teaspoon whole fenugreek seeds

1 pound trimmed and finely chopped fenugreek greens (leaves only)

½ pound trimmed, cleaned, and finely chopped spinach

1 cup unhulled and split mung beans *(chhilke vali moong dal)*, picked over, washed in several changes of water, and drained

¼ teaspoon ground turmeric

1½ teaspoons salt, or to taste

1 tablespoon chickpea flour mixed slowly with 5 tablespoons cold water

2 thin slices of peeled fresh ginger, cut into fine slivers

2 tablespoons very fine half rings of peeled onion

2 to 4 fresh hot green chiles

Put 2 tablespoons of the oil in a heavy-bottomed pot and set over medium-high heat. When hot, put in the cumin seeds. Ten seconds later, put in the asafetida and fenugreek seeds. Stir once and quickly put in the fenugreek greens, spinach, the split beans, turmeric, and 4 cups of water. Stir and bring to a boil, watching carefully so that the contents of the pot do not boil over. Partially cover, leaving the lid very slightly ajar. Turn the heat down to low and cook very gently for 50

(recipe continues)

minutes, or until the beans are tender. Add the salt and stir to mix. Stir the chickpea flour mixture and add it to the beans. Stir and cook over very low heat for another 10 minutes.

Put the remaining 3 tablespoons of oil in a small frying pan and set over medium-high heat. When hot, put in the ginger, onion, and whole green chiles. Stir and fry until the onion turns brown, then empty the contents of the frying pan into the pot with the split beans. Stir to mix.

Note: The whole chiles should be eaten only by those who know what they are doing.

SERVES 4 TO 6

Mung Bean Pancakes

INDIA

Cheela

These nutritious pancakes may be eaten as a bread or they may be served at breakfast with a fresh chutney, a dipping sauce, or a yogurt relish.

1 cup hulled and split mung beans *(moong dal)*

¼ to ¾ teaspoon cayenne

1 teaspoon salt

¼ teaspoon ground turmeric

½ teaspoon whole cumin seeds

2 scallions, cut into very fine rounds (use all of the white and the lower half of the green sections)

1 medium tomato, peeled, seeded, and chopped, and placed in a strainer to drain

2 tablespoons finely chopped fresh cilantro

7 to 8 tablespoons peanut or canola oil

Pick over and wash the split beans and then soak them for 6 to 7 hours in water to cover by about 5 inches. Drain, disarding the soaking liquid.

Put the soaked beans into a blender and blend until they are pastelike. Add ½ cup of water, the cayenne, salt, turmeric, and cumin seeds. Blend until the mixture is smooth and light. Empty the batter into a bowl.

Just before cooking, stir in the scallions, tomato, and cilantro.

Spread 1 teaspoon of oil in an 8-inch nonstick frying pan and set over medium-low heat. When hot (this will take a few minutes), stir the batter well. Ladle ⅓ cup into the center of the heated pan. Let it sit there for 3 to 4 seconds. Now place the rounded bottom of an old-fashioned soup spoon or a ladle lightly on top of the batter and, using a slow, gentle, continuous spiral motion, spread the batter outward to make a pancake that is 5½ inches in diameter. Dribble ½ teaspoon oil on top of the pancake and another ½ teaspoon just outside its edges. Using a plastic spatula, spread out the oil on top of the pancake and also smooth out any ridges or bumps. Cover the pan and let the pancake cook for 2 minutes. The bottom should be a nice reddish color. Turn the pancake over and cook, uncovered, another 1½ minutes, or until the second side has a few red spots. Remove the pancake and keep covered. Continue making pancakes this way, being sure to stir the batter from the bottom each time.

A stack of pancakes may be wrapped in foil and heated in a medium oven for 15 minutes. You may also zap individual pancakes in a microwave oven for 1 minute each.

MAKES ABOUT 9 PANCAKES

Durupadi Jagtiani's
Fritters Made with Hulled and Split Mung Beans INDIA
Moong Dal Bhajjia

Serve these highly addictive fritters with any dipping sauce you like, even tomato ketchup! They are wonderful as a snack or as an accompanying dish at mealtime. You may use any leftover fritters to make Mung Bean Dumplings in a Spicy Tomato Sauce (page 82).

1 cup hulled and split mung beans *(moong dal),* picked over, washed, and drained

1 teaspoon finely grated peeled ginger

2 garlic cloves, peeled and crushed to a pulp

½ to ¾ teaspoon salt

¼ teaspoon cayenne

½ teaspoon baking powder

1 teaspoon finely chopped fresh hot green chile (optional)

½ teaspoon whole cumin seeds

2 tablespoons chopped fresh cilantro

Peanut or canola oil for deep-frying

Place the split beans in a bowl with water to cover by 5 inches. Leave to soak for 6 to 7 hours.

Drain the beans (discard the soaking liquid) and put them into the container of a food processor. Blend, adding the ginger, garlic, salt, cayenne, and baking powder,

(recipe continues)

until you have a coarse paste. Slowly add 5 to 6 tablespoons of hot water, processing all the while, until the paste has a droppable consistency. It should also look light and airy but remain slightly grainy. Empty into a bowl. Add the green chile, if using, cumin, and cilantro and stir to mix.

Pour about 1 inch of oil into a deep-frying pan or wok and set it over medium heat. Wait until the oil gets very hot. Now work fast. Stir the batter gently and remove a heaped teaspoon. Using a second teaspoon, release the batter into the oil. (The fritters will be about 1¼ × ¾ inch.) Keep doing this until the frying pan is full. Fry for about 1 minute at medium heat, turning the fritters over as they become golden, and then turn the heat down to low. Continue to fry for another 6 minutes or so, turning the fritters now and then. They should have an even, rich, golden-red color and be cooked through. Use a slotted spoon to remove the fritters and drain on paper towels. Make all the fritters this way, remembering at the start of each batch, to *(a)* turn the heat back to medium and get the oil very hot again and *(b)* stir the batter once very gently from the bottom up. Serve the fritters ideally as soon as they are made.

Leftover fritters may be stored in a closed container in the refrigerator.

MAKES 30 TO 35 FRITTERS

Durupadi Jagtiani's
Mung Bean Dumplings in a Spicy Tomato Sauce

INDIA

Dal Ki Kachori

Combining cooked fritters with a light but spicy tomato sauce is typical of the Sindh region of what was Western India before its partition. As they absorb the sauce, the fritters turn wonderfully soft and fluffy. Care should be taken to cook the fritters in the sauce only briefly, as they will eventually fall apart. Serve this dish with flatbreads or even over pasta.

3 tablespoons peanut or canola oil

1½ teaspoons whole brown mustard seeds

15 fresh curry leaves (use fresh basil leaves as an alternative)

2 garlic cloves, peeled and finely chopped

1 (1-pound, 12-ounce) can tomatoes with liquid, ground up in a blender

2 tablespoons tomato paste

1¾ teaspoons salt

¼ teaspoon ground turmeric

2 teaspoons garam masala (page 723)

¼ teaspoon cayenne

1 recipe Fritters Made with Hulled and Split Mung Beans (page 81)

Put the oil in a large pan and set over medium-high heat. When hot, put in the mustard seeds. As soon as the mustard seeds begin to pop, a matter of seconds, put in the curry leaves, then add the garlic. Stir once briefly and add the ground tomatoes and tomato paste. Stir to mix, then put in the salt, turmeric, garam masala, cayenne, and 1 cup of water. Stir and bring to a boil. Cover, turn the heat down to low, and simmer gently for 20 minutes. Add the fritters to the sauce and bring to a simmer. Cover and simmer gently for 10 minutes, or until the fritters have just softened. Serve immediately.

SERVES 4 TO 6

Shiu-Min Block's

Sweet-and-Sour Mung Bean Sprouts CHINA

Chow Do Ya

Use good, crisp fresh mung beans sprouts for this.

7 cups fresh mung bean sprouts, well washed
 and drained

5 teaspoons soy sauce

1 tablespoon sugar

1 tablespoon red wine vinegar

¼ teaspoon salt

2 tablespoons peanut or canola oil

1 scallion, cut into 1½-inch lengths (both
 white and green parts, the white sections
 halved lengthwise)

3 large slices of peeled fresh ginger

2 garlic cloves, lightly crushed and peeled but
 left whole

1 teaspoon oriental sesame oil

Put the sprouts in a heatproof bowl. Pour boiling water over them and drain immediately. Leave in the strainer or colander. Combine the soy sauce, sugar, vinegar, and salt in a small bowl; set aside.

Put the oil in a large wok or frying pan and set over high heat. When hot, put in the scallion and ginger. Stir and fry for 30 seconds. Add the bean sprouts and garlic and stir for 30 seconds. Put in the soy sauce mixture and stir for another 30 seconds. Add the sesame oil, stir, and turn off the heat. Remove the ginger slices and garlic and serve immediately.

SERVES 4

Shiu-Min Block's

Mung Bean Thread Salad

Liang Ban Fen Si

CHINA

You may serve this light salad as a first course, a quick lunch, or as part of a meal. Try to cut all the cucumbers and pepper into strips of the same size. Serve this at room temperature or chilled.

1½ cups fresh mung bean sprouts

Dressing

1 tablespoon peanut oil

2 scallions, cut into 2-inch lengths, then cut lengthwise into thin strips

4 thin slices of peeled fresh ginger

2 tablespoons Chinese light soy sauce or Japanese soy sauce

4 teaspoons rice wine vinegar

1 tablespoon sugar

2 teaspoons oriental sesame oil

¼ teaspoon salt

1 garlic clove, lightly mashed and peeled but left whole

2 (1.8-ounce) packages mung bean threads (also called cellophane noodles)

½ large red bell pepper, cut into thin, long julienne strips

2 (6-inch) cucumbers, peeled, seeded, and cut into fine julienne strips

6 to 7 tablespoons coarsely chopped roasted peanuts

2 teaspoons roasted sesame seeds (page 734)

2 to 3 tablespoons chopped fresh cilantro

Put the bean sprouts in a bowl. Pour boiling water over them and let stand for 1 hour. Drain.

While the sprouts soak, put the oil in a medium frying pan and set over medium-high heat. When hot, put in the scallions and ginger. Stir for a few seconds and put in ½ cup of water, the soy sauce, vinegar, sugar, sesame oil, salt, and garlic. Turn the heat down to low and cook gently for 2 to 3 minutes, stirring now and then. Allow to cool. You may strain this mixture if you like.

Put the bean threads in a bowl. Pour boiling water over them. As soon as they soften (this could take less than a minute), drain them and rinse under cold water. Drain again.

Spread the bean threads out on a serving platter. Top with the bean sprouts and then with the bell pepper and cucumber strips. If not eating immediately, cover well and refrigerate.

Just before serving, pour the soy sauce dressing evenly over the salad. Sprinkle the peanuts and sesame seeds over the top and then top with the cilantro.

SERVES 4 TO 6

Mung Bean Sprouts Stir-Fried with Ginger

Kong Namul

You may serve this hot, with plain rice, or at room temperature or chilled, as a salad.

5 cups fresh mung bean sprouts

2 tablespoons peanut or canola oil

1 (1-inch) piece of peeled fresh ginger, thinly sliced and cut into very fine slivers

1 garlic clove, peeled and cut into fine slivers

½ to 1 fresh hot green chile, seeds removed and cut into fine, long slivers

1 scallion, cut into quarters lengthwise, then into 2-inch lengths

¼ teaspoon salt

2 teaspoons soy sauce

1 teaspoon rice vinegar

2 teaspoons roasted sesame seeds (page 734)

1 teaspoon oriental sesame oil

Bring a large pot of water to a rolling boil. Drop in the sprouts. Bring the water to a boil again and drain immediately. Run the sprouts under cold water and leave in the strainer.

Put the oil in a wok or large frying pan and set over medium heat. When hot, put in the ginger, garlic, chile, and scallion. Stir for a minute, then add the drained sprouts and salt. Toss once and turn off the heat. Add the soy sauce, vinegar, sesame seeds, and sesame oil. Toss again and serve hot, warm, at room temperature, or chilled.

SERVES 4

Pigeon Peas, also *Toovar* and *Arhar Dal*

Once thought to be of African origin and now traced to possible roots in south-western India, these round, dull yellow peas with their earthy, dark flavor are used in the Caribbean in their whole form and throughout India in their hulled and split forms. The plants vary slightly in northern and southern India; when hulled and split the northern variety is sold in Indian shops as *arhar dal* and the southern as *toovar dal*. For all cooking purposes, however, they are interchangeable.

Toovar dal is a staple of South Indian cuisine, especially among vegetarians, and is eaten there from breakfast to dinner. Every day, a different stew is prepared with it, sometimes with the addition of browned, whole shallots, sometimes pumpkins, sometimes tomatoes, and sometimes green squashes.

In the Indian state of Gujarat (western India), families buy *toovar dal* in bulk at harvest time. It is picked over, rubbed with castor oil—a trick meant to keep insects at bay—and then stored in large canisters for the rest of the year. You can buy this "oily *toovar*," with its slightly translucent look, in Indian shops as well. It needs to be washed very thoroughly before being cooked, but otherwise it is prepared just like the regular *toovar.*

Cooking whole pigeon peas: Pick over the peas and wash them well. Drain. Soak the peas overnight in water to cover by 5 inches. Drain. Alternatively, you may use the Quick-Soak Method (page 6). Drain, discarding the soaking liquid.

Put the peas in a medium pan along with water to cover them by 2 inches and bring to a boil. Cover partially, turn the heat down to low, and simmer gently until the beans are tender, 1¼ to 1½ hours.

Pressure cooker method for pigeon peas Pick over, soak, and drain the peas as suggested above. Put the peas in a pressure cooker and cover with water by ½ inch. Put the lid on and bring up to pressure. Cook for 15 minutes. Allow the pressure to drop by itself. (If the recipe requires that you drain the peas, save the cooking liquid for soup.)

Basic Recipe for Hulled and Split Pigeon Peas (*Arhar* or *Toovar Dal*)

In India, these split peas are always cooked with the addition of a little turmeric. Salt is added at the very end. Once cooked, lightly boiled or sautéed vegetables may be added. For Indian dishes, a final tarka *(page 7) is also essential, unless you are feeding the sick, the elderly, or young children.*

1 cup hulled and split pigeon paste *(toovar dal),* picked over, washed in several changes of water, and drained

¼ teaspoon ground turmeric
1 to 1¼ teaspoons salt

Put the split peas and 4 cups of water in a heavy-bottomed pan and bring to a boil. Watch carefully to prevent the contents of the pot from boiling over. Skim off the froth that rises to the top. Add the turmeric and stir once. Cover partially, turn the heat down to low, and cook very gently for 1 hour, or until the beans are tender. (Older beans may take up to 1½ hours.) Add the salt and stir to mix.

SERVES 4

Sweet-and-Sour *Toovar Dal*

Khatti Meethi Toovar Dal

Split peas cooked in the Gujarati style get a bit of sweetness from sugar and tartness from tamarind, plus a hint of cloves and cinnamon. Serve with rice or eat with a spoon and flatbreads. Salad and yogurt dishes may be served on the side.

1 cup hulled and split pigeon peas *(toovar dal),* cooked according to the basic recipe (page 86)

1 tablespoon brown sugar

1 tablespoon thick tamarind paste (page 737) or 2 teaspoons fresh lemon juice

⅛ to ¼ teaspoon cayenne

Salt, if needed

2 tablespoons peanut or canola oil

4 to 5 whole cloves

1 (2-inch) cinnamon stick

Combine the cooked *dal,* sugar, tamarind, and cayenne in a medium pan and bring to a simmer over medium-high heat. Turn the heat down to low and simmer for 10 minutes, stirring now and then. Taste for the balance of sweet, salt, and sour.

Put the oil in a small frying pan and set it over medium heat. When very hot, put in the cloves and cinnamon. Stir once or twice and quickly empty the oil and spices into the pan with the *dal.* Stir to mix.

Note: The whole spices are not meant to be eaten.

SERVES 4

Toovar Dal with Sliced Shallots and Carrots

Sambar

The sambars *of southern India have certain things in common. They are soupy stews, made with* toovar dal *and seasoned with a fiery spice mixture called* sambar *powder, which happens to contain, among other things, fried and ground split peas and split beans. Generally, they are sour and hot, the sourness contributed frequently by tamarind paste, though tomatoes may also be used. Other than that, the sky is the limit. Almost any vegetable from eggplant and radishes to kohlrabi may be added.*

This particular sambar *is quite a simple one in which sliced shallots and carrot sticks are*

(recipe continues)

lightly sautéed before being added to the cooked split peas. Serve this over rice with vegetables or with a salad on the side.

You may make your own sambar *powder, following the recipe on page 708, or else buy it ready made from an Indian grocer.*

3 tablespoons peanut or canola oil

4 medium shallots, peeled and cut into long, thin slivers

1 small carrot (2 ounces), peeled and cut into 1 × ¼ × ¼-inch sticks

1 cup hulled and split pigeon peas *(toovar dal),* cooked according to the basic recipe (page 86)

2 tablespoons *sambar* powder (page 708)

2 tablespoons thick tamarind paste (page 737) or 1½ tablespoons fresh lemon juice plus a pinch of sugar

Salt, if needed

½ teaspoon whole brown mustard seeds

1 dried hot red chile

10 fresh curry leaves (if unavailable use fresh basil leaves as a different but interesting substitute)

Put 2 tablespoons of oil in a medium frying pan and set over medium heat. When hot, put in the shallots and carrot. Stir and sauté them until they just start to brown. Combine the shallots, carrot, their cooking oil, all of the cooked *toovar dal,* the *sambar* powder, and tamarind paste in a medium pan. Stir and bring to a simmer. Simmer gently on low heat for 10 to 15 minutes, or until the carrot is tender. Taste for salt, adding more if needed.

Put the remaining 1 tablespoon oil in a small frying pan and set over medium-high heat. When very hot, put in the mustard seeds. As soon as the mustard seeds begin to pop, a matter of seconds, put in the dried chile. When the chile darkens, another few seconds, add the curry leaves and stir once. Pour the contents of the frying pan over the *toovar dal* and stir to mix.

SERVES 4

Pinto Beans

These medium beans with a mottled beige and brown color are sisters to red kidney beans and native to the Americas. Sadly, they lose their mottled effect when cooked and turn a dull brown. They can be prepared almost exactly like red kidney beans but because of their smaller size, they may end up cooking a bit faster. You may use them for all the recipes in the red kidney bean section.

For general directions on cooking pinto beans, see page 47.

Tex-Mex Pinto Bean Stew with Ancho Chiles

This spicy stew may be served with heated corn tortillas or over rice. If you like, grated Parmesan cheese may be sprinkled over the top of each serving.

1¼ cups dried pinto beans, picked over, washed, and drained

2 dried ancho chiles

3 tablespoons olive oil

1 celery stalk, cut into ⅛-inch dice

1 small onion (4 ounces), finely chopped

1 carrot, peeled and cut into ⅛-inch dice

3 garlic cloves, peeled and finely chopped

6 canned plum tomatoes, finely chopped, plus 1 cup liquid from the can

2 bay leaves

1½ teaspoons ground and roasted cumin seeds (page 724)

½ teaspoon dried oregano

1½ teaspoons salt, or to taste

1¾ cups (7 ounces) green beans, cut into 1-inch sections

Soak the beans overnight in water to cover them by 5 inches. Drain. Alternatively, you may Quick-Soak them according to general directions on page 6. Drain, discarding the soaking liquid.

Put the beans and 4 cups of fresh water in a medium pot and bring to a boil. Cover, leaving the lid slightly ajar. Turn the heat down to low and cook gently for 1½ to 2 hours, or until the beans are tender.

Meanwhile, put the chiles and 1 cup of water in a small pot and bring to a boil. Cover, turn the heat down to low, and simmer gently for 5 minutes. Turn off the heat and let the pot sit, covered, until the chiles are cool enough to handle. Lift the chiles out of the liquid (save the liquid) and remove the stem area and seeds. Put the chiles in a coarse sieve set over a bowl and push out as much pulp as you can. Mix the liquid used for cooking the chiles with the pulp and set aside.

Put the olive oil in a large frying pan and set over medium-high heat. When hot, put in the celery, onion, carrot, and garlic. Stir and sauté for about 5 minutes, or until the onions soften a bit and just start to turn brown. Add the tomatoes, their liquid, bay leaves, cumin, oregano, and the ancho chile puree. Stir and bring to a simmer. Cover, turn the heat down to low, and simmer gently for 10 minutes.

When the beans are tender, stir in the contents of the frying pan. Add the salt and green beans, stir, and bring to a simmer. Cover, turn the heat down to low, and cook gently for another 20 minutes.

SERVES 6

Soybeans

It has recently become quite fashionable at expensive, trendy restaurants to offer gratis, as a very, very first course, a small bowl of what look like hairy boiled pea pods. These are soybeans in their green form, either boiled plain and served with a little coarse salt, the Japanese way, or boiled with a little salt and a couple of whole star anise pods, the Chinese way. Rather like peanuts, these legumes are irresistible; once you start peeling and nibbling, it is hard to stop.

Because soybean plants have roots that trap nitrogen, essential to the fertility of the soil, they were initially grown in the United States in the late nineteenth century for the sole purpose of being plowed under as "green manure" to enrich the soil. The plants were still plowed under in the early twentieth century, but the beans were also used to extract oil, mainly to use in soaps. The remaining roughage from the crushed beans was fed to cattle. This is pretty much how soybeans are still used in the West today, though the demand for bean curd (made from soybeans) has increased enormously.

Today almost every supermarket in America—to say nothing of every single health food shop—carries bean curd and sometimes even vegeburgers and "hot dogs" made from soybeans. (Of course, the best vegeburgers are the ones you make at home. See page 94 for soybean patties and page 103 for Bean Curd Vegeburgers.)

In the East—in China particularly—soybeans have been cultivated perhaps for as long as five thousand years, with clear records going back at least 2500 years. There it is understood that soybeans offer some of the cheapest usable protein—more than any other legume (34 to 38 percent) and are rich in iron and vitamins B1 and B2. In all of East Asia they are a staple (though sometimes the soybeans have to be imported from America, which remains the world's top producer) and used not for their oil as in the West but in dozens of other ways, starting with the green pods. These pods begin to appear in the early summer, gladdening many a heart (including mine). In the West, these pods are sold only by Chinese grocers.

Once the beans are mature and dried, they look like small yellow balls. These may be soaked (soaking elongates the beans) and then sprouted or else dried off a bit and either fried or roasted like peanuts. Of course, they may be cooked in water like other beans and then mixed with seasonings. While peanuts are ground into peanut "butter," soybeans are the only legumes that may be "milked" (soy milk) and then set into "cheese" (bean curd). Throughout China, Korea, Japan, the Philippines, and Indonesia, soybeans are fermented for long-term use, and made into all manner of soy sauces and soybean pastes. What is more, soybeans can be exposed to a mold *(Rhizopus)* and then left to ferment to create the protein-rich *tempeh,* which is found mainly in Indonesia as well as our own health food shops and some supermarkets.

Cooking soybeans: Soybeans have thick skins and take time to tenderize. They require either long, slow cooking or some time in the pressure cooker. Remember that once the beans have been cooked, they will still need to be finished off in some way.

You may Quick-Soak the beans before cooking them according to directions on page 6, but you will have more uniform results if you soak them overnight.

Pick over, wash, and drain 1 cup soybeans. Soak the beans in water to cover by at least 5 inches and leave overnight, about 10 hours. Drain and rinse well.

Put the beans in a medium pan. Add 7 cups of water and bring to a boil. Turn the heat down so as to maintain a low simmer, cover partially, and cook for 2 hours. Now add 1 cup of water and return to a simmer. Cover partially and cook gently for another hour. Add another cup of water, bring back to a simmer, cover partially, and cook another hour. Now add another 1 cup of water and simmer, partially covered, for 1½ hours, or until the soybeans are very tender.

Pressure cooker method Pick over, wash, and drain 1 cup soybeans. Soak the beans overnight in water to cover by at least 5 inches and leave overnight, about 10 hours. Drain and rinse off.

Put the beans into a pressure cooker with just enough water to cover them and 1½ teaspoons peanut or corn oil. Cover and bring up to pressure (15 pounds); lower the heat while maintaining the pressure and cook for 25 minutes. (Young beans may take a little less time and older ones a minute or two more.) Allow the pressure to drop by itself. You will be left with almost no liquid. If you need more, you may add a little water or stock.

Soybean sprouts: These are not as widely available as mung bean sprouts and in the West are found mainly in Chinese and Korean groceries. They look like slightly larger, coarser versions of mung bean sprouts. The Chinese like to remove the tips (the seed end) and the wispy tails before cooking them, but Koreans often cook them with the bean attached. Because of their firmer texture, they are excellent in salads, stir-fries, and even cooked along with rice.

Making soybean sprouts To make about 3 cups, pick over and wash ½ cup of whole soybeans and then soak them in plenty of water for 12 hours. Drain and rinse them gently a few times. Drain thoroughly again. Now put them into a sprouting jar (you can get this in a health food or gardening shop), cover the jar with its mesh lid, and then leave it on its side in a dark, warm, draft-free area (such as an oven in a warm kitchen). Four times every day for the next 6 days or so, remove the jar, gently fill it with water without tilting it too much, and then empty the water out again. Do this until the sprouts have grown to 3 inches. Remove the sprouts from the jar and put them in a large bowl. Cover well with water to allow the skins to float to the top. Pour all the water and the skins out.

The sprouts may be refrigerated, covered with water, for 4 to 5 days. Change the water every day.

Soy milk: As many children in East Asia are lactose-intolerant, they are raised on soy milk, which is often sold fresh in cartons and plastic bags in supermarkets. In the West, we have to go to health food shops or special Chinese grocers. Soy milk may be drunk cold and plain but it is often heated and seasoned either with sugar or with soy sauce, scallions, and a little sesame oil and eaten from a Chinese bowl with a soup spoon. Sometimes pieces of the deep-fried, savory Chinese cruller *yu thiau* are floated in the milk.

Making soy milk To make about 3½ cups, pick over and wash 1 cup of whole soybeans and then soak them for 10 hours in water that covers them well. Drain and rinse several times. Drain again. Now measure the beans in volume and use just the same volume of warm water to blend them thoroughly in a blender until you have as smooth a puree as possible.

Line a colander with an old, clean pillowcase or large muslin bag and set the colander on top of a large pot or bowl.

Bring 1 cup of water to a boil in a medium pan and when it is boiling, pour it into the puree. Bring it to a boil again and immediately pour the mixture into the lined colander. Close up the pillowcase and, using the bottom of a jar or a potato masher, press out as much liquid as possible. Open the pillowcase, add ¾ cup of warm water, and squeeze out some more milk.

Put the milk into a clean pan and bring it to a boil. As soon as the milk begins to rise, turn the heat down to low and simmer gently for 10 minutes. The soy milk may be used immediately or refrigerated for 2 to 3 days.

Bean curd: Just as cheese is made from milk after it has been made to curdle, so bean curd, in all its infinite varieties, is made from soy milk that has been curdled with solidifiers such as magnesium chloride, calcium chloride, magnesium sulfate, or even very fresh seawater, and then weighted down. As with all soybean products, bean curd is protein rich and is reputed to have the added benefit of helping older women replace lost estrogen.

The most common varieties of fresh bean curd include very soft, medium, and firm bean curd. These come in blocks of varying sizes and densities and are commonly found in water-filled containers in health food shops, supermarkets, and all East Asian groceries. There is also a very soft variety, known as silken bean curd, which I have not used in this chapter.

Storing fresh bean curd The best way is to put the block of bean curd in a bowl, cover it with fresh water, and then refrigerate it. Change the water daily. It should last for 3 to 4 days.

Fried bean curd: This consists of firm bean curd that has been pressed lightly to get rid of some of its moisture and then deep-fried (when done professionally, it is fried twice, first at a low and then a high temperature), allowing it to become brown and crisp on the outside, spongy, and very absorbent. Only East Asian grocers carry it and it is sold in the form of large cakes or smaller cubes; sometimes it is sold frozen as well. Japanese and Korean stores sell it embedded with vegetables and sesame seeds or in the form of little pouches that may be filled. It lasts 2 to 3 days in the refrigerator.

Pressed bean curd: This is available both plain and flavored in the refrigerated compartments of Chinese groceries. These bean curd cakes have been pressed for much longer than "firm" bean curd, making them hard enough to be cut into fine julienne strips that hold their shape. The cakes are generally about 3 × 3 × ¾ inch in size and yellowish-brown or brown in color (the darker ones have been flavored with soy sauce and spices). Each weighs anywhere from 3½ to 4 ounces. They may be stored in a plastic container in the refrigerator for 4 to 5 days.

Fermented bean curd: This smells and tastes like a very ripe soft cheese and the small cubes are sold in glass bottles, almost like a pickle. You will find it both plain and in many "flavors." The seasonings can include crushed red chiles. It is quite salty, and a little bit is wonderful mashed into a dressing the same way you would add a cheese (the Thais make dressings that contain lime juice, chiles, and fermented bean curd). It is frequently added to stir-fried vegetables, such as spinach. Sold only by Chinese grocers, it lasts for months in the refrigerator.

Tempeh: Once found only in Indonesia, tempeh is now commonly sold in most health food shops. It is a kind of miracle food containing almost as much protein as chicken, vitamin B12 (which few vegetarian foods have), no cholesterol, no salt, and few calories. Visually, it does not look promising, but then neither does a chicken. It looks like a slim rectangle coated with white film. Generally, it is made from cooked soybeans (or other legumes, grains, and seeds) that are allowed to ferment with the help of a mold *(Rhizopus)* that eventually envelops them in a white, cottony shroud. Tempeh is sold in cakes that are about ¾ inch thick. It should be wrapped in a plastic bag and then stored in the refrigerator, where it will last 3 to 5 days. You may also freeze it.

Tempeh is generally sliced and fried before being incorporated into dishes. To get the slices nice and crisp, two things help: cutting the slices as thin as possible and deep-frying. After this preliminary step, the strip lends a wonderful meaty presence to dozens of dishes. You will find two of my favorites on pages 107 and 108.

Soybeans with Brown Sugar

Rather like baked beans, this lightly sweetened and very nutritious dish may be served with rice or on toast. I often add reconstituted hijiki, *a dried seaweed rich in calcium and iron that is available in health food stores, to the soybeans to increase their food value.*

2 tablespoons dried *hijiki*

2 tablespoons peanut or canola oil

½ teaspoon peeled and very finely diced fresh ginger

2 scallions, cut crosswise into very fine rings (both white and green sections)

1 small carrot, peeled and cut into small dice

1 cup soybeans prepared according to the basic method (page 91), cooking liquid reserved

2 tablespoons brown sugar

1 teaspoon salt

1 teaspoon oriental sesame oil

Set the *hijiki* to soak in a large bowl of warm water for 30 minutes, or until it is soft. Lift it out of the water, leaving any grit behind, and chop it into ½-inch pieces.

Put the oil in a medium pan and set over medium-high heat. When hot, put in the ginger, scallions, and carrot. Stir for 30 seconds and add the *hijiki*, drained soybeans plus 1 cup of their cooking liquid or water, the brown sugar, and salt. Stir and bring to a simmer over medium heat. Turn the heat to low and simmer, partially covered, for 30 minutes, or until you have a thick, syrupy mass of beans. Taste for the seasonings and adjust. Turn off the heat and stir in the sesame oil. Serve hot.

SERVES 4

Spicy Soybean Patties with Mint

INDIAN-AMERICAN

Soybean Shami Kabab

Few cooks in India use soybeans. I have come up with a quite delicious recipe that tastes very much like the shami kababs *of North India and Pakistan. I like to serve the patties with paper-thin rings of onion that have been separated and soaked in cold water for 1 hour and then drained and patted dry. I just scatter these over the top as they do in India.*

    As the patties already have rice and some vegetables in them, all you need to serve on the side are some fresh vitamin- and flavor-rich chutneys (such as the Delhi-Style Cilantro and Mint Chutney, page 660), salsa, or even tomato ketchup. A green salad would complete the meal.

    I like to use freshly cooked white rice, as it keeps the patties light. If I have leftover cooked rice, I reheat it with a little water in the microwave oven or in a frying pan.

1 cup dried soybeans, picked over, washed, and drained

1½ cups cooked plain white rice

6 to 8 tablespoons peanut or canola oil

3 scallions, cut crosswise into very fine rings (use all of the white and the lower half of the green sections)

5 thin slices of peeled fresh ginger, finely chopped

2 to 3 garlic cloves, peeled and finely chopped

1 medium carrot (3 ounces), peeled and coarsely grated

1 to 2 fresh hot green chiles, finely chopped

3 to 4 tablespoons chopped fresh cilantro

2 tablespoons finely chopped fresh mint

2 teaspoons garam masala (store-bought will do here)

½ teaspoon cayenne, or to taste

1 teaspoon salt

Freshly ground black pepper

1 egg, beaten

¼ cup dry bread crumbs, or as needed

Cook the soybeans according to the directions on page 91. Drain them and mash well until they are pastelike. Add the rice. Mix and set aside in a bowl.

Put 2 tablespoons of the oil in a large frying pan and set over high heat. When hot, put in the scallions, ginger, garlic, carrot, and green chiles. Stir and fry for 3 to 4 minutes, or until very lightly browned. Empty the contents of the frying pan into the bowl with the beans and rice. Add the cilantro, mint, garam masala, cayenne, salt, and pepper to taste. Mix well and taste for seasonings, adding more of anything you like. Put in the egg and bread crumbs. Mix well. The mixture should be firm enough to form into balls or patties. Add a little more bread crumbs if necessary. (This mixture can be kept, covered with plastic, in the refrigerator for up to 3 days.)

Divide the "dough" equally into 16 parts and form 16 patties, about 3 inches in diameter.

Heat 3 tablespoons of the remaining oil in a large, preferably nonstick frying pan over medium-high heat. When hot, lay in as many patties as the pan will hold easily in a single uncrowded layer. Fry them for about 2 minutes on each side, or until they develop a rich, dark, reddish-brown crust on both sides. Remove and drain briefly on paper towels and serve hot if you can or hold in a warm oven. Make the remaining patties exactly the same way, adding a little more oil to the frying pan as you need it.

MAKES 16 MEDIUM PATTIES; SERVES 4

(recipe continues)

Variation
Stuffed Spicy Soybean Patties with Mint   INDIAN-AMERICAN
Bharva Soybean Shami Kabab

Make the soybean mixture or "dough" as in the previous recipe. Cover and refrigerate until ready to cook. Make the stuffing by combining about 7 tablespoons finely chopped shallots, 4 tablespoons finely chopped cilantro, 2 to 3 fresh hot green chiles, finely chopped, ½ teaspoon salt, and 4 teaspoons fresh lemon juice in a bowl. Mix and set aside. Divide the dough into 16 portions. Pick up one part. Make a rough ball, flatten it into a rough 3-inch patty, and put a scant tablespoon of the stuffing in the center of it. Bring the ends of the patty together to make a ball again. Flatten the ball carefully to make a neat 3-inch patty. Make all the patties this way and then cook as in the previous recipe.

Bean Curd with Asparagus and Chinese Mushrooms   HONG KONG

This is an easy way with bean curd, made even easier by the seemingly year-round availability of asparagus. Serve with plain rice.

12 dried Chinese black mushrooms, left soaking in 1 cup of hot water for 30 minutes

½ pound asparagus, trimmed, peeled (page 133), and cut into 1½-inch pieces, then left to soak in water to cover for 20 to 30 minutes

1 pound firm or medium-firm bean curd, cut into 1-inch cubes, put in a bowl, and soaked in boiling water to cover for 15 minutes

2 tablespoons Chinese Shao Hsing wine or dry sherry

3 tablespoons soy sauce (Chinese light soy sauce is ideal)

¾ teaspoon sugar

2 teaspoons cornstarch

1 teaspoon oriental sesame oil

1 teaspoon chili paste with soybean or chili paste with garlic (page 717)

¼ teaspoon salt

3 tablespoons peanut oil

1 garlic clove, lightly crushed and peeled but left whole

2 thin slices of fresh ginger, lightly crushed

2 scallions, cut crosswise into very fine rings (use both white and green sections)

Lift the mushrooms out of their soaking liquid, reserving the liquid. Cut off and discard the tough stems. Halve the mushroom caps if they are large. Strain the mushroom liquid through a fine cloth and set aside.

Drain the asparagus. Drain the bean curd.

In a small bowl, combine the wine, soy sauce, sugar, cornstarch, sesame oil, chili paste, salt, and 4 tablespoons of the mushroom-soaking liquid. Mix well and set aside.

Heat the oil in a wok or large frying pan over high heat. When hot, put in the garlic and ginger. Stir for 30 seconds, then add the asparagus. Stir another 30 seconds. Now put in the bean curd, mushrooms, and half of the sliced scallions and stir for a minute. Pour in 4 tablespoons of the mushroom-soaking liquid, cover, turn the heat down to low, and cook for 3 minutes. Remove the cover, stir the seasoning mixture, and pour it in. Mix gently. Stir in the rest of the scallions. As soon as the sauce thickens, about 1 minute, remove from the heat and serve.

SERVES 4 TO 6

Chris LaBrusciano's
Ginger-Garlic Bean Curd UNITED STATES

This recipe is adapted from a dish I had at the Hungry Mountain Co-op in Montpelier, Vermont. The chef, Chris LaBrusciano, told me that it is not possible to make it with fresh ginger and garlic and that only the powdered versions would do. Here is his version—it is just as good as it is simple. It calls for nutritional yeast, a yellow powder rich in protein with all the essential amino acids and all the B vitamins, sold in all health food shops.

3 tablespoons peanut or canola oil

1 pound firm bean curd, cut into ¾-inch cubes

1 teaspoon garlic powder

1 teaspoon ginger powder

2 tablespoons tamari

1 tablespoon nutritional yeast

Put the oil in a large, preferably nonstick frying pan or wok and set over high heat. When hot, put in the bean curd. Stir and fry for 5 minutes, or until lightly browned on all sides. Add the garlic and ginger powder. Turn down the heat slightly and cook, stirring, another minute. Add the tamari. Turn the heat down to low. Stir and cook another 2 minutes. Sprinkle the nutritional yeast over the top, stir to mix, and turn off the heat.

SERVES 4

Meera Jaffrey's
Bean Curd with Tomatoes and Cilantro

This recipe comes from my daughter, who spent a great deal of time in China. She often adds spinach to the dish as well. If you wish to do that, use about 10 ounces of chopped, blanched, and drained spinach (it could be the frozen kind) and add it just after the tomatoes. Serve with plain rice.

1 pound medium bean curd, cut into 1-inch cubes

4 tablespoons peanut oil

2 scallions, cut crosswise into fine rounds (keep white and green parts separate)

1 (1½-inch) piece of fresh ginger, peeled and very finely chopped

4 medium garlic cloves, peeled and very finely chopped

5 to 6 medium mushrooms, sliced

1 well-packed cup (2 ounces) coarsely chopped fresh cilantro

3 medium tomatoes (14 ounces)

2 tablespoons soy sauce

½ teaspoon salt

1 to 2 teaspoons chili paste with soybean (or chili paste with soybean and garlic, page 717)

1 teaspoon rice vinegar

½ teaspoon sugar

1 cup (5 ounces) fresh or frozen defrosted peas

1 teaspoon oriental sesame oil

Spread a double layer of paper towels out on a board and lay the bean curd cubes on it in a single layer. Put another double layer of paper towels on top and then invert a large plate over the bean curd cubes to press out some of the water. Leave for 30 minutes.

Put 3 tablespoons of the oil in a nonstick frying pan and set over medium heat. Put in the bean curd cubes. Sauté, turning the cubes around for 6 to 7 minutes, or until they are golden on most sides. Remove with a slotted spoon. Add the remaining tablespoon of oil to the frying pan. When hot, put in the white slices of scallion, ginger, and garlic. Stir for 40 seconds. Put in the mushrooms. Stir for 30 seconds. Put in the cilantro. Stir and fry for a minute. Now put in the tomatoes, soy sauce, salt, and chili paste. Stir for a minute. Put in the bean curd cubes, the vinegar, sugar, and peas. Stir a few times and bring to a simmer. Cover, lower the heat, and simmer gently for 5 minutes. Add the green portion of the scallions and the sesame oil. Toss and turn off the heat.

SERVES 4 TO 6

Shiu-Min Block's

Cold Bean Curd Salad CHINA

Liang Ban Dofu

Even though normally made with the firm variety, for this dish you may use almost any kind of fresh bean curd—soft, medium, or firm; the texture will simply be different. If soft bean curd is used, the dish will need to be served in a bowl, perhaps over steaming hot rice. It may be served as part of any oriental meal. Long Beans with Fermented Black Beans (page 209) would make a good accompaniment.

1 pound fresh bean curd

2 tablespoons Chinese Soy Sauce Salad Dressing (page 677)

2 tablespoons Crunchy Sichuan Garlic Relish (page 664) (or a combination of another tablespoon of the Chinese Soy Sauce

Salad Dressing mixed with 1 to 2 teaspoons chili paste with soybean and garlic, page 717)

Salt, if needed

8 tablespoons chopped fresh cilantro

Bring a medium pot of water to a boil. Add the bean curd and simmer 2 minutes. Drain. Let the bean curd cool a little and then crumble it with your fingers. Add the Chinese Soy Sauce Salad Dressing and the Crunchy Sichuan Relish. Mix and taste. Add a little salt if needed, then add cilantro and mix again. Serve at room temperature or cold.

SERVES 4 TO 6

Shiu-Min Block's

Bean Curd with Hot Sauce

CHINA

La Jiao Chieng Chow Dofu

This is a spicy bean curd dish to be eaten with rice and other Chinese-style vegetables.

5 teaspoons soy sauce

1½ teaspoons chili paste with garlic (page 717)

1 teaspoon sugar

1 teaspoon oriental sesame oil

3 tablespoons vegetable stock or water

2 tablespoons canola oil

2 scallions, cut crosswise into fine rings (both white and green sections)

3 slices of peeled fresh ginger, very finely diced

2 garlic cloves, lightly mashed and peeled but left whole

1 pound firm bean curd, cut into ⅓-inch dice

1 tablespoon finely chopped fresh cilantro

Combine the soy sauce, chili paste, sugar, sesame oil, and stock in a small bowl. Stir to mix.

Put the oil in a wok or frying pan and set over high heat. When hot, add the scallions, ginger, and garlic and stir for 30 seconds. Now put in the bean curd. Stir for 30 seconds, then add the soy sauce mixture, stir, and bring to a boil. Cover, turn the heat down to low, and simmer gently for 5 minutes. Add the cilantro and stir to mix.

SERVES 4

Bean Curd with Mushrooms

CHINA

Mo Gu Dofu

I use ordinary, medium white mushrooms here but any fresh mushrooms would work well. Serve with plain rice.

½ pound firm bean curd

For the batter

2 egg whites, lightly beaten

1 tablespoon Chinese Shao Hsing wine or dry sherry

¼ teaspoon salt

¼ cup cornstarch

Peanut or canola oil for frying

For the sauce

2 tablespoons cornstarch

5 tablespoons vegetable stock

1 tablespoon Chinese Shao Hsing wine or dry sherry

½ teaspoon sugar

¼ teaspoon salt

1 teaspoon oriental sesame oil

You also need

2 dried hot red chiles

1 garlic clove, peeled and finely chopped

1 teaspoon very finely minced fresh peeled ginger

½ pound white mushrooms, thickly sliced

Scant ½ teaspoon salt

1 scallion, cut crosswise into thin rounds (both green and white sections)

Cut the bean curd into rectangles about 3 inches long × ¾ inch wide × ¼ inch thick. Lay them in a single layer on a double thickness of paper towel that has been placed on a clean counter or board. Cover with another double thickness of paper towel and then put another board on top. Place some weights on the top board (I use 4 full wine bottles) and let stand for 30 minutes. Remove the weights and pat the bean curd dry with fresh paper towels.

Put the egg whites, wine, salt, and cornstarch into a wide, shallow bowl and mix well. Add the bean curd and gently coat the pieces with the batter.

Pour oil to a depth of ¾ inch in a medium frying pan and set over medium heat. When hot, slip in the bean curd pieces, one at a time. Fry for about 1½ minutes, or until one side is golden. Turn the pieces over and fry until the second side is golden as well, another 1½ minutes or so. Remove with a slotted spoon and drain on clean paper towels. (This much may be done ahead of time.)

Combine the sauce ingredients in a small bowl and set aside.

Heat 3 tablespoons of the oil used to fry the bean curd in a large frying pan or wok over high heat. When hot, put in the red chiles. Stir until they swell and darken, a matter of seconds, then add the garlic and ginger and stir once. Put in the mushrooms and stir briskly for a minute. Add the bean curd. Stir for another minute, then add the salt and stir again. Take the pan off the heat, stir the sauce mixture, and pour it in. Place the pan back over low heat and cook for about 30 seconds, stirring gently, or until the sauce thickens. Sprinkle the scallion over the top, stir once, and serve immediately.

SERVES 3 TO 4

Bean Curd with
Black Bean Sauce

CHINESE-AMERICAN

Here bean curd is lightly browned and then cooked quickly and easily with a coarse paste that includes salted black beans, ginger, and garlic. It requires no more that a green vegetable and rice to complete the meal. The dish is also elegant enough to serve at dinner parties.

For the sauce

½ cup vegetable stock

1 teaspoon cornstarch

2 teaspoons Chinese Shao Hsing wine or dry
   sherry

1 teaspoon oriental sesame oil

½ teaspoon salt

Freshly ground black pepper

You also need

3 tablespoons peanut oil

1 pound firm bean curd, cut into ¾- to 1-inch
   cubes

1 to 2 fresh hot green chiles, cut crosswise at
   a slight angle into ¼-inch-thick slices

4 scallions, cut crosswise at a slight angle into
   ¼-inch-thick oval slices (both white and
   green sections)

2 tablespoons salted black beans, rinsed
   thoroughly and very finely chopped

2 garlic cloves, peeled and very finely
   chopped

2 teaspoons finely minced ginger

Combine the sauce ingredients in a small bowl, mix well, and set aside.

Put the oil in a large wok or nonstick frying pan and set over high heat. When the oil is hot, put in the bean curd cubes. Stir gently for 5 minutes, or until the pieces are lightly browned on most sides. Remove to a plate with a slotted spoon. Put in the chile and scallions and stir and fry for 30 seconds, scraping up any bean curd that might have stuck to the bottom. Quickly add the black beans, garlic, and ginger and stir and fry for 10 seconds. Return the bean curd to the pan and toss for 10 seconds. Stir the sauce, pour it in over the bean curd, and stir gently over low heat, until the sauce is thick. Serve immediately.

SERVES 4

Bean Curd Vegeburgers

These are easily some of the best bean curd and vegetable patties I have ever eaten. They are light in texture and very easy to prepare. You can serve them simply, with a little tomato ketchup and a very thin slice of raw onion on top, either sandwiched in a bun or between slices of toast, or you may offer them with a salad and bread on the side.

1 pound firm bean curd

5 tablespoons peanut or canola oil

3 scallions, cut crosswise into very fine rings (use all the white and the lower half of the green sections)

4 large shiitake mushrooms (caps only), cut into ⅛-inch dice (use 5 plain medium mushrooms as a substitute)

1 smallish carrot (3 ounces), peeled and cut into ⅛-inch dice

2 tablespoons celery cut into ⅛-inch dice

½ to 2 fresh hot green chiles, finely chopped

4 tablespoons chopped fresh cilantro or parsley

2 tablespoons tamari soy sauce, or to taste

Freshly ground black pepper

1 egg, beaten

About ½ cup dry bread crumbs

Put the bean curd on a double layer of paper towels. Cover with another double layer of paper towels. Put a board or large plate on top and put a weight such as a 1-pound can on top of that. Leave for an hour. Crumble the bean curd into a mixing bowl, mashing and crumbling it further until it is like ground meat.

Put 2 tablespoons of the oil in a large frying pan and set on high heat. When hot, put in the scallions, mushrooms, carrot, celery, and chile. Stir and fry for 3 minutes, then add these to the bowl with the crumbled bean curd. Stir in the cilantro, tamari, and pepper to taste. Mix well and taste to see if there is enough salt. Now add the egg and about 5 tablespoons bread crumbs, or enough to form patties. Mix well and make 7 to 8 patties. Put the remaining bread crumbs in a large plate. Dredge the patties in the bread crumbs to cover them lightly on all sides. (The breaded patties can be refrigerated for 3 to 4 hours or cooked immediately.)

Heat the remaining 3 tablespoons of oil in a large, nonstick skillet over medium-high heat. Place all the patties in the pan and cook for 3 to 4 minutes on each side, or until they are well browned. Drain on paper towels and serve immediately.

MAKES 7 TO 8 PATTIES

(recipe continues)

Variation I

Curried Bean Curd Vegeburgers

Make the vegeburgers according to the master recipe but with this difference: After the 2 tablespoons oil is hot, put in 1 teaspoon whole cumin seeds. Stir them for 10 seconds before putting in the scallions, mushrooms, carrot, celery, and chile. Stir and fry for 3 minutes. Add 1 tablespoon curry powder (My Curry Powder, page 707, would be ideal, but any hot curry powder will do) and stir for 10 seconds, then proceed with the recipe. These may be served with a salad for a light meal or in a bun, like a hamburger, with a dollop of hot chutney on top.

Vegeburgers in Brown Mushroom Sauce

Sometimes I like to serve vegeburgers in a more elegant mode, accompanied by a sauce made with fresh shiitake and dried porcini mushrooms. I serve some plainly cooked vegetables (such as grilled tomatoes, boiled potatoes, lightly sautéed spinach) on the side. Make the sauce before the burgers, as it can be reheated easily.

This sauce may be ladled over noodles (perfect for ½ pound), polenta, even over cooked beans or chickpeas. It may also be used to briefly simmer a pound of fresh bean curd cubes.

6 to 7 slices of dried porcini mushrooms or about 1½ tablespoons if they are in small pieces

7 to 8 fresh shiitake or white mushrooms

1 vegetable bouillon cube

1½ teaspoons cornstarch

2 tablespoons olive or canola oil

3 tablespoons peeled and finely chopped shallots

1 smallish carrot (3 ounces), peeled and finely chopped

3 tablespoons dry vermouth

1 small tomato (4 ounces), peeled, seeded, and chopped (see page 300)

4 teaspoons soy sauce

½ teaspoon sugar

Freshly ground black pepper

1 recipe vegeburgers (page 103)

Soak the dried porcini in 1½ cups of hot water and set aside for 1 hour, or until well softened. Lift the mushrooms out of the liquid and, if the slices are large, cut them into fine slivers. Strain the soaking liquid if necessary.

Discard the stems of the fresh shiitake mushrooms and cut the caps into fine slivers.

Heat 1 cup of the mushroom liquid with the bouillon cube until dissolved. Combine the remaining ½ cup of mushroom liquid with the cornstarch and set aside.

Heat the oil in a large frying pan over medium-high heat. When hot, put in the shallots and carrot. Stir and fry for 1½ minutes, or until the shallots just start to turn brown. Add the dried and fresh mushrooms. Stir and fry for another 1½ minutes. Add the vermouth and cook, stirring now and then, until all the vermouth is absorbed and the pan appears dry. Add the stock, the tomato, soy sauce, sugar, and pepper to taste. Stir and bring to a simmer. Cook very gently over low heat for 5 minutes. Stir the cornstarch mixture and pour it into the pan. Stir to mix and simmer gently until the sauce has thickened, about 1 minute. Turn off the heat.

Make the vegeburgers according to the master recipe, reheat the sauce if necessary, and serve hot.

SERVES 4

Shiu-Min Block's
Pressed Bean Curd Braised
with Five Flavorings   CHINA
Wu Shiung Dofu Gun

I have not indicated how many people this recipe serves because once prepared, there are many things you can do with these full-flavored bean curd cakes, each resulting in a different number of servings: You may slice some of the bean curd cakes and serve them with drinks, plain or with a dipping sauce; you may slice or shred them and stir-fry them with vegetables (see Pressed Bean Curd Stir-Fried with Hot Peppers, page 106); slices may be put into a leafy green salad; julienned pieces may be combined with finely julienned endive and cucumber, moistened with a French salad dressing, and served as a first course; fine shreds may be combined with blanched bean sprouts and then dressed with the Chinese Soy Sauce Salad Dressing (page 677); and of course, slices may be eaten plain with rice.

You need pressed and "flavored" bean curd for this recipe. You will see it in the refrigerated compartments of Chinese grocery and health food stores. These cakes are about 3 ×3 ×¾ inch in size and yellowish-brown or brown in color. Each weighs anywhere from 3½ to 4 ounces.

Once braised, the bean curd cakes will hold for about 2 weeks in the refrigerator if kept in a sealed container without their braising liquid. They are very useful to have on hand.

(recipe continues)

2 teaspoons peanut oil

3 thin slices of fresh ginger, cut crosswise off the root

4 whole scallions, cut into 2½-inch segments, the white parts halved lengthwise

3 tablespoons Chinese dark soy sauce

2 tablespoons Chinese light soy sauce

2 teaspoons Chinese Shao Hsing wine or dry sherry

½ teaspoon salt

4 to 5 whole star anise

8 pieces (about 1¾ to 2 pounds) pressed flavored bean curd

Put the oil in a good-sized pot (large enough to hold all the bean curd easily) and set over medium-high heat. When hot, add the ginger and scallions and stir for 30 seconds. Put in 2 cups of water, the dark soy, the light soy, the Shao Hsing wine, salt, and star anise and stir to mix. Put the bean curd cakes into this liquid, cover, and bring to a boil. Boil vigorously for 2 minutes, then turn the heat to medium-low and cook, covered, for another 40 minutes, turning the cakes over now and then or else basting them occasionally with the sauce. Remove the cakes from the sauce, cool, and store in a closed container in the refrigerator. The sauce may now be discarded.

Shiu-Min Block's

Pressed Bean Curd Stir-Fried with Hot Peppers

CHINA

Dofu Gan Chaw Ching La Jiao

This stir-fry may be made with the yellowish-brown or brown flavored pressed bean curd sold by Chinese grocers (see details on page 93) or with the Pressed Bean Curd Braised with Five Flavorings (page 105). You will need only 2 cakes. Eat it with rice and either another vegetable, such as Broccoli Stir-Fried with Ginger and Garlic (page 146), or a simple green salad.

You will also need medium-hot peppers such as the long Italian kind, long Korean peppers, or the light green kind that the Greeks use for making pickled peppers. If you want the dish to have no heat whatsoever, you may use one large green or red bell pepper instead of the long hot peppers. Cut it in half lengthwise and then core and seed. Cut the halves crosswise into thin strips about ⅛ inch in width.

3 tablespoons peanut oil

3 scallions, white and green parts, cut into 2-inch lengths, then cut lengthwise into fine strips

3 thin slices of peeled fresh ginger, cut into fine strips

2 cakes pressed flavored bean curd or 2 cakes Pressed Bean Curd Braised with Five Flavorings (page 105)

6 to 7 ounces medium-hot peppers (see recipe introduction), stem end removed (but not seeds) and then cut on the diagonal into ⅛-inch slices

2 garlic cloves, lightly crushed and peeled but left whole

¾ teaspoon salt

1 teaspoon oriental sesame oil

Put the vegetable oil in a large wok or frying pan and set over high heat. When hot, put in the scallions and ginger and stir for 10 seconds. Put in the bean curd and hot peppers, stir for 10 seconds, then add the garlic and salt. Stir for 2 minutes. Add 1 tablespoon water, cover, turn the heat to medium-low, and cook 2 minutes. Turn off the heat, add the sesame oil, and stir to mix.

SERVES 6

Fried Spiced Tempeh

INDONESIA

Tempeh Goreng

Here is one of the many simple versions of fried and spiced tempeh. It may be served as a snack or as part of the main meal. Instead of hard-to-find Indonesian kenari *nuts, I have used almonds.*

3 garlic cloves, peeled and coarsely chopped

3 medium shallots, peeled and coarsely chopped

2 blanched almonds, finely chopped

1 tablespoon ground coriander

1 teaspoon salt

½ teaspoon coarsely ground black pepper

¼ teaspoon cayenne

8 ounces tempeh

Peanut or canola oil for deep-frying

Combine the garlic, shallots, almonds, and ½ cup of water in a blender. Blend until you have a smooth paste. Add the coriander, salt, pepper, and cayenne and blend again for a second to mix. Empty into a large bowl.

Cut the slab of tempeh crosswise into ⅛-inch-thick slices. Score the slices lightly on both sides in a cross-hatch pattern at ¼-inch intervals.

(recipe continues)

Heat enough oil to have about 1½ inches in a deep frying pan or about 3 inches in the center of a wok over medium heat. When hot, put half the tempeh slices into the bowl with the seasonings, stir the pieces around quickly to coat them, then lift them out, shaking off extra liquid, and put them into the hot oil. Stir and fry for about 6 minutes, or until the tempeh slices are crisp and golden. Remove with a slotted spoon and drain on a paper towel. Make a second batch the same way. Serve while still hot and crisp.

SERVES 3 TO 4

From the home of Pia Alisjahbana

Sweet-and-Sour Tempeh with Peanuts

INDONESIA

Sambal Goreng Tempeh Kering

This dish was part of a superb banquet I had in Jakarta that concluded with generous servings of one of my favorite fruits, the durian. Serve with plain rice by itself or with some Southeast Asian vegetables such as Cabbage with Garlic and Shallots (page 152). Any fruit, such as mangoes or sliced oranges, can always conclude the meal.

4 to 5 dried red chiles, seeds removed and soaked in ¼ cup hot water for 30 minutes

¾ cup coarsely chopped shallots

1 (1-inch) piece of fresh ginger, grated to a pulp

3 garlic cloves, peeled and coarsely chopped

Peanut oil for deep-frying

½ cup raw skinned peanuts

8 ounces tempeh, cut into 1½ × ¼ × ¼-inch matchsticks

10 fresh curry leaves, if available, or 8 fresh basil leaves, torn in rough pieces

4 teaspoons thick tamarind paste (page 737)

1 teaspoon salt

2 teaspoons light brown sugar

In a blender, combine the chiles and their soaking liquid, the shallots, ginger, and garlic and blend until a paste forms, pushing down with a rubber spatula as necessary.

Heat enough oil to have about 1½ inches in a deep frying pan or about 3 inches in the center of a wok over medium heat. When hot, add the peanuts and fry just until they start to color; remove them with a slotted spoon and drain on paper towels. Now put in half of the tempeh. Stir and fry for about 6 minutes, or until the matchsticks are reddish-gold and crisp. Remove and drain on paper towels. Fry the remaining tempeh in the same way, draining on paper towels.

Remove all but 4 tablespoons of oil from the frying pan or wok. Put in the spice paste from the blender as well as the curry leaves. Stir and fry on medium heat for 7 to 8 minutes, or until the paste loses its watery look. Stir in the tamarind paste, salt, and sugar, then add the tempeh and peanuts. Stir gently to mix.

SERVES 4

Split Peas

Split peas, green and yellow, need almost no introduction. They are found in most supermarkets in areas as disparate as India, Greece, Morocco, Malaysia, and the United States, indeed around much of the world. The variety of the dried peas may vary slightly but the cooking methods remain the same. They are transformed into spicy stews in Trinidad, thick, earthy purees in Algeria, Tunisia, Cyprus, and Morocco, and rich smoky soups in the United States. I have reserved green split peas exclusively for use in the soups chapter; the recipes that follow are for yellow split peas, which can also be made into delicious soups but here are used for purees and stews.

The earliest peas, so far, have been discovered in Thailand, dating back to almost 10,000 B.C. We also know that they were eaten by the ancients Greeks and Romans, almost always in their dried form. I find it very interesting that a common staple in northern England—not too far from the very Roman Hadrian's Wall—is "mushy peas," dried green peas cooked coarsely into a thick puree. This "pease porridge" (as in "Pease-porridge hot, pease-porridge cold, pease-porridge in the pot, nine days old") probably dates back to antiquity.

Dried peas are skinned and split in order to make cooking faster—or more accurately, in order to avoid the soaking process. The method of cooking these skinned and split peas varies according to what you want to do with them, so it is best to follow individual recipes.

Melle Derko Samira's

Moroccan Yellow Split Pea Puree   MOROCCO

Bissara

This is one of the simplest of bissaras *or legume purees to be found in Morocco. Generally, a shallow soup plate is filled with this puree, paprika, ground cumin, and ground cayenne are sprinkled over the top, and enough good-quality virgin olive oil is poured over the surface to provide a generous film. Diners dip pieces of Everyday Moroccan Bread (page 460) into the* bissara. *Some lemon juice may be squeezed over the top, or, if you so wish, Moroccan or Indian preserved lemon may be served with it.*

This dish is sometimes served as a second course in an elaborate Moroccan meal, preceded by Moroccan salads and followed by stews and couscous. In the villages, it is often the main dish, accompanied by vegetables and salads.

1 cup yellow split peas, picked over, washed in several changes of water, and drained

3 whole garlic cloves, unpeeled

¼ teaspoon ground turmeric

¾ teaspoon salt

6 to 9 tablespoons extra-virgin olive oil

1 teaspoon ground cumin

1 teaspoon ground paprika

About ½ teaspoon cayenne

4 lemon wedges (optional)

Combine the split peas, garlic, turmeric, and 3 cups of water in a medium pot. Bring to a boil over medium heat without allowing it to boil over. Turn the heat down to low and partially cover the pan. Cook gently for 40 to 50 minutes, or until the split peas are very tender.

Using a potato masher, mash the garlic cloves against the sides of the pan and remove their skins. Now mash the peas until you have a thick, coarse puree. Add the salt, 1 tablespoon of the olive oil, ¼ teaspoon cumin, ¼ teaspoon paprika, and ⅛ teaspoon cayenne. Stir well. The puree should be thick enough to pick up with a piece of bread, but not so thick that it feels solid. If it is too thick, thin out with a few extra tablespoons of water.

To serve, ladle the split peas into 3 soup plates or wide, shallow bowls, spreading it out and leveling it with the back of a soup spoon. Sprinkle ¼ teaspoon cumin, ¼ teaspoon paprika, and ⅛ teaspoon cayenne evenly over each of the servings. Cover each serving with a thin layer of olive oil. Each serving should be shared by 2 people. (The puree can also be served in a single bowl, to be put in the center of the table and shared by all diners, the way it often is in Morocco.) Serve hot, accompanied by wedges of lemon, if desired.

SERVES 6

From Tiffin's, Port of Spain

Yellow Split Peas with Thyme and Cumin

TRINIDAD

Dholl

This dish of the Trinidad Indians is often eaten with rice, a vegetable such as Curried Long Beans (page 210) or Spinach Bhaji (page 230), and a relish. Trinidadian Pepper Sauce (page 771) is always on the table!

Though very similar to an Indian dal, *the difference lies in the use of the earthy, sweet, yellow split peas, which are not found in India, and the use of thyme and chives, which came to Trinidad with Mediterranean immigrants.*

You may wish to eat this dish in the Eastern Mediterranean and North African manner, with flatbreads. Ladle some out into a bowl when it has cooled somewhat and thickened. Dribble some olive oil over the top to prevent a film from forming, and place it in the center of the table for all to share and dip their bread pieces into. Other salads and cheeses may be served at the same time to form the appetizer course or a full, light meal.

1½ cups yellow split peas, picked over, washed in several changes of water, and drained

Scant ½ teaspoon ground turmeric

½ cup very finely chopped onion

1 tablespoon very finely chopped chives

2 to 3 teaspoons very finely chopped fresh hot red or green chiles or ¼ Scotch bonnet, finely chopped

1 tablespoon very finely chopped parsley

1 teaspoon finely chopped fresh thyme leaves or ¼ teaspoon dried thyme leaves

1¼ teaspoons salt

3 tablespoons peanut or canola oil

½ teaspoon whole cumin seeds

1 garlic clove, peeled and crushed to a pulp

Combine the drained split peas and 5 cups of water in a heavy pot and bring to a boil, making sure that the contents do not boil over. Add the turmeric, stir, turn the heat down to low, and cover partially, leaving the lid just very slightly ajar. Cook gently for 35 minutes. Add the onion, chives, chiles, parsley, thyme, and salt. Stir, cover partially again, and continue to cook gently for another 20 minutes, or until the split peas are tender, stirring now and then. Turn off the heat.

Put the oil in a small frying pan and set over medium-high heat. When very hot, put in the cumin seeds. Let them sizzle for 10 seconds and then put in the garlic. Stir for a few seconds until it turns golden, then pour the contents of the pan over the split peas. Stir to mix.

SERVES 6

Urad Beans, Whole and Split
(Ma, Urad Dal)

As a child, I seemed to favor foods that were slightly glutinous. The two that fit the bill, and which I often ate together with much passion, were okra and split *urad* beans. Among all the beans and split peas, *urad* is the only one I know that is slightly viscous, allowing it to qualify, in my mind at least, as super comfort food.

An ancient bean of Indian origin, *urad* is believed to be a sister to the mung bean and to have developed from the same basic form. Remains dating back 3500 years have been found in central India.

Rather like mung beans, whole *urad* beans (*ma* or *sabut urad* in Indian shops) are small and somewhat cylindrical in shape. However, unlike mung beans, which have a shiny, green skin, *urad* beans are a dull black. Once hulled and split, they reveal a very pale yellow, almost cream-colored interior.

In their whole form they are a staple in the Punjab in India, where they are called *ma* and often cooked in combination with red kidney beans in order to get a wonderful contrast in texture and color. Once tender, they are lubricated with generous tablespoons of homemade white butter, which is plentiful in that dairy-rich state, and served in the poorest of villages, the most egalitarian of temples, and the palaces of the richest maharajas. While Punjab may well lay claim to the greatest use of the whole *urad* bean, the entire subcontinent delights in the hulled and split version, *urad dal*. North Indian Muslims love to cook it so each grain stays separate and in South India it is soaked, ground, mixed with soaked and ground rice, and allowed to ferment. This basic batter is then used to make dozens of different types of savory pancakes *(dosas)* and steamed cakes *(idlis)*.

Also, it should be kept in mind that of all the legumes, it is *urad* that is richest in the phosphorus compound phytin, necessary in the making of *poppadums,* the crispbreads that appear miraculously at the start of every Indian restaurant meal. Since ancient times, it has been the legume of choice in India for the making of all manner of fine wafers and dumplings.

To cook whole unhulled *urad* beans *(ma)*: see azuki beans (page 8).

To cook hulled and split *urad* beans *(urad dal)*: The beans are cooked rather like hulled and split mung beans, although the cooking time is a little longer. The basic recipe follows.

Basic Recipe for Hulled and Split Urad Beans

INDIA

Basic Urad Dal

When the beans are to be finished off with a tarka, *as suggested in the next two recipes, they may be cooked according to this procedure and refrigerated a day or two before reheating.*

1 cup hulled and split *urad* beans *(urad dal),* picked over, washed in several changes of water, and drained

¼ teaspoon ground turmeric

1 to 1¼ teaspoons salt

Put the split beans and 4 cups of water in a heavy-bottomed pot and bring to a boil. Watch carefully that the contents of the pot do not boil over. Remove the froth that rises to the top. Add the turmeric and stir once. Cover partially, turn the heat down to low, and cook very gently for 1 hour, or until the beans are tender. Add the salt and stir to mix.

You may do the *tarka* right away or at a later time. If the beans have been refrigerated, add just enough water to prevent them from sticking to the pan, usually just a few tablespoons, and stir over medium-high heat until hot.

SERVES 4 TO 6

Split Urad Beans in the Delhi Style

INDIA

Dilli Ki Urad Dal

Serve this with a flatbread, some salads, and a vegetable. A yogurt dish would complement the meal.

1 cup hulled and split *urad* beans *(urad dal),* cooked according to the basic recipe, above

3 tablespoons *ghee* (page 723) or peanut oil

½ teaspoon whole cumin seeds

Generous pinch of ground asafetida

2 whole dried hot red chiles

¼ cup peeled, seeded, and chopped tomato (if you need directions, see page 300)

(recipe continues)

Heat the *urad dal* and keep it warm.

Put the *ghee* or oil in a small frying pan and set over medium-high heat. When hot, put in the cumin seeds and asafetida and let the cumin seeds sizzle for 10 seconds. Now put in the red chiles. As soon as they darken, a matter of seconds, put in the tomato. Stir twice, then empty the contents of the frying pan into the pan with the beans. Stir to mix and serve. (The whole red chiles should be eaten only by those who know what they are doing.)

SERVES 4

Split Urad Beans Cooked in the Lucknow Style   INDIA
Lucknavi Urad Dal

This dish, very traditional and very simple at the same time, is eaten mainly by the Muslim families from Lucknow in Uttar Pradesh.

Here the split beans are soaked first and then cooked in a small quantity of water, which allows them to retain their shape. Fresh green and dried red chiles add their own special flavors and aromas, and the browned onions that grace the very top add crispness. If you like, you may remove the garlic clove before serving. Diners may also squeeze a little lime juice over the portion in their plates.

Eat these split peas with flatbreads, vegetable dishes, and salads. You could even roll them into a flatbread with lettuce and tomatoes for a very satisfying wrap sandwich.

1 cup hulled and split *urad* beans *(urad dal)*, picked over and washed

3 tablespoons peanut or canola oil

½ teaspoon whole cumin seeds

1 fresh hot green chile

1 garlic clove, peeled and split in half lengthwise

⅛ teaspoon ground turmeric

¾ teaspoon salt

1 dried hot red chile

1 small onion (2 ounces), peeled, halved lengthwise, then very thinly sliced

Soak the split *urad* beans in water to cover by 5 inches for 4 hours. Drain.

Heat 1 tablespoon of the oil in a medium pan and set over medium-high heat. When hot, put in the cumin. Stir for a few seconds, then put in the green chile and garlic. Stir until the garlic is golden and put in the beans. Stir for a few seconds. Now put in 1 cup of water, the turmeric, and salt. Stir and bring to a boil. Cover tightly, turn the heat down to low, and cook very gently for 25 minutes.

Just before serving, heat up the beans gently and put them in a serving dish. Leave in a warm place. Heat the remaining 2 tablespoons of oil in a small frying pan over medium-high heat. When hot, put in the red chile and stir until it darkens, a matter of seconds. Now put in the onion, stirring and frying until the onion slices turn reddish-brown and crisp. You will need to lower the heat a bit as they brown. Pour the contents of the frying pan over the cooked beans. Serve immediately.

SERVES 3 TO 4

Whole Urad Beans Cooked in the Punjabi Style
INDIA
Ma

A hearty bean dish from rural Punjab in the northwest of India, this can be eaten with flatbreads and some greens. A yogurt or cheese dish should ideally be part of the meal.

This dish is made with whole black urad *beans, sold in Indian shops as whole* urad (sabut urad) *or* ma. *The slightly glutinous bean is often combined with red kidney beans for a contrast of textures and colors. The long cooking time reflects the traditional method for making this dish in Punjabi villages, where* tandoors *(large clay ovens) are used in the daytime to cook breads and sometimes meats. The leftover hot ashes are not wasted. In the late evening, earthen pots are filled with these beans and water, buried in the smoldering ashes, and left to cook slowly overnight.*

1 cup dried whole *urad* beans *(ma)*

½ cup dried red kidney beans

2 to 2¼ teaspoons salt

3 tablespoons peanut or canola oil

⅔ cup finely chopped onions

2 tablespoons finely grated ginger

¾ cup finely chopped very ripe tomatoes

¼ teaspoon cayenne

Soak the *urad* beans and kidney beans overnight in 7 cups of water or Quick-Soak them in the same amount of water, using the directions on page 6. Drain in a colander, discarding the soaking liquid.

Return the beans to the pot with 6 cups of fresh water and bring to a boil. Cover and cook on low heat for 1 hour. Uncover and continue cooking gently for an additional hour. Add salt to the beans and stir to mix. Leave on very low heat.

(recipe continues)

Meanwhile, put the oil in a medium frying pan and set over medium-high heat. Add the onions and stir and fry until the onions just begin to brown. Put in the ginger and stir once or twice. Then add the tomatoes and cayenne. Cook for 2 minutes, or until the oil begins to separate from the tomato mixture. Empty the contents of the frying pan into the pot with the cooked beans and stir to mix well. Turn the heat down to low and simmer gently for 1 to 2 minutes to marry all the flavorings. Serve hot.

SERVES 6 TO 8

Cashew Nuts

Cashew nuts may be native to Brazil or other parts of the tropical Americas, but it is India, more specifically western, coastal India, where they were introduced by the Portuguese in the early sixteenth century and where 90 percent of the world's crop is now grown, that has created substantial dishes where they play starring roles.

My own exposure to cashew nuts came early in life. My mother loved to cook but her large kitchen staff made it quite unnecessary. Still, she could not resist stepping up to the charcoal-fired stove to make special things. Anything my father adored fell into this "special" category, as did all religious foods, which my mother felt were essential to our salvation but which my father routinely ignored.

Every evening, my father sat down in a comfortably upholstered chair to enjoy his whiskey and soda. The ritual varied according to the season but in the winter, a fire was lit, the whiskey poured, and assorted nuts were set out on the coffee table as accompaniments. These included the season's new walnuts from Kashmir (these had to be *kagzi,* or the "paper-shell" variety, which could be cracked between the palms of two hands), which were always eaten with golden raisins from Afghanistan, lest we get a sore throat, according to my mother. There were also almonds (brain food, my mother said), also from Kashmir, and cashews from somewhere in the south, an area my parents knew little about.

The cashews were always freshly fried by my mother. Though I watched her do it hundreds of times, I do not quite remember the actual frying; it was probably boring. But the next step was not. She removed the cashews with a slotted spoon when they were just perfectly golden and spread them out on brown paper. (We always had brown paper. It was used to cover every single textbook and notebook. My mother did all that for us, and oh, so neatly.) Then, while the cashews were still hot, coarse salt and black pepper were sprinkled over them, the nuts put into the prettiest bowls made out of coconut shells (my mother had found them at some national exhibition and they stayed with her until she died), and the offering brought before my father while it was still hot. I now use a microwave oven and very little oil to make a similar dish (page 118).

We ate cashews as snacks, as much of the Western world does today. We knew nothing about cashews as major dishes at a meal. That was a world I had yet to discover.

Cashews like to grow where there is no hint of a freeze, where there are balmy seas and possibly a few unthreatening, sandy hills—in short, where most of us would like to be. India's southwestern coast, all the way up to Goa, fits the bill perfectly. In Goa today, there is a store that no tourist should miss in the capital city, Panaji, that sells only the best, freshest cashews in all grades. That is what I bring home when I go to Goa. You do not know what a good cashew can be until you have tasted their largest and plumpest. They are sold with their reddish-brown, slightly bitter skin on (purists, some of my best friends among them, will eat no other) and off. All cashews that are sold have gone through an initial roasting, even the "raw" ones.

The cashew is a nut that needs to be understood. It grows on what seems to be a slightly misshapen tree, attached to the bottom of what looks like an apple-like fruit that is not really a fruit. Actually it is the cashew that is the true fruit but it does not know it. The false fruit, the red or yellow cashew apple, is pretty, pleasant in flavor, and rich in vitamin C. It is eaten out of hand in most of the tropical world and is even made into wines and hard liquors. The nut is removed but cannot be eaten immediately as it is poisonous. (It belongs to the same family as poison ivy, mangoes, and pistachios.)

It has two "skins" that hold between them acids that can burn the mouth and lips. These acids are drained out in an initial roasting and used to make varnishes and termite treatments. All cashews we get as raw, skinned cashews have gone through this treatment. If they have been "roasted" or "fried," that is a second step in the processing of the cashews.

All along the western coast of India and in Sri Lanka as well, cashews are cooked like vegetables and beans. For vegetarians, it is important to remember that aside from their delicious taste, they, like most nuts, contain some protein and are high in cholesterol-reducing polyunsaturated and monounsaturated fats, fiber, copper, folacin (which prevents birth defects), magnesium, phosphorus, vitamin B6, and lots of vitamin E. In other words, when mixing and matching ingredients for a meal, cashews can play an important part.

In order to cook cashews as you would dried beans, it is best to soak "raw" cashews overnight. Then they are ready for any seasonings you wish to throw at them. What follow are mostly traditional dishes from western, coastal India and Sri Lanka, the area where cashews are grown and eaten regularly. You should feel free to experiment and create dishes of your own, as I have done.

Storing raw cashews: Raw cashews are best stored in the freezer. Once cashews have been roasted or fried, they are best kept in tightly closed jars and tins.

Niru Row Kavi's
Quick Cashews Zapped in the Microwave

I often wondered what a microwave was good for other than reheating food until a friend in India gave me this recipe, which puts the microwave to good use.

This is a very easy way to roast cashews with any spices or seasonings that you like. I have used just salt and a little cayenne, but you could add a generous pinch of thyme or perhaps a little cumin. The cashews are quite soft when they come out of the microwave. Just give them about 10 minutes to harden up.

I have a high-powered microwave with a turntable. You might need to make adjustments in time if you have any other kind.

½ cup whole raw cashews

1 teaspoon peanut or canola oil

¼ teaspoon salt

⅛ teaspoon cayenne

Place the cashews in a bowl large enough to fit them in a single layer. Add the oil and toss well. Sprinkle with the salt and cayenne and stir to mix. Put in the microwave oven and cook on High for 3 minutes. Stir and cook for 3 to 4 minutes longer, stopping to stir at least once. Let the cashews cool completely, about 10 minutes. Sprinkle with additional salt and cayenne as desired.

SERVES 4 AS AN APPETIZER

Cashews in a Mediterranean Tomato Sauce

Here is a recipe that I have created, cooking cashews not in the traditional way, with Indian spices, but with herb-filled Mediterranean seasonings. Serve with a green salad and bread.

1½ cups whole raw cashews

2 tablespoons olive oil

2 garlic cloves, peeled and finely chopped

1 cup finely chopped tomatoes

1 teaspoon dried oregano

¼ teaspoon dried thyme

1¼ teaspoons salt

Pinch of sugar

Soak the cashews overnight in water to cover by at least 3 inches. Drain, discarding the soaking liquid.

Put the oil in a frying pan and set over medium-high heat. When hot, put in the garlic. Stir once or twice, until the garlic just begins to brown, then add the tomatoes, oregano, and thyme. Turn the heat to medium, stir, and cook for 1 minute.

Now put in the cashews, salt, and sugar. Stir to mix well and bring to a simmer. Cover and cook over low heat for 3 to 5 minutes. Serve hot.

SERVES 6

Niru Row Kavi's

Cashews in a Green Spice Paste   INDIA

This dish from the Konkan coast of western India may be served with Indian breads or rice. It could be accompanied by other Indian or Middle Eastern–style vegetables and some yogurt relish.

1½ cups whole raw cashews

2 fresh hot green chiles

¾ cup chopped fresh cilantro

¼ cup freshly grated coconut (page 722) or
  2 tablespoons desiccated unsweetened
  coconut soaked in 2 tablespoons hot water
  for 1 hour

2 tablespoons peanut or canola oil

1 teaspoon whole brown mustard seeds

15 to 20 fresh curry leaves (optional)

1 garlic clove, peeled and finely chopped

1 tablespoon thick tamarind paste (page 737)

1¼ teaspoons salt

Soak the cashews overnight in water to cover by at least 3 inches. Drain, discarding the soaking liquid.

Put the green chiles, cilantro, and coconut into the container of a blender. Add ¼ cup of water and puree, pushing down the mixture with a rubber spatula when necessary. Set the spice paste aside.

Put the oil in a frying pan and set over medium-high heat. When hot, put in the mustard seeds. As soon as the mustard seeds begin to pop, a matter of seconds, toss in the curry leaves, if using, and stir once. Immediately add the garlic and stir a few times until the garlic just begins to brown. Quickly put in the green spice paste and the tamarind, salt, and drained cashews. Stir to mix well. Turn the heat down to low, cover, and simmer for 4 to 5 minutes. Serve hot.

SERVES 6

Niru Row Kavi's

Indian-Style Cashew and Green Pea Bhaji

INDIA

This is a simple everyday dish very commonly eaten along western India's Konkan coast, where cashews grow prolifically. Serve with an Indian bread and a selection of Indian legumes and relishes.

1½ cups whole raw cashews

3 tablespoons peanut or canola oil

1 teaspoon whole brown mustard seeds

15 to 20 whole fresh curry leaves (use fresh basil leaves as an interesting substitute)

1 fresh hot green chile, cut into long slivers (do not remove seeds)

1 cup fresh or frozen defrosted peas

1¼ teaspoons salt

Soak the cashews overnight in water to cover by at least 3 inches. Drain, discarding the soaking liquid.

Put the oil in a frying pan and set over medium-high heat. When hot, put in the mustard seeds. As soon as the mustard seeds begin to pop, a matter of seconds, put in the curry leaves and stir once or twice. Add the cashews, chile, peas, salt, and ¼ cup of water and stir to mix well. Turn the heat down to low, cover, and cook gently for 5 minutes. Serve hot.

SERVES 6

Peanuts

Peanuts, which are not a nut at all but a legume that grows underground, are native to Central and South America. Ancient pottery vessels shaped like the peanut have been found among Inca artifacts. Spanish and Portuguese explorers took this legume to Africa and Asia, where they took root. The peanut's food value was discovered quickly and it was used in the making of sauces and stews, added to stir-fries and salads, and made into oil. (Today India and China account for more than half the world's production.) African slaves brought the peanut back to the Americas—to North America this time, where it was virtually unknown. It had a slow start in the South but eventually won over the nation in the form of peanut butter.

This legume, which is rich in protein, the B vitamins, vitamin E, fiber, and unsaturated fats, is sold in many forms. If you live in a peanut-producing nation, there is nothing like fresh peanuts whose shells are still soft. These peanuts may be boiled, shell and all, with any flavorings of your choice and then just peeled and eaten. The flavoring penetrates the shell and goes into the nut.

In New York, I can find fresh peanuts only in the autumn in Chinatown and a few Indian groceries, but I am always so happy when they appear in the market. Dried peanuts may be bought roasted and dry-roasted in jars and tins. They are also sold raw, both with their reddish skins and without them. In much of the Far East, they are bought this way and then roasted at home in a wok. The skins, now very crisp, are just rubbed and blown away.

To store peanuts: Raw shelled peanuts may be stored in the freezer for 6 months and in the refrigerator for 3 months. All roasted nuts should be kept in tightly lidded jars and tins in cool, dry places.

Boiled Peanuts, Indonesian Style   INDONESIA

Once, while on my way to film in the courtyard of an Indonesian temple, I was stopped at the entrance by a peddler hawking paper cones filled with what seemed to be some kind of food. Unable to resist, I bought a cone and found it filled with these peanuts. They had been boiled very simply with salt and red chiles. I found them utterly delicious and could hardly be kept from eating them all through the filming! They make for a very healthy snack food.

¾ cup raw peanuts, preferably skinned

½ to ¾ teaspoon salt

2 whole dried hot red chiles

Put the peanuts in a medium bowl. Cover with boiling water and set aside for 20 to 30 minutes. Drain, discarding the soaking liquid.

Peel off the red skin, if any, from the peanuts. Put the peanuts into a small pot. Add 1¼ cups of water, the salt, and dried chiles. Bring to a boil. Cover, turn the heat down to low, and simmer for 20 minutes. Drain and pat dry. Serve at room temperature.

SERVES 4

Shiu-Min Block's

Peanuts Boiled with Five Flavorings CHINA

Wu Shiung Hwa Shung

These peanuts make excellent munch food—and that is exactly what they are supposed to be. Fresh, raw peanuts in their semisoft shells come to market in the autumn. All you need to do is boil them, shell and all, until they are tender, then spread a newspaper on the table and begin peeling and eating. I just love them. In the peanut-growing areas of America, fresh peanuts are always available in season. In New York, I find them easily in Chinatown.

1 teaspoon peanut or canola oil

3 thinish slices of fresh ginger

2 whole scallions, cut into 2½-inch segments, the white segments cut again in half lengthwise

2 tablespoons Chinese dark soy sauce

2 tablespoons Chinese light soy sauce

2 teaspoons salt

3 whole star anise

2 pounds fresh raw peanuts in their shells

Put the oil in a pot large enough to hold all the peanuts easily and set over medium-high heat. When hot, put in the ginger and scallions and stir for 30 seconds. Put in the dark and light soy, stir once, then add 3 cups of water, the salt, and star anise. Stir to mix. Add the peanuts to the pot and bring to a boil. Cover, turn the heat down to low, and cook gently, stirring occasionally, until the peanuts are tender, 30 to 45 minutes, depending upon size. Drain, cool, and serve at room temperature or chilled.

SERVES 6 TO 8

From the Spring Deer Restaurant in Hong Kong

Chinese "Pickled" Peanuts

HONG KONG

Despite their name, these peanuts are not so much pickled as they are boiled and seasoned in a Chinese style. In Hong Kong's Spring Deer Restaurant, famous for its North Chinese cuisine, these are placed on the table as diners come in. A cold beer or a whiskey, a few of these popped into your mouth, and waiting for dinner becomes quite a pleasurable affair.

I often pass these around with drinks. As the nuts have a little sesame oil on them, I give each person a small spoon and a plate of their own to put the spoon on when they finish.

¾ cup raw peanuts, preferably skinned

⅓ celery stalk, cut into ¼-inch dice
    (2 tablespoons)

⅓ good-sized carrot, cut into ¼-inch dice
    (2 tablespoons)

½ to ¾ teaspoon salt

1 teaspoon oriental sesame oil

Put the peanuts in a medium bowl, cover with boiling water, and set aside for 20 to 30 minutes. Drain and peel off the red skin, if any, from the peanuts.

Put the peanuts into a small pot. Add the celery, carrot, 1¼ cups of water, and the salt and bring to a boil. Cover, turn the heat down to low, and simmer for 20 minutes.

Drain the peanuts and pat dry. Transfer to a bowl and add the sesame oil, tossing until the peanuts are evenly coated. Serve at room temperature.

SERVES 4

Vegetables

Artichokes   126

Asparagus   133

Beets   138

Belgian Endive   142

Broccoli   144

Cabbage   147

Carrots   154

Cauliflower   161

Celery   166

Chinese Chives   168

Corn   169

Daikon (White Radishes)   175

Eggplants   176

Fava Beans   198

Fiddlehead Ferns   200

Green Beans   201

Greens   210

Jerusalem Artichokes   234

Kohlrabi   237

Leeks   241

Mushrooms   242

Okra   250

Peas   256

Peppers and Chiles   262

Potatoes and Sweet Potatoes   268

Pumpkins and Winter Squashes   286

Summer Squashes   294

Tomatoes   300

Turnips   305

Mixed Vegetable   308

Savory Fruit Dishes   315

I feel I have been spoiled. When I was growing up in India we raised all our own vegetables so I had the choice of grabbing them straight off the plants, vines, or shrubs that produced them and devouring them raw. I could shell and peel, eat with salt, chile, or sugar—or with nothing. I could invite my friends and neighbors along and play hostess or loll about lazily on the perfectly mowed lawns consuming our considerable bounty by myself. Peas and tomatoes were always at the top of my list, with kohlrabi, cauliflower, radishes, carrots, beans, and chickpea shoots following closely behind. Once the vegetables went into the kitchen, they went into my mother's and the cook's domain. But in the garden, under the blue winter sky, all the vegetables were mine.

I knew exactly how I liked my tomatoes—hard and crisp but red ripe. As I plucked and ate them I could smell and almost taste the green sepals they wore like little crowns. To this day, I associate a good fresh tomato with the smell of the greenery that hosts the fruit.

While tomatoes were always in my life from the first day I can remember, kohlrabis were not. My father sent for the seeds or seedlings, I cannot recall which, when I was about six. What was this wild thing? I wondered.

It was the gardener's custom to bring my mother a whole basket of the garden's produce at about eleven o'clock in the morning. She would sit on the diwan in the verandah, surrounded by bolsters and cushions, and decide which vegetables should go to the kitchen (and how they would be cooked), which needed to be made into juice immediately (most of our overabundant tomatoes were juiced for our midmorning snack), and what we should eat raw, right away.

The day the gardener brought a basket of kohlrabis was one I shall never forget. The gardener was new to them, so the cook was sent for. The cook was baffled and kept shaking his head. My mother called my father at the office and the message that came back was that since it was a cabbagelike vegetable, the leaves should be given to the cook to prepare in a cabbagelike manner. Once the cook took away the leaves, we were left with the little "knot" that had connected them. My mother, ever adventurous, sent for a paring knife, which came, napkin and all. She peeled the "knot." It looked promising. She cut it. One look at the crisp, pale green inside, and we knew that once again my father had grown a winner.

Chickpeas were never planted for the beans they might produce, but rather for their greens. We ate them as little feathery shoots, either raw in salads or stir-fried with a little ginger and green chile. They had all the promise of green chickpeas in them just as snow pea shoots carry hints of the peas that will soon droop from their stems.

Cauliflowers were eaten when they were small and their stems still pale green. They had no odor of age, so unlike the plastic-covered, giant specimens we find in our supermarkets today. My mother had them cooked in different ways but

I loved them best when the florets were lightly browned and then stir-fried with our little new potatoes. You will find a similar recipe here.

We picked our okra young as well. The small pods were either stuffed or cooked with tomatoes. They were also thinly sliced and fried until crisp. We just loved them.

Over the years I seem to have traveled to most corners of the world. I greet young fresh vegetables, wherever I find them, like lost siblings. In Australia, where I taught a series of cooking classes, I stayed with my friend Di Holuigue. Each night before the start of my classes, Di prepared a family dinner, and I looked down into a dish one day and there they were, tiny okra, just like the ones we had grown. She cooked them so differently—and so beautifully—in a Chinese-Australian style, a quick stir-fry with garlic, a red chile, soy sauce, and sesame oil. They were out of this world.

In the mountains of Greece, another hostess, Elena Everoff, picked some spinach from her garden and cooked it with a small amount of rice (which helps absorb all the spinach juices), olive oil, and lemon juice. Where had this dish been all my life?

Here you'll find an Iranian ratatouille that combines the usual suspects—onions, carrots, tomatoes, eggplant, and zucchini—with fresh fruit and dried fruit to make a delightfully grand casserole. Such a delicate sweet-and-sour mélange could only come from Iran.

To organize this rather large chapter, I have arranged the vegetables alphabetically. Greens, however, are bunched together and mixed vegetables come at the very end. When fruit is the main ingredient—pineapple, mango, plantain—they'll sit under the benign heading of "Savory Fruit Dishes." There are simple dishes for all vegetables—what would we do without them?—and those that are less than simple but well worth the minor effort. I have selected about two hundred vegetable dishes from around the world that I like, hoping you will like them too.

Artichokes

I love all vegetables but I seem to love the prickly, globular artichoke above all others.

It could well be that the difficulty in getting to the limited edible portions makes the heart grow fonder. It is also true that I was introduced to the artichoke at a rather romantic, adventurous stage of my life. I was young, straight out of a London drama school, and coming to America for the very first time on the *Queen Mary*. Right there on the high seas, I fell in love with the taste and texture of the artichoke heart.

Even though my own exposure to artichokes is associated with America, first on the voyage over and then in my several trips to Castroville on the West Coast, which advertises itself as the "artichoke capital of America," artichokes actually originated in the Mediterranean. According to Waverly Root, Mediterraneans eat two hundred times more artichokes per capita there than we do in the United States. For one thing, artichokes are cheaper in the Mediterranean and considered everyday food. Many markets sell fully cleaned fresh hearts sitting in pans of acidulated water. I would give my eyeteeth for that!

In Turkey, apart from the pleasure they give, artichokes are revered for their medicinal value and considered perfect food for all manner of liver ailments. One of my hostesses in Istanbul informed me that the best diet for hepatitis sufferers was a steady, monthlong diet of mainly artichokes.

I have eaten stewed artichokes in Morocco, fried, thinly sliced artichoke hearts in Italy, and artichokes cooked with white wine and coriander seeds in Cyprus. Syrian hostesses have served me artichokes in a sweetened pomegranate sauce and Greek nuns have offered me artichokes cooked with peas and dill. You will find many of these recipes here.

Buying and storing artichokes: Look for green, crisp artichokes without brown spots or dried-out tips. Buy heads with stems attached. Store in a perforated plastic bag or in the vegetable bin in the refrigerator.

Basic Preparation for Boiled Artichokes

Baby artichokes, 2 to 4 ounces Baby ones, when you can find them, need little done to them. Wash them well. Trim the stem bottoms. A good inch of the stem may be left on. The artichokes may now be boiled in water for no longer than 10 minutes, or until a lower leaf pulls off easily. They may also be quartered lengthwise and boiled quickly in stock. Most parts may be eaten. Just discard the few sections that seem too coarse, such as the tips of the outer leaves.

Larger artichokes, 6 to 12 ounces These require somewhat different treatment. The simplest way to cook these artichokes is to just boil them. Trim away their stems so they can sit flat on a plate and then lower them into a large pot of boiling, salted water. Cover and boil for anywhere from 15 to 35 minutes, depending upon the size of the artichoke. Small ones cook fairly quickly. To check if an artichoke is ready, tug at one of the lower leaves; if it pulls off easily, the artichoke is ready. Drain the artichokes, then drain further by turning them upside down. They may now be eaten hot, chilled, or at room temperature.

Eating boiled artichokes: Boiled artichokes are generally served with what may be called a dip. For hot or warm artichokes, this can consist of melted butter with a generous squeeze of lemon juice and a hint of salt, or a hollandaise sauce. For cold artichokes, a vinaigrette or a mayonnaise works well. To eat them, just pull off the petal-like leaves starting at the bottom, dip their lower, fleshy sections in any of the suggested "dips," and then put this section in your mouth while still holding on to the tip end of the leaf. Clamp your teeth down on the center of the leaf. Keeping your teeth shut, pull out the leaf, thus scraping off these fleshy parts. Discard the hard, coarser section of the leaf. Turn to the next leaf and eat it the same way. The leaves will get softer and you will be able to eat a bit more of each. Soon you will come to the fuzzy choke. Scrape this choke away with a knife or a spoon and eat all the rest—which is the heart— with a knife and fork, again dipping every forkful in the prepared sauce or dressing. This is what you have been waiting for. The heart is the best part of the artichoke.

Trimming artichokes: For a more formal presentation, the thorny, prickly parts of the artichokes are often removed. As artichokes darken wherever they are cut, they need to be kept in acidulated water, that is, water with lemon juice added to it, about 3 tablespoons to every 4 cups of water. Have this water ready. First cut off most of the stem so that the artichoke can stand up. Pull off and remove some of the lower leaves that are very near the stem. Now lay the artichoke on its side and cut off about ¾ to 1 inch of the very top, depending upon size. Using a sharp pair of scissors, cut the top third off all the remaining leaves. Keep dipping the artichoke in acidulated water as you do this. You may, if you wish, remove the choke at this stage as well. Pull the leaves apart as if you wanted to peer inside. Then use a grapefruit spoon to scrape away all the choke. Once an artichoke is prepared, put it in the bowl of acidulated water. The more artichokes you prepare, the more acidulated water you will need.

Preparing medium to large raw artichoke hearts: Some recipes call for just the hearts. You need large artichokes for this. Unless you want the whole heart to sit firmly on the plate, it is best to leave at least 1 inch of the stalk attached. The core of the stalk is just an extension of the heart itself and should be eaten. Get your acidulated water ready as above. Have a cut lemon half near you as well. Now, starting with the first outer ring of leaves near the stem, bend each leaf back one by one, as close to the base as possible, and snap it off. Rub the lemon over all the cut surfaces. When you begin to see the paler green leaves, lay the artichoke on its side and, using a sharp stainless steel knife, cut off and discard the upper ⅔ of the artichoke. Rub the lemon all over the cut surfaces. Using a grapefruit spoon, scrape out all the choke. Rub the cut lemon inside or dip the artichoke in acidulated water. You now have what could be called a rough cut of the artichoke heart. Use a sharp, stainless steel paring knife and peel the stem. Continue upward neatly, as if you were still peeling, and remove all the dark green sections. You should be left with just the very pale green heart. Drop the heart into the bowl of acidulated water. The heart may be left whole, cut into quarters or 6 or 8 parts, or it may be sliced according to the recipe. Keep the parts in acidulated water until you are ready to cook them. Pat dry just before you start cooking.

Precooking medium to large whole artichoke hearts: There are times when you might want to have fully cooked artichoke hearts ready to be used later in a mixed salad or as beds for poached eggs, dressed vegetables, or dried beans. Here is how to do it:

2 tablespoons unbleached all-purpose white
    flour

2 tablespoons fresh lemon juice

1 teaspoon salt

3 to 4 medium raw artichoke hearts, trimmed
    as above

Put the flour in a medium bowl. Slowly add 5 cups of water, stirring with a whisk as you do so. Add the lemon juice and salt. Empty into a wide pan and bring to a simmer. Turn the heat down to low and simmer gently for 5 minutes. Lay the artichoke hearts in the pan in a single layer and simmer gently for 15 to 20 minutes, or until the tip of a knife pierces the flesh easily. Let the hearts cool in the liquid. They will need to be rinsed off just before they are used in a dish.

Artichokes Stewed with Potatoes   MOROCCO

Artichokes are cheap and plentiful in much of the Mediterranean region and used in everyday meals. This dish may be eaten hot as a stew or chilled as a salad or first course. It is generally accompanied by Everyday Moroccan Bread (page 460), though any other bread will suffice.

3 raw hearts from large artichokes, cut
    crosswise into $1/2 \times 1$-inch pieces, stored in
    acidulated water (page 128)

1 medium red waxy potato, peeled and cut
    into 1-inch dice

3 tablespoons olive oil

1 tablespoon fresh lemon juice

1/2 teaspoon ground cumin

1/2 teaspoon paprika

1/8 teaspoon cayenne (optional)

3/4 teaspoon salt

Freshly ground black pepper

Put all the ingredients in a wide-bottomed pot. Add 1 cup of water and mix well. Bring to a boil. Cover, turn the heat down to medium-low, and cook for 15 to 20 minutes, stirring now and then, or until the potatoes are tender. Serve hot, warm, or at room temperature.

SERVES 2 TO 3

Androche Markidis'

Artichoke Hearts with
Wine and Coriander Seeds

CYPRUS

Tiganites Aginares

*This may be made with just artichoke hearts or with a combination of artichoke hearts and pota-
toes (the potatoes stretch out the artichokes, I was told by the two delightful ladies in Nicosia who
gave me this recipe). Ideally the artichoke hearts should be deep-fried first and so should the potatoes. However, in my effort to lower the oil content of the dish, I have come up with a slightly
different version.*

*Serve with crusty bread and bean dishes, such as Black-Eyed Peas with Swiss Chard
(page 20). Some cheese or a yogurt salad should be served on the side.*

4 large raw artichoke hearts in acidulated
    water (page 128)

2 medium potatoes (12 ounces)

¼ cup olive oil

1½ tablespoons coriander seeds, lightly
    crushed in a mortar so each seed breaks
    into 2 to 3 pieces

¾ cup dry white wine

¾ teaspoon salt, or to taste

2 teaspoons fresh lemon juice

1 teaspoon good-quality extra-virgin
    olive oil

Cut the artichoke hearts into 4 to 8 parts, depending upon size, rather like a
pizza. Put back into the acidulated water.

Peel the potato and cut it into pieces similar in size to the artichokes. Put the
potatoes into a small pot, cover well with water, and bring to a boil. Cover and
turn the heat down to low. Boil for 5 minutes and drain. The potatoes will be half
cooked. Rinse them under cold water and pat dry.

Remove the artichokes from the acidulated water and pat dry.

Put the oil in a large frying pan or large sauté pan and set over medium-high heat.
When hot, put in the artichokes and potatoes. Stir and fry until the artichokes and
potatoes have browned lightly. Now put in the coriander seeds, wine, and 1 cup of
water. Turn the heat to high. Cook on high heat, stirring frequently, until there is
very little liquid left and the vegetables are tender, 10 to 12 minutes. If you run
out of liquid, add another ½ cup of water and keep cooking rapidly until there is
very little liquid left. (This process may be repeated.) Add the salt and lemon
juice. Toss to mix. Dribble the extra-virgin olive oil over the top when serving.

SERVES 4

Artichokes with Peas

Carciofi con Piselli

This dish is my idea of heaven. Use fresh young tender peas in season. Otherwise the frozen petite pois, or extra fancy petite peas as they are sometimes called, work very well. The only tomatoes to use here are the Oven-Dried Plum Tomatoes (page 305). If you have not laid up a supply of these, do without them. The artichokes and peas will still taste wonderful. Do not use store-bought sun-dried tomatoes as they are far too intense for something this delicate.

For the same dish served with pasta, a family favorite, see page 484.

The artichoke hearts themselves may be prepared several hours ahead of time, sliced, and then left in acidulated water. Make sure to pat them very dry on paper towels before cooking. The entire dish may be prepared ahead of time. Do not cover it once the peas go in as they tend to discolor.

2 cups fresh or frozen tender peas (see note above)

4 raw hearts from large artichokes, prepared according to directions on page 128, then sliced crosswise into ¼-inch-thick slices. Slice through the stem when you come to it and keep in acidulated water.

6 tablespoons olive oil

3 to 4 garlic cloves, lightly crushed and peeled but left whole

Salt

½ cup vegetable stock or water

3 tablespoons dry white wine (dry white vermouth is fine)

6 tablespoons finely chopped fresh Italian parsley (use just the leaves, washing and drying them before chopping)

1 tablespoon fresh lemon juice

Freshly ground black pepper

6 Oven-Dried Plum Tomato halves (page 305), cut lengthwise into fine slices (optional)

Bring 4 cups of water to a boil. Drop in the peas and boil until just barely tender (the peas should be slightly undercooked—for petite peas, this takes about 1 minute). Drain and rinse under cold water. Drain again and set aside.

Just before cooking, dry off the artichoke heart slices between layers of paper towels.

Put the oil in a large frying pan and set over medium-high heat. When very hot, put in the garlic and the artichoke heart slices. Fry, stirring gently, until golden brown, 3 to 4 minutes. Sprinkle in about ¼ teaspoon salt, add the stock and wine, and bring to a boil. Cover, turn the heat down to low, and simmer gently for 5 minutes, or until the artichokes are just tender. Uncover, add the peas, parsley, lemon juice, black pepper to taste, and another ½ to ¾ teaspoon salt (taste as you

(recipe continues)

go). Turn the heat up, stir, and bring to a simmer. Turn the heat to medium-low and simmer, stirring gently, for 2 minutes. Add the tomatoes, if using. Stir for another 30 seconds and turn off the heat. (Leave uncovered, even when reheating.)

SERVES 4

Fried Artichokes   Italy
Carciofi Fritti

One winter four couples who had known each other over at least three decades and now lived in different parts of the world met up in Italy and shared a villa just outside Sienna in Tuscany. We generally cooked dinners at home or went out together to dine in some recommended restaurant but during the day we all wandered freely, reporting to the others any discovery that seemed unique or even sensational. One day a couple reported having eaten lunch at a restaurant in the tiny, fortified, hilltop town of Montereggioni that included a plate of fried artichoke hearts. Needless to say, my husband and I were there the next day. I warned my husband in advance that I would not share my artichokes with him and that if he wanted any, he would have to order a plate for himself. He did!

In Italy, artichokes are fried in different ways. Medium or smaller ones are first trimmed (page 128) and then often quartered lengthwise, though some recipes leave them whole. Chokes are removed, if necessary. Sometimes only slices of the heart from large or medium artichokes are used. Before frying, the slices or quarters may be dipped in just flour or first flour and then egg.

What I like best are just the hearts, cut into slices, dipped in flour and then water, and then fried. (This technique of dipping quickly in water removes extra flour that would eventually sink to the bottom of the cooking utensil and start to burn.) Once cooked, I season with salt and pepper plus a little lemon juice and serve immediately.

Peanut or canola oil for shallow frying

4 raw artichoke hearts (from large or medium artichokes), prepared according to directions on page 128, cut crosswise into 1/8-inch-thick slices, and left in acidulated water

1 to 1½ cups unbleached all-purpose white flour, spread out in a large, shallow bowl

Salt

Freshly ground black pepper

Lemon wedges

Pour the oil to a depth of 1 inch in a medium frying pan and set over medium-low heat. Allow it to get hot (a piece of bread should sizzle as soon as it hits the oil). This will take a little time.

Meanwhile, remove the artichoke slices from the acidulated water (save the water) and pat dry. Put the slices in the flour and coat thoroughly.

When the oil is hot, remove a small handful of artichoke heart slices (I use both hands and so have 2 small handfuls), shake off a little of the flour, dip them very quickly in the acidulated water in one quick in-and-out motion, shake again, and then put them into the frying pan. Stir and fry 3 to 4 minutes, or until golden brown. Remove and drain on paper towels and keep in a warm place. Do all the artichoke hearts this way. Put on a large serving dish, sprinkle with salt and pepper, and serve. Those who desire lemon juice should squeeze some over their portion.

SERVES 4

Asparagus

There is nothing like fresh, seasonal asparagus, white or green, thick or thin, though these days, the season seems to go on forever!

The classic French cooking method is to trim off the woody ends, peel the bottom halves, and then tie up the spears into bundles. The bundles are then placed standing up in tall pots filled with rapidly boiling, salted water and cooked until crisp-tender. The bundles are then removed and the asparagus spears served immediately with butter or a sauce such as hollandaise. The spears could also be cooled quickly and served with mayonnaise or doused in a vinaigrette.

This tried-and-true system works, and I do use the French method of cooking and serving frequently. But there is another method of basic preparation that I have now come to prefer. I like to cook asparagus lying down in just a few table-spoons of water, which eventually gets absorbed in the cooking. This way not a drop of flavor is lost in the water and the asparagus retains its intensity of taste. I do, however, believe passionately in peeling asparagus so that the entire spear can really be enjoyed.

Buying and storing asparagus: The crisper the asparagus, the better it will be. Cook as quickly as possible, but if you need to store it, stand it up in a bowl with a little water at the bottom.

To prepare asparagus: Cut off the lower woody section and discard it. Keep the upper 6 inches or so. Peel the lower 2 to 3 inches of each spear with a good peeler (I use a short Swiss peeler) or a paring knife. The spears may be left whole or they may be cut—into thirds or even smaller pieces—if the recipe requires it. Smaller pieces are better if stirring is required. You may now soak the asparagus in water for 15 to 30 minutes. This keeps it crisp. Drain it well before cooking it.

Basic Asparagus, My Way

This method may be used for all kinds of asparagus, thick or thin, white or green, cut into segments or whole. What will vary is the cooking time. Thicker asparagus will take longer to cook, about 4 minutes, and the very thin kind may be done in 2 minutes.

1 pound fresh asparagus, trimmed, peeled, left whole or cut into thirds, and then left to soak according to directions on page 133

1 tablespoon bland olive or peanut oil

¼ teaspoon salt

2 teaspoons oriental sesame oil (optional)

Drain the asparagus well.

Put the olive oil in a large frying pan and set over medium-high heat. When hot, put in the asparagus. Stir quickly until the asparagus is coated with the oil, using tongs to turn the whole stalks. Add 3 tablespoons of water and the salt. Cover, turn the heat down to low, and cook 2 to 4 minutes, or until the asparagus is just cooked through. Remove the cover, add the sesame oil if you like its aroma, and turn the heat up to boil away most of the liquid.

If you wish to serve the asparagus chilled, spread it out on a clean plate and allow to cool. Now put in a covered container and refrigerate.

SERVES 2 TO 3

Shiu-Min Block's

Cold Asparagus with a Chinese Dressing

CHINA

Liang Ban Hsu Sun

Prepared in this fashion, the asparagus remains very crisp and green.

1 pound fresh asparagus, peeled, cut into thirds at a slight diagonal, and then left to soak according to directions on page 133

For the dressing

4 teaspoons soy sauce

1 teaspoon sugar

1 teaspoon Chinese Shao Hsing wine or dry sherry

2 teaspoons red wine vinegar

1 teaspoon oriental sesame oil

1 garlic clove, lightly crushed and peeled but left whole

Drain the asparagus well.

Bring a large pot of water to a rolling boil. Drop in the asparagus for just 1 minute. Drain and run under cold water. Drain again. Leave in a colander.

Mix all the ingredients for the dressing and set aside.

Just before serving, put the asparagus into a bowl. Remove the garlic from the dressing, stir, and pour it over the asparagus.

SERVES 4

Cold Asparagus with a Korean Dressing

KOREA

Spicy and cooling, this is a wonderful way to serve asparagus. Sesame seeds flavor the dressing best if they are freshly roasted and go straight from the hot pan into the liquid dressing with a sizzle.

1½ pounds fresh asparagus, trimmed, peeled, cut into thirds at a slight diagonal, and then left to soak according to directions on page 133

For the dressing

3 tablespoons soy sauce

1 teaspoon sugar

⅛ teaspoon cayenne

1 tablespoon red wine vinegar

1 tablespoon oriental sesame oil

1 garlic clove, peeled and crushed to a pulp

1 tablespoon freshly roasted sesame seeds, still hot from the pan (see page 734)

Drain the asparagus well.

Bring a large pot of water to a rolling boil. Drop in the asparagus and boil for 2 to 3 minutes, or until just tender. Drain and run under cold water. Drain again. Leave in a colander.

Mix all the ingredients for the dressing and set aside.

Just before serving, put the asparagus into a serving bowl. Remove the garlic from the dressing, stir well, and pour it over the asparagus.

SERVES 6

Asparagus with Pine Nuts

This may be served by itself as a first course or as part of a meal. The pine nuts should be mixed in at the last minute.

2½ pounds fresh asparagus, trimmed, peeled, cut into thirds, and then left to soak according to directions on page 133

2 tablespoons olive oil

3 tablespoons pine nuts

2 scallions, cut into very fine rounds all the way up their green sections

1 to 1½ teaspoons very finely chopped fresh hot green chile

½ teaspoon salt

¾ teaspoon sugar

2 teaspoons fresh lemon juice

¼ teaspoon soy sauce

2 tablespoons oriental sesame oil

Drain the asparagus well.

Put the olive oil in a large sauté or frying pan and set over medium heat. When very hot, put in the pine nuts. Stir once or twice until the pine nuts are golden and then remove them with a slotted spoon and spread on paper towels. Quickly put the scallions and chile into the oil. Stir once and put in the asparagus, 3 tablespoons of water, and the salt. Stir gently to mix and bring to a simmer. Cover and cook on medium heat for 3 minutes, or until the asparagus is just done. Uncover and add the sugar, lemon juice, soy sauce, and sesame oil. Stir to mix, boiling away most of the liquid as you do this. Add the pine nuts, toss, and serve immediately.

SERVES 6

Asparagus with Romesco Sauce   SPAIN

Romesco Sauce, a beautiful orange-red, is just perfect with asparagus. Its color contrasts stunningly with the shaded greens of the vegetable and its flavors—roasted peppers, garlic, good olive oil, and vinegar—complement the delicate taste and texture of the asparagus. (Sometimes I serve asparagus with two sauces, a neat trick I first saw at Moulin de Mougin in the south of France. Roger Verge's sauces were both white. I like to have one white, a hollandaise, and the other red, the Romesco.)

Use either the Classic Romesco Sauce (page 669) or the Simple Romesco Sauce (page 670). Both of these Spanish sauces are excellent.

The asparagus may be steamed until just tender when pierced with the tip of a knife or else poached with just enough liquid to cook it. I like the second method.

This dish may be served hot as soon as it is made, at room temperature after it has sat for an hour, or chilled after it has been refrigerated. It should not be reheated.

2 pounds fresh asparagus, trimmed, peeled, left whole, and then left to soak according to directions on page 133

1 tablespoon extra-virgin olive oil

Scant ½ teaspoon salt

3 to 4 tablespoons Romesco Sauce (see recipe introduction) per person

Drain the asparagus well.

Put the olive oil in a large frying pan and set over medium-high heat. When hot, put in the asparagus. Stir quickly until the asparagus is coated with oil, using tongs to move the spears around. Add 3 tablespoons of water and the salt. Cover, turn the heat to low, and cook 3 to 4 minutes, or until the asparagus is just cooked through. Uncover and turn up the heat to boil away most of the liquid.

Serve the hot asparagus immediately in individual plates with a dollop of Romesco Sauce across the middle or on the side. You could also allow the asparagus to cool on a platter, then cover, refrigerating, if necessary. Serve the room-temperature or chilled asparagus the same way, either on individual plates or in a large platter with a wide ribbon of sauce going across the center.

SERVES 4 TO 6

Asparagus Stir-Fried with Ginger and Red Pepper HONG KONG

Asparagus has now become a much favored vegetable in the top Hong Kong restaurants. Serve them with rice and a bean curd dish or with other vegetables.

2 pounds fresh asparagus, trimmed, peeled, cut into thirds, and then left to soak according to directions on page 133

2 tablespoons peanut or canola oil

2 thin slices of peeled ginger, lightly mashed

5 garlic cloves, peeled and lightly mashed

1 dried hot red chile, coarsely crumbled

¼ cup vegetable stock

1 tablespoon soy sauce

¼ teaspoon salt

¼ teaspoon sugar

1 teaspoon oriental sesame oil

Drain the asparagus well.

Put the vegetable oil in a large wok or frying pan and set over high heat. When hot, put in the ginger and garlic. Give a few quick stirs. Put in the red chile, stir

(recipe continues)

once, and quickly put in the asparagus. Stir until the asparagus turns deep green and is coated with oil. Add the stock, soy sauce, salt, and sugar. Stir and bring to a boil. Cover, turn the heat to low, and cook 3 to 4 minutes, or until the asparagus is just tender. Uncover and boil away most of the liquid. Add the sesame oil, stir once, and serve.

SERVES 4 TO 6

Beets

Rich in potassium and calcium, these red marvels are much underused. Apart from being boiled or roasted and used in salads, they may be stir-fried, made into cold dishes, and made into curried dishes. If you grow your own, look for the small, very sweet striated Italian variety known as chioggia, which may be used for any of the beet recipes in this book. Needless to say, their natural sweetness will add its own dimension. They are also not as violently red as common beets and so give off a gentler color.

How to buy and store beets: Beets are generally sold with their leaves, which can be cooked with the root or separately (see beet greens, page 211). Look for juicy, unwithered roots and bright green leaves. Store in the vegetable bin of the refrigerator.

Boiling beets: Cut off the beet stalks in such a way that you leave at least ½ to 1 inch of the stalks still attached (this holds the skin together). Wash the roots well and put them in a pan with enough water to cover them generously (as you would when boiling potatoes). Bring to a boil. Cover, turn the heat down to low, and simmer gently for 20 to 60 minutes (depending upon the size), until the tip of a knife may be inserted easily. Drain. Cut off the stalk area and peel the beets. They are now ready to be used in all dishes that require boiled beets.

Roasting beets in aluminum foil: I absolutely loathe potatoes that have been roasted in foil. This process steams them in the most undesirable fashion, leaving the flesh somewhat gooey and the skins leathery and soft. However, the same method is perfect for beets, whose skin is inedible anyway. The beet flavor gets concentrated (nothing is lost in the water) and the root gets beautifully tender.

To roast beets, preheat the oven to 375°F. Cut off the beet stalks in such a way that you leave at least ½ to 1 inch of the stalks still attached. Wash the roots well. Wrap each beet in foil and set on a baking tray in a single layer. Bake for 40 to 60 minutes, depending upon size. The tip of a knife should be inserted easily. Take the beets out of the oven and remove the foil. Cut off the stalk area and peel the beets. The beets are now ready to be used in any recipe that requires beets roasted in aluminum foil.

Grated Beets with Shallots

This is one of the quickest ways of cooking beets. The grating can be done in a food processor and the cooking takes only about 10 minutes. I generally make this quite spicy but you could easily leave out the green chile altogether. With the beets picking up the taste of the fried shallots, this is really an exquisite dish.

3 tablespoons olive oil

½ teaspoon whole brown or yellow mustard seeds

2 large shallots, peeled and cut into fine slivers

1 fresh hot green chile, cut crosswise on a sharp diagonal into thin slices

1 pound beets, peeled and coarsely grated

1 teaspoon salt

1 tablespoon fresh lemon juice

Put the oil in a wide pan or a large frying pan and set over medium-high heat. When hot, put in the mustard seeds. As soon as the mustard seeds begin to pop, a matter of seconds, put in the shallots and green chile. Stir and fry for 30 seconds. The shallots should turn a little brown. Now put in the beets and stir for a minute. Put in the salt and ½ cup of water. Bring to a boil. Cover, turn the heat to low, and cook gently for 10 minutes. Uncover, turn the heat up to medium, and add the lemon juice. Stir to mix and turn off the heat.

SERVES 4

Elena Averoff's

Boiled Beets and Beet Greens with a Horseradish Dressing

GREECE

Pantzarosalata

It is unusual to have both the root and the leaves in the same dish but here they are in a delicious pairing. You may serve this with virtually all meals. The horseradish gives it an extra kick.

The coarse stems should be trimmed off the leaves. Generally, the leaves should be left whole, but if they are very large, they can be cut on a diagonal into wide ribbons.

3 good-sized beets (about 12 ounces)

8 ounces trimmed beet greens

¼ cup olive oil

2 teaspoons red wine vinegar

2 teaspoons prepared horseradish

¼ teaspoon salt, or to taste

1 very small garlic clove, peeled and crushed to a pulp

(recipe continues)

139

Put the beets to boil in a large pot with water to cover them by several inches. Boil until they are tender, 30 to 40 minutes.

Prod with the tip of a knife to test doneness. Peel. Cut in halves lengthwise and then crosswise into ⅓-inch-thick slices.

Bring 12 cups of water to a rolling boil. Drop in the beet greens and boil about 12 minutes or until they are just tender. Drain.

Combine the beets and greens in a shallow serving dish. Mix the remaining ingredients and pour the dressing over the beets and greens. Mix gently and serve warm, at room temperature, or chilled.

SERVES 4

From the Ormylia Monastery in Macedonia

Pureed Beet Salad
GREECE

Pantzarosalata II

Rather like the chickpea puree popularly known as hummus and the eggplant puree known generally as baba ghanouj, this more unusual puree of beets is eaten in a very similar way. It is served as part of the appetizer course, a meze, to be eaten with bread or used as a sauce for fritters, such as the Crisp Zucchini Fritters (page 298). It is also quite wonderful on boiled or baked potatoes. Because it has walnuts in it, it is nutritionally quite substantial. This recipe was given to me by a charming young nun named Protokliki, "First Called."

1 good-sized beet (about 6 ounces) or
   2 smaller ones

4 tablespoons chopped walnuts

1 slice of stale white bread (you could use a
   small boiled potato instead)

1 garlic clove, peeled and coarsely chopped

6 tablespoons olive oil

2 tablespoons red wine vinegar

½ teaspoon salt, or to taste

Cover the beet well with water and boil until it is tender, about 40 minutes. Drain. Peel and chop coarsely.

In the container of an electric blender or food processor, combine the beet, walnuts, bread, garlic, olive oil, vinegar, and salt. Blend until smooth.

SERVES 6

From the home of the Raja of Mahmudabad in Lucknow

Beets with Mint and Yogurt

INDIA

Chukandar Dahi

Until I starting making this myself, I had had this dish only once in my life—in the royal, shabby-genteel mansion that the Raja of Mahmudabad called home. The grandeur of bygone days hung in the air like a ghost. I was led up what was once a grand staircase but now seemed to barely hold itself up. The family had wisely retreated to a tiny suite in the mansion. While all other rooms seemed almost bare, the door to the suite, opened by a retainer, revealed a room that could have come straight out of an aristocrat's home in England: a cold study (it was winter) with very English fraying chairs, very English fraying books, and a very English fireplace with blazing logs; oriental carpets on the floor (Was there a dog? I cannot remember); and a young, handsome raja with a very English Oxbridge accent, the "proper" accent of another era now rarely heard in Oxbridge circles. The raja's hospitality and grace matched the era of his accent. I was led to the dining room (also on its last legs) as if I were being led to the annual ball. And the lunch was about as grand as a Muslim nobleman could produce. This beet dish was among many on the table. I asked for the recipe after the very first bite.

A word of warning: I have a friend who at first refused to eat this dish because of its color, a wild, alarming fuchsia. He complained that it did not look "natural." Since then he has been persuaded. The taste, he says, won him over.

This is generally served at room temperature or chilled.

1 (8-ounce) beet or 2 smaller ones, boiled or roasted in foil (page 139)

2 cups plain yogurt

¾ to 1 teaspoon salt

Freshly ground black pepper

⅛ to ¼ teaspoon cayenne (optional)

2½ tablespoons finely chopped fresh mint

1 tablespoon vegetable oil (I like to use olive oil)

3 small garlic cloves, peeled (or 1 large garlic clove, cut lengthwise into 3 sections)

Peel the beet and grate it coarsely.

Put the yogurt in a bowl and beat it lightly with a fork or a whisk until it is smooth and creamy. Add the salt, pepper to taste, and cayenne, if using. Mix. Add the mint and beet. Mix gently.

Put the oil and garlic in a small frying pan and set over medium-high heat. The garlic will eventually begin to sizzle. Press down on the garlic with a spatula and let it sizzle some more, turning the pieces once or twice, until they turn a medium brown. Now pour the flavored oil and garlic into the bowl with the yogurt and mix.

SERVES 6 TO 8

Beet and Mushroom Curry

Shorvedar Chukandar Aur Khumbi

This is a simple curry made with raw beets and mushrooms that may be served with rice and a split pea dish. Yogurt relishes and chutneys or salads may be served on the side.

3 tablespoons peanut or canola oil

½ teaspoon whole cumin seeds

½ teaspoon whole yellow or brown mustard seeds

6 ounces medium mushrooms, halved lengthwise

14 ounces beets, peeled and cut into ¾-inch dice

2 teaspoons peeled and grated ginger

2 large garlic cloves, peeled and crushed to a pulp

1 fresh hot green chile, very finely chopped

1 cup canned tomato sauce

1 teaspoon salt

Put the oil in a medium pan and set over medium-high heat. When hot, put in the cumin and mustard seeds. As soon as the mustard seeds begin to pop, a matter of seconds, put in the mushrooms. Give the mushrooms a quick stir and put in the beets. Stir and fry the beets for 2 minutes. Now put in the ginger, garlic, and chile. Stir and fry, still on medium-high heat, for another 2 minutes. Now put in the tomato sauce, 1 cup of water, and the salt. Stir to mix and bring to a boil. Cover, turn the heat down to low, and cook gently for about 40 minutes, or until the beets are tender.

SERVES 4

Belgian Endive

This once-exotic vegetable has slim, sleek, elongated whitish leaves that bunch around each other tightly like some pale, effete but stylish lettuce. As with white asparagus, the leaves never see the light of day, growing without benefit of sun in fairly cool earth. Belgian endive is known both for its crispness and its slightly bitter taste. In its original form, the plant has fairly bitter green leaves and, by the nineteeth century, was grown partly for these leaves and partly for its roots (it is also known as chicory), which were ground and either mixed with coffee or used as a coffee substitute. Endive as we know it was discovered accidentally in the last century in Belgium when roots left in dark storage began to sprout yellowish-white leaves.

Endive is most commonly used in salads. But it makes a superb cooked vegetable, delicate in flavor and quite worthy of its somewhat excessive price. If possible, buy it wrapped in its dark paper as this keeps it from taking on color and turning bitter. Cut off the bottom end if you want to separate the leaves for salads or else cut the whole heads lengthwise into halves or quarters for braising. Wash quickly under running water and pat dry. Soaking in water only makes the leaves more bitter. My favorite way of cooking endive is also the simplest: I brown it first and then let it bake, covered, in its own juices—of which it has plenty.

Storing Belgian endive: Wrap in paper and store in the vegetable bin.

Browned Belgian Endives Cooked in Their Own Juices

This dish is as glorious as it is simple. I often serve it as a course by itself. This recipe may easily be doubled. In that case, you may have to brown the endive in two batches but you will still be able to bake it all in one dish. You should not need to increase the oil or butter.

Endive heads come in various widths. If they are very fat (the last heads I got weighed 1/2 pound each), then you will need to quarter them lengthwise. If they are slim, just halve them lengthwise.

1 pound Belgian endives

3 tablespoons olive oil

Scant 1/2 teaspoon salt

Freshly ground black pepper

1 tablespoon unsalted butter

Preheat the oven to 350°F.

Trim the very bottom of the endive heads, making sure that there is enough base left to hold the leaves together. Now cut the heads lengthwise into halves or quarters, depending upon width (see recipe introduction).

Put the oil in a wide flame- and ovenproof dish and set over medium-high heat. When hot, put in the endive pieces in a single layer and brown them well on all sides. This will take 6 to 7 minutes. Sprinkle the salt and pepper over the top and dot with the butter. Cover well (you may use foil here) and bake in the oven for 20 minutes, or until tender.

SERVES 2 TO 3

(recipe continues)

Variation

Belgian Endives with Bread Crumbs and Parmesan Cheese

Brown the endives according to the preceding recipe and then lay the pieces in a gratin dish. Cover well with foil and bake as in the preceding recipe. Remove the foil and dust the top with a mixture of 3 tablespoons fresh bread crumbs and 3 tablespoons freshly grated Parmesan cheese. Dribble a little melted butter or olive oil over the top and place under the broiler until lightly browned. Serve immediately.

Broccoli

This cancer-fighting vegetable, rich in calcium and vitamin C, is available everywhere. It may be blanched and combined with sauces, stir-fried, and put into risottos and pasta dishes as well as salads.

How to buy broccoli: Look for tight green heads with firmly closed buds. Yellowing buds are an indication of aging. Avoid broccoli with very split, woody stems.

Cutting and washing broccoli: In our family, we waste very little, eating both the head and stem. The main stem, which tastes very much like kohlrabi, is cut off and peeled, to be eaten out of hand as the cooking proceeds. (It may also be sliced on a slight diagonal and used in stir-fries or salads.) The main head is broken into florets of the size needed, each stem peeled individually with a paring knife. This allows for even cooking and leaves no hard, chewy segments. I like each floret to have at least an inch of stem so that it holds together elegantly. Wash in a sink of lukewarm water to which you have added some salt. (This gets rid of little creatures.) Lift out of the water and drain. If the broccoli is a little limp, you can soak the florets in cold water for 30 minutes and drain.

Blanching broccoli: This is one of the fastest methods of cooking this vegetable. Bring 4 quarts of water to a rolling boil over high heat. Add 2 tablespoons salt and stir. Put in the broccoli florets and let the water come to a boil again. Boil, uncovered, for 2 to 3 minutes, or until the broccoli is just tender. Drain. Either use immediately (the broccoli is at its best now) or rinse under cold water to preserve its color, drain, and set aside for later use.

Broccoli with Walnut Sauce

Blanched broccoli is so good when served with Caucasian walnut sauce. Its food value increases, too, as walnuts have almost as much protein as meat. If the sauce seems too thick, just save a tablespoon or two of the water used for cooking the broccoli and thin it out.

I used 1 large broccoli head for this dish.

6 well-packed cups broccoli florets, blanched according to directions on page 144 and drained

Walnut Sauce (page 684)

Put the drained broccoli in a serving dish. Pour the sauce over the top, toss gently, and serve immediately.

SERVES 4

Broccoli with Spinach
Broccoli Ka Saag

INDIAN-AMERICAN

Broccoli is a very uncommon vegetable in India, though it has been adopted with much love by the Indians who have settled in the United States. In our inspired New World recipe, Indians combine it with spinach, making two vegetables taste like an as-yet-unknown third one. Serve it with any South Asian or Western meal, or have it on toast as one of my daughters does.

For this recipe I bought ¾ pound of spinach. After cleaning and trimming, I was left with ½ pound. I used the florets of a good-sized broccoli head. Each floret had only about 1 inch of stem. (Save the rest of the stems for another recipe.) If a hot red chile is not available, use a green one.

Salt

½ pound washed trimmed spinach

6 cups broccoli florets (see above)

¼ cup olive oil

½ smallish onion (1 ounce), peeled and very finely chopped

1 garlic clove, peeled and very finely chopped

2 thin slices of peeled ginger, very finely chopped

½ to 1 fresh hot red chile, seeds removed, if preferred, very finely chopped

1 teaspoon ground cumin

Bring a large pot of water (about 4 quarts) to a rolling boil. Add 2 tablespoons salt. Now put in the spinach and broccoli florets and bring to a boil again. Boil

(recipe continues)

rapidly for 3 to 4 minutes, or until the broccoli and spinach are tender. Drain in a colander. Run cold water over the greens. Let them drain naturally, but do not squeeze any liquid out. Chop very finely.

Put the oil in a large, preferably nonstick frying pan and set over medium-high heat. When hot, put in the onion, garlic, ginger, and chile. Stir and fry until the onion bits turn brown at the edges. Put in the cumin. Stir once and quickly put in the broccoli-spinach mixture. Stir once or twice and turn the heat to medium. Now put in 1 teaspoon salt. Stir and cook gently until the broccoli-spinach mixture has just heated through. Serve.

SERVES 4 TO 6

Shiu-Min Block's

Broccoli Stir-Fried with Ginger and Garlic

CHINA

Chow Chia Lan

Normally made with kailan, *or Chinese broccoli, this may just as easily be prepared with the plain broccoli we can buy in our supermarkets. To cook the broccoli evenly, all the stems need to be peeled and sliced and the head cut into delicate florets.*

1 large head of broccoli (about 1½ pounds)

2½ tablespoons peanut or canola oil

2 thin slices of fresh ginger

1½ teaspoons salt

3 garlic cloves, peeled and lightly crushed

3 tablespoons vegetable stock, liquid from soaking dried mushrooms, or water

1 teaspoon oriental sesame oil

Cut the broccoli head into slim, 1½-inch lengths. Peel the larger stems and cut them crosswise into ⅛-inch slices.

Put the oil in a large wok or frying pan and set over high heat. When hot, put in the ginger. Stir once and put in the broccoli, salt, and garlic. Stir vigorously for a minute, or until the broccoli turns bright green. Add the stock, cover, and cook on high heat for about 1½ minutes. Turn off the heat. Add the sesame oil and stir to mix. Serve immediately.

SERVES 4 TO 6

Broccoli with Potatoes

Here is a simple dish I make with seasonings from both India and Trinidad.
I bought a large, 1½-pound head of broccoli and was left with ¾ pound of florets, about 6
cups. Amchar masala *may be bought from a West Indian grocer or you can make your own.*

6 cups broccoli florets

Salt

1 waxy potato (8 ounces) or 2 smaller ones,
    boiled, drained, and cooled

3 tablespoons peanut or canola oil

Generous pinch of ground asafetida

½ teaspoon whole brown or yellow mustard
    seeds

1 fresh hot green chile, with its tip cut off

10 fresh curry leaves (use fresh basil leaves as
    a different but interesting substitute)

1 teaspoon *amchar masala* (page 706)

Blanch the broccoli florets in salted water according to directions on page 144. Drain and if not cooking immediately, refresh under cold water. Leave in a colander.

Peel the potato and cut into chunky dice, the same size as the broccoli florets.

Just before eating, put the oil in a large, preferably nonstick frying pan or sauté pan and set over medium-high heat. When hot, put in the asafetida and, a second later, the mustard seeds. As soon as the mustard seeds begin to pop, a matter of seconds, put in the green chile and the curry leaves. Stir once and put in the potatoes. Stir and fry for about 4 minutes, or until the potatoes are very lightly browned. Sprinkle them with a scant ½ teaspoon salt. Toss to mix. Now put in the broccoli and *amchar masala*. Turn the heat to medium and stir for 1 to 2 minutes, until the broccoli has heated through. Turn off the heat and serve.

SERVES 4

Cabbage

Perhaps ancient Greeks and Romans knew what they were doing when they devoured cabbage. And so do contemporary Koreans, who consider the cabbage pickle, *kimchi,* their national dish and eat it at every meal. Cabbage is rich in cancer-preventative magic and vitamin C. It may be stir-fried, steamed, braised, pickled, and used in stuffings for savory turnovers and dumplings or the leaves may be stuffed themselves. Many recipes for cabbage are scattered throughout this book. All cabbage cooks down considerably.

Buying cabbage: When shopping for any cabbage, look for crisp, unblemished leaves. Signs of withering or yellowing indicate staleness and age.

Types of cabbages: First of all, there is regular cabbage. It has lovely green leaves, which can be fairly dark on the outside but turn quite pale near the core. Red cabbage is associated with Germanic, sweet-and-sour winter stews, though it can be cooked in many other equally interesting ways. I have worked out a curried red cabbage that is as festive as it is good. As this cabbage is fairly tough, stewing or braising it slowly in the oven is the best approach. Savoy cabbage, popular in France and Belgium, has crinkled skin and may be used for all the regular cabbage dishes. Then there are all the Chinese cabbages. I have decided to keep bok choy, which is also of the cabbage family, in the greens section but celery cabbage, with its pale, slim, elongated leaves, and the similar but chunkier, heavier napa cabbage certainly belong here.

Shiu-Min Block's
Sweet-and-Sour Cabbage
Tang Chu Bow Pai Tsai

CHINA

With its unusual hint of bitter oranges, this is both a vegetable dish and a condiment. It is particularly wonderful served with plain rice, bean curd, or bean dishes and any other vegetable of your choice. It may be served with all Chinese meals and goes well with many Mexican and Indian ones as well.

The cabbage needs to be cut into chunky 1-inch pieces—squares, rectangles, and triangles. I use a large wok or 14-inch frying pan to make this.

2 tablespoons distilled white vinegar

2 tablespoons sugar

2 tablespoons light soy sauce

2 tablespoons marmalade

¼ teaspoon salt

2 tablespoons peanut or canola oil

2 thin slices of fresh ginger, cut on the diagonal, 2 inches long

¾ medium green cabbage (18 ounces)

2 medium garlic cloves, lightly crushed and peeled but left whole

½ teaspoon oriental sesame oil

Combine the vinegar, sugar, soy sauce, marmalade, and salt in a bowl. Mix well.

Set a wok over high heat. When hot, swirl the oil into it and put in the ginger. Stir for a few seconds and put in the cabbage. Stir and fry for 2 minutes. Now put in the sauce. Stir and cook for a minute. Add the garlic, stir once, and cover. Cook 2 minutes. Add the sesame oil, stir, and turn off the heat.

SERVES 2 TO 4

Vali Manuelides'

Cabbage with Rice and Currants

Tembel Dolma

I am just as lazy as the next person and am forever looking for delicious dishes that cook quickly. In Turkey I sat around for hours watching housemaids stuffing leaves (chard, cabbage, grape) and preparing many-layered desserts, which would later be consumed by masters and mistresses of the house. Would I ever come back to New York and make these things, I wondered. Then in Greece I ran into Payanis Manuelides, a Greek from Turkey, who told me of tembel dolma, *or the "lazy man's stuffed cabbage." His mother, Vali, provided the recipe. This was a dish after my own heart. Here it is.*

The cabbage and rice are layered and once cooked, they may be inverted like a cake into a serving dish.

Salt

½ large head of fresh green cabbage (1 pound in all), cored and shredded

3 tablespoons peanut or canola oil

1 medium onion, peeled and cut into fine half rings

2 tablespoons pine nuts

1½ cups long-grain rice (I like to use Thai jasmine rice)

2 tablespoons dried red currants

½ well-packed cup (1½ ounces) finely chopped fresh dill

¼ teaspoon ground cinnamon

Freshly ground black pepper

1 tablespoon sugar

Bring 2½ quarts of water to a rolling boil over high heat. Add 1 tablespoon salt and stir. Now put in the cabbage and bring to a boil again. Boil for 1 minute, or just until the cabbage wilts. Drain immediately and run under cold water. Drain again and leave in a strainer.

Put the oil in a large frying pan and set over medium-high heat. When hot, put in the onion. Stir and fry about 4 minutes, or until the onion has browned a bit. Put in the pine nuts. Stir and fry for 30 seconds. Turn the heat to medium-low and put in the rice, currants, dill, cinnamon, black pepper to taste, and 1½ teaspoons salt. Stir and sauté for 2 minutes. Turn off the heat.

Divide the cabbage into 3 portions and the rice into 2. Put one portion of the cabbage in the bottom of a heavy, medium pan, spreading it out evenly. Cover with a layer of seasoned rice. Cover the rice with a second layer of cabbage, then another layer of rice and a final layer of cabbage. Add 3 cups of water and the sugar. Find

(recipe continues)

a plate that you can fit, upturned, on top of the cabbage. Turn the heat to medium-high and bring the pot to a boil. Cover tightly, turn the heat down to low, and cook for 30 minutes. Turn off the heat. Leave the pot undisturbed in a warm place for another 30 minutes or a bit longer. Just before eating, remove the lid and the plate inside the pan. Take a knife and go around the edges of the pan. Now upturn a large serving plate and place it on top of the pan. Invert the pan so that the plate is now under it. The rice should just slide out. Serve hot.

SERVES 4 TO 6

Mrs. Sanuar's

Stir-Fried Green Cabbage with Spicy Red Paste

INDONESIA

Sambal Kol

This spicy Sumatran specialty may be made with the coarser dark green outer leaves of green cabbage, kohlrabi leaves, or young collard greens. You will need about 1 pound of just leaves. Serve with rice and any bean or split pea dish.

3 garlic cloves, peeled and chopped

6 shallots, peeled and coarsely chopped

1 smallish red bell pepper, seeds removed and coarsely chopped

¼ to ½ teaspoon cayenne

5 tablespoons peanut or canola oil

Dark outer leaves of cabbage mixed with some inner ones to make up 1 pound, washed and very finely shredded into long, thin strips, about 6 well-packed cups

¾ to 1 teaspoon salt

Put the garlic, shallots, red pepper, cayenne, and 3 to 4 tablespoons of water in the container of an electric blender or food processor and blend until you have a coarse paste.

Put the oil in a large wok or pan and set over high heat. When hot, put in the spice paste. Stir and fry for 5 to 6 minutes, or until it turns dark. Add the cabbage and salt and stir to mix. Cover tightly, turn the heat down to low, and cook for 10 minutes. Sprinkle with a little water if the cabbage seems to stick.

SERVES 4

Curried Red Cabbage with Cranberry Juice

I grew up with neither red cabbage nor cranberry juice. America has taught me to use both. I came up with this combination one Christmas when I wanted to braise red cabbage with Indian seasonings. I also did not want to use any red wine, whose tartness and color helps to keep the red cabbage red. And so I came up with the idea of substituting cranberry juice and was very happy with the results. I now serve this cabbage dish both hot and cold. (It makes for a very good, slawlike salad when cold.) The fennel seeds add a very special, sweet flavor, which I have loved since childhood.

The shredding of the cabbage may be done in a food processor or you may cut long, very fine slices by hand.

Serve this with mushroom dishes, eggplants, and beans.

3 tablespoons olive or peanut oil

1 teaspoon whole cumin seeds

$1/2$ teaspoon whole fennel seeds

2 medium onions (about 8 ounces), peeled and cut into fine half rings

3 garlic cloves, peeled and finely chopped

1 teaspoon peeled and finely grated fresh ginger

2 tablespoons curry powder (you may use My Curry Powder, page 707)

1 red cabbage ($2 1/2$ pounds), cored and finely shredded

1 cup pure unsweetened cranberry juice (see Note)

1 cup vegetable stock

2 tablespoons sugar

$1 1/4$ teaspoons salt (more if the stock is unsalted)

Preheat the oven to 350°F.

Put the oil in a large, ovenproof, casserole-type pan and set over medium-high heat. When hot, put in the cumin and fennel seeds. Stir for 5 seconds and put in the onions. Stir and fry for about 5 minutes, or until the onion pieces begin to brown at the edges. Put in the garlic and ginger. Stir and fry for another minute. Put in the curry powder. Stir and fry for 20 seconds. Put in the cabbage, cranberry juice, stock, sugar, and salt. Bring to a boil. Cover and bake in the oven for $1 1/4$ hours, stirring now and then.

Note: I used unsweetened cranberry juice, which is sometimes sold as "Just Cranberry." It is exceedingly sour. If you cannot find that, you may use the sweetened cranberry juice or cranberry apple juice. Just cut down on the sugar or use none at all. Taste the cabbage halfway through the cooking and adjust the sweetness to what you like. The dish should be sweet-and-sour.

SERVES 6 TO 8

Cabbage with Garlic and Shallots INDONESIA

Tumis Kol

The younger and greener the cabbage, the better this dish will taste.

3 tablespoons peanut or canola oil

4 to 5 medium shallots, peeled and cut into long, fine slivers

2 garlic cloves, peeled and cut into long, thin slivers

1 fresh hot green chile, cut into long, fine slivers

4 scallions, first cut into 2-inch lengths and then into long, fine strips

1¾ pounds fresh green cabbage (about ½ large head), with its hard core removed and then cut lengthwise into very fine strips

3 to 4 tablespoons chopped Chinese celery leaves or plain celery leaves

¼ cup vegetable stock

1 teaspoon salt, or to taste

Put the oil in a large, wide pan or large wok and set over medium-high heat. When hot, put in the shallots and garlic. Stir and fry for a minute. Put in the green chile and stir for another 30 seconds. Now put in the scallions, cabbage, and celery. Stir and fry for 3 minutes. Add the stock and salt. Stir once and bring to a simmer. Cover, turn the heat to medium, and cook for 5 to 7 minutes, or until the cabbage has wilted completely. Uncover, turn the heat up a bit, and stir for another minute or two. Taste for salt and serve.

SERVES 4

South Indian Cabbage INDIA

Dakshini Band Gobi

Many South Indian foods get their very special flavoring from a mixture of spices that include split peas (used as a spice), fenugreek, mustard seeds, and curry leaves. Here is a common South Indian way of cooking cabbage. Have all the spices measured and ready before you start, as they go into a hot pan in quick succession.

¼ cup peanut or canola oil

Generous pinch of ground asafetida

1 teaspoon whole brown mustard seeds

1 teaspoon *urad dal, chana dal,* or yellow split peas

5 to 6 whole fenugreek seeds

2 to 3 whole dried hot red chiles

10 fresh curry leaves, if available (use fresh basil leaves as a substitute)

1¾ pounds fresh green cabbage (about ½ large head), with its hard core removed and then shredded (as in coleslaw)

1 to 1¼ teaspoons salt

Put the oil in a large wok or large, wide pan and set over medium-high heat. When hot, put in the asafetida. A second later, put in the mustard seeds and *urad dal.* As soon as the mustard seeds start to pop, a matter of seconds, put in the fenugreek seeds and red chiles. Allow the *dal* to get red and the chiles to turn dark. Now put in first the curry leaves and then the cabbage and give a few quick stirs. Add the salt. Stir and cook for a minute. Cover, turn the heat to low, and cook for 6 to 8 minutes, or until the cabbage has wilted completely. (You may add a sprinkling of water, if needed.) Uncover and taste for salt. Stir and cook for another minute or two.

SERVES 4

Shiu-Min Block's

Stir-Fried Celery Cabbage with a Gingery Milk Sauce

CHINA

Nai Yo Bai Tsai

This is an unusual Chinese dish which may be served as part of a Chinese meal with rice or with Peas and Mushrooms in a Green Curry Sauce (page 258) and mashed potatoes.

1 pound celery cabbage

1½ cups light salted vegetable stock

½ cup milk

2 teaspoons cornstarch dissolved in 1 tablespoon milk and 1 teaspoon oriental sesame oil

2 tablespoons peanut or canola oil

2 scallions, cut crosswise into very fine rings (white part only)

2 thin slices of peeled fresh ginger

½ teaspoon salt

Freshly ground white pepper

(recipe continues)

Separate all the cabbage leaves and wash them. Shake off as much water as possible. Stacking several leaves together, cut them crosswise into 1½-inch segments. Again stacking several segments together, cut them lengthwise, into halves.

Heat the stock in a large frying pan. When boiling, put in the celery cabbage. Boil for 3 to 4 minutes, stirring the leaves, until almost cooked. Remove with a slotted spoon. (The stock may now be saved for some other use.)

Combine the milk with the cornstarch mixture and set aside.

Clean off the frying pan and wipe it dry. Put in the oil and set it over medium-high heat. When hot, put in the scallions and ginger. Stir a few times and put in the celery cabbage. Stir for 30 seconds. Take off the heat. Stir the milk mixture and pour it in. Add the salt and pepper to taste, mix, and return to low heat. When bubbling, cook for a minute, stirring now and then. Serve immediately.

SERVES 3 TO 4

Carrots

In India, I grew up with many varieties of carrots. There was the almost black carrot used in preserves, the dark wine-colored "bleeding" carrot used in water pickles (it bled like a beet and colored everything it was cooked with), and the more common reddish-orange carrot, a stiff sturdy thing and winter staple that we grew in our kitchen garden. Most of the time we ate it raw, either out of hand, or in salads. But it was cooked in two ways that I loved: It was grated and made into carrot halvah, a dessert, that was eaten with mounds of clotted cream; and it was diced and cooked with fenugreek greens and green chiles. I was addicted to this too and devoured it with fresh breads.

As carrots are meant to have originated in Afghanistan, it is not surprising that India, a neighbor, has many of the early varieties that are not found in the West at all. It is the hybridized orange carrot that is most commonly available here. Like all carrots, it is rich in cancer-fighting beta-carotene that helps to make vitamin A in our bodies. It is strange that small, baby carrots used by many of our chefs are the least nutritious of all and that large, even somewhat old ones have the greatest concentrations of sweetness and flavor.

Choose carrots with good color and clear skin. Do not buy those with sprouting hair or mold.

Preparing carrots: Carrots are best peeled with a vegetable peeler. After trimming the top and bottom, they are ready to be grated or cut.

Unless the recipe suggests otherwise, it is best to grate carrots on the coarsest part of the grater so you get long shreds. The grating attachment on a food processor may also be used.

To make carrot olives, cut off the very thin end of the peeled carrot and save it for soups. Cut the remaining carrot crosswise into 1-inch chunks. Now take a paring knife and round off all cut edges by trimming them away. What you will actually be doing is peeling away a thin strip from the outer edge of the top and bottom of each chunk of carrot.

Julienned carrots are carrots cut into strips or sticks. The size of the sticks can vary. First cut the peeled carrot crosswise into 3 to 4 pieces. (This will determine the length of the sticks.) Now stand up one piece after the other and cut it lengthwise into 3 to 4 slices. (The thickness of the slices will determine the width of the sticks.) Now lay down a few slices at a time and cut them lengthwise into sticks of the thickness you desire.

For dice, cut julienned sticks crosswise, a few at a time, into squares. For larger, chunky dice, cut the thinner part of the carrot in half lengthwise and the fatter part of the carrot into quarters lengthwise. Now lay down the long slices and cut them crosswise into the size of dice you want. For carrot ovals or oval slices, slice the carrot crosswise at a slight or sharp diagonal, depending upon the length of slice you want. You can vary the thickness of the slices according to what is required.

Quick Glazed Carrots with Ginger

UNITED STATES

Here is how I make glazed carrots. It is a fast method that also keeps the carrots firm the way I like them. The ginger here should be grated to a pulp either on a Japanese ginger grater or on the finest part of an ordinary grater. This may be served with green vegetables and dried beans as well as some bread.

1 pound carrots, peeled and cut into 1-inch "olives" (see above for directions)

1 cup vegetable stock

1/8 teaspoon salt

1 teaspoon very finely grated peeled fresh ginger

2 tablespoons unsalted butter

2 tablespoons brown sugar

Combine the carrots, stock, salt, ginger, butter, and sugar in a medium pot and bring to a boil over medium-high heat. Cook, stirring gently but fairly frequently, for 5 to 6 minutes, turning the heat down a bit if the liquid gets too low. You should be left with just a little thick syrup at the bottom.

SERVES 4

Carrots, Mushrooms, and Onions à la Grecque

MEDITERRANEAN

Almost a salad, these mixed vegetables are served at room temperature or chilled. In the summer, I often put them out with sliced tomatoes, a bean dish, some cheese, and some good, crusty bread for a simple lunch. These vegetables may be refrigerated in their liquid and kept for a week.

If you cannot get pearl onions or small shallots, you may use a medium onion, peeled and cut into 1/2-inch-thick half rings.

7 tablespoons olive oil

4 tablespoons fresh lemon juice

2 teaspoons whole coriander seeds

1 teaspoon whole peppercorns

1 teaspoon whole fennel seeds

2 bay leaves

4 garlic cloves, very lightly mashed and
    peeled but left whole

1 teaspoon salt

Freshly ground black pepper

1/2 teaspoon sugar

1 pound carrots, peeled and cut crosswise into
    1/2-inch-thick slices (the wider slices from
    the top of the carrots may be halved
    lengthwise)

1 cup (4 ounces) pearl onions or very small
    shallots, peeled and left whole but with
    tiny crosses cut at the root end

8 medium white mushrooms, quartered
    lengthwise

In a stainless steel pan, combine the olive oil, lemon juice, coriander seeds, peppercorns, fennel seeds, bay leaves, garlic, salt, pepper to taste, sugar, and 2 cups of water. Bring to a boil. Cover, turn the heat down to low, and simmer gently for 30 minutes. Strain and pour the flavored liquid back into the pan. Add the carrots, onions, and mushrooms and bring to a boil. Cover, turn the heat down to medium-low, and simmer for 10 to 15 minutes, or until all the vegetables are tender. Uncover and let the vegetables cool in the liquid.

Refrigerate the vegetables in their liquid and use as needed. Remove the vegetables with a slotted spoon and serve.

SERVES 4

Sautéed, Lightly Sweetened Carrots with Herbs

You may sauté these julienned carrots in olive oil or, as I prefer, in a mixture of olive oil and a little butter. The fresh herbs may be used singly or in combination. I love to eat this with slightly bitter greens and either potatoes or bread.

2 tablespoons olive oil

1 tablespoon unsalted butter

1 pound carrots, peeled and cut into
  $2 \times \frac{1}{4} \times \frac{1}{4}$-inch julienne strips

1 tablespoon finely chopped fresh herbs
  (thyme, tarragon, and sage) or 1 teaspoon
  dried herbs

Scant $\frac{1}{2}$ teaspoon salt

1 teaspoon sugar

Put the oil and butter in a frying pan or sauté pan and set over medium-high heat. When hot, put in the carrots, herbs, and salt. Stir and fry for 3 to 4 minutes, or until the carrots are crisp-tender. Add the sugar. Stir to mix and turn off the heat.

SERVES 4

Stir-Fried Carrots and Ginger with Mustard Seeds

Gajar No Sambharo

This is a very light and refreshing approach to carrots. I love to stuff this into pita breads along with beans, roasted peppers, and whatever else looks good in the refrigerator.

3 tablespoons peanut or canola oil

$\frac{1}{2}$ teaspoon whole yellow or brown mustard
  seeds

1 pound carrots, peeled and coarsely
  grated

2 inches of fresh ginger, peeled and coarsely
  grated

$\frac{1}{2}$ teaspoon salt

$\frac{1}{4}$ teaspoon cayenne

1 teaspoon fresh lime juice

Put the oil in a large frying pan, sauté pan, or wok and set over medium-high heat. When hot, put in the mustard seeds. As soon as the mustard seeds begin to pop, a matter of seconds, put in the carrots, ginger, salt, cayenne, and lime juice. Stir and fry for 2 to 3 minutes.

SERVES 4

Mrs. Chanchal Kapoor's

Village-Style Carrots with Potatoes and Peas

INDIA

Gajar Aloo Matar

A dish from the villages of the Punjab in northwestern India, this is cooked up in open courtyards in the morning and then taken to the farmers in the fields at midday, along with breads, pickles, and yogurt or fresh buttermilk. In India, where the peas are much firmer, they are generally put in to cook at the same time as the carrots and potatoes. I have used frozen peas here. If you wish to use fresh peas, could put them in with the carrots. However, if they seem very tender, you might put them in after the carrots and potatoes have cooked for 10 minutes.

I noticed in the Punjab that when a quick fresh tomato puree is required, the tomato is simply grated. All the skin stays behind and you are left with a coarse, natural puree. It has seeds in it, but for this dish that does not matter.

3 tablespoons peanut or canola oil

1 medium onion (5 ounces), peeled and finely chopped

1 (1-inch) piece of fresh ginger, peeled and cut into minute dice

2 medium tomatoes (11 ounces), grated

1¾ to 2 teaspoons salt

½ to 1 teaspoon cayenne

2 teaspoons garam masala (store-bought garam masala should be used here, or if using my recipe, page 723, use only 1 teaspoon)

¼ teaspoon ground turmeric

1 pound carrots, peeled and cut into ½-inch chunky dice (page 155)

1 pound boiling potatoes, peeled and cut into ½-inch dice

1 cup (5½ ounces) defrosted frozen peas

Put the oil in a wide pan or deep frying pan and set over medium-high heat. When hot, put in the onion. Stir and fry for 4 to 5 minutes, or until the onion starts to brown at the edges. Now put in the ginger and stir for another minute. Put in the grated tomatoes, salt, cayenne, garam masala, and turmeric. Stir and fry, still on medium-high heat, for 3 to 4 minutes, or until the tomato mixture has thickened a bit. Now add the carrots and potatoes. Stir for a minute. Add ½ cup of water, stir, and bring to a simmer. Cover, turn the heat down to low, and cook gently for 15 to 20 minutes, or until the potatoes are tender. Add the peas, stir, and cover again. Cook another 4 to 5 minutes, or until the peas are cooked through.

SERVES 6

Carrots with Fresh Fenugreek or Fresh Cilantro

Gajar Methi

Fenugreek greens, a seasonal favorite in India, are fed to camels in Morocco, which always makes me laugh! One country's delicacy is another country's animal fodder! (In the same way, India, which grows tons of lemongrass, uses it only medicinally and, in only western India, as an herbal flavoring for tea.)

In this very traditional dish, made in every Delhi home and sold in the bazaars of the old city, carrots are diced and cooked with tender fenugreek leaves. Whole stalks of this rather strong-smelling herb are now sold in the Indian markets that have sprung up in major cities. The leaves need to be taken off the stems, washed thoroughly, and then chopped. If you cannot get fenugreek (called fresh methi *by the Indians), you may use cilantro.*

Serve with breads, bean dishes, chutneys, and relishes.

3 tablespoons peanut or canola oil

Generous pinch of ground asafetida

½ teaspoon whole cumin seeds

1 pound carrots, peeled and cut into ½-inch chunky dice (page 155)

8 tablespoons finely chopped fenugreek greens *(methi)* or cilantro

1 fresh hot green chile, finely chopped

⅛ teaspoon cayenne

½ teaspoon salt

1 teaspoon garam masala

1 teaspoon ground *amchoor* or ¾ teaspoon fresh lemon juice

Put the oil in a large, nonstick frying pan and set over medium-high heat. When hot, put in the asafetida. Five seconds later, put in the cumin seeds and let them sizzle for 15 seconds. Now put in the carrots and stir a few times. Turn the heat to medium. Add the fenugreek or cilantro, chile, cayenne, salt, garam masala, and *amchoor* or lemon juice. Stir for a minute. Add 3 tablespoons of water, cover, and turn the heat down to low. Cook for about 5 minutes, or until the carrots are tender. There should be no liquid left and the greens, now quite dark, should cling to the carrots.

SERVES 4

Persian-Style Carrots with Dried Apricots

I love the Persian way of combining savory foods with the sour and the sweet and of putting dried fruit into grain and vegetable dishes. Here are carrots cooked in that manner. I came up with this recipe one Christmas and served it with Red Peppers Stuffed with Herbed Rice in the Persian Manner (page 264). Indeed, this dish is as perfect for feasts as it is for everyday eating.

I used whole, seeded Turkish apricots here. They tend to be a little sweeter than the California apricot halves but just a bit more fibrous. Use whichever you can find easily but adjust the sugar as needed.

2 tablespoons olive oil or a mixture of
    1 tablespoon olive oil and 1 tablespoon
    unsalted butter

1 smallish onion (3 ounces), peeled, halved
    lengthwise, and then cut crosswise into
    ⅛-inch-thick half rings

4 medium carrots (10 ounces), peeled and cut
    crosswise but at a slight diagonal into
    ¼-inch-thick oval slices

6 seeded dried Turkish apricots, split into
    halves, or 12 dried California apricot
    halves

1 tablespoon sugar

¼ teaspoon salt

½ cup plus 2 tablespoons vegetable stock

Put the oil or oil and butter in a large, preferably nonstick frying pan and set over medium-high heat. When hot, put in the onion, carrots, and apricot halves. Stir and sauté for about 5 minutes, or until all the ingredients just start to brown. Put in the sugar and salt and stir for 10 seconds. Put in the stock and bring to a boil. Cover and cook on medium-high heat for about 4 minutes, or until the liquid is absorbed and the carrots are tender.

SERVES 4

Cauliflower

When I was growing up, family weddings in India went on for days. Caterers set up their cooking tents in an open area, such as a courtyard, that was not being used for the wedding itself or for serving meals. It was here that all the cooking, from breakfast to dinner, was done. Cauliflower—young, crisp, and succulent— was a wedding staple. Winter weddings were popular because of the cooler climate and cauliflower was the queen of winter vegetables. It was cooked in vast quantities. At one meal hundreds of us devoured the florets and, so as to throw nothing away, we ate the coarse stems at the next. The caterers, all famous locally for their "good hand," transformed these stems into spice-encrusted wonders that we ate rather like artichoke hearts, pulling away the soft flesh in the center between our teeth and leaving the coarse skins behind.

As a result, I have always thought of cauliflower as two vegetables, the soft florets and the sturdy central stem. Unfortunately, I can never get enough stems together to attempt that now mythic wedding delicacy.

How to buy and store cauliflower: The fresher and younger the cauliflower, the better it will be. Look for crisp white heads without black spots and with crisp green outer leaves. Yellowing leaves are an unpleasant indication of age. In American supermarkets, cauliflower heads average 1½ to 2 pounds, including some outer leaves, which yield very roughly 4 to 5 cups of florets. It is best to buy cauliflower the day you are to eat it. If you must store it, wrap it in a dish towel and then put it in a large plastic bag that is left open.

How to cut cauliflower into florets: Many of my recipes call for cutting the cauliflower into delicate florets. Here is how you go about this: First, remove the leaves and cut off the thick central stem as high up near the head as you can. Now begin to break off the outside florets with as much stem attached to them as possible. It is the stem that provides the elegance to florets. The outside florets tend to be large and chunky. As you get to the inside of the head, the florets will get smaller and so will the stems. Use a small paring knife and cut the center section lengthwise into as many sections as needed so that you have a head no wider than 1 inch and a stem about 1½ to 2 inches long. In some cases you will be creating a stem with what is actually the core of the cauliflower. Now go back to the chunky outside florets. Each can be divided into 2, 3, or 4 delicate florets of the same size that you prepared earlier but start cutting lengthwise from the stem up. This will ensure that you have a reasonable stem for each little head.

To blanch and refresh 4 to 5 cups (about 1 pound) of cauliflower florets: Bring 4 quarts of water to a rolling boil in a large pot. Add 2 tablespoons salt and stir. Now put in the florets and bring to a boil again. Boil rapidly for 3 to 4 minutes, or until the florets are just tender. Drain. You may serve these florets very simply with butter or with some extra-virgin olive oil, lemon juice, and freshly ground black pepper sprinkled over them. If I am going to put a cold dressing on them, I do it while they are still hot so it gets absorbed quickly. If the florets are not to be used immediately, rinse them under cold running water until they have cooled off completely.

Cauliflower Stir-Fried with Ginger and Cilantro

A simple, refreshing stir-fry that is good hot but also chilled.
    Pick off the cilantro leaves, wash them well, and then spin dry them. This will make it much easier to chop them finely.

¼ cup olive oil

4 thin slices of fresh ginger

1 head of cauliflower (1¾ pounds), cut into
    delicate florets according to directions on
    page 161

¾ teaspoon salt, or to taste

Freshly ground black pepper

4 tablespoons very finely chopped fresh
    cilantro

Generous squeezes of lemon juice

Put the oil in a large wok or sauté pan and set over medium-high heat. When hot, put in the ginger. Stir for 10 seconds, pressing down upon the ginger. Now put in the cauliflower and salt. Stir and fry for 2 to 3 minutes. Add 4 tablespoons of water and cover. Cook on medium-high heat for 2 to 3 minutes, or until the cauliflower is crisp-tender. Uncover and boil away extra liquid if there is any. Add the black pepper to taste, cilantro, and lemon juice. Stir to mix and turn off the heat. Serve. (The ginger may be removed before serving.)

SERVES 4 TO 6

Benita Kern's
Cauliflower with Ginger and Cream

INDIAN-AMERICAN

A most unusual dish and completely new to me, this comes from an Indian friend living in the States who got it from another Indian friend in the States. It may be served with almost any meal. I have even had it as a topping for a baked potato! It is simplicity itself to prepare and quite heavenly.

I used a 12-inch-wide sauté pan to make this. You need to give the cauliflower a chance to spread out and absorb the sauce at the same time.

1 head of cauliflower (2¼ pounds), cut into delicate florets according to directions on page 161

1 (1-inch) piece of fresh peeled ginger, cut into minute dice

1 to 2 fresh hot green chiles, very finely chopped

4 tablespoons very finely chopped fresh cilantro

1 cup heavy cream

½ cup milk

1 teaspoon salt

Combine all the ingredients in a heavy, wide sauté pan and set over medium-high heat. Bring to a boil. Cover, turn the heat down to low, and cook 10 minutes, stirring now and then and replacing the cover each time. Remove the cover and turn the heat to medium-high. Stir gently and cook another 2 to 3 minutes, or until the cauliflower is just done to your taste and the sauce has thickened slightly.

SERVES 4

Promila Kapoor's

Punjabi-Style Cauliflower and Potatoes with Ginger INDIA

Aloo Gobi

This everyday cauliflower and potato dish is generally eaten with flatbreads (rotis or parathas) as well as a yogurt relish and some pickles. You may serve it as a part of any meal, along with greens, beans, and rice or bread.

Peanut or canola oil for shallow frying

1 pound boiling potatoes, peeled and cut into thick 2×1×1-inch fries

1 head of cauliflower (1¾ pounds), cut into delicate florets according to directions on page 161

1 tablespoon peeled finely chopped fresh ginger

¼ teaspoon ground turmeric

¾ to 1 teaspoon salt

¼ teaspoon cayenne

1 teaspoon ground cumin

1 teaspoon ground coriander

2 to 3 tablespoons coarsely chopped fresh cilantro

(recipe continues)

Put the oil in a large frying pan and set over medium heat. When it is hot, put in the potatoes and fry until they are golden and almost tender, about 10 minutes. Lift the potatoes out with a slotted spoon and drain on paper towels. Turn the heat to medium-high, put in the cauliflower florets, and fry for 3 to 4 minutes, until they are golden brown. Lift the cauliflower out with a slotted spoon and drain on paper towels. Turn the heat off. Remove all the oil from the frying pan except for 2 tablespoons (the extra oil can be strained and reused). Turn the heat to medium-high and put in the ginger. Stir for 10 seconds. Now return the potatoes and cauliflower to the pan. Turn the heat down to medium. Put in the turmeric, salt, cayenne, cumin, and coriander. Stir gently to coat the vegetables with the spices. Add 3 tablespoons of water. Stir once and cover the pan. Turn the heat down to low and cook very gently for 4 minutes. Add the cilantro and toss gently. Serve hot.

SERVES 4

Cauliflower and Green Beans in a Red Chile Dressing
INDONESIA

Gudangan

On every visit to Yogjakarta, I have had a different version of this dish. It is always served at room temperature there and, in one case where I bought it from a hawker in the market, consisted of lightly blanched cauliflower, long beans, and mung bean sprouts, all tossed together in a sour and spicy dressing that had fresh red chiles and fresh coconut.

For the dressing

1 to 2 fresh long hot red chiles, seeded and chopped (or ½ medium red pepper, seeded, cored, and chopped, plus ½ teaspoon cayenne)

1 garlic clove, peeled and chopped

4 teaspoons lime juice

⅓ teaspoon salt, or to taste

Freshly ground black pepper

½ cup (2 ounces) freshly grated coconut or 5 tablespoons (1 ounce) unsweetened dessicated coconut soaked in 4 tablespoons hot water for 1 hour

1½ teaspoons dark brown sugar (more may be added)

You also need

Salt

1 head of cauliflower (2 pounds), cut into delicate florets according to directions on page 161

5 long beans or 16 green beans, cut into 1½-inch lengths

1 packed cup fresh mung bean sprouts

Combine all the ingredients for the dressing and set aside. Taste for the balance of seasonings. (The dressing may be refrigerated, if you like.)

Bring 4 quarts of water to a rolling boil in a large pot. Add 2 tablespoons salt and stir. Now put in the cauliflower florets and beans and bring to a boil again. Boil rapidly for 3 to 4 minutes, or until the florets are just tender. Throw in the sprouts, stir once, and drain immediately.

Put the well-drained, still hot vegetables into a bowl, pour the dressing over the top, and stir to mix. Serve immediately. (You may also refrigerate the dish and serve it chilled.)

SERVES 4

Cauliflower Fritters INDIA
Gobi Bhajjia

I love these extra crisp fritters, which may be served all by themselves as a snack (the chickpea flour in them makes them extra nutritious as do the egg whites) or as part of a meal. Eat them as soon as they are made with Trinidadian Pepper Sauce (page 771), Indonesian Peanut Sauce (page 667), or Afghani Sour Cherry Chutney (page 659). They are equally good with tomato ketchup! If you are cooking the fritters in several batches, it is really ideal to eat each batch as it gets done.

For the batter

2 cups chickpea flour

1 teaspoon salt

Freshly ground black pepper

1/2 teaspoon dried thyme

1 teaspoon ground cumin or whole cumin
     seeds

1 teaspoon ground coriander

1/2 teaspoon cayenne

2 egg whites

Peanut or canola oil for deep-frying

1 head of cauliflower (1 1/2 pounds), broken
     into delicate florets according to
     directions on page 161

Sift the chickpea flour into a bowl. Slowly add about 2 cups or a little less water, mixing with a wooden spoon as you go. Add the salt, pepper, thyme, cumin, coriander, and cayenne and mix. You should end up with a smooth batter of medium thickness. Beat the egg whites to a very light froth with soft peaks and set them aside.

Put the oil in a large wok to a depth of 3 inches or large sauté pan to a depth of 1 1/2 inches and set over medium heat. When hot (this will take a few minutes),

(recipe continues)

fold the egg whites into the batter and then, one at a time but moving quickly, dip the florets into the batter and put them in the oil. Put in only as many as the utensil will hold easily. Stir and fry for 5 to 6 minutes, or until the fritters are crisp and golden-red. Remove with a slotted spoon and drain quickly on a plate lined with paper towels. Do more batches as needed the same way.

SERVES 3 TO 4

Celery

Most of us enjoy this ancient Mediterranean vegetable raw, simply munching on those heavenly, crisp stalks or adding chopped pieces to cold salads. At the home of my American in-laws, celery stalks were always set out on oval plates on either side of the candlesticks at both Thanksgiving and Christmas. They were consumed with generous sprinklings of salt well before dinner started. And remember when we all thought that celery stalks filled with cream cheese were God's gift to man? Fortunately our tastes seem to have moved on to find more interesting uses for this versatile vegetable.

When cooked, celery is almost a different vegetable. Of course it may be used as a seasoning in soups, stews, and bean dishes, providing them with a complex, flavorful base, but celery is wonderful cooked by itself, especially when it is stir-fried or braised.

How to buy celery and store celery: Celery is generally sold two ways, in whole bunches and as "hearts," which are the inner, more tender stalks. Needless to say, you should look for clean, crisp, unblemished stalks. When storing, it is best to keep them in a slightly open plastic bag. Slightly tired celery may be restored if put in a bowl of icy water for a couple of hours.

Preparing celery: It is a good idea to remove the strings from the coarser outside stalks before cooking. To do this, lay a stalk with its hollow side down and cut crosswise across the very bottom but not all the way through. Now draw the cut sections backward toward the top, pulling the strings as well. You may have to pull off a few strings individually, using the same technique.

Celery Gratin with Fennel and Black Pepper

An elegant celery dish, this has a final coating of nicely browned Parmigiano-Reggiano cheese mixed with crushed fennel seeds and crushed black peppercorns.

2 heads of celery (about 1¾ pounds)

Salt

2 tablespoons olive oil

2 tablespoons unsalted butter

1 small onion, quartered

1 medium carrot, peeled and cut into ½-inch-
   thick rounds

2 cups rich vegetable stock (I use stock cubes
   here)

¼ cup dry vermouth

4 tablespoons grated Parmigiano-Reggiano
   cheese

½ teaspoon coarsely ground black pepper

1 teaspoon lightly crushed fennel seeds
   (you could whir them for a second in a
   clean coffee grinder or use a mortar and
   pestle)

Remove the coarser outer stalks of the celery. Cut off the top, leaving about 7 inches. Trim away a very thin slice at the bottom, making sure that the stalks stay attached. Wash the celery well and then cut each head in half lengthwise.

Bring about 1 gallon of water to a rolling boil over medium-high heat. Add 2 tablespoons salt and stir. Put in the celery. Continue to boil for 10 minutes, or until the celery is completely limp. Drain carefully.

Put the oil and butter in a wide pan and set over medium-high heat. When bubbling, put in the onion and carrot. Stir and sauté for 3 minutes, or until very lightly browned. Arrange the celery neatly in a single layer and pour the stock and vermouth over the top. Bring to a boil. Cover, leaving the lid very slightly ajar, and cook 45 minutes, or until the celery is quite tender. Gently lift out the celery and put it in a single layer, cut side down, in a gratin dish. Strain the remaining liquid and boil it down until you have 5 to 6 tablespoons left. Dribble this over the celery. Combine the cheese, pepper, and fennel and sprinkle this over the top.

Heat the broiler and put the gratin dish under the heat just long enough to brown the top. Serve immediately.

SERVES 4

Celery Stir-Fried with Snow Peas

Here's a light, crunchy vegetable dish that would be the perfect accompaniment to something with a softer texture such as eggplants or bean curd.

Do not use the very coarse outer celery stalks for this. You will need 1 large celery head or 1½ to 2 of the smaller "hearts."

The snow peas should be destringed before being cut. (Snap off the stem end and pull it backward over the top of the pea, along with the string. See page 256 for details.)

1 tablespoon peanut or canola oil

3 slices of fresh peeled ginger

1 scallion, cut crosswise into ¼-inch-wide rings

2¾ cups (9 ounces) celery stalks, cut crosswise at a very slight diagonal into ¼-inch-wide strips

1½ cups (4 ounces) snow peas, cut crosswise at a very slight diagonal into ¼-inch-wide strips

½ teaspoon salt, or to taste

Freshly ground black pepper

Put the oil in a large frying pan and set over high heat. When hot, put in the ginger and scallion. Stir for 30 seconds. Now put in the celery and snow peas. Stir for about 3 minutes. Put in the salt and pepper to taste. Stir and mix for another 30 seconds. Turn off the heat. Remove the ginger slices before serving.

SERVES 3 TO 4

Chinese Chives

These chives, sold only in Chinese markets, come two ways. Flat chives *(juo tsai)* are sold tied in bundles and look like flat blades of grass that meet at the bottom like a scallion. The other chives, known as flowering chives *(juo tsai hwa),* are slightly tubular, rather like western chives but double the length, and have a closed bud at the top. These also come in bundles. The first may be cut and used in scrambled eggs or stir-fried. The latter are excellent when they are stir-fried all by themselves. The bud and stem are eaten. Both types have a strong chive flavor with a hint of garlic.

To buy and store fresh Chinese chives: In Chinese markets there is generally no danger of getting anything but very fresh chives. The flat chives tend to be floppier than the flowering ones, but they should both look alert and green. Rather like radish tops, they do not last well in the refrigerator. Wrap them up in newspaper or brown paper without washing and then put them in the vegetable bin. Plan on using them up quickly.

To clean Chinese chives: The flat variety are cleaned rather like scallions. Pull away any drooping blades and any brown section near the root end and wash well. The flowering chives need only be trimmed at the bottom and washed.

Shiu-Min Block's

Stir-Fried Chinese Chives CHINA

Chow Juo Tsai

This dish of chives gives a wonderful accent to an Asian meal. Even though I used the flat variety of Chinese chives here, you may use the flowering variety, cutting them in half lengthwise.

¾ pound flat Chinese chives, cleaned and
    well washed according to directions
    above
3 tablespoons peanut or canola oil

2 thin slices of fresh ginger, cut into fine
    shreds
1 teaspoon salt
½ teaspoon oriental sesame oil

Cut the chives crosswise into ½-inch segments, keeping the white sections separate.

Put the oil in a large frying pan or wok and set over high heat. When hot, put in the ginger and the white part of the chives. Stir for 10 seconds and then put in the green parts of the chives. Stir and add the salt. Stir for about 1½ minutes. Add the sesame oil and toss.

SERVES 3 TO 4

Corn

It is mainly fresh corn that I am concerned with here. (For dried corn and corn-meal, see Grains, pages 332 to 356.) The ears we get to eat in America are so hybridized that they require just a few minutes of cooking. We are so spoiled. For those of us who are by the sea in August or near farms, we have access to sweet corn that has just been picked that morning or afternoon. We take it home, shuck it, and put it into a covered pot of boiling water well before any sugar in the ears has converted to starch. Here it stays for a mere 5 minutes when it is rescued with tongs, slathered with sweet butter—and salt and pepper for those who desire it— and then eaten, in rows or in a circular pattern, as years of habit dictate. (I do without salt, pepper, or butter, maintaining that with a good ear of corn, nothing else is required.)

When I was growing up in India, the corn we ate was really young maize. During the rainy season little charcoal stoves mushroomed up along the roadsides. Our tougher corn was perfect for grilling. The ears were put on the glowing charcoal while the sellers squatted beside it, fanning the flames. Once done, the kernels would be golden brown, even black in spots. Some would pop and flower into popcorn. Salt, pepper, chili powder, and lime juice were rubbed all over. (I always liked mine plain.) Cars would pull up. Money would go out of a rolled-down window and the hot ears of corn would go in. Then the car would move on. How I loved this corn! I would remove each kernel and store them in my pocket like a squirrel. Then, for the rest of the day, I would eat the kernels, one by one, depleting my treasure as slowly as I could possibly manage.

I have looked in vain for maize in the farms around our country house. My local farmer used to grow multicolored "Indian" corn, the kind that is sold dried and tied in bunches in the autumn. He used to sell me some when it was young, though he never quite understood why I wanted it. That corn was excellent for grilling. But now, in order to preserve it for the months to come, the farmer needs to spray it early; so I have lost my source. A good edible product lost to decoration!

Our modern sweet corn may also be grilled, but in a different manner and with totally different results. It needs to be soaked whole and then grilled with its husk still on. See page 171 for a recipe.

Buying and storing corn: Where we are in upstate New York, apart from the yellow sweet corn, there is Silver Queen, which has all white kernels, and Butter and Sugar, which has both white and yellow kernels. Just buy the freshest ears you can find, with pale green, damp stems, and try to eat them quickly. If you cannot, put them in the refrigerator bin immediately. If they do not fit—this happens to me so often—remove the husks, pull off the silk, and store in perforated plastic bags.

To remove kernels from fresh corn: Shuck the corn as suggested. Stand the corn at a slight angle on a chopping board and, using a sharp knife and working from top to bottom, cut the kernels off in rows. Make sure you do not cut into the hard cob itself.

Frozen and canned corn: Out of season, I frequently use frozen corn kernels. While nothing like fresh corn, they are a good substitute in stews and soups. I had never bought canned corn until a year ago. A friend in England suggested that I try it for one of her recipes. "But," she added, "get only Green Giant." I followed her advice and was most pleasantly surprised, so I am passing this information on.

Grilled Sweet Corn

This is one of the traditional Native American ways of preparation, perfect for warm summer days when corn is in season and outdoor grills are smoking. Do not shuck the corn for this recipe, at least not until the corn is cooked.

As I have said before, I never put butter on my corn. But my husband, who puts butter on whatever he can, insists that the best way of buttering corn, a way he picked up along the route somewhere, is to tear off a piece of bread, dab a big chunk of butter on it, and then move it up and down the steaming-hot ear. Of course, he eats the bread when he is done buttering the corn!

8 ears of sweet corn with husks   Butter, salt, pepper, and cayenne (optional)

Soak the unhusked ears of corn in water for 2 to 3 hours.

Meanwhile, light your outdoor grill (or use your indoor broiler, with the tray set about 5 inches from the source of heat) and grill, turning the ears frequently for 15 to 20 minutes, or until the husks are charred and the kernels are cooked through. Peel away the husk and silk and serve with the butter and a light sprinkling of the seasonings, if desired.

SERVES 4 TO 8

Corn with Ginger

Here is a fine way to cook midseason corn. I make this with fresh ears of white Silver Queen corn but any corn kernels, even frozen ones that have been defrosted or good-quality drained canned ones, will do. If you wish to serve this hot, you will find it surprisingly good over a bowl of steaming polenta (corn over corn, yes, but very good) or stuffed into pita bread. It goes well with dried bean dishes and green vegetables. This corn may also be served cold, as a salad.

2 tablespoons peanut or canola oil

1 teaspoon whole cumin seeds

1 teaspoon finely chopped peeled fresh ginger

1½ cups (12 ounces) peeled and chopped very ripe tomatoes or canned tomatoes with a little of their juice

1 teaspoon salt

½ teaspoon sugar

3 cups (1 pound) corn kernels taken from 3 to 4 ears of freshly shucked corn (preferably Silver Queen), frozen defrosted corn kernels, or canned drained corn kernels

1 fresh hot green chile, finely chopped (optional)

3 tablespoons coarsely chopped fresh cilantro

(recipe continues)

Put the oil in a medium frying pan or sauté pan and set over medium-high heat. When it is hot, put in the cumin seeds and let them sizzle for a few seconds. Stir in the ginger and cook for 30 seconds. Put in the tomatoes and stir for 5 minutes, letting the tomatoes reduce slightly. Add the salt, sugar, corn, and optional green chile. Reduce the heat to low and cook, stirring now and then, for 5 minutes, or until the corn is just done. Finally, add the cilantro and toss to mix well. Serve hot, at room temperature, or chilled.

SERVES 4 TO 6

Panna Thakrar's

Corn Cooked in Yogurt INDIA

Dahi Valu Makai Nu Shaak

This is normally eaten with Indian breads but any flatbread would be suitable. I find it almost impossible to tackle the corn pieces with a knife and fork. As with all corn-on-the-cob dishes, it is best to eat this the Indian way, with the hands. It is slightly messy. Just keep some paper napkins handy!

4 ears of fresh sweet corn, husked

1 garlic clove, peeled and coarsely chopped

1 to 2 fresh hot green chiles, coarsely chopped

1 (1½-inch) cube of fresh ginger, peeled and finely chopped

3 tablespoons plus 2 cups plain yogurt

1 teaspoon salt

¼ teaspoon ground turmeric

4 tablespoons raw shelled and skinned peanuts

3 tablespoons peanut or canola oil

½ teaspoon whole brown or yellow mustard seeds

Generous pinch of ground asafetida, if available

10 fresh curry leaves (fresh basil leaves make an interesting alternative)

3 to 4 tablespoons chopped fresh cilantro

In a large pot, bring about 2 inches of water to a boil over high heat. Put in the corn, bring to a boil again, and cover. Boil about 3 minutes, or until the corn is just cooked. Drain. Scrape off all the kernels from 2 of the ears of corn. Cut the remaining 2 ears crosswise into 1-inch pieces.

Put the garlic, green chile, ginger, and 3 tablespoons yogurt into an electric blender. Blend, pushing down with a rubber spatula, if necessary, until you have a smooth paste. Add the salt and turmeric and blend to mix.

Put the 2 cups yogurt into a large bowl and mix with a fork until smooth and creamy. Empty the garlic paste into the same bowl. Add the corn kernels and the corn pieces, mix well, and leave to marinate for 4 to 8 hours.

The peanuts need to be crushed to the size of large mustard seeds. This may be done in a spice grinder or clean coffee grinder, using the stop-and-start pulsing method, or with a pestle in a mortar. Set aside.

Put the oil in a large nonstick frying pan or wok and set over medium-high heat. When hot, put in the mustard seeds. As soon as the mustard seeds begin to pop, a matter of seconds, put in the asafetida and the curry leaves. Stir once, turn the heat down to low, and put in the peanuts. Stir and fry for a minute, or until the peanuts turn golden. Put in the corn and all the marinade in the bowl. Turn the heat to medium. Bring the contents of the pot to a simmer, stirring gently all the time. Cover, turn the heat down to low, and cook 10 minutes. Add the cilantro and stir. Serve hot.

SERVES 4

Panna Thakrar's

Corn with Cauliflower INDIA

Phulawar Makai Nu Shaak

This is a superb dish that may be served with breads, greens, and yogurt relishes. You may also serve it with a green salad and a crusty bread.

Panna, a Gujarati Indian who lives in London, cooks the dish year-round and uses canned corn that has been drained. You may use fresh cooked corn taken off the cob if you like or frozen cooked and drained corn kernels. You will need 1½ cups of cooked corn.

1 (¼-inch-thick) slice of peeled fresh ginger, finely chopped

2 fresh hot green chiles, finely chopped

3 tablespoons peanut or canola oil, or *ghee* (page 723)

1 teaspoon whole cumin seeds

1 head of cauliflower (2 pounds), trimmed and cut into delicate florets according to directions on page 161

2 small onions (each about 2 ounces), peeled, quartered, and the layers separated

1 (15¼-ounce) can corn, drained (see recipe introduction)

⅛ teaspoon ground turmeric

1¼ to 1½ teaspoons salt

3 to 4 tablespoons chopped fresh cilantro

(recipe continues)

Put the ginger, green chiles, and 2 tablespoons of water in an electric blender. Blend to a puree, pushing down with a rubber spatula when necessary. Set the puree aside.

Put the oil in a large wok or frying pan and set over medium-high heat. When hot, put in the cumin seeds. Stir once and put in the cauliflower. Stir and fry the cauliflower for 2 minutes. Cover, turn the heat down to medium-low, and cook another 2 to 3 minutes, stirring now and then. Add the onions. Stir and cook, uncovered, on medium-low heat for 2 minutes. Cover and cook on medium-low heat for 2 minutes, stirring now and then. Uncover and add the corn, turmeric, and salt. Stir and cook for 1 minute. Add the ginger-chile paste, stir, and cook another minute. Add the cilantro and toss. Serve hot.

SERVES 6

Panna Thakrar's

Spicy Corn with Sesame Seeds and Tomatoes

INDIA

Tamatar Varu Makai Nu Shaak

This spicy corn dish is excellent with breads. It may be rolled inside a tortilla or an Indian chapati or stuffed into a pita bread along with some Tahini Sauce (page 737). You may serve it with greens, beans, and tortillas. I often have leftovers on toast with a little green salad on the side.

It is very good. You may use fresh cooked corn taken off the cob or canned drained corn if you like or frozen cooked and drained corn kernels. You will need 1 1/2 cups of cooked corn.

2 tablespoons peanut or canola oil

1/2 teaspoon whole brown or yellow mustard seeds

1/4 teaspoon whole cumin seeds

Generous pinch of ground asafetida

1 garlic clove, peeled and finely chopped

1 fresh hot green chile, finely chopped

1 1/2 tablespoons sesame seeds

1 smallish onion (3 ounces), peeled and finely chopped

1/2 large green bell pepper (about 3 ounces), cut into 1/2-inch dice

1 (15 1/4-ounce) can corn, drained (see recipe introduction)

1 teaspoon salt

1/2 teaspoon garam masala (page 723)

1/8 teaspoon ground turmeric

1/2 teaspoon ground cumin

1/2 teaspoon ground coriander

1 teaspoon paprika

4 to 5 canned plum tomatoes with some of their liquid, put in a blender and liquefied (enough to have 1 cup)

3 to 4 tablespoons chopped fresh cilantro

Put the oil in a large nonstick frying pan and set over medium-high heat. When hot, put in the mustard and cumin seeds. As soon as the mustard seeds begin to pop, a matter of seconds, put in the asafetida. Stir once and put in the garlic and green chile. Stir once or twice and put in the sesame seeds. As soon as the sesame seeds turn golden and/or pop, a matter of seconds, put in the onion and green pepper. Stir and fry for 5 minutes. Add the drained corn, salt, and garam masala. Stir and cook for a minute. Add the turmeric, ground cumin, coriander, and paprika. Stir and cook for a minute. Add the liquefied tomatoes and bring to a simmer. Cover, turn the heat down to low, and simmer gently for 10 minutes. Uncover, add the cilantro, and stir to mix. Serve hot.

SERVES 4

Daikon (White Radishes)

Known generally by its Japanese name, daikon, this long white radish can grow to more than a foot in length and become as wide as a man's forearm. In Asia it is used for all manner of pickles but it is also used in soups, where it becomes beautifully translucent, or simmered slowly with soy sauce and sugar in the technique that the Chinese call "red-cooking," which makes it delightfully succulent.

How to buy and store daikon: Daikon are sold mainly by East and South Asian grocers. Unless you need very thick radishes, look for those that have a diameter of about 2 inches and that look crisp and white. It is awful to end up with limp, dried-out, cottony ones. It is almost worth it to break one in half and look at the insides right in the store. As with red radishes, opaque white spots inside indicate dryness. You may have to buy the one you snapped but at least you will be buying only one! Store in a perforated plastic bag in the refrigerator.

How to prepare daikon: Wash them off first and then peel them deeply with a peeler. There are almost two layers of skin, and you need to get through both. If a julienne of daikon is required, you may, of course, use one of those amazing Japanese mandolines that have razor-sharp teeth but are much lighter than their bulkier French counterparts. You could also use the East Asian method: First cut slices of the thickness you need. Now spread the slices in an overlapping row in front of you like a deck of cards. Using a cleaver or a large knife, start cutting the strips at one end and keep going until you have reached the other. Peeled radishes may also be grated, either to a pulp or coarsely, or roll-cut (page 179) or diced. As they contain a lot of water, they are often salted before they are pickled.

Shiu-Min Block's

Stewed or "Red-Cooked" Daikon CHINA

Hung Shao Lo Bo

This is one of my most favorite ways of cooking the large, chunky daikon. Serve it with rice and greens. The daikon needs to be roll-cut. If you cannot manage that, just cut it into 1-inch chunks.

1 pound chunky daikon, about 2 inches in diameter

2 tablespoons peanut or canola oil

2 scallions, cut into 1½-inch lengths (both white and green sections), white sections halved lengthwise as well

2 slices of peeled fresh ginger

2 tablespoons soy sauce

1 teaspoon sugar

2 garlic cloves, lightly crushed and peeled but left whole

1 teaspoon oriental sesame oil

3 tablespoons finely chopped fresh cilantro

Peel the daikon and roll-cut it according to directions on page 179. When you get to the top section, which is much thicker, you might need to halve some of the chunks.

Put the oil in a wide pan and set over medium-high heat. When hot, put in the scallions and ginger. Stir for 30 seconds. Now put in the daikon and stir once or twice. Add the soy sauce, sugar, garlic, and ¾ cup of water. Bring to a boil. Cover, turn the heat down to low, and cook for 15 minutes, or until the daikon is tender. Stir now and then during this period. Uncover, turn up the heat, and boil away all but about 4 tablespoons of the liquid. Stir now and then during this period. Add the sesame oil and cilantro and stir to mix. Serve hot or at room temperature. The daikon may be reheated in its own liquid.

SERVES 4

Eggplants

Eggplants, which are thought to have originated in India, come in many sizes and colors. Tiny little green ones, the size of peas and quite raw, are floated on top of Thai curries, adding a certain in-your-face, wake-up astringency to each morsel. Larger green ones, the size of substantial pomegranates, sometimes with whitish stripes, are hollowed out and stuffed in South and Southeast Asia or else sliced and fried or used in stir-fries. In India, they are cut into small dice and cooked along with other vegetables, such as diced potatoes. White ones, some the shape and size of golf balls, others larger and slightly elongated, have their own pale and creamy taste. They have a fine texture and cook quite fast.

However, the two colors of eggplants most commonly seen in Western markets are purple and pinkish-mauve.

Purple eggplants: Most supermarkets tend to carry the large, plump, somewhat oval, purple eggplants that weigh approximately ¾ pound to 1½ pounds. Very small ones, the size and shape of eggs, may be found in Indian and sometimes Chinese markets. Larger long, slim, dark purple ones, often called Italian eggplants, are sold by Italian grocers and sometimes by supermarkets. These vary in length from 4 to 6 inches.

Pinkish-mauve eggplants: Sold in America as Japanese eggplants, these can be found in most South and East Asian markets and in many West Coast supermarkets. Slim and long—they range from 6 to 9 inches—these are delicate in both texture and flavor. They are perfect for poaching and steaming. In Japan they are often served with a miso sauce or else dipped in a tempura batter and deep-fried. If you cannot get them, look for the substitutes suggested in individual recipes.

Many people believe that eggplants help prevent cancer and that they also inhibit the growth of fatty deposits in the arteries. They are certainly low in calories, with a cupful of the cooked vegetable proudly weighing in with fewer than 40 calories. Unfortunately, oil is their natural partner. They turn slithery, satiny, attractively brown, and positively sensuous when stir-fried or, better still, deep-fried.

But the amount of oil their greedy bodies soak in can be controlled in various ways. One is by cutting the vegetable into segments and either salting it or letting it soak in salty water for at least 30 to 40 minutes. This draws out some of their natural liquid, making them less dry and spongelike.

Instead of deep-frying them before cooking with sauces and seasonings, I have also taken to rubbing slices lightly with oil and broiling them until they are lightly browned on both sides.

Of course, eggplants may also be steamed, poached, or roasted before they are dressed. There are dozens of recipes for them scattered throughout this book not only because I love them but because they are so versatile and provide the dark, meaty accents often missing in meatless meals.

To buy and store eggplants: Look for shiny smooth skins without brown spots. It is best if the sepals and stem are still attached. Cook as soon as possible and, if you need to store, keep in the vegetable bin of your refrigerator.

Roasting eggplants: There are many recipes—from southern Asia, the Middle East, and the Mediterranean—that require eggplants to be roasted before being made into salads, dips, and entrées.

Traditionally, much of this roasting used to be done in hot ashes. Eggplants, usually of the large variety, were buried in hot ashes and removed when they were charred on the outside and soft inside. The skin was then peeled off and the pulp used as desired. This is still done in the villages of South Asia, the Middle East, and some of the Mediterranean. In Santorini, a Greek island, I witnessed another method.

I had gone some considerable distance to see a man considered to be the best local baker. I intended to watch, learn, and hopefully get some bread recipes. Well, no recipes were forthcoming. The man was cagey, fobbing the most dubious information off on me. Perhaps he thought I might open a competing Greek bakery in New York! However, the day was saved by two sightings. The first was a lovely green vine that cascaded down the baker's house, a vine of the large Santorini capers with their nasturtium-like leaves, and the second was a large tray of big, fat eggplants—there must have been at least a dozen of them—all nicely browned and covered with ash, coming out of the bread oven. The baker used the still-heated oven to roast his own and his neighbor's vegetables once the breads were done! An eggplant salad, the baker's fresh bread, and some fava (yellow split peas here) would probably be dinner for much of the village.

Whichever method you wish to use for roasting eggplant, it is best to prick holes in them with a fork first so they do not split and splatter. They are done when they turn very soft and flabby. Once that happens, you should peel them. This will be very easy to do by hand; no knife will be required. Once peeled, you can cut off their stem ends. They are now ready to be finely chopped or mashed with a fork, pulled into shreds, or even put into the blender if that is what the recipe requires.

1. *Top-of-the-Stove Method (for a gas range)* This is my preferred way of roasting a single large or medium eggplant. If I have more than one, I use another method.

First of all, try and buy an eggplant with a stem. This helps in the handling. It is a good idea to line your burner with foil to protect it from drips.

A 1½-pound eggplant will take 35 to 40 minutes to cook this way. A smaller one may take a little less time and a bigger one more.

Prick the eggplant (about 12 times) with a fork and stand it over a low gas flame on the stove, stem end up. If it tends to topple over, hold it by the stem or with a pair of tongs. When the bottom has charred, lay it down. Move it as needed so as to char one side completely. Now turn the eggplant just a little bit and start to char the adjacent section. Keep doing this until the entire vegetable is charred and turns soft and pulpy. You will need to hold it by its stem end or it will come apart at this stage.

Remove the eggplant from the flame. Now peel the skin off and quickly wash the eggplant under running water to remove any clinging charred bits. Pat it dry with paper towels. You may now chop the flesh coarsely into pieces and proceed with the recipe.

A 1½-pound eggplant will yield 2 cups of chopped flesh.

2. *Oven Roasting Method (good when there are many eggplants or when there is an electric range)* Preheat the oven to 450°F. Prick the eggplants all over with a fork first and lie them down in a baking tray lined with foil. Bake, turning every 15 minutes. One pound of eggplants will take about an hour. They should flatten and turn very soft inside. Then peel the eggplants by hand, chop off the stem end, and chop or mash as needed.

3. *Fireplace Method (good for medium-large eggplants)* In our country house, where we often make wood fires, another method I use is to stand the eggplants fairly close to the fire in the fireplace. Then, as I knit or read, I turn the eggplants every now and then with tongs to roast all sides evenly. Once they are charred thoroughly on the outside and pulpy inside, I peel them, sometimes washing off little bits of the charred skin under cold running water. I then pat these dry and cut off their stem ends. The eggplants may now be shredded or mashed. This method gives a nice smoky aroma to the flesh.

4. *Electric or Gas Broiler Method (good for all sizes and shapes)* It is best to broil the eggplants slowly under the lowest heat you can manage. Prick them first and lay them on a foil-lined baking tray. Place under the broiler. As one side chars, turn the eggplants just a little bit. Keep doing this until all the skin has charred. Always hold the eggplant by its stem end, especially as it turns soft. Now peel and mash as in the fireplace method.

Roll-Cutting: Some recipes, particularly some Chinese ones, require that vegetables such as eggplants daikon, zucchini, carrots, or cucumbers be roll-cut. This gives them a large cut, skinless surface that can absorb flavors easily and cook fast.

The technique for all is the same as described below. To roll-cut long, slim eggplants or any long vegetable, lay one eggplant in front of you so its stem end faces left and the bottom end faces right. Make the first cut about 1½ inches from the bottom end at a steep diagonal that goes to the right. Now roll the eggplant slowly toward you until the cut end faces up. Make another steep diagonal cut that goes to the left. The cuts should meet and form a V. Roll the eggplant toward you again until the last cut end faces up. Make another steep diagonal cut to the right. Keep doing this until you have cut the entire eggplant.

Cold Eggplants with a Soy Sauce Dressing

HONG KONG

You may, if you like, make this dish with zucchini. It will need to steam for just 3 to 5 minutes. Serve as part of a Chinese meal or as a summer vegetable dish.

4 small Italian or Japanese eggplants (10 ounces), about 6 inches long

For the sauce

1 large garlic clove, peeled and crushed to a pulp

1 scallion, cut crosswise into very fine rounds

1 (½ × ½-inch) piece of fresh ginger, peeled and very finely chopped

1 Chinese celery stalk or ½ celery stalk, cut into very small dice

1 tablespoon finely chopped fresh cilantro leaves

1 tablespoon Chinese light soy sauce

1 tablespoon oriental sesame oil

1 teaspoon distilled white vinegar

2 teaspoons tomato ketchup

⅛ teaspoon sugar

2 tablespoons vegetable stock, such as Dried Mushroom Stock (page 577), or water

You also need

2 teaspoons finely diced fresh cilantro stems

Quarter the eggplants lengthwise and then cut them crosswise into 3-inch segments. Steam over high heat for 10 to 15 minutes, or until tender. (General steaming instructions are on page 736.)

Meanwhile, combine the garlic, scallion, ginger, celery, and cilantro leaves in a small bowl. Cover and set aside. In another bowl, combine the soy sauce, sesame oil, vinegar, ketchup, sugar, and vegetable stock or water. Stir to mix, then set aside.

When the eggplants are tender, gently lift them out and arrange them neatly in a single layer on a large platter. Empty the contents of the bowl that contains the garlic mixture into the bowl that contains the soy sauce mixture. Stir the sauce. Pour the sauce evenly over the eggplants. Sprinkle the cilantro stems over the top and serve at room temperature or chilled.

SERVES 2 TO 4

Variation

Deep-Fried Eggplants with a Soy Sauce Dressing

For dinner parties, instead of steaming the eggplants, I often deep-fry them. Then, while they are still hot, I douse them with the room-temperature sauce and serve them immediately. Have the sauce ready before you start the frying.

To deep-fry, cut the eggplants as suggested above. Sprinkle them lightly with salt and set aside for 30 to 40 minutes. Pat dry.

Meanwhile, pour oil into a wok or deep-frying pan to a depth of 2 to 3 inches. Set over medium-high heat. When hot, put in as many eggplant pieces as the pan will hold easily and fry, turning when needed, until the pieces are a rich medium-brown. Remove with a slotted spoon and drain on paper towels. Fry all the eggplants this way, place them in a serving dish, and douse with the sauce.

Cold Eggplants with
Spicy Chinese Peanut Dressing HONG KONG

4 small Italian or Japanese eggplants (10 ounces), about 6 inches long

For the sauce

4 teaspoons freshly made peanut butter from a health food shop or 4 tablespoons roasted peanuts ground to a paste in a clean coffee grinder

4 teaspoons soy sauce

4 teaspoons distilled white vinegar

2 teaspoons Chinese rice wine or dry sherry

1 tablespoon oriental sesame oil

2 teaspoons sugar

½ teaspoon salt

¼ to ½ teaspoon chili paste with soybean or chili paste with garlic (page 717), optional

½ teaspoon very finely chopped ginger

4 tablespoons finely chopped fresh cilantro leaves

You also need

4 teaspoons finely diced fresh cilantro stems

Quarter the eggplants lengthwise and then cut them crosswise into 3-inch segments. Steam over high heat for 10 to 15 minutes, or until tender. (General steaming instructions are on page 736.)

Meanwhile, combine all the ingredients for the sauce, except the cilantro leaves, in a bowl and mix well.

When the eggplants are tender, gently lift them out and arrange them neatly in a single layer on a large platter. Stir the sauce. Add the cilantro leaves to it and mix again. Pour the sauce evenly over the eggplants. Sprinkle the cilantro stems over the top and serve at room temperature or chilled.

SERVES 2 TO 4

Poached Eggplants with a Korean Hot Sauce

Khaji Namul

I have poached the eggplants here, but they could just as easily be steamed for 10 to 15 minutes instead (see page 736 for general steaming instructions). Serve hot with rice and a bean curd dish or at room temperature or chilled as a salad.

You may make this ahead of time and refrigerate it.

1 pound long, slim, eggplants, preferably the pinkish Japanese variety, or else the long, slim, purple Italian ones or slim white ones

2 teaspoons *kochu jang* (or 2 teaspoons fine brown miso mixed with ½ teaspoon cayenne)

½ cup vegetable stock

2 teaspoons any Japanese, Korean, or Chinese rice wine (such as sake or Shao Hsing) or dry sherry

1½ teaspoons soy sauce

2 teaspoons oriental sesame oil

1 tablespoon peanut or canola oil

1 large garlic clove, peeled and finely chopped

2 scallions, cut into fine rings all the way up their green sections

1 (½-inch) cube of fresh ginger, peeled and very finely chopped

Salt (optional)

1 tablespoon roasted sesame seeds (page 734)

Quarter the eggplants lengthwise and then cut them crosswise into 3-inch segments. Put in a large frying pan. Add enough water to cover the bottom of the pan by about ½ inch and bring to a boil. Cover, turn the heat down to medium-low, and poach for 10 to 15 minutes, turning gently once or twice, until the eggplant pieces are just tender. Drain carefully and arrange in a single layer in a shallow serving dish.

Put the *kochu jang* in a small bowl. Slowly add the stock, dissolving the paste as you go. Now add the rice wine, soy sauce, and 1 teaspoon of the sesame oil. Mix.

Put the vegetable oil in a frying pan and set over medium-high heat. When hot, put in the garlic, scallions, and ginger. Stir for 30 seconds. Put in the sauce from the bowl. Stir once and taste for salt, adding some, if needed. Bring to a boil. Throw in the sesame seeds. Now quickly pour this sauce over the eggplants. Serve hot, chilled, or at room temperature.

SERVES 4

Creamed Eggplant
Baba Ghanouj

There are hundreds of recipes for this dish to be found throughout Greece, Turkey, and the Middle East. This is perhaps the lightest and creamiest of them all. Serve this smoky delicacy with any crusty bread or with pitalike breads as part of a meal, a dip, or a first course.

1 large eggplant (about 1⅓ pounds), roasted, peeled, and coarsely chopped according to directions on pages 178 and 179

3 tablespoons olive oil

1 tablespoon fresh lemon juice

¾ to 1 teaspoon salt

Put the coarsely chopped eggplant into the container of an electric blender. Add the olive oil, lemon juice, and salt. Blend briefly for 5 to 6 seconds until creamy. Serve at room temperature or chilled.

SERVES 4

Smoked Eggplant
Bharta

Much of India's northwestern state of Punjab is vegetarian, a great many of its villages almost totally so. This is a popular village dish. The eggplant, usually the larger purple variety, is put whole into the hot ashes of outdoor stoves and allowed to char and blacken on the outside. The inside, now nicely soft and smoky, is removed, mashed, and cooked along with onions, ginger, and tomatoes. A village meal might well consist of this bharta, *some mustard greens, flat whole wheat breads (rotis), and a tall glass of buttermilk or* lassi, *a milk and yogurt drink (page 656).*

Bharta *also makes a very good spread. I often eat it over toast. If you keep it soft, it also makes a good dip for triangles of pita bread.*

4 to 5 tablespoons peanut or canola oil (olive oil may be used here)

1 cup finely chopped onions

1 (2 × 1-inch) piece of fresh ginger, peeled and grated to a pulp

1 cup peeled and chopped very ripe tomatoes

1½ teaspoons ground cumin

⅛ to ¼ teaspoon cayenne

¾ teaspoon salt

1 large eggplant (1½ pounds), roasted, peeled, and coarsely chopped according to directions on pages 178 and 179

2 to 3 tablespoons coarsely chopped fresh cilantro

(recipe continues)

Put the oil in a frying pan, preferably nonstick, and set over medium-high heat. When hot, add the onions. Stir and fry until the onions are brown around the edges. Put in the ginger and stir for 1 minute. Add the tomatoes. Stir and fry until slightly reduced, 3 to 5 minutes. Add the cumin, cayenne, and salt. Stir to mix. Now stir in the eggplant. Turn the heat to medium and cook for another 10 to 15 minutes. Add the cilantro and mix well. Serve hot if serving as part of the main course, at room temperature as a dip, and chilled as a spread.

SERVES 4

Stuffed Baby Eggplants TURKEY
Imam Bayeldi

These melt-in-the-mouth eggplants may be served with any Mediterranean bean dish and some crusty whole wheat bread. A yogurt relish on the side would complete the meal. If you cannot get small eggplants, use 4 larger ones and bake them until they are tender.

8 small Italian eggplants (about 3 ounces each), 4 to 5 inches long, preferably with sepals attached

A little peanut or canola oil

Salt

3 tablespoons olive oil

½ large onion (3½ ounces), finely chopped

2 teaspoons peeled and very finely chopped garlic

2 large tomatoes (1 pound), peeled and finely chopped

1 teaspoon salt

Freshly ground black pepper

4 tablespoons very finely chopped parsley

Preheat the oven to 350°F.

Peel 3 strips about ⅓ inch wide down each eggplant, so they have a striped appearance. Rub generously with oil and salt and place in a baking dish. Cover with a lid or foil and bake for 1 hour, or until softened and cooked through.

Meanwhile, make the filling. Put the olive oil in a frying pan and set over medium heat. When hot, put in the onion and garlic. Stir and cook for about 4 minutes, or until the garlic and onion have softened. Put in the tomatoes, salt, and pepper to taste. Stir and bring to a simmer. Turn the heat down to low and simmer gently for 7 to 8 minutes, until the tomatoes have softened and the liquid has thickened. Add the parsley, stir once, and turn off the heat.

Remove the eggplants from the oven and arrange prettily in a serving dish. Cut a pocket in each eggplant this way: Starting ¼ inch from the top, cut a long slit that stops ¼ inch from the bottom. The slit should be deep but not go all the way through. In order to widen the slit, push the eggplant very gently from the top and the bottom toward the center. Ladle ⅛ of the filling into each pocket. Serve hot or chilled.

SERVES 4

Stir-Fried Eggplants with Tomato and Parmesan Cheese

This recipe is my own creation but it was inspired by what a friend had cooked in a Tuscan kitchen. It should perhaps be labeled "Italian inspired." You may serve it with pasta and a green salad or just with bread and some greens.

1 eggplant (about 1 pound)

Salt

¼ cup olive oil

3 garlic cloves, lightly crushed and peeled but
　　left whole

½ teaspoon dried oregano

2 teaspoons fresh lemon juice

⅛ teaspoon cayenne

1 good-sized tomato, peeled, seeded, and
　　chopped (page 300)

Freshly ground black pepper

3 tablespoons grated Parmesan cheese

2 tablespoons finely chopped fresh parsley,
　　preferably flat-leaf

Quarter the eggplant and then cut the sections crosswise into ½-inch-wide pieces. Put 5 cups of water in a wide bowl. Add 1 tablespoon salt and stir to mix. Put in the eggplant pieces. Upturn a smallish plate on top of the eggplant pieces to keep them submerged. The plate should stay inside the bowl. Set aside for 40 minutes. Drain and pat the eggplant pieces as dry as possible with a clean dish towel.

Put the oil in a large, preferably nonstick frying pan and set over high heat. When hot, put in the garlic and a second later, the eggplant. Turn the heat down just a bit to medium-high. Stir and fry until the eggplant pieces are lightly browned on both sides, about 4 minutes. Put in ½ teaspoon salt, the oregano, lemon juice, and cayenne. Stir to mix and then put in ½ cup of water. Cover, turn the heat down to low, and cook very gently for 10 minutes, or until the eggplant pieces are tender.

Uncover, put in the tomato and pepper to taste, and turn the heat up to medium-high. Stir and fry for 1 to 2 minutes. Turn off the heat. Add the Parmesan cheese and parsley. Toss, check for salt, and serve immediately.

SERVES 3 TO 4

Birdie's
Eggplant and Tomato "Choka"   TRINIDAD

Somewhere between a salad and a main vegetable, this dish may be served with any meal, along with bean and grain dishes. It may also be served as a first course to be eaten with pita breads or tortilla chips. It is not unlike a salsa and may be served hot, at room temperature, or chilled.

The eggplants may be roasted using any of the methods given on pages 178 to 179. Birdie, whose recipe this is, roasts both the eggplants and tomatoes together in the oven so I have done the same. Just remember that larger tomatoes and eggplants will take longer to roast than smaller ones. (For more on Trinidadian chokas see Tomato "Choka," page 301.

1 medium eggplant (about 1 pound)

3 medium tomatoes (about 12 ounces)

4 garlic cloves, peeled and crushed (keep
    1 crushed clove aside)

½ cup very finely chopped onion

1 teaspoon salt

Lots of freshly ground black pepper

½ to 1 fresh hot red or green chile, finely
    chopped (optional)

For the final "choka"

2 tablespoons olive or any other vegetable oil,
    preferably peanut or canola oil

½ teaspoon whole cumin seeds

Preheat the oven to 450°F.

Line a baking tray with foil and spread out the eggplant and tomatoes on it. Bake for 25 minutes. Remove the tomatoes and put in a bowl. Rotate the eggplant slightly and continue to bake it another 35 minutes or longer, rotating it every 6 to 7 minutes, until it has flattened and turned soft.

The tomatoes should now be cool enough to handle and a little liquid should have accumulated under them. Discard the liquid. Peel the tomatoes and remove the cores. Chop the tomatoes coarsely. Peel the eggplant—the peel should come off in strips—and remove its stem end. Now chop it coarsely. Put the eggplant and tomato in a bowl. Add 3 of the crushed garlic cloves, the onion, salt, pepper, and hot chile if you wish to use it. Mix well.

Put the oil in a small frying pan and set over medium-high heat. When hot, put in the cumin seeds. Ten seconds later, put in the remaining crushed garlic clove. Stir until the garlic turns golden, a matter of seconds. Now pour the contents of the frying pan, oil and seasoning, over the eggplant and tomato mixture. Serve warm, at room temperature, or chilled.

SERVES 6

Eggplants and Shiitake Mushrooms Cooked in a Japanese Sauce

JAPAN

This is a simple preparation to be eaten with plain rice (either Japanese or any long-grain variety) and perhaps a bean curd dish. Use long, slim eggplants for this, either the pinkish-purple Japanese variety or the purple Italian or Indian ones. Shorter ones should be cut into fewer segments.

9 dried shiitake mushrooms

¾ pound slim Japanese eggplants, about 8 inches long (see recipe introduction)

Peanut or canola oil for deep-frying

2 tablespoons Japanese soy sauce

1½ tablespoons mirin

1 teaspoon oriental sesame oil

1 teaspoon sugar

Soak the mushrooms in ½ cup of hot water for 30 minutes.

Peel two ½-inch-wide strips down opposite sides of each eggplant to expose part of their flesh. Cut each eggplant crosswise into 3 to 4 pieces, i.e., into about 2-inch-long segments.

Pour oil to a 2-inch depth for deep-frying into a wok, deep frying pan, or deep-fryer and set over medium heat. When it is hot, put in the eggplants and fry until they are golden brown, 6 to 7 minutes. Lift the eggplants out with a slotted spoon and drain on paper towels.

Remove the mushrooms from their soaking liquid. Strain the soaking liquid through a sieve lined with a paper towel or clean dishcloth. Save the soaking liquid. Cut off the coarse mushroom stems and discard.

In a medium-wide pot, combine the mushroom soaking liquid, soy sauce, mirin, sesame oil, and sugar. Set over medium heat and bring to a simmer. Put in the eggplants and mushrooms. Spoon the sauce over them and cook gently for 3 to 4 minutes. Leave the vegetables in the sauce until you are ready to serve them. Serve hot, warm, or at room temperature.

SERVES 3 TO 4

Hot and Spicy Sichuan-Style Eggplants   CHINA

These eggplants are generally fried before being sautéed with the hot bean paste. Here, in order to make them lighter, I have steamed them instead.

This is a spicy, fiery dish that should be served with rice and other crunchy, Chinese-style vegetables.

The ideal eggplants to use here are the long, slim ones sold in America as Japanese eggplants. They are a pinkish-purple color. Long, slim Italian eggplants are also good. They need to be "roll-cut." If that is too difficult, simply cut them crosswise at a diagonal at 1½-inch intervals. If you cannot get Japanese or Italian eggplants, use regular large eggplants. First quarter them lengthwise and then cut them crosswise at 1-inch intervals.

1 pound eggplants (see recipe introduction)

2 tablespoons peanut or canola oil

2 scallions, cut crosswise into fine rings (both white and green sections)

3 thin slices of peeled ginger, cut into fine dice

3 garlic cloves, peeled and finely chopped

5 teaspoons soy sauce

2 to 3 teaspoons chili paste with soybean (page 717)

2 teaspoons sugar

2 teaspoons red wine vinegar

Salt, if needed

1 teaspoon oriental sesame oil

3 tablespoons chopped cilantro

Roll-cut the eggplants according to directions on page 179.

Put the eggplants in a colander or on a steaming tray and steam for 15 to 17 minutes, or until tender (for general steaming directions, see page 736).

Put the oil in a large, nonstick wok or frying pan and set over high heat. When hot, put in the scallions, ginger, and garlic. Stir for a minute. Put in the eggplants. Stir for a minute. Now put in the soy sauce, chili paste with soybean, sugar, and vinegar. Stir and cook for 3 minutes. Taste and add a little salt, if needed. Add the sesame oil and stir once. Turn off the heat. Sprinkle the cilantro over the top before serving.

SERVES 4

Sri Lankan Eggplant Curry

Vambotu Curry

Serve this with plain rice. You may make it as hot as you like. The original recipe called for 2 tea-spoons of cayenne! Normally the eggplant is fried. I have tried to cut down on the oil by broiling it instead.

I have used the large variety of purple eggplant for this dish. Fennel and mustard seeds may be ground at home in a clean coffee grinder. For this recipe, each needs to be ground separately.

1 pound eggplant

2 tablespoons peanut or canola oil

Salt

Freshly ground black pepper

1 teaspoon ground cumin

1 teaspoon ground coriander

¼ teaspoon ground turmeric

½ teaspoon ground fennel

½ teaspoon cayenne, or more as desired

4 teaspoons fresh lime or lemon juice

1 small cinnamon stick

15 fresh curry leaves (use fresh basil leaves as an interesting substitute)

1 small onion (2 ounces), peeled and cut into fine half rings

¾ cup coconut milk from a well-stirred can

2 teaspoons ground brown mustard seeds

Preheat the broiler, placing a shelf about 6 inches away from the source of heat.

Cut the eggplant crosswise into ½-inch-thick round slices and put the slices in a broiling tray. Rub 1 tablespoon of the oil on both sides of the slices and then sprin-kle both sides lightly with salt and pepper. Place the tray under the broiler and cook one side for about 4 minutes and the other side for about 3 minutes, or until both sides are a pretty, reddish color. Remove and quarter each slice. Put the sec-tions in a bowl and sprinkle with ½ teaspoon salt, the cumin, coriander, turmeric, fennel, cayenne, and lime juice. Toss gently to mix.

Put the remaining 1 tablespoon oil in a large, preferably nonstick frying pan and set over medium-high heat. When hot, put in the cinnamon stick and a second later, the curry leaves. Stir once and put in the onion. Stir and fry for about 2 minutes, or until the onion has browned a bit. Put in the seasoned egg-plant. Stir and toss for 4 minutes. Combine the coconut milk and the mustard seeds and pour the mixture over the eggplant. As soon as it starts bubbling, turn the heat to medium-low and cook, uncovered, for 3 minutes, stirring gently now and then. Check for the balance of salt, cayenne, and lime, adding more of what-ever you need. Serve hot.

SERVES 3 TO 4

Eggplants with Spicy Shallot-Tomato Sauce

Sambal Terong

If you cannot get slim Japanese or Italian eggplants, use the larger variety and cut it into 1-inch squares. In Indonesia, instead of red bell peppers, fresh hot red chiles would be used. If you can find them, you may use them but they will make the dish very hot. My dish is medium hot.
Serve with rice and any bean or bean curd dish.

1¼ pounds Japanese eggplants, about 8 inches long, cut crosswise into ¾-inch-wide chunks

1 teaspoon salt

For the sauce

½ large red bell pepper (3 ounces), seeded, cored, and coarsely diced

4 medium shallots, peeled and coarsely chopped

3 garlic cloves, peeled

¼ teaspoon ground turmeric

½ teaspoon cayenne

3 tablespoons vegetable oil, preferably peanut or corn oil

2 medium tomatoes (about 10 ounces), finely chopped

½ teaspoon salt

You also need

Vegetable oil, preferably peanut or corn oil, for deep-frying

Put the eggplants in a bowl. Sprinkle salt evenly over the top. Toss and set aside for 30 to 60 minutes.

Meanwhile, make the sauce. Put the red pepper, shallots, garlic, turmeric, cayenne, and 4 tablespoons of water into a blender. Blend to a paste. Set the spice paste aside.

Put 3 tablespoons of oil in a large, nonstick frying pan and set over medium-high heat. When hot, put in the spice paste. Stir and fry for 7 minutes, or until the paste loses most of its moisture. Add the tomatoes and stir for an additional 4 minutes. Add the salt and ½ cup of water. Turn the heat down to low, cover, and simmer for 3 to 4 minutes. Turn the heat off and set aside.

Drain the eggplants and place them on paper towels in a single layer. Pat the tops dry with more paper towels.

Pour oil to a 2-inch depth for deep-frying in a wok, deep frying pan, or deep-fryer and set over medium heat. When it is very hot, put in enough eggplants to fit in a single layer. Cook for about 7 minutes, or until they are golden brown on both sides. Lift the eggplants out with a slotted spoon and drain on fresh paper towels. Fry all the eggplants this way. (The oil can be strained and reused.)

Set the sauce over medium-low heat. When hot, put in the eggplants. Stir gently, folding the slices into the sauce. Serve hot, warm, or at room temperature.

SERVES 4 TO 6

From Victor Matiya's Jerusalem Restaurant in Toronto

Buttery Soft Slices of Deep-Fried Eggplant with Garlic   PALESTINE

Bentinjen M'li

The first time I sampled this simple, melt-in-the-mouth creation was in Toronto. It was made by a Palestinian who explained that the dish is common to most Arabs in the Eastern Mediterranean. Serve very hot as a part of any meal from South Asia and all points west.

Salt

1¼ pounds eggplant, peeled and cut into
    ¾-inch-thick round slices

1 tablespoon olive oil

1 to 2 garlic cloves, peeled and crushed to a
    pulp

Peanut or canola oil for deep-frying

Freshly ground black pepper

1 lemon, cut in half

2 tablespoons finely chopped fresh parsley

1 teaspoon very finely chopped fresh hot
    green chile (no seeds)

Put 2 quarts of water in a large bowl. Add 2 tablespoons salt and mix until the salt has dissolved. Soak the eggplant slices in this solution for 3 to 4 hours or more.

Put the olive oil and garlic in a very small pot and set over medium heat. The garlic will begin to sizzle. Let it sizzle until it turns golden. Take the oil off the heat and set aside.

Take the eggplant slices out of their soaking liquid and pat them as dry as possible.

Just before eating, put oil to a depth of 2 inches for deep-frying in a wok or deep-fryer and set over medium heat. When very hot, gently lower as many eggplant slices into the oil as will fit in a single layer. Fry until one side is reddish-brown, about 3 minutes. Turn the slices over and fry until the other side is the same color, another 3 minutes. Lift the slices out with a slotted spoon and drain well on paper towels. Fry all the slices this way.

(recipe continues)

Now work quickly. Put the slices in a single layer in a serving dish. Dribble a little of the garlic oil over each slice. Sprinkle lightly with salt and pepper. Squeeze a little lemon juice over each slice and then scatter the parsley and chile over the top. Serve hot.

SERVES 4

Promila Kapoor's

Deep-Fried Eggplant Slices　　　INDIA

Baigan Kachri

This popular dish from the Punjab is served in India sometimes as a snack at teatime and sometimes with meals. It is made with the large purple eggplant.

1 1/4 pounds eggplant, washed and cut into
    1/2-inch thick, slices

Salt

Freshly ground black pepper

1/4 teaspoon cayenne

1 teaspoon ground coriander

1 teaspoon ground cumin

1 cups sifted whole wheat flour

1 teaspoon ground cumin

1 cup (5 oz /140 g) sifted whole wheat flour
    (preferably Indian chapati flour, which
    does not need sifting)

Vegetable oil for deep-frying

Lay the eggplant (aubergine) slices on a flat surface in a single layer. Pat them dry with paper towels. Sprinkle salt generously on them as well as the black pepper, and half of the cayenne pepper, coriander, and cumin. Pat the seasonings in. Turn the slices over and do the same on the other side. Place the slices on a flat dish and let them soak up the spices for 30 minutes.

Dredge the slices in the flour, covering both sides well. Shake off excess flour.

Put the oil for deep frying in a wok or deep-fryer and set over medium heat. When very hot, gently lower as many eggplant (aubergine) slices into the oil as will fit in a single layer. Fry until one side is golden brown, about 2-3 minutes. Turn the slices over and fry until the second side is golden brown, another 2-3 minutes. Lift the slices out with a slotted spoon and drain well on paper towels. Fry all the slices this way. Serve immediately.

SERVES 4

Eggplant with Minty Tomato Sauce and Yogurt

AFGHANISTAN

Badenjan Boorani

This is a superb party dish from Afghanistan—rounds of eggplant freshly fried, and topped first with a tomato sauce and then with a dollop of creamy yogurt. Serve rice on the side. You may also serve a single round of eggplant as a first course.

If you wish to use fresh tomatoes, you will need 1½ cups of peeled and chopped tomatoes.

The frying of the eggplant slices should be done at the last minute. It takes 6 to 7 minutes for one batch. You might need to do two batches. Allow yourself another couple of minutes to let the oil heat.

1¼ pounds eggplant (the large variety)

1¼ teaspoons salt

For the tomato sauce

¼ cup peanut or canola oil

1 medium onion, very finely chopped

3 garlic cloves, peeled and very finely chopped

8 plum tomatoes from a can, finely chopped, plus ¼ cup of the can liquid

1¼ teaspoons salt

3 tablespoons chopped fresh mint leaves

1 teaspoon ground cumin

½ teaspoon ground coriander

¼ teaspoon cayenne

Freshly ground black pepper

You also need

½ cup plain yogurt

Peanut or canola oil for deep-frying

Extra mint sprigs or leaves for garnishing

Trim the very ends of the eggplant and cut it crosswise into 1-inch-thick slices. Put the slices in a single layer in a large platter or lasagna-type dish. Sprinkle the salt over both sides, rubbing it in well. Set aside for 1 hour.

Meanwhile, make the tomato sauce. Put the oil in a large, nonstick frying pan and set over medium-high heat. When hot, put in the onion. Stir and fry for 2 to 3 minutes, or until the onion pieces begin to brown at the edges. Put in the garlic. Stir for a few seconds. Now put in the tomatoes and their liquid as well as all the remaining ingredients for the tomato sauce. Stir to mix. Cover, turn the heat to low, and cook gently for 10 minutes. Set aside in a warm place.

Make the yogurt sauce. Put the yogurt in a small bowl and beat lightly with a fork.

Just before you sit down to eat, put oil to a depth of 2 to 3 inches for deep-frying in a wok or deep-fryer and set over medium heat. Take the eggplant slices from the platter and dry them off well with paper towels.

(recipe continues)

When the oil is hot, drop in as many slices as the utensil will hold easily and fry, turning now and then, for 6 to 7 minutes, or until both sides are a medium brown color. Drain well on paper towels. Do a second batch, if needed.

To serve, arrange the eggplant slices in a single layer on a large platter. Top each slice with a dollop of the tomato sauce and then with a tablespoon of the yogurt. Garnish with the mint sprigs or leaves. Serve immediately.

SERVES 3 TO 4

Sweet-and-Sour Eggplants INDIA
Khatte Meethe Baigan

Frying does something miraculous to eggplants. It makes their flesh satiny. I rest the fried segments on paper towels to remove most of the oil before simmering them with a selection of Indian spices. Serve with rice or bread, a green vegetable, and salads.

1⅛ pounds whole, slim Japanese or small Italian eggplants—do not remove sepals or stem

Peanut or canola oil for deep-frying

¾ teaspoon salt

¼ teaspoon ground turmeric

1 teaspoon ground coriander

1 teaspoon ground cumin

¼ teaspoon garam masala (page 723)

1 teaspoon ground *amchoor* (page 711)

A combination of ¼ cup warm water,
      2 teaspoons fresh lemon juice, and
      2 teaspoons brown sugar

Quarter the eggplants lengthwise in such a way as to leave them whole at the stem end.

Heat oil to a depth of 2 inches for deep-frying in a wok, deep frying pan, or deep-fryer over medium heat. When it is hot, put in the eggplants and cook until they are lightly browned, about 5 minutes. Lift the eggplants out with a slotted spoon, drain on paper towels, and let them cool. (The oil can be strained and reused.)

Meanwhile, mix the salt, turmeric, coriander, cumin, garam masala, and *amchoor* in a bowl. Sprinkle the spice mixture on the inside and outside of the eggplants and rub it in.

Lay the eggplants down in a single layer in a clean frying pan. Pour the combination of the water, lemon juice, and sugar over the eggplants and bring to a simmer. Cover, turn the heat down to very low, and simmer gently for 5 minutes, turning the eggplants gently once or twice. (To turn, hold the top, uncut end with a pair of tongs.) Serve hot.

SERVES 4

Sour Fennel-Flavored Eggplant   PAKISTAN
Khatte Baigan

A superb Pakistani dish to be eaten with South Asian breads or with pita bread, this goes particularly well with Chickpeas and Chana Dal Cooked Together in a Mint Sauce (page 34). Simple relishes made with raw tomatoes and onions may be served on the side. I use the large purple eggplant for this dish. The Bengali spice mixture used here consists of fennel seeds, cumin seeds, mustard seeds, fenugreek seeds, and nigella (kalonji) *mixed sometimes in equal proportions and sometimes with more of the first three seeds and less of the last two. This mixture, already prepared, is sold by most Indian grocers.*

1 eggplant (about 1 pound)

Salt

4 tablespoons vegetable oil (I use olive oil)

1¼ teaspoons *panchphoran* (page 731)

1 teaspoon ground *amchoor* (page 711) or 1 tablespoon fresh lemon juice

⅛ to scant ½ teaspoon cayenne

3 tablespoons plain yogurt

Quarter the eggplant lengthwise and then cut the sections crosswise into ½-inch-wide pieces. Put 5 cups of water in a wide bowl. Add 1 tablespoon of salt and stir to mix. Put in the eggplant pieces. Upturn a smallish plate on top of the eggplant pieces to keep them submerged. The plate should stay inside the bowl. Set aside for 40 minutes. Drain and pat the eggplant pieces as dry as possible with paper towels.

Put the oil in a large, preferably nonstick frying pan and set over high heat. When hot, put in the *panchphoran* and a second later, the eggplant pieces. Turn the heat down just a bit to medium-high. Stir and fry until the pieces are lightly browned, about 4 minutes. Put in ½ teaspoon salt, the *amchoor*, and cayenne. Stir to mix and then put in ½ cup of water. Cover, turn the heat down to low, and cook very gently for 10 minutes, or until the vegetable pieces are tender. Uncover, put in the yogurt, and turn the heat up to medium-high. Stir and fry gently for 1 to 2 minutes, or until the yogurt is absorbed.

SERVES 3 TO 4

Spicy Eggplant Stew with Potatoes, Mushrooms, and Chickpeas

INDIA

Shorvedar Baigan Aur Aloo

This is a hearty stew filled with chunky vegetables. You may serve it with bread, salads, and yogurt relishes. Or, serve it as I often do, in big, old-fashioned, individual soup plates with hunks of crusty French or Italian bread and green salad. Eat it with a spoon and a fork. For dessert, fruit and cheeses are both simple and good.

Okra may be added to the stew, if you like. Stir-fry 12 to 16 small whole okra pods in a little oil over medium-high heat for 3 to 4 minutes until lightly browned, sprinkle them with a little salt, and add them to the stew 15 minutes before the cooking time is over. Let them simmer along with the other vegetables until everything is tender.

You may cook your own chickpeas (page 26) or use canned ones. Just remember that a 20-ounce can generally yields about 2¼ cups of drained cooked chickpeas.

¼ cup peanut or canola oil

⅛ teaspoon ground asafetida

1½ teaspoons whole cumin seeds

3 whole dried hot red chiles

2 garlic cloves, lightly crushed and peeled

¾ pound potatoes, peeled and cut into 1- to 1½-inch chunks

¾ pound long, slim Japanese or Italian eggplants, cut crosswise into 1- to 1½-inch chunks

¾ pound large white mushrooms, cut into halves or quarters to match the size of other vegetable pieces

¼ teaspoon ground turmeric

1 teaspoon ground coriander

1 cup tomato puree

2¼ teaspoons salt

¾ well-packed cup (3 ounces) very finely minced fresh cilantro (leaves, stems, and roots)

2¼ cups drained cooked chickpeas

Put the oil in a large, wide pot and set over high heat. When hot, put in the asafetida and cumin. Let them sizzle for 10 seconds. Put in the red chiles. As soon as they swell and darken, a matter of seconds, put in the garlic and potatoes. Stir and fry for a minute. Put in the eggplant chunks. Stir and fry for 2 minutes. Put in the mushrooms. Stir and fry another 2 minutes. Now put in the turmeric and ground coriander. Stir once and put in the tomato puree, 4 cups of water, salt, cilantro, and chickpeas. Bring to a boil. Cover, turn the heat down to low, and cook gently for 35 to 40 minutes, until the vegetables are tender.

SERVES 4 TO 6

Cheryl Rathkopf's
Sri Lankan Eggplant "Pickle"
Vambotu Pahi

SRI LANKA

Somewhere between a condiment and a vegetable dish, this very mustardy dish may be served with almost any meal.

I have used the large variety of purple eggplant, although ideally you should use the very small variety sometimes sold as baby eggplants. If you can get them, cut each into quarters lengthwise.

If you cannot get fresh lemongrass, just leave it out.
You may keep this dish 4 to 5 days in the refrigerator.

1 pound eggplant

Salt

Freshly ground black pepper

¼ teaspoon ground turmeric

Peanut or canola oil for shallow frying

1 small cinnamon stick

15 fresh curry leaves (use fresh holy basil or basil leaves as a different but equally interesting substitute)

1 fresh lemongrass stick (use the bottom 6 inches, cut into 2 pieces—crush the root end lightly)

1 medium onion (4 ounces), peeled and very finely chopped

1 to 3 fresh hot green chiles, cut crosswise into ¾-inch segments

1½ tablespoons brown mustard seeds, ground in a clean coffee grinder or other spice grinder

1 teaspoon cayenne

2 teaspoons sugar

3 garlic cloves, peeled and crushed to a pulp

2 teaspoons very finely grated peeled fresh ginger

2 tablespoons distilled white vinegar

Cut the eggplant crosswise into ½-inch-thick round slices. Sprinkle both sides lightly with salt, pepper, and turmeric. Set aside for 30 minutes. Pat dry with paper towels. Quarter each slice.

Heat the oil for shallow frying in a large frying pan over medium-high heat. When hot, put in as many pieces of eggplant as will fit easily and fry until both sides are reddish-brown. Remove with a slotted spoon and drain on paper towels. Do all the eggplant this way.

Remove all but 2 tablespoons of the oil from the frying pan and set the pan once again over medium-high heat. (The remaining oil may be strained and saved for

(recipe continues)

future use.) When hot, put in the cinnamon stick and a second later, the curry leaves. Stir once and put in the lemongrass, onion, and green chiles. Stir and fry for about 4 minutes, or until the onion is soft and has browned a bit. Allow to cool.

Combine 1 teaspoon salt, the mustard seeds, cayenne, sugar, garlic, and ginger in a large bowl. Mix. Add the vinegar and mix again. Put in the fried eggplants and the onion mixture. Stir to mix. Cover and refrigerate overnight. Reheat gently. Remove the lemongrass and cinnamon stick before serving. (In warm weather, this may be served at room temperature.)

SERVES 3 TO 4

Fava Beans

Fresh fava beans, although very common in Europe, are still hard to find in American supermarkets and when located in specialty stores, may be purchased only at what seems like a fairly high price. Oddly enough, even though fava beans probably originated in Europe, they are now cheap and plentiful in the Middle East and much of China.

America, for some reason, has never taken to them. This is a shame as the beans, with their dark earthy taste and buttery texture, are so good and do not need to be the rare specialty items that they are.

Of a medium green shade, the large, bulbous pods need to be opened up first. Lying inside on top of a white flannel-like lining are large flat seeds. The size depends on the time of year. The seeds tend to be small in the early summer and swell to their maximum in the late summer when they start to turn slightly yellow. The first thing to do is to shell the pods.

You need to buy lots of bean pods to get a handful of beans. Two pounds of pods bought in the spring yielded 1¾ cups (½ pound) of skinned beans. Two and three-quarter pounds pods bought in the summer yielded 3 cups (¾ pound) of beans and just about served 4 people.

Once the pods are shelled—and you shell them just as you would shell pea pods—the beans need to be cooked quickly and then peeled. Each bean is covered with a leathery skin that does not make very pleasant eating. The Chinese like to cook the beans with their skins and then pop each open as they eat. I find this too much of a chore and prefer to do the skinning beforehand. Let me assure you that this initial double trouble is well worth the effort.

For all the recipes here, the shelled but not yet skinned beans are boiled quickly in water, cooled off, and their leathery skins then peeled away. The peeled beans need little done to them. They may be served as is with a dollop of butter or a little good olive oil poured on them. They may be quickly sautéed or stir-fried, or used in pilafs, risottos, and salads. One of my favorite recipes in this book is the Artichoke Heart and Fresh Fava Bean Salad (page 612).

How to prepare 2¾ pounds of fava beans: Shell the fava bean pods. Bring 8 cups of water to a rolling boil. Add 4 teaspoons salt and stir to mix. Now put in the shelled beans. Depending upon the size of the beans, cook for 2 to 5 minutes, or until the beans are just tender. Drain quickly and rinse off under cold water. Now peel the beans, removing the leathery skin. The beans may now be served as is, heated with a little butter or oil, or cooked further according to the recipes that follow.

Fresh Fava Beans Sautéed with Garlic and Thyme

MEDITERRANEAN

Instead of thyme, you may use the same quantity of finely chopped fresh sage leaves or finely chopped oregano leaves.

2¾ pounds fava bean pods, about
   3 cups shelled

2 tablespoons olive oil

2 garlic cloves, very lightly mashed and
   peeled but left whole

1 teaspoon fresh thyme leaves or ¼ teaspoon
   dried thyme leaves

¼ teaspoon salt

Freshly ground black pepper

1 to 2 teaspoons fresh lemon juice

Cook and peel the beans according to directions above.

Put the oil and garlic in a large frying pan and set over medium-high heat. When the garlic begins to sizzle, stir it around for a few seconds. Now put in the thyme and stir for a few seconds. Put in the beans, salt, pepper to taste, and lemon juice. Stir briefly until the beans have heated through. Turn off the heat.

SERVES 4

Stir-Fried Fava Beans with Ginger

CHINA

Sung Jiang Chow Tsan Do

Fava beans are eaten over much of China, especially in the West where even fermented bean pastes are made with it. Here is a simple stir-fry.

2¾ pounds fresh fava bean pods, about
    3 cups shelled

2 tablespoons peanut or canola oil

2 garlic cloves, very lightly crushed and
    peeled but left whole

3 thin slices of fresh ginger

Scant ½ teaspoon salt

Freshly ground black pepper

1 teaspoon sugar

1 tablespoon Chinese Shao Hsing wine or dry
    sherry

1 tablespoon vegetable stock or water

2 scallions, cut crosswise into fine rings (use
    both white and green sections)

1 tablespoon oriental sesame oil

Cook and peel the beans according to directions on page 199.

Put the oil in a wok or large frying pan and set over high heat. When hot, put in the garlic and ginger. Stir once or twice, pressing down on the garlic and ginger. Now put in the shelled beans and stir once. Put in the salt, pepper, sugar, wine, and stock. Stir for 30 seconds, or until the liquid is absorbed. Add the scallions and stir for 10 to 20 seconds. Dribble the sesame oil over the top and stir to mix. Turn off the heat. Remove the garlic and ginger before serving.

SERVES 4

Fiddlehead Ferns

These come into season for just 2 to 3 weeks of the year, shyly curled, embryonic heads that will transform, if left alone, into proud, upright ferns. With their asparagus-like flavor and a very slightly glutinous texture, they are, for me, a harbinger of spring, a food not to be missed. While they sell for big bucks in the fancy stores, my local farmers market sells them for almost nothing, especially at the end of the day. I include no major recipes for them as they are best just boiled. But there is a trick to boiling them well.

How to buy and prepare fiddlehead ferns: Look for crisp, green fiddleheads and cook them soon after bringing them home. Wash them in cold water, removing any bits of brown casings that might still be clinging to them.

Bring a large pot of water to a rolling boil. When boiling, drop in the fiddle-heads. Bring the water to a boil again and then immediately drain the fiddle-heads. This water will be somewhat brown. Wash the fiddleheads under cold water as you bring another large pot of water to a rolling boil. Drop in the fiddleheads once again and boil rapidly for 4 to 8 minutes, or until the fiddleheads are just tender but still firm (rather like asparagus). Drain. The fiddleheads may now be served hot with just a pat of butter or "dressed" with a vinaigrette and served at room temperature or chilled.

Green Beans

The Chinese call them *si ji do,* or "four season beans," because they are available in all seasons; the Japanese, who got them from China and who seem to have lost a season somewhere, call them *sandomame,* or "three times beans," because they are harvested thrice yearly; the Indians (in India) call them *france bean,* or French beans, because we may well have gotten them from French colonizers; and the French call a slim, young version of the bean haricot vert, with the word *haricot,* which most of us think of as quintessentially French, being in fact a corruption of the Aztec word *ayacotl.*

The green bean, which can be found all year in all parts of the world today, started its life in the New World more than nine millennia ago.

There are many varieties of green beans but for the recipes in this section, I have used mostly the rounded string beans—about ¼ inch around—(which are now, on the whole, stringless) that are commonly found in much of the world. The recipes may, however, be used for flat beans, though those may take a bit longer to cook. Where the slim and delicate haricot vert might be ideal or can easily be sub-stituted, I have suggested that in the recipe.

Long Beans: Some recipes call for long beans which, though still very beanlike, have a darker, earthier flavor all their own. They are a separate species that prob-ably originated in India, though they are now found in most of southern and east-ern Asia. Known also as yard-long beans or asparagus beans, these are about a foot or more in length and can come in both dark and lighter shades of green. The colors make little difference to the flavor or texture, though I do find the darker ones to be a bit more crisp and dense. Long beans are found in Indian, Chinese, and Caribbean markets.

Once, more than a decade ago, I was in Hong Kong, watching Wili Mark, a local food historian, prepare these long beans. While standing around, I idly picked up a bean and began nibbling on it. I have always loved its taste. All the Chinese in that tiny kitchen were aghast. It was then that it struck me that the

Chinese never eat raw vegetables, possibly because night soil used to be a traditional fertilizer. Even iceberg lettuce is quickly passed through hot oil in a wok before it is served. On the other hand, these long beans are routinely served raw in much of Thailand and Malaysia as saladlike greens to be munched along with bites of searingly hot foods. One of my favorite ways of eating them raw involves first cutting them into very fine rounds and then scattering them over fried rice. They add a unique taste and a decidedly welcome crunch.

It goes without saying that any beans you buy should be bright green and crisp. Wash them and then trim them at both ends. Cut them further according to the recipe.

Many recipes require that you blanch the green beans first. Here is how you go about it:

To blanch and refresh 1 pound regular green beans or haricots verts: Bring 4 quarts of water to a rolling boil in a large pot. Add 2 tablespoons salt and stir. Now put in the beans and bring to a boil again. Boil rapidly for 4 minutes, or until the beans are just tender. Drain the beans. If the beans are not to be used immediately, rinse them under cold running water until they have cooled off completely. Note: Haricots verts should boiled for just 2 minutes.

Green Beans with Cumin and Fennel   INDIA

These spicy green beans go particularly well with split pea and dried bean dishes, potato and sweet potato dishes, and eggplant dishes. Breads or rice may be served on the side. To complete the meal, yogurt drinks or relishes or perhaps a paneer *or cheese dish may also be served.*

3 tablespoons peanut or canola oil

1 teaspoon whole cumin seeds

1 teaspoon whole fennel seeds

2 good-sized shallots or 1 small onion (about 1½ ounces), peeled and cut into fine slices

1 garlic clove, peeled and cut into fine slices

1 (1-inch) piece of fresh ginger, peeled and cut into very fine slivers

1 pound green beans, cut into 1-inch pieces

1 teaspoon ground coriander

1 teaspoon ground cumin

¼ teaspoon ground turmeric

¼ teaspoon cayenne

1¼ teaspoons salt

1 small tomato (2 ounces), chopped

3 tablespoons finely chopped fresh cilantro

Put the oil in a large frying pan and set over medium-high heat. When very hot, add the whole cumin and fennel seeds. Stir for a few seconds. Quickly add the shallots, garlic, and ginger. Stir for about a minute, or until lightly browned. Add the beans and stir for another 2 minutes. Add the coriander, cumin, turmeric, and cayenne and stir a few times. Add ½ cup of water and the salt and bring to a simmer. Stir and cover. Turn the heat down to low and cook gently for 5 minutes. Add the tomato and cilantro. Stir, cover, and cook for another 4 to 5 minutes, or until the beans are tender.

SERVES 4 TO 6

From the Çiragan Hotel in Istanbul

Green Bean Salad

TURKEY

Taze Fassoulia Salata

This dish is generally served chilled or at room temperature either as is or with a further "dressing" of the walnut-rich Circassian Sauce, which makes it much more nutritionally sound and adds new flavors to it. Serve with bread and possibly other salads.

¼ cup olive oil

1 medium onion, peeled and cut into fine half rings

4 garlic cloves, peeled and finely chopped

1 pound fresh or canned tomatoes, finely chopped

1 pound fresh green beans, with tops and tails removed but otherwise left whole

1 teaspoon salt

1 cup Circassian Sauce (page 684), optional

Put the oil in a large frying pan and set over medium-high heat. When hot, put in the onion and garlic. Stir and cook for 2 to 3 minutes, or until the onion just begins to soften. Put in the chopped tomatoes and their liquid. Stir and cook on medium heat, breaking up the tomatoes further, for another 7 to 8 minutes. Add the beans, salt, and 1 cup of water. Bring to a boil. Cover, turn the heat down to low, and simmer gently for 20 minutes, or until the beans are tender. Uncover, turn the heat up, and boil down most of the sauce. Let the beans cool. Now, if you wish to add the Circassian Sauce, fold it in gently. Serve at room temperature or chilled.

SERVES 4

Shiu-Min Block's

Stir-Fried Dry Green Beans
with Tien Jing Preserved Vegetable   CHINA
Gun Chow Si Ji Do

The Tien Jing preserved vegetable comes tightly packed in earthen crocks, which, when empty, I like to use as vases in the country—they look wonderful with wildflowers. The vegetable is already cut up into small segments. It can be used straight out of the crock.

If you cannot get the preserved vegetable, use 1 tablespoon of tamari soy sauce.

1 pound string beans

¾ cup peanut or canola oil

2 teaspoons finely chopped peeled fresh
   ginger

1 dried hot red chile, crumbled coarsely

2 whole scallions, cut crosswise into very fine
   rounds (both white and green sections)

3 tablespoons Tien Jing preserved vegetable
   (page 742)

¼ teaspoon salt

2 garlic cloves, lightly crushed and peeled but
   left whole

1 teaspoon oriental sesame oil

Trim the beans at the ends but otherwise leave them whole. Wash and pat dry.

Heat a large wok on high and put in the oil. (If using a large frying pan, put the oil in first and then set on high to heat.) When very hot, put in all the beans. Stir and fry them for about 5 minutes, or until blistered and lightly browned. Remove with a slotted spoon. Remove all the oil except 1 tablespoon. (This oil may be reused for another dish.) Still on high heat, put in the ginger and chile. Stir once and put in the scallions and preserved vegetable. Stir a few times and put in the beans, salt, and garlic. Stir gently to mix. Add the sesame oil. Toss and serve.

SERVES 3 TO 4

Green Beans with Garlic and Preserved Lemon

Preserved lemons have a distinctive flavor that just cannot be duplicated. I always have some sitting in the refrigerator. Here, you may use either the Salted Lemons, Moroccan Style (page 689) or else the Simple Lemon Pickle (page 690). Only about ¼ lemon is required. This is one of the most refreshing bean dishes.

1 pound green beans

Salt

3 tablespoons olive oil

1 dried hot red chile

3 to 4 garlic cloves, lightly mashed and peeled but left whole

¼ preserved lemon, rind only, washed, patted dry, and very finely chopped

Freshly ground black pepper

A little fresh lemon juice

Trim the beans at both ends and cut into 1-inch segments. Blanch and drain according to directions on page 202.

Put the oil in a large frying pan or sauté pan and set over medium-high heat. When hot, put in the red chile. Stir once or twice until it is dark red. Quickly put in the garlic. Stir and fry for a few seconds. Add the drained beans and the preserved lemon and turn the heat to medium-low.

Stir and mix. If the beans are no longer hot, heat them through. Sprinkle a little salt and some black pepper over the top. Add the lemon juice. Toss to mix and taste for salt. Serve immediately.

SERVES 3 TO 4

Variation

Green Beans with Roasted Red Pepper and Preserved Lemon

I sometimes add a roasted red pepper to the beans. Roast the pepper according to directions on page 262 and cut into pieces about the same size as the beans. Add at the same time as the beans.

Green Beans with Mushrooms

Sem Aur Khumbi

This is a simple Indian way with green beans. You may stuff these beans into a pita bread, along with a chutney or yogurt relish. You may also eat them with other vegetables, yogurt dishes, and dried beans.

6 tablespoons peanut or canola oil

1 teaspoon whole cumin seeds

1 medium onion, cut in half lengthwise and then crosswise into very thin slices

5 to 6 garlic cloves, peeled and very finely chopped

1 (1½-inch) piece of fresh ginger, peeled and cut into very fine rounds, then stacked and cut into very fine slivers

10 ounces white mushrooms, cut into thick slices lengthwise

1½ pounds green beans, cut into 1-inch segments

1 tablespoon ground coriander

2 teaspoons ground cumin

½ teaspoon ground turmeric

1 teaspoon garam masala (page 723)

1 teaspoon cayenne

1½ teaspoons salt

Put the oil in a large wok, frying pan, or sauté pan and set over medium-high heat. When hot, put in the cumin seeds. Let them sizzle for 10 seconds and then put in the sliced onion. Stir and fry until medium brown. Add the garlic and ginger and fry for a few seconds, or until the garlic turns golden. Put in the mushrooms. Stir and fry until the mushrooms lose their raw look and turn shiny. Add the beans, coriander, ground cumin, turmeric, garam masala, cayenne, and salt. Stir to mix. Add ½ cup of water and bring to a boil. Cover, turn the heat down to low, and cook gently for 15 minutes, or until the beans are tender. Stir once about halfway through this period. Uncover and boil away most of the liquid, turning the beans gently as you do so. (The beans may be easily reheated.)

SERVES 4 TO 6

Green Beans with Browned Shallots

Browned shallots give these beans a very intense taste. I usually start browning the shallots immediately after I throw the beans into the boiling water. The beans take about 4 minutes to cook, which is enough time to brown the shallots. You could, of course, do the two things consecutively if you find that easier.

1 pound green beans or haricots verts

Salt

3 tablespoons olive oil

2 good-sized shallots (2 ounces), peeled and cut into fine slivers

Freshly ground black pepper

Trim the beans at both ends but leave them whole. Blanch and drain them according to directions on page 202.

Put the oil in a large frying pan or sauté pan and set over medium-high heat. When hot, put in the shallots. Stir and fry for 2 to 3 minutes, or until the shallots are browned. Add the drained beans and turn the heat to medium-low. Stir and mix. If the beans are no longer hot, heat them through. Sprinkle a little salt and lots of black pepper over the top. Toss to mix and taste for salt. Serve immediately.

SERVES 3 TO 4

Bengali-Style Green Beans   INDIA

Serve these lightly pungent green beans with rice or couscous. Legumes and dairy dishes should be served on the side.

It is best to grind the mustard seeds in a clean coffee grinder or other spice grinder.

2 tablespoons whole brown or yellow mustard seeds (or a combination of the two)

3 tablespoons mustard oil or any vegetable oil (olive oil makes a good substitute)

1 medium onion (5 ounces), quartered lengthwise and thinly sliced

¾ pound green beans, cut into 1-inch-long pieces

1¼ teaspoons salt

½ cup (1 ounce) chopped fresh cilantro

1 fresh hot green chile, cut into long slivers (do not remove the seeds)

Put the mustard seeds in a clean spice grinder and grind to a fine powder. Empty into a small bowl. Add ¾ cup of water and let soak for 20 to 30 minutes. Do not stir. Set the mustard mixture aside.

Put the oil in a frying pan and set over medium-high heat. Add the onion. Sauté on medium heat until the onion is soft and just begins to take on color. Put in the beans, salt, cilantro, and green chile. Stir for 1 minute. Carefully pour the watery top of the mustard mixture over the green beans, making sure to leave all the thick paste behind (you do not need the thick paste). Stir to mix well. Bring the beans to a boil. Turn the heat down to low and cover. Simmer very gently for 25 minutes, or until the beans absorb all the spices and lose some of their wetness. Serve hot.

SERVES 4 TO 6

Cheryl Rathkopf's

Green Bean and Potato Curry   SRI LANKA

Bonchi Curry

This is a simple curry to be served with rice, pickles, and chutneys.
The green beans in Sri Lanka are cut on a steep diagonal at ¼-inch intervals. If you are not up to that, cut them crosswise at 1-inch intervals.

2 medium potatoes (about ½ pound), peeled
    and cut into ¾-inch dice

½ teaspoon ground turmeric

3 tablespoons peanut or canola oil

15 fresh curry leaves (substitute fresh holy
    basil or basil leaves for a different but
    equally interesting flavor)

1 cup very finely chopped shallots or red
    onion

3 garlic cloves, peeled and very finely chopped

½ teaspoon very finely chopped peeled fresh
    ginger

3 small fresh hot green chiles, cut crosswise
    into fine rings

¾ pound green beans, cut as suggested above

4 teaspoons Sri Lankan Raw Curry Powder
    (page 707)

1 cup canned coconut milk (shake the can
    before using)

1 (3-inch) cinnamon stick

1¼ to 1½ teaspoons salt

2 tablespoons fresh lime juice

In a medium pot, combine the potatoes, enough water to cover them well, and ¼ teaspoon turmeric. Bring to a boil. Cover partially, turn the heat down a bit, and cook until the potatoes are almost done but still hold their shape well. Drain.

Put the oil in a large sauté pan or frying pan and set over medium-high heat. When hot, put in the curry leaves. Ten seconds later, put in the shallots, garlic, ginger, and green chiles. Sauté for 2 to 3 minutes. Put in the green beans and sauté for another minute. Put in the curry powder and stir once. Now put in the coconut milk, 1 cup of water, the remaining ¼ teaspoon turmeric, the cinnamon stick, salt, and potatoes. Stir and bring to a boil. Cover, turn the heat down to low, and cook about 15 minutes, or until the beans are just tender. Add the lime juice and stir it in.

Remove the cinnamon stick and serve.

SERVES 4 TO 6

Shiu-Min Block's

Long Beans with Fermented Black Beans

CHINA

Don Sher Chaw Gan Do

If you wish to make this dish a little hot, put in only 3 teaspoons of fermented black beans. Then, just when you add the water, put in 1 teaspoon of chili paste with soybean (page 717). Serve with rice.

The beans required here are sold in Asian markets as long beans, or even yard-long beans. If you cannot find them, ordinary green beans or haricots verts may be used.

4 teaspoons fermented black beans (page 713)

2 tablespoons peanut or canola oil

2 slices of peeled fresh ginger, cut into fine shreds

½ pound long beans, trimmed at the ends and cut into 1-inch pieces

1 garlic clove, lightly crushed and peeled but left whole

1 teaspoon salt

½ teaspoon oriental sesame oil

Rinse out the fermented black beans and then chop them finely.

Put the oil in a wok or frying pan and set over high heat. When hot, put in the black beans. Stir once and put in the ginger. Stir for 10 seconds. Put in the long beans and stir for a few seconds. Add the garlic, salt, and 2 teaspoons of water. Stir and cook over high heat for 2 minutes. Turn off the heat. Put in the sesame oil and stir. Serve immediately. (The garlic may be removed before serving.)

SERVES 4

From Tiffin's, Port-of-Spain

Curried Long Beans

TRINIDAD

Curry Bodi

In Port-of-Spain, these curried long beans were generally eaten at lunchtime with roti, a flatbread either plain or stuffed with split peas (page 448). If long beans are not available, use any other rounded green beans (but not the flat ones).

If you want to use the habanero-type Scotch bonnet hot chiles commonly found in Trinidad, I would recommend using just a half or a quarter of one. I have used the green chiles more commonly found in supermarkets. They vary in strength, so use your judgment.

3 tablespoons peanut or canola oil

1 smallish onion (3 ounces), peeled and very
    finely chopped

2 garlic cloves, peeled and very finely chopped

1 to 2 fresh hot green chiles, very finely
    chopped (see recipe introduction)

4 teaspoons curry powder

1¼ pounds long green beans, cut into
    1½-inch segments

1½ teaspoons salt

½ teaspoon *amchar masala* (page 706)

1 teaspoon ground roasted cumin seeds
    (page 724)

Put the oil in a deep frying pan or a wide saucepan and set over medium-high heat. When hot, put in the onion, garlic, and chiles. Stir and fry until the onion is medium brown. Put in the curry powder, stir once, and add 1 cup of water, the beans, and the salt. Stir. Cook on medium heat, uncovered, for 5 to 6 minutes, stirring now and then. Turn the heat down to low and cook another 4 to 5 minutes, or until the beans are tender and there is almost no liquid left. Put in the *amchar masala* and the cumin. Stir and cook another minute.

SERVES 3 TO 4

Greens

When my children were small, they hated all greens. But my husband and I continued to cook and eat them with relish, insisting only that the children taste a little bit of everything we had prepared. From my husband's Kentucky father we had learned to cook collard greens and kale the Southern way. These quickly became—and still are—Thanksgiving and Christmas staples. From a cousin who married a Kashmiri, I had learned to cook collards the Kashmiri way, with asafetida, so that became a part of our repertoire as well. In my travels around the world I fell in love with Greek mixed greens, including some very bitter ones, all dressed with olive oil and lemon juice. The buttery snow pea shoots I tasted in Hong Kong were instantly added to the family repertoire. Trinidad had its recipes to offer, as did Sri Lanka. And of course, there was always Italy, with its broccoli rabe. Whether cooked just with garlic or served on a bed of mashed fava beans, this substantial vegetable was always pungent, slightly bitter and exquisite.

Our children's attitude toward greens changed dramatically when each reached the age of thirteen. (I remember the demarcation line well as it seemed also to be the time when instead of groaning through museums, they began to ask on their own to see, say, the Impressionists.) At thirteen, they began to *ask* for greens and to this day, our children, who now have their own children, eat them with a passion. We assume this passion is being passed along.

Vitamin- and mineral-rich greens are so essential to our well-being. The beta-carotene in them helps us to battle cancers while the large amounts of calcium they contain helps preserve our bones. Many of these greens may be combined or used interchangeably in the recipes that follow.

Buying greens: Look for crisp greens without slimy dark spots. All greens cook down considerably in bulk, the exact amount varying according to the green and its age. So look at specific recipes for quantities to use.

Storing greens: If not using immediately, store greens without washing, wrapped in brown paper or a lightly dampened dishcloth. You can put the whole bundle in a plastic bag, but leave it open and then put it in a drawer in the refrigerator.

Washing greens: Greens are generally coated with grit and mud, so start by filling a large sink with lukewarm water and dunking them all in. Bunched-up leaves should be pulled apart and separated. Coarse stems may be cut away at this stage and either peeled if they have tender innards or discarded. As they float, push them up and down in the water a few times. If you have a second sink, fill it with cold, not lukewarm, water and transfer the greens. Otherwise, lift out the greens (leaving all grit on the bottom of the sink) and put the leaves in a colander. Wash out the sink and fill it up again. Put in the greens, pushing them in and out of the water again, and let them float free briefly. Wash a third time the same way, each time lifting the greens out of the sinkful of water. Never let the water drain with the greens still in the sink. Put the greens in a colander.

For most greens, a little water clinging to them does not hurt. Sometimes it even helps. However, when I want to stir-fry soft greens, such as spinach, I often spin-dry them first in my salad dryer.

Beet greens: How you prepare beet greens depends upon their size. For someone like myself who does not grow them but depends upon the marketplace, there are two types of greens available. There are the baby greens that are very expensive, sold in specialty stores and used mainly in salads. Then there are the leaves we break off the top of our beets when we buy them. The latter go from midsize that take 10 to 15 minutes to cook to very large ones that take almost 30 minutes before they are tender. I like to sauté the greens briefly and then cook them in the minimum amount of water. You will need to check the greens as they cook, adding a tiny bit more water if they seem to dry out.

Bok choy: This is a Chinese green whose bottom end looks a bit like a smooth white or pale green, curvaceous celery stalk but as the eye travels upward the stems turn into deep green leaves that resemble young collard greens. To cook it, you need to separate the white part and cut it at a slight diagonal into $1/2$-inch-wide strips. You could also blanch the white and green parts together for a minute in boiling water and then stir-fry them with garlic and ginger. A soy-based sauce may be poured over the top. Baby bok choy is just a young, small version of the same thing. It is sold in Chinese markets and specialty shops. The small heads may be split in halves or quarters lengthwise, washed well between the still-attached layers, and then blanched briefly before being stir-fried just like the larger bok choy.

Broccoli rabe (rapini): These slightly bitter greens with a few, small, broccoli-like flowers are used quite commonly in Italy. I was introduced to them about three decades ago, when they were still quite rare and only found in Italian-American markets. Now even supermarkets carry them. They cook quickly and, for me, are the perfect foil for dried beans and grains, as they cut through their starchy texture.

To prepare them, first separate the stalks (with leaves attached). The very coarse parts of the stalks may be cut off and discarded. The rest of the stalks may be left attached and peeled, which makes them totally edible. I like to blanch the leaves in boiling salted water for 2 minutes and then rinse them in cold water to fix their color. They may now be sautéed quickly with a little oil and garlic or with any other choice of seasonings.

Chinese broccoli *(gailan/kailan):* Very similar to broccoli rabe but without the bitterness and with much smoother stalks and leaves. Sold mainly in Chinese markets, it is an excellent green that may be used as a substitute in all the broccoli rabe recipes. Peeling the stalks is recommended with this green.

Collard greens: These greens are very popular in the American South and are a staple in the Indian state of Kashmir. Generally, I like to stew them slowly in a mixture of oil, garlic, and vegetable stock. The cooking time and the amount of liquid will vary according to the size and age of the greens. I have never seen young tender collard greens in New York. The kind I get—large dark leaves on heavy stalks—take 1 to $1\frac{1}{2}$ hours to cook. I have to add that I see many recipes—

even some attached to the collard greens themselves—that suggest that these greens may be cooked in 10 minutes. Some even suggest that I steam them for 5 minutes. That has never proved an accurate estimation. Even though collards have a chewy texture, they need to be tender enough to chew. So use your discretion and cook them for as long as needed to get them to your preferred degree of tenderness. Also, when you bring the greens home, it is customary to cut the very coarse ends of the stalks off. Many people, myself included, go further and cut off the entire stems and then core the leaves before cutting them into fine shreds. My husband, having grown up with a Southern father whose childhood was spent on a farm, will not hear of it. He likes to use a good section of the stalk, which he chops coarsely, and the whole leaf, which he cuts into very coarse strips. He says he prefers the texture his way.

Escarole: Looks like a large head of lettuce with coarser leaves. The taste is sweet but with a hint of bitterness. It is best to blanch the leaves in boiling salted water for a few minutes until quite wilted and then refresh in cold water. Just before serving, sauté the greens as you would broccoli rabe.

Kale: The curly heads of this green, extra rich in calcium, are available from early summer right through much of the winter. The flavor gets more intense and the color darkens with the passing months. To prepare kale for cooking, cut off the main, heavy stem at the bottom and separate the leaves. Wash well. Now cut off the coarse individual stems. The heavy central vein may be removed or not, as you like. The leaves may be cut crosswise into fine or coarse strips and then steamed or stewed. The cooking time increases with age, and though I have seen many recipes that suggest cooking times of 5 minutes, I have never come across such tender kale. My cooking times range from 15 minutes to 1 hour.

A new kale has begun to appear in specialty markets, the black Tuscan kale called *cavolo nero* in Italy. It is so nutty and delicious, that if you see it, disregard its price and buy it just once to taste it. The elongated leaves are so dark green they appear almost black. Remove the stems, stack several leaves together, and cut crosswise into very fine strips. Braise or steam just like regular kale. In New York, I never see whole heads of Tuscan kale, just the leaves, so there is very little waste.

Kohlrabi greens: These greens, similar in taste and texture to collard greens, are the leafy tops of kohlrabis though unlike collards they are rarely sold on their own. They are best braised or stewed. Remove the very coarse ends of the stalks before cooking. Tender leaves may be cooked whole while coarse ones may be cut crosswise into ribbons first.

Mustard greens: These have a little pungency to them and may be cooked like collards. In India, mustard greens and spinach are traditionally combined, braised, then pureed and later thickened with a little cornmeal. This is standard winter fare in the villages of the Punjab. The coarse stalks should be removed and the greens cut into fine ribbons before braising. Look for mustard greens in Indian stores as *sarson ka saag*.

Snow pea shoots: I had my first snow pea shoots in Hong Kong more than a decade ago. They were satiny soft in the mouth and tasted as if all the young shoots in this world had been combined and given an extra blessing from pea heaven for good measure. Quite extraordinary! You can imagine my thrill when I walked into New York's Chinatown and found, for the first time, young snow pea shoots, tendrils and all. I bought a pound of them and stir-fried them very simply with garlic and ginger. Well, they were tough and unfriendly, a tangled mass that I could not even pick up easily. Perhaps I had bought old shoots, I thought. I bought them a second and third time with the same results.

Then my friend Shiu-Min showed me how to cook them and I realized what I was doing wrong. The tendrils, however pretty, were part of the problem. "Remove the tendrils," my friend said, "as they make all the stalks entangle." She also told me to break up the stalk into pieces about 3 inches long, each with some leaves on it. "If the stalks are very coarse, remove them altogether and use just the leaves," my friend suggested. So *that* was it!

In southwestern China where these shoots abound, an order of noodle soup generally comes with a topping of lightly blanched snow pea shoots and some chopped cilantro. Then all you have to do is pour on the hot sauce and dig in with your chopsticks.

These shoots are sold in Chinese markets and can now also be found in fancy food shops. They should be washed and then dried off before being stir-fried. A salad spinner is very useful for this.

Sorrel: Also known as sour grass; the leaves resemble young spinach and have a markedly sour flavor. Sorrel is generally used to flavor sauces but may be combined with other greens for a tart accent. Trim away the stems before cooking.

Spinach: There are basically two types of spinach on the market: the curly-leafed spinach and the smooth-leafed one. Their taste and texture, once cooked, are similar. Many bunches are sold with parts of the roots still attached. These need not be discarded. For many dishes the roots can be peeled and left on. Most stalks may be chopped and cooked; they turn as tender as the spinach. Spinach lends itself to being stir-fried (spin it dry first) or braised.

Swiss chard: These days one can find both green and red Swiss chard. The leaves of both are green, but one has white stalks and veins and the other, red ones. They cook identically but have a different look. Generally, it is a good idea to cut off the thick stalks and the central veins that seem to be an extension of the stalks.

These should be cut further as needed and either cooked separately or put in the pot first as they are a little bit tougher than the green part and take slightly longer to cook.

As white veins discolor very quickly after cutting, many people like to blanch them for 2 minutes in a mixture of flour, water, lemon juice, and oil. This treatment does not improve their flavor and is therefore not necessary. I must admit that I hardly ever do it. But if you do want a pristine pale color for the veins and stalks, gradually add 6 cups of water to 4 tablespoons plain white flour, using a whisk to get a smooth texture. Now add 2 tablespoons lemon juice, 1 tablespoon vegetable oil, and a little salt. Bring to a boil and then simmer gently for 2 minutes. Drop the cut white chard veins and stems into this liquid. Simmer for 2 minutes and leave in the liquid. Drain just before using.

Rinse well and pat dry. You may now proceed with any chard recipe. Red veins do not need this treatment.

Turnip greens: Treat like mustard greens.

Watercress: This western salad green that grows near streams or in them is used frequently for sauces and soups in the West in addition to being eaten raw. It has also been adopted by the Chinese, who have subjected it to their own culinary rules that require that all vegetables be cooked, however briefly, before they are eaten. Because long stems become a sorry tangled mess in stir-frying, watercress is either broken up into smaller pieces or finely minced before it enters the wok.

Stir-Fried Beet Greens with Ginger and Green Chiles INDIA
Chukandar Ka Saag

In the Delhi region, many greens are cooked with this simple seasoning of fresh ginger and chiles.
If the beet leaves are young and small, you may leave them whole. They will also cook much faster. The leaves I used here were large and mature, so they needed to be cut into fine ribbons. They came off 3 bunches of large beets.

3 tablespoons peanut or canola oil

1 fresh hot green chile, cut into long, fine slivers

3 slices of fresh ginger cut into long, fine slivers

1 pound beet greens (no stems), cut crosswise into fine ribbons

⅓ teaspoon salt, or to taste

(recipe continues)

215

Put the oil in a large pan and set over medium-high heat. When hot, put in the chile and ginger. Stir a few times and put in the beet greens. Stir a few times and then cover the pan. Turn the heat down to low and cook until the leaves have wilted. Add the salt and stir a few times. Add 4 tablespoons of water, bring to a simmer, and cover. Cook on low heat for about 30 minutes, or until the greens are tender. Stir every now and then during this period.

SERVES 3 TO 4

Baby Bok Choy with Chinese Mushrooms   CHINESE-AMERICAN

You may also make this with regular bok choy and with the Chinese green known as gailan. *Cut the bok choy as suggested on page 212. Trim away the coarse* gailan *stems and peel what remains of them. Otherwise leave the* gailan *stalks whole, with leaves and flowers attached.*

For the stock in the recipe, I use whatever is left of the mushroom soaking liquid, which I strain, and enough water to make up the amount needed. To this I add a vegetable stock cube. I heat the stock to dissolve the cube and then let it cool off before combining all the ingredients for the sauce. This dish may be served with plain rice and a bean curd dish.

12 Chinese dried black mushrooms

2 teaspoons cornstarch

1 cup vegetable stock

1 tablespoon tamari soy sauce

1 tablespoon Chinese Shao Hsing wine or dry sherry

1½ teaspoons sugar

2 teaspoons oriental sesame oil

1 pound baby bok choy, cut lengthwise into halves or quarters according to size

2 tablespoons peanut or canola oil

3 garlic cloves, lightly crushed and peeled but left whole

4 thin slices of fresh ginger

¼ teaspoon salt, or to taste

Soak the mushrooms in 1 cup of hot water for 30 minutes. Lift the mushrooms out. (The soaking liquid should be strained and saved for stock.) Cut the hard stems off the caps and halve them.

Put the cornstarch in a bowl. Slowly add the stock, mixing as you go. Add the soy sauce, wine, sugar, and sesame oil. Stir to mix and set aside.

Bring 4 quarts of water to a rolling boil. Drop in the bok choy and bring to a boil again. Boil, uncovered, for 1 to 2 minutes, or until crisp-tender. Drain. If not using immediately, rinse under cold water and set aside.

Put the vegetable oil in a large frying pan or sauté pan and set over medium-high heat. When hot, put in the garlic and ginger. Stir, pressing down upon them, for about 15 seconds. Now put in the mushrooms and stir for 10 seconds. Put in the bok choy and salt and stir another 30 seconds. Turn the heat down to low, stir the reserved sauce, and pour it into the pan. Stir gently to mix. Turn up the heat to medium and let the sauce thicken, stirring gently now and then. Turn off the heat and serve immediately.

SERVES 4

Broccoli Rabe with Garlic   ITALY/UNITED STATES

One of the simplest—and also, to my mind, one of the best—ways of cooking this slightly bitter Italian green is to blanch it first in boiling water and then sauté it with garlic. If you want to put it over fettuccine or linguine—it is excellent that way—make sure you are generous with olive oil as you do want to lubricate your pasta. This quantity of greens is just right for a pound of pasta. This recipe may be used for Chinese gailan *and escarole. For escarole, separate the leaves and wash them well first, then proceed with the blanching and sautéing.*

1¼ pounds broccoli rabe	¼ cup olive oil
Salt	3 garlic cloves, peeled and finely chopped

Cut off the coarse stems of the broccoli rabe and wash well. Bring a large pot of water to a rolling boil. Put a tablespoon of salt into the water and then put in the broccoli rabe. Cover, bring to a boil again, and boil rapidly for 2 minutes, or until just tender. Drain and rinse immediately under cold running water. Drain and set aside until just before eating.

Put the oil and garlic into a large frying pan and set over medium heat. When the oil begins to sizzle and the garlic turns a light golden color, put in the broccoli rabe. Sprinkle in about ½ teaspoon salt and stir gently to mix. Turn the heat down to low. Turn the broccoli rabe pieces over gently until heated through.

SERVES 4

Variation
Broccoli Rabe with Garlic and Chile Flakes

Follow the preceding recipe but when sprinkling in the ½ teaspoon salt toward the end, sprinkle in ¼ to ½ teaspoon crushed chile flakes as well.

Broccoli Rabe Served on a Bed of Fava Beans

ITALY/UNITED STATES

Fava beans were quite a staple in ancient Greece and Rome. I like to think this simple way of serving it, greens cooked with garlic and olive oil served on a puree of dried beans, is as old as it is good. If broccoli rabe is unavailable, spinach or chard may be substituted. However, the sharp, somewhat pungent taste of broccoli rabe marries perfectly with the intensity of dried fava beans.

For the fava beans

1¼ cups split and skinned dried fava beans, picked over, washed, and drained

½ medium onion (3 ounces), finely chopped

2 whole garlic cloves, peeled

2 bay leaves

1 teaspoon salt

For the broccoli rabe

1½ pounds broccoli rabe, coarse stems removed and remaining thick stems peeled

¼ cup olive oil

2 teaspoons finely chopped garlic

¾ teaspoon salt

Combine the fava beans, onion, 2 garlic cloves, bay leaves, and ¾ cup of water in a medium pot and set over a medium-high flame. Bring to a boil. Cover, turn the heat down to low, and simmer gently for 15 minutes, or until the beans are soft. Add 1 teaspoon salt and mash the beans to a puree. Keep warm in a double boiler set over boiling water.

Bring a large pot of water to a rolling boil. Drop the broccoli rabe into the water and boil, covered, for about 3 minutes, or until it is just tender. Drain.

Put the ¼ cup of oil in a large frying pan and set over medium heat. Add the 2 teaspoons garlic, stir once or twice, then quickly add the greens and the ¾ teaspoon salt. Stir once and turn the heat to medium-low. Stir, cook for another minute, and then turn off the heat.

To serve, divide the fava puree into 4 to 6 portions. (This will depend on the number of diners.) Put each portion into an old-fashioned soup plate or a medium plate, spreading it evenly. Divide the broccoli rabe into the same number of portions. Using a slotted spoon, lift each portion out of the frying pan and heap it onto the center of each plate of fava beans. Whatever liquid is left in the frying pan should be drizzled over the exposed section of fava beans on each plate. Serve immediately.

SERVES 4 TO 6

Broccoli Rabe Sautéed
with Mustard Seeds

Here broccoli rabe is cooked Indian style, with mustard seeds.

1½ pounds broccoli rabe, coarse stems
    removed and remaining thick stems
    peeled

¼ cup olive oil

1 teaspoon whole brown or yellow mustard
    seeds

1 to 2 fresh whole hot green chiles, split
    slightly in the center

2 garlic cloves, lightly crushed and peeled but
    left whole

1 shallot, peeled and cut into long, fine slivers

¾ teaspoon salt

Bring a large pot of water to a rolling boil. Drop the broccoli rabe into the water
and boil, covered, for about 3 minutes, or until it is just tender. Drain.

Just before eating, put the oil in a large frying pan and set over medium-high
heat. When hot, put in the mustard seeds. As soon as they start to pop, a matter
of seconds, put in the chile, garlic, and shallot. Stir once or twice and turn the
heat to medium. Stir and sauté until the shallot slices are golden. Add the greens
and the salt. Stir once and turn the heat to medium-low. Stir and cook for another
minute and then turn off the heat. Discard the chile and garlic cloves before serving, if you wish.

SERVES 3 TO 4

Collard Greens with Browned Onions   INDIA
Karam Ka Saag

*This dish is made by the Muslims of Kashmir. If the collard leaves are young and tender, they may
be left whole. I bought a little over 1½ pounds of collard greens and after trimming was left with
1⅛ pounds.*

(recipe continues)

1½ pounds collard greens

¼ cup mustard or olive oil

2 medium onions (9 ounces in all), peeled and
  sliced into fine half rings

3 garlic cloves, peeled and finely chopped

1 (1-inch) piece of fresh ginger, peeled and
  cut into minute dice

1 smallish tomato (2 ounces), peeled by
  dropping into boiling water for 10 seconds
  and then finely chopped (a canned plum
  tomato may be used)

1¼ teaspoons salt

¼ to ½ teaspoon cayenne

Remove the coarse stalks and central rib from all the leaves and cut them cross-wise into very fine ribbons.

Put the oil in a large, wide pot and set over medium-high heat. When hot, put in the onions. Stir and fry until the onions are a medium brown color, about 8 minutes. Put in the garlic and ginger. Stir and cook 1 minute. Put in the tomato. Stir and cook 1 minute. Now put in the greens, 2 cups of water, the salt, and the cayenne. Stir to mix and bring to a boil. Cover, turn the heat down to low, and cook for 1 to 1½ hours, or until the greens are very tender. There should be very little liquid left at the bottom of the pot. If there is more, uncover and boil it away, stirring as you do so.

SERVES 4 TO 5

Collard Greens with Asafetida   INDIA

Haak

This is a Kashmiri way of cooking these greens. This staple is always eaten with plain rice and cooked in mustard oil. For those who would rather use another oil, extra-virgin olive oil provides an equally strong flavor, though the tastes are of course quite different. A lighter olive oil may be used if a milder taste is desired. The asafetida gives the greens a wonderful aroma reminiscent of both garlic and truffles. Only the Hindus of the region use asafetida, so this is a Hindu recipe.

Traditionally, these greens are flavored with the Kashmiri spice combination suchvari. *This is not a powder. Rather, it consists of hard patties made by combining split pea flour, spices, and mustard oil, forming flat discs with holes in the center and then drying them in the sun. Most Kashmiri Hindu homes have large jars filled with these discs, often made annually by venerable women—grandmothers, mothers, and mothers-in-law. Whenever some spices are required, a piece is broken off and ground or crushed to a powder. I have simplified matters by putting in some curry powder instead.*

In Kashmir, collard leaves are used whole. Older, coarser leaves, the kind I usually get in New York, take longer to cook, so I help matters along by cutting them into fine strips. If yours are young and tender, cut down on the cooking time and, if you want, leave them whole.

3 pounds collard greens

¼ cup mustard or olive oil (see recipe introduction)

⅛ teaspoon ground asafetida

1 whole fresh hot green chile

1 whole dried hot red chile

1 teaspoon ground cumin

1 teaspoon ground coriander

½ teaspoon ground turmeric

1 tablespoon curry powder

1¼ to 1½ teaspoons salt

Remove the coarse stalks and central rib from all the leaves and cut them crosswise into very fine ribbons. (There should be 1½ to 1¾ pounds of greens left.)

Put the oil in a large pot and set over medium-high heat. When hot, put in the asafetida and, a second later, the green and red chiles. Stir for a few seconds until the red chile turns dark. Put in 2 cups of water and bring to a boil. Now put in the greens, cumin, coriander, turmeric, curry powder, and salt. Stir to mix and bring to a boil again. Cover, turn the heat down to very low, and cook gently for 1 to 1½ hours, or until the greens are very tender. There should be very little liquid left at the bottom of the pot. If there is more, uncover and boil it away, stirring as you do so.

SERVES 6

Summer Kale with Leek

Here I used two 1-pound heads of pale green summer kale that had turned a lovely pink in the center. Serve this with a sweet potato or pumpkin dish and a dish of dried beans. (Winter kale may take longer to cook and may require a little more stock.)

2 pounds summer kale

1 good-sized leek

3 tablespoons olive oil

3 garlic cloves, peeled and cut into fine slivers

2 cups vegetable stock

Salt

Prepare the kale according to directions on page 212, washing it well and cutting the leaves crosswise into ¼- to ⅓-inch ribbons.

(recipe continues)

Cut off and discard the very green section of the leek. Cut the remaining white and pale green parts into halves lengthwise and then crosswise into ¼- to ⅓-inch slices. Wash thoroughly in a sinkful of water. Lift out of the water, leaving all dirt behind, and put in a colander to drain.

Put the oil and garlic into a wide, medium pan and set over medium-high heat. As soon as the garlic begins to sizzle, put in the leek. Stir and sauté for a few minutes, or until the garlic and leek are golden. Now put in the kale. Stir once or twice. Put in the stock and bring to a boil. Cover, turn the heat down to low, and cook 20 to 25 minutes, or until the kale is tender. Taste for salt, adding as much as you need. (This will depend upon the saltiness of your stock.) If there is too much liquid in the pan, turn up the heat and boil it away, stirring as you do so.

SERVES 4

Black Tuscan Kale *(Cavolo Nero)* with Raisins

If you cannot get Tuscan kale, use ordinary green kale here. Once cooked, you may add a cupful of ricotta cheese to this dish and use it to make turnovers with any pastry dough of your choice. You may also serve this as a topping for mashed or baked potatoes.

1 pound black Tuscan kale or ordinary green
  kale
3 tablespoons olive oil
1 whole dried hot red chile

3 garlic cloves, lightly crushed and peeled but
  left whole
3 to 4 tablespoons raisins
2 cups vegetable stock
Salt

Remove the coarse stalks from the kale leaves, wash them well, and then cut the leaves crosswise into very fine strips.

Put the oil, chile, and garlic in a wide, medium pan and set over medium-high heat. The garlic will soon start sizzling. Stir until the garlic is golden on both sides. Now put in the raisins and stir once. Put in the kale and stir a few times. Put in the stock and bring to a boil. Cover, turn the heat down to low, and simmer 20 to 30 minutes, or until the kale is tender. Uncover and if there is any liquid left at the bottom, turn up the heat to high and boil it away. Taste for salt, adding as much as needed. Stir to mix. Remove the chile before serving.

SERVES 4 TO 6

Kohlrabi Greens Cooked with Garlic

Kohlrabi leaves, especially the tender ones, can be quite delicious if cooked very simply the Spanish way with olive oil, garlic, and a dried red chile. (To cook the kohlrabi itself, see pages 236 to 239) You can cook collard greens and mustard greens this way, too. The cooking times will vary according to the tenderness of the leaves. The lovely pot liquor is delicious, too, served over plain rice. All you need to complete the meal is a stew of beans—chickpeas, black-eyed peas, or lentils.

2½ pounds kohlrabi greens (taken from 6
  kohlrabi and weighed after all coarse
  stems have been removed)

3 tablespoons olive oil

1 to 2 dried hot red chiles

4 to 5 garlic cloves, peeled and finely chopped

¾ teaspoon salt

Wash the kohlrabi leaves well. Arrange several kohlrabi leaves on top of each other and cut crosswise into fine ribbons.

Put the oil in a large pot and set over medium-high heat. When hot, put in the red chile. Stir once. It should darken immediately and puff up slightly. Add the garlic and stir once or twice. Put in all the kohlrabi leaves, salt, and 4 cups of water and bring to a boil. Cover, turn the heat down to low, and simmer gently until the leaves are tender, cooking about ¾ hour to 1½ hours, depending upon the toughness of the leaves. Stir occasionally. Serve hot.

SERVES 6

Shiu-Min Block's

Stir-Fried Snow Pea Shoots   CHINA

Chow Shway Do Miao

Here is the perfect way to cook snow pea shoots—or any other pea shoots for that matter. If you grow your own peas, you can take the tips off your own plants. Unfortunately, it does take a pound of pea shoots—an armful—to cook enough for four people!

These may be served as the green vegetable with almost any meal.

1 pound snow pea shoots, washed and dried

3 tablespoons peanut or canola oil

2 slices of peeled fresh ginger

2 garlic cloves, lightly crushed and peeled

¾ teaspoon salt

1 teaspoon oriental sesame oil

(recipe continues)

Remove all the tendrils from the shoots and then break them into 3-inch pieces as suggested on page 214.

Put the oil in a very large pot and set over high heat. When hot, put in the ginger and garlic. Give a few quick stirs. The garlic should get golden. Now put in the shoots and the salt. Stir and cook for about 3 minutes, or until the shoots have wilted completely. Put in the sesame oil and toss. Serve immediately.

SERVES 4

Cheryl Rathkopf's
Sri Lankan Greens
Mallum

SRI LANKA

I cannot tell you what a discovery these simply prepared greens were for me. Almost any green, leafy vegetable may be used, including taro leaves (known in the West Indies as eddo *or* dasheen leaves *and in India as* arvi ka patta*),* kang kung *(water spinach or swamp cabbage), red leaf spinach (found in most Chinatowns), passion fruit leaves, and manioc (yucca, cassava) leaves.*

The most important thing is to cut the vegetable into very fine shreds—even brussels sprouts, if you are using them. Coarse stems should be discarded. If the leaves are tough, water may need to be added and the dish cooked a bit longer. Most of the softer greens need no water at all; just the water from washing them suffices to cook them through.

Serve with any South Asian meal.

3 tablespoons peanut or canola oil

15 fresh curry leaves, if available

1 medium onion (4 ounces), peeled and cut into very fine half rings

1 to 2 fresh hot green chiles, split in half lengthwise

1 pound green cabbage, collards, kale, mustard greens, taro leaves, dasheen, or spinach, well washed and cut into fine shreds (7 well-packed cups)

¾ to 1 teaspoon salt

¼ teaspoon ground turmeric

2 tablespoons desiccated unsweetened coconut or 3 tablespoons grated fresh coconut (page 718)

Put the oil in a large wok or frying pan and set over medium-high heat. When hot, put in the curry leaves, onion, and green chile. Stir and fry for about 4 minutes, or until the onion has browned a bit. Put in the shredded vegetable, salt, and turmeric. Stir and cook until the vegetable has wilted somewhat. Cover, turn the heat down to low, and cook 10 minutes, or until the vegetable is tender. Uncover, add the coconut, and stir again. Turn off the heat.

SERVES 2 TO 4

Sautéed Spinach with Dill and Onion   TURKEY
Zeytin Yagli Ispanak

Here is a simple yet very refreshing and light Turkish approach to spinach. Serve with almost any meal. It is particularly good with a nicely baked potato and some sliced summer tomatoes or with Stuffed Baby Eggplants (page 184), known in Turkey as imam bayeldi, and some good, crusty bread.

1½ pounds spinach (¾ pound cleaned weight)

2 tablespoons olive oil

1 tablespoon unsalted butter

1 large onion (6 ounces), finely chopped

2 garlic cloves, peeled and finely chopped

2 tablespoons finely chopped fresh dill

½ cup vegetable stock or water

¾ to 1 teaspoon salt

For the yogurt sauce

½ cup plain yogurt

¼ teaspoon salt

1 garlic clove, mashed to pulp

¼ teaspoon paprika

Bring 12 cups of water in a large pot to a rolling boil over high heat. Put in the spinach and bring to a boil again. Allow to boil rapidly for 2 to 3 minutes. Drain the spinach in a colander. Run water over the spinach to cool it down. Squeeze out all the moisture by cupping small amounts of spinach between your palms and pressing. Chop the spinach finely.

Put the oil and butter in a medium frying pan and set over medium heat. When the oil and butter are hot, add the onion and garlic. Cook, uncovered, for 6 to 7 minutes, or until the onion is soft and translucent. Lower the heat if the onion starts to brown. Add the spinach, dill, vegetable stock or water, and salt. Simmer gently, uncovered, for 10 to 12 minutes.

Make the yogurt sauce. Put the yogurt in a little bowl and beat lightly with a fork until creamy. Add the salt and garlic and mix well.

Put the spinach in a serving dish and ladle the yogurt mixture over its center in a generous dollop. Sprinkle paprika over the yogurt and serve.

SERVES 4

Durupadi Jagtiani's
Spinach with Sorrel
Patla Palag

This is a simple but unusual dish from what was once the Indian state of Sindh but which now is a part of Pakistan. When the spinach and the sorrel are cooked, they are mashed by hand (I use a wooden potato masher), thickened with a little whole wheat flour, and flavored with oil and garlic. I like to do the thickening with yellow cornmeal. If you do not have a wooden potato masher, once the cornmeal or whole wheat flour has done its job of thickening, you could puree the spinach in an electric blender. This removes some of the texture but does the job of pureeing. Very interestingly, Sindhis serve this sour spinach and sorrel dish on cold winter days with a sweet Sindhi flatbread called loli *(page 450).*

2 pounds fresh spinach, trimmed and well washed in several changes of water, then chopped

½ pound fresh sorrel, stems trimmed away and leaves well washed in several changes of water, then chopped

1 medium onion, peeled and finely chopped

1 fresh hot green chile, finely chopped

1 teaspoon salt

2 teaspoons yellow cornmeal (or 2 teaspoons whole wheat flour slowly mixed in a small bowl with 2 tablespoons water)

3 tablespoons vegetable oil (I like to use olive oil)

3 to 4 garlic cloves, peeled and lightly mashed but left whole

In a good-sized pan, combine the spinach, sorrel, onion, chile, salt, and 1 cup of water. Bring to a boil. Cover, turn the heat down to low, and simmer for about 15 minutes. The spinach and sorrel should have completely wilted by this time. Move the lid so it sits slightly ajar, turn up the heat to medium-low, and cook another 15 minutes. Uncover and either put in the cornmeal slowly or the whole wheat flour mixture. Stir and mash the greens with a wooden potato masher as you do this. You should end up with a coarse puree.

Put the oil in a small frying pan and set it over medium-high heat. Put in the garlic. As the oil heats, the garlic will begin to sizzle. When it has turned golden on all sides, empty the contents of the frying pan, oil and garlic, into the pan with the spinach. Stir to mix.

SERVES 4

Elena Averoff's
Spinach with Rice

GREECE

Spanakorizo

I was served this at my first meal in Metsovo and just fell in love with it. Going to Metsovo, a quaint little town nestling in the hills of the Epirus region, was for me like going to one of the Indian hill stations. While Athens had been hot, here, walking in the narrow cobbled streets or sitting in the Averoffs' traditional wooden house, it was deliciously cool. Spanakorizo is made all over Greece and Cyprus and there are many variations. This is Mrs. Averoff's version. She makes it with spinach and scallions that she picks from her own kitchen garden. While many people chop up the spinach, Mrs. Averoff keeps her leaves whole. I also found it very interesting to watch Mrs. Averoff snipping the fresh dill into the spanakorizo *with a pair of scissors!*

For those who have never eaten this, let me explain that it contains more spinach than rice. The rice acts almost like a sauce, helping to "unify" the spinach. I like the dish best when it is served hot, but I have had it warm and at room temperature as well. I have seen it served with a dollop of thick Greek yogurt on top or with a generous squeeze of lemon juice. All versions are good.

For a simple Greek meal, you could serve this dish with some kalamata olives, some goat or sheep's milk cheese (the cheese can be drizzled with olive oil and sprinkled with fresh or dried oregano or thyme), a bean dish, and some crusty bread.

1½ pounds fresh spinach

6 scallions, cut crosswise into fine rings all the way up to the green section

5 tablespoons olive oil

Salt

3 tablespoons Italian risotto rice or any medium-grain rice

2 tablespoons finely chopped fresh dill

1 tablespoon fresh lemon juice (or more, if desired)

Trim the spinach and separate the leaves. Wash well and drain. Bring 12 cups of water to a rolling boil and drop in the spinach leaves. Cook for 1 to 2 minutes, or until they are just wilted. Drain. Run under cold water and drain in a colander.

Put 2 cups of water in a wide pot and bring to a boil. Put in the scallions, oil, ½ teaspoon salt, and the rice. Cook on medium-high heat, stirring now and then, for 10 to 12 minutes, or until the rice is just done and the liquid in the pot is reduced to a little thick sauce. Put in the spinach and another ½ teaspoon salt. Stir and cook for 2 to 3 minutes. Add the dill and lemon juice and stir to mix. Serve hot.

SERVES 4

Spinach with Tomato

INDIA

Saag

Serve with flatbreads, beans, and yogurt relishes.

¼ cup peanut or canola oil

1 to 2 hot fresh green chiles, very finely
   chopped

2 medium onions, peeled and very finely
   chopped

3 garlic cloves, peeled and very finely chopped

1 ripe tomato (4 ounces), peeled after
   dropping into boiling water for 15 seconds,
   and then peeled and finely chopped

3 pounds spinach, cut crosswise into very fine
   strips

1 teaspoon salt, or to taste

1 teaspoon garam masala (page 723)

Put the oil in a large, wide pot and set over medium-high heat. When very hot, put in the chile, onions, and garlic. Stir and fry until the onions turn medium brown. Add the tomato. Stir and fry for 2 minutes. Now put in the spinach and salt. Cover, allowing the spinach to wilt. Stir, turn the heat to medium, cover again, and cook for 25 minutes. Uncover, add the garam masala, and stir. Cook, uncovered, another 5 to 6 minutes, or until almost no liquid is left at the bottom of the pan. Turn up the heat during this period, if needed.

SERVES 6

From Casa Ruiz in Triana, Seville

Spanish-Style Spinach with Chickpeas   SPAIN

Known as espinacas con garbanzos *and served in tapas bars across Seville, this dish is usually eaten with pieces of fried bread. It is an appetizer, to be enjoyed with many glasses of dry sherry or wine. This very Moorish creation may also be served as part of a meal with rice or couscous, some Moroccan salads, and perhaps some cheese to finish off the meal.*

I like using dried chickpeas because their natural broth is so sweet and delicious. You might want to consider cooking the chickpeas in a pressure cooker if you are in a hurry (page 26). If you wish to use canned chickpeas, drain a 20-ounce can. Rinse the chickpeas to get rid of their tinny taste. When you put them into the pot, add ¾ cup stock or water as well. Go light on the salt, as canned chickpeas are generally salted already.

¾ cup (5 ounces) dried chickpeas

¼ cup olive oil

5 garlic cloves, peeled and finely chopped

2 pounds fresh spinach, washed and cut into
     wide, ribbonlike shreds

2 teaspoons ground cumin

1 teaspoon ground coriander

1½ teaspoons paprika

⅛ to ¼ teaspoon cayenne or crushed red
     pepper flakes

1¼ teaspoons salt

Soak the chickpeas overnight in cold water to cover by about 3 inches. Drain.

In a medium pot, bring the chickpeas and 2½ cups of water to a boil. Cover, lower the heat, and simmer for 2½ to 3 hours, or until the chickpeas are tender.

Put the oil in a wide, medium pot and set over medium-high heat. When hot, put in the garlic and stir once or twice. Add the spinach and stir until the spinach has wilted. Add the chickpeas with their cooking liquid, the cumin, coriander, paprika, cayenne, salt, and 1 cup of water. Mix well. Cook on medium heat, uncovered, for 20 to 30 minutes. Stir occasionally. There should be a little thick juice left at the bottom of the pan. Serve hot or at room temperature.

SERVES 4 TO 6

Spinach with Browned Onions   INDIA

Musalmani

This very simple Muslim approach to cooking spinach is common in North India.
*   You may use vegetable oil to make this dish,* ghee *(clarified butter), or a mixture of the two.*
(I tend to use olive oil but the most commonly used North Indian oil is peanut oil.)

3 tablespoons olive oil

3 tablespoons *ghee* (page 723)

2 to 3 whole dried hot red chiles

3 smallish onions (10 ounces), peeled, cut into
     halves lengthwise and then into very fine
     half rings

3 pounds spinach, cut crosswise into very fine
     strips

1 teaspoon salt, or to taste

Put the oil or combination of oil and *ghee* in a large, wide pot and set over medium-high heat. When very hot, put in the chiles. Stir quickly for a few seconds, or until

(recipe continues)

the chiles darken. Now put in the onions. Stir and fry until the onions turn a deep brown. Now put in the spinach and salt. Cover, allowing the spinach to wilt. Stir, turn the heat to medium, cover again, and cook for 25 minutes. Uncover and stir. Cook, uncovered, another 5 to 6 minutes, or until almost no liquid is left at the bottom of the pan. Turn up the heat during this period, if needed.

Note: The whole red chiles should be eaten only by those who know what they are doing. It may be a good idea to just remove them.

SERVES 6

From Tiffin's, Port-of-Spain
Spinach Bhaji

TRINIDAD/INDIA

This may be eaten with any South Asian or Trinidadian-Indian meal. In Trinidad, it is often served in homes with Yellow Split Peas with Thyme and Cumin (page 111), rice, and Trinidadian Mango Curry (page 321).

¼ cup vegetable oil, prefereably peanut or corn oil

1 to 2 hot red or green chiles, very finely chopped

2 medium onions, peeled and very finely chopped

3 garlic cloves, peeled and very finely chopped

3 pounds spinach, cut crosswise into very fine strips

1 teaspoon salt, or to taste

Put the oil in a large, wide pot and set over medium-high heat. When very hot, put in the chile, onions, and garlic. Stir and fry until the onions turn medium brown. Now put in the spinach and salt. Cover, allowing the spinach to wilt. Stir, turn the heat to medium, cover again, and cook for 25 minutes. Uncover and stir. Cook, uncovered, another 5 to 6 minutes, or until almost no liquid is left at the bottom of the pan. Turn up the heat during this period, if needed.

SERVES 6

Young Swiss Chard with Sesame Seeds

JAPAN/KOREA/UNITED STATES

This dish, with slight variations, may be found in Japan, Korea, and now in many parts of the United States as well. The sesame seeds add to the already nutritious chard.

If you cannot get young chard, with the leaves and stalks together no longer than 10 inches, cut up mature stalks crosswise and at a slight diagonal into fine strips and cut mature leaves crosswise into ¼-inch-wide ribbons. When your pot of water is boiling, throw in the stalks first and then, a minute later, throw in the leaves and boil rapidly for another 3 to 4 minutes before draining. Then follow the recipe.

Serve this with rice and a bean curd dish or even as a first course by itself.

1½ pounds young Swiss chard (see recipe introduction), well washed but left whole

2 tablespoons soy sauce

2 teaspoons sugar

2 tablespoons oriental sesame oil

2 tablespoons roasted and very lightly ground sesame seeds (page 734)

1½ tablespoons Chinese Shao Hsing wine or dry sherry

Bring a large pot of water to a rolling boil. Drop in the chard and bring back to a boil. Cover partially and boil rapidly for 3 to 4 minutes, or until the stems are just tender. Drain and rinse under cold water. Squeeze out as much water as possible and put the chard in a bowl. Separate the leaves, which will be like strands now.

Combine the soy sauce, sugar, sesame oil, sesame seeds, and wine. Mix well. Pour the dressing over the chard and toss to mix. Serve at room temperature or chilled.

SERVES 4

Swiss Chard with Tomatoes and Chickpeas

This Italian dish may also be made with any of the softer greens, such as spinach, broccoli rabe, and beet greens. After washing, each needs to be treated somewhat differently. Cut spinach into 1-inch-wide, ribbonlike strips; cut off and discard the coarser, lower stems of broccoli rabe and cut the leafy section crosswise at 1-inch intervals; cut off and discard the stems of beet leaves and then slice the leaves crosswise like the spinach. (If the beet leaves are very young—the kind that are sold for salads in fancy markets—they may be left whole.) With red or green Swiss chard, I always like to separate the stems from the leaves. Both are edible; I just like to cook the stems a bit longer.

I like using dried chickpeas because their natural broth is so sweet and delicious. You might want to consider cooking the chickpeas in a pressure cooker if you are in a hurry (page 6). If you wish to use canned chickpeas, rinse and drain a 20-ounce can. When you put them into the pot, put in ¾ cup of water or stock as well. Go light on the salt as canned chickpeas are generally salted already.

I find it very interesting that a similar, but very Moorish, dish may be found today in Spain. It is the seasonings that make the difference. See Spanish-Style Spinach with Chickpeas (page 228). You may serve this with crusty bread, cheeses, and roasted red peppers (page 262).

¾ cup (5 ounces) dried chickpeas

¼ cup olive oil

5 garlic cloves, finely chopped

4 to 5 fresh sage leaves, peeled and finely chopped

6 canned plum tomatoes, drained and finely diced

2 pounds fresh Swiss chard, washed, the stems cut crosswise into ¼-inch strips and the leaves cut into wide 1-inch ribbons

1¼ teaspoons salt

1 teaspoon good-quality extra-virgin olive oil

Soak the chickpeas overnight in cold water to cover by about 3 inches. Drain.

In a medium pot, bring the chickpeas and 2½ cups of water to a boil. Cover, lower the heat, and simmer for 2½ to 3 hours, or until the chickpeas are tender.

Put the oil in a wide, medium pot and set over medium-high heat. When hot, put in the garlic and sage and stir for about 20 seconds. Add the tomatoes and stir for a minute. Put in the chard stems and stir for 2 minutes. Put in the chard leaves and stir until they wilt. Add the chickpeas with their cooking liquid, the salt, and ¾ cup of water. Mix well. Cook on medium heat, uncovered, for 20 minutes. Stir occasionally. There should be a little thick juice left at the bottom of the pan. Serve hot or at room temperature. Drizzle the extra-virgin olive oil over the top just before serving.

SERVES 4 TO 6

Greek Mixed Greens

Horta

We were at a terrace restaurant that overlooked Athens. I had heard and read so much about the Greek love of mixed bitter greens and was wondering aloud if I would need to go into a Greek home to eat them when my hostess, Aglaia Kremezi, suggested that we could order horta *right there. It arrived at the table, simply boiled and then dressed with good olive oil and some lemon juice. It had a slight hint of bitterness and was incredibly good. As I traveled through Greece, I had it in pies and savory pastries as well as in combination with lentils and dried beans.*

In Greek markets, you find a variety of greens, some bitter and some not. They are generally cooked in combination. For my horta, *I combine Swiss chard, the tops of radishes, and dandelion greens. In all, I have 1½ pounds of trimmed greens, with more Swiss chard than the other two. After boiling, I sauté the mixed greens very briefly.*

Salt

1½ pounds mixed greens (see recipe introduction), well-washed, trimmed, and coarsely chopped

¼ cup olive oil

5 scallions, cut crosswise into fine rings

2 garlic cloves, lightly crushed and peeled but left whole

4 teaspoons fresh lemon juice

1 tablespoon extra-virgin olive oil

Bring a large pot of water to a rolling boil, as if you were boiling pasta. Add enough salt to make the water feel slightly salty (about 1 tablespoon). Drop in the greens and boil for about 10 minutes. Drain.

Put the ¼ cup of olive oil in a large frying pan or sauté pan and set over medium-high heat. When hot, put in the scallions and garlic. Stir and fry for a minute. Add the greens and about ½ teaspoon salt (taste as you go) and mix well. Turn off the heat. Put the contents of the pan into a serving dish. Dribble the lemon juice and extra-virgin olive oil over the top and serve immediately.

SERVES 4

Shiu-Min Block's

Stir-Fried "Foreign Vegetable," i.e., Watercress

CHINA

Chow Si Yang Tsai

A very simple dish of greens acknowledged as foreign to China (having come in from the West), this watercress stir-fry is nonetheless well liked. It may be served with all meals. There are no tendrils to deal with here, but, as with the snow pea shoots, it is important that the watercress stalks be properly broken up into smaller segments.

2 bunches watercress (10 ounces), well-washed and dried off

2 tablespoons peanut or canola oil

2 slices of peeled fresh ginger

2 garlic cloves, lightly crushed and peeled but left whole

½ teaspoon salt, or to taste

1 teaspoon oriental sesame oil

Break the watercress stalks into 3-inch pieces.

Put the oil in a large wok or pot and set over high heat. When hot, put in the ginger and garlic. Give a few quick stirs. The garlic should turn golden. Now put in the watercress and the salt. Stir and cook for about 3 minutes, or until the watercress has wilted completely. Put in the sesame oil and toss. Serve immediately.

SERVES 2 TO 3

Jerusalem Artichokes (also called Sunchokes)

They look like irregular potatoes and have a parsnippy-sweet taste and a texture that, once cooked, is somewhat like that of turnips. They are all-American yet rarely cooked in the nation of their origin. Great for soups, for roasting whole, for stir-frying, stewing, and salads, these are, of course, Jerusalem artichokes that are neither from Jerusalem nor artichokes. In reality, they are the starchless tubers of a sunflower (a *girasole,* which turns with the sun, hence its confused name), which the Native Americans called sun-roots.

How to buy and store Jerusalem artichokes: They are at their best in the late autumn and winter. The smoother their skins, the easier they are to peel. They should be firm and taut, with as few knobs as possible. Try to get all of the same size, especially if you plan to roast them whole. Store in a bin in the refrigerator.

How to clean and prepare Jerusalem artichokes: The skins may be eaten, so scrub well with a brush and get all the grit out. Peel, if needed, with a paring knife, cutting deeper than you do potatoes so as to get a somewhat rounded exterior. As cut surfaces discolor fast, drop the chokes into water to which you have added a little lemon juice or vinegar (acidulated water) as soon as you have peeled or otherwise cut them.

What to watch out for: When cooking the chokes remember that, unlike potatoes, they can turn soft in the center rather suddenly, so keep testing them. Chokes can cause flatulence in some people, so start by eating just a few.

Roasted Jerusalem Artichokes

This is my favorite method of cooking these artichokes. You do not have to bother with peeling them; the outside stays crisp and the inside can soften all it wants. Each artichoke transforms into a parsnip-flavored popover or Yorkshire pudding! You just cut it open while it is still hot, put butter on it if you like (I do not bother), put a little salt and pepper (I do not bother), and devour it.

If the Jerusalem artichokes are larger or smaller, you will need to adjust the cooking time.

8 Jerusalem artichokes (about 2½ ounces each)

A little vegetable oil for rubbing on the artichokes

Butter, salt, and pepper (optional)

Preheat the oven to 400°F.

Scrub the artichokes well to remove all the dirt. Pat them dry, rub with oil, and then put them in a single layer on a baking tray. Bake 40 to 45 minutes, or until just tender. Prick with the point of a knife to check. The whole artichoke will just begin to give a little. Serve immediately. To eat, cut in half and dot with butter and sprinkle lightly with salt and pepper if desired.

SERVES 4

Jerusalem Artichokes with Cumin and Shallots

Here, with slow stir-frying, the Jerusalem artichokes turn slightly chewy. They are soft enough to eat but not so soft that they break up. They are wonderful served with greens, bean dishes, and rice.
My artichokes were about 2½ ounces each and I quartered them. If yours are larger or smaller, make the necessary adjustments.

8 Jerusalem artichokes (about 2½ ounces each)

3 tablespoons vegetable oil (I use olive oil)

¼ teaspoon whole cumin seeds

1 medium shallot, peeled and cut into long, very fine slivers

½ teaspoon salt

Freshly ground black pepper

Pinch of cayenne (optional)

Peel and quarter the artichokes and leave them in acidulated water (page 234).

Put the oil in a large frying pan and set over medium heat. When hot, put in the cumin seeds. Stir once and put in the quartered artichokes. Now stir and fry slowly for 10 minutes. By this time the artichoke pieces should have browned lightly on all sides. Turn the heat down to low and cook another 5 minutes. Now put in the shallot slices, letting them fall into the bottom of the pan wherever there is room. Stir and fry another 5 minutes. The shallot slivers should turn brown. Add the salt, pepper to taste, and cayenne, if desired. Stir for 1 to 2 minutes to mix well.

SERVES 3 TO 4

Kohlrabi

As worthy as turnips and as delicious as cauliflower, kohlrabi nevertheless remains an almost unknown vegetable in most of America. Supermarkets, if they carry them at all, tend to carry oversized, woody ones, often without their precious leaves attached, making it impossible for us to fall in love with them. But when they are young and tender, I could, all by myself, polish off half a dozen raw at a single sitting for lunch and then cook up all their leaves together for my dinner later.

Kohlrabi is of the cabbage family and is really two vegetables in one. In India we call them *gant-gobi,* or knotted cabbages, because the bottom part is turnip shaped and therefore knotlike. If you could take the best part of a broccoli stem and blow it up into a turnip shape, you would get a good sense of both the taste and texture of the bottom half of a kohlrabi. Rather like broccoli stems, this half requires deep peeling. In Vietnam, a peanut-encrusted salad made from them is a wedding staple. In India, they may be stewed with tomatoes or corn. In China, they are often "red-cooked" with rock sugar, soy sauce, and a host of root vegetables or just stir-fried. These turnip-shaped heads may also be sautéed and braised.

The second part of the vegetable is the green leaves, which sprout up from the sides and the top. Of a medium green color, they are rather like collard greens and may be cooked exactly like them.

Buying and storing kohlrabi: Look for young kohlrabies where the heads are no bigger than 2 to 2½ inches in diameter. This is the ideal size, though larger ones that are a crisp, light green color all over will do as well. When you get them home, break off the leaves just near the head and store them separately in a perforated plastic bag. Store the round heads in a separate perforated plastic bag.

Preparing kohlrabi for eating: The kohlrabi head needs to be peeled before it is eaten raw or cooked. Rather like broccoli stems, the skin is coarse and tough, especially at the root end. So peel deeply with a paring knife, especially at the root end where you can actually cut off a thick slice and discard it. I often cut off a good ⅛ of the head at the bottom end. Peel lightly at the top where the skin is thin and the flesh at its most tender. When serving raw kohlrabi, I like to cut kohlrabi lengthwise so every slice has some of the tender portion and some of the coarser part. (For kohlrabi leaves, look in the Greens section, page 213.)

Sautéed Kohlrabi

This is a James Beard recipe. I do not believe this great American chef ever put it down in any of his cookbooks but he did ask me to make it one day when we were all preparing an informal meal for ourselves in his kitchen. We agreed that both broccoli stems or kohlrabi could be used here as their taste and texture was almost interchangeable. He suggested I use only butter for the cooking. Those were different times. I have used a combination of butter and olive oil in this recipe. The kohlrabi cooks very quickly and is both delicate and quite delicious. Serve with a black-eyed pea recipe or Refried Beans (page 12) and a baked potato.

2 large kohlrabi heads (1¼ pounds weight
    without leaves)
2 tablespoons olive oil

2 tablespoons unsalted butter
½ teaspoon salt
Freshly ground black pepper

Cut off about ⅛ of each kohlrabi at the bottom end. This end is fairly coarse. Peel the rest and cut into ⅛-inch-thick slices. Stacking the slices together, cut into fine julienne strips.

Put the oil and butter in a large frying pan and set over medium heat. When the butter has melted, put in the kohlrabi. Stir and sauté on medium-low heat for 6 to 7 minutes, or until the kohlrabi is just tender. Add the salt and pepper to taste. Serve immediately.

SERVES 4

Stir-Fried Kohlrabi

This is a simple stir-fry, best served with a bean curd dish and rice.

2 large kohlrabi heads (1¼ pounds, weight
    without leaves)
2 tablespoons peanut or canola oil
1 dried hot red chile
1 to 2 garlic cloves, peeled and finely chopped
¼ teaspoon salt

Freshly ground black pepper
2 teaspoons soy sauce
2 teaspoons oriental sesame oil
1 scallion, quartered lengthwise and then cut
    into 2-inch lengths

Cut off about ⅛ of each kohlrabi at the bottom end. This end is fairly coarse. Peel the rest and cut into ⅛-inch-thick slices. Stacking the slices together, cut into ⅛-inch julienne strips.

Put the oil in a large wok or frying pan and set over medium-high heat. When the oil is hot, put in the chile. Stir and fry for a second, or until the chile has darkened. Put in the garlic. Stir once and put in the kohlrabi, salt, and pepper to taste. Toss. Turn the heat to medium-low. Stir and cook for 6 to 7 minutes, or until the kohlrabi is just tender. Add the soy sauce, sesame oil, and scallion. Toss a few times. Serve immediately.

SERVES 4

Spicy Kohlrabi with Corn   INDIA

I like to make this when both fresh kohlrabi and corn are in season but if it is more convenient, frozen corn may be used. Serve with rice or any bread, along with salads and relishes.

1 (1-inch) piece of fresh ginger, peeled and coarsely chopped

2 garlic cloves, peeled and coarsely chopped

1 fresh hot green chile, coarsely chopped

1 teaspoon distilled white vinegar

3 tablespoons peanut or canola oil

1 teaspoon brown mustard seeds

1 medium tomato, finely chopped

4 cups fresh corn kernels (1¼ pounds)

2 medium kohlrabies, peeled and cut into ¼-inch dice

1 teaspoon salt

Freshly ground black pepper

1 tablespoon fresh lemon juice

½ teaspoon garam masala (page 723)

2 to 3 tablespoons finely chopped fresh cilantro

Put the ginger, garlic, green chile, vinegar, and 4 tablespoons of water in an electric blender or food processor. Blend until you have a paste.

Put the oil in a medium frying pan and set over medium-high heat. When hot, put in the mustard seeds. As soon as they start to pop, a matter of seconds, put in the paste from the blender. Stir and fry until the oil seems to separate, about 1 minute. Add the tomato. Turn the heat to medium and cook until the tomato is soft. Add the corn and kohlrabies as well as 1 cup of water, the salt, and pepper to taste. Stir and bring to a simmer. Cover and turn the heat down to low. Cook gently for 10 to 12 minutes. Add the lemon juice, garam masala, and cilantro. Stir

(recipe continues)

to mix and taste for the balance of seasonings. Cook gently, uncovered, for another 2 to 3 minutes, stirring now and then.

SERVES 4 TO 6

Spicy Kohlrabi Stew with Tomatoes   INDIA

This pungent stew is best eaten with rice (or a flatbread) and a dried bean or split pea dish from India, the Mediterranean, or Mexico.

You may substitute 1 to 2 cloves of finely chopped garlic for the asafetida if you wish, putting it into the oil at exactly the same time as the quartered kohlrabi.

2 pounds kohlrabi heads (about 6 good-sized ones, weight without leaves)

2 tablespoons peanut or canola oil

½ teaspoon whole cumin seeds

Generous pinch of ground asafetida

1 to 4 dried hot red chiles (according to desired heat)

5 medium tomatoes, peeled and finely chopped, or 3 to 4 medium canned tomatoes, finely chopped, plus ½ cup liquid from the can

¼ teaspoon ground turmeric

¾ teaspoon salt

¼ teaspoon sugar (if the tomatoes are sour)

Cut off about ⅛ of each kohlrabi at the bottom end. This end is fairly coarse. Peel the rest and cut into chunky quarters just as you would quarter an apple.

Put the oil in a medium pan and set over medium-high heat. When hot, put in the cumin seeds. A second later, put in the asafetida and the red chiles. Stir briefly until the chiles turn dark, a matter of seconds. Now put in the kohlrabi. Stir once or twice and quickly put in the tomatoes, turmeric, ¾ cup of water, salt, and sugar. Stir and bring to a boil. Cover, turn the heat down to low, and simmer very gently for 30 to 35 minutes, or until the kohlrabi is tender (pierce with a tip of a knife— it should go in easily).

Note: The whole red chiles should be eaten only by those who know what they are doing. It may be a good idea to just remove them.

SERVES 4 TO 6

Leeks

Stalwarts of the onion family and commonly used in Europe, leeks remain expensive and underused in America. We know that their sweetness adds a gentle glow to soups and stews, but they may also be braised whole, eaten as cold main dishes flavored with oil and lemon, or transformed into savory tarts. I have watched such tarts being made in both Greece and Italy.

It was mid-September in the mountains of northern Greece and the last of the autumn crops were being harvested—peppers, eggplants, and tomatoes. The leeks, on the other hand, were to be left in the ground through the winter where a mound of earth around the whites of each stalk would protect them from inclement weather. The leeks would be pulled out as the kitchen required them. Their tops, however, were being harvested for pies, as "leeks do not need their tops to survive," I was told. I found this unusual, since most people find the green tops fairly tough and discard them. But this was the countryside where frugal farmers wasted nothing. I learned these simple country pies were eaten throughout the war when wheat flour and most vegetables were scarce. The leek tops were shredded with a pair of scissors and salted, then mixed with feta cheese, oil, and a little trahana, a dried, bulgurlike wheat grain cured with sheep's milk. This was the filling that was put between layers of plain cornmeal. Olive oil was dribbled over the top and once the natural liquids had soaked through the cornmeal, the pie—the *prassopita*—was baked in a hot oven. It was plain and delicious.

I have only one recipe in this section, perhaps my favorite leek dish in the world, which also happens to be of Greek origin. Leeks, however, are used in other chapters; see Summer Kale with Leek on page 221.

How to buy and store leeks: Look for crisp, unblemished white stalks with fresh green leaves. Depending upon what you are making, try and buy leeks of the same width. They run from very slim ones used in Japanese cooking to widths of 1½ inches. We often have no choice, the leeks being sold in bunches where thin and fat ones are lumped together! Store the leeks, unwashed, in a perforated plastic bag in the vegetable bin of your refrigerator.

How to wash and prepare leeks: The dark green part of the leeks should first be cut off (these leaves may be used to flavor stocks), leaving only the very pale green and white sections. All leeks are filled with dirt and need a thorough washing. If whole leeks are required, cut a slit along one length, fan out the leek, and wash it well under running water, making sure you go between each layer. Generally, you can cut the leek in half lengthwise. Now fan out one half at a time and wash it under running water. The leeks can now be cut further as needed.

Marina Liveriadou's

Leeks with Rice

GREECE

Prassorizo

Somewhere between a risotto and a vegetable dish, this is a scrumptious lemony creation in which the rice helps to bind the leeks together. You may serve it either as a first course or as part of a Mediterranean meal. If you like, some sliced carrots and celery may be added to the leeks.

6 good-sized leeks (2 pounds)

½ cup Arborio rice or any medium-grain rice

½ cup olive oil

1 to 1¼ teaspoons salt

Freshly ground black pepper

2 tablespoons fresh lemon juice

Cut off and discard the dark green section of the leeks. Cut the remaining white and pale green parts into halves lengthwise and then crosswise into ¼- to ⅓-inch slices. Wash thoroughly in a sinkful of water; put in a colander to drain.

In a wide pot, combine the leeks and 3 cups of water. Set over high heat and bring to a boil. Turn the heat down to medium-high and cook for about 15 minutes, or until the leeks are tender. Add the rice, oil, salt, pepper, lemon juice, and another ½ cup of boiling water. Cook on medium-high heat, stirring now and then, for another 15 minutes, or until the rice is just tender. Serve hot.

SERVES 4

Mushrooms

I know little about foraging for wild mushrooms and though I have participated in country mushroom hunts, I was always led by someone "in the know." More often, I pick my fresh mushrooms from baskets in specialty food shops and farm markets! Other than the common, cultivated white mushroom, the varieties that we can now buy seem to change and grow. Remember the tiny enoki mushrooms from Japan? Well, their day seems to have come and gone.

What seems to have stayed, I hope for good, are the large and meaty portobello mushrooms, the delicate shiitake mushrooms (which also have a dried version, called dried shiitake or Chinese black mushrooms, found in East Asian stores), the tender, pale, anemone-like oyster mushrooms (also available in cans in Chinese groceries), and of course the very seasonal, spongelike morels and cèpes (called porcini in Italy). We can also get dried porcini and dried morel mushrooms, perfumed with their smoky, earthy aroma. These may be added to regular white mushrooms for added depth and flavor.

The world has still more mushrooms to offer. In Indonesia, I have eaten the most exquisite fresh straw mushrooms steamed in banana leaves with shallots and chiles. (Canned straw mushrooms are sold in East Asian markets.) In northern Thailand I have feasted on the trufflelike black mushrooms that spring up only in the early summer; these hard and crunchy little balls are often deep-fried. And in India, I grew up with a satiny, slim monsoon mushroom, the likes of which I have never seen outside India, that, when it appeared, was stewed with cilantro and cumin. There are also the delicate and silky Chinese abalone mushrooms that I have only seen in cans in Chinese markets. All are delicious and worth seeking out.

How to buy and store fresh mushrooms: Look for crisp mushrooms without wet black spots. They should not be withered or dried out, nor should they smell "high" or be in the least bit slimy. Store mushrooms, unwashed, in a paper bag in the vegetable bin of the refrigerator and use them as quickly as possible.

How to prepare mushrooms: Fresh mushrooms are best left unwashed. Brush away all dirt and then wipe them with damp paper towels. Cut off the ends of the stems if they are woody or dirty. They are now ready to be used.

Reconstituting dried mushrooms: Dried mushrooms need to be soaked in hot water for 15 to 30 minutes, or until they are soft. Lift them out of the water (this leaves grit behind), and then follow the recipe, as some dried mushrooms have tough stems that need to be cut off and others do not. The mushroom-soaking liquid can be strained and used for stocks.

Mushrooms with Sesame Seeds

It is amazing how good these simple mushrooms are. You may serve them on toast or as part of a meal that includes bread, beans, and other vegetables.

½ pound white mushrooms	Salt
3 tablespoons olive oil	Freshly ground black pepper
2 teaspoons sesame seeds	2 tablespoons finely chopped fresh parsley

Cut the mushrooms lengthwise into thick slices.

Put the oil in a large frying pan and set over medium-high heat. When hot, put in the sesame seeds. As soon as the sesame seeds begin to pop, a matter of seconds, put in the mushrooms. Stir and fry for a few minutes, or until the mushrooms lose their raw look. Add salt and pepper to taste. Stir again. Add the parsley. Stir to mix and turn off the heat.

SERVES 2 TO 3

Lalit Jaggi's

Simple Stir-Fried Mushrooms

INDIA

Simple and good, this is a favorite in my sister's household.

1 pound medium white mushrooms

¼ cup olive oil

1 teaspoon whole cumin seeds

12 scallions, white parts only, cut crosswise
    into very fine slices

1¼ teaspoons salt

2 teaspoons fresh lemon juice

⅛ teaspoon cayenne (optional)

Wipe the mushrooms off with a damp cloth and slice thinly and evenly.

Put the oil in a large frying pan or wok and set over high heat. When hot, put in the cumin seeds. The seeds will sizzle. Let them sizzle for 10 seconds and then put in the scallions. Stir for 1 to 2 minutes. Put in the mushrooms and salt. Stir and fry until the mushrooms have wilted. Stir in the lemon juice and the cayenne.

SERVES 3 TO 4

Shiu-Min Block's

Three Kinds of Mushrooms

CHINA

Shin Young Gu

I love to serve these mushrooms on top of the Pan-Fried Noodles (page 476). They may also be served accompanied by plain rice and a bean curd dish. Use a light vegetable stock here.

15 medium dried Chinese black mushrooms

1½ cups hot vegetable stock

1½ tablespoons peanut or canola oil

3 garlic cloves, lightly mashed and peeled but
    left whole

6 thin slices of peeled fresh ginger

4 scallions, cut into 1½-inch lengths (both
    green and white sections)

1 (15-ounce) can Chinese abalone
    mushrooms, drained

1 (15-ounce) can Chinese oyster mushrooms,
    drained

2 tablespoons soy sauce

2 tablespoons Chinese Shao Hsing wine or dry
    sherry

2 teaspoons sugar

10 snow peas

2 teaspoons cornstarch, dissolved in
    2 teaspoons water and 1 teaspoon oriental
    sesame oil

Soak the dried mushrooms in the hot stock for 30 minutes. When the mushrooms have softened, lift them out and save the liquid. Cut the hard stems off the mushrooms and halve any very large caps. Line a strainer with a thin, clean cloth or paper towel and then strain the mushroom broth. Set it aside.

Put the oil in a large frying pan and set over medium-high heat. When hot, put in 2 of the garlic cloves. Stir and fry until they turn golden. Now put in the ginger and scallion pieces. Stir once or twice. Add the mushrooms and stir once or twice. Put in the remaining garlic, the mushroom broth, soy sauce, wine, and sugar. Stir and bring to a simmer. Cover and simmer very gently for 8 to 10 minutes. Put in the snow peas and the cornstarch mixture. Stir to mix and cook another minute.

SERVES 4

Portobello Mushrooms Stuffed with Bean Curd

This will make a very elegant main course for 2 at a meal that starts off with a soup (the Simple Pumpkin Soup, page 589) and follows the mushrooms with a substantial salad (how about the Artichoke Heart and Fresh Fava Bean Salad, page 612?). It makes a superb appetizer as well.

I used portobello mushrooms for this as they are now so readily available. Any large mushroom will do—field mushrooms, porcini, or even large white ones. You will just need more of them if they are smaller. Mine had very large caps, about 4½ inches in diameter.

The sauce may be made ahead of time, but make sure you toast the sesame seeds right before you put them into it. The hot seeds sizzle as they go into the cold sauce, creating even more flavor.

½ pound firm bean curd

1 egg, beaten

2 scallions, both white and green sections, cut crosswise into very fine rounds

1 teaspoon peeled and finely grated ginger

4 large portobello mushrooms

6 tablespoons olive oil

6 tablespoons tamari soy sauce

2 tablespoons red wine vinegar

1 tablespoon freshly roasted sesame seeds

Few sprigs of fresh cilantro for garnishing (optional)

Lay the bean curd on a double thickness of paper towel that has been placed on a clean counter or board. Cover with another double thickness of paper towel and then put a plate on top. Put some weights on the plate (I use a heavy can of juice). Set aside for 30 minutes. Remove the weights and pat the bean curd dry with

(recipe continues)

fresh paper towels. Crumble the bean curd finely. To do this, you can either push it through a coarse sieve or press down on it with the back of a fork and crumble it further with your fingers.

Put the bean curd in a bowl. Add the egg, scallions, and ginger. Mix well.

Wipe the outside of the mushroom caps with a damp towel. Turn them over. Gently break off the stems right at the point where they are attached to the cap. Divide the stuffing into 4 parts. Pat one portion of the stuffing firmly into each of the caps.

Unless you have a super-large frying pan that can hold all caps, put 2 tablespoons of oil in each of 2 large frying pans and set both over medium-high heat. Put 2 caps, stuffing side up, in each of the pans. Fry for a minute. Now turn the heat to medium and fry more gently another 3 to 4 minutes, or until the caps have browned at the bottom. Put another tablespoon of oil in each pan and cover them. Turn the heat down to low and cook 3 to 4 minutes. Turn off the heat.

Meanwhile, combine the soy sauce, vinegar, and sesame seeds in a bowl. While they are still very hot, put 2 mushrooms in the center of 2 dinner plates. Spoon about 1½ tablespoons of sauce over each mushroom. Garnish with the cilantro, if using, and serve immediately. Offer the little bit of sauce left in a tiny bowl with a small spoon in case more is required.

SERVES 2 TO 4

Mushrooms with Coriander and Cumin   INDIA
Khumbi

In India we made this with delicate monsoon mushrooms, but ordinary white mushrooms will do. Serve with crusty bread or pita bread. Cheese and salads may be served on the side.

¾ pound medium white mushrooms

3 tablespoons peanut or canola oil

½ teaspoon whole cumin seeds

3 garlic cloves, peeled and finely chopped

1 (1-inch) piece of peeled fresh ginger, grated to a pulp

1 teaspoon ground coriander

1 teaspoon ground cumin

¼ teaspoon ground turmeric

⅛ to ¼ teaspoon cayenne

1 medium tomato, grated to a puree (see page 300 if you need directions)

¾ teaspoon salt, or to taste

Freshly ground black pepper

3 tablespoons finely chopped fresh cilantro (use parsley as a substitute)

Wipe off the mushrooms with a damp cloth and cut them in halves lengthwise. Put the oil in a large wok or sauté pan and set over medium-high heat. When hot, put in the cumin seeds. Ten seconds later, put in the mushrooms. Stir and fry them until they look silken. Now add the garlic, ginger, coriander, cumin, turmeric, and cayenne. Continue to stir and fry for another 2 to 3 minutes. Add the tomato and stir a few times. Now add the salt, black pepper to taste, and ½ cup of water and bring to a boil. Cover, turn the heat down to low, and simmer gently for 10 minutes. Sprinkle the cilantro over the top before serving.

SERVES 4

Marios Mourtezis'

Mushrooms with Wine and Coriander Seeds   CYPRUS

Maniteria Efelia

I discovered this recipe in Nicosia and fell in love with mushrooms prepared this way. Large, firm, white mushrooms are ideal, and while the original recipe called for just mushroom caps, I can rarely bear to throw away the good part of the stems. Finely chopped green parsley may be sprinkled over the top. Also, you could sauté a little garlic before you put in the mushrooms.

Serve hot, at room temperature, or chilled as an accompanying vegetable or as a salad.

Whole coriander seeds should be crushed lightly in a mortar, each seed splitting into 2 to 3 pieces. This crushing will release a wonderful aroma.

Use a good, dry, drinking white wine here. The rapid boiling down of the wine helps all the alcohol to evaporate.

5 tablespoons olive oil

1 pound large white mushrooms, wiped with a damp cloth and quartered lengthwise (medium mushrooms should be halved)

1 tablespoon coriander seeds, lightly crushed

½ cup dry white wine

½ teaspoon salt, or to taste

Freshly ground black pepper

1 tablespoon fresh lemon juice

Put the oil in a large frying pan and set over high heat. When hot, put in the mushrooms. Stir and fry for 3 minutes, or until the mushrooms appear glazed. Put in the coriander and wine. Cook, stirring, on high heat, until there is very little liquid left in the pan, about 5 minutes. Add the salt, black pepper, and lemon juice. Stir to mix and turn off the heat.

SERVES 4

Mushroom and Potato Stew

This is a wonderful stew to which I sometimes add cubes of lightly browned bean curd or cooked beans. Serve with a crusty bread or rice and a green salad.

¾ pound medium white or porcini
    mushrooms

¼ cup olive oil

1 medium onion, peeled and finely chopped

3 garlic cloves, peeled and finely chopped

2 celery stalks, peeled and finely chopped

1 medium carrot, peeled and finely chopped

2 large tomatoes, peeled (see page 300 for
    directions, if needed) and finely chopped

2 medium potatoes (¾ pound), peeled and
    cut into ¾-inch dice

1 teaspoon finely chopped fresh rosemary or
    ½ teaspoon dried rosemary, well crumbled

1 teaspoon chopped fresh thyme or
    ½ teaspoon dried thyme

1 cup dry white wine (dry vermouth works
    well here)

1 to 1¼ teaspoons salt

Freshly ground black pepper

Wipe off the mushrooms with a damp cloth and cut each in half lengthwise.

Put the oil in a wide pan set over medium-high heat. When hot, put in the onion, garlic, celery, and carrot. Stir and fry until they soften, turning the heat down a bit if they seem to brown. Now put in the mushrooms and stir for a minute. Add the tomatoes, potatoes, rosemary, thyme, wine, salt, and pepper to taste and bring to a boil. Cover, turn the heat down to low, and simmer gently for 30 minutes, or until the potatoes are tender.

SERVES 4

From Pinocho in Barcelona

Spanish-Style Grilled Portobello Mushrooms

SPAIN

This dish is generally made in Barcelona with boleto (porcini) mushrooms. Since I cannot easily find them here, I use portobello mushrooms. For this recipe, I used one very large portobello mushroom.

1 large portobello mushroom (5 ounces)

2 tablespoons olive oil

Salt

About 1 tablespoon Spanish-Style Garlic and
    Parsley-Flavored Olive Oil (page 665)

1 tablespoon finely chopped fresh parsley

Cut off the mushroom stem and wipe the outside section of the mushroom cap with a damp paper towel. Cut the mushroom cap crosswise and at a diagonal into ¼-inch-thick slices.

Set a cast-iron griddle or frying pan over medium heat. Put 1 tablespoon of oil into the pan. When hot, put in enough mushroom slices to fit in a single layer. Cook for 2 minutes. Turn the mushroom slices over, add 1 tablespoon more oil to the pan, and cook for another 2 minutes. Remove from the pan and arrange the slices in a single layer on a large platter.

When the mushrooms are all cooked, lightly sprinkle salt over the slices. Dribble the Spanish-Style Garlic and Parsley-Flavored Olive Oil evenly over the top. Finally, sprinkle on the parsley and serve immediately.

SERVES 2

Stir-Fried Fresh Shiitake Mushrooms

These exquisite mushrooms may be served as a first course or as part of a meal. You may even serve them on buttered toast. As they cook very fast, it is best to make this at the last minute.

12 fresh shiitake mushrooms

¼ cup olive oil

1 teaspoon whole brown mustard seeds

15 fresh curry leaves (use fresh holy basil or
    fresh basil leaves as a substitute)

1 to 2 garlic cloves, and peeled lightly crushed

Salt (about ¼ teaspoon or less)

Freshly ground black pepper

Generous pinch of cayenne

1 to 2 teaspoons fresh lemon juice

Cut off the mushroom stems and wipe the caps with a damp cloth.

Put the oil in a large frying pan and set it over medium-high heat. When it is very hot, put in the mustard seeds. As soon as they begin to pop, a matter of seconds, put in the curry leaves. Stir for a few seconds and add the garlic. Stir until the garlic turns golden and then add the mushrooms. Stir the mushrooms around for 1 to 2 minutes, or until they soften and are just cooked through. Add the salt, black pepper, cayenne, and lemon juice according to your taste, though rough amounts are suggested. Toss to mix. Remove the garlic before serving, if desired.

SERVES 2 TO 3

Okra

I grew up with okra. According to my mother, the two foods I took to most after leaving her breast at age two were both mucilaginous—okra was one and *urad dal,* yellow split peas, the other. What is more, I liked to eat them at the same meal.

I still love okra in all its forms—those where its mucilaginous, thickening quality is encouraged, such as soups (Kallaloo, page 585), those where this mucilaginous quality is successfully and deliberately disguised, such as all the dishes where okra is well sautéed or fried, and, needless to say, everything in between as well.

Whether okra originated in Africa or Asia matters little here. Today, the best vegetarian okra dishes seem to come from India, Pakistan, the Middle East, Turkey, Greece, and the Caribbean. Strangely enough, Australia, where Chinese and Vietnamese farmers are growing beautiful vegetables, is creating delicious hybrid recipes of its own. You will find one of those here as well.

Buying okra: Look for small, crisp, all-green pods. Generally speaking, the smaller pods (3 to 4 inches) are more tender and contain more delicate seeds. If you find pods even smaller than that in the market, grab them and cook them whole or sliced. I have seen some slim, 6-inch-long pods that were very good, but that has only been on rare occasions. Large, hard seeds (rather like large, tough seeds in a cucumber) are fairly unpleasant and pods containing them are best avoided. The greener the pods, the fresher they are. Browning occurs in spots over time, but a little bit of it does not hurt.

Cleaning okra: It is a good idea to wipe whole, uncut okra pods with a damp cloth and then let them dry off completely before slicing them. This discourages the mucilage from "weeping." If for some reason the pods are very dirty, rinse them off quickly and then pat them dry. Leave the okra in an airy place to dry off some more before any trimming or cutting is done. In the eastern Mediterranean, okra is rinsed out with vinegar and then allowed to dry off completely in the sun before it is cooked. This is supposed to decrease the mucilage.

Preparing okra for cooking: Generally, one needs to remove the very tip and the slightly conical top. The tip—just the tiny tail-like end—may be snipped off. The top, however, is cut in different ways by different people. My mother peeled the conical top, thereby keeping its shape. Some people cut the whole cap off. Many people cut the cap off but just above its base line so no mucilage escapes. You may do as you wish.

Frying okra: Okra is stunning when shallow- or deep-fried and allowed to turn very crisp. All its mucilage disappears entirely. It can be fried plain and then served with a sprinkling of salt and pepper, or it can be fried with a variety of seasonings such as curry leaves or onions. It can even be fried in a batter. When frying okra, you need to give the slices enough time to cook through and turn crisp without turning very dark. I like to start at a medium temperature and then turn the heat down as the okra cooks. It should be drained well and served immediately or it turns leathery.

Fried okra may be served at most meals. It may also be served with an omelet for lunch or breakfast, as a topping for soup (I sprinkle a few slices over my Kallaloo, page 585), or as a snack. It disappears very fast!

Okra with Potatoes   INDIA

This Gujarati specialty may be served with any Indian meal that includes a bean or split pea dish and either rice or an Indian bread. A yogurt relish would be a perfect accompaniment.

4 medium garlic cloves, peeled

1 (1-inch) piece of fresh ginger, peeled and coarsely chopped

¼ to ½ teaspoon cayenne

2 teaspoons ground cumin

1 teaspoon ground coriander

½ teaspoon ground turmeric

3 tablespoons peanut or canola oil

½ teaspoon whole cumin seeds

½ teaspoon brown mustard seeds

14 ounces fresh okra, trimmed at the ends and cut into ¾-inch pieces

9 to 10 ounces waxy red potatoes, boiled, peeled, and cut into 1-inch cubes

2 medium tomatoes (½ pound), cut into 1-inch dice

1 teaspoon sugar

1½ tablespoons fresh lemon juice

1 teaspoon salt

1 tablespoon finely chopped fresh cilantro leaves

Put the garlic, ginger, and 4 tablespoons of water into a blender and blend to a puree. Empty into a small bowl. Add the cayenne, ground cumin, ground coriander, and turmeric and mix well.

Put the oil in a 9-inch frying pan and set over medium heat. When the oil is hot, add the cumin and mustard seeds. As soon as the mustard seeds begin to pop, a matter of seconds, turn the heat down to medium-low and add the spice paste. Stir and fry for 30 seconds. Add the okra, potatoes, tomatoes, sugar, lemon juice, salt, and ½ cup of water. Stir well and bring to a gentle simmer. Turn the heat down to low, cover, and cook very gently for 10 to 12 minutes, or until the okra is tender. Stir. Garnish with cilantro and serve hot.

SERVES 4 TO 6

Diane Holuigue's

Okra Cooked in an Australian Manner

AUSTRALIA

Di Holuigue runs a cooking school in Melbourne, Australia. She teaches part of the time and the rest of the time features teachers she has brought in from around the world. Those of us who are lucky enough to have been invited are often treated to family meals in her charming red dining room. This okra dish was thrown together quickly one evening for the group to share. This recipe reflects the influence of Far Eastern ingredients, which are becoming quite commonplace in Australia today.

It is best to use tender young okra for this dish.

1 pound young okra, trimmed and left whole

2 tablespoons peanut or canola oil

2 whole dried hot red chiles

2 garlic cloves, peeled and cut into long slices

1½ to 2 tablespoons soy sauce

1 teaspoon oriental sesame oil

Pinch of sugar

Wipe the okra off with a damp cloth and leave to dry in a single layer.

Put the oil in a frying pan and set over medium-high heat. When it is hot, put in the red chiles. Let them cook for a few seconds until they puff up. Add the garlic and stir once. Now toss in the okra and cook until it turns bright green, 1 to 2 minutes. Turn the heat down to low and continue cooking, with the pan uncovered, for another 10 to 15 minutes, until the okra is tender. You will need to stir or shake the pan every now and then. Finally, add the soy sauce, sesame oil, and sugar. Cook and stir another 2 to 3 minutes. Serve hot.

SERVES 4 TO 6

Fried Okra with Fresh Curry or Basil Leaves

INDIA

Tali Bhindi

In Kerala (South India), seasonings such as salt and turmeric are blended in a water solution and sprinkled over all manner of chips and crisps as they are frying. Somewhat magically, the seasonings go right into the food. It is this technique that I have used here for the crisply fried okra.

Even though curry leaves give the okra a special Indian aroma, I often use the fresh basil leaves that grow so easily in my garden for a different taste. Thai holy basil leaves may also be used. Serve with any Indian or Western meal.

¼ teaspoon salt

¼ teaspoon ground turmeric

Peanut or canola oil, for shallow frying

½ pound fresh young okra, tops and tails
    removed and then cut crosswise into
    ⅛-inch-thick rounds

10 fresh curry leaves (use fresh basil leaves or
    holy basil leaves as a substitute)

Freshly ground black pepper

Pinch of cayenne (optional)

Combine the salt, turmeric, and 1½ teaspoons of water in a small bowl and set aside.

Put the oil to a depth of ¾ inch in a 7- to 8-inch frying pan and set over a medium flame. When hot (a piece of okra should sizzle when dropped in), put in the okra and curry or basil leaves. Stir once and then sprinkle the turmeric mixture evenly over the top. Stir and fry for about 5 minutes. Now turn the heat down just a bit and continue to fry until the okra is crisp. If it begins to darken, turn the heat down just a little bit more. The frying should take about 12 minutes. Remove the okra and leaves with a slotted spoon and drain on paper towels. Taste and then sprinkle with extra salt, if needed, as well as some black pepper and, if you like, cayenne over the top. Toss to mix and serve.

SERVES 3 TO 4

Okra with Tomatoes
Mayai Wara Bhinda

THE INDIANS OF UGANDA

This dish may be served plain, the way it is here, or, as is more common among those of Indian-Muslim descent in Uganda, with a topping of scrambled eggs or even an omelet. In its plain version, it is generally served with flatbreads or any crusty bread, dried bean or split pea dishes, yogurt relishes, and fresh chutneys.

¼ cup peanut or canola oil

1 pound fresh okra, tops and tails removed
    and then cut crosswise into ¼-inch-thick
    rounds

3 medium tomatoes (12 ounces), peeled
    (page 300) and chopped

2 medium garlic cloves, peeled and mashed to
    a pulp

2 tablespoons fresh lime juice

½ teaspoon ground coriander

½ teaspoon ground cumin

⅛ teaspoon ground turmeric

⅛ to ¼ teaspoon cayenne

¾ teaspoon salt, or to taste

Freshly ground black pepper to taste

(recipe continues)

Put the oil in a large, preferably nonstick frying pan and set over medium-high heat. When hot, put in the cut okra. Stir and fry for 7 to 10 minutes. When the okra starts to brown, turn the heat down to medium and cook, stirring, another 3 to 4 minutes. The okra will have browned a bit more. Turn the heat down to low and cook 2 to 3 minutes, or until the okra is almost tender. Now put in all the remaining ingredients. Stir gently and cook on low heat for 4 to 5 minutes, or until all the flavors have melded and the tomatoes have dried a little. Check for salt, adding more if you need it.

SERVES 3 TO 4

Nasreen Rehman's

Fried Okra with Onions   PAKISTAN

Tali Hui Bhindi

In this Pakistani recipe, okra is cut into longer, somewhat diagonal strips and then fried along with finely sliced onions. When crisp, the combination is drained and tossed with popped mustard seeds and browned whole chiles. Serve with any South Asian, Middle Eastern, Greek, or Turkish meal.

Peanut or canola oil for shallow frying

2 dried hot red chiles

1½ teaspoons whole brown mustard seeds

½ pound fresh young okra, tops and tails removed and then cut on a diagonal into ⅛-inch-thick rounds

1 smallish onion (3 ounces), peeled, halved lengthwise, and then cut crosswise into very thin slices

Salt

Freshly ground black pepper

Put the oil to a depth of ¾ inch in an 8- to 9-inch frying pan and set over a medium flame. When hot, put in the red chiles. As soon as they darken, use a slotted spoon to transfer them to a small bowl. Put the mustard seeds into a long-handled metal cooking spoon, hold it with a dish towel or oven mitt, and lower it into the oil. As soon as the mustard seeds begin to pop, a matter of seconds, remove the spoon, pouring back as much oil as you can into the frying pan but retaining all the mustard seeds. Put the mustard seeds into the little bowl with the chiles. Now put the okra and onion into the frying pan. Stir and fry for about 5 minutes. Turn the heat down just a bit and continue to fry until the okra and onion are crisp. If they begin to darken too much (the onion should turn a reddish-brown), turn the heat down just a little bit more. The frying should take about 12 minutes. Remove the okra and onion with a slotted spoon and drain well on paper towels before putting in a serving bowl. Sprinkle with salt, black pepper, and the popped mustard seeds. Throw in the red chiles, toss to mix, and serve.

Note: The chiles should be eaten only by those who know what they are doing.

SERVES 3 TO 4

Nasreen Rehman's

Batter-Fried Okra   PAKISTAN

Tali Hui Besan Wali Bhindi

These crisp okra fritters may be served with a meal but they make a wonderful first course as well, served in a Western manner, perhaps with a dipping sauce (try them with any of the fresh chutneys).

The interesting element in this Pakistani recipe is that the okra is not cut crosswise, as it is normally, but lengthwise, into thin strips. All the seeds are removed before the slices are dipped in a very light chickpea flour batter, making the fritters uncommonly elegant. Ideally, they should be eaten as soon as they are made.

½ pound fresh okra

¾ cup chickpea flour (also called *besan* or gram flour in Indian shops)

1¼ teaspoons salt

¼ to ½ teaspoon cayenne (the former gives a mild heat, the latter a medium heat)

Generous pinch of ground turmeric

Peanut or canola oil for deep-frying

Cut off the very tops and tips of the okra pods and then cut each lengthwise into ⅛-inch-thick slices, removing all the seeds with the tip of a paring knife.

Put the chickpea flour in a bowl. Slowly add ¾ cup plus 2 tablespoons of water, mixing as you go, or enough to have a smooth, thinnish, flowing batter (rather like a crepe batter). Add the salt, cayenne, and turmeric and mix well.

Put the oil to a depth of 1½ inches in a large, deep frying pan and set over medium-low heat. Allow to get hot. This takes a little time. Meanwhile, put all the okra slices in the batter. When the oil is heated, work swiftly and put the okra slices, one at a time, into the hot oil, trying not to overlap the slices too much. Fry for about 7 minutes, or until the slices are golden at the bottom and fairly crisp. Turn the okra pieces over and cook another 5 to 6 minutes. Turn the okra over a few more times, frying for 17 to 18 minutes in all, until the fritters are crisp and the okra is cooked through. Remove with a slotted spoon and leave to drain on paper towels for 2 minutes. Change the paper towels and drain another minute. Serve hot.

SERVES 3 TO 4

Peas

When I was a child, I preferred raw peas to cooked ones as our garden produced the sweetest, tenderest varieties that my father could order from the Suttons Seed Catalogue mailed out from Calcutta. We had such an abundance that after the season's first peas had been consumed raw, we had to find other ways to use up the rest. We gave basketsful to friends and relatives. The rest we cooked. We ate them in hundreds of dishes that required them to be shelled, of course, but my mother also cooked the smaller peas whole much as we cook sugar snap peas today. Their skins were not entirely edible, so we pulled the whole pea between our teeth like artichoke leaves, eating not just the peas but the soft flesh on the shells as well.

Today, there are three main types of peas on the market: green peas, sugar snap peas, and snow peas. We should perhaps say that there are four types, frozen peas being the fourth. Peas freeze better than most vegetables and, out of season, are the best alternative to fresh ones. They are also much cheaper. I use them frequently in dishes that require peas to be cooked along with other foods.

When buying any kind of fresh peas, make sure their color is bright and their texture crisp. They should ideally have no black or brown spots.

Green peas: Generally speaking, 3 pounds of green peas in the pod yield about 3½ cups (14 ounces) of shelled peas, just enough for 4 people. However, the number and size of peas can vary and my recipes reflect it. If you wish to boil the peas, throw them into a pot of boiling, salted water for 3 to 5 minutes, or until they are tender. Drain. Either eat them immediately with a little butter or olive oil or rinse them under cold water and reserve them for later use.

I generally prefer to steam-cook peas in a few tablespoons of water: I sauté them briefly before adding a few tablespoons of water, some salt and sugar, and then covering and cooking them until the peas are just tender. These peas may be served simply, the way they are, or flavored as they cook with almost any herb, from tarragon to mint. A little oriental sesame oil dribbled over them in the last seconds of cooking also helps to bring out their flavor. Remember that pea pods may be saved for soups.

Sugar snap peas: These are small, very sweet peas that have edible pods so no shelling is required. Both pea and pod are eaten together. However, the pods do have tough strings that run on both sides and these need to be removed before cooking. The best way to do this is to snap the stem—or the end on the stem side—backward and then pull along the back. The string will pull away. Do the same with the tip of the pea. Snap it backward and pull it along what might be considered the belly of the pea. Wash the peas. They are now ready to be cooked.

These peas may be boiled whole, just like ordinary peas, or steamed. However, as with shelled peas, I prefer to steam-cook them in just a little water and oil with a touch of salt and sugar. Unfortunately, once you string sugar snap peas on both sides a few will open up, but that never bothers me.

Snow peas: These flat, tender pods with undeveloped seeds were once used only in Chinese cookery but have now become quite mainstream. The pods are cooked whole but need to have their strings removed. Luckily, they have tough strings on the upper side only. Remove them using the same method as the one used for sugar snap peas. I like to stir-fry snow peas very briefly, either alone or with other vegetables, and then steam-cook them in just a little water.

Many recipes in this book recommend defrosted frozen peas as a substitute for fresh ones. To defrost them, just put the amount you need in hot water to cover and, once separated, drain them.

Peas with Ginger and Sesame Oil

Here is a simple way to cook fresh summer peas.

I bought 3 pounds peas and was left with 3 1/2 cups (14 ounces) after shelling. If you end up with more or less, adjust the recipe.

1 tablespoon peanut or canola oil

4 slices of fresh ginger

3½ cups (14 ounces) shelled fresh peas

1 teaspoon salt

1½ teaspoons sugar

1 tablespoon oriental sesame oil

2 teaspoons roasted sesame seeds (page 734), optional

Put the oil in a large frying pan and set over medium heat. When hot, put in the ginger slices. Stir and fry for 10 seconds, pressing down on the ginger. Put in the peas, salt, and sugar. Stir until the peas turn bright green. Add 4 tablespoons of water and bring to a simmer. Cover and cook on medium heat for about 5 minutes, or until the peas are tender. Uncover, add the sesame oil, and boil away any extra liquid. Sprinkle the sesame seeds on top, if desired, and serve immediately.

SERVES 4

Peas and Mushrooms in a Green Curry Sauce

A simple curry to be served with rice, this can also be eaten with pita breads or with any Indian or North African bread. If using fresh peas, you will need about 2¾ pounds in the pod.

1 fresh hot green chile, coarsely chopped

1 cup (1 ounce) fresh cilantro leaves

2 garlic cloves, peeled

1 × 1-inch piece of fresh ginger, peeled and coarsely chopped

¼ teaspoon ground turmeric

3 cups shelled peas (frozen may be used)

2 tablespoons peanut or canola oil

1 teaspoon whole cumin seeds

2½ cups or 10 medium white mushrooms, sliced lengthwise

1 to 1¼ teaspoons salt

¼ cup heavy cream

Put the green chile, cilantro, garlic, ginger, and turmeric in an electric blender. Add 4 tablespoons of water and blend to a puree, pushing down the mixture with a rubber spatula when necessary. Set the green spice mixture aside.

Now toss 1 cup of peas into the blender. Add 4 tablespoons of water and blend to a puree. Set the pea paste mixture aside.

Put the oil in a large nonstick frying pan and set over medium-high heat. Put in the cumin seeds. Let them sizzle for 10 seconds, shaking the pan occasionally. Put in the mushrooms and sauté for 1 minute. Remove the mushrooms from the pan with a slotted spoon. Add the green spice mixture to the pan and stir for 2 to 3 minutes. Put in the mushrooms, the rest of the peas, the pea paste, salt, heavy cream, and ¼ cup of water. Turn the heat to medium, stir gently, cover, and cook for 3 to 4 minutes. Serve hot.

SERVES 4 TO 6

Green Peas with Coconut and Cilantro

Vatana Bhaji

From the state of Maharashtra in India, this is a delicious way to serve both fresh or defrosted frozen peas. If using fresh peas, you will need about 2 pounds.

If you cannot get fresh curry leaves, use either Thai holy basil leaves or ordinary basil leaves for a different but equally interesting flavor. If you cannot get fresh coconut, soak 8 tablespoons desiccated, unsweetened coconut in ¾ cup of hot water for an hour.

3 tablespoons peanut or canola oil

Generous pinch of ground asafetida (optional)

1 teaspoon whole brown mustard seeds

½ teaspoon whole cumin seeds

15 fresh curry leaves (use holy basil or basil leaves as a substitute)

2½ cups shelled fresh or defrosted frozen peas

1 to 2 fresh hot green chiles, finely chopped

1 teaspoon salt

1 teaspoon sugar

¼ teaspoon ground turmeric

½ teaspoon ground cumin

½ teaspoon ground coriander

¾ cup (3 ounces) freshly grated coconut

3 tablespoons very finely chopped fresh cilantro

Put the oil in a large frying pan and set over medium-high heat. When hot, put in the asafetida, if using, and, a second later, the mustard and cumin seeds. As soon as the mustard seeds begin to pop, a matter of seconds, put in the curry leaves. Stir for a second and put in the peas, chiles, salt, sugar, turmeric, ground cumin, and coriander. Stir for a minute until the peas turn bright green. Add 4 tablespoons of water and bring to a boil. Cover, turn the heat down to low, and simmer gently for 5 minutes, or until the peas are tender. Uncover, turn the heat up to medium-high, and add the coconut and cilantro. Stir, boiling away any extra water. Serve immediately.

SERVES 3 TO 4

Sugar Snap Peas with Dried Mint

Mint is used in much of the Muslim world of the Middle East and South Asia, in both fresh and dried forms. They have somewhat different flavors and are really not interchangeable. This recipe is normally made with shelled peas, but I love it with crisp, green sugar snaps, which are now becoming so easy to find. It is important to crumble the dried mint to a coarse powder before adding it to the recipe; this is generally done by rubbing it between the palms.

1 tablespoon olive oil

1 tablespoon unsalted butter

¾ pound fresh sugar snap peas, strings removed (page 256)

¾ teaspoon salt, or to taste

½ teaspoon sugar

1 teaspoon dried mint

Put the oil and butter in a large frying pan or wok and set over medium heat. When medium-hot, put in the peas. Stir briskly a few times. Now put in the salt, sugar, and mint. Stir once, add 3 tablespoons of water, and bring to a vigorous simmer. Cover quickly, turn the heat down to low, and cook for 3 minutes, or until the peas are almost done. Uncover, turn the heat up to high, and quickly boil away all the liquid in the pan as you stir gently. Serve immediately.

SERVES 4

Sugar Snap Peas with Cumin and Thyme

I have based this recipe on one of my mother's in which she stir-fried whole peas with hot and sour spices. With sugar snap peas, of course, the whole pod may be eaten. I came up with this recipe while summering in Martha's Vineyard, when the sugar snaps were as fresh as they could be and the spices in my cupboard somewhat limited!

2 tablespoons peanut or canola oil

½ teaspoon whole cumin seeds

½ teaspoon whole brown or yellow mustard seeds

¾ pound fresh sugar snap peas, strings removed (page 256)

¾ teaspoon salt, or to taste

2 teaspoons finely chopped fresh thyme or ½ teaspoon dried thyme

Generous pinch of cayenne (optional)

Freshly ground black pepper

1 tablespoon fresh lemon juice

Put the oil in a large frying pan or wok and set over medium heat. When hot, put in the cumin seeds and mustard seeds. As soon as the mustard seeds begin to pop, a matter of seconds, turn off the heat. When the oil has cooled to medium, put the pan back on medium heat and put in the peas. Stir briskly a few times. Now put in the salt, thyme, and 3 tablespoons of water. Bring to a simmer. Cover quickly, turn the heat down to low, and cook for 3 minutes, or until the peas are almost done. Uncover and add the cayenne, black pepper to taste, and lemon juice. Turn the heat to high and quickly boil away all the liquid in the pan as you stir gently to mix the seasonings. Serve immediately.

SERVES 4

Stir-Fried Snow Peas with Scallions   CHINA
Ching Chao Shway Do

This simple stir-fry is very good with rice and bean curd dishes.

2 tablespoons peanut or canola oil

3 thin slices of ginger

2 garlic cloves, lightly crushed and peeled but left whole

¾ pound snow peas, strings removed (page 256) and halved crosswise at a fairly steep diagonal

1 medium carrot, peeled and cut into fine julienne strips about 2½ inches long

1 teaspoon salt

½ teaspoon sugar

3 scallions, both green and white sections, first cut crosswise into 2½-inch lengths and then lengthwise into fine strips

2 teaspoons oriental sesame oil

Put the oil in a wok or large frying pan and set over medium-high heat. When hot, put in the ginger and garlic. Stir and fry 10 seconds, pressing down on the garlic. Put in the snow peas and carrot. Stir and fry for 10 seconds. Put in the salt and sugar, stir once, and add 2 tablespoons of water. Cover, turn the heat down to low, and cook 2 minutes, or until the vegetables are just done. Uncover, turn the heat to medium-high, and add the scallions and sesame oil. Stir for 20 seconds. There should be no liquid left at the bottom; if there is, cook a few seconds longer. Serve.

SERVES 4

Peppers and Chiles

Peppers and chiles, which were brought from the New World to the Old World and are today eaten in both worlds, if such divisions still hold, come in many colors—red, green, yellow, orange, and even purple. Raw, they may be put into all manner of salads. Cooked, they are known to enhance rice dishes, soups, and bean dishes and are wonderful when stuffed or used in sauces.

In this section, you will find recipes for sweet bell peppers and for the larger Mexican varieties of chiles.

Buying and storing peppers: Look for thick-skinned peppers, especially if you are going to roast them. They should look crisp and have no rotted spots. Store them unwrapped in the vegetable bin of your refrigerator.

Roasting peppers and chiles: Most peppers and large chiles are superb when they are roasted and peeled. They caramelize slightly as some of their moisture evaporates, their taste intensifies as they turn soft and slithery, and many, especially red bell peppers, become miraculously sweet as well. I almost always serve roasted peppers in some form or another when I do a large dinner party.

Much of the Mediterranean and Central America have recipes that require the roasting and peeling of peppers. There are various methods for achieving this: using top-of-the-stove roasters, grilling, broiling, and baking. All of these methods work.

I especially like to arrange segments of peeled, roasted peppers in a slightly overlapping pattern on a large plate and serve drizzled with either a bit of balsamic vinegar or ¼ cup or so of Spanish-Style Garlic and Parsley-Flavored Olive Oil (page 665).

Method I The easiest way to roast peppers—I saw this in Metsovo, Greece, where they were getting ready to put up the autumn harvest as it was coming in—is to roast them in the oven. A convection oven is more efficient, but any oven will do. This method works well for both large and small quantities.

Preheat the oven to 425°F.

Lay out the whole peppers in a tray, as many as it will hold easily, and put in the upper third of the oven. (If you have a lot of peppers to roast, use several trays and all the shelves. Just keep moving the trays around from the top to the bottom shelves.) You will need to roast the peppers for about 25 minutes in all. After 10 minutes, turn the peppers over. Continue to roast, turning the peppers a little bit every 5 minutes, or until all the sides are roasted evenly. Take the tray(s) out of the oven and cover with a dish towel for 10 minutes. You can now core the peppers, removing the stem area, and peel them. Slice them as needed.

Method II If you require sectioned peppers as well as a roasted taste, here is one of the best methods:

Preheat the broiler.

Quarter the bell peppers and remove the seeds, core, and stem area. Lay the pepper sections out in a single layer, skin-side up, on a baking tray. Broil about 6 inches from the heat source, until the outside has charred. You will need to move the pepper pieces around, tilting them this way and that, so they char evenly. This will take anywhere from 10 to 13 minutes. When they are done, lift the pepper pieces up with tongs, put them in a brown paper bag, and close the bag. Set aside for 7 to 10 minutes. Alternatively, you could cover the baking tray with a dish towel and set aside for 10 minutes. (I find this much easier and have given up the paper bag method entirely.) You can now peel the peppers.

Once the peppers are peeled, store them in a jar or plastic container, covered with olive oil. The peppers will keep this way in the refrigerator for 3 to 4 days. Remove from the oil and serve.

Shiu-Min Block's

Stir-Fried Hot Peppers with Ginger and Garlic
CHINA

Chow Ching La Jiao

For this dish, which is somewhere between a condiment and an accompanying vegetable, you need long hot peppers of medium heat. In much of America, this would mean buying Italian hot peppers or long Korean hot peppers. Fresh Greek hot peppers, the kind that are pickled, will also do when available.

10 ounces fresh Italian hot peppers (or any long peppers of medium heat—see recipe introduction)

3 tablespoons peanut or canola oil

2 thin slices of peeled fresh ginger, finely chopped

2 scallions, white and green parts, cut into fine rounds

2 garlic cloves, peeled and lightly crushed

2 tablespoons light Chinese soy sauce

1 teaspoon salt

1 tablespoon oriental sesame oil

(recipe continues)

Halve the peppers lengthwise and slice them thinly crosswise.

Put the oil in a large frying pan and set over high heat. When hot, put in the ginger and scallions. Stir for 10 seconds and put in the garlic. Stir once or twice and put in the peppers. Stir for a minute and add the soy sauce and salt. Stir another minute and turn off the heat. Add the sesame oil and stir to mix.

SERVES 4

Roasted Red Bell Peppers with Mustard Seeds

I do have a passion for roasted red bell peppers and once, after an afternoon concert in the country at which my husband had played some beautiful Schubert in a sextet, we invited the musicians and many other friends from the audience to stop off and dine with us before driving home. Almost everything had to be prepared beforehand. I wanted the meal to have an Indian flavor, though nothing needed to be too traditional. One of the dishes I made was this one. It was so easy to make ahead of time.

These peppers may be prepared up to 24 hours in advance, covered with plastic wrap, and refrigerated. Serve them chilled, or better still, at room temperature.

3 red bell peppers, sliced, roasted, and peeled according to the directions on page 262

Salt

Freshly ground black pepper

6 tablespoons olive oil

½ teaspoon brown or yellow mustard seeds

10 to 15 fresh curry leaves (substitute fresh holy basil or basil leaves for a different but equally interesting flavor)

4 garlic cloves, lightly crushed and peeled but left whole

⅛ teaspoon cayenne (optional)

Lay the pepper slices out in slightly overlapping layers on a large serving platter. Sprinkle lightly with a little salt and pepper.

Put the oil in a small frying pan and set over medium-high heat. When very hot, put in the mustard seeds. As soon as the mustard seeds begin to pop, a matter of seconds, put in the curry leaves and garlic. Stir for 20 to 30 seconds and take the pan off the heat. Immediately put in the cayenne, if desired, and then quickly pour the oil and seasonings evenly over the pepper slices. Serve at room temperature or chilled. To store, cover the dish with plastic wrap and refrigerate.

SERVES 4 TO 6

Shamsi Davis'

Red Peppers Stuffed with Herbed Rice in the Persian Manner   IRAN

Dolmeh Ye Felfel Germer

This dish may be made with eggplants and green peppers, but I have chosen to make it here with red peppers only, as they are the sweetest.

Red peppers seem to be getting bigger by the minute. Try to get medium ones that can sit firmly without toppling over. Also, try to make sure that each pepper has a stem, as they look so much prettier.

Two of these peppers served with a green salad are a meal for me. They also make a wonderful dish for parties where you might like to make a whole platter of both red and green peppers. (This would be particularly appropriate for a Christmas dinner.) You could accompany the peppers with a platter of Persian-Style Carrots with Dried Apricots (page 160) and some broccoli rabe.

1 cup basmati rice

½ cup red lentils *(masoor dal)*

8 red bell peppers (4 pounds)

3 tablespoons olive oil

1 medium onion, peeled and finely chopped

2 garlic cloves, peeled and finely chopped

1 large shallot, peeled and finely chopped

Salt

1½ well-packed cups (1½ ounces) very finely chopped fresh parsley

¾ cup (1 ounce) very finely chopped fresh chives

2 tablespoons very finely chopped fresh tarragon

2 tablespoons very finely chopped fresh basil

4½ tablespoons tomato paste

1 tablespoon sugar

Combine the rice and red lentils in a bowl and wash in several changes of water. Cover well with water and leave to soak for 30 minutes. Drain.

While the rice and lentils are soaking, prepare the peppers. Cut a neat cap off the top of each one, rather like a big plug. Now clean the insides of all seeds and ribbing. Cut off any seeded area that is attached to the caps.

Once the soaking is over, put the oil in a large, nonstick sauté pan and set over medium-high heat. When hot, put in the onion, garlic, and shallot. Stir and fry for about 5 minutes, or until the onion is soft and golden. Now put in the drained rice and lentils and stir gently for a minute. Now add ½ cup of water and ½ teaspoon salt. Stir gently, staying on medium-high heat until all the water is absorbed,

(recipe continues)

about 2 minutes. Add another ½ cup of water and another ½ teaspoon salt and stir very gently until all the water is absorbed, being very careful not to break the rice grains. Repeat this one more time, putting in just a scant ½ teaspoon of salt the last time around. Once the water is absorbed, put in the parsley, chives, tarragon, and basil. Stir to mix and turn off the heat. Taste, adding more salt if you need it.

Put the tomato paste in a bowl. Add the sugar and 1½ teaspoons salt. Slowly add 3 cups of water, stirring as you go.

Preheat the oven to 350°F.

Stand the peppers in a baking tray. Fill each one ¾ full with the rice mixture. Stir the tomato mixture and pour 4 tablespoons into each pepper. Now close each pepper with its own cap. Pour a few tablespoons of the tomato mixture at the bottom of the pan and put the peppers in the oven. Bake about 1¼ to 1½ hours, or until the peppers are soft. Baste frequently with the tomato mixture, adding more to the bottom of the pan when it is needed. Serve hot or at room temperature.

MAKES 8 STUFFED PEPPERS

From George Nikolaides in Porto Carras

Red Peppers Stuffed with Feta Cheese GREECE
Piperia Florina

The Florina red pepper is long in shape and very sweet, but any red pepper will do. You may serve these stuffed peppers as a first or main course. If serving as a main course, a bulgur dish and a green salad would complete the meal.

6 large red peppers (about 2½ pounds in all)

¾-pound block of imported feta cheese cut into ¼-inch-thick slices (use goat cheese as a substitute)

6 tablespoons olive oil, preferably good-quality extra-virgin

2 tablespoons chopped fresh thyme or 2 teaspoons dried thyme

For garnishing

1 to 2 tablespoons finely chopped fresh parsley

A few fresh thyme sprigs (optional)

Roast the peppers whole according to Method I on page 262; core and seed them but leave them whole.

Spread the cheese slices out on a plate in a single layer and pour the oil over them. Sprinkle half the thyme over the top and turn the slices over. Sprinkle the remaining thyme over the second side. Set aside for 30 minutes.

Slide the cheese slices inside the peppers in a single layer, arranging each on a baking tray as you go. You may need to cut the slices to fit inside the peppers. Dribble some of the oil used for marinating the cheese over the top.

Just before serving, preheat the broiler, setting the shelf 5 to 6 inches below the heat source. Broil for 3 to 4 minutes, or until the cheese has melted a bit and the peppers are lightly browned in spots. Sprinkle the parsley over the top and garnish with fresh thyme sprigs. Serve immediately.

SERVES 6

Rosario Guillermo's

Mexican Poblano Peppers with Cheese

MEXICO

Rajas con Queso

This spicy cheese-chile combination from Puebla is a wonderful spread to put on warm wheat or corn tortillas. It may also be eaten on toast. At a party you may serve it as a dip for tortilla chips. If Monterey Jack cheese is unavailable, use twice as much Cheddar cheese.

4 fresh poblano peppers (12 ounces)

1 tablespoon unsalted butter

2 tablespoons heavy cream

½ teaspoon salt

¾ cup (2 ounces) grated Monterey Jack cheese

¾ cup (2 ounces) grated Cheddar cheese

Broil the peppers whole according to directions on page 262. Remove the stem and seeds of the peppers. Peel and cut lengthwise into ½-inch-wide strips.

Put the butter in a nonstick frying pan over medium heat. When hot, put in the peppers. Stir and sauté for 3 minutes. Add the cream and salt. Stir and cook gently until all the cream has been absorbed, 2 to 3 minutes. Turn the heat down to low and add the 2 cheeses. Stir gently until the cheese melts and serve immediately.

SERVES 4

Potatoes and Sweet Potatoes

POTATOES

When potatoes were first introduced to India by colonizing Europeans, locals embraced them with a passion. A few went so far as to declare that they were the only good thing that the West had given the East! The Indians already had many tubers and roots in their culinary repertoire, some of native origin and others having made much earlier journeys from the coast of East Africa. When the potato was added to the list, new recipes were created for it almost instantly. Today, I can say without exaggeration, that there must be at least a few thousand potato recipes in the nation. Indeed, when I teach classes on spices, I use the potato as a base to demonstrate the ability of spices to transform—one vegetable yielding, in my class alone, 30 to 40 dishes.

Here, I must add an odd fact. While nearly all Hindu Indians eat potatoes several times a week, either by themselves or in mixed vegetable dishes, on high holy days and fasting days potatoes are not considered auspicious. I am convinced that this has something to do with their origins as interlopers. On holy days old cultures seem to return fiercely to old roots (in every sense of the word)!

There are, of course, recipes for this tuber in this section from the different regions of India. But there are also recipes here from Peru, the home of potatoes, and many other regions across the globe.

Potatoes have complex carbohydrates—the kind that provide slow-release, long-term energy—and are filled with vitamins, minerals, and protein. Most of their nutrients lie just beneath the skin, so ideally it is best to cook them with their skins on and peel them later if needed.

There are many new varieties—which are actually old varieties—of potatoes on the market now. My own farmers market in Union Square, New York, now has them in flesh shades of purple, yellow, and black, as well as the more regular beige-white ones, and in shapes that go from small marbles and little uneven, gingerlike fingers (fingerlings) to ¾-pound ovals. The Incas, we are told, feasted on more than two hundred varieties in their high Andean abodes. Having first lost or ignored most of them, we will hopefully resurrect more and more as time goes on.

In the meantime, what most markets offer us are new potatoes (young, early-season potatoes), which have thin, sometimes peeling skins and moist, waxy flesh, and older potatoes (mid- and late-season potatoes) with drier flesh and leathery skins.

Other than that basic difference in age, in America, we can buy crumbly baking potatoes filled with starch that makes them ideal not just for baking whole but also for fluffy mashed potatoes and crisp French fries, or we can buy smooth-fleshed, waxy boiling potatoes with less starch that can be sliced for potato salads without crumbling or used in stews without breaking up.

Buying and storing potatoes: Buy healthy potatoes that are not shriveled, have no rotted spots and not too many eyes, and that are not sprouting. Ideally, potatoes should be stored in a cool cellar. Yes, I love reading that in books, too. Not many of us have cool root cellars, much as we would like them. I tend to buy no more than a week's worth of potatoes. I then put them into an airy basket that I hang in a dark, cool spot in the house with every intention of using them up as quickly as possible. If they start to go, I quickly make a large soup!

To prepare potatoes: Scrub the potatoes well and remove any eyes. Peel if you have to, using a good peeler or a paring knife. As potatoes discolor when their flesh is exposed, put them into a bowl of water as soon as they are cut. The water will draw away some of their starch. This does not matter except when you are making a dish where you want sliced potatoes to hold together, as in the Crisp Potato Cake with Herbs (page 276). Here it is a good idea to peel potatoes and put them whole into a bowl of water. Slice them just before you need to cook them. Less starch will be lost this way.

To boil potatoes: Cover scrubbed potatoes, peeled or unpeeled, whole or cut, with cold water and bring to a boil. Cover partially, turn the heat to a simmer, and cook until the tip of a knife may be inserted with ease. Drain immediately. If potatoes have been cooked unpeeled, you may peel them now. This is not needed for new potatoes; old skin, however, does not taste good and I always remove it. If you want the potatoes to cool off for the purpose of dicing them neatly later, leave the potatoes in their skins as they cool, refrigerating them once they have cooled, if needed. Dicing will become much easier.

Potatoes may also be boiled in salted water, if you like. Just add about $1\frac{1}{2}$ teaspoons for every quart of water. You may also boil them in vegetable stock or in water flavored with garlic and onion, or whole spices such as cinnamon, bay leaves, and cloves. The liquid may be used later to make stock.

To steam potatoes: Put the scrubbed potatoes in a steaming basket and steam until the tip of a knife may be inserted easily. This will depend upon the size of the potatoes and the quantity, anywhere from 13 to 20 minutes. General steaming directions are on page 736. I use this method for small new potatoes that I am cooking in small amounts.

To bake potatoes: After large baking potatoes (such as russets) have been scrubbed, prick them well with a fork and put them in an oven preheated to 400°F. Bake for 45 minutes to 1 hour, or until the tip of a knife may be inserted easily. Do not bake in foil as it produces damp skin and an unpleasant aroma.

Baked potatoes may be split open, lightly salted and peppered, and then served with a topping of any sauce you like, such as the Simple Romesco Sauce (page 670) or any vegetable dish, such as the Cauliflower with Ginger and Cream (page 162). See also Baked Potatoes, the Greek Way (page 277).

SWEET POTATOES

Botanically speaking, sweet potatoes are not related to potatoes at all. In fact, they are not even tubers, but roots. They are also not yams, although they are often mislabeled thus. What they *do* have in common with the potato is that they are both underground products of the Americas. Peru had both sweet potatoes and potatoes around the birth dates of Christ. Unlike potatoes, though, sweet potatoes originated in a tropical climate. They have long been associated with one another; the very word *potato* is derived from the Spanish word *patata*, which itself is derived from the Arawak Indian word for sweet potatoes, *batatas*. Confused? All you really need to remember is that sweet potatoes are delicious. They are also rich in vitamin A.

Buying and storing sweet potatoes: Look for smooth-skinned specimens without cuts, bruises, or mold, preferably of the same size, especially if you plan to boil or roast them. Do not refrigerate. Instead, store in an airy basket.

Preparing sweet potatoes: Scrub them well if they are to be cooked in their skins, otherwise wash. Peel and cut as required.

Boiling sweet potatoes: It is best to boil them whole, in the skin. Cover with water and bring to a boil. Cover partially, turn the heat down to low, and cook until a knife tip may be inserted easily, about 30 minutes for a medium sweet potato. Once boiled, the sweet potato may be peeled and cut as required. If further cooking is required, as for baked, sweetened dishes, undercook the sweet potato slightly.

Baked sweet potatoes: After scrubbing, prick holes in the sweet potatoes with a fork. Then lay them down on a foil-lined tray and bake in an oven preheated to 400°F. for 45 minutes to 1 hour, or until the tip of a knife may be inserted easily. I love these both for their taste and for their simplicity in preparation.

Shiu-Min Block's

Stir-Fried Sweet-and-Sour Potato Shreds

CHINESE-AMERICAN

Tien Suong Tu Do

This is a new, unusually delicious creation. The potatoes here remain very crunchy—almost raw. You do need to make a very fine julienne of potatoes first. To do this, my Chinese friend first slices large boiling potatoes lengthwise—making 1/16-inch-thick even slices—and then she stacks the slices and cuts long, fine slivers. You may use a mandoline or that wonderful new Japanese slicing gadget that sells under the name "Benriner."

This dish may be served hot, as soon as it is made, at room temperature, or chilled. It should not be reheated. I sometimes serve it with a collection of other saladlike vegetable dishes for lunch.

1 pound large boiling potatoes

2 tablespoons peanut or canola oil

2 scallions, cut first into 2-inch segments (both white and green portions) and then each segment cut lengthwise into fine strips

2 slices of peeled fresh ginger, cut into fine julienne strips

4 teaspoons soy sauce

4 teaspoons red wine vinegar

1/3 teaspoon salt, or to taste

1 tablespoon sugar

2 garlic cloves, lightly mashed and peeled but left whole

1 teaspoon oriental sesame oil

Peel the potatoes and cut them into fine julienne strips (see recipe introduction). Put them into a bowl of water. Shake them around in the water so they release their starch. Pour out the starchy water. Repeat this a few times and drain thoroughly.

Put the oil in a large, nonstick wok or frying pan and set over high heat. When hot, put in the scallions and ginger. Stir for 30 seconds. Now put in the potatoes. Stir for 30 seconds. Add the soy sauce, vinegar, salt, sugar, and garlic. Stir and fry for 2 minutes. Turn off the heat. Add the sesame oil and stir to mix. Remove the garlic cloves and empty into a serving dish. Serve immediately. You may also serve it later at room temperature.

SERVES 4

Gisella Orjeda's

Peruvian Potatoes in the Huancayo Style

Papas a la Huancaina

This dish, in which boiled potatoes are served with a rich, spicy cheese sauce, comes from Huancayo, which is in the Andes, about six hours east of Lima, the Peruvian capital. Yellow potatoes are used here (Solanum gonyiocalix), *but any freshly boiled potatoes will do. I like to use Yukon Gold.*

Feta cheese is the best substitute for the local cheese used in Peru. The sauce is yellow, a color which comes from yellow chiles. As we cannot get them easily, I like to use half of a yellow bell pepper and then a couple of hot green chiles for the heat. If you cannot even get the yellow pepper, just leave it out and use only the green chiles. Turmeric will provide the color.

These potatoes are generally served garnished with lettuce, hard-boiled eggs cut into long quarters, and olives, making them into a complete meal. You may easily double the recipe if you like.

1¼ pounds even-sized boiling potatoes (see recipe introduction), well washed

1 egg yolk

1 cup milk, or a bit more

½ pound feta cheese, crumbled

½ cup peanut or canola oil

½ yellow bell pepper (about 3 ounces), seeds and veins removed and finely chopped

1 to 1½ fresh hot green chiles, seeds and veins removed and finely chopped

1 garlic clove, peeled and finely chopped

¼ teaspoon ground turmeric

1¼ teaspoons flour

Salt (optional)

For the garnish

A few crisp romaine lettuce leaves

2 hard-boiled eggs, peeled and quartered lengthwise

8 olives of your choice

Cover the potatoes with water and set to boil.

While they are cooking, make the sauce. Put the egg yolk, 1 cup of milk, and the cheese into a blender and blend until you have a smooth paste. Leave in the blender.

Put the oil in a medium frying pan and set over medium heat. When hot, put in the yellow pepper, the hot green chile, garlic, and turmeric. Sauté for a minute or two until softened. Add the flour and stir a few times. Now put in the paste from the blender and turn the heat to low. Stir until the sauce is thick, about 2 minutes. Taste for salt. Pour back into the blender and blend briefly again, adding more milk if needed to get the consistency of heavy cream.

Peel the potatoes while they are still hot and put in a serving dish, cutting them into halves or quarters if they are too large. Pour the sauce over the top. Tuck a few lettuce leaves on the sides. Decorate with the eggs and olives. Serve immediately.

SERVES 2 TO 4

Niru Row Kavi's

Gujarati-Style Hot Sweet-and-Sour Potatoes

INDIA

Khatta-Mittha Batata

We generally eat this family favorite with parathas, *chapatis, or any crusty bread. Other vegetables, legumes, and yogurt dishes are served on the side. This dish from the western Indian state of Gujarat is hot, sweet, and sour and has a little sauce. I like to serve it in individual bowls.*

2½ cups (1 pound) potatoes, peeled and cut into ½-inch dice and put in a bowl of cold water

¾ to 1 teaspoon salt

½ teaspoon cayenne

¼ teaspoon ground turmeric

½ teaspoon ground coriander

½ teaspoon ground cumin

¼ cup peanut or canola oil

10 to 15 fresh curry leaves, if available (use fresh holy basil or basil leaves for a different but equally interesting flavor)

1½ to 2 tablespoons thick tamarind paste (page 737)

½ cup peeled and chopped very ripe tomatoes

1 tablespoon brown sugar

Drain the potatoes, pat them dry, and put them in a bowl. Add the salt, cayenne, turmeric, coriander, and cumin. Toss well.

Put the oil in a large frying pan and set over medium-high heat. When hot, put in the potatoes. Stir and fry until they are lightly browned on all sides. Add 1 cup of water, the curry leaves, tamarind paste, tomatoes, and sugar. Bring to a boil. Turn the heat down to low and simmer gently until the potatoes are soft, about 10 minutes. Stir occasionally. Serve hot. (If the sauce is not thick enough, you may crush 1 or 2 potato pieces in the pot and stir.)

SERVES 4

(recipe continues)

Potatoes Cooked with Fennel Seeds INDIA

Aloo Ki Lonji

In the streets of North India where it is commonly sold, this wonderfully spicy potato dish is known as aloo ki lonji. *It is best enjoyed with Indian breads, particularly with* parathas *and* pooris. *Green vegetables, pickles, and yogurt relishes should be served on the side.*

1 pound boiling potatoes

2 tablespoons peanut or canola oil

1 to 2 whole dried hot red chiles

¼ teaspoon whole fennel seed

⅛ teaspoon whole fenugreek seeds

¼ teaspoon nigella *(kalonji)*

½ teaspoon brown mustard seeds

½ teaspoon whole cumin seeds

¾ cup peeled and chopped very ripe tomatoes
   (see page 300 if you need directions)

1¼ teaspoons salt

¼ teaspoon ground turmeric

⅛ to ¼ teaspoon cayenne

Boil the potatoes in 6 cups of water until tender. Drain. Peel and break by hand into roughly 1-inch pieces. Set aside.

Heat the oil in a medium pot over medium-high heat. When hot, put in the red chiles and stir once. They should darken immediately and puff up slightly. Add the fennel, fenugreek, nigella, mustard seeds, and cumin seeds. The mustard seeds should begin to pop within seconds. Immediately put in the tomatoes, salt, turmeric, and cayenne. Stir in the potatoes. Add 1¾ cups of water and stir to mix well. Bring to a boil. Turn the heat down to low, cover, and cook gently for 20 minutes. Stir occasionally. If you like the sauce thicker, crush 1 or 2 potato pieces against the sides of the pot and mix in with the sauce. Serve hot.

SERVES 3 TO 4

Variation

Potatoes with Ginger and Fennel Seeds

Aloo Ki Lonji

Peel a 1-inch piece of fresh ginger and either grind it to a pulp or else chop it and then liquidize it in a blender with a few tablespoons of water.

Proceed as above, adding the ginger as soon as the mustard seeds have popped. Stir for a few seconds. Now put in the tomatoes, salt, turmeric, and cayenne and proceed with the recipe.

Potato Cooked in a Punjabi Village Style

Punjabi Aloo

Here is a dish very commonly eaten by the farmers of Punjab in northwestern India. Serve with Indian, Middle Eastern, or North African breads. Yogurt drinks and green vegetables may be served on the side.

3 tablespoons peanut or canola oil

¾ cup finely chopped onions

1 tablespoon finely grated ginger

3 garlic cloves, peeled and mashed to a pulp

½ cup finely chopped very ripe tomatoes

1 fresh hot green chile, finely chopped

¼ teaspoon ground turmeric

¼ teaspoon cayenne

1 teaspoon salt

1 pound waxy red potatoes, peeled, cut into 1-inch dice and put in a bowl of cold water

1 teaspoon garam masala (page 723)

Put the oil in a large frying pan or wide pan and set over medium-high heat. When hot, put in the onions. Stir and fry until they are medium brown. Put in the ginger and garlic. Stir for 1 minute. Add the tomatoes, green chile, turmeric, cayenne, and salt. Turn the heat to medium and stir for 2 minutes. Drain the potatoes and put them in. Add 1½ cups of water. Stir to mix and bring to a boil. Cover, turn the heat down to low, and simmer gently until the potatoes are tender, cooking about 20 minutes. Stir occasionally. Uncover, turn the heat to medium, and cook another 10 minutes, or until the sauce has slightly reduced and is thick. Sprinkle the garam masala over the top and stir gently to mix. Serve hot.

SERVES 4

Moroccan Potato Stew with Turmeric

This is a gentle stew that I love to eat with Black-Eyed Peas with Herbs (page 18), Moroccan Tomato Salad (page 636), and a Middle Eastern or North African bread. To complete the meal, some green salad and cheese should be served before or after.

2 tablespoons olive oil

½ medium onion (3 ounces), finely chopped

½ cup peeled, seeded, and finely diced tomato (page 300)

1⅛ pounds waxy red potatoes, peeled and diced into 1-inch pieces

¼ teaspoon ground turmeric

½ teaspoon ground cumin

1 teaspoon paprika

⅛ teaspoon cayenne (optional)

2 tablespoons finely chopped fresh cilantro

1¼ teaspoons salt, or to taste

Put the oil in a medium pot and set over medium-high heat. Add the onion. Turn the heat down to medium and sauté until the onion is soft and translucent, about 5 minutes. Add the remaining ingredients and stir. Pour in 2 cups of water and mix well. Turn the heat up to high and bring to a boil. Cover the pot, turn the heat down to low, and cook gently for 20 to 30 minutes, or until the potatoes are tender. If you wish to make the sauce thicker, crush 1 or 2 of the potato pieces in the pot and stir. Serve hot.

SERVES 4

Crisp Potato Cake with Herbs

There are so many herbs growing in my garden that I am always looking for ways to use them. I created this for my friend and fellow chef, Michael James.

2½ pounds baking potatoes

About 6 tablespoons olive oil

Salt

Freshly ground black pepper

2 teaspoons chopped fresh thyme or
    1 teaspoon dried thyme

2 teaspoons chopped fresh rosemary or
    1 teaspoon dried crumbled rosemary

2 teaspoons chopped fresh oregano or
    ½ teaspoon dried oregano

Peel the potatoes and keep them in water.

Preheat the oven to 400°F.

In a large nonstick frying pan with an ovenproof handle, pour 4 tablespoons of the oil and place over medium-low heat. At the same time, pick up a potato, dry it, and cut it into ⅛-inch-thick slices. Lay the slices in the pan in a slightly overlapping layer, starting at the outside working toward the center in a spiral. Continue until you have covered the bottom of the pan. Lightly salt and pepper the potatoes. Sprinkle some of the herbs over the top and dribble a little oil on top as well. Continue making layers the same way until all the potatoes and seasonings are used up, sprinkling seasonings and dribbling oil over each layer. Press down on the top with a large spatula. If you feel that the potatoes have browned a bit at the bottom (the edges will show this), cover well with foil and put the pan in the oven. Bake for 35 to 40 minutes, or until the potatoes are tender. Uncover and put the pan under the broiler briefly to brown the top.

Loosen the sides and bottom gently with a spatula, then slide the cake out onto a large, round plate. Cut into wedges and serve.

SERVES 6

Elena Averoff's

Baked Potatoes, the Greek Way   GREECE

Patata Psiti

This recipe comes from the hills of the Epirus region where I feasted on superb baked potatoes dressed with olive oil and garden seasonings.

Young green garlic is called for here but since I can only get that for about 3 weeks of the year at my farm market, you may use chives and a little regular garlic as a substitute. If you grow your own garlic, use about 1 tablespoon of a mixture of both white and green parts.

½ cup extra-virgin olive oil

1 garlic clove, lightly crushed and peeled but
    left whole

2 teaspoons very finely chopped fresh oregano
    or ½ teaspoon dried oregano

1½ tablespoons very finely sliced fresh chives

4 large baking potatoes, freshly baked
    according to directions on page 269

Salt

Freshly ground black pepper

Put the oil into a bowl. Add the garlic clove and press it down to release its juices. Remove the garlic. Add the oregano and chives and mix.

Split open the hot baked potatoes lengthwise. Lightly salt and pepper them. Pour the olive oil mixture over the top and serve immediately.

SERVES 4

Spicy Hash Brown Potatoes

A greasy spoon classic is given an Eastern spin with the addition of whole spices and a dash of cayenne. I love to serve these with eggs or with some grilled tomatoes and mushrooms.

1 pound boiled potatoes, peeled

3 tablespoons peanut or canola oil

¼ teaspoon whole cumin seeds

¼ teaspoon whole brown or yellow mustard
    seeds

¼ teaspoon sesame seeds

½ medium onion, peeled and chopped (about
    ¼-inch dice)

¾ to 1 teaspoon salt

Freshly ground black pepper

⅛ to ¼ teaspoon cayenne

Crumble the potatoes so you have a very coarse mash.

Put the oil in a large, nonstick frying pan and set over medium-high heat. When hot, put in the cumin, mustard, and sesame seeds. As soon as the seeds begin to pop, a matter of seconds, put in the onion. Stir for 30 seconds and put in the potatoes, salt, pepper to taste, and cayenne. Stir the potatoes around for a minute and mix well. Then spread them out evenly in the pan, mashing them down a little, and turn the heat to medium. When the potatoes have turned reddish-brown at the bottom, turn them over and brown the opposite side as well. Serve immediately.

SERVES 4

Anna Elena Martinez'

Mexican Potato Cake   MEXICO

Pay de Papa

A delicious layered cake of mashed potatoes and sautéed vegetables, enriched with egg and milk, this is a meal in itself and may be served with a large green salad.

    If you cannot get a poblano chile, use the combination of ¹/₂ green bell pepper, sliced, and 1 fresh hot green chile, finely chopped.

    I like to cook the vegetables in a heavy cast-iron frying pan over high heat. This browns them the way I like. Use any heavy pan or heavy wok.

For the vegetable layers

3 tablespoons peanut or canola oil

1 medium onion, peeled and chopped

8 medium white mushrooms, cut lengthwise
   into ¼-inch-thick slices

2 medium zucchini, cut in half lengthwise and
   then crosswise at ¼-inch intervals

1 large poblano chile (about 3½ ounces),
   cored, halved lengthwise and cut
   crosswise into ¼-inch-thick slices

2 medium tomatoes, peeled (page 300) and
   chopped

1 teaspoon salt

Freshly ground black pepper

For the mashed potatoes

2 pounds potatoes

2 tablespoons unsalted butter, cut into
   thin pats

1 cup milk

2 eggs, beaten

1¾ to 2 teaspoons salt

Freshly ground black pepper

A dash of grated nutmeg

You also need

A little butter for greasing

3 tablespoons dry bread crumbs

To make the vegetables, put the oil in a large cast-iron or other heavy, wide pan or wok and set over high heat. When hot, put in the onion. Stir and fry for 1 minute. Now put in the mushrooms. Stir and fry for another minute. Put in the zucchini and poblano chile. Stir and fry for 4 to 5 minutes. Add the tomatoes. Stir and fry for 2 to 3 minutes. Now turn the heat to low and cook, stirring, another 5 to 6 minutes, or until all the vegetables are cooked through. Add the salt and pepper and stir to mix. Turn off the heat.

Scrub the potatoes and put them in a pot with water to cover. Boil the potatoes and when done, peel them while they are still hot and mash them coarsely with the butter. Using an electric beater or a whisk, slowly add the milk and then the eggs, salt, pepper to taste, and nutmeg. Beat until smooth.

Preheat the oven to 350°F.

Butter a 4-cup ovenproof soufflé dish and dust it well with 2 tablespoons of the bread crumbs. Divide the mashed potato into 3 parts and the vegetables into 2 parts. Line the bottom of the soufflé dish evenly with a layer of the potatoes. Top that with a layer of vegetables, then another layer of potatoes, another layer of vegetables, and a final layer of potatoes. Dust the top with the remaining 1 tablespoon bread crumbs. Put the soufflé dish in the top third of the oven and bake for 40 minutes.

SERVES 6

Mitthan Bhabi's

Crumbled Potatoes with Peas

INDIA

Aloo Matar

Very similar to Potatoes Cooked with Fennel Seeds (page 274), this spicy potato dish is best enjoyed with Indian breads, particularly with parathas *and* pooris. *In our family, it was always served at religious functions. Offer green vegetables, pickles, and yogurt relishes on the side.*

1 pound boiling potatoes

3 tablespoons peanut or canola oil

¾ teaspoon whole cumin seeds

⅛ teaspoon whole fenugreek seeds

¾ cup peeled and chopped very ripe tomatoes

2 teaspoons ground coriander

1 teaspoon ground cumin

¼ teaspoon ground turmeric

1 teaspoon garam masala (page 723)

1 cup (4 ounces) shelled fresh or defrosted
   frozen peas

1¼ teaspoons salt, or to taste

¼ to 1 teaspoon cayenne

Boil the potatoes in 6 cups of water until tender. Drain. Peel and break by hand into roughly ¾-inch pieces. Set aside.

Put the oil in a medium pot and set over medium-high heat. When hot, put in the whole cumin and fenugreek seeds. Ten seconds later, put in tomatoes, ground coriander, ground cumin, turmeric, and garam masala. Stir and cook until the liquid from the tomatoes has almost completely cooked off and you can see the oil. Add the potatoes, peas, salt, and cayenne. Stir gently a few times, then add 1¾ cups of water and stir to mix well. Bring to a boil. Turn the heat down to low, cover, and cook gently for 20 minutes. Stir occasionally. If you like the sauce thicker, crush 1 or 2 potato pieces against the sides of the pot and mix into the sauce. Serve hot.

SERVES 4

MASHED POTATOES:
A HALF DOZEN INTERPRETATIONS

This quintessential comfort food is eaten in almost every country of the world. There is little variation in the basic boiling and mashing procedure; it is the seasonings added later that make all the difference.

Note: When beating potatoes to make them airy, use a whisk or electric beater. Never use a food processor, as it makes potatoes gummy.

Basic Mashed Potatoes

2¼ pounds potatoes (preferably baking potatoes), peeled and cut into large chunks

1¼ teaspoons salt

Freshly ground black pepper

Boil the potatoes with water to cover as directed on page 269. Drain but save the cooking water in case you wish to thin out the potatoes. Either put through a ricer (this is the easiest) or use a potato masher to mash the potatoes. Add the salt and pepper to taste and mix well. Keep warm in a covered double boiler.

SERVES 4

Variation I
Mashed Potatoes My Husband's Old-Fashioned Way

Boil and mash the potatoes according to the basic recipe. Quickly add ¾ cup plus a little more hot milk, 4 to 6 tablespoons butter, cut in small pats, the salt, and pepper to taste. Beat with a whisk, fork, or electric beater until light and fluffy.

Variation II
Mashed Potatoes with Garlic the New-Fashioned Way

Put 5 to 6 garlic cloves into the cooking water with the potatoes. When tender, mash the potatoes with the garlic cloves according to the basic recipe. Quickly add 4 tablespoons good-quality extra-virgin olive oil, the salt, and pepper to taste. Beat with a whisk, fork, or electric beater until light and fluffy.

(recipe continues)

Variation III

Mashed Potatoes with Mustard Oil and Ground Mustard Seeds from Orissa in East India

Grind 2 teaspoons whole yellow or brown mustard seeds in the container of an electric coffee grinder. Put 4 tablespoons mustard oil or extra-virgin olive oil in a shallow bowl. Add the ground mustard seeds and beat well. Finely chop a fresh hot green chile. Now boil and mash the potatoes according to the basic recipe. Quickly add the oil-mustard combination, the chile, salt, and pepper to taste. Mix well.

Variation IV

Mashed Potatoes the South Indian Way

Boil and mash the potatoes according to the basic recipe, adding the salt and pepper to taste and mixing well.

Put 4 tablespoons peanut oil in a small frying pan. When hot, put in 1 teaspoon of *chana dal* or yellow split peas. Stir and fry until they start to turn red. Now put in a pinch of ground asafetida, 1 teaspoon whole brown or yellow mustard seeds, and 1 to 2 whole dried hot red chiles. Stir once. As soon as the mustard seeds pop, a matter of seconds, empty the oil and seasonings over the potatoes. Mix well.

Variation V

Mashed Potatoes the Maharashtrian Way from West India

Boil and mash the potatoes according to the basic recipe, adding the salt, pepper to taste, and 1 teaspoon sugar.

Put 4 tablespoons peanut oil in a medium frying pan over medium-high heat. When hot, put in 1 teaspoon whole brown or yellow mustard seeds. As soon as they pop, a matter of seconds, add 1 to 2 dried hot red chiles. Stir once or twice and throw 10 fresh curry leaves or fresh basil leaves into the pan. Stir once and add 2 tablespoons very lightly crushed raw peanuts. Stir once or twice or until the peanuts are golden. Quickly pour the oil and seasonings over the potatoes. Stir to mix.

Variation VI

Mashed Potatoes the North Indian Way

Boil and mash the potatoes coarsely. (See the basic recipe.) Add the salt, pepper to taste, ¼ teaspoon cayenne, 1 teaspoon ground roasted cumin seeds, 3 tablespoons finely chopped fresh cilantro, and 1½ tablespoons lime juice. Stir to mix.

Durupadi Jagtiani's

Potato Patties

INDIA

Aloo Tikki

These are a favorite teatime snack, eaten with chutneys—or even tomato ketchup! At Dawat, our restaurant in New York, we offer them as an appetizer with a wonderful fresh red pepper chutney. Three of them, served with a salad, would make a very delicious meal.

4 large baking potatoes (2½ pounds)

3 thick slices (4 ounces) crusty Italian bread broken into small pieces (about 2 cups) and soaked in water until the crust has softened, about 15 minutes

2½ teaspoons salt

½ cup dry bread crumbs

½ teaspoon cayenne

¾ teaspoon whole cumin seeds

½ teaspoon freshly ground black pepper

1½ teaspoons finely chopped fresh hot green chile

2 tablespoons finely chopped fresh cilantro leaves

Peanut or canola oil for deep-frying

Put the whole potatoes into a large pot, cover with water, and bring to a boil over high heat. Lower the flame to medium and cook for 35 minutes, or until the tip of a knife easily slips into each potato. Remove from the water and immediately peel and run through a ricer or mash.

Squeeze the bread between your hands until it is quite dry. Pat dry one more time with a paper towel. Break the bread up to remove any clumps and run through a ricer or mash. Add the bread to the potato.

Then add the salt, bread crumbs, cayenne, cumin seeds, black pepper, fresh hot green chile, and the fresh cilantro. Mix well.

Lightly oil your hands. Make balls of the mixture the size of clementines. Flatten them into patties that are 3 inches in diameter and ½ to ¾ inch thick.

Put the oil for deep-frying in a wok or Indian *karhai* (page 740) and set over high heat. Allow the oil to get very hot. (It should just start smoking.) While you are waiting for the oil to heat up, line a plate with paper towels for draining the patties after they have been fried. Cooking 1 patty at a time, slide the patty carefully into the oil, fry for 10 seconds, flip over gently and fry for another 10 seconds, flip over and fry 5 seconds, and flip over and fry a final 5 seconds. Remove with a slotted spatula. Allow to drain on the paper towel–lined plate. Make all patties this way. Serve hot.

SERVES 6 TO 8

Sakina El Alaoui's

Sweet Potatoes with Raisins and Cinnamon

MOROCCO

Patates Douces

This heavenly dish, with its caramelized onions and plump raisins, may be served with dark greens, rice, and any dish of beans or split peas. It also offers a unique possibility at Thanksgiving time for those looking for variations on the theme of candied sweet potatoes.

Some people like to sprinkle a generous pinch of ground cinnamon over the top before serving.

5 tablespoons olive oil

1 (2-inch) cinnamon stick

1 medium onion (6 ounces), peeled, cut in
   half lengthwise and crosswise into very
   fine half rings

3 medium sweet potatoes (18 ounces), peeled
   and cut into chunky slices, about 1 inch
   thick × 1 inch wide × 1½ inches long

½ teaspoon salt

½ teaspoon ground ginger

3 tablespoons golden raisins

⅛ to ¼ teaspoon cayenne

1 to 2 teaspoons sugar

Put the oil in a wide sauté pan or large frying pan and set over medium-high heat. When hot, put in the cinnamon stick and the onion.

Sauté for about 3 minutes, or until the onion has lost much of its water. Add the sweet potatoes and stir. Continue to sauté another 6 to 7 minutes, or until the onion begins to turn light brown and the sweet potatoes have also picked up a little color. Add ¾ cup of water, the salt, ginger, raisins, cayenne, and sugar. Bring to a boil. Turn the heat down to low, cover, and cook gently for 7 to 9 minutes, or until the sweet potatoes are tender. There should be almost no liquid left in the pan, except for a little oil. (If there is, uncover and boil the liquid off.) Serve hot.

SERVES 3 TO 4

Cheryl Rathkopf's

Sri Lankan Sweet Potatoes
with Cardamom and Chiles   SRI LANKA
Bathala Theldala

As good as the preceding Moroccan sweet potatoes, this dish is spicier, more aromatic, and chock-full of caramelized onions. I love it with dark greens, Tomato Sambal (page 302), and any combination of either rice and beans or rice and split peas.

2 very large sweet potatoes (about 2½ pounds)

¼ teaspoon ground turmeric

5 tablespoons peanut or olive oil

3 whole dried hot red chiles, broken into halves

2 whole cardamom pods

1 (3-inch) cinnamon stick

20 fresh curry leaves (substitute fresh holy basil or basil leaves for a different but equally interesting flavor)

3 good-sized onions (about 1¼ pounds), cut into halves lengthwise and then into very fine half rings

1 to 3 teaspoons coarsely crushed dried hot red chiles

1¼ to 1½ teaspoons salt

1½ tablespoons fresh lime juice, or to taste

Peel the sweet potatoes and quarter lengthwise. Now cut crosswise at ¾-inch intervals to get chunky pieces. Put the sweet potato pieces in a large pot and cover well with water. Add the turmeric and bring to a boil. Stir well to mix in the turmeric. Boil, uncovered, for 5 to 6 minutes, or until the sweet potatoes are tender but still firm. Drain.

Put the oil in a large frying pan and set over medium-high heat. When hot, put in the red chiles. Stir once and when the chiles darken, a matter of seconds, put in the cardamom and cinnamon. Stir once or twice and put in the curry leaves. Stir once and put in the onions. Stir and cook the onions for 5 to 6 minutes, or until they are lightly browned. Put in the sweet potatoes. Stir and fry for 5 minutes. Put in the crushed red chiles, salt, and lime juice. Stir and cook, lowering the heat as needed, until the sweet potatoes are tender enough for your taste.

Remove the cinnamon stick and cardamom pods before serving.

SERVES 6

Pumpkins and Winter Squashes

I refer here to anything with a hard skin and an orange flesh, rich in vitamin A, beta-carotene, potassium, and fiber, vegetables that help us wage our wars against cancers, immune diseases, night blindness, and even common colds—vegetables known for their sweetness that can be picked in the early winter and eaten one, two, even four months later. In Korea, pumpkins are considered very good for mothers who have just given birth in reducing abdominal swelling. A cap is cut off near the top of the pumpkin and honey is poured inside. Then the entire pumpkin is steamed until the flesh is soft. This tender flesh is then strained and served to the new mother. Pumpkins are also combined with azuki beans and rice, cooked slowly, and served as a *conjee* or porridge. Included here would be the orange-skinned pumpkin (such as the sugar pumpkin, but not the watery Halloween variety), green-skinned pumpkins with orange flesh, dark green, fluted acorn squashes with pale orange-yellow flesh, pale putty-colored butternut squashes that are slim at the top but round off into balls at the bottom, the very large, elongated melon-shaped Hubbard squash whose skin seems harder than that of a nut, and many more.

Why are the biggest and best of them, such as the large, thick-fleshed eating pumpkins and Hubbard squashes, so hard to find in our supermarkets and, even when found, why are they always sold whole, more for decorative purposes than for eating? Who would buy a whole pumpkin? Why do we need to go to ethnic markets to find the best of them cut into user-friendly chunks? Why is it that in a nation where pumpkins perhaps originated and are certainly celebrated, the only access the public has to their flesh is in cans and that too in a mashed form? Pumpkin flesh can be steamed, stir-fried, made into fritters and soups, put into risottos and pilafs, into savory and sweet pies, and into yogurt relishes. So why can it not be found at our local grocer as it is in much of the world?

Around Thanksgiving time one year, I was most surprised to find at a local supermarket in the western Massachusetts countryside packaged sections of pumpkin, Hubbard squash, and butternut squash that had been cut, had their seeds removed, and peeled. It was almost like a mirage. I rushed to the manager of the supermarket—Guido's in Great Barrington, Massachusetts—to express my gratitude and to try and ensure that this would be a permanent feature of the store. It would only last through the "holiday season," I was told. What is the best way to break open a Hubbard squash, I wanted to know, having struggled with it on numerous occasions. "Drop it from the roof," I was told, not in jest. And how do you peel a butternut squash, I asked, knowing the difficulties involved. "We have worked out a method that requires the use of a lathe," was the answer.

So, while it is possible to bake halved portions of the smaller squashes in their skins, recipes that require skinned, uncooked segments for stir-fries, fritters, stews, risottos, and the like are somewhat of a challenge. But the challenge can be overcome.

Buying and storing winter pumpkins and winter squashes: Whole acorn and butternut squashes are available throughout the late autumn and winter months. If you are looking for good, thick-fleshed pumpkins, you need to locate a source that carries them beyond November/December. I find that Chinese and Hispanic markets are a good source, as are some Indian ones. Look for clean, hard skins with no soft spots. Whole, firm pumpkins and squashes (with stems still attached) may be stored in cool airy places for 1 to 4 months. (In Indian temples where hundreds of people are fed at a time, hard-skinned squashes, pumpkins, and gourds are slipped into very wide-meshed rope bags—more rope than bag—and then suspended from what looks like a series of clotheslines in a shaded verandah or courtyard. Stored this way, they last for months.)

Stored pumpkins and squashes should not be allowed to freeze or get too warm, so a temperature that hovers around 50 to 55°F. is ideal. Once cut, sections of large pumpkins and squashes may be stored in the refrigerator, loosely covered with a cloth or plastic wrap. They should last for at least a week.

How to peel and cut up hard-skinned pumpkins and squashes: I wish more supermarkets would do this work for us. We would then eat them for much of the year. Until that happens, here is the best way I know to go about the task. For a pumpkin or large squash, using a heavy, sharp knife, cut it in half, going from the stem down. Now cut wedges that are 1 to 1½ inches at the widest point. Remove the seed-filled center. (Save the seeds—just the seeds, not the pulp around them. Spread the seeds out on a paper towel–lined tray—or several trays—and let them dry out for 24 hours in an airy, sunny spot. They can now be peeled and eaten. I just love them.) Lay the wedges on their sides and, still using a heavy, sharp knife, cut off the skin in sections. The wedges may now be cut as needed. For smaller pumpkins and squashes, halve or quarter the vegetable as needed. Remove and discard the seeded area. If the skin needs peeling, use a potato peeler. Now cut the sections up if the recipe requires it.

Having said this, let me add that Hubbard squashes are very tough to open up and may require a carefully aimed hatchet or dropping from a height! You might even try a wedge and a hammer, as if you were splitting wood. (Be sure to nestle the squash in a hollow so it does not slide around.) These squashes taste quite wonderful and every bit of effort is well worth the trouble!

Generally speaking, a section of winter squash or pumpkin will lose anywhere from a third to half its weight in skin and seeds. In other words, if you have 1½ pounds of pumpkin section with skin and seeds, expect to be left with no more than 1 pound after skinning and removing the seeded area. Roughly speaking,

1½ pounds of peeled and diced pumpkin or hard squash is the equivalent of about 4 cups.

Depending upon the density of pumpkin or squash flesh, it will cook down from two-thirds to half its volume. Winter squashes and pumpkins that have been stored for several months reduce much less when cooked than those picked and cooked in the early autumn. They tend to have very firm flesh and concentrated flavor. Pumpkin flesh that has been cooked to a pulp may be frozen. It will last in the freezer for six months.

Butternut Squash with Sage

I love the Italian way with pumpkin, when it is cooked beautifully with fresh sage leaves. One autumn, just around Thanksgiving, my frost-defying sage bush was still holding its head up in the herb garden and in the local supermarket, there were peeled butternut squashes, which are so much like pumpkin. I put the two together to make what has now become a family favorite; we eat it frequently with rice, greens, and some kind of beans. At the Thanksgiving table, this dish has become a "must."

Any peeled winter pumpkin or orange-fleshed winter squash may be substituted for the butternut squash, and you may also use sweet potatoes.

3 tablespoons olive oil

1 large shallot (about 2 ounces), peeled and cut into fine slivers

10 fresh sage leaves

1½ pounds peeled butternut squash (or any winter squash or pumpkin), cut into ¾- to 1-inch cubes (4 cups)

½ teaspoon salt

1 tablespoon sugar

Put the oil in a wide pan or deep frying pan and set it over medium-high heat. When hot, put in the shallot slivers and sage leaves. Stir and fry until the shallot slivers are golden. Put in the squash and stir until the pieces turn a little brown at the edges and the shallot slivers turn a rich reddish-brown. Add the salt and sugar. Give a few quick stirs to caramelize the sugar and then add ½ cup of water. Bring to a boil. Cover, turn the heat down to low, and simmer gently for 15 to 20 minutes, or until the squash is just tender.

SERVES 4

Pumpkin or Hubbard Squash Cooked with Bengali Seasonings

INDIA

Bangali Kaddu

I make this with both pumpkin and Hubbard squash. From a 3-pound segment with skin, I am usually left with about 2 pounds of seedless, skinless flesh.

You may serve this with most Indian meals. For a more elaborate meal with an international feel, I like to put this dish together with Palestinian Rice with Lentils and Browned Onions (page 404), Sliced Tomatoes in a Tomato Sauce (page 303), some greens, such as Sautéed Spinach with Dill and Onion (page 225), and a yogurt relish or cheese dish.

¼ cup mustard oil or olive oil

½ teaspoon whole cumin seeds

½ teaspoon whole brown mustard seeds

¼ teaspoon nigella *(kalonji)*

¼ teaspoon whole fennel seeds

⅛ teaspoon whole fenugreek seeds

2 bay leaves

2 to 3 whole dried hot red chiles (of the cayenne type)

About 2 pounds pumpkin or Hubbard squash flesh (from a 3-pound segment), cut into 1- to 1½-inch cubes

¾ to 1 teaspoon salt

1½ tablespoons light brown sugar

Put the oil in a large, wide, preferably nonstick pan and set over medium-high heat. When hot, put in the cumin and mustard seeds. As soon as the mustard seeds begin to pop, a matter of seconds, put in the nigella, fennel, fenugreek, bay leaves, and red chiles. Stir once or twice quickly and put in the pumpkin or squash. Stir for a minute. Cover, turn the heat down to low, and cook for 40 to 45 minutes, or until just tender, stirring now and then and replacing the cover each time. Uncover and add the salt and sugar. Stir gently, mashing the pumpkin lightly so that you retain some texture. Serve hot.

Note: The whole chiles should be eaten only by those who know what they are doing. If you like, you could remove the bay leaves and chiles, though I find their presence both decorative and authentic.

SERVES 4 TO 6

Mitthan Bhabi's
Pumpkin Cooked in the Delhi Style INDIA
Parhezi Kashiphal

I make this with either pumpkin or Hubbard squash. My family in India—and this is a family recipe—uses the green pumpkin, a variety I have never seen here. This is probably, technically speaking, a gourd. The local name for it is kashiphal, *or "the fruit of the holy city of Benares." I find that a plain pumpkin or any hard-skinned yellow squash works just as well.*

This dish was cooked chiefly on holy days and certain types of fasting days. We ate it with flatbreads, a yogurt dish, a potato dish such as Crumbled Potatoes with Peas (page 280), and some pickles and chutneys. It can also be served with the same accompaniments as Pumpkin Cooked with Bengali Seasonings (page 289).

¼ cup peanut or canola oil, or *ghee* (page 723)

½ teaspoon whole cumin seeds

¼ teaspoon nigella *(kalonji)*

¼ teaspoon whole fennel seeds

⅛ teaspoon whole fenugreek seeds

½ teaspoon whole black peppercorns

2 to 3 whole dried hot red chiles (preferably cayenne)

About 2 pounds pumpkin or Hubbard squash flesh (from a 3-pound segment), cut into 1- to 1½-inch cubes

¾ to 1 teaspoon salt

1½ tablespoons light brown sugar

2 teaspoons ground *amchoor* (page 711) or fresh lemon juice

Put the oil in a large, wide, preferably nonstick pan and set over medium-high heat. When very hot, put in the cumin seeds. Ten seconds later, put in the nigella, fennel, fenugreek, peppercorns, and red chiles. Stir once or twice quickly and put in the pumpkin or squash. Stir for a minute. Cover, turn the heat down to low, and cook for 40 to 45 minutes, or until just tender, stirring now and then and replacing the cover each time. Uncover and add the salt, sugar, and *amchoor.* Stir gently, mashing the pumpkin lightly so that you retain some texture. Serve hot.

Note: The whole chiles and peppercorns should not be eaten.

SERVES 4 TO 6

Lola's
Trinidadian Pumpkin

This may be made with pumpkin, butternut squash, or Hubbard squash. From 3 pounds, with skin, I am usually left with about 2 pounds of seedless, skinless flesh.

The very fiery Congo peppers were used in this dish in Trinidad. Of the habanero family, they are also called Scotch bonnets and look like little lanterns. If you decide to use these, use only about a quarter without seeds. I have used the plainer green chile. I have also used cilantro instead of the more commonly used culantro leaves.

Serve with any Indian, Trinidadian, or North African meal.

3 tablespoons olive oil

1 medium onion, peeled and finely chopped

3 garlic cloves, peeled and finely crushed

1 fresh hot green chile, sliced into very thin rings

1 teaspoon fresh thyme or ½ teaspoon dried thyme

2 tablespoons finely chopped cilantro

About 2 pounds pumpkin or Hubbard squash flesh (from a 3-pound segment), cut into 1- to 1½-inch cubes

¾ to 1 teaspoon salt

1½ tablespoons light brown sugar

Put the oil in a large, wide, preferably nonstick pan and set over medium-high heat. When very hot, put in the onion. Stir and fry until the onion is lightly browned. Put in the garlic, chile, thyme, and cilantro. Stir for a few seconds until the garlic is golden and put in the pumpkin or squash. Stir for a minute. Add 3 tablespoons of water, cover, turn the heat to low, and cook for 40 to 45 minutes, or until just tender, stirring now and then and replacing the cover each time. Uncover and add the salt and sugar. Stir gently, mashing the pumpkin lightly so that you retain some texture. Serve hot.

SERVES 4 TO 6

Pumpkin Fritters

Kaddu Ki Bajjia

For this dish, I used a section of pumpkin that weighed 1½ pounds. After removing the seeds and peeling it, I was left with 1 pound of flesh. Any orange-fleshed squash such as Hubbard or butternut, may be used instead of pumpkin.

These fritters may be served as a snack with tea and a savory chutney or as a part of a meal. They are best when eaten as soon as they are made.

For the batter

½ cup chickpea flour

½ cup rice flour

¼ teaspoon baking soda

¼ teaspoon ground turmeric

¼ to ½ teaspoon cayenne

¾ teaspoon salt

Peanut or canola oil for shallow frying

1 pound orange pumpkin flesh (see recipe introduction), coarsely grated

½ medium-small onion (1½ ounces), peeled and cut into very fine half rings

1½ tablespoons sesame seeds

Put the chickpea flour, rice flour, baking soda, turmeric, cayenne, and salt into a bowl. Slowly add water (you will need about 7 ounces, plus another tablespoon), mixing as you go, to make a smooth batter of medium thickness.

Just before you get ready to eat, pour the oil to a depth of ½ inch into a large frying pan and set it over medium-low heat. Wait until the oil is hot; this can take several minutes. Stir the batter and put in the grated pumpkin, sliced onion, and sesame seeds. Mix gently. Now pick up a handful of the pumpkin mixture, enough to make a patty about 2½ inches in diameter and about ½ inch thick on the palm of one hand. Slide this patty into the hot oil. Make several such patties, just enough to fill the frying pan in a single layer. Fry the patties for about 3½ minutes on one side. Turn them over and cook for another 3½ minutes on the second side, or until reddish-brown and crisp. Remove with a slotted spoon and set down on paper towels to drain. Make all patties this way and serve as soon as possible.

SERVES 6

Kassiani's
Savory Greek Pumpkin Pie
Kolokithopita

The pitas *of Metsovo, a stunning little town in the hills of the Epirus region, are a world unto themselves. They are large round pies, about 15 inches in diameter, filled with anything from pumpkin, zucchini, or eggplant to leeks or just cheese.*

On chilly evenings, families return to their traditional wooden houses and settle down on rug-covered divans set before the fireplace. Trays bearing the pitas *are brought in. If these are old, carved, traditional trays of great value, the* pitas *will not have been cut into diamond shapes with a knife, as this would mark the trays. Instead, they will be cut with scissors or broken by hand.*

The pastry part of a normal pita *is a kind of filo, only it is rolled out at home with long, dowel-like rolling pins and is not as thin as the filo we get from the freezer cases of our supermarkets. Each* pita *requires 10 to 11 sheets as well as patience and practiced dexterity. Some proper Greek grocers outside Greece do sell this thicker filo for* pitas *so do use it if you can find it, but my recipe calls for the easy-to-find supermarket variety. My pie is also much smaller than the traditional Metsovo version.*

For this recipe, the pumpkin flesh needs to be grated. This is done with great ease in a food processor. Early autumn pumpkins tend to be more watery than ones held for a few months. If your pumpkin is very watery, add 1 to 2 tablespoons of bulgur wheat as you are stirring and frying it. This is a common Metsovo trick.

16 sheets of frozen filo pastry, defrosted

4 tablespoons plus about ¾ cup olive oil

1 good-sized onion (5 ounces), peeled and cut into fine half rings

About 6½ cups (2½ pounds) coarsely grated pumpkin flesh (from a 3-pound segment)

2 teaspoons salt

2 to 3 tablespoons sugar

Freshly ground black pepper

1 egg, beaten

6 ounces imported feta cheese, crumbled

Defrost the frozen pastry following package directions. Once it is defrosted, put the entire package in the refrigerator.

Heat the 4 tablespoons of oil in a large, preferably nonstick pan over medium-high heat. When hot, put in the onion. Stir and fry until soft, turning the heat down if necessary. Put in the pumpkin. Turn the heat back to medium-high. Stir and fry for 8 to 10 minutes, or until the pumpkin is soft. Stir in the salt, sugar, and black pepper to taste. Allow to cool. Stir in the beaten egg and crumbled feta cheese.

Preheat the oven to 400°F.

(recipe continues)

Generously oil a metal baking pan that is $9 \times 9 \times 1\frac{1}{2}$ inches.

Work quickly with the filo now. Spread out 1 sheet on a clean, dry surface and brush it generously with oil. Lay it inside the baking tray, leaving about $1\frac{1}{2}$ to 2 inches sticking out on all sides. (The rest can be cut or folded over.) Put 3 more sheets over the first, each brushed with oil, in exactly the same way. Fold a damp towel lengthwise and put it like a ring around the edges of the pastry that are sticking out to prevent them from drying. Divide the pumpkin mixture into 4 parts. Spread one part over the last filo sheet. Now put 2 sheets of filo over the pumpkin mixture, just as you had the earlier sheets, brushing each with oil and trimming them or folding them in but leaving a little sticking out of the pan. Cover the edges that stick out with the damp towel. Spread another quarter of the stuffing over the top. Keep repeating this until all the stuffing is used up. End with 4 more layers of filo. Brush the top with oil. Now roll in the pastry ends that were sticking out to form a neat edge all around. Brush the edges with oil. Using a knife, cut rows about $2\frac{1}{4}$ inches apart. Now cut rows at a diagonal, also $2\frac{1}{4}$ inches apart to form diamonds. Put the pie in the oven and bake for 45 minutes, or until golden brown. Serve hot or warm.

SERVES 6

Summer Squashes

This is the section for summer's bounty, the soft-skinned squashes and gourds that fill our gardens and our markets the world over. I have confined myself here to one representative of the western world, the zucchini, and one of the eastern, the bitter melon. But you should feel free to substitute and experiment with other varieties when you come across them.

ZUCCHINI

They can be grilled, sautéed, made into fritters, and put into soups and breads. The only danger in cooking them is that they can quickly turn to mush, so cook them briefly. If you are putting them in soup, put them in just a few minutes before the end of the cooking period.

How to buy and store zucchini: Look for crisp specimens that are all green and have no brown spots. Store in the vegetable bin of the refrigerator.

How to prepare zucchini: Wash and trim the ends. Young zucchini may be left the way it is, but older ones need to have their pulpy seeds removed. The best way to do this is to cut them in half lengthwise and scrape the seeds out with a spoon (a grapefruit spoon works well), leaving just the walls. As they are full of water and slices often stick to each other, stir-frying is difficult. It is because of this that many recipes suggest that slices be salted and squeezed before any cooking is done. This draws much of the water out.

BITTER MELONS

Bitter melon, which can be really bitter, is credited in Asia with many medical virtues, even the prevention of cancer. It is greatly loved. Green in color, it looks squashlike but has very knobbly alligator skin. Inside, buried in a somewhat hollow pith, are crunchy seeds that may be scraped out but that many people love. It may be sliced and sautéed with onions, it can be stuffed, and it can also be cooked with other vegetables.

How to buy and store bitter melons: You will find these only in East and South Asian markets, where two main varieties are generally available: the small, dark green ones from India, generally no longer than 4 to 5 inches with tiny bumps, and the paler green, much larger ones (a few are 9 inches) with rows of big bumps. As with other squashes, look for crisp, clean specimens without brown spots. Store in the vegetable bin of the refrigerator.

How to prepare bitter melons: After washing, slit open and salt them inside to remove just a little of their bitterness. (The Chinese do not do this.) After salting, they are often left on a slanted board to drain and then washed inside and out before cooking. Very often the bumps are scraped away with a knife (at least my mother always did this—perhaps to be able to brown them more evenly).

Simple "Grilled" Zucchini
UNITED STATES/MEDITERRANEAN

You will find versions of this recipe throughout the Mediterranean and in much of America. I give it here just in case some of you are unfamiliar with it; it is so good and so simple you really should have this in your repertoire. It's wonderful prepared outdoors over charcoal in the summer but I make it indoors all year round as zucchini now seem to be available in all seasons. I use the grill that is built into my stove but you could use a large cast-iron frying pan instead.

Once the zucchini are cooked, it is best to serve them right away. If you want to serve this dish as a salad, arrange the slices in slightly overlapping layers on a large platter and allow them to cool. Just before serving, dribble 4 tablespoons of a simple oil-and-vinegar or oil-and-lemon dressing over the top.

(recipe continues)

About 2 tablespoons olive oil

2 medium zucchini (12 ounces), cut diagonally into ⅓-inch-thick slices

Salt

Freshly ground black pepper

2 tablespoons finely chopped fresh parsley

Set a cast-iron griddle or cast-iron frying pan over high heat. Let it get hot. Dribble just enough olive oil, about 1 tablespoon, to grease it lightly. When the oil is very hot, a matter of seconds, lay down enough zucchini slices to cover the bottom in a single layer. Do not overcrowd. Cook for about 2 minutes, or until the bottoms of the slices turn a rich medium brown. You may need to move the slices around so they all cook evenly. Turn the slices over. Cook for another 2 minutes, or until the second side turns medium brown. Remove the slices from the pan and arrange in a single layer on a large platter. Cook all the zucchini slices this way. With each batch, remember to add enough oil to keep the pan lightly greased.

When the zucchini are all cooked, lightly sprinkle salt and pepper over the slices. Sprinkle the parsley over the top and serve.

SERVES 4

From Pinocho in Barcelona
Spanish-Style Grilled Zucchini   SPAIN
Calabacitas a la Plancha

Known as zucchini cooked "a la plancha," or on a hot griddle, this is a specialty that I had first in a Barcelona market, La Boqueria, at a "restaurant" named Pinocho. Pinocho turned out to be a very simple stall with dozens of people sitting at a counter on high stools with more people waiting. It was obviously popular, and I surmised that it was also good. It was. Most of what I ate was freshly grilled on a large griddle. A garlicky olive oil was sprinkled over the top as well as lots of finely chopped parsley. We ate our vegetables with chunky, toasted bread that had also been rubbed with garlic oil as well as with a cut tomato. The combination was quite extraordinary.

2 tablespoons olive oil

2 medium zucchini (12 ounces), cut diagonally into ¼-inch-thick slices

Salt

About 2 tablespoons Spanish-Style Garlic and Parsley-Flavored Olive Oil (page 665)

1 tablespoon finely chopped fresh parsley

Set a cast-iron griddle or cast-iron frying pan over high heat. Let it get hot. Dribble just enough olive oil, about 1 tablespoon, to grease it lightly. When the oil is very hot, a matter of seconds, lay down enough zucchini slices to cover the bottom in a single layer. Do not overcrowd. Cook for about 2 minutes, or until the bottoms of the slices turn a rich medium brown. You may need to move the slices around so they all cook evenly. Turn the slices over. Cook for another 2 minutes, or until the second side turns medium brown. Remove the slices from the pan and arrange in a single layer on a large platter. Cook all the zucchini slices this way. With each batch, remember to add enough oil to keep the pan lightly greased.

When the zucchini are all cooked, lightly sprinkle salt over the slices. Dribble the flavored oil evenly over the top, sprinkle on the parsley and serve.

SERVES 4

Niloofar Haeri's
Puree of Zucchini   IRAN
Qalye Kadu

Here is a mildly spiced and unusually fresh way of cooking zucchini. Serve with breads and with dishes of beans or split peas and yogurt.

3 tablespoons olive oil

1⅓ cups finely chopped onion

3 garlic cloves, peeled and finely chopped

¼ teaspoon ground turmeric

4 medium zucchini (about 2¾ pounds), peeled and cut into ¼-inch dice

1 teaspoon salt

1 teaspoon ground cumin

⅛ teaspoon cayenne

Freshly ground black pepper

1½ teaspoons tomato paste

Put the olive oil in a medium frying pan or wide sauté pan and set over medium-high heat. When hot, put in the onion and garlic. Stir and sauté for 10 to 12 minutes, until the onion is soft. You may need to reduce the heat to prevent browning. Add the turmeric and stir once. Remove a third of the onion-garlic mixture and set aside. Add the zucchini and salt to the frying pan and return the heat to medium-high. Stir and cook for 1 to 2 minutes, or until the zucchini begins to release a little liquid. Cover, turn the heat down to low, and cook gently for 10 minutes, or until the zucchini is soft. Uncover, add the cumin, cayenne, black pepper to taste, and tomato paste. Mash the zucchini with a potato masher right in the frying pan, allowing it to cook gently as you do so. Keep cooking and mashing for a minute or two, or until you have a coarse, well-mixed puree. Add the reserved onions and mix well. Serve hot, warm, at room temperature, or chilled.

SERVES 4 TO 6

From the Ta Nissia Restaurant in Salonica

Crisp Zucchini Fritters

GREECE

Kolokithi Tiganito

In Greece these are generally served as a first course along with a yogurt salad such as Soft Yogurt Cheese with Cucumber (page 558) or Soft Yogurt Cheese with Feta (page 559) or else with the Pureed Beet Salad (page 140). You may, of course, have them as a snack with tomato ketchup. That always works! They are exquisitely crisp, the result of a neat trick that I learned in Salonica whereby the zucchini slices are first dipped in flour, then quickly in water, and then deep-fried in very hot oil.

2 medium zucchini (about 10 ounces in all)

½ teaspoon salt

Peanut or canola oil for shallow frying

1 cup unbleached all-purpose white flour

Cut off the very ends of the zucchini and then cut either round or diagonal slices that are ⅓ inch thick. Put them in a bowl. Add the salt and toss gently. Set aside for 1 hour. Drain thoroughly. Spread the slices out on a dish cloth or strong paper towel. Spread another cloth or paper towel on top and press down to dry off the slices.

Just before eating, pour the oil to a depth of ½ to ¾ inch into a large frying pan and set the pan over high heat. Give it time to heat up. Meanwhile, put the flour in a large plate and spread it out. Put some cold tap water in a bowl and keep it nearby. Dip the vegetable slices in the flour, first on one side and then the other, and then line them up against the sides of a baking tray.

The next step needs to be carried out speedily. Dip one slice at a time in the water and then put it immediately into the hot oil. Put as many slices into the hot oil as the pan will hold easily in one layer. Fry, turning when needed, for 3 to 4 minutes, or until the slices are golden brown on both sides and crisp. Remove with a slotted spoon and spread out on a plate lined with paper towels. Fry all the slices this way. Serve immediately.

SERVES 3 TO 4

Bitter Melons Stuffed with Onions and Pomegranate Seeds

Bhara Hua Karela

There is no doubt about it. Bitter melon is an acquired taste. I happen to love them. Throughout Asia, where bitter flavors are not only loved but considered medicinal, bitter gourds are a part of every child's heritage. Here they are stuffed and may be served with any Indian meal that includes legumes, breads, and yogurt relishes.

4 small bitter melons (10 ounces), 5 to
    6 inches long

1¼ teaspoons salt

¾ tablespoon *anardana* (dried pomegranate
    seeds, page 715)

1 teaspoon whole fennel seeds

½ cup finely chopped onion

⅛ to ¼ teaspoon cayenne

½ teaspoon ground cumin

½ teaspoon ground coriander

2 tablespoons peanut or canola oil

Using a paring knife, scrape the rough skins off the bitter gourd so thoroughly that almost all the ridges are removed. Cut a slit along the length of each bitter gourd, making sure not to pierce the skin on the opposite side. Rub ¼ teaspoon of salt all over the skin and the insides of each bitter gourd. When done, stand all the bitter gourds in a bowl. Set aside for 5 to 6 hours. Run each bitter gourd under running water, washing off the salt as much as possible. Pat dry.

Put the *anardana* and fennel seeds in a clean spice grinder and grind to a coarse powder. Empty into a bowl. Add the onion, cayenne, cumin, coriander, and the remaining ¼ teaspoon salt. Mix well. Stuff the bitter gourds with the spice mixture.

Put the oil in a frying pan and set over medium-low heat. Place the bitter gourds, stuffed side down, into the pan. Cook until the bitter gourds are brown on one side. Keep turning until all sides are browned and the bitter gourds are cooked through, 20 to 25 minutes.

SERVES 4

Tomatoes

These days tomatoes seem to come in all shapes and colors. I wish I could say that I cared. All I ask for is flavor and texture, and sadly, those remain elusive. Markets now have tomatoes from Holland, from Israel, from Mexico, but the best ones are our own local tomatoes, which make an appearance in the summer and then vanish for the rest of the year.

Once, on the almost barren, dry island of Santorini, a single tomato bush was pointed out to me. It seemed to be growing on sand. All its leaves were yellow. And yet, a few, very red, slightly shriveled cherry tomatoes clung to the stems. I was told to pluck one and eat it. It was extraordinary, seemingly made up of a sun-ripened essence of tomato. That is what I am always aiming to find, that tomato of my childhood, which grew in my garden and which I plucked and ate—sweet-and-sour, full of crunch and juice.

How to buy and store tomatoes: Search for the best tomatoes you can find. Red-ripe is what you want, not overripe and rotted and not pink and cottony. Once you bring the tomatoes home, leave them unrefrigerated, in a single layer in your kitchen, until they are fully ripe. Sometimes this can take a whole week or even longer.

How to peel, seed, and chop tomatoes: For certain dishes, where you want raw, diced tomatoes, you might want to peel very ripe tomatoes with a vegetable peeler or a paring knife. Otherwise, the easiest way to peel a tomato is to drop it in boiling water for 15 seconds and then peel the skin away. To seed the tomato, cut it in half crosswise. Now hold the cut side down over a bowl or sink and, with a light hand, squeeze out all the seeds. The shell is ready to be diced.

How to grate a tomato: When a coarse tomato puree is required, the easiest way to get it is to hold a ripe tomato over a bowl and grate it on the coarsest part of a grater. The skin stays in your hand while the puree collects in the bowl. Sometimes the tomato slides along the grater and does not engage with the sharp holes. In such cases all you do is cut a thin slice off the tomato. This will get it going.

From Kay at Tiffin's, Port-of-Spain
Tomato "Choka"   TRINIDAD

The chokas *of the Trinidadian Indians are so interesting in their evolution and history, much of which can only be deduced. It is likely, however, that they came with the indentured laborers drawn from the northern Indian states of Uttar Pradesh and Bihar after 1846.*

The name of this dish gives this emigration pattern away. Choka *is obviously a corruption of the Hindi word* chhownk *(which has the same meaning as* bhagaar *and* tarka—*for more on this, see tarka, page 737). This is the name for a common Indian technique used to flavor dishes: Seasonings are sprinkled into very hot oil, where they quickly intensify in taste or change character, and then the newly flavored oil as well as the seasonings are poured over a cooked food to give it an extra fillip.*

So, what in India might have been chhownka timatar *or "tomatoes with a chhownk" has now turned into Tomato* Choka *for a people who no longer speak Hindi or even understand it —forget about the hard-to-pronounce consonants like* chh—*and whose common language, along with all the other immigrants, is Caribbean English. The dishes, as well as their seasonings, are simple, giving further proof that the villages that were abandoned in the nineteenth century for an uncertain future in the Western world were poor but that as in all the villages of India even today, the food that was eaten was utterly delicious.*

In Trinidad, tomatoes are sometimes roasted very simply by sticking a fork into them at the stem end and holding them over a low flame until the skin is burnt off and the flesh turns soft. You may use that method or the oven-roasting method that I have used here.

This is sometimes eaten on bread, with lashings of Trinidadian Pepper Sauce (page 717). At other times, hard-boiled eggs are put into a dish of Tomato "Choka" and the two are eaten together. And of course, it is also eaten plain with Roti (page 448) and Spinach Bhaji (page 230) or with a dish of chickpeas.

4 red, ripe tomatoes, about 1¼ pounds

2 small garlic cloves, peeled

½ to 1 fresh hot red chile, seeds removed, cut into minute dice

1 teaspoon salt, or to taste

For the final "choka"

2 tablespoons vegetable oil (use olive oil)

2 small garlic cloves, peeled and mashed to a pulp

Preheat the oven to 450°F.

Line a baking tray with foil and lay the tomatoes on it. Bake for 25 minutes. Remove the tomatoes and put in a bowl. Let them cool off a little so they can be handled. A little liquid should have accumulated under them. Discard the liquid. Peel the tomatoes and remove the cores. Chop them coarsely and put them back in the bowl. Mash the garlic, red chile, and salt together in a mortar or on a cutting board with the flat side of a knife. Add to the tomatoes and stir to mix. Taste for the balance of seasonings.

Put the oil and crushed garlic in a small frying pan over medium-high heat. Stir until the oil heats up and the garlic turns golden. Now pour the contents of the frying pan, oil and garlic, over the tomato mixture. Serve warm, at room temperature, or chilled.

SERVES 4 TO 6

Gwen Silva's

Tomato Sambal

Takkali Sambola

A Silva family recipe, this is part condiment, part vegetable dish. It may be served with most South Asian, Middle Eastern, North African, and Mexican meals. Sri Lankans tend to make their own chili powder from dried red chiles at home. It is very red, has delicious flavor, and is not so fiery that it blows a hole through the roof of your mouth. Many specialty stores sell hot paprika. You could use that or a chile powder from an Indian, Korean, or Sri Lankan grocer as a substitute.

Use good, ripe tomatoes here. If you have access to fresh screw pine leaves (daun paan-daan/rampe), you can put in a 1-inch piece at the same time as the curry leaves.

1 pound red, ripe tomatoes, cut crosswise into thin slices

2 teaspoons salt

1½ tablespoons good-quality chili powder (i.e., powdered chiles—see recipe introduction)

6 tablespoons peanut or canola oil

4 garlic cloves, unpeeled and lightly crushed, and 4 garlic cloves, peeled and finely sliced lengthwise

15 fresh curry leaves (use holy basil or basil leaves as a different but equally interesting substitute)

1 (3-inch) cinnamon stick

2 medium onions, peeled and cut into very fine round slices

2 tablespoons fresh lime juice

1½ to 2 teaspoons sugar

Put the tomatoes on a large plate, nicely spread out in layers. Sprinkle the salt and chili powder over the top.

Put the oil in a large frying pan and set over medium-high heat. When hot, put in the 4 crushed garlic cloves. Stir and fry them until they turn dark brown. Put in the curry leaves and cinnamon. Stir once or twice and put in the onions. Stir and fry until they are golden brown. Add the sliced tomatoes and sliced garlic. Stir and cook for 2 minutes, or until the tomatoes begin to soften and are at a simmer. Lower the heat and cook gently for 15 to 20 minutes, or until the tomatoes are soft and the dish has the appearance of a pulpy sauce. Add the lime juice and sugar. Stir to mix and taste for the balance of seasonings.

Remove the cinnamon stick and whole garlic before serving.

SERVES 6

From Victor Matiya's Jerusalem Restaurant in Toronto

Sliced Tomatoes in a Tomato Sauce   PALESTINE

Bandora M'li

I do not know what it is about this simple dish, but I absolutely must have it every time I visit Toronto. I was introduced to it by Bonnie Stern, who runs a cookery school a convenient walking distance from the Jerusalem Restaurant where this Arab specialty is served. The menu there calls the dish Fried Tomatoes. They are much more than that. The delicious sauce may be soaked up with bread or any rice dish. These tomatoes may also be served with fried eggs.

2 medium tomatoes

Salt

Freshly ground black pepper

5 teaspoons olive oil

1 garlic clove, peeled and well crushed

½ to 1 teaspoon very finely chopped fresh hot green chile (jalapeños are used in the restaurant)

¾ cup canned tomato juice

1 tablespoon finely chopped fresh parsley

Take skin-thin slices off the very top and bottoms of the tomatoes and discard them. Cut the tomatoes crosswise into 3 slices each. Lightly salt and pepper the slices on both sides.

Put the oil, garlic, and green chile into a medium, nonstick frying pan set over medium-high heat. When the garlic begins to sizzle, put in the tomato slices in a single layer and fry lightly, about a minute on each side. Now put in the tomato juice and parsley and bring to a boil. Turn off the heat and serve.

SERVES 2

Tomatoes Stuffed with Lentils and Rice

Tomatoes make great containers for almost any kind of stuffing. Here I've used Cypriot Lentils with Rice. You will need just half the recipe, so just halve all the quantities; the cooking times will remain the same. The browned onions for garnishing the lentils should be saved to garnish the tops of the tomatoes. You can, if you like, mix 8 heaping tablespoons of grated Parmesan cheese with the lentils before stuffing them into the tomatoes. Serve with any greens of your choice and perhaps the Trinidadian Pumpkin (page 291).

Only 8 of the tomatoes are to be stuffed. The other 2 provide the lids.

(recipe continues)

10 firm, flat-bottomed medium-large
    tomatoes

Salt

Freshly ground black pepper

1 teaspoon sugar

½ recipe Lentils with Rice (page 63)

8 tablespoons finely chopped fresh parsley

2 tablespoons finely chopped fresh mint plus
    8 large mint leaves for garnish

1 tablespoon extra-virgin olive oil

Preheat the oven to 400°F.

Using a sharp, pointed paring knife, cut a cone-shaped cap at the stem end of 8 of the tomatoes. Using a teaspoon, scoop out all the pulp and seeds, making sure that you do not go through the shells. Sprinkle a little salt inside each of these hollowed-out tomatoes and carefully rub it on the inside walls. Let the tomatoes sit like this for 10 minutes. Now turn the tomatoes over and let them drain for another 10 minutes. Turn the tomatoes over again so they are right side up and sprinkle the insides once again with just a little salt, some pepper, and a little sugar.

Combine the Lentils with Rice, parsley, and chopped mint. Mix gently. Stuff the tomatoes with this mixture, making sure not to overstuff. Stuff all 8 tomatoes this way. Put the tomatoes in a baking tray, cut side up. Cut the remaining 2 tomatoes crosswise into ¼-inch-thick slices. Place 1 slice on top of each tomato. Sprinkle the slice with a little salt and pepper. Place a mint leaf on top of each slice and then dribble a little olive oil over the top. Place the baking tray in the oven and bake 12 to 15 minutes, or until the tomatoes have softened. Put in a serving dish carefully and top each tomato with a few crisp browned onions. Serve immediately.

SERVES 4 TO 8

Oven-Dried Tomatoes

I was recently in Australia to teach a set of cooking classes at Diane Holuigue's Melbourne cookery school, which is also her home. Before each class we sat down to a family meal. At one of the meals, a bowl of tomatoes appeared, nicely drizzled with olive oil. They had an intense, concentrated flavor and yet they were like nothing I had eaten previously. Well, these tomatoes had been dried overnight in her oven, partially dried so they were still somewhat juicy. They had none of the sharpness of the sun-dried tomatoes sold in our specialty shops and were utterly delicious, with the intense, sun-baked flavors of the tomatoes I had sampled on Santorini.

    You can oven-dry cherry tomatoes or plum tomatoes. These may then be used in salads, pasta dishes, or eaten on their own with bread. In the summer, I put them out at all meals.

    The best time for drying these tomatoes is at night. I put them in the oven before I go to sleep and they are done when I awake!

A little peanut or canola oil to brush on the
  baking tray
1 pound cherry tomatoes
¼ teaspoon salt

⅓ teaspoon sugar
1 to 2 teaspoons olive oil (you can use the
  Spanish-Style Garlic and Parsley-Flavored
  Olive Oil, page 665, if you wish)

Preheat the oven to 175°F. (or the lowest temperature on the oven).

Brush a baking tray or baking sheet lightly with oil. (A nonstick tray is ideal.) Cut each cherry tomato in half crosswise and place the halves very close to each other in a single layer on the baking tray, cut sides up. Sprinkle the salt, sugar, and olive oil over the top. Place the tray in the oven and leave it there for about 8 hours. (Check after 7.) The time can vary slightly according to the quality of the tomatoes and the oven.

The tomatoes should not dry out completely but should be chewy. If a tomato is beginning to dry out, remove it and continue with the others. These tomatoes may now be put in a container and stored in the refrigerator, where they will hold for 4 to 5 days. They can also be covered with olive oil before being refrigerated. This way they will last about 2 weeks.

ABOUT 1 CUP OVEN-DRIED CHERRY TOMATOES

Variation
Oven-Dried Plum Tomatoes

Halve 2 pounds of plum tomatoes and arrange on a prepared baking tray as above. Sprinkle with 1 teaspoon salt, ¾ teaspoon sugar, ½ teaspoon dried thyme, and 1 tablespoon of olive oil. Bake as above for 12 hours, checking after 11.

ABOUT 3 CUPS OVEN-DRIED PLUM TOMATOES

Turnips

Like daikon, turnips are excellent for pickling. In India we pickle them with mustard seeds either in water (even the water turns incredibly delicious) or in mustard oil. These spicy pickles are then enjoyed throughout the cold winter months.

They are also superb when they are stewed or gently braised, either in the western style with butter and stock or in the East Asian way with soy sauce, stock, and sugar. An excellent Indian trick with small whole turnips is to peel them, prick holes in them, and leave them to soak in salty water. This draws out a lot of the natural liquid in them and gives them more texture. The turnips are then browned and cooked in a spicy sauce. If you cannot find small turnips, you may use larger turnips cut into chunky dice.

How to buy and store turnips: There are so many varieties of turnips. For the purposes of this chapter, I have used only the regular white turnip edged with purple. In our markets, it is hard to find the root with its leaves attached. I find that such a pity as I love turnip greens and was raised with dishes where the roots and their sprouting greenery were diced small and cooked together. But roots do have a much longer life on their own, so our local markets are probably doing only what is expedient! However, most farmers markets do offer bunches of turnips complete with greens, and they are worth searching for.

Small turnips are ideal. These are best, both nutritionally and in terms of flavor, if they are consumed raw in salads and pickles. Older turnips are best cooked, but here, too, small turnips have the best taste and texture. Look for roots that have crisp, clean, bright skins. Store in the vegetable bin of your refrigerator.

How to prepare turnips: Wash them well. Rather like daikon, turnips need deep peeling, as they almost have a double skin. You may do this with a vegetable peeler or a paring knife. Sprinkling the peeled sections with salt—or else putting them in salted water—helps draw out their abundant liquid.

Turnips Braised with Soy Sauce and Sugar

Here I have combined Chinese and Japanese ways of cooking turnips. I think these go particularly well with dark greens, dried beans, and rice.

The turnips I used weighed about 8 ounces each. I used 4 of them and cut each into 8 pieces. If your turnips are larger or smaller, make the necessary adjustments.

2 tablespoons peanut oil or canola oil

2 pounds turnips, peeled and cut into 1½-inch dice

1 cup vegetable stock

2 tablespoons tamari soy sauce

1 tablespoon sugar

½ teaspoon oriental sesame oil

Put the oil in a large frying pan and set over medium-high heat. When hot, put in the turnips. Stir and fry until the turnips are lightly browned on all sides, about 5 minutes. Add the stock, soy sauce, and sugar. Bring to a boil. Cover, turn the heat down to low, and simmer gently for 15 minutes, or until the turnips are tender. Turn every now and then so the turnips color evenly. Sprinkle the sesame oil over the top and toss. These turnips may be made ahead of time and reheated.

SERVES 4 TO 6

Turnips with Yogurt and Tomato

Shaljam Lajavaab

Here the turnips have a much denser texture than those in the preceding recipe, as they are first left in salted yogurt to get rid of some of their moisture. Serve with any bean or split pea dish and a green vegetable. Rice or bread may be served on the side.

The turnips I used weighed about 8 ounces each. I used four of them and cut each into 8 pieces. If your turnips are larger or smaller, make the necessary adjustments.

The yogurt is best if it is sour. I often leave it unrefrigerated overnight to allow this to happen. (Here is a good opportunity to use up yogurt that has been sitting in the refrigerator for a while.)

Yogurt curdles as it cooks. The secret lies in boiling all the yogurt-tomato mixture away so the sauce, such as it is, clings to the turnip pieces, making them absolutely scrumptious.

1 cup plain yogurt

1 teaspoon salt

2 pounds turnips, peeled and cut into
   1½-inch dice

3 tablespoons peanut or canola oil

½ teaspoon whole cumin seeds

2 large shallots (about 1½ ounces), peeled
   and cut lengthwise into fine slivers

2 medium tomatoes (8 ounces), peeled and
   chopped

⅛ to ¼ teaspoon cayenne

Put the yogurt and salt into a large bowl. Beat lightly with a fork or whisk until the yogurt is smooth and creamy.

Pierce the turnip pieces on all sides with a fork and then put them into the bowl with the yogurt. Mix well and set aside for at least 3 hours. (You can leave the turnips in the yogurt for up to 8 hours, but refrigerate them after 3 hours.) Strain, but save the yogurt. Leave the turnips in the strainer.

Put the oil in a large, preferably nonstick frying pan and set over high heat. When hot, put in the strained turnips. Stir and fry until the turnips are lightly browned on all sides, about 5 minutes. Remove with a slotted spoon and set aside. Turn the heat down to medium-high. Quickly put in the cumin seeds. Stir once and put in the shallots. Stir and fry 1 to 2 minutes, or until the shallots are lightly browned. Put in the tomatoes and cayenne. Stir and fry for 1 minute. Put in the turnips and reserved yogurt. Bring to a boil. Cover, turn the heat to medium, and cook, covered, for 10 minutes, stirring every now and then. Now turn the heat down to low and cook another 10 minutes, stirring every now and then. Do not allow the turnips to stick to the bottom of the pan. If necessary, sprinkle a little water if they seem too dry.

SERVES 4 TO 6

Mixed Vegetables

Draupadiji's
A Delicious Puree of Mixed Vegetables INDIA
Sai Bhaji

Very often, when my husband and I want a one-pot meal, we eat a mélange of spinach, potato, carrot, beans, tomato, zucchini, and split peas. There are many versions of this dish in India. This one, which I have acquired recently, is the one I like the most. It is meant to be eaten with crusty bread (that is what they do in Sindh, where this dish is from). As we cannot get the local yeast breads here, we get a French baguette and start at one end, breaking off pieces as we pick up the spicy puree with a fork or spoon. On the side, I always have a simple salad of chopped-up tomatoes and onions dressed with salt, pepper, and lemon juice, a common standby in India.

Very few seasonings are used here, just garlic, green chile, and a lot of dill, which is the main flavoring. I bought a 5-ounce bunch of dill and after I had removed the stems and chopped the feathery leaves, I was left with 1 well-packed cup (3 ounces). Indian chana dal, *sold only by Indian grocers, has a much gentler flavor than yellow split peas, though they look similar. However, if you cannot get the first, use the second. Many people like to use an electric blender for the puree. I prefer to mash by hand to get a coarser texture.*

¼ cup peanut or olive oil

4 garlic cloves, peeled and chopped

1 fresh hot green chile, chopped (use more or
    less, as desired)

1 medium onion, peeled and finely chopped

10 ounces fresh spinach, trimmed, well
    washed in several changes of water, and
    chopped

10 green beans, cut crosswise into fine rounds

1 medium carrot, peeled, halved lengthwise
    and then cut crosswise into fine slices

1 medium potato (about 8 ounces), peeled
    and cut into small dice

2 large tomatoes (12 to 14 ounces), peeled
    (see page 300 for instructions, if needed)
    and chopped

1 medium zucchini, cut into small dice

1 very well-packed cup (3 ounces) chopped
    fresh dill

½ cup (3 ounces) *chana dal* (page 25) or yellow
    split peas

2 teaspoons salt

Put the oil, garlic, and chile into a wide, medium pan and set over medium-high heat. As the oil heats, the garlic will begin to sizzle. Stir it and when it is golden, put in the onion, spinach, green beans, carrot, potato, tomatoes, zucchini, dill, *chana dal,* and 3 cups of water. Stir and bring to a simmer. Cover, turn the heat down to low, and simmer gently for 30 minutes. Turn the heat up very slightly to medium-low, uncover partially, and continue to cook for another 30 minutes. Add the salt and mix. Now mash the vegetables and split peas with a wooden (or any other) potato masher until you have a coarse puree.

SERVES 4 TO 6

Melle Derko Samira's

Moroccan Casserole of Vegetables   MOROCCO

Tagine of Vegetables

A tagine is a round, casserole-type dish made of clay. As it sits on the top of the stove, its conical clay lid causes steam to rise and then fall gently down the sloping sides as condensation, allowing for cooking with a minimum of water. Instead, I use a casserole with an 8-cup capacity, which is roughly 8 ×8 ×2¹/₂ inches and has a lid. I place it in the oven for slow baking.

This gentle vegetable medley may be served with couscous, rice, or bread. A bean dish should be served on the side to complete the meal.

2 medium zucchini (13 ounces), cut into ¹/₈-inch-thick rounds

4 medium carrots (8 ounces), peeled and cut into ¹/₈-inch-thick rounds

1¹/₂ teaspoons peeled and very finely chopped garlic

1¹/₂ teaspoons ground cumin

1¹/₂ teaspoons paprika

2 tablespoons finely chopped fresh cilantro leaves

4 tablespoons finely chopped fresh parsley

1¹/₂ teaspoons salt

Freshly ground black pepper

2 waxy red potatoes (10 ounces), peeled and cut into ¹/₈-inch-thick rounds

¹/₂ head green cabbage (10 ounces), shredded (6 cups in volume)

1 large onion (6 ounces), cut into ¹/₈-inch rounds

2 large tomatoes (15 ounces), cut into ¹/₄-inch-thick rounds

1 medium green bell pepper (6 ounces), seeded and cut into ¹/₄-inch-thick rounds

¹/₄ cup olive oil

Set an oven rack in the middle of the oven. Preheat the oven to 350°F.

To assemble the casserole, arrange the zucchini in a single, slightly overlapping layer at the bottom of an ovenproof dish (see recipe introduction). Over this, arrange the carrots, also in an overlapping layer. Now sprinkle ¹/₄ teaspoon garlic, ¹/₄ teaspoon cumin, ¹/₄ teaspoon paprika, 1 teaspoon cilantro, 2 teaspoons parsley, ¹/₄ teaspoon salt, and pepper to taste.

(recipe continues)

Arrange the potatoes in a single overlapping layer on top of the carrots. Again sprinkle ¼ teaspoon garlic, ¼ teaspoon cumin, ¼ teaspoon paprika, 1 teaspoon cilantro, 2 teaspoons parsley, ¼ teaspoon salt, and pepper to taste over the potatoes.

Spread the cabbage on top of the potatoes and over it sprinkle ¼ teaspoon garlic, ¼ teaspoon cumin, ¼ teaspoon paprika, 1 teaspoon cilantro, 2 teaspoons parsley, ¼ teaspoon salt, and pepper to taste.

Carefully arrange the onion rounds in a single overlapping layer over the cabbage. Some of the onion rings may come apart, but try to maintain their shape as best you can. Sprinkle ¼ teaspoon garlic, ¼ teaspoon cumin, ¼ teaspoon paprika, 1 teaspoon cilantro, 2 teaspoons parsley, ¼ teaspoon salt, and pepper to taste.

Arrange the tomatoes in a single overlapping layer over the onion slices. Sprinkle ¼ teaspoon garlic, ¼ teaspoon cumin, ¼ teaspoon paprika, 1 teaspoon cilantro, 2 teaspoons parsley, ¼ teaspoon salt, and pepper to taste.

Finally, arrange the green peppers in an overlapping layer over the very top. Sprinkle ¼ teaspoon garlic, ¼ teaspoon cumin, ¼ teaspoon paprika, 1 teaspoon cilantro, 2 teaspoons parsley, ¼ teaspoon salt, and pepper to taste. Evenly pour the oil and ½ cup of water over the vegetables.

Cover and bake for 50 to 60 minutes. During the last 20 minutes, baste frequently with the juices that accumulate at the bottom. A bulb baster is ideal for this. If you don't have one, you may carefully tilt the dish, spoon up the juices, and pour them over the top. Cover the dish and put it back into the oven each time. Baste 3 to 4 times during the last 20 minutes. Serve hot.

SERVES 6

Escalivada (Salad of Broiled and Roasted Vegetables)

There is nothing more beautiful than a large platter of roasted vegetables done the Spanish way. Offer plain or toasted pieces of French bread with them or serve with one of the two Romesco Sauces (pages 669 and 670). A little vinegar may be added to the olive oil, if desired.

All the vegetables here require different roasting methods and times. I put them all in together. The small eggplants and red peppers will both grill in about 10 minutes but the eggplants need to be turned over halfway during this time. The red pepper quarters will just need to be moved around (not turned over) so their outsides char evenly. As for the onions, I turn them around for the first 10 minutes so all sides char and then, after removing all the other vegetables, I turn the oven to 350°F and cook the onions gently for another 45 minutes or until they are soft inside.

3 large red bell peppers (22 ounces)

5 small Italian or Japanese eggplants (12 ounces), about 7 inches long

3 medium onions (18 ounces)

Salt

Freshly ground black pepper

5 tablespoons olive oil (extra-virgin preferred)

2 tablespoons finely chopped parsley

Heat the broiler.

Quarter the peppers lengthwise and remove the stem and seeds. Lay the peppers, skin side up, in a baking tray. Spread the eggplants beside them. Place under the broiler, 4 to 5 inches from the heat source. Broil for 7 to 10 minutes, or until the outside skins are quite charred. Turn the eggplants over after 4 to 5 minutes of broiling. Broil the other side. For the red peppers, you will need to move them around and also turn the tray frequently so that the skins are evenly charred. Put the red peppers in a paper bag. Close the bag and set it aside for 10 minutes.

Meanwhile, put the onions under the broiler. Broil, turning frequently, for 10 minutes, or until the outside is charred. Set the oven to bake at 350°F. Bake the onions for 30 to 45 minutes, or until they have softened inside.

Peel away the eggplant skins as soon as they are cool enough to handle. Leave the eggplants whole. Peel away the red pepper skins when they have finished resting in the paper bag. Peel the onions and cut or break into quarters.

Arrange all the vegetables in a single layer on a large platter. Sprinkle with salt and pepper to taste. Dribble the olive oil over the top. Garnish with parsley and serve at room temperature.

SERVES 4 TO 6

Shamsi Davis'

Persian Sweet-and-Sour "Ratatouille" of Fruit and Vegetables

IRAN

Taskabab Bedunay Gosht

A sweet-and-sour mélange of fresh fruit (quince and apple), dried fruit (apricots and prunes), and fresh vegetables (onions, carrots, tomatoes, eggplant, and zucchini), this delightful Persian creation may be baked and served in the same casserole dish. On the other hand, if you really wish to impress, you may bake the dish in a nonstick, oven- and flameproof pan and once done, slip the now molded mélange onto a large, round serving platter. The diameter of your cooking utensil, whatever you use, should be around 10 inches and the height around 4 inches. You may halve the recipe and use a smaller pan, if you prefer.

I like to serve this with any dish of chickpeas, some flatbreads (or rice), and a generous dollop of spread made with feta cheese.

If you do not wish to make the Persian Spice Mix, just combine ½ teaspoon ground cinnamon, ½ teaspoon ground cardamom, and ¼ teaspoon ground cumin.

¼ cup olive oil

2 very large onions (1¼ pounds), peeled and cut into ⅛-inch-thick rounds

Salt (about 2 teaspoons in all)

Freshly ground black pepper

3 garlic cloves, peeled and very finely chopped

1 eggplant (1 pound), peeled and cut crosswise into ¼-inch-thick round slices

2 large quinces (about 1¼ pounds) or the same weight in green cooking apples, peeled, quartered, cored, and then cut into ⅛-inch-thick slices

2 medium zucchini (about 14 ounces), cut crosswise at a diagonal into ⅛-inch-thick oval slices

3 medium carrots, peeled and cut crosswise at a slight diagonal into ⅛-inch-thick oval slices

2 large tomatoes (1¼ pounds), cut crosswise into ⅛-inch-thick rounds

2 large boiling potatoes (about 14 ounces), peeled and cut crosswise into ⅛-inch-thick rounds

16 dried apricots, very coarsely chopped

12 pitted prunes, very coarsely chopped

1¼ teaspoons Persian Spice Mix (page 706 or see recipe introduction)

¼ teaspoon ground turmeric

1 tablespoon fresh lime or lemon juice

1 cup tomato juice (canned will do)

2 tablespoons very finely chopped parsley

Put the oil in a flame- and ovenproof nonstick pan or casserole-type dish. Cover the bottom with a slightly overlapping layer of onions. (Some onion slices will be left over.) Sprinkle salt, pepper, and some chopped garlic over this first layer. Cover the onions with a slightly overlapping layer of eggplant slices. (Not all the eggplant slices will be used up.) Sprinkle salt, pepper, and a little garlic over this second layer. Cover with a slightly overlapping layer of quince and sprinkle on more salt, pepper, and garlic. Follow this with an overlapping layer of zucchini. Sprinkle salt, pepper, and garlic over the top. Next, add a layer of carrots. These slices will not overlap. Sprinkle on the salt, pepper, and garlic. The next layer should alternate the leftover eggplant and onion slices. Sprinkle with salt, pepper, and garlic. Now cover with a slightly overlapping layer of tomatoes and more salt, pepper, and garlic. Then follow with a slightly overlapping layer of potatoes. Sprinkle with salt, pepper, and the remaining garlic. Scatter the apricots and prunes evenly over the top. Sprinkle lightly with just salt and pepper.

Preheat the oven to 350°F.

Combine the Persian spice mix, turmeric, and lime juice in a small bowl. Add the tomato juice and mix again.

Put the pan or casserole dish over medium heat. Allow it to heat up for 10 minutes. The onions will pick up a little color. Now pour the tomato juice mixture evenly over the top. Cover the pan or casserole dish and put it in the oven for 1¾ hours.

Remove from the oven. Uncover and let the mélange settle for 10 minutes. Now find a plate that will just fit inside your pan or casserole dish. Upturn the plate and place it on top of the fruit and vegetables. While pressing down on the plate slightly, tilt the cooking pan enough so you can pour out all the accumulated liquid into a smaller saucepan. Boil down the sauce until you have about 1 cup. Taste for salt, adding more if you need it.

If you are serving this Persian "ratatouille" in the casserole dish, just sprinkle parsley over the top and take it to the table. The sauce may be passed on the side. If you wish to serve it like a "cake," put a large plate over the pan and then quickly turn the pan upside down so the vegetables land in the plate. Now put a second large serving plate very firmly over the vegetables and quickly flip one more time so the prunes and apricots are on top again. (Tidy up if there are slight mishaps.) Sprinkle the parsley over the top and serve. The sauce may be passed on the side.

SERVES 6 TO 8

Mixed Grilled Vegetables, Indian Style

INDIAN-AMERICAN

Everyone in my family loves to barbecue. Here is one of the dishes I enjoy in the summer. I came up with the marinade a few years ago when I was preparing an outdoor dinner for a large party. It requires a mixture of vegetables with different textures and colors plus some cheese. Indian-style Homemade Cheese Flavored with Black Pepper, Roasted Cumin Seeds, and Roasted Ajwain Seeds (page 563) is ideal, but plain Homemade Indian Cheese (page 561) or, in a pinch, a feta or goat cheese will do. While any Indian-style cheese requires marination, the European-style cheeses, which are sour, salty, and well flavored, do not and may be put directly on the grill.

For the vegetables I like to use green and red peppers, some cherry tomatoes, both broccoli and cauliflower, some fresh shiitake or portobello mushrooms, zucchini, pumpkin or hard squash, potatoes, snow peas, and part of a large onion. All the vegetables need some sort of preparation, with a few needing boiling or parboiling. You will need to marinate the vegetables for 3 to 4 hours, though longer does not hurt.

With this, I like to serve a chickpea dish and some good crusty bread.

For the marinade

2 tablespoons red wine vinegar

1 tablespoon Dijon mustard

1½ tablespoons sugar

1½ teaspoons salt

2 tablespoons Tabasco sauce

2 tablespoons peeled and finely chopped fresh ginger

1 tablespoon ground roasted cumin seeds (page 724)

1 tablespoon peeled and finely chopped fresh garlic

¼ cup tomato juice (canned will do)

4 tablespoons chopped fresh cilantro

You also need

4 pieces of peeled pumpkin (or any hard winter squash), each about 1½ inches square

4 chunky cauliflower florets

4 chunky broccoli florets

4 snow peas

1 large potato, freshly boiled in its jacket, peeled, and quartered lengthwise

4 fresh large shiitake mushrooms, stems removed

¼ very large onion, peeled and its layers separated

1 medium red pepper, quartered lengthwise, seeds and veins removed

1 medium green pepper, quartered lengthwise, seeds and veins removed

1 medium zucchini, cut crosswise at a slight diagonal into ½-inch-thick slices

4 cherry tomatoes

4 pieces of Homemade Cheese Flavored with Black Pepper, Roasted Cumin Seeds, and Roasted *Ajwain* Seeds (page 563), each about 1½ inches square

Put all the marinade ingredients into an electric blender. Blend until you have a smooth paste. Strain and set aside.

Bring a large pot of lightly salted water to a rolling boil. When boiling, put in the pumpkin pieces. Twenty seconds later, put in the cauliflower and broccoli. Twenty seconds after that, put in the snow peas. Boil rapidly for 10 more seconds and drain thoroughly.

Spread all the vegetables and cheese pieces out in a large, stainless steel roasting pan, or a large lasagna-type dish, or a large, slightly deep platter. Pour the marinade evenly over the top. Massage the vegetables and cheese very gently with the marinade. Cover with plastic wrap and refrigerate for 3 to 4 hours (or even overnight).

An hour or so before eating, get your charcoals heated up and set the grill 5 to 6 inches from the heat source. Once the charcoal has turned ashen in color, put the potatoes and pumpkin on the grill. Next, add the cauliflower, broccoli, mushroom caps (upturn them), zucchini, the larger onion sections (discard the smaller ones), and the peppers (skin side down). Keep moving and turning the vegetables so they cook evenly. As soon as the vegetables get done, start to remove them. Put the cheese, tomatoes, and snow peas on the grill last. As soon as the cheese, tomatoes, and snow peas get a few brown spots, they are ready. Arrange the vegetables and cheese on a platter and serve immediately.

SERVES 4

Savory Fruit Dishes

Many fruits are used in what might be called main or side dishes. Among these are mangoes, pineapples, and plantains. I've included a few of my favorites in this section.

MANGOES

There are so many varieties, each with its own taste, texture, and color. Most varieties in the northern hemisphere ripen in the summer, from late April to July, so that would be the best time to buy them. Generally, mango skins are green when raw and turn yellow to red as they ripen. However, it is important to know that in some varieties, the skin stays green even when the mango is fully ripe.

In this book, mangoes have been used in three of their forms: unripe, semi-ripe, and fully ripe.

Unripe mango: This has dark green skin and greenish-white or white flesh that is very hard and sour. The stone in the center, while fairly hard, may be cut with a sharp knife. It often separates into two parts. The outside wall of the stone stays attached to the flesh but the inside "nut" often dislodges and may be discarded. It is this unripe mango that is used for mango chutneys and mango pickles. (See the section on Sauces, Fresh Chutneys, and Condiments page 658.) Sometimes these mangoes are peeled and sometimes they are not. If they are meant to be used unpeeled, scrub them well and then dry them off before use. These mangoes are sold only by Indian grocers and can vary in size from small ones the size of prunes to large ones the size of grapefruit.

Semiripe mangoes: Here the flesh has started to turn yellow and sweet but is still hard. These mangoes are good for certain cooked dishes but should not be eaten raw as their taste is still undeveloped. You may, if you like, serve them raw the Thai way, with a dip that is a mixture of sugar, salt, black pepper, and cayenne, giving back to the mango some of the intensity of flavor it lacks. I have to add that many chefs in the United States—even some of the best ones—use tasteless semiripe mangoes in dishes that cry out for fully ripe ones.

Fully ripe mango: The flesh here is yellow or yellowish orange, soft, sweet, juicy, and, at its best, smooth-textured and nonfibrous, rather like a meltingly soft peach.

In the West, mangoes are generally sold hard and underripe. (I do not refer to them as semiripe as the degree of ripeness varies.) Here it is good to know that even in their land of origin, which is probably India, mangoes are always picked underripe and are meant to ripen off the tree. In India, as in most of southern and southeastern Asia, the shopkeepers often do the job for you in baskets lined with straw. In the West, we have to do the job ourselves.

Buying and storing mangoes: When buying mangoes, smell them at the stem end, and if they seem to have the potential of being sweet, make the purchase. You will be taking a bit of a chance, but if it works out once, look for the same variety again. When you get home, wrap the hard mango in newspaper and put it in a basket or an open cardboard box. (Do not refrigerate it.) You can ripen several mangoes together in this way, wrapping each one separately in newspaper first. In Thai villages, baskets of mangoes are left to ripen in straw under the bed. When the perfume becomes overwhelming, the household knows that the mangoes are ready to be eaten! Examine your mangoes every day. They should eventually yield very slightly to the touch, but should *not* have black spots on them. You may now refrigerate the mangoes.

To peel and cut a mango: A green, unripe mango and even a semiripe one may be peeled with a peeler, but a ripe mango is best peeled with a paring knife. The mango usually has two flatter sides. Cut a thick slice lengthwise off each of these sides as close to the stone as you can. Now cut 2 slices off the sides of the stone, as close to it as possible. You can now dice the slices as required.

PLANTAINS

Plantains, which look like large bananas, are found everywhere in the Tropics and, whether green or ripe, are always cooked before being eaten. Rich in potassium, vitamin C, and good carbohydrates, they are a healthy addition to our diets. I love their starchy texture and, as they ripen, their increasingly sweet-and-sour flavor.

In much of the West, they are sold by South Asian, Latin American, and Caribbean grocers. I know one West Indian grocer in Brooklyn who lines them up according to ripeness—or according to color, which is the same thing. At one end are the very green, unripe plantains. Next are the barely ripe ones, which are a dull yellow, and then there are the very ripe ones, which are almost black. Of course there are all the stages in between as the plantains keep ripening.

Green plantains: These are like starchy, slightly glutinous potatoes in their taste and texture. Very little sweetness has developed in them at this early stage. They need to be peeled with a knife, cut as needed, and then used quickly or else put in water as they begin to darken, just as potatoes do. Green plantains make perfect plantain chips, which are quite delicious. Great discipline is required to eat them in small quantities! They may also be diced and boiled in salted water and then used in stir-fries, curries, soups, and salads. Wonderful soups are served on the wharf in Port of Spain, Trinidad, containing chunks of plantains. Their cooking time is not unlike that of potatoes. Plantains cut in 1/2-inch dice and boiled like potatoes will be done in about 15 minutes. In South India, well-scrubbed plantains are sometimes diced, skin and all, boiled, and put into dozens of coconut- or yogurt-flavored curries.

Barely ripe plantains: These yellowish ones (with a few black patches), may be shallow-fried, deep-fried, sautéed, or baked in their skins. These have already begun to develop a sweet-and-sour taste. I like nothing better than to cut them into "fingers" and sauté them in just a little oil. They cook quickly this way and are quite delicious. Yellow plantains peel almost like bananas, though you do need to start them off with a paring knife and use the paring knife in odd places whenever the peeling gets difficult. Another way to peel them is to cut the ends off and then cut the plantain into 3 equal sections crosswise. Peel each section separately: Cut a slit lengthwise that goes through just the skin from top to bottom. Now fold the skin away, going around the flesh.

Ripe black plantains: These are the sweetest of all. They can generally be peeled just like a banana. Even though they are very ripe, unlike bananas they will retain their shape well in cooking and may be sliced and browned in a little butter or oil. They may also be used in desserts.

PINEAPPLES

Even though pineapples were introduced to Asia from the New World and were initially an object more of curiosity than love (South Indians called them the "jack-fruit of the donkey"), they seem to have taken hold, particularly in the cuisines of Malaysia and Singapore. Here, the juice of sour, unripe pineapples is often used in curry sauces while ripe pineapples are not only eaten out of hand but cooked.

How to buy a pineapple: Smell it. It should smell sweet. Look at its color—the yellower it is, the riper it will be. Feel its very top, near the leaves, and its bottom—it should have a little give. Make sure that there are no soft, mushy, rotten patches.

How to peel and prepare a pineapple: To peel the pineapple, lay it down and cut off its very top with the leaves and slice off the bottom. Now stand it up again and, using a large knife, peel downward in strips. There will still be some dark "eyes" left. To remove these "eyes," you may either remove each eye separately with a corer (like a potato corer) or—and I think this is much easier—remove the eyes in diagonal, V-shaped strips. For those who have never done this, I will explain further. The eyes run in a kind of pattern, a pattern that is somewhat in the eye of the beholder. The pattern that most people choose to see conveniently runs diagonally, in slightly swirling curves. Holding a large knife at a slight angle with the sharp end of the blade facing left, cut from the right of a row of eyes to a depth of about ⅓ inch. Now move the knife to the left of the row of eyes. Hold the knife at an angle so the sharp end of the blade faces somewhat to the right. Cut again to the same depth. You should now be able to remove the whole row of eyes. Keep doing this until all eyes are removed. Now stand the pineapple up again and cut it lengthwise into 4 to 6 parts. Cut off the hard cores, which run along the center. Lay each wedge down and cut it crosswise into slices.

From the Rasa Restaurant in London

Yogurt with Plantain and Mango INDIA

Moru Kachiathu

South Indians love cooling yogurt dishes, which they eat with plain rice. The yogurt is generally quite thinned out and watery. Sometimes buttermilk is used instead of yogurt. To eat such a flowing, liquid meal, I generally find it much easier to put the soupy yogurt in a bowl, add a little plain rice to it, and then eat the whole thing with a spoon. It makes a perfect summer meal.

This is my version of a specialty served at the Rasa restaurant in London. This all-vegetarian establishment concentrates on foods from the South Indian state of Kerala.

The ideal plantain to use here is a yellow one that has a few black marks on it, although a green or semigreen one will do. You will need about 3 inches of the plantain, peeled and cut into ¾-inch dice (see page 317 for details).

Mangoes come in many sizes. What is most important is that the mango should be fully ripe and have as little fiber as possible. (At the Rasa restaurant, where this dish is served all year round, slices of canned Indian Alphonso mangoes are used.) I bought a large, delicious, 1-pound mango and used about half of it.

If you like, you may do without the plantain and use all mango instead. Just double the quantity of mango.

3 inches of yellow plantain, peeled and cut into ¾-inch dice

1½ cups plain yogurt

½ teaspoon salt

1 tablespoon peanut or canola oil

1 teaspoon *chana dal* or yellow split peas

1 teaspoon whole brown mustard seeds

2 dried hot red chiles, halved

15 fresh curry leaves (use fresh basil leaves as an interesting alternative)

1 medium shallot, peeled and cut into fine slivers

3 thin slices of peeled fresh ginger, cut into fine shreds

1 cup (4 to 5 ounces) peeled mango, cut into ¾-inch dice (page 316)

Put the diced plantain into a small pan with water to cover well and bring to a boil. Cover, turn the heat down to low, and cook about 15 minutes, or until the plantain is tender. Drain.

Put the yogurt in a bowl and beat lightly with a fork or whisk until smooth and creamy. Slowly add 1 cup of water and the salt. Stir to mix.

Put the oil in a small frying pan and set over medium heat. When hot, put in the *chana dal.* Stir until the grains just start to turn reddish. Put in the mustard seeds. As soon as the seeds begin to pop, a matter of seconds, put in the red chiles. Stir once and put in the curry leaves. Stir once or twice and put in the shallot and ginger shreds. Turn the heat to medium-low. Stir and fry the shallots and ginger for 2 minutes, or until golden. Pour the oil and spices into the yogurt and stir to mix. Add the diced plantain and mango and stir to mix. Serve at room temperature or chilled.

SERVES 4

Yogurt with Mango and Coconut

INDIA

Manga Pacchadi

As in the following recipe, this is made with thinned-out yogurt or buttermilk. It is eaten in its Indian state of origin, Kerala, with rice and other bean and vegetable dishes. You may also serve it in a bowl all by itself.

I got this recipe from an Indian who has settled in America. She often makes it with canned Indian Alphonso mangoes (sold by Indian grocers) or even with canned or very ripe fresh peaches. Of course all canned fruit needs to be drained thoroughly first.

I used 1 large (1 pound) mango here. Since you need chunky pieces, it is best to cut the mango slices (see page 316 if you need directions) into roughly 1½-inch squares.

4 tablespoons unsweetened desiccated
    coconut

⅛ teaspoon ground turmeric

½ teaspoon whole cumin seeds

2 whole dried hot red chiles, broken up

¾ teaspoon salt

1 tablespoon peanut or canola oil

1 teaspoon whole brown mustard seeds

4 to 5 whole fenugreek seeds

1¾ cups (9 ounces) peeled and diced mango
    (1½-inch squares)

1½ cups plain yogurt

Put a small cast-iron pan over medium heat. When it is hot, put in the coconut. Stir it around until it browns slightly. Put in the turmeric, stir once, and empty the roasted coconut into a plate. Wipe off the frying pan and put it back on the heat. Put in the cumin seeds and chiles. Stir them around just until they turn a shade darker. Put them on top of the coconut. Allow to cool slightly and then put these seasonings into an electric coffee grinder or other spice grinder. Grind as finely as possible. Put this mixture into a small pan with ½ cup of water and ¼ teaspoon salt and bring to a boil. Turn the heat down to medium-low and simmer somewhat vigorously for 6 to 7 minutes, or until the mixture has thickened.

Heat the oil in a medium frying pan over medium-high heat. When hot, put in the mustard seeds. As soon as the mustard seeds begin to pop, a matter of seconds, put in the fenugreek seeds. Stir once and put in the diced mango. Stir and cook for 1 to 2 minutes and then pour in the coconut mixture. Stir once and turn off the heat. Allow to cool.

Meanwhile, put the yogurt in a bowl. Beat lightly with a fork or whisk until smooth and creamy. Slowly add 1 cup of water and ½ teaspoon salt. Stir to mix.

When the mango-coconut mixture has cooled, put it into the bowl with the yogurt and mix. Serve at room temperature or chilled.

SERVES 4

From Tiffin's, Port of Spain

Trinidadian Mango Curry

TRINIDAD

Curry Mango

Somewhere between a curry and a sweet chutney, this dish may be served with all South Asian, Malay-style, and Middle Eastern meals.

You need half-ripe mangoes here. Since these are what most commonly pass for mangoes in the Western world, they should not be hard to find. Each mango should be hard with yellow or pale orange flesh.

For the curry powder, I like to use Bolst's hot version. Ready-made amchar masala *is sold by Caribbean grocers, though you can easily make your own and store it.*

1 medium onion, peeled and chopped

3 garlic cloves, peeled and chopped

1 to 4 fresh hot green chiles, chopped

4 teaspoons curry powder

2 teaspoons *amchar masala* (page 706)

1 teaspoon ground cumin

¼ cup peanut or canola oil

3 half-ripe mangoes (about 1 pound each), peeled, the flesh taken off the stone and cut into ¾-inch squares

5 tablespoons dark brown sugar

1½ teaspoons salt

Put the onion, garlic, and green chiles into an electric blender. Add 4 to 5 tablespoons of water and blend until you have a smooth paste. Set aside.

Combine the curry powder, *amchar masala,* and cumin in a small bowl. Add 4 tablespoons of water, mix, and set aside.

Heat the oil in a large, nonstick frying pan over high heat. When hot, put in the paste from the blender. Stir and fry for 8 minutes, or until it has browned a bit. Turn the heat to medium and put in the curry powder paste. Stir for a minute and put in the mango pieces. Stir once or twice to mix. Now put in 1½ cups of hot water, the sugar, and salt and bring to a simmer. Stir now and then and simmer gently, uncovered, for 15 minutes.

SERVES 4 TO 6

Malaysian Pineapple Curried with Cinnamon and Star Anise

Pineapple Pacchadi

Even though pacchadis *originated in South India and in their motherland are fruit- or vegetable-based yogurt dishes, once they traveled East with migrants, they began to take new forms. This half relish, half curry, is one of them. It has no yogurt in it at all. This may well be because many East Asians, being lactose-intolerant, have no milk-based dishes in their culture. What this* pacchadi *does have is a sweet-and-sour taste and a pronounced aroma of cinnamon, cardamom, star anise, and cloves.*

I used half of a large fresh pineapple here. Once the pineapple had been peeled, cored, and cut, I had 4 cups (1¼ pounds). You may easily double the recipe. Remember that when you are cutting the pineapple in halves and quarters, you should cut lengthwise (see page 318 for details). If you cannot get fresh pineapple, you may use canned slices that have been quartered. You will probably need less sugar as the slices are generally very sweet already.

In Malaysia, whole fresh hot red chiles are used in the spice paste. As they are not always easy for me to find, I used 2 dried hot red chiles, but they need to be softened first in order to be ground properly.

2 dried hot red chiles

5 medium shallots, peeled and chopped

1 (1-inch) piece of fresh ginger, peeled and finely chopped

2 garlic cloves, peeled and chopped

4 tablespoons peanut or canola oil

½ of a large peeled, prepared fresh pineapple, cut into wedges (page 318) and left to drain in a colander

2 (2-inch) cinnamon sticks

6 whole cardamom pods

2 pieces broken off a star anise flower

3 to 4 whole cloves

2 tablespoons superfine sugar

2 tablespoons fresh lemon juice

¾ teaspoon salt

Put the chiles in a small bowl with 5 tablespoons of hot water and either zap them in the microwave for 2 minutes or let them soak for 3 hours until they are soft.

Empty the chiles and their soaking liquid into an electric blender. Add the shallots, ginger, and garlic and blend, pushing down with a rubber spatula, if necessary, until you have a smooth paste.

Put 3 tablespoons of oil in a large frying pan and set over high heat. When hot, put in the drained pineapple. Fry, turning now and then, until all slices are lightly browned, 8 to 9 minutes. Remove the pineapple pieces with a slotted spoon and keep in a bowl. Turn the heat down to medium-high, add the remaining table-spoon of oil, and put in the cinnamon, cardamom, star anise, and cloves. Stir a few times and put in the paste from the blender. Stir and cook on medium-high heat for 4 minutes, or until the paste browns a bit. Turn off the heat. While the paste is still hot, put back the pineapple slices. Add the sugar, lemon juice, and salt and stir to mix. Serve hot, lukewarm, or at room temperature.

SERVES 3 TO 4

Sautéed Yellow Plantain   MOST OF THE TROPICS

Barely ripe yellow plantains with a few black marks are generally cut into fingers and shallow-fried in almost every tropical nation that I have traveled in. Instead of shallow-frying, I sauté them in just a few teaspoons of olive oil in a nonstick pan. Because of the natural sugar in them, they brown and caramelize beautifully. I love their sweet-sour flavor and their starchy, chewy texture.

In Latin America, they are generally eaten with rice and beans. I have also seen them served for Sunday brunches with eggs. They also make a perfect accompaniment to a meal of salads. Very often, in the summer, I make lunches that consist of a variety of salads. Some salads are of Mediterranean origin—I almost always have roasted peppers and Tabbouleh (page 424). Some salads, such as the ones made with yogurt, are Indian. I would certainly have some tomato salad, and something made with eggplants. I almost always add these sautéed plantains to this spread.

When buying the plantain, look for one that has a yellowish color (it will be a dark, dull yellow, not like that of an eating banana, with some dark, blackish patches) and a fairly firm texture. Do not get one that is all black.

1 barely ripe but firm plantain

2 to 3 teaspoons olive oil

Salt

Freshly ground black pepper

With a sharp paring knife, cut off the stem end of the plantain. Start peeling it downward with a knife and then try and pull the skin off in strips. Use a knife wherever the skin is firmly attached. Cut the plantain crosswise into 3 equal sections. Now cut each section lengthwise into 4 "fingers."

Put the oil in a medium nonstick frying pan and set over medium heat. When very hot, put in the plantain pieces in a single layer. As one side turns a rich reddish-gold, turn it over. Keep sautéing until all sides are golden red, 6 to 7 minutes. Remove from the pan with a slotted spatula, drain on paper towels, and put in a serving dish. Sprinkle lightly with salt and pepper and serve hot.

SERVES 2 TO 3

Grains

Barley   325

Buckwheat   328

Corn   332
   Dried Corn and Hominy 337
   Polenta   341
   Corn Flours and Meal   348

Millet   357

Oats and Oat Flour   361

Quinoa   366

Rice   370
   Rice with Spices   379
   Rice with Vegetables   383
   Rice with Fruit or Dairy   396
   Rice with Beans   399
   Risotto   405
   Rice Flour   411

Wheat and Spelt Wheat   416
   Wheat and Spelt Berries   420
   Bulgur   423
   Wheat Flatbreads   429
   Sindhi Flatbreads and Bakes   451
   Wheat and Semolina Flour Breads   460
   Pancakes   466
   Noodles and Pasta   474
   Semolina "Risottos"   488
   Couscous   494
   Wheat Gluten/Seitan   505

Wild Rice   506

It was the cultivation of grains that civilized man, forcing even the most rootless to seek permanent residence. As I looked at a four-thousand-year-old furrowed field in the West Indian desert of Rajasthan, I had a clear sense not only of my own past but of our endless toil to feed ourselves in ever better ways. Grains and beans sustained us then, just as grains and beans sustain much of the world today. Even the most avid meat eaters of the West are being forced to rethink what they are consuming, based on the new food pyramid presented by nutritional experts, in which grains form the solid base. We have come full circle.

This chapter takes a close look at the major grains—wheat, rice, and corn—and at some less-used grains as well. Corn reigns in the Americas, wheat lies at the heart of many European, West Asian, and North Indian meals, while rice belongs to Asia. Of course, there is much intermarriage and cross-fertilization.

You will find here the most exquisite Irani rice dishes with saffron-colored potato crusts and flavoring of dried limes and barberries as well as simple ways to cook the elegant Chinese black rice that gives off purple-black juices as if it were a crushed blueberry. There are South Indian pancakes made with easy, non–South Indian batters and new breads with pistachios and cardamom.

It is best to begin. I proceed alphabetically.

Barley

Perhaps the most ancient of grains, barley is today used in the West mostly in soups and of course in the making of beers and whiskeys. In Asia, I have seen it used in other ways. Koreans, who probably had no rice at all in their early history, often cook a flattened barley with rice, combining their past with their present. Their daily infusion is barley tea, made out of whole barley grains that have been toasted (you may buy these from a Korean grocer—ask for *bori cha*). In Bhutan, roasted barley flour, *tsampa,* is eaten with a salty, souplike tea enriched with yak's butter.

Pearled barley: This is the type of barley most commonly found in most Western supermarkets. A highly polished grain that has lost a lot of its nutrients, including the germ, it is used most frequently in soups. Although it takes only about 30 minutes to become edible, it is generally allowed to simmer much longer to a more melting texture. The organic pearled barley sold in health food shops has a little more bran on it and must cook about 1 hour to become tender. This is the one I mostly use.

To cook pearled barley: Put 1 cup of barley in a heavy saucepan, add 3 cups of water, and leave to soak for 1 hour. Add 1 teaspoon of salt and bring to a boil. Cover, turn the heat down to very low, and cook for 1 hour. Makes 4 to 6 cups.

You may eat pearled barley by itself, but I find it heavy going. I usually make a batch to mix into soups and stews over the course of several days. It keeps very well in the refrigerator.

Pressed barley: Available only in Korean shops, it looks like rolled oats and once soaked for 30 minutes, cooks happily along with soaked and drained rice.

Barley with Spinach and Shallots

Here I have cooked the barley with spinach using a technique I learned in Greece. I often serve it with a large baked potato over which I dole out either a mushroom or a tomato sauce (for the mushroom sauce see the mushroom ragout in Fettuccine with a Mushroom Ragout, page 484; the two tomato sauces are on pages 679 and 680). You could also serve it with Stuffed Baby Eggplants (page 184).

I bought a little more than 2 pounds of spinach for this recipe and after trimming was left with 1¾ pounds. I left the leaves whole but trimmed away the stems.

You will need cooked barley here. If it is cold from being in the refrigerator, just break up the lumps and lightly separate the grains.

Salt

1¾ pounds trimmed and well-washed spinach
    leaves

5 tablespoons olive oil

2 large shallots (3 ounces in all), peeled and
    cut into fine half rings

½ cup cooked organic pearled barley
    (page 325)

1 cup vegetable stock

1½ tablespoons fresh lemon juice

Salt as needed

Freshly ground black pepper

Bring 5 quarts water to a rolling boil. Add 1 tablespoon salt and stir to mix. Drop in the spinach leaves and bring to a boil again. Boil rapidly for 2 to 3 minutes or until the leaves are completely wilted. Drain. Run under cold water and, with a light hand, squeeze out most of the water. Separate the leaves and set aside in a colander.

Put the oil in a large sauté pan or frying pan and set over medium heat. When hot, put in the shallots. Sauté the shallots for about a minute or until they soften. Stir in the spinach and barley. Add the stock, stir, and bring to a simmer. Cover, turn heat to low, and simmer gently for 5 minutes. Uncover, add the lemon juice, and taste for salt, adding some if you need it. Turn the heat up and boil away some (but not all) of the liquid; a thick sauce should remain. Add some black pepper, stir, and serve.

SERVES 4

Barley Stew

This cold Caucasian-style barley stew can be made very easily if you have some cooked barley in the refrigerator.

1 tablespoon olive oil

3 mushrooms, thinly sliced lengthwise

2 scallions (white and green parts), cut into fine rounds

1 small carrot, peeled and cut into ¼-inch rounds

1 celery stalk, cut crosswise into ¼-inch slices

3 cups vegetable stock

1 medium tomato (6 ounces), peeled, seeded, and chopped (page 300)

½ cup cooked organic pearled barley (page 325), well crumbled so there are no lumps

Salt and freshly ground black pepper

¾ cup plain yogurt

1 tablespoon finely chopped fresh dill

Put the oil in a medium saucepan and set over medium-high heat. When hot, put in the mushrooms. Stir for a minute, or until they are shiny. Now put in the scallions, carrot, and celery. Stir for 2 minutes, then add the vegetable stock, tomato, and barley and bring to a boil. Cover, turn the heat down to low, and simmer for 15 minutes. Add salt and black pepper as needed. Stir to mix and allow to cool completely.

Put the yogurt in a bowl and beat lightly with a fork until creamy. Slowly add about 4 tablespoons of the broth from the stew. Now pour the yogurt into the pan and stir. Taste again for salt. Add the dill, mix, and serve at room temperature or chilled.

SERVES 2

Japanese Rice with Sesame Seeds, Nori, Mushrooms, and Pressed Barley   KOREA
Honsik Bab

This is a simple rice that may be served with an omelet and Stir-Fried Chinese Chives (page 169) or by itself with a crisp salad.

    This tastes best if the sesame seeds are freshly roasted.

(recipe continues)

2 cups Japanese short-grain rice

½ cup pressed barley

1 tablespoon peanut or canola oil

2 medium white mushrooms, thinly sliced

Salt

1 sheet nori

1 tablespoon roasted sesame seeds (page 734)

Wash the rice in several changes of water and then set aside in a strainer to drain for 1 hour.

Wash the barley in several changes of water. Drain and return to a bowl. Cover generously with water and set aside for 30 minutes. Drain.

Put the oil in a heavy pan and set over medium-high heat. When hot, put in the mushrooms. Stir for a minute, or until the mushrooms are shiny, sprinkle a little salt over the top, and stir. Add the rice, barley, and 2½ cups of water. Cover tightly and bring to a boil. When you see the steam escaping from under the lid, turn the heat down to very low and cook for 20 minutes. Turn the heat up to high for just a minute and then remove the pan from the heat. Let the pan sit, covered and undisturbed, for another 15 minutes.

Meanwhile, wave the sheet of nori over a flame to toast it briefly on both sides. Then cut it into fine strips that are about 1 inch long. When the rice is ready, gently fold in the nori and sesame seeds. Serve hot.

SERVES 4 TO 6

Buckwheat

Buckwheat, which is not officially classified as a grain at all but as an herb, most probably originated in central Asia. In our world today, it is eaten in many parts of Europe (think of blini pancakes and kasha—cracked buckwheat—in Russia, buckwheat crepes in Brittany, France, and buckwheat polenta in northern Italy).
It is most popular in the United States in the form of spongy pancakes that are devoured happily by the entire nation with lots of butter and maple syrup. In East Asia, it is mostly made into noodles that are eaten with dips, sauces, and broths.

Most health food shops sell triangular kernels of whole buckwheat as well as buckwheat flour. Buckwheat noodles are available from Japanese and Korean grocers.

Buckwheat is an excellent source of magnesium, potassium, zinc, vitamin B16, iron, folic acid, and calcium as well as lysine. It is very easy to digest, making it a grain that older people can eat as well.

Store buckwheat, both the grain and the flour, in airtight containers in a cool, dry place.

Plain Whole Buckwheat

Serve this in place of rice or potatoes.

1 cup peanut or canola oil

1 cup whole buckwheat

½ teaspoon salt

Put the oil in a heavy pan and set over medium heat. When hot, put in the buckwheat. Stir and roast the grains until they are fragrant, 2½ to 3 minutes. Add 2 cups of water and the salt and bring to a boil. Cover tightly, turn the heat down to very low, and simmer gently for 30 minutes. Turn off the heat and let the pan sit, covered, for another 15 minutes. Fluff up the buckwheat and serve.

SERVES 4

Stir-Fried Buckwheat

Buckwheat stir-fried in the South Indian manner is spicy and very good. Serve it with yogurt relishes and pickles or simply on its own.

2 tablespoons peanut or canola oil

½ teaspoon whole brown or yellow mustard seeds

10 to 15 fresh curry leaves, if available

1 teaspoon *chana dal* or yellow split peas

2 whole dried hot red chiles

1 scallion, cut into fine rounds (both green and white sections)

1 cup green peas, parboiled by dropping in boiling water for 2 minutes, then drained

Plain Whole Buckwheat, cooked according to the preceding recipe

Salt

Freshly ground black pepper

Put the oil in a large, nonstick frying pan and set over medium-high heat. When hot, put in the mustard seeds. As soon as they begin to pop, a matter of seconds, put in the curry leaves. Stir once and put in the *chana dal*. Stir and fry until the *chana dal* is red. Put in the chiles and stir once or twice. Add the scallion and stir a few times. Add the peas and stir a few times, then add the cooked buckwheat. Stir and toss until heated through. Sprinkle with salt and pepper, stir to mix, and serve.

SERVES 4

Buckwheat Pancakes

These very fluffy yeast pancakes must be eaten while still very hot. You may have them with butter, sugar, and lemon juice; butter and jam; sour cream and jam; or butter and maple syrup—they are good every way!

2¼ cups very warm milk

1 (¼-ounce) package active dry yeast

1 teaspoon plus 2 tablespoons sugar

1 cup unbleached all-purpose white flour

1 cup buckwheat flour

½ teaspoon salt

1 egg, beaten

2 to 3 tablespoons unsalted butter, softened

Put ¼ cup of the warm milk in a cup. Sprinkle in the yeast and 1 teaspoon of the sugar, stir, and set aside for 10 to 15 minutes. The yeast should bubble up.

Combine the 2 flours, salt, and the remaining 2 tablespoons sugar in a bowl. Make a well in the center and pour in the yeast mixture. Stir it in with a wooden spoon. Slowly add the remaining milk, stirring it in as you do so. Cover the bowl loosely and leave in a warm place to rise for 1½ hours. Add the beaten egg and stir it in. Let the batter rest, covered, in a warm place for another 30 minutes.

Just before you sit down to eat, set a cast-iron griddle, large cast-iron frying pan, or large, heavy nonstick frying pan over medium-high heat. Brush with the softened butter. Using a ladle, scoop up about ½ cup of the batter at a time and drop as many pancakes as the pan can hold easily. Cook one side for 1½ minutes, or until a nice reddish-brown. Turn and cook the second side the same way for another 1½ minutes. Remove the pancakes to a plate and serve right away. Repeat with the remaining batter.

MAKES ABOUT 12

Cold Buckwheat Noodles   JAPAN
Zaru Soba

One of the joys of a Japanese summer is chilled buckwheat noodles. In restaurants, they might appear in baskets nesting over ice; on airplanes they come in plastic trays. A restaurant I visited near Kyoto served nothing but these noodles. It had been built on a ledge beside a mountain stream. Diners could sit on a shady bridge that straddled the tumbling waters and slurp up icy noodles. What a way to celebrate the essence of the season!

For this dish the noodles are served plain and eaten with a dipping sauce and condiments.

Prepare the condiments before you cook the noodles. Instead of putting the seven-spice season-ing in the dipping sauce, you may do what many Japanese chefs do: They poke a hole in the center of the cut end of a large daikon radish and then insert a seeded fresh hot red chile into the hole. They let the radish sit for an hour, then they grate it. Lo and behold, they end up with a hot, pink mass!

For the dipping sauce

2½ cups Dried Mushroom Stock (page 577)

4 to 6 tablespoons soy sauce

6 tablespoons mirin

Dash Japanese Seven-Spice Seasoning
    (shichimi) (page 725)

For the noodles

½ pound soba (Japanese buckwheat noodles)

1 to 2 sheets nori, cut into fine shreds

Other condiments

2 scallions, cut into fine rounds (white and
    green portions), soaked in cold water for
    30 minutes, then drained and squeezed
    dry in a cloth

About 1 teaspoon grated Japanese wasabi
    horseradish or prepared wasabi paste

4 tablespoons grated peeled daikon

Combine the stock, soy sauce, and mirin in a pan. Taste for balance of seasonings —the sauce should be a little salty. Bring it to a boil, then turn the heat down to low and simmer very gently for 5 minutes. Turn off the heat and let the sauce cool off. Add the seven-spice seasoning and then refrigerate it.

Bring 4 quarts of water to a rolling boil in a large pot. Drop in the soba noodles and stir. When the water returns to a boil, pour in a cup of cold water. Let the water come to a boil yet again and pour in another cup of cold water. Do this 2 or more times, or until the noodles are just cooked through but not hard in the center. Drain and immediately rinse under cold water. Rub the noodles gently under cold running water to get rid of all their gumminess. Drain well and coil the noodles evenly on 4 separate plates. Scatter the nori over the top.

Pour the dipping sauce into 4 bowls. Ideally, every diner should have individual little bowls of condiments. If that is not possible, there can be common bowls to share.

To eat, diners should put some scallions, a pinch of wasabi, and some grated daikon into their bowl of dipping sauce and mix them in. They should then pick up some noodles, dip them in the sauce, and eat.

SERVES 4

Corn

Corn belongs to the Americas. However, I have been to parts of the world that believe otherwise. On a remote Eastern Indonesian island where rice cannot survive in the dry volcanic soil, corn, brought by the Spaniards and Portuguese five hundred years ago, is not only the chief source of sustenance but also has been so intricately woven into the island's mythology and culture that locals assume it was always there. The women don mannish hats and dance corn dances on the black earth under the banyan tree, miming the sowing, reaping, drying, and even the "popping" of the grain in undulating motions. Corn has caused the habitants of older mythologies (such as spirits on the banyan tree) to intertwine with the not-so-old. Corn has entered the islanders' souls.

In the Punjab in India, where corn flatbreads and mustard greens might as well be painted on the state flag, I was once scolded by a college professor for suggesting that corn might have come, relatively recently, from another world. No, no, he insisted, corn was always here. What *was* "always here" were flatbreads, made mainly from wheat, that date back to the same period as corn tortillas in Mexico. The new grain was used just the way the old one was, to make rotis and chapatis (flatbreads). Though it is hard to make flatbreads from finely ground, dried corn (in Mexico, they use cooked corn, which is somewhat easier to work with), the Punjabis manage it easily. There is not a single home that does not cook *makki di roti* (corn flatbread), which is eaten with generous smears of homemade white butter.

Corn gruels were probably the easiest ways to cook and eat this dried grain in ancient times, and even today the popularity of these comfort foods continue unabated. Africans feel as close an affinity to their *mielie meel* as Caribbeans do to their *coo-coo,* the latter being a mush of cornmeal and okra with a distinct African ancestry. In South Africa, for example, *mielie meel* is eaten for breakfast, lunch, and dinner. At breakfast, it is cooked thinner, like cereal, and then eaten with sugar and milk if they are available. For main meals it is cooked thicker, formed into balls, and eaten with meats and sauces.

Northern Italians feel just as attached to their polenta. There, corn easily replaced other grain gruels made successively with millet, spelt, barley, buckwheat, and wheat. In the hills of northern Greece I have had leek pitas (pies) that were made not with the more common, rolled-out flour-pastry sheets, but with layers of cornmeal strewn in a large pie tin with alternating layers of sautéed leeks. Once baked, the cornmeal formed layers of mush, not unlike layered polenta. I was told that corn was used during the war when wheat was scarce and although it is still associated with poverty, like polenta in Italy and *coo-coo* in the Caribbean, it has now become quite a darling of the fashionable world and is even seen in pricey restaurants.

While all the world now loves corn, its origins lie deep in southern Mexico,

Honduras, and Guatemala, where it has been traced back more than eight thousand years. From there it spread both north and south, eventually becoming the premier grain of the Americas. Spanish and Portuguese conquerors of the New World then took it in their ships and spread it throughout the Old World. We are talking, of course, of maize. Sweet corn, as we now know it, is but one of the many varieties of maize and was discovered in the late eighteenth century, being grown by the Iroquois in central New York. It has been further hybridized in the last century.

When Cortez arrived in Mexico, he found the locals eating flatbreads (tortillas) made from dried maize that had been cooked with hardwood ashes (or ground limestone), an alkaline that helped remove the hull, add a little leavening, and mysteriously make the niacin in corn more readily usable. When I was in Mexico, one of my favorite cheap meals was a bowl of the red or green posole to be found in large steaming kettles at local weekend fairs. This stew was made with large grains of white corn (also called posole) that had been cooked first with an alkaline and dried, and then cooked again slowly with pork and chiles until they softened and opened up like flowers. You will find a vegetarian version of the dish on page 338.

Many years ago, my husband gave me a 1907 photograph of kneeling Native American women, their hair parted in the center and then curled like big shells around their ears, bent in a row over grinding stones. Betty Fussell, in her excellent book *I Hear America Cooking*, seems to explain my picture, saying that by A.D. 1000, Native Americans had set up communal "factories." Several women would gather to grind corn on grinding stones *(metates)*. They would divide up in sets of three, with the first person grinding the corn coarsely into grits and the others grinding finer and finer until they had a fine corn flour.

Here follows a look at the edible corn products available for cooking purposes, all made from dried corn and used as grains. (For fresh corn, see pages 169 to 175.) Dried corn is generally sold in two colors, yellow and white. While blue corn is grown in the Southwest of the United States and in some parts of Mexico, and other colors (dark red, rose, purple, brown, black, as well as variegated cobs) are also to be found in the Americas, it is the white and yellow that are most readily available.

Dried corn kernels, also called dried seed corn: Yellow or white, they are just whole dried kernels with the rich germ still inside them. It is these that are used to make the spicy, Indonesian soup-stew from Sulawesi, *bubur Manado*. In their whole state they may be added to any stew but must be allowed to cook slowly and long by themselves first as they take several hours to become tender. The times vary with the size and type of grain. Store the dried kernels in the refrigerator as the germ is very perishable. It is these kernels that are ground to make cornmeal and/or corn flour.

Popping corn These also consist of dried corn kernels but of a special variety that can hold a lot of moisture within its starchy center. Once exposed to heat, the moisture turns to steam, causing the kernels to expand, explode, and expose their innards, rather like buds that are forced to flower fully at command.

Cornmeal, corn flour, and polenta: Cornmeal consists of dried corn kernels, yellow or white, ground to a consistency that can vary from coarse to fine. Unless you buy the stone-ground, whole grain cornmeal sold by specialty stores, the highly perishable (and very nutritious) germ will have been removed, giving the ground meal an extended shelf life. Whole grain cornmeal with the germ included (this has telltale black or dark red specks in it) should be stored in the refrigerator where it will hold for a year. It may also be frozen almost indefinitely. Sometimes "stone-ground" cornmeal is mistakenly called "water-ground," as it was once customary to run massive grinding stones with waterpower.

Corn flour can mean different things. In the United States and most of the world, it consists of dried corn kernels that have been very finely ground to a powdery flour. In India this is sold as *makki ka ata* and is used in the making of flat Punjabi corn breads. However, in the United Kingdom, corn flour is the white starch derived from corn kernels and used as a thickener. It is the same thing that we, in America, call cornstarch.

"Polenta," according to Giuliano Bugialli, the Italian food authority, refers only to a *cooked* mush of cornmeal and water; the ground grain used to make it is sold in Italy as *farina gialla,* or "yellow flour." However, as I have found, the ground grain is sometimes sold as polenta even in Italy. In the rest of the world, the ground grain is sold as either "polenta" or "Italian cornmeal" and can be bought from specialty shops. So, for the purposes of this book, I shall call the uncooked grain "Italian yellow cornmeal." It is sold in both fine and coarse grinds and may be bought mixed with other grains such as buckwheat. Most of what we get has had the germ removed, but it is possible, here and there, to find organic, whole grain Italian cornmeal (Bergamasca's branata polenta is the one brand I know). Giuliano insists that we use only Italian cornmeal to make the cooked polenta as it is less sour and pasty, perhaps because of the nature of the corn itself. (One miller I know says that he sifts out all the very fine powdery flour, which may eliminate some of the pastiness for the polenta he packages.) However, according to Betty Fussell, one of America's leading corn experts, polenta is just the Italian name for cornmeal, in spite of all the hype. Remember to store organic, whole grain cornmeal in the refrigerator or freezer.

Posole/hominy: Called posole in Mexico and hominy in the United States, these are dried grains of large field corn that have been cooked with an alkali and had their hulls removed. Very often the germ is removed as well but you can buy whole grain hominy in specialty stores. Posole/hominy is sold canned or dried. Canned posole or hominy needs to be drained and rinsed thoroughly. Though fully cooked, you will probably want to braise or stew it briefly to let it absorb flavors. Dried posole/hominy needs slow cooking. Rinse it well first. Then, for every 1 cup (6 ounces) of posole/hominy, add about 5 cups of water, bring to a boil, cover, and then cook gently for about 2½ hours, or until the grains are tender. They will also open up like flowers. If the water dries up in the cooking, a little more boiling water may be added. Posole is used in Mexico to make a long-simmered stew of the same name. It is also used to make the following:

Hominy grits Generally just called "grits," this very coarsely ground hominy, generally white, is eaten in the southern United States for breakfast, along with eggs. It cooks in boiling water like a cereal, generally taking about 20 minutes. Instant varieties are also available.

Masa harina This is a fine flour made from dried hominy. It is sometimes sold with a little wheat flour mixed in. It is this flour that is used in the making of Mexican tortillas. It needs to be mixed with water and made into a dough first.

Masa This is the dough made directly from soaked and ground hominy. It makes the best—and softest—tortillas. Unfortunately, it may only be purchased from tortilla factories. Some cities in the United States (such as Chicago and Los Angeles) are lucky enough to have them, usually in the Mexican section of town. Masa has a one-day shelf life and is best kept in the refrigerator.

Masa harina "precocida": In South America, unlike Mexico, corn is generally not cooked with an alkali before being dried and ground. However, it does go through a cooking process in plain water, after which it is dried and made into a special fine "precooked" cornmeal. Both yellow and white corn may be treated this way. This meal is in turn used to make the special English muffin–shaped Colombian breads called *arepas*. It is also very good in muffins. It is much less grainy, when cooked, than cornmeal. Look for "Masarepa" in the stores.

Amina de Freitas'

Cornmeal and Okra Mold

TRINIDAD

Coo-Coo

I have had many versions of this popular Caribbean Creole dish, some made with water, others with milk, and yet others with coconut milk. Sometimes sautéed onions and grated coconut are added and at other times, it is flavored with a mélange of Mediterranean herbs. The two ingredients that remain constant, however, are yellow cornmeal and okra. (You may use frozen okra here.)

As in Creole gumbos, okra provides the glue—and glutinous texture—that holds the dish together and gives it its African texture and taste. As soon as the corn mush is made, it is molded. It sets very quickly. It is then cut into slices and served with soups, stews, vegetables, and beans. I even like to serve the slices, like polenta, with a topping of tomato sauce.

Leftovers may be refrigerated. Once cold and very firm, my favorite way of eating coo-coo *is to cut off ¹/₂-inch-thick slices, brown them well on both sides in a little oil, and serve them with a topping of sautéed broccoli rabe or with a green salad and cold vegetables.*

A little unsalted butter to grease a mold

1 teaspoon salt

8 fresh okra pods, wiped off, trimmed, and cut crosswise into ¼-inch-thick rounds

¼ teaspoon dried thyme

2 tablespoons very finely sliced fresh chives

1 cup (5¾ ounces) yellow cornmeal

Grease a 4-cup mold or dish with butter and set aside.

In a heavy, medium pan, combine 3¼ cups of water, the salt, and the okra. Bring to a boil. Turn the heat down to low and simmer 20 minutes, or until the okra is tender. Strain the liquid (but save the okra). You should have 3 cups of liquid. If not, add water or remove some liquid so you have the correct amount.

Put 1 cup of this liquid back in the pan. Put the okra back in the pan as well and add the thyme and chives. Bring to a simmer over medium heat. When the water begins to bubble, pour in the cornmeal in a slow and steady stream, stirring with a wooden spoon as you do so. Slowly, over the next 15 minutes, add the remaining 2 cups of liquid, stirring all the time. Continue to stir and cook another 5 minutes. Take the pan off the heat and pour the mush into the greased mold or dish, making sure you get all of it out with a rubber spatula. Smooth the top and set aside for 5 minutes until set. Unmold and cut into slices or squares. Serve as suggested in the recipe introduction.

SERVES 6

Grits with Mushrooms

I hereby offer a new recipe to the world of grits.

Grits, an American southern favorite, are generally cooked with boiling water like a cereal, and then served with butter as an accompaniment to eggs. They have always been a great favorite of my husband, whose father was a southerner.

One day I decided to cook our grits in another *southern manner—the manner of southern India. Instead of the coarse semolina that is normally used for the Indian* uppama, *I substituted grits. The results were superb. Even my husband, who does not take kindly to any meddling with tradition, just loved them. "What are you going to call this dish?" he worried. "Why, the Jaffrey grits of course," I teased. Here they are. Serve them with eggs or as the starch with any meal.*

2 tablespoons peanut or canola oil

½ teaspoon whole brown or yellow mustard seeds

15 to 20 fresh curry leaves (omit if unavailable)

1 large shallot, peeled and finely chopped

8 medium white mushrooms, sliced ⅛ inch thick

¾ cup old-fashioned grits

¾ teaspoon salt

Bring a kettle of water to a boil and keep nearby over low heat. Have a measuring cup nearby as well.

Put the oil in a large nonstick frying pan and set over medium-high heat. When hot, put in the mustard seeds. As soon as the mustard seeds begin to pop, a matter of seconds, put in the curry leaves. Stir once and add the chopped shallot. Stir for 30 seconds and put in the mushrooms. Stir and fry the mushrooms for a minute, or until they turn satiny. Now put in the grits. Stir and cook until the grains are golden, about 2 minutes. Turn the heat to medium-low. Quickly fill the measuring jug with 3½ cups of boiling water and begin to pour it slowly into the pan as you stir gently, breaking up all the lumps. When all the water has been added, put in the salt. Stir again to mix and bring to a boil. Cover, turn the heat down to low, and cook 20 minutes, stirring now and then.

SERVES 4

Green Posole

Posole Verde

This was one of my best-loved dishes in Mexico City. Tart and hot, this meal-in-a-bowl was served in earthenware containers, with generous sprinklings of chopped onion, avocados, and dried oregano. Sometimes sliced radishes, cucumbers, and finely shredded cabbage or lettuce were also added. There was always a hot green salsa on the table as well. (See Green Tomatillo Salsa, page 679.) Crisply Fried Tortillas (tostadas) were served on the side. (You may use crusty bread or pitas instead.) There were cut limes, of course, to squeeze over the top. The mixture of the deeply soothing soft corn made fiery with chiles, the sourness of the lime, the saladlike crunch of fresh vegetables, and crisp tostadas was quite unforgettable.

When I had the dish in Mexico, it had been made with a pork base. I use white beans and mushrooms instead, which works surprisingly well. To get some of the dense flavor, I have resorted to vegetarian bouillon cubes. Use Knorr or Maggi.

You will need a mixture of hot and not-so-hot green chiles such as poblano and jalapeño, and the husk-covered, sour green tomatillos for this dish. There is no real substitute for the tomatillos, which are like lime juice–sprinkled tomatoes. They are available in cans in Mexican and specialty shops (see Resources). You may use a mixture of green tomatoes and 1 tablespoon lime juice or extra green peppers (roasted) and 1 tablespoon lime juice. If you cannot get the poblanos, use the same weight of ordinary sweet green peppers and substitute 2 to 3 plain fresh hot green chiles for the jalapeño.

My recipe uses dried posole. You may use dried whole hominy or canned posole or canned hominy. For canned pasole/hominy, drain, rinse well, and drain again. You should end up with 3 cups. Add this to the boiled beans at the same time as the cooked posole in this recipe.

1 cup (6 ounces) dried posole

1 cup (6 ounces) dried cannellini beans (or dried Great Northern or navy beans), picked over, washed, and drained

1 pound mild poblano chiles (about 6 to 8)

3 tablespoons peanut or canola oil

3 garlic cloves, peeled and finely chopped

5 medium tomatillos (6 ounces), husks removed, washed and finely chopped (see recipe introduction)

6 scallions, very finely sliced into thin rounds (both green and white sections)

1 to 2 jalapeño chiles, finely chopped

1 teaspoon ground cumin

12 medium white mushrooms, quartered

2 large or 8 small good-quality vegetable bouillon cubes

1 tablespoon chopped fresh oregano or 1 teaspoon dried

½ cup finely chopped cilantro

¾ to 1 teaspoon salt

For the topping (you do not need all—mix and match at will)

3 scallions, very finely sliced into thin rounds (both green and white sections)

Dried oregano (about ¼ teaspoon per bowl)

1 ripe avocado, peeled and diced at the last minute

1 medium cucumber, peeled and diced

Generous handful each of shredded cabbage and iceberg or other crisp lettuce

Fresh lime wedges

Green Tomatillo Salsa (page 678)

18 Crisply Fried Tortillas (page 354)

Put the dried posole in a pan with 5 cups of water and bring to a boil. Cover, turn the heat down to low, and simmer gently for 2 to 2½ hours, or until the posole is tender. Keep an eye on the posole. If the water in the pan seems to be cooking away, add a little more boiling water. When the posole is cooked, drain, reserving the liquid, if any, in a measuring cup.

Put the beans in a pan with 3 cups of water and bring to a boil. Boil rapidly for 2 minutes, then cover, turn the heat off, and let the pan sit, covered, for 1 hour. Drain. Cover the beans with 3 cups of fresh water and bring to a boil again. Cover, turn the heat down to low, and cook gently for about 40 minutes, or until the beans are just tender. Drain, saving the cooking liquid in the same measuring cup as the posole liquid.

Roast the poblano chiles. Lay them out in a broiling tray in a single layer and place under a heated broiler about 5 inches from the heat source. Roast, turning the chiles often, until all sides are lightly charred; this should take 5 to 6 minutes. Remove the tray from the heat and cover it with a towel for 10 to 15 minutes. Now peel, seed, and finely chop the chiles.

Put the oil and garlic in a good-sized pan and set over medium-high heat. When the garlic begins to sizzle and turn golden, put in the tomatillos, scallions, and the jalapeño. Stir and sauté for about 5 minutes. Add the cumin and stir once. Put in the mushrooms and stir for 2 minutes. Add the chopped poblano chiles and stir for a minute. Now put in the drained posole, beans, crumbled bouillon cubes, oregano, and the cilantro. Add enough water to the reserved bean and posole liquid in the measuring jar to make 5 cups. Bring to a simmer. Mix well and taste for salt (the bouillon cubes are already salted, so add only what you need). Add to the pot, cover, lower the heat, and simmer very gently for 1¼ hours, stirring now and then.

Serve with a generous sprinkling of the toppings. If you like, offer Green Tomatillo Salsa and Crisply Fried Tortillas on the side.

SERVES 6

Indonesian Corn, Rice, and Vegetable Stew

INDONESIA

Bubur Manado

This dish is really an Indonesian posole! I can only guess at how it evolved.

We are at the tail end of the fifteenth century. Rice gruels already exist in every Asian country where there is rice, with local names like kanji, congee, jook, *and* bubur. *Sometimes the rice is combined with beans and vegetables to make even more nutritious soup-gruel-stews. Relishes, sauces, and condiments are added to these, often at the table, to give them more flavor and interest.*

At this stage Spanish and Portuguese ships begin to sail into Asian waters bearing New World marvels like corn, tomatoes, squashes, yucca, pumpkins, and chiles. The corn, maize, is dried, the kernels removed for storage and then used whole in these stews, just as rice was.

This particular stew is actually from the northern part of Sulawesi. It gets its name from the capital city of the region, Manado. It is cooked very slowly, without many seasonings (but with many aromatics), and then eaten with a sour and fiery sambal *(relish) made with roasted tomatoes, shallots, chiles, and lime juice.*

You need whole, dried corn kernels here, sometimes called seed corn. Most health food stores carry it as do Latin American and Southeast Asian grocers. Dried corn cooks slowly, over several hours, lending its own sweetness and mellowness to the dish. You may also substitute dried posole.

This dish may be made a day ahead of time and then stored in the refrigerator. If it thickens too much, thin it out with vegetable stock or water. Serve it in old-fashioned soup plates, pasta plates, or bowls. The sambal *should be offered separately, with every diner dribbling just as much as desired over the top of his/her serving.*

2 fresh lemongrass stalks (bottom 6 inches only)

1 cup (5 ounces) dried corn kernels

6 tablespoons raw rice (I like to use jasmine rice)

3 large or 12 small vegetable bouillon cubes

2 heaping cups peeled pumpkin or butternut squash, cut into ¾-inch dice (page 287)

2 medium (10 ounces) boiling potatoes, peeled and cut into ¾-inch dice

6 scallions, cut crosswise into very fine rounds (both white and green sections)

4 to 5 tablespoons fine strips of holy basil leaves (use basil as a substitute)

8 ounces red or green Swiss chard, cut crosswise into fine strips (keep stems and leaves separated)

10 ounces spinach, cut crosswise into fine strips

Salt to taste

For serving

Sambal with Roasted Tomatoes, Shallots, and Chiles (page 681)

Crush the bulbous end of the lemongrass stalks lightly, then combine with the corn and 10 cups of water in a large pot and bring to a boil. Cover, turn the heat down to low, and simmer 2½ hours or longer, until the corn is tender enough to be chewed. Remove the lemongrass and discard. Add 2 cups of boiling water and the rice, and bring to a boil. Cover, turn the heat down to low, and cook another 30 minutes.

Put in the bouillon cubes, pumpkin or squash, potatoes, scallions, holy basil, and the Swiss chard stems. Stir well and bring to a boil. Cover, turn the heat down to low, and cook another 30 minutes, stirring now and then. Add 3 cups of boiling water, stir, and bring to a boil. Put in the chard leaves and spinach and stir well from the bottom, mixing the leaves in. Keep the heat on low and cook 15 minutes, uncovered, stirring frequently. Taste for salt.

Serve hot, with the *sambal* on the side.

SERVES 6

POLENTA

The first time that I had polenta was not in Italy but New York, in James Beard's town house on 12th Street, about twenty years ago. It had been cooked by a mutual friend, Marion Cunningham (whose work on *The Fannie Farmer Cookbook* is now legendary). There were just four of us for dinner, Jim, Marion, my husband, and myself. Jim and I had just taught a cooking class and were lounging about with glasses of red wine. Marion served the polenta with a plain tomato sauce. I was in awe of the simplicity, the satiny texture, and the deeply soothing nature of the dish. I asked Marion for the recipe immediately.

Since then, I have traveled to Italy numerous times and eaten polenta in many forms, in many places. I have seen it baked in layers, like lasagna; I have seen it swirled over cheese while it was still soft and flowing or served on the side with a dab of butter and a sprinkling of Parmesan cheese; and I have seen it allowed to cool, then sliced and either fried or grilled and used as a base for other cooked foods. It was always good.

Organic whole grain Italian cornmeal is the ideal one to use (see page 334), but it is not always easy to find. The next best is any Italian coarse-grained yellow cornmeal (polenta).

The hardest aspect of cooking polenta in the traditional manner is the constant, arm-breaking stirring it requires for about 45 minutes. If you want soft, satiny polenta, there is no other option. (Once all the cornmeal is in the pan, I hand over the wooden spoon to my violinist husband, who uses his bowing arm and never seems to tire!) Use a very large, heavy, preferably nonstick pan to make it. It bubbles and heaves as it cooks, so you need to allow room for that and for the grains of cornmeal to swell. You might want to wear oven gloves, as the thick, hot gruel tends to spatter. Once the polenta is cooked, the pan used should be soaked in water immediately. It then becomes quite easy to clean.

There is another method of cooking polenta in the oven. Here the mixing of cornmeal and water is simplified (you mix the cornmeal in cold water) and most of the stirring is eliminated. The results are very good, though not quite as smooth as in the more laborious way. And it does save a lot of time and effort. Both methods are given below.

You will find serving suggestions for soft, freshly made polenta and for polenta that has been cooled and allowed to firm up in the recipes that follow.

The Classical Method of Cooking Polenta   ITALY

1 tablespoon salt

2 cups coarse-grained Italian yellow cornmeal (also sold as polenta)

Bring 8½ cups of water to a boil in a very large, heavy, preferably nonstick pan. Turn the heat down to medium-high. Add the salt. Using a long-handled wooden spoon, keep stirring with one hand while you pick up a fistful of cornmeal at a time with the other and let it flow through your fingers into the water in a slow but steady stream. You may also empty the cornmeal into a jug and pour it out from the spout in a very slow, steady stream. When all the cornmeal is in, continue the constant stirring for 40 to 45 minutes, breaking up any lumps that might form and scraping away from the bottom and the sides. In the end, you should have a thick, smooth mass that comes away from the sides.

If you want your polenta soft and creamy, serve it immediately.

Polenta sets fast. If you are not going to eat it immediately or if there are leftovers after the first serving, it should be immediately emptied into a flat-at-the-bottom, squarish container or even a bowl that has been rinsed out with cold water. Flatten the top of the polenta with a wet rubber spatula, cover, and refrigerate. It will last in the refrigerator for 4 to 5 days. When cold, the polenta will settle into the shape of the container and may be unmolded and cut into thick slices. To reheat the slices, sprinkle them with water, cover, and heat either in a microwave oven or in a nonstick frying pan. These slices may also be toasted or fried (see Toasted Polenta Slices, Fried Polenta Slices, opposite).

SERVES 4

Polenta Cooked in the Oven

2 cups coarse-grained Italian yellow cornmeal (also sold as polenta)

Dab of unsalted butter or vegetable oil

1 tablespoon salt

Put the cornmeal into a bowl. Slowly add 3 cups of water, stirring with a wooden spoon as you do so.

Preheat the oven to 400°F. Butter or oil an 8×8×4-inch or similar-sized baking dish.

Put 4½ cups of water into a large pan and bring it to a boil over medium-high heat. Add the salt. Stir the cornmeal mixture again and then slowly pour it into the boiling water, stirring with a wooden spoon as you do so. Bring to a boil, stirring all the time. The mixture will thicken very quickly into a homogeneous paste. Quickly pour this paste into the baking dish, smooth over the top with the back of a wooden spoon, cover, and bake for 50 minutes.

Serve as is (with a topping of butter and grated Parmigiano-Reggiano cheese, if desired) or cool, cover, and refrigerate. The polenta is now ready to be used in the same way as the cool, firm, more traditionally cooked polenta. Once cooled, the polenta may be toasted or fried.

SERVES 4

Variation I

Toasted Polenta Slices

Cut firm, cold polenta (made by either of the above methods) into as many ½-inch slices (rectangular, square, or diagonals) as you need. Brush the slices lightly with butter or olive oil and lay in a broiling tray, slightly separated from each other as they tend to stick. Set the tray about 5 inches away from the source of heat. As soon as the slices are lightly browned on both sides, remove them from the heat and serve with any topping you desire such as the Tomato Sauce with Mushrooms (page 680) or the Mushroom Ragout in Fettuccine with a Mushroom Ragout (page 484).

Variation II

Fried Polenta Slices

Cut the firm, cold polenta (made by either of the above methods) into as many ½-inch slices (rectangular, square, or diagonals) as you need.

(recipe continues)

Put about 2 tablespoons of olive oil in a frying pan, preferably a nonstick one, and set over medium-high heat. Let the oil get really hot. Put in as many slices as the pan will hold in a single layer, slightly separated from each other as they tend to stick. Let the slices brown lightly on one side, about 2 minutes. Turn the slices over and brown the second side. Add a little more oil if needed and brown the remaining slices. Serve at once with a topping of your choice, such as Tomato Sauce with Mushrooms (page 680) or the Mushroom Ragout in Fettuccine with a Mushroom Ragout (page 484), or as an accompaniment.

Soft Polenta Mixed with Cheese and Butter

This is one of the simplest ways of serving soft polenta. You may either serve it as an accompaniment to a Mediterranean bean dish and some greens or you could top it with some greens and quickly sautéed mushrooms. If you have access to fresh white truffles, you could grate them over the top. For a humbler meal, serve it topped with Sautéed Spinach with Dill and Onion (page 225) or with sautéed broccoli or Simple Tomato Sauce (page 679).

A freshly made recipe of soft polenta cooked according to the classical method or in the oven (pages 342 to 343)

2 to 3 tablespoons unsalted butter, cut into small pats

⅔ cup (2 ounces) grated Parmigiano-Reggiano cheese

As soon as the polenta is made, stir in the butter and cheese. Mix and serve immediately.

SERVES 4 TO 6

Polenta with Asparagus

This may be eaten as a first course (in which case, it will serve 6 to 8) or as the main course with a salad to follow. The asparagus should be kept hot, while the Romesco Sauce should be at room temperature or warmed lightly.

Soft Polenta Mixed with Cheese and Butter, freshly made according to the recipe above

Asparagus with Romesco Sauce, freshly made according to the recipe on page 669

Put a generous portion of the hot polenta on a plate, top with a portion of asparagus, and then drizzle the Romesco Sauce generously over the top. Serve immediately.

SERVES 4

Polenta with Broccoli Rabe ITALY

Polenta con Broccoli Rapini

Almost any greens are good over polenta, but broccoli rabe, with its slight bitterness, is scrumptious. Those who cannot get this Italian green may use chard, spinach, or even broccoli florets, blanched first in salted water and then sautéed in olive oil with garlic.

Soft Polenta Mixed with Cheese and Butter, freshly made according to the recipe on page 344, or Fried Polenta Slices (page 345), freshly prepared

Broccoli Rabe with Garlic, freshly made according to the recipe on page 217

Put a portion of the polenta on a plate and top with a portion of the hot broccoli rabe. Serve immediately.

SERVES 4

Polenta with a Mushroom and Potato Stew

This may be eaten as a first course or as the main course with a salad to follow.

Mushroom and Potato Stew, freshly made according to the recipe on page 248

Soft Polenta Mixed with Cheese and Butter, freshly made according to the recipe on page 344, or Fried Polenta Slices (page 343) or Toasted Polenta Slices (page 343)

Heat up the stew and crush a few of the potato pieces against the side of the pan in order to thicken it a bit. Cook for another 5 minutes.

Serve portions of polenta topped with the hot stew.

SERVES 4

Polenta with Tex-Mex Chili

This is a meal in itself. I love to serve the polenta in a large, relatively shallow earthen bowl, topped with the chili, which in turn is topped with flecks of chopped fresh cilantro. I stick some corn chips in, even a few slim hot green chiles for those who want them.

The chili can, of course, be made a day ahead. Do not make the chili too thick. It should flow with ease. Add a little extra water if you need to as you are reheating it.

Soft Polenta Mixed with Cheese and Butter, freshly made according to the recipe on page 344

Tex-Mex Vegetarian Chili (page 64), reheated

For the garnish

About 2 tablespoons finely chopped fresh cilantro

A few handfuls of corn chips

Follow the directions above for serving.

SERVES 4 TO 6

Soft Polenta Draped over Cheese

Here freshly made polenta is ladled over cheese, dotted with butter, and then served quickly while it is still soft and hot. This may be served both as a first course or as a main course with a salad on the side.

Because the cheese is salty, you may put 2 teaspoons instead of the 1 tablespoon salt in the water when cooking the polenta.

¾ cup (4 ounces) fontina cheese, diced into ¼-inch pieces

8 tablespoons (1½ ounces) coarsely grated Parmigiano-Reggiano cheese

2 tablespoons unsalted butter, divided in 4 parts

A freshly made recipe of soft polenta cooked according to the classical method or in the oven (pages 342 to 343)

Divide the cheeses into 4 parts each. Put the fontina in the center of 4 plates and top with the Parmigiano-Reggiano. Ladle the hot polenta over them and top each plate of polenta with one part of the butter. Serve immediately.

SERVES 4

Polenta Lasagna

Here polenta is layered with cheese and spinach as well as with a mushroom and tomato sauce before it is baked. This is a meal in itself and requires only a salad on the side.

For this dish, I usually cook the polenta using the classical method. The tomato sauce and the spinach should be prepared first (make the tomato sauce slightly thicker than you would for pasta). The cheeses should be kept chopped and grated. The dish for the baking should be buttered and kept ready. Only when all the preparations are done should you start making the polenta.

If you wish to make this dish ahead of time, cool and cover it until needed, refrigerating if necessary. To reheat, sprinkle with water, cover, and either heat in a microwave oven or in an ordinary oven at 350°F. for 20 minutes.

2 tablespoons olive oil

1 large shallot or 2 medium ones (1 ounce), peeled and cut into fine long slivers

About 12 ounces trimmed, well-washed, and dried spinach leaves or 1 package frozen whole leaf spinach, thawed

Salt

About 2 tablespoons unsalted butter

A freshly made recipe of soft polenta cooked according to the classical method (page 342) *but using only 2 teaspoons salt in the water*

1 cup (3 ounces) coarsely grated Parmigiano-Reggiano cheese

½ cup (3 ounces) fontina cheese cut into ¾-inch dice

1¼ cups Tomato Sauce with Mushrooms (page 680)

Put the oil in a large pan and set over high heat. When hot, put in the shallot. Stir and fry for 1 to 2 minutes, or until lightly browned. Put in the spinach. Stir and fry for 5 minutes. Add ¼ teaspoon salt and stir it in. Let the spinach cool. Now chop it well and set aside.

Lightly grease an ovenproof 8×8×4-inch baking dish, using a little of the butter.

Make sure the Tomato Sauce is ready and all other preparations are done. Make the polenta now. Stop long enough in your stirring to preheat the oven to 425°F.

Quickly ladle ⅓ of the polenta into the baking dish, spreading this layer out with a wet rubber spatula. Sprinkle the Parmigiano-Reggiano over it, followed by the spinach and then the fontina cheese. Spread another ⅓ of the polenta over the fontina, again spreading and evening it out with the help of a wet spatula. Now spread the layer of Tomato Sauce with Mushrooms and follow it with the final layer of polenta. Smooth out the top and dot with bits of butter. Bake, uncovered, for 45 minutes. Serve immediately.

SERVES 4 TO 6

Corn Tortillas

MEXICO

For an Indian like me, corn tortillas, the mainstays of Mexican food, are just like chapatis, only they are made out of corn instead of whole wheat. The word chapatis *implies that these flatbreads were originally patted into rounds by hand (*chapat *means "to slap"), though now they are generally (though not always) rolled out. Tortillas, too, were once slapped into shape between the palms of two hands, though now the use of tortilla presses is becoming quite common.*

I love the tortilla press. Tortillas are impossible to roll out as the crumbly dough begins to fray at the edges and patting them into shape takes years of practice. For most mortals, the only answer is the tortilla press, which is sold at reasonable prices in all Mexican markets. (Indian markets call the same thing a poori or chapati press!) It consists of two heavy metal discs connected on one side with a hinge. There is a handle that brings one disc down over the other, pressing anything placed between them into a thin round in a matter of seconds. Pressure determines the thickness.

*It is important to have the correct flour to make the tortillas. If you are lucky enough to live near one of the several mechanized tortilla factories (*tortellerias), *which do exist in cities like Chicago and Los Angeles, you can buy ready-made dough. Ask for the masa for tortillas. White corn, already boiled with lime (known at this stage as* nixtamal *or wet hominy), has been ground into a dough by machines (it used to be ground on a grinding stone). If you can get this, it will last for 24 hours and should be refrigerated if not used within a few hours. But most of us have no access to this dough. The next best choice is masa harina, the flour made from dried hominy.*

Generally, any good Latin American supermarket will offer a bewildering array of masa harinas. My guide and teacher for all things Mexican, Juanita Jarillo, led me through this maize to the Maseca brand. She said it was a very fine flour, pale in color, and that it made the best tortillas. Grainy, often yellow, meal-like flours should be left for other preparations.

There is nothing as rewarding as a soft, homemade tortilla. It may be eaten with all manner of foods, such as eggs, beans, and vegetables. If it is rolled around these foods along with some spicy salsa, it turns into a taco. If it is folded over foods like a turnover, it may be called a quesadilla. Day-old tortillas may be layered to make the Red Kidney Bean Casserole (page 50). Day-old tortillas can also be dried off slightly and then fried to make crisp tostadas, which may be eaten with soups (or put into soups) or eaten dipped in spicy salsas.

2 cups masa harina (see recipe introduction)

Put the masa harina into a wide bowl. Slowly add about 1⅓ cups of hot tap water, mixing as you go. You should end up with a soft, puttylike dough, as soft as you can make it without it being sticky. Add more water if you need it. Knead well and form a smooth ball. Put the ball in a plastic bag and set aside for 30 minutes or longer.

Divide the dough into 16 smooth balls. Flatten the balls slightly to make small, smooth patties. Keep them covered or in a plastic bag.

Set up the tortilla press. Cut out 2 pieces of heavy plastic about the same size as the 2 disclike parts of the tortilla press. (Zip-lock bags have the perfect thickness for cutting up. For small amounts of tortillas, wax paper will do.)

Put a cast-iron griddle, cast-iron frying pan, or Indian *tava* on medium-high heat. Give it time to heat up.

Make a small wad with a cloth or paper toweling (as if you were going to polish furniture). Set aside.

Open up the tortilla press. Lay one piece of plastic on the lower disc. Put one patty of dough in its center. Cover with another piece of plastic. Now bring the top down and press to get a tortilla about 5 inches in diameter. Open up the press. You should have a tortilla. Remove the top layer of plastic. Slide one hand under the second layer of plastic and then overturn the tortilla onto your free hand. Now slap the tortilla onto the griddle or frying pan, overturning it again. Remove the plastic. Let it cook for 30 seconds. Turn it over with a spatula and cook another 30 seconds. Turn the tortilla again. Both sides should have a few pale brown spots. Now, using your wad, press down on one section of the tortilla as you give it a slight turn. Do this with speed, quickly going all around the whole tortilla. It should puff up. Turn after 20 seconds and do this again if it has not puffed up. Keep turning the tortilla over every 15 seconds or so, until the tortilla has a few brownish spots and has cooked 2 to 2½ minutes in all. Remove and keep covered in a thick towel. Turn the heat down to medium-low as you press out the next tortilla. When it is formed, turn the heat up to medium-high again and slap it on the griddle. Make all tortillas this way, stacking them on top of each other and keeping them covered. Let them rest for 15 minutes and then either eat them immediately or put them, covered in the towel first and then in foil, in a warming oven where they should stay warm for an hour.

To reheat homemade or store-bought cold corn tortillas, set up a steamer with a perforated steaming tray and just an inch or less of water at the bottom. The water should not touch the tray. Bring the water to a boil. Put 12 to 16 tortillas, wrapped in a towel, into the tray. Cover. When the water comes to a rolling boil again and steam comes out from under the lid, steam for about 2 minutes and then remove the towel-wrapped bundle. Let it sit for 15 minutes and serve immediately or keep hot in a warming oven the same way as freshly made tortillas.

MAKES 16

Adela Lorenzo's

Corn Tortillas Stuffed with Cheese

EL SALVADOR

Papoosa de Queso

These are a delight. They are served with a spicy Cabbage Salad with Oregano, page 616 (curtido), and are a favorite with adults and children alike. Just as American children enjoy stopping off for a hamburger with fries, children in El Salvador beg their mothers for a papoosa *with* curtido.

You may use well-crumbled Mexican cheese queso fresco here if you can get it or else use coarsely grated Monterey Jack or pale, mild Cheddar.

For helpful hints on making tortillas and what kind of flour to buy, read the preceding recipe. Just remember that a papoosa *is only a tortilla with a stuffing in the center.*

2 cups masa harina

1 teaspoon salt

About 2 loosely packed cups (8 ounces) coarsely grated cheese (see recipe introduction)

About 4 tablespoons peanut or canola oil

To serve on the side

Cabbage Salad with Oregano (page 616)

Put the masa harina and salt into a wide bowl. Slowly add about 1⅓ cups of hot tap water, mixing as you go. You should end up with a soft, puttylike dough, as soft as you can make it without it being sticky. Add more water if you need it. Knead well and form a smooth ball. Put the ball in a plastic bag and set aside for 30 minutes or longer.

Divide the dough into 10 smooth balls. Flatten the balls slightly to make small, smooth patties. Keep them covered or in a plastic bag. Divide the grated cheese into 10 portions. Keep a bowl of lukewarm water nearby.

Cup one palm slightly and dampen it with the lukewarm water. Take one piece of dough and put it in the dampened palm. Press down on it until you have a 3-inch round, which is slightly cupped because of the shape of your palm. If the edges break, fix them with dampened fingers. Now put about 2 to 3 tablespoons of the grated cheese into the cup. Bring the edges of the cup together over the top of the cheese and form a ball again. Press down on the ball gently to make a patty. Make 9 other cheese-filled patties in a similar manner and keep covered on a sheet of wax paper.

Now, using a tortilla press, proceed to make the stuffed tortillas or *papoosas* in exactly the same way as the tortillas in the preceding recipe (page 348) but with these differences: 1. The *papoosas* should be just slightly thicker than the tortillas. 2. Grease the griddle or frying pan very lightly with oil before you cook each *papoosa*. 3. They will puff up less.

Make all the *papoosas,* stacking them on top of each other and keeping them covered. Serve them while they are still hot, if possible, with the cabbage salad.

The best way to reheat *papoosas* is to heat a cast-iron griddle or cast-iron frying pan over medium-high heat. When it is really hot, slap on as many *papoosas* as it will hold in a single layer and then heat them for about 30 seconds on each side. You could also wrap all of them in foil and put the whole bundle into a preheated 350°F. oven for 15 minutes.

MAKES 10

Variation I

Corn Tortillas Stuffed with Potatoes and Green Pepper
EL SALVADOR

Papoosa de Papa

Make these exactly as the *papoosas* in the preceding recipe, except, instead of the cheese, substitute a mixture of 2 cups boiled, cooled, peeled, and coarsely grated potatoes, ½ teaspoon salt, and, if you like, ½ to 1 teaspoon finely chopped hot or mild green chiles.

Variation II

Anna Montes'

Corn Tortillas Stuffed with Cheese and Refried Beans
EL SALVADOR

Papoosa de Queso con Frijoles Refritos

Make these *papoosas* exactly as in the master recipe for Corn Tortillas Stuffed with Cheese but with this difference: For the stuffing, you will need only half the cheese and about 10 tablespoons of well-crushed, cooled Refried Beans (page 12). Stuff each *papoosa* with about 1½ tablespoons of the cheese and about 1 tablespoon of the beans.

Rosario Guillermo's

Quesadilla with Cheese

A simple, everyday dish, this consists of folded-over corn tortillas filled with cheese that are allowed to cook briefly so the cheese can melt. You might call them Mexican melted cheese sandwiches topped with a spicy salsa.

You may make these quesadillas with store-bought corn tortillas, though they will never be quite as good as those made with homemade ones. Just steam the tortillas briefly so they are soft and pliable. You may also make these with freshly made Wheat Tortillas (page 445), which tend to be larger so use just 6, or with freshly made Indian Griddle Flatbreads (page 444).

4 cups (about 1 pound) grated Monterey Jack or mild white Cheddar cheese

Vegetable oil, preferably peanut or corn oil, for greasing

12 corn tortillas, freshly made or freshly warmed up according to directions in the recipe for Corn Tortillas (page 348)

Simple Red Salsa (page 683)

12 tablespoons sour cream (optional)

Divide the grated cheese into 12 portions.

Set a large cast-iron griddle or cast-iron frying pan over medium heat. Let it heat up and then grease it lightly with oil. Place as many of the tortillas as will fit in a single layer on it. Work with speed now. Spread a portion of the grated cheese on top of each, spread it out, and allow it to melt. Fold the tortillas over and press down on them lightly with a spatula. Cook them very briefly, turning them over a few times, until fully heated through and slightly crisp on the outside. Serve immediately, with a topping of Simple Red Salsa and a dollop of sour cream, if desired. Make all the quesadillas this way, greasing the griddle or frying pan each time.

SERVES 4 TO 6

Rosario Guillermo's

Quesadilla with Mushrooms   MEXICO

If jalapeño chiles or chiles serrano are unavailable, any other fresh or canned hot green chile may be used. The amount can be varied according to your taste. This is really a corn tortilla sandwich. Heat the tortillas according to directions in the recipe for Corn Tortillas (page 348).

3 tablespoons vegetable or olive oil

1 medium onion (6 ounces), cut into very fine half rings

2 fresh or canned chiles serrano or jalapeño chiles, finely chopped

2 garlic cloves, peeled and finely chopped

10 ounces white mushrooms, cut into ⅛-inch-thick slices

5 to 6 leaves of fresh epazote or 1 tablespoon finely chopped fresh cilantro

½ teaspoon salt

Freshly ground black pepper

4 freshly heated corn tortillas

Guacamole (page 613), optional

Put the oil in a medium frying pan and set over medium heat. When hot, put in the onion and the chiles. Stir and fry until the onion turns light brown at the edges. Put in the garlic and cook until it turns golden brown. Add the mushrooms, epazote or cilantro, salt, and black pepper to taste. Sauté for 4 minutes, or until there is no liquid at the bottom of the pan.

Put a hot tortilla on a plate. Spread a quarter of the mushroom mixture over one half of the tortilla. Gently fold the empty side of the tortilla over the filled side. Fill all the tortillas this way. Serve hot or warm, with a dollop of Guacamole on the side, if you like.

SERVES 2 TO 4

Crisply Fried Tortillas MEXICO

Tostadas

Tostadas, whole fried tortillas, are best made with store-bought tortillas, which tend to be much flimsier. To get the tortillas to turn nice and crisp, it is best to dry them out well. In order to keep them flat and not curl up during the drying, it is a good idea to keep them covered with a light cloth.

They may be served with Green Posole (page 338) and all manner of bean and vegetable dishes, along with salads and salsas.

You may make your own tortilla chips by cutting the tortillas into 6 wedges with scissors. Dry then fry, a few at a time, as below.

12 store-bought tortillas   Peanut or canola oil for deep-frying

Spread the tortillas out in a single layer in a dry, warm, and airy spot, such as a table covered with a cloth. Cover with muslin or cheesecloth and leave for 5 to 6 hours, or until leathery.

Heat about 2 inches of oil in a deep sauté pan over medium-high heat. When hot, put in 1 tortilla. Hold it down for 30 seconds. Turn it and let it cook another 30 seconds. It should be golden brown. Remove it and drain well on paper towels. Fry all the tortillas this way.

MAKES 12

Flat Indian Corn Breads INDIA

Makki di Roti

This is the bread that no one in the northwestern Indian state of Punjab can live without, especially in the cold winter season. It requires a very fine flour made with dried and ground yellow corn kernels. It is best to get this from an Indian grocer who sells it as makki ka ata.

These flatbreads are best cooked on an Indian tava *or cast-iron griddle. You may use a cast-iron frying pan as well. In the Punjab, freshly cooked breads are generously dotted with homemade butter and served with another winter favorite, mustard greens. You may serve them with any beans and greens of your choice. Yogurt salads or drinks may be served on the side.*

These breads, like the tortillas of Mexico, require hot water to form the dough. Also, like tortillas, they are generally not rolled out but made by hand as the dough cracks easily. They are thicker than the average tortillas and easy to form once you have learned the knack.

3 cups (14 ounces) Indian corn flour *(makki ka ata),* plus extra for dusting

1 teaspoon salt

Unsalted butter

Combine the flour and salt in a bowl. Slowly add about 1¾ cups plus 1 tablespoon of hot tap water, just bearable to the touch, mixing as you go, until you have the texture of soft Play-doh. Knead for about 10 minutes. Form a smooth ball, put it in a plastic bag, and set aside for 30 minutes or longer.

Divide the dough into 8 smooth balls. Flatten the balls into 8 smooth patties. Cover them with plastic wrap or a cloth.

Make a small wad with a cloth or paper toweling (as if you were going to polish furniture). Set aside.

Put a cast-iron griddle or frying pan on medium-high heat and then give it time to heat up. Meanwhile, take a patty and dip it in the extra flour. Roll the edges in the flour as well as if it were a wheel. Now put the patty down on a floured work surface, such as your counter. Press down repeatedly on the patty with the palm of one hand, all the while turning the patty a little. This will keep flattening it and thinning it out. Keep your other hand at the edge of the patty and push it in slightly to keep the edges from breaking. Dip the patty in flour a second time if you need to. When you have a disc that is about 6½ inches in diameter, lift it up carefully on the palm of one hand and then overturn it with a slap onto the hot griddle. Let it sit for a minute. Turn it over and cook on the second side for 40 seconds. Turn it over again and cook for 30 seconds. This time, using your wad, press down on one section of the bread as you give it a slight turn. Do this with speed, quickly going all the way around. The bread should puff up. Turn it over again and cook for 30 seconds, pressing down with the wad again if it has not puffed fully. Turn and cook another 30 seconds. The bread should have attractive brown spots and be cooked through. If not, turn one more time. Remove from the heat. Pinch the top a few times and put a generous dollop of butter on it (as generous as your diet allows). Keep in a covered dish.

Make all the breads this way and eat them while they are still hot.

MAKES 8

Corn Bread with Sesame Seeds   UNITED STATES

This is really my mother-in-law's recipe, to which I have added carrots and sesame seeds. It is light and cakelike. Perhaps that is why I like it so much.

Unsalted butter for greasing a baking pan

1 cup (5¾ ounces) yellow cornmeal

1 cup (5 ounces) unbleached all-purpose white flour

4 teaspoons baking powder

¾ teaspoon salt

¼ cup (1¾ ounces) extra-fine sugar

2 large eggs

1 cup milk

2 tablespoons peanut or canola oil, or melted shortening

2 carrots, peeled and grated

2 tablespoons sesame seeds

Preheat the oven to 425°F. Lightly butter a 9×9×2-inch baking pan.

Combine all the dry ingredients—cornmeal, flour, baking powder, salt, and sugar—and sift them. Put the eggs in a large bowl and beat them. Add the milk and oil. Mix lightly. Fold in the dry ingredients. Add the grated carrots and fold them in as well. Pour the mixture into the buttered baking pan. Sprinkle the sesame seeds evenly over the top and bake 20 to 25 minutes, or until a toothpick inserted inside comes out clean.

SERVES 6 TO 8

Teresa Ayuso's

Ecuador-Style Corn Muffins   EQUADOR

Eat these light and delicate muffins with a smear of butter at mealtime or at teatime and break-fast, with both butter and jam.

¼ cup unsalted butter, melted, plus extra for buttering the muffin pans

1¼ cups (5 ounces) cake flour

½ cup (2 ounces) yellow or white *masarepa* (page 335)

½ teaspoon salt

1 tablespoon baking powder

3 tablespoons sugar

1 cup heavy cream

1 egg, lightly beaten

Preheat the oven to 375°F.

Butter the muffin pans.

Mix the cake flour, *masarepa*, salt, baking powder, and sugar in a large bowl. Add the cream, egg, and butter, stirring just enough to wet the flour. Do not overmix. Spoon into the buttered muffin pans, filling them until they are about ⅔ full. Bake for 20 to 25 minutes.

MAKES 9

Millet

Once in a while, in the dead of our North Indian winter, my mother served millet flatbreads. Loaded with homemade white butter and sometimes topped with coarse sugar but mostly with crumbled jaggery freshly made right on our sugar-cane fields, they were a delight to us children. In Delhi, we ate these breads relatively rarely. However, in western India, they are quite a staple, especially among some of the nomadic communities in the desert. Today India is the largest producer of millet, which comes in many varieties and colors.

Millet may well have originated in Ethiopia or elsewhere in western Africa and then drifted into Asia and southern Europe by sea more than four thousand years ago. Perhaps it was actually carried in Arab dhows. Some people feel that it originated in Asia and then went west. What we know for sure is that it did take root among early civilizations in much of Asia and North Africa.

A tiny round grain, millet has protein that is superior to that of rice, wheat, and corn. Rich in magnesium as well, it is easy to digest and is thought to reduce blood cholesterol.

Today, millet is available in several forms.

Millet flour: You may buy this in health food shops and Indian groceries (where it is called *bajray ka ata* or *bajra* flour). Millet flour is singularly lacking in gluten and needs to be combined with wheat flour for yeast breads. Even the making of flatbreads requires a special technique that is closer to the making of *papoosas*—the flat corn breads of El Salvador—than anything else.

Millet grains: While mostly yellow millet grains are found in the West, in other parts of the world gray, white, and even reddish ones are fairly common. East Asia also produces a glutinous millet.

Millet grains may be cooked somewhat like rice, though they require roasting and presoaking to be tender and fluffy. They may also be roasted first and then combined with other grains, such as rice, or cooked by themselves with a variety of seasonings and vegetables.

Storing millet: Store millet grains and millet flour in a tightly closed container in a cool, dark, dry spot.

Plain Millet

Plain millet may be served instead of rice at any meal. Once cooked and fluffy, it can easily be converted into a salad just like soaked bulgur or used to stuff vegetables.

1 tablespoon olive or canola oil

1 cup millet

½ teaspoon salt

Have 2 cups of boiling water ready.

Put the oil in a heavy pan and set over medium-high heat. When hot, put in the millet. Stir and fry for about 3 minutes, or until the millet smells roasted and just begins to turn color (it will first turn paler and then just start to turn golden). Quickly pour in the boiling water, cover, and set aside for 1 hour. Uncover, add the salt and another 2 tablespoons of water, mix, and bring to a boil again. Cover tightly, turn the heat down to very low, and cook gently for 40 minutes. Turn off the heat. Leave covered for at least 15 minutes. If left covered in a warm place, the millet will stay hot for a good hour.

SERVES 3 TO 4

Millet with Cumin, Browned Onions, and Green Beans   INDIA

Bajray ki tahiri

Serve with a simple yogurt relish or with other vegetables and bean dishes.

3 tablespoons canola oil

1 cup millet

½ teaspoon whole cumin seeds

1 small onion (2 ounces), peeled and cut into fine half rings

About 20 green beans, cut crosswise into ¼-inch rounds

1 medium tomato, peeled, seeded, and finely diced

1 teaspoon salt

⅛ to ¼ teaspoon cayenne

1 tablespoon fresh lemon juice

Have 2 cups of boiling water ready.

Put 1 tablespoon of the oil in a small, heavy frying pan and set over medium-high heat. When hot, put in the millet. Stir and fry for about 3 minutes, or until the millet smells roasted and just begins to turn color (it will first turn paler and then just start to turn golden). Quickly pour in the boiling water, cover, and set aside for 1 hour.

Put the remaining 2 tablespoons of oil in a heavy pan and set over medium-high heat. When hot, put in the cumin seeds. Ten seconds later, put in the onion. Stir and fry until the onion has browned. Now put in the green beans and stir a few times. Put in the tomato and stir for a minute. Now add the salt, cayenne, and lemon juice as well as the millet and its soaking liquid. Stir and bring to a boil. Cover, turn the heat down to very low, and cook 40 minutes. Turn off the heat. Leave covered for at least 15 minutes. If left covered in a warm place, the millet will stay hot for a good hour.

SERVES 3 TO 4

Millet with Sesame Seeds, Carrot, and Chard
KOREAN-STYLE

Serve this millet dish with Spicy Soy Korean Sauce (page 676). You need just the green portion of the chard leaves. Save the white sections for another dish.

3 tablespoons peanut or canola oil

1 cup millet

2 teaspoons sesame seeds

2 scallions, cut crosswise into very fine rounds (both white and green sections)

1 medium carrot (3 ounces), peeled and cut into ¼-inch dice

3 to 4 large Swiss chard leaves, cut into fine strips

1 tablespoon soy sauce

2 teaspoons oriental sesame oil

1 teaspoon sugar

Have 2 cups of boiling water ready.

Put 1 tablespoon of the oil in a small, heavy frying pan and set over medium-high heat. When hot, put in the millet. Stir and fry for about 3 minutes, or until the millet smells roasted and just begins to turn color (it will first turn paler and then just start to turn golden). Quickly pour in the boiling water, cover, and set aside for 1 hour.

Put the remaining 2 tablespoons of oil in a heavy pan and set over medium-high heat. When hot, put in the sesame seeds. Stir. As soon as the sesame seeds start to

(recipe continues)

pop, a matter of seconds, put in the scallions and carrot. Stir and fry for a minute. Now put in the chard. Stir and cook until the chard wilts, lowering the heat if needed. Now add the soy sauce, sesame oil, and sugar. Give a few good stirs. Add the millet and its soaking liquid as well as 2 more tablespoons of water. Bring to a boil. Cover, turn the heat down to very low, and cook gently for 40 minutes. Let the pan sit, covered, for 10 minutes before serving.

SERVES 4

Millet Flatbreads   INDIA
Bajray Ki Roti

There is some solace in knowing that these breads were probably cooked in exactly this way four thousand years ago. They belong to the unchanging part of India. They are very simple and basic. Whenever I eat them, I am overwhelmed by an eerie sense of continuity.

The everyday breads of wandering shepherds in the deserts of western India, they are, on special occasions, served in a sweetened form, with butter and either crumbled jaggery or sugar. This is that version. These breads need to be cooked as soon as the dough is made. Generally, only a little dough is made at a time and the breads slapped out by hand.

½ cup (2¼ ounces) millet flour

½ cup (2¼ ounces) chapati flour (page 419)

¼ teaspoon salt

2 tablespoons unsalted butter

8 teaspoons granulated sugar or well-crumbled jaggery

Cut out a round piece of wax paper that is about 6 inches in diameter.

Set a cast-iron griddle, frying pan, or Indian *tava* on medium-low heat.

Combine the 2 flours and salt in a bowl. Slowly add a little less than ½ cup of warm water, mixing as you go, to form a medium-soft dough. Form a roll with the dough and then divide it into 4 parts. (Kneading is not necessary.) Make 4 balls.

Spread out the wax paper in front of you. Put a ball of dough down in the center and then, with a hand dipped in warm water, pat it down evenly until you have a 5-inch round.

Turn the heat under the griddle to medium. Lift up the wax paper and invert it onto the griddle. Peel the wax paper away, leaving the flatbread behind. Let the flatbread cook for about 40 seconds. Ease a spatula under it and turn it over. Cook it for another 40 seconds. Turn it again. This time cook each side for 15 seconds. Now begin to turn every 5 seconds until the bread has cooked for about 3 minutes in all. Put the bread on a plate. (Turn the heat down to low.) Prod the bread all over with the tip of a knife and then spread a quarter of the butter over it. Top with about 2 teaspoons of sugar or jaggery. This bread should be eaten immediately, but if that is not possible just butter and cover it with an inverted plate; the sweetening can be sprinkled on later. Make the remaining 3 breads the same way, remembering to turn the heat up to medium just before you slap the bread on the griddle.

MAKES 4

Oats

Consistently important in northern European nations such as Scotland and Ireland, oats have been little more than a very occasional breakfast food in the rest of the world. Now, newly aware of the fiber in the grain, fine oatmeal is being added to mixed grain breads and almost no granola is made without rolled oats. More oat cakes are being made in homes and eaten both in sweet and savory forms. It is worth noting that lightly salted porridges are eaten in Scotland and Ireland with cream or buttermilk but often without sugar. (Berbers in Morocco, who rightfully claim couscous as their national dish, often eat that in just the same way, with milk or buttermilk.)

No recipes for making porridges will be given here, as they appear on the boxes and cans that contain good-quality oatmeal. I will say here that the best oatmeal porridge I ever had was in John Tovey's inn and restaurant on Lake Windermere, in England's Lake District. It had been left to simmer in a slow cooker all night and was served hot and steaming the next morning with local heavy cream and brown sugar. I have had a similar creamy porridge at Ballymaloe, in County Cork, Ireland, where we followed it with local tayberries (a gorgeous cross between raspberries and loganberries). My husband and I eat oatmeal regularly in the winter. We cook it slowly in a double boiler which also gives very satisfying results.

The recipes in this book use oats in one of two forms:

Rolled oats: These are hulled oats that have been steamed, put under rollers to flatten them, and then dried. They are wonderful in granola where they are wetted and then roasted slowly. They may also be put into breads or dusted on top of loaves before baking.

Oat flour: I love the sweet, earthy taste of oat flour and use it frequently in my cooking. I throw it in when I am baking yeast breads and use it for making Indian-style chapatis. Whole grain oat flour is now sold by health food stores. It is low in gluten so most bakers recommend using no more than 25 percent oat flour in any yeast bread. Oats contain a natural antioxidant, which helps breads made with them stay fresh longer.

Granola

Even though our local health food store offers more than a dozen varieties of granola, none of them is quite right for me. One has too much coconut, another dried blueberries, a third has vanilla and cashews, and so on. I like my granola quite simple—just rolled oats, sunflower seeds, almonds, sesame seeds, and raisins. That's it. With a little cold milk poured on top, it is heaven.

4½ cups (14 ounces) rolled oats

1 cup (2½ ounces) sliced, blanched almonds

1 cup (4 ounces) untoasted sunflower
    seeds

½ cup (2 ounces) sesame seeds (the beige
    kind)

½ cup canola or peanut oil, plus a little extra
    for greasing the tray

1 cup honey

1 tablespoon dark brown sugar

¼ teaspoon salt

1 cup (4 ounces) raisins

Preheat the oven to 350°F.

Put the oats, almonds, sunflower seeds, and sesame seeds in a large baking tray lined with greased foil.

Combine 1 cup of water, ½ cup oil, the honey, sugar, and salt in a small pan and bring to a simmer. Stir to mix and turn off the heat. Slowly pour this mixture over the oats, nuts, and seeds, mixing and moistening thoroughly as you go. Spread the granola out in the tray and then place the tray in the oven. Bake for 15 minutes. Toss well. Turn the heat down to 275°F. and bake another 45 minutes, tossing every 10 to 15 minutes. Turn the heat down to 250°F. and bake for another 30 minutes or so, tossing every 10 minutes. Now turn the heat down to 225°F. and bake for a further 20 to 30 minutes, tossing after every 10 minutes, until the mixture appears dry. Remove the tray from the oven. Add the raisins. Toss the granola every now and then until it has cooled thoroughly. Store in a tightly closed jar.

MAKES 9 CUPS

Oat Flatbreads
Indian-Style Oat Chapatis

I make this flatbread smaller and thinner than regular chapatis. Sometimes I make it plain but at other times I throw in some spices, which change both its color and taste.

    Eat these flatbreads with jam or cheese or like tortillas, rolling them around a mixture of cooked beans, salads, and salsas (or chutneys) and even melting cheese on them.

½ cup whole grain oat flour

½ cup chapati flour (page 419)

¼ teaspoon salt

Butter or extra-virgin olive oil (optional)

Combine the two flours and salt in a bowl. Slowly add about 7 tablespoons of water, just enough to gather the dough together and make a very soft ball. Knead the dough well for 10 minutes. Make a smooth ball. You can make the flatbreads right away if you like or put the dough in a bowl and leave it covered with a lightly dampened cloth.

Set a cast-iron frying pan or griddle on medium-high heat. Allow it to heat up. Make a small wad with a cloth or paper towel.

Divide the dough into 8 balls. Take one ball of dough and dust it well with flour, keeping the rest covered as you work. Roll the ball out into a 4½- to 5-inch round on a floured surface. Lift it up and slap it back and forth between your palms to shake off the extra flour. Slap the chapati onto the hot griddle and let it cook for 40 seconds. Turn it over and cook the second side for another 30 seconds. Turn it over again and cook 5 to 6 seconds longer, pushing down on it with the wad of toweling and rotating it a little with each push. This helps the flatbread to puff up.

Put the cooked chapati on a plate and butter or oil it lightly if desired. Cover with an upturned plate. Make all the chapatis this way, making sure to wipe off the cast-iron pan with a paper towel after each one is made. If it takes you a while to roll out the next chapati, turn the heat under the cast-iron pan to low while you roll it and then turn it up again. Stack the chapatis one on top of the other and keep covered.

These chapatis are best as soon as they are made. But they can be made ahead and kept in a plastic bag in the refrigerator or freezer. Reheat foil-wrapped chapatis in a medium oven for 15 minutes. You can also sprinkle a little water on an individual chapati and then either heat it in a microwave oven for 20 to 30 seconds or slap it onto a hot, lightly greased griddle for a few seconds on each side.

MAKES 8

Variation

Spicy Oat Flatbreads

Make these exactly as in the preceding recipe but with this difference: When combining the two flours, increase the salt to ½ teaspoon and also put in ½ teaspoon ground cumin, ½ teaspoon ground coriander, ¼ teaspoon cayenne, and ⅛ teaspoon ground turmeric. Mix well before adding the water.

I love to roll these around cooked beans or Spicy Hash Brown Potatoes (page 278), along with some lettuce and tomato and a hot chutney.

Oat Bread with Sesame Seeds

I like to make this bread almost entirely in my electric mixer, as the dough is quite soft. You could also make it by hand. I give both methods.

The top of the bread is covered with sesame seeds in a manner beloved in the Middle East.

1 package active dry yeast

1 teaspoon brown sugar

¼ cup honey

1 tablespoon salt

About 4 cups unbleached all-purpose
    white flour

2 cups whole wheat flour

1½ cups whole grain oat flour

Oil for greasing

1 egg yolk, beaten

2 tablespoons plain yogurt, lightly mixed to a
    creamy consistency with a fork

3 tablespoons sesame seeds (the beige kind)

Combine the yeast and sugar with ¼ cup of very warm water in a cup or small bowl. Mix and set aside to "proof"—bubble up.

Empty the bubbling yeast into the bowl of a large mixer or a large bowl. Add 3 cups of warm water, the honey, salt, 2 cups of the white flour, and 1 cup of the whole wheat flour. Mix well either with the paddle attachment of the mixer or with a wooden spoon until smooth. Cover and set aside in a warm spot for 1 to 2 hours or until doubled in bulk and spongy.

Using the electric dough hook or a wooden spoon, slowly incorporate the remaining 1 cup of whole wheat flour and the oat flour. Now begin to add the remaining white flour, only as much as you need to make a really soft dough. If using the electric mixer, the dough will come off the sides of the bowl and climb up the dough hook. Remove it from the mixer bowl and form a soft ball with floured hands. If making by hand, the dough will soon become too hard to move around with a spoon. Empty it out onto a floured work surface and begin to knead the dough, incorporating more white flour if you need it. Your dough should be smooth, but as soft as you can manage. Knead well for 10 minutes and form a ball.

Put the ball of dough into a well-greased bowl, turning it around until it is well coated. Cover with a towel or plastic wrap and set aside in a warm place for 1½ hours or until doubled in bulk. Punch the dough down so it deflates and knead briefly on a floured surface.

Divide the ball of dough into two and form into loaves. Put the loaves into 2 well-greased 9×5×3-inch loaf pans. Cover with oiled plastic wrap and leave in a warm place for 1 hour or until doubled in bulk.

Preheat the oven to 375°F.

The dough will now have filled the pans and risen above them. Remove the covering carefully. Combine the egg yolk with the yogurt and brush the tops of the loaves with this mixture. Sprinkle the sesame seeds very generously over the top. Using a single-edged razor blade or the point of a knife, cut 3 diagonal slashes on the top of each loaf, going about ½ inch deep. Put the loaf pans in the oven to bake for 40 to 50 minutes or until golden brown and hollow-sounding when tapped. Remove the loaves from the pans immediately (go around them with a knife if they resist) and cool on a rack.

Once thoroughly cooled, the breads may be wrapped and either kept in a bread box for eating or frozen for future meals.

MAKES 2 LOAVES

From Bob's Red Mill in Portland

Oat Cakes SCOTLAND

These are wonderful with butter and jam as well as with cheese. As a variation, I sometimes add ½ teaspoon of coarsely crushed black peppercorns to the flours as I am mixing them.

¾ cup oat flour

¼ cup unbleached all-purpose white flour,
    plus a little more for dusting

⅓ teaspoon sugar

⅛ teaspoon salt

⅛ teaspoon baking powder

2 tablespoons melted butter, plus a little
    extra for greasing

Preheat the oven to 325°F.

Combine the oat flour, white flour, sugar, salt, and baking powder in a bowl. Add the butter and mix well with a fork. Slowly add about 3 tablespoons of hot water and mix again with the fork, gathering the dough together against the sides of the bowl. Form a ball and then flatten it.

Flour your work surface lightly and roll the dough out until it is ⅛ inch thick. Using a cookie-cutter, cut out 3-inch rounds. Gather the scraps and roll them out again until you have used up all the dough.

Put the oat cakes on a greased baking sheet and bake 25 minutes. Cool on a rack, then store in a resealable plastic bag for up to 2 days.

MAKES 8

Quinoa

A grain we hardly knew just a decade ago, this tiny, millet-sized seed (pronounced "keen wa") can now be found in all health food shops and many supermarkets. It has become a fashionable darling to our star chefs, who are using it in ever newer ways. I love it myself. And with good reason. It cooks fast, has a sweet, nutty taste, retains its shape and crunchy texture, may be used in stuffings and salads, and, what is best, is richer in calcium than milk, has more protein than most cereals (with well-balanced amino acids) and lots of phosphorous (more than a banana), magnesium, and iron. It is a grain to be reckoned with.

South American Indians knew that. It was the premier grain in the Andes mountains before the invasions of the Spanish conquerors. Incas called it their "mother seed" until laws were passed by their new rulers prohibiting its cultivation. All quinoa fields were destroyed by order and eventually the entire quinoa culture virtually disappeared for several centuries, only to reappear in the last few decades at the urging of interested Americans.

Washing and draining quinoa: Quinoa needs to be very well washed as the seeds are covered with saponin, a slightly bitter, soapy substance. Put the quinoa in a bowl and cover with water. Toss the grains in the water, rubbing them against each other, and then pour most of the water out. Do this several times until the water runs clear. Now put the grains in a fine sieve and drain thoroughly. Set the sieve over an empty bowl until you are ready to cook.

Cooking quinoa: Quinoa should be cooked in double its volume of water.

To serve 4, put 1 cup (6 ounces) of quinoa and 2 cups of water in a small, heavy pan. Add 1 teaspoon of salt if desired. Stir and bring to a boil. Cover tightly, turn the heat down to very low, and cook gently for 20 minutes. Set the pan aside in a warm place, covered and undisturbed, for another 15 minutes. (This helps the grains dry out and fluff up.) Fluff the grains and serve.

Plain quinoa is excellent for using in salads, for stir-frying with vegetables, and for layering in tomatoes and peppers (with grated cheese and herbs, for example) as part of the stuffing.

You may cook the quinoa in vegetable stock instead of water if you like.

Quinoa with Green Beans and Carrot

This spicy quinoa dish may be served hot, at room temperature, or cold. Here the rice is used like a spice; it gives an interesting roasted flavor.

I often serve this at brunch with a wedge of Persian Egg Pie with Herbs (page 537). Yogurt and cheeses may also be served on the side.

It also makes a wonderful stuffing for tomatoes or peppers.

As the ingredients go into the pan in very quick succession, it is a good idea to have them all ready when you start to cook.

2 tablespoons olive oil

½ teaspoon whole brown or yellow mustard seeds

1 teaspoon raw rice (jasmine or any long-grain rice)

1 dried hot red chile, crumbled

15 fresh curry leaves (use 10 fresh basil leaves as a different alternative)

10 green beans, cut crosswise into ¼-inch sections

¼ cup peeled carrot, cut into ¼-inch dice

1 cup (6 ounces) quinoa, washed and drained

1 teaspoon salt

1 tablespoon fresh lemon juice

Put the oil in a small, heavy pan and set over medium-high heat. When very hot, put in the mustard seeds. As soon as the mustard seeds begin to pop, a matter of seconds, put in the rice. Stir until the rice swells, whitens, and then browns lightly—which will happen fast. Quickly put in the red chile and stir once. Put in the curry leaves and give a stir or two. Put in the beans and carrot, stir once, and turn the heat to medium-low. Stir for 30 seconds, then add the quinoa and stir for a minute. Now put in 2 cups of water, 1 teaspoon salt, and the lemon juice and bring to a boil. Cover tightly, turn the heat down to very low, and cook for 20 minutes. Set the pan aside in a warm place, covered and undisturbed, for another 15 minutes. Fluff the grains and serve.

SERVES 4

Quinoa with Mushroom and Mustard Seeds

Quinoa can be combined with almost any seasoning or vegetable. Here I have chosen mushrooms and mustard seeds, which complement it beautifully. Serve with greens and beans, a yogurt cheese, or a bean curd dish.

1 tablespoon olive oil

½ teaspoon whole brown or yellow mustard seeds

1 large white mushroom, cut into small dice

1 thin slice of peeled fresh ginger, cut into minute dice

1 scallion, cut into very fine rings (both white and green portions)

1 cup (6 ounces) quinoa, washed and drained according to instructions on page 366

2 cups vegetable stock or water

Salt

Put the oil in a small, heavy pan and set over medium-high heat. When very hot, put in the mustard seeds. As soon as the mustard seeds begin to pop, a matter of seconds, put in the diced mushroom and ginger. Stir twice and turn the heat to medium-low. Put in the scallion and stir for a minute. Add the quinoa and stir for a minute. Now put in the stock or water and about 1 teaspoon salt if your stock is unsalted (otherwise adjust and use less) and bring to a boil. Cover tightly, turn the heat down to very low, and cook for 20 minutes. Set the pan aside in a warm place, covered and undisturbed, for another 15 minutes. Fluff the grains and serve.

SERVES 4

Quinoa with Tomato and Thyme

This dish is best made in the summer when the tomatoes are really red and sweet. I use fresh thyme from my garden but dried thyme will also do. Serve hot, at room temperature or cold.

2 tablespoons olive oil

½ teaspoon whole cumin seeds

1 garlic clove, peeled and very finely chopped

1 medium tomato (6 to 7 ounces), peeled, seeded, and finely chopped (for directions, see page 300)

1 teaspoon fresh thyme and ½ teaspoon dried

1 cup (6 ounces) quinoa, washed and drained according to instructions on page 366

2 cups vegetable stock or water

Salt

⅛ teaspoon cayenne (optional)

Put the oil in a small, heavy pan and set over medium-high heat. When very hot, put in the cumin seeds. Ten seconds later, put in the garlic. Stir once and quickly put in the tomato. Stir for 30 seconds and turn the heat to medium-low. Put in the thyme and stir for a minute. Add the quinoa and stir for a minute. Now put in the stock or water, about 1 teaspoon of salt if your stock is unsalted (otherwise adjust and use less), and cayenne.

Stir and bring to a boil. Cover tightly, turn the heat down to very low, and cook for 20 minutes. Set the pan aside in a warm place, covered and undisturbed, for another 15 minutes. Fluff the grains and serve.

SERVES 4

Quinoa with Corn and Potatoes

Did the Incas ever cook quinoa with corn? Or with potatoes? Did they ever cook it with its own very edible leaves even though the season for the leaves probably came well before the harvesting of the grain? We can only guess at all this. Here is a dish I have created to honor Inca and other native American ingredients. I have used sweet corn, which was probably not known then.

Frozen corn works well enough for this recipe; if you cannot get tomatillos, use green or red tomatoes. Serve with greens and beans.

3 tablespoons peanut or canola oil

1 smallish potato (3 ounces), peeled and cut into ½-inch dice

2 medium tomatillos (3 ounces in all), husks removed, washed and finely chopped

1 cup corn kernels, either frozen (defrosted) or fresh

½ to 1 teaspoon finely chopped fresh hot green or red chile (optional)

2 tablespoons finely chopped culantro (use fresh cilantro as a substitute)

1 cup (6 ounces) quinoa, washed and drained according to instructions on page 366

1¼ teaspoons salt

Put the oil in a heavy, medium pan and set over medium-high heat. Put in the potato and stir and cook for 2 to 3 minutes, or until the potato pieces have browned lightly on all sides. Add the tomatillos and stir and cook for 2 to 3 minutes, or until they soften. Add the corn, chile, and culantro. Stir for another minute. Add the quinoa and stir for a minute. Now add 2 cups of water and the salt. Stir and bring to a boil. Cover tightly, turn the heat down to very low, and cook gently for 20 minutes. Set the pan aside in a warm place, covered and undisturbed, for another 15 minutes. Fluff the grains and serve.

SERVES 6

Rice

There was a time when a trip to a New York supermarket led to only three kinds of rice: long-grain, short-grain, and parboiled. As for the health food stores, all they carried rather stolidly was a generic brown rice. What changes have been wrought in so short a time!

My local health food shop has shelves stocked with Bhutanese red rice, "forbidden" black rice (subtitled "the emperor's exclusive grain"), brown basmati rice, short-grain brown rice, long-grain brown rice, medium-grain brown rice, and organic basmati rice. Today our markets are brimming with jasmine rice, instant rice, Japanese short-grain rice, Turkish medium-grain rice, glutinous rice, several varieties of Italian risotto rice, and all manner of rice mixes that blend rice with nuts, beans, and seasonings.

Rice is the grain that feeds more people than any other cereal in this world. And it has been journeying steadily westward. It was the Arabs who spread it across Europe. From there, the British brought it to North America. But where did it originate?

Rice grains dating to 6000 B.C. have been found in northern Thailand. In North India, archaeological digs have revealed grains that have been radiocarbon-dated to 5000 B.C. Rice, from the wild plants gathered by hermits to the much valued aromatic and long-grain rices in cultivation, are mentioned in ancient Indian texts that date back four thousand years. There are terraced fields in Kashmir that date to 10,000 B.C. What were they used for? While rice may have developed simultaneously on several continents, its earliest cultivation seems to have been in northern India and the triangle that connects Burma, Thailand, Laos, Vietnam, and South China.

When Aristobolus of Kassandrelia accompanied Alexander the Great to India, he found what for him was a strange, highly productive plant standing in formal, water-filled beds. Rice was already North India's premier grain. It was ground into flour, made into dry wafers, pressed, puffed, made into pancakes and dumplings, stuffed into leaves, and made into wines and liquors.

In ancient India, rice was cooked with sesame seeds, jaggery, and milk and even made into a soup with pomegranate juice flavored with dried ginger and long pepper (see page 580 for my stab at this). Brides threw parched rice into the sacred fire as symbols of fertility and infants were fed it at the *annaprassana* ceremony, when a child is given his first solid food. (This ceremony remains the same today.) Rice and *ghee* are supposed to bring glory to the child. In some regions a full measure of rice is placed strategically near the door for a bride to knock over as she enters her new home, signifying a future with plenty.

Four thousand years ago China too had declared rice to be one of its premier grains. In many parts of India, Japan, China, Indonesia, and Thailand, a meal and rice are almost synonymous. I have Indonesian friends who might eat a hamburger in town at 7 P.M. but not consider themselves to have dined until they go home and eat their rice. Japanese men will eat and carouse in town until midnight and then go home and have rice with their wives as a symbol of having a dutiful meal at home. Buddha, when he was fasting, limited himself to just a few grains of rice a day in order to discipline his body. He was having his meal, only in a minuscule portion.

In all of Asia and many parts of the Mediterranean I find it remarkable that everybody prefers their own rice. If you are used to eating rice, you are used to eating a particular rice and nothing else quite satisfies. It is only in America, where rice is still not in the blood, that every new rice is embraced as the wonder of the day. In Bali, you will hear that the only perfect rice is the plump Balinese one, grown under the watchful eye of the goddess Sri. The Japanese, who could export cheap rice from California, will pay six times as much for their own because they insist it is sweeter and has more texture. The Italians prefer their own risotto rice, while the Greeks and Turks, who have similar rices, will prefer to eat what they grow. In India, much of the west coast thinks that the best daily rice is their partially milled red rice and in the south, it is "boiled rice," a parboiled, medium-grain rice that sits on every single plate and banana leaf.

While rice is a grain that needs little done to it before eating other than husking and boiling, many people in the West are wary of cooking it. There are a few simple tricks that are easily learned. Each rice has its own idiosyncrasies and once they are understood, the cooking is quite manageable. Remember that, generally speaking, a 1-cup measure of rice will, in volume, yield about 3 times as much cooked rice. This might feed 4 westerners, but only 1 to 2 Asians.

All rices need to have their outer hulls removed to be edible. What is then left is brown rice (or black or red rice, depending upon the color of the original hull). If the next layer, which is bran, is also removed, you end up with white milled rice.

Rices are classified according to size and shape. Short-grain rices are the shortest. They are also starchy and tend to be sticky when cooked. They are mostly recommended for desserts. Medium-grain rices are plump, a little bigger, and a little less starchy. Long-grain rices are the least starchy and the grains are more able to remain separate after cooking. They are ideal for pilafs.

It is important that all rices be cooked in heavy pans with an even distribution of heat. Tight-fitting lids are essential if you are using the absorption method. If you do not have a tight-fitting lid, put a piece of well-crimped foil between the top of the pot and the lid. Also, the size of the pan should be just about right for the amount of rice being cooked. Remember that rice will expand about 3 times. Your pan should ideally be no larger than 5 to 6 times the volume of the raw rice.

Here are some of the rices and rice products that I have used in this section (See also the color section for a photograph of these rices.):

Brown rice: The grains at this stage are covered with bran. Bran, as we know, fights cholesterol and is also full of nutrients such as thiamine, riboflavin, and niacin. Brown rice, which is now sold in all sizes, takes longer to cook than white rice and has a chewy texture. It is not suitable for all meals as it is fairly dense. Generally, I like to wash brown rice and then soak it in double the volume of water. After that I cook the brown rice in the soaking liquid for 35 minutes. I let the pan rest for another 10 minutes before uncovering it. All brown rices—including brown basmati—may be cooked this way. The textures will be different, of course. Let me say here and now that Indians never eat brown basmati rice. Basmati rice, the white milled kind, is considered an expensive delicacy, eaten at special occasions when the health benefits of bran are rarely a consideration.

White basmati rice: Although various aromatic rices were known in ancient India, the name *basmati*—meaning "one with a good smell"—seems to have come into usage around the seventeenth century. It was a special long-grain rice grown in the foothills of the Himalayas where the sun and the snow-fed rivers provided just the right nourishment. (I find it quite baffling that a commercial American rice company is attempting to get the patent on the word *basmati*. The production of basmati to supply the world's growing market is a great source of revenue for a developing nation like India. To try and take the name away seems a little like stealing.)

Aromatic rices—and there are several in this world, including several more in India—have been prized through history. Their aromas vary. One of my earliest childhood memories is the sweet smell of basmati rice cooking in our family kitchen. Even today in my Manhattan apartment, the aroma still brings back the feel of the sun, the chirping of the green parrots, the view of the river which we could see from the dining room, the feel of my mother's sari, the touch of my grandfather's beard—in short, wherever I am, it brings back my childhood in Delhi.

Other than aroma, one of the chief characteristics of the basmati rice grain is that it is slim and curves slightly upward. Once cooked, the entire grain elongates and grows to 3 times its original length. The thickness changes little. It is this elegance, along with its aroma, that makes basmati rice so prized. When bought at auction by wholesalers, the best grades have few broken pieces and a uniform creamy white color. The best basmati rice is also aged.

In India there are some communities that will buy the rice in bulk as soon as it is harvested. Then they store it at home and eat it the following year. For most other people, the rice is aged in airy stacks by the wholesalers for at least nine months. The aging mellows the rice, hardens it, and also, as ancient Indian texts have maintained, makes it more digestible. Ibn Batuta, a Moroccan traveler who came to India in A.D. 1340, was shown the sultan's rice, which was stored in the walls of the city of Delhi for ninety years. It had turned black but was still edible!

Japanese rice: Used for both Japanese and Korean meals, this is a short-grain plump rice that is slightly sticky when cooked, ideal for eating from a bowl with chopsticks. It is washed before cooking and then left in a strainer for an hour to absorb the water clinging to it. After that it is cooked for about 20 minutes by the absorption method. The proportion of water to rice is 1¼:1.

Risotto rice: Arborio, Carnaroli, and Vialone Nano are three varieties of the rounded, medium-grain Italian rice used for risottos. It is generally not washed as the starchiness in the grain and outside it is very desirable. For more on this rice, see page 405.

Glutinous or sweet rice: This is an opaque white short-grain rice that is used mainly for the making of East Asian desserts. It is, however, the daily rice for the inhabitants of northern and eastern Thailand as well as for some people in Laos, Cambodia, and Vietnam.

The rice is washed and then soaked for 6 to 8 hours in cold water or 2 to 3 hours in hot water. After that it is generally steamed, though it can be cooked in a double boiler as well. In the markets of northeastern Thailand, this rice is cooked on the pavements for all who wish to buy it for their dinner. Large conical baskets filled with soaked rice are stuck into the narrow mouths of large steaming vessels. The basket is lifted and the rice tossed repeatedly so all the grains can cook evenly. Once cooked, buyers take the shiny grains home in plastic bags but the minute the rice reaches the kitchen, it is transferred into very traditional covered baskets. Here it stays soft and warm for several hours. It is these baskets that are taken to the dining table. Everyone serves themselves a little rice on their plates. To eat it they form a ball and then dip it in the daily stew or spicy salad.

Small-grain "forbidden" Chinese black rice: I have been eating black rice in East Asia for decades. My favorite dish remains a dessert I had one hot afternoon in Malaysia: a bowl of very cold, sweetened black rice soup topped with equally cold coconut milk. Heaven. Its color is deceptive. Rather like some "black" tulips, it is not black at all but a deep purple. When you cook it you might be confused into thinking that you are cooking blueberries as the rice oozes a purple-red liquid. Black rice generally needs an overnight soak but this special, small, shiny variety is fast cooking and a 1-hour soak is enough.

Red Bhutanese rice: This is a partially milled rice where the bran color is red. It cooks with a little less water than most brown rices and has a very pleasing earthy flavor. Red rices are found in the western Indian regions of Goa and Maharashtra as well, which I feel are of better quality than the Bhutanese rice available to us.

Washing rice: Many milled rices have food additives that are tossed with cornstarch and added to the grains. They only serve to make the rice gummy. I almost always wash them off. The rice sometimes has other impurities. It always has milling dust that needs to be removed.

Put the rice in a bowl and fill the bowl with water. Gently cup your hands under the rice and turn it over a few times. Quickly pour most of this cloudy water out by tilting the bowl. If you are slow, the rice will absorb the unclean starchy water. Quickly fill the bowl again with fresh water and wash the rice again the same way. Do this several times until the water is almost clear.

Soaking and draining rice: Soaking the rice helps to keep the grains separate, if that is the end you seek. Cover the rice very generously with fresh water and leave it to soak for 30 minutes. Longer does not hurt. It will swell and turn opaque. After soaking, drain the rice thorougly and leave it in a colander.

Cooking white basmati rice and other good-quality long-grain rices: There are dozens of ways to cook these rices, each with a slightly different result, so check the recipes individually. Here are some of the possibilities: baking, the absorption method (just enough water to be absorbed by the rice), parboiling and then baking, stir-frying and then using the absorption method, and boiling and then baking. Generally, when you cook long-grain rice by the absorption method, the ratio of water to rice, in volume, should be $1\frac{1}{3}:1$.

Rice flours: Rice flours are made from both plain rice and glutinous rice. They are used in the preparation of sweets, savories, pancakes, and noodles.

Storing rice and rice flours Store rice and rice flours in tightly closed jars.

Rice noodles: In Asia, rice noodles can be got fresh or dried, in all types of thicknesses. In a Bangkok rice noodle factory, I have watched rice flour dough being extruded from a showerhead poised above a vat of boiling water. As long noodles fell in, they were moved around to firm up and then quickly pushed out to have a cold water bath after which they were drained and made into small coils. These coils were swiftly arranged in overlapping layers on banana-leaf-covered baskets and immediately sent out for sale. Their life was just 24 hours. They would be served with all manner of coconut sauces and as stir-fried dishes.

In South India, housewives make their own rice noodles with small, hand-held wooden presses. As they push out a dough of rice flour and hot water, the noodles fall into oiled saucers or else on to a piece of muslin stretched over boiling water. They are steamed and eaten, sometimes with just lightly sweetened coconut milk flavored with cardamom or with a mixture of oil and spices.

In the West, fresh rice noodles are hard to find. What is easier to get are dried noodles. The very fine ones are sold as *rice sticks* and the slightly wider ones as *banh pho*. Rice sticks can be dropped into boiling water until just tender (a matter of a few minutes—you will need to watch them) and then rinsed under cold water. They can also be given a dip in water, shaken, and then deep-fried in hot oil. This makes them expand and turn into a puffy, tangled mass, wonderful for garnishes. *Banh pho* should be soaked for 30 minutes and then dropped into boiling water for less than a minute (again you will need to test them). They should be drained and rinsed. If you need them hot, they can be dropped into boiling water for a second again, just before eating. A little oil helps to keep the noodles from sticking to each other.

Plain Basmati Rice
Saaday Basmati Chaaval

INDIA

This is the everyday rice at our restaurant Dawat in New York. It is plain basmati rice cooked by the absorption method, except that we throw a few cardamom pods into the cooking water for their exquisite aroma.

2 cups basmati rice, washed in several changes of water and drained (see page 374 for details, if needed)

5 whole cardamom pods

Put the rice in a bowl, cover generously with water, and leave to soak for 30 minutes. Drain thoroughly.

In a heavy pan, combine the drained rice, 2⅔ cups of water, and the cardamom pods. Bring to a boil. Cover very tightly, turn the heat down to very, very low, and cook for 25 minutes. Leave the pot covered and undisturbed for 10 minutes or more. Remove the cardamom and serve.

SERVES 4

Plain Long-Grain Rice

Sometimes we are all in a big rush. There is no time to wash and soak rice. Here is a simple method of cooking rice under those conditions. It is best to use American-style long-grain rice here. It would be a pity to waste the basmati.

2 cups long-grain rice

1 teaspoon unsalted butter (optional)

¾ teaspoon salt (optional)

Put the rice in a heavy pan. Add the butter and salt, if you want. Now pour in 3 cups of water, stir, and bring to a boil. Cover, turn the heat down to very, very low, and cook for 25 minutes. Leave the pan covered and undisturbed for another 10 minutes.

SERVES 4

Plain Brown Rice

Brown rice takes longer to cook than white rice. Soaking reduces the cooking time.

2 cups long- or medium-grain brown rice, washed in several changes of water and drained

1 teaspoon olive oil

¾ teaspoon salt (optional)

Lots of freshly ground black pepper (optional)

Put the rice in a bowl, cover with 4 cups of water, and leave to soak for 1 hour.

Put the rice and its soaking liquid in a heavy pan. Add the oil as well as the salt and pepper, if you want them. Bring to a boil. Cover, turn the heat down to very, very low, and cook for 35 minutes. Leave the pan covered and undisturbed for another 10 minutes.

SERVES 4 TO 6

Clockwise, from lower right:
Instant Korean Cabbage Pickle, Simple South Indian Mango Pickle, Delhi-Style Peach Chutney, Sweet and Sour Lemon Chutney, Moroccan-Style Salted Lemons, Delhi-Style Cilantro and Mint Chutney

ABOVE
Chickpea Pizza with Rosemary, Tomato, and Parmesan Cheese

BELOW
Azuki and Whole Mung Beans, Crushed and Sauteed, in a yin/yang pattern with, *from left to right:* **cellophane noodles, unhulled whole mung beans, unhulled split mung beans, hulled and split mung beans, mung bean sprouts, azuki beans.**

Top to bottom:
**Flavored pressed
bean curd, tempeh,
firm bean curd, soft
bean curd, dried soy
beans, sprouted soy
beans, soy milk**

Polenta with Tex-Mex Chili

Masa harina

Masa

Hominy

Popping corn

Cornmeal

Polenta

Posole

Grits

Fresh corn kernels

Masa harina "precocida"

Corn flour

Dried corn kernels

Clockwise, from left:
Eggplant with Minty Tomato Sauce and Yogurt, Eggplants with Spicy Shallot-Tomato Sauce, Cold Eggplants with Spicy Chinese Peanut Dressing

Spelt

Moroccan couscous

Coarse bulgur wheat

Semolina

Seitan

Skinned wheatberries

Lebanese couscous

Whole wheat couscous

Whole wheatberries

Fine bulgur wheat

Israeli couscous

TOP
**South Indian
Pancakes with Onion
and Tomato, Sweet
Mango Lassi**
CENTER
**Soft Spongy Pancakes,
Moroccan Mint Tea**

BOTTOM
**Israeli Couscous
with Asparagus and
Fresh Mushrooms**

Sprouted black-eyed peas

Split fava beans

Black turtle beans

Chickpea flour

Sprouted lentils

Chana dal

Whole fava beans

Sprouted chickpeas

Dried chickpeas

Red lentils (masoor dal)

Canned chickpeas

French lentils

Whole green lentils

Black-eyed peas

Red kidney beans

Pinto beans

Cannellini beans

Yellow split peas

Giant white beans

Split pigeon peas (toovar dal, Arhar dal)

Navy (great northern) beans

Whole pigeon peas

Split urad beans

Whole urad beans (urad dal)

**Persian Pilaf with
Lime and Green Beans**

**Lime and Ginger
Syrup, Sour Cherry
Syrup, Caribbean
Seasoning Sauce**

Red Bhutanese rice

Long-grain brown rice

"Forbidden" Chinese black rice

Basmati rice

Japanese rice

Glutinous rice

Risotto rice

Long-grain white rice

Wild rice

Kallaloo

Top to bottom:
Beet and Mushroom Curry, Boiled Beets and Beet Greens with a Horseradish Dressing, Grated Beets with Shallots

Plain "Forbidden" Black Rice

This is such an unusual rice that you almost need to create a meal around it. I have served it surrounded by grilled red peppers that had been dotted with one of my Romesco Sauces (pages 669 and 670). That was a superb combination. I have also served it surrounded by sliced summer tomatoes and mozzarella—with fresh basil and extra-virgin olive oil, of course.

1 cup "forbidden" black rice, washed in several changes of water and drained

¾ teaspoon salt

Put the rice in a bowl and cover with 1¾ cups of water. Leave to soak for 1 hour. Put the rice, its soaking liquid, and the salt in a heavy pan and bring to a boil. Cover, turn the heat down to low, and cook for 35 minutes. Let the pan rest, covered and undisturbed, for 10 minutes.

SERVES 4

Bhutanese Red Rice   **BHUTAN**

This is a simple, peasant-style rice dish.

1 cup red Bhutanese rice, washed in several changes of water and drained

Put the rice in a bowl and cover with 1¾ cups of water. Leave to soak for 45 minutes. Put the rice and its soaking liquid in a heavy pan and bring to a boil. Cover tightly, turn the heat down to very low, and cook gently for 35 minutes. Leave the pot covered and undisturbed for 15 minutes.

SERVES 3 TO 4

Plain Japanese Rice

Sometimes when I am very hungry, I just roll a ball of freshly cooked Japanese rice in toasted sesame seeds, wrap the ball in nori seaweed, dip it in soy sauce, and then just devour it. To me, this is the essence of Japan. Here is the basic rice. You might choose to do other things with it.

2 cups Japanese short-grain rice

Wash the rice in several changes of water and then leave to drain in a strainer for 1 hour.

Put the rice in a heavy pan. Add 2½ cups of water and cover tightly. Bring to a boil. When you see the steam escaping from under the lid, turn the heat down to very low and cook for 20 minutes. Turn the heat to high for just a minute and then remove the pan from the heat. Let the pan sit, covered and undisturbed, for another 15 minutes.

SERVES 4

Steamed Plain Glutinous Rice

In northern Thailand, glutinous rice is eaten with spicy salads and stews. It is also wonderful with fresh fruit, especially if you dribble coconut milk and sugar on it!

1½ cups glutinous rice, washed in several
changes of water and drained

Soak the rice in water that covers it well for 6 to 8 hours. Drain.

Set up the steaming equipment (page 736). The steaming tray should be perforated. Lay a piece of muslin or a tea cloth on it and then spread the rice over the top. Put the tray in the steamer, cover, and steam for about 25 minutes, or until the rice is tender. Transfer the rice to a closed container (in northern Thailand, this would be a special tall basket with a lid).

SERVES 4

Spicy Brown Rice with Sprouted Spelt

You may use sprouted wheat instead of the spelt, if you like.

2 cups long-grain brown rice, washed in
    several changes of water and drained

1 tablespoon peanut or canola oil

1 teaspoon whole brown or yellow mustard
    seeds

½ to 1 fresh hot green chile, finely chopped

1 scallion, cut into fine rings (white and green
    portions)

2 tablespoons finely chopped cilantro

½ cup sprouted spelt (page 417)

1 teaspoon salt

Put the rice in a bowl, cover with 4 cups of water, and leave to soak for 1 hour.

Put the oil in a heavy pan and set over medium-high heat. When hot, put in the
mustard seeds. As soon as the mustard seeds begin to pop, a matter of seconds,
put in the chile and scallion. Stir once or twice and put in the cilantro. Stir once
and put in the spelt. Give a few stirs and put in the rice with its soaking liquid
and the salt. Bring to a boil. Cover, turn the heat down to very, very low, and cook
for 35 minutes. Leave the pan covered and undisturbed for another 10 minutes.

SERVES 4

Parsi Rice with Cloves and Cinnamon   INDIA
Parsi Pullao

This rice dish can be served with almost any meal.

2 cups basmati rice

1½ tablespoons sugar

¼ cup peanut or canola oil

8 cloves

2-inch piece of cinnamon

1 medium onion, cut in half lengthwise and
    then into very fine half rings

1 teaspoon salt

Wash the rice in several changes of water. Drain. Cover well with water and leave
to soak for 30 minutes. Drain well.

(recipe continues)

Put the sugar in a small, heavy pan and set over medium-low heat. Allow the sugar to melt, caramelize, and brown without stirring. Now pour in 1 cup of water. Be careful, as it will bubble. Stir. Pour into a measuring jug. Add more water to make 2⅔ cups and set aside.

Put the oil in a heavy pan and set over medium-high heat. When hot, put in the cloves and cinnamon. Stir once or twice and put in the onion. Stir and fry until the onion has browned. Now put in the rice and salt. Stir gently to coat all the rice grains with oil. Now pour in the caramel water and bring to a boil. Cover, turn the heat down to very low, and cook gently for 25 minutes. Remove the cloves and cinnamon before serving.

SERVES 4 TO 6

Lemon Rice

INDIA

Elamcha Saatham

In South India, this rice is flavored with lime juice. At our New York restaurant, Dawat, we do a simpler version using both the juice and rind of lemons instead. This has proved to be very popular.
Serve Indian style, with vegetable dishes, any bean dish, poppadums, a yogurt relish, and pickles, of course, or Western style with beans, grilled vegetables, and salads.
This is served at room temperature in South India, where it is generally quite balmy. In the colder West, I like to serve it hot.

2 cups basmati rice

1 teaspoon salt

2 tablespoons peanut or canola oil

1 teaspoon whole brown mustard seeds

15 fresh curry leaves (use fresh basil or holy basil leaves as an interesting substitute)

2 to 3 teaspoons fresh lemon juice (put in 2 teaspoons first and then taste)

2 teaspoons finely grated lemon rind

Wash the rice in several changes of water. Drain thoroughly. Combine the rice, salt, and 3 cups of water in a medium pot and bring to a boil. Cover tightly, turn the heat down to very low, and cook for 25 minutes.

Put the oil in a large frying pan and set over medium-high heat. When hot, put in the mustard seeds. As soon as the seeds begin to pop, a matter of seconds, put in the curry leaves. Stir once and then empty the contents of the frying pan over the rice. Add the lemon juice and rind. Mix gently with a fork or slotted spoon. Mix once again when emptying into a serving dish.

SERVES 6

Saffron-Orange Rice

Zarda

This slightly sweet Muslim-style, North India rice dish is served with meals and not as dessert. Serve it with stuffed vegetables such as the Stuffed Baby Eggplants (page 184) from Turkey.

Although you could dry your own orange skins in strips (make sure that the oranges have not been sprayed with pesticides), you could also buy dried strips from Chinese grocers.

1 teaspoon saffron threads

2 tablespoons hot milk

1 cup basmati rice

4 tablespoons *ghee* (page 723) or unsalted butter, melted

6 whole green cardamom pods

2 tablespoons whole raw cashews, split in halves lengthwise

1 tablespoon blanched slivered almonds

1 tablespoon golden raisins

5 slices of dried orange skin

7 tablespoons sugar

½ teaspoon salt

Put the saffron in a very small cup or bowl. Add the milk and set aside for 2 to 3 hours.

Wash the rice in several changes of water. Drain. Put the rice in a bowl, add water to cover by 2 inches, and set aside for 30 minutes. Drain.

Preheat the oven to 325°F.

Put the *ghee* or butter in a heavy flame- and ovenproof pot and set over medium-high heat. When it is hot, put in the cardamom pods, cashews, almonds, and raisins. Stir until the almonds are golden. Put in the rice and stir gently for a minute. Add the orange skin, sugar, saffron and milk, salt, and 1⅓ cups of water. Stir gently to mix and bring to a boil. Cover, first with a piece of foil and then with a lid, and place in the oven. Bake for 30 minutes. Stir gently before serving.

Removed the whole cardamom pods before serving, as they are not meant to be eaten.

SERVES 4

Santha Ramanujam's

South Indian Coconut Rice INDIA

Tengai Saadam

This is a very pleasant rice dish that should be made when fresh coconut is available. I happen to love it with Malaysian Pineapple Curried with Cinnamon and Star Anise (page 322) and any dried bean dish.

This dish is served at room temperature in a part of the world where the mercury seems stuck at "balmy." In the colder West, it is best to serve it lukewarm. If the rice cools off too much, you could zap it briefly in a microwave oven after sprinkling it lightly with water and covering it.

1 tablespoon hulled and split *urad dal* (page 112)

2 cups long-grain rice (not basmati)

3 tablespoons canola oil or a combination of canola oil and *ghee* (page 723)

1 teaspoon whole brown mustard seeds

2 whole dried hot red chiles, each broken in 2

Generous pinch of ground asafetida

2 tablespoons raw cashew nuts, broken up (1 cashew nut into about 6 pieces)

15 fresh curry leaves (use fresh basil or holy basil leaves as an interesting substitute)

1½ cups (6 ounces) freshly grated coconut (page 718)

1½ teaspoons salt

Soak the *urad dal* in boiling water to cover and set aside for 1 hour. Drain and pat dry.

While the *dal* soaks, make the rice. Combine the rice and 3 cups of water in a medium pot and bring to a boil. Cover tightly, turn the heat down to very low, and cook 25 minutes. Turn off the heat and let the rice sit, covered and in a warm place, until the *dal* has finished soaking. Now, empty the rice out into a large, shallow bowl or dish to cool off a bit.

Put the oil in a large frying pan and set over medium-high heat. When hot, put in the mustard seeds. As soon as the seeds begin to pop, a matter of seconds, put in the red chiles and asafetida. As soon as the chiles begin to darken, put in the cashew nuts and curry leaves. When the cashews turn golden, put in the drained *dal*. Stir until the *dal* turns red. Now put in the coconut. Stir and cook for 2 minutes. Then turn the heat down to medium-low. Keep stirring and frying until the coconut has browned a bit. Turn off the heat. Empty the contents of the frying pan over the rice. Add the salt and mix thoroughly (a slightly wet wooden paddle is ideal for this).

SERVES 4 TO 6

Rice with Spinach

Roz eb Sabanigh

SYRIA

Serve this elegant rice dish with Middle Eastern or Indian bean and vegetable dishes. Yogurt relishes go well with it, too. If you wish to use frozen spinach, get leaf spinach and cook it according to package directions, then squeeze out all the water and chop finely.

For this dish, I bought 1 pound of untrimmed spinach. After trimming, I had about 14 ounces.

I like to use basmati rice here, but any good-quality long-grain rice will do. I have even made it with Thai jasmine rice.

2 cups basmati rice

14 ounces trimmed fresh spinach (see recipe introduction), well washed

¼ cup olive oil

2 (2-inch) cinnamon sticks

½ cup finely chopped onion

1½ teaspoons salt

Rinse the rice in several changes of water. Drain. Cover the rice well with water and leave to soak for 30 minutes. Drain.

Meanwhile, bring a large pot of water to a rolling boil. Drop in the spinach and bring to a boil again. Boil rapidly for 3 to 4 minutes, or until the spinach has wilted completely. Drain and refresh under cold water. Squeeze out all the moisture by cupping small amounts of spinach between your palms and pressing. Chop the spinach finely.

Put the oil in a medium, heavy-bottomed pan and set over medium-high heat. When hot, put in the cinnamon. Stir once and put in the onion. Stir and fry for about 3 minutes, or until the onion has browned at the edges. Put in the spinach. Stir and fry for about 3 minutes, or until most of the water in the spinach seems to have disappeared. Turn the heat down to medium-low. Continue to stir and sauté the spinach for another 7 to 8 minutes. The spinach will now be a few shades darker. Put in the drained rice and salt. Stir and sauté gently for 2 minutes. Add 2⅔ cups of water and bring to a boil. Cover very tightly, turn the heat down to very low, and cook gently for 25 minutes. Fluff gently before serving.

SERVES 6

Shamsi Davis'

Persian Pilaf with Lime
and Green Beans

IRAN

Lubia Polo

This is one of the best vegetarian pilafs I have ever eaten. It comes to the table almost like a cake, a slightly collapsed cake, but still very cakelike. The top, all reddish-gold and encrusted, consists of a layer of sliced potatoes, now all beautifully crisp. Below it is a layer of white rice. Below that is a layer of green beans stewed with shallots and tomatoes that have been flavored with the highly aromatic Persian dried limes and with cinnamon. There follow more layers of rice and green beans.

Persian dried limes are a world unto themselves. Once you have discovered them, you will wonder how you ever lived without them. (Look for mail-order sources of Middle Eastern foods at the back of the book.) When you buy them, they are as hard as rocks, feel hollow, and look quite unprepossessing. You need to hit them with a well-aimed mallet so they break into 3 to 4 pieces. The insides are blackish and just as unprepossessing as the outsides. You need to pull or scrape the insides out and collect them in a bowl, making sure you discard the bitter seeds. Now grind the black gold that you have collected in a clean coffee grinder and store it in a jar. Do just 2 to 3 limes at a time. If all this sounds arduous, it isn't. It took me less than 5 minutes to do 2 limes, which was more than I needed, but you need to do that amount to make the grinder run properly. Besides, you could always use fresh lime juice as a substitute.

It is best to do the final cooking of the rice in a nonstick pan. A 3-quart size is ideal. If you double the recipe—and I often do for parties—double the size of the pan and the ingredients. The cooking times remain the same.

This rice is such a favorite that I cook it for family dinners and for entertaining. With it, I serve a dish of some beans or chickpeas, such as the Cypriot dish, Black-Eyed Peas with Swiss Chard (page 20), and an Irani boorani, such as the Yogurt with Eggplant and Walnuts (page 552). At a dinner party, you may add other vegetable dishes and salads.

2 cups basmati rice, picked over, washed, and drained

¼ cup peanut or canola oil

2 to 3 large shallots (3 ounces), peeled and finely chopped (red onion may be substituted)

2 cups (8 ounces) green beans (dwarf or French beans), cut into 1-inch pieces

1 teaspoon tomato paste

3 plum or any other smallish tomatoes (about 5 to 6 ounces), peeled, seeded, and finely chopped (canned tomatoes may be used)

¾ teaspoon ground cinnamon

Salt

1 teaspoon ground dried lime (see above) or 1 tablespoon fresh lime juice

2 tablespoons butter

Generous pinch of ground turmeric

1 large boiling potato

Soak the rice for 30 minutes in lukewarm water that covers it generously. Drain.

While the rice is soaking, put the oil in a medium pan and set over medium-high heat. When it is hot, add the shallots. Stir and fry for 3 to 4 minutes, or until the shallots are lightly browned. Put in the green beans and stir them around for 3 minutes. Now add the tomato paste and tomatoes as well as 3 tablespoons of water (or liquid from the can of tomatoes), ¼ teaspoon cinnamon, and ¾ teaspoon salt. Stir and bring to a simmer. Cover, turn the heat down to low, and simmer gently for 12 to 13 minutes, or until the beans are tender. Add the lime and stir to mix. Set aside.

Put 10 cups of water into a large pot and bring to a rolling boil. Add 1½ table-spoons salt and mix in. Scatter the rice into the boiling water and bring to a boil again. Boil rapidly for 5½ minutes, or until the rice is almost done but still has a very slim hard core in its very center. (To test remove a grain and press it between the fingers.) Drain the rice immediately and leave in a sieve or colander.

Put the butter in a nonstick pan (see recipe introduction) and set it over low heat. Add 2 tablespoons of water and the turmeric. Peel the potato and cut it crosswise into ⅛-inch-thick rounds. Lay a round in the center of the pan. Surround it with the other rounds until you have no more space left. You can cut some of the rounds if needed to almost cover the bottom. A few blank spaces are fine. As soon as all the butter has melted, divide the rice into 3 parts and spread one part over the potatoes. Top this rice with half of the green beans, spreading them out evenly. Sprinkle ¼ teaspoon cinnamon over the beans. Spread the second part of the rice over the beans. Top this rice with the remaining beans, once again spreading them out and sprinkling ¼ teaspoon cinnamon over them. Cover the beans with the final layer of rice. Cover the pot and turn the heat to medium-high. After 4 minutes, turn the heat down to medium-low. After another 4 minutes, lift the cover and quickly drape a dish towel over its underside and then put it back on the pan. (The towel will be between the pan and the lid.) Flip the ends of the towel on top of the lid so they do not burn. Turn the heat down to very low and cook 30 minutes.

To serve, have a large, warm serving plate ready. Remove the cover and slide a knife along the inside of the pan to loosen the rice. Put the serving plate on top of the pan of rice. Now upturn it and invert its contents, rice and crust, onto your serving plate. The "cake" will crumble a little, spreading out at the bottom, but this is as it should be. Serve immediately. Cut the crust as you serve.

Alternatively, empty just the rice into the serving plate, scooping it out gently with a slotted spoon. Now remove the crust from the pan and, with a knife or a pair of kitchen scissors, cut it into even wedges. You may arrange the wedges, crusty browned side up, around the rice or put them on a separate plate.

SERVES 4

Shamsi Davis'

Persian Pilaf with a Potato Crust   IRAN

Polo Ba Tahdig Seeb Zameeni

This is a plain saffron rice with a potato crust. You may leave out the optional saffron mixture if you so desire and instead mix together ¼ teaspoon turmeric with 2 tablespoons boiling water and 2 tablespoons hot melted unsalted butter.

It is best to do the final cooking of the rice in a nonstick pan. A 2-quart size is ideal. If you double the recipe, double the size of the pan and the ingredients. The cooking times remain the same.

For the optional saffron mixture

1 sugar cube

1 teaspoon saffron threads

2 tablespoons unsalted butter, melted

2 tablespoons boiling water

2 cups basmati rice, picked over, washed, and drained

Salt

2 tablespoons unsalted butter

1 large boiling potato or 2 medium ones

Put the sugar cube into a small mortar. Put the saffron threads on top of it. Using the pestle, crush the 2 ingredients into as fine a powder as possible. Empty into a small cup. Add the melted butter and the boiling water. Set aside for 3 hours.

Soak the rice for 30 minutes in lukewarm water that covers it generously. Drain.

Put 10 cups of water into a large pot and bring to a rolling boil. Add 1½ tablespoons salt and mix in. Scatter the rice into the boiling water and bring to a boil again. Boil rapidly for 5½ minutes, or until the rice is almost done but still has a very slim hard core in its very center. (The way to test this is by removing a grain and pressing it between the fingers.) Drain the rice immediately and leave in a sieve or colander.

Put the butter in a nonstick pan (see recipe introduction) and set it over low heat. Add 2 tablespoons of water plus a teaspoon of the saffron mixture. Peel the potato and cut it crosswise into ⅛-inch-thick rounds. Lay a round in the center of the pan. Surround it with the other rounds until you have no more space left. You can cut some of the rounds if needed to almost cover the bottom. A few blank spaces are fine. As soon as all the butter has melted, empty the rice over the potatoes. Cover the pot and turn the heat to medium-high. After 4 minutes, turn the heat down to medium-low. After another 4 minutes, lift the cover and quickly dribble the remaining saffron mixture over the rice. Drape a dish towel over the underside of the lid and then put it back on the pan. (The towel will be between the pan and the lid.) Flip the ends of the towel on top of the lid so they do not burn. Turn the heat down to very low and cook for 25 minutes.

To serve, have a large warm serving plate ready. Remove the cover and slide a knife along the inside of the pan to loosen the rice. Put the serving plate on top of the pan of rice. Now upturn it and invert its contents, rice and crust, onto the serving plate. The "cake" will crumble a little, spreading out at the bottom, but this is as it should be. Serve immediately. Cut the crust as you serve.

Alternatively, empty just the rice into the serving plate, scooping it out gently with a slotted spoon. Now remove the crust from the pan and, with a knife or a pair of kitchen scissors, cut it into even wedges. You may arrange the wedges, crusty browned side up, around the rice or put them on a separate plate.

SERVES 4 TO 5

Shamsi Davis'
Persian Pilaf with Fresh Green Herbs   IRAN
Sabzi Polo

This is another exquisite vegetarian pilaf from Iran. As in the preceding recipe, this also comes to the table like a slightly collapsed cake. The top, all crisp and reddish, is encrusted with herbs. Below it is a layer of white rice. Below that is a layer of green herbs. There follow more layers of rice and herbs. The herbs themselves—chives, dill, parsley, and cilantro—are used generously and, when combined, turn into a strange new vegetable, much more exciting than the sum of the parts. The very bottom of the cake is often tinted with saffron. (I only use saffron when I am entertaining.)

In Iran, this is eaten on Nawrooz, *the first day of the New Year, the day of the spring equinox, when it is garnished with fresh young garlic shoots and served with fish. I serve it with a dish—any dish—of black-eyed peas instead. It amuses me to think that I am thus combining two traditions for New Year's Day, one borrowed from Iran and the other from the African Americans of the southern United States. Of course this is not just a New Year's Day treat for me. It is often on the menu when I cook for the family or entertain.*

It is best to do the final cooking of the rice in a nonstick pan. A 3-quart size is ideal. If you double the recipe—and I often do for parties—double the size of the pan as well. The cooking times remain the same.

If you wish to use saffron, put ¾ teaspoon chopped saffron threads and 1 tablespoon boiling water into a very small cup. Set aside for 2 to 3 hours. Dribble 1 teaspoon of the mixture at the bottom of the pan when you are putting in the yogurt. Dribble the remaining mixture, including the threads, over the last layer of rice.

It is a good idea to dry the herbs before chopping them. I dry my parsley, dill, and cilantro in a salad spin-dryer though paper towels will do.

(recipe continues)

2 cups basmati rice, rinsed and drained

1⅓ lightly packed cups chopped fresh dill

1⅓ lightly packed cups chopped fresh cilantro

1¾ lightly packed cups chopped fresh parsley

5 tablespoons very finely chopped fresh chives

2 garlic cloves, peeled and very finely chopped

1½ tablespoons salt

3 tablespoons peanut or canola oil (or a mixture of oil and butter)

1½ tablespoons plain yogurt

1 tablespoon clarified butter, melted butter, or more canola oil

Soak the rice for 30 minutes in lukewarm water that covers it generously. Drain.

Combine the dill, cilantro, parsley, chives, and garlic in a bowl. Toss to mix and set aside.

Put 10 cups of water into a large pot and bring to a rolling boil. Add the salt. Scatter the rice into the boiling water and bring to a boil again. Boil rapidly for 5½ minutes, or until the rice is almost done but still has a very slim hard core in its very center. (The way to test this is by removing a grain and pressing it between the fingers.) Drain the rice immediately and leave in a sieve or colander.

Put the oil in a nonstick pan (see recipe introduction) and set it over low heat. Add 3 tablespoons of water and the yogurt and stir to mix. Add 3 tablespoons of the mixed herbs and distribute them evenly around the bottom of the pan. Now divide the rice into 3 portions and spread one portion evenly over the herbs. Top this rice with half of the remaining green herbs, spreading them evenly. Spread the second portion of the rice over the herbs. Top this rice with the remaining herbs, spreading them evenly. Cover the herbs with the final layer of rice. Dribble the clarified butter, butter, or oil over the rice. Cover the pot and turn the heat to medium-high. After 4 minutes, turn the heat down to medium-low. After another 5 minutes, lift the cover and quickly drape a dish towel over its underside and then put it back on the pan. (The towel will be between the pan and the lid.) Flip the ends of the towel on top of the lid so they do not burn. Turn the heat down to very low and cook 30 minutes.

To serve, have a large, warm serving plate ready. Remove the cover and slide a knife along the inside of the pan to loosen the rice. Put the serving plate on top of the pan of rice. Now upturn it and invert its contents, rice and crust, onto your serving plate. The "cake" will crumble a little, spreading out at the bottom, but this is as it should be. Serve immediately. Cut the crust as you serve.

Alternatively, empty just the rice into the serving plate, scooping it out gently with a slotted spoon. Now remove the crust from the pan and, with a knife or a pair of kitchen scissors, cut it into even wedges. You may arrange the wedges, crusty browned side up, around the rice or put them on a separate plate.

SERVES 4 TO 6

Shamsi Davis'
Persian Rice with Currants

Zareshk Polo

Just think of it: the aroma of orange saffron that, in terms of taste, has been sweetened lightly with sugar, the green crunchiness of pistachio nuts, and the sweet and lemony-sour quality of tiny, crimson Persian currrants (dried barberries). All this combined with good-quality, long-grain rice. This heady combination could only come from Iran.

What is more, this rice has a crust. It is not, in this case, a rice crust but one made with pita bread, which lines the bottom of the pan. The bread turns crisp on the outside and spongy inside, as well as sweet-and-sour, and it picks up all the fragrances and tastes of the rice medley. I could eat the bread part all by itself.

Because this is very much a party dish, I have made it in party proportions. At a four-course meal, I have even fed ten people with it. (I served Tabbouleh, a Salad Made with Bulgur and Arugula, page 422, with any of the Romesco Sauces on the side as a first course, pages 669 to 670, Kallaloo, the Trinidadian soup, page 585, as a second course, this rice with the Aromatic Cuban White Bean and Pumpkin Stew, page 54, and fresh fruit as the final course.)

For serving, plain white plates are preferred in Iran, as they show up the colors in the rice. You may of course use any serving dish of your choosing.

If you cannot get Persian currants (for sources of Middle Eastern specialties, see page 00), use ordinary currants; however, as they are already quite sweet, cook them for 2 minutes in 4 table-spoons lemon juice instead of the sugar and water. Drain them and then use them as the recipe suggests.

It is best to do the final cooking of the rice in a nonstick pan. A 3½-quart size is ideal.

For the saffron mixture

1 sugar cube

1 teaspoon saffron threads

2 tablespoons unsalted butter, melted

2 tablespoons boiling water

4 to 5 tablespoons raw unsalted pistachios, shelled

3 cups basmati rice, picked over, rinsed, and drained

1 cup Persian currants (dried barberries or *zareshk*), lightly rinsed and drained (to use currants, see recipe introduction)

1 tablespoon sugar

2½ tablespoons salt

4 tablespoons (½ stick) unsalted butter

1 pita bread

(recipe continues)

Put the sugar cube into a small mortar. Put the saffron threads on top of it. Using the pestle, crush the 2 ingredients into as fine a powder as possible. Empty into a small cup. Add the melted butter and the boiling water. Set aside for 3 hours.

Soak the pistachios for 3 hours in boiling water that covers them generously. Removing a few at a time, peel them and quarter them lengthwise. Set aside.

Soak the rice for 30 minutes in lukewarm water that covers it generously. Drain.

Separate the currants if they are clumped up and put them into a small pan along with the sugar and ¼ cup of water. Stir to mix. Bring to a boil, then turn the heat down to low and simmer gently for 2 minutes, stirring once or twice. Drain and set aside.

Put 14 cups of water into a large pot and bring to a rolling boil. Add the salt and mix in. Scatter the rice into the boiling water and bring to a boil again. Boil rapidly for 5½ minutes, or until the rice is almost done but still has a very slim hard core in its very center. (The way to test this is by removing a grain and pressing it between the fingers.) Drain the rice immediately and leave in a sieve or colander.

Put the butter in a good-sized nonstick frying pan and set over low heat. Add 3 tablespoons of water and 1 teaspoon of the saffron mixture. Split the pita bread open so you have 2 equal rounds. Once the butter has melted, lay one round right in the center of the pan, its browner side facing up. If extra space is left around it, cut the second pita round neatly to fill those spaces. Spread 2 tablespoons of the currants on top of the bread. Now layer about a third of the rice on top. Top the rice with half of the pistachios and half of the remaining currants. Put a second layer of rice on top of the currants to be followed by a layer of the remaining pistachios and the remaining currants. Top this with a final layer of rice. Cover, turn the heat to medium-high, and cook for 4 minutes. Turn the heat down to medium-low and cook another 4 minutes.

Remove the cover and dribble the remaining saffron mixture over the rice. (Save the saffron cup—the little bit of saffron clinging to it will be used later.) Quickly drape a dish towel over the inside of the lid and put the lid on the pot. (The towel will be between the pot and the lid.) Flip the ends of the towel on top of the lid so they do not burn. Turn the heat down to very low and cook 30 minutes.

To serve, have a large warm serving plate ready. Remove the lid and slide a knife along the inside of the pan to loosen the rice. Empty just the rice into the serving plate, scooping it out gently with a slotted spoon. Take a tablespoon of this cooked rice and put it into the cup that held the saffron. Turn the rice around in the cup so it picks up all the remaining saffron. Put this "extra-saffroned" rice right in the center, on top of the regular rice. Now remove the crust from the pan and, with a knife or a pair of kitchen scissors, cut it into even wedges. You may arrange the wedges, crusty browned side up, around the rice or put them on a separate plate.

Alternatively, put the serving plate on top of the pot of rice. Now upturn it and invert its contents, rice and crust, into the serving plate like a cake. The "cake" will crumble a little and spread out at the bottom, but this is as it should be. Serve immediately. Cut the crust as you serve.

SERVES 6 TO 8

Shiu-Min Block's

Emerald Fried Rice

Fay Chway Chow Fan

CHINA

This is a rice that both tastes and looks good.

The Chinese green that is used here is sold as kailan *in Chinese markets. Only the leaves are needed for this recipe; the stems and flowers should be used for something else.*

If you cannot get kailan, *use 15 dark green Swiss chard leaves (cut out and discard the pale inner vein) or 25 spinach leaves.*

The best fried rice is made with leftover rice that has been refrigerated or at least cooled thoroughly. Regular long-grain or jasmine rice is best. Do not *use easy-cook, parboiled, or basmati rice.*

1½ cups lightly salted vegetable stock

1 medium carrot (3 ounces), peeled and cut into ⅛-inch dice

About 25 *kailan* leaves, cut crosswise into fine ribbons

3 tablespoons peanut or canola oil

2 eggs, lightly beaten

3 scallions, cut into fine rings (green and white portions)

4 cups cooked cooled (preferably refrigerated) rice

½ to ¾ teaspoon salt

Freshly ground black pepper

Put the stock in a large frying pan and bring to a boil over medium-high heat. When bubbling, put in the carrot. Blanch the carrot for 2 minutes and then remove with a slotted spoon. Put in the *kailan* leaves and blanch for about 1 minute, pushing the leaves about in the stock. Remove the *kailan* with a slotted spoon when it has wilted. (Save the stock for some other use.) Chop the *kailan* as finely as possible and squeeze out all the liquid.

(recipe continues)

Put 2 tablespoons of the oil in a large, preferably nonstick wok or a large nonstick frying pan and set over high heat. When hot, put in the beaten eggs. Stir them about and scramble very lightly. Remove with a slotted spoon. Add the remaining tablespoon of oil and put in ⅔ of the sliced scallions as well as the blanched carrot and *kailan*. Stir for a minute. Crumble in the rice. Stir and fry, breaking up any lumps with the back of a slotted spoon, until the rice has heated through. Put in the eggs, salt, and pepper and stir quickly to mix. Empty the rice into a serving dish. Scatter the remaining scallion rings over the top and serve.

SERVES 4

Spicy Brown Rice with Green Beans and Fresh Herbs

If you have Caribbean Seasoning Sauce (page 675) sitting in your refrigerator, you may use 2 tablespoons of that instead of the fresh herb mixture and lemon juice. The herbs and beans help perk up and lighten the brown rice, which can be rather stolid by itself.

2 cups long-grain brown rice, washed in several changes of water and drained

2 tablespoons olive oil

1 medium shallot, peeled and finely chopped

20 green beans, cut crosswise into ½-inch rounds

1 teaspoon finely chopped fresh oregano

1 tablespoon finely chopped fresh chives

1 teaspoon finely chopped fresh thyme

1 to 2 teaspoons finely chopped fresh hot green chile, with seeds

1 teaspoon ground cumin

1¼ teaspoons salt

1 tablespoon fresh lemon juice

Put the rice in a bowl with 4 cups of water and leave to soak for 1 hour.

Put the oil in a heavy pan and set over medium-high heat. When hot, put in the shallot. Stir and fry until the shallot pieces just begin to brown at the edges. Add the green beans, oregano, chives, thyme, chile, and cumin and stir for a minute. Now put in the rice and its soaking liquid, salt, and lemon juice. Bring to a boil. Cover, turn the heat down to very, very low, and cook for 35 minutes. Leave the pan covered and undisturbed for another 10 minutes.

SERVES 4 TO 6

Rosario Guillermo's

Green Rice with Stuffed Poblano Chiles

MEXICO

Arroz Verde con Chiles Relleños

Green parsley-flavored rice cooked with a topping of roasted poblano chiles filled with cheese makes a spicy dish that is a meal by itself—all that is needed is icy cold beer. If you cannot get poblano chiles, use small green bell peppers and rub the insides with a little cayenne after they have been peeled.

4 poblano chiles (12 ounces), roasted according to instructions on page 262

2 ounces Cheddar or Monterey Jack cheese

2 loosely packed cups parsley, leaves only

½ medium onion, coarsely chopped

3 garlic cloves, peeled and coarsely chopped

3 tablespoons peanut or canola oil

2 cups long-grain rice

1½ teaspoons salt

3 cups milk

Remove the stem and seeds of the chiles. Peel them and open them up so they lie flat. Cut the cheese into ⅛- to ¼-inch-thick slices. Lay a slice of cheese along one half of a chile. Fold the other half of the chile over the cheese to re-form the chile shape. Do this with the remaining chiles and set aside.

In a blender, combine the parsley, onion, garlic, and ⅓ cup of water. Blend thoroughly.

Put the oil in a medium, heavy-bottomed nonstick pot and set over medium-high heat. When hot, put in the rice and salt. Turn the heat down to medium-low and stir and sauté for 6 to 7 minutes, or until the rice is golden. Add the parsley mixture and bring to a simmer. Turn the heat down to low and cook, stirring very gently, without breaking the rice grains, for 4 to 5 minutes. Add the milk and bring to a boil. Cover, turn the heat down to very low, and cook for 25 minutes. Lift the cover and very quickly lay the poblano chiles over the rice in a single layer. Cover and keep cooking gently until the cheese has melted, a matter of minutes.

Invariably, a little bit of the rice at the bottom will brown; do not worry.

To serve, remove the chiles carefully and set them to one side. Take out the rice with a slotted spoon and transfer to a serving dish, leaving any browned bits behind. Arrange the chiles over the top and serve.

SERVES 4

From Billur Selvi at Zeynep Fadilligolu's aunt's house

Swiss Chard Leaves Stuffed with Sweet-and-Sour Rice

TURKEY

Pazili Dolmasi Zeytinagli

You have probably had dolmas before—vine leaves stuffed with rice. In this particular Turkish house, which sits grandly on the Bosporus in Istanbul, they do make the more usual dolmas with vine leaves but they also make what for me was delightfully different: Swiss chard leaves stuffed with a combination of rice, currants, pine nuts, dill, mint, sugar, and allspice. Lemon juice was squeezed on the cold dolmas when they were served.

Though these are often served as appetizers, I love to serve them for lunch, accompanied by a bean salad as well as a salad of greens and tomatoes.

The rice normally used in the stuffing is short-grain Turkish rice. Use any short-grain rice or even jasmine rice, if you like.

Chard leaves come in different sizes. The ideal size for stuffing is about 4 × 6 inches or a wee bit larger. However, if the leaves are too large, as mine usually are, it is a good idea to remove the central white part of the leaf altogether, therefore splitting it into 2 halves. For this recipe, I bought a 12-ounce bunch of chard, which had 8 big leaves.

For the stuffing

¼ cup olive oil

1 medium red onion (4 ounces), finely chopped

½ cup short-grain rice

1 tablespoon currants, washed and drained

1 tablespoon pine nuts

1 teaspoon crushed dried mint (don't use fresh here)

2 tablespoons finely chopped fresh dill

½ teaspoon salt

Freshly ground black pepper

½ teaspoon ground allspice

1½ tablespoons sugar

About 12 ounces fresh Swiss chard

A few lettuce leaves

¼ cup olive oil

2 tablespoons fresh lemon juice, plus lemon wedges for serving

¼ teaspoon salt

Make the stuffing. Put the oil in a medium pan and set over medium heat. When hot, put in the onion. Stir and fry for a minute, then add the rice. Stir and cook another 30 seconds. Add the currants, pine nuts, mint, dill, salt, pepper to taste, and allspice and stir a few times. Add ½ cup of water and bring to a simmer, then cover tightly, turn the heat down to very low, and cook gently for 10 minutes. Add the sugar and stir once. Turn off the heat. Set aside to cool off.

Fill a medium, very wide pan or even a deep frying pan with about 2 inches of water and bring it to a boil. Lower the heat so the water is at a bare simmer. Take a chard leaf and cut off the stem entirely (save it for another use). If the leaf is small, take a paring knife and peel off the back of its white central vein. A very thin skin should pull off after an initial snip. If the leaf is large, remove the central vein altogether. Consider the 2 resulting halves as 2 leaves.

Working with just 2 to 3 leaves at a time, drop 1 leaf into the barely simmering water and let it lie there for about 2 minutes, or until it has wilted completely. Spread it out on a work surface. Do the same with another 1 or 2 leaves. Now fill and roll as follows: Put about ½ tablespoon of the rice mixture on the leaf, a little in from either the center of the long side of a leaf or the wide side of the leaf, spreading it out about 2½ inches. Fold that edge of the leaf over the rice. Now bring the left side of the leaf over the rice and then the right side over it. Roll the rice up into a cylinder that is about 2½ inches long and about 1½ inches in diameter. Put this dolma, seam side down, in a small, preferably nonstick pan lined with lettuce leaves. Make all the dolmas this way, arranging them neatly in the pan in tight rows. Make a second layer over the first as needed. If any oil is left in the rice pan, pour it over the rolls. Place a small inverted plate on top of the rolls (I use a saucer) to keep them from unraveling and then pour in ¾ cup of water mixed with the ¼ cup olive oil, 2 tablespoons lemon juice, and ¼ teaspoon salt. Bring to a simmer. Cover, turn the heat down to very low, and simmer gently for 45 minutes, removing the plate now and then to baste the rolls with the pan juices if they no longer remain covered. Allow to cool with the plate still on top. Remove the plate. Carefully lift out the dolmas and refrigerate them in tight rows in a covered container until ready to serve.

MAKES 15 TO 16

Rice with Yogurt and Apple

INDIA

Bhakala Bhat

There are hundreds of variations of this cooling, soothing, saladlike dish, known popularly as curd rice in South India. It is perfect for a summer's day.

My version includes a mixture of fruit and vegetables, among them sour, crisp green apples. We seem to get them all year round now, with the different hemispheres providing never-ending gifts to each other.

2 cups long-grain rice, washed in several
    changes of water

Salt

½ cup finely diced carrot

About 15 green beans cut crosswise into
    ¼-inch dice

2 to 4 tablespoons cold milk

2 cups plain yogurt, lightly beaten

½ cup tart green apple, peeled, cored, and
    cut into ¼-inch dice (keep in salted water
    to prevent discoloring)

½ cup finely diced peeled cucumber

1 fresh hot green chile

3 tablespoons chopped fresh cilantro

½-inch piece of fresh ginger, peeled and very
    finely diced

1 tablespoon peanut or canola oil

½ teaspoon *urad dal* (page 112) (use *chana dal*
    page 25 if you happen to have that
    instead)

½ teaspoon whole brown mustard seeds

10 fresh curry leaves, if available

Soak the rice for 30 minutes and drain.

Put the drained rice in a small, heavy pan. Add 3 cups plus 2 tablespoons of water and bring to a boil. Cover, turn the heat down to low, and cook for 30 minutes.

While the rice boils, bring a large pot of salted water to a rolling boil. Drop in the carrot and green beans and boil rapidly for 3 to 4 minutes, or until just tender. Drain and rinse under cold water, then drain again.

Once the rice has cooked (it will be soft), empty it into a large wide bowl. Add 2 to 3 tablespoons of the milk and mix it in, mashing the rice a bit as you do. Add more milk if needed to get a porridgelike consistency. Once lukewarm, stir in the yogurt, then add the carrot and beans as well as the drained apple, cucumber, chile, cilantro, ginger, and about 1½ teaspoons salt, or to taste. Mix gently.

Put the oil in a small frying pan and set over medium-high heat. When hot, put in the *urad dal*. As soon as it turns red, put in the mustard seeds. When the mustard seeds pop, a matter of seconds, add the curry leaves and stir once. Quickly pour the oil and spices over the bowl of rice and yogurt. Stir gently to mix. Serve at room temperature.

SERVES 6

From the home of Anand Sarabhai
Rice with Yogurt and Fresh Pomegranate Seeds INDIA

In the intense heat of summer, there is nothing more cooling and refreshing than a plate of rice mixed with yogurt and fruit. I had come across many versions of this in South India but nowhere else. Then I found this very unusual one in the West Indian state of Gujarat, where bright-fruited pomegranate trees stand out as welcoming beacons in the beige, sandy land. It was served beautifully too, studded with the red pomegranate seeds and a few fried whole red chiles.

2 cups long-grain rice

2 tablespoons cold milk

2 cups plus 2 tablespoons plain yogurt, lightly beaten

1½ teaspoons salt

1 tablespoon finely chopped fresh cilantro

2 teaspoons peanut or canola oil

1 teaspoon whole brown mustard seeds

2 to 3 whole hot dried red chiles

6 to 8 fresh curry leaves, if available

1 cup fresh pomegranate seeds

Rinse the rice in several changes of water. Drain. Cover well with water and leave to soak for 30 minutes. Drain well again. Put the rice in a medium pot. Add 3 cups of water and bring to a boil. Cover tightly, turn the heat down to very low, and cook for 30 minutes. Empty the rice into a large bowl and mash lightly, allowing it to cool a little bit as well. Add the cold milk and stir to mix, then add the yogurt, salt, and cilantro. Mix again.

Put the oil in a small frying pan and set over medium-high heat. When hot, put in the mustard seeds. As soon as the mustard seeds start to pop, a matter of seconds, put in the red chiles. Stir the chiles for a few seconds until darkened. Now put in the curry leaves, if you have them. Leave them for a few seconds, then take the pan off the heat. Remove the chiles and pour the remaining contents of the pan, oil and seasonings, over the rice mixture. Stir to mix.

Allow the rice mixture to cool completely. Put into a serving dish. Stud neatly with the red chiles and pomegranate seeds. Serve at room temperature or lightly chilled.

SERVES 6

Mexican-Style Rice Casserole with Corn, Sour Cream, and Cheese

This wonderful dish originated with my friend Zarela Martinez and then traveled to me through another friend, Catherine Brandel, who teaches at the Culinary Institute of America in the Napa Valley. This is the only recipe using converted rice in my book. I have never developed a taste for it, perhaps because I was raised with what I call real *rice. However, I make an exception for just this dish. Here is an easy, casserole-type dish that can be made for multitudes or for just the family. What is even better, it can be assembled ahead of time and then set to bake half an hour before you sit down to eat.*

In season use fresh corn taken off the cob, tossing it in the pan with the green chiles and onion for a minute instead of adding it at the time of the final assembly.

If you cannot get poblano chiles, roast one green pepper instead and then throw in 1 to 2 chopped fresh hot green chiles as well. This way you will get both the texture and the heat.

2 tablespoons peanut or canola oil

1 medium onion (5 ounces), peeled and chopped

2 garlic cloves, peeled and finely chopped

2 poblano chiles, roasted, peeled, seeded, and cut into ¼-inch dice (for directions, see page 262)

2 cups sour cream

6 tablespoons finely chopped fresh cilantro

6 cups cooked converted rice (from 2 cups raw rice)

1¾ cups corn kernels, fresh (see note above), thawed frozen, or canned

1½ lightly packed cups grated Cheddar cheese

Put the oil in a large sauté pan or other wide pan and set over medium-high heat. When hot, put in the onion and garlic. Stir and sauté until the onion is translucent, about 3 minutes, turning the heat down if necessary. Add the roasted diced poblanos and stir another minute. Let everything cool off. Combine the sour cream, ½ teaspoon salt, and the cilantro. Stir to mix and set aside.

Stir the rice and corn into the poblano mixture, then add the sour cream and blend it in. Finally, blend in the grated cheese. Put this mixture into a 3-quart casserole dish and cover it. You may now refrigerate it for up to 24 hours.

Preheat the oven to 350°F.

Bake the casserole for 45 minutes or until heated through.

SERVES 6

Azuki Beans and Rice with Sesame Salt

JAPAN/KOREA

Sekihan

Several versions of this festive dish are served in both Korea and Japan, almost always made with glutinous rice or glutinous rice powder, both of which need to be steamed for a proper consistency. I have simplified the recipe by substituting plain Japanese rice, such as Kokuho Rose, and a few tablespoons of glutinous rice, a combination that does not require steaming. When it is served, it is sprinkled with Sesame Salt, a mixture of roasted salt and sesame seeds. You may also crumble lightly toasted nori seaweed over the top. Serve with vegetables and a bean curd dish or with a large salad.

1 cup red azuki beans, picked over, washed, and drained

¼ cup glutinous rice, washed and drained

1¾ cups Japanese rice

Sesame Salt (page 704), to taste

Combine the beans with 3 cups of water and either soak overnight or follow the Quick-Soak Method on page 6. Drain.

Put the glutinous rice in a bowl. Cover generously with hot water and set aside for 2 hours. Drain.

Put the Japanese rice in a separate bowl and wash well in several changes of water. Drain and set aside for 1 hour in a sieve or colander. Drain.

Once the beans have been soaked and drained, put them in a pan with 3 cups of water and bring to a boil. Cover, turn the heat down to low, and simmer gently for 40 minutes, or until the beans are just tender enough to be eaten but still hold their shape. Drain the beans, reserving the cooking liquid.

Combine the drained beans and the 2 drained rices in a heavy pan. Add enough water to the cooking liquid to make 3 cups and add to the pot. Bring to a boil, then cover tightly, turn the heat down to very low, and cook for 30 minutes.

Serve with a sprinkling of Sesame Salt.

SERVES 4

Rakhi Sarkar's

Delicious "Risotto" of Rice and Split Peas

INDIA

Khichri

Indians have not stopped eating khichri, *ancient India's nutritious mixture of rice and beans, for more than four thousand years. In this wonderful Bengali version, vegetables are cooked along with the rice-bean mixture to make a one-pot meal. In India, diners add dollops of* ghee.

    I love to serve the "risotto" in individual, old-fashioned soup plates with a liberal sprinkling of garam masala, finely cut strips of ginger, thin slices of hot green chile, cilantro leaves, some crisply fried onions, and a good squeeze of lime or lemon juice.

For the basic risotto

¾ cup hulled and split mung beans
    (moong dal)

1 tablespoon peanut or canola oil

1 cinnamon stick

3 cardamom pods

3 cloves

2 bay leaves

¾ cup basmati rice, washed in several
    changes of water and drained

1 medium potato (7 ounces), peeled and cut
    into ½-inch dice (1½ cups)

1 cup (4 ounces) fresh or frozen shelled peas

2¼ cups (8 ounces) small cauliflower florets

4 teaspoons salt, or to taste

For the seasoning

3 tablespoons peanut or canola oil

3 teaspoons whole cumin seeds

1 bay leaf

½ large onion (3½ ounces), very finely
    chopped

1-inch piece of fresh ginger, peeled and
    grated to a pulp

1 ripe medium tomato (6 ounces), finely
    chopped (out of season use a canned
    tomato)

½ teaspoon ground turmeric

¼ teaspoon cayenne

½ teaspoon garam masala (page 723)

For the final garnish

2-inch piece of fresh ginger, peeled and cut
    into very fine rounds, the rounds stacked
    and cut into very fine slivers

2 fresh hot green chiles, cut into very fine
    rounds

A generous handful of fresh cilantro leaves

1 tablespoon garam masala (page 723)

8 lime or lemon wedges

Put the split mung beans in a medium cast-iron frying pan and set over medium heat. Stir and roast for about 4 minutes, or until the beans turn golden red. Remove from the frying pan and wash in several changes of water. Drain.

Put the 1 tablespoon of oil in a large pot, preferably nonstick, and set over medium-high heat. When hot, put in the 1 stick cinnamon, 3 cardamom pods, 3 cloves, and 3 bay leaves. Stir for 10 seconds and add 6¼ cups of water. Bring to a boil. Add the mung beans, rice, potato, peas, and cauliflower. Bring to a boil again. Cover, lower the heat, and simmer very gently for 30 minutes. Uncover, and add the salt and 2 cups of boiling water. Mash the mixture coarsely as you stir to mix. Keep cooking gently for another 20 to 30 minutes, stirring and mashing periodically. Do not allow the grain and vegetable mixture to scorch or stick at the bottom. It should end up with a thick porridgelike consistency. Turn off the heat when done and keep covered.

Prepare the seasoning (this may be done while the risotto cooks). Heat the oil in a medium frying pan over medium-high heat. When hot, put in the cumin and bay leaf. As soon as the bay leaf darkens a little bit, a matter of seconds, put in the onion. Stir and sauté until the onion turns brown at the edges. Add the ginger and stir for about 30 seconds. Put in the tomato, turmeric, cayenne, and ¼ cup of water and bring to a simmer. Turn the heat to medium and cook, uncovered, for 2 to 3 minutes, or until the tomato pieces have softened. Empty the contents of the frying pan into the pot with the risotto. Add ½ teaspoon garam masala and stir to mix. Heat the "risotto" gently over a low flame, stirring as you do so.

To serve, ladle a portion of the "risotto" into an old-fashioned soup plate. Sprinkle a few shreds of ginger, a few slices of green chile, a few cilantro leaves, a generous pinch of garam masala, and some squirts of lime or lemon juice over each portion. Serve immediately.

SERVES 8

Simple "Risotto" of Rice and Split Peas

INDIA

Khichri

This simpler version of khichri *is comfort food, eaten all over the country by the very young and very old alike. It is a great favorite of my little grandson, Cassius, who is all of one year old. In India, dollops of* ghee *(clarified butter) are added at the table; for Cassius, I sometimes stir in a small pat of butter. His mother always looks askance at this—she hated butter as a child and still does—but I put it in anyway. Also, for Cassius and his little friends, I sometimes put in a sliced carrot and some finely sliced green beans about half an hour before the cooking is done.*

As a variation, you may stir 1 to 2 tablespoons of grated Parmesan cheese into each portion before you serve or else pass the cheese and black pepper around the table. A green salad may be served on the side.

(recipe continues)

For the basic "risotto"

½ cup (3 ounces) hulled and split mung
 beans *(moong dal)*, picked over, rinsed in
 several changes of water, and drained

¾ cup basmati rice, rinsed in several changes
 of water and drained

¼ teaspoon ground turmeric

2 thin slices of fresh ginger

8 cups vegetable stock or water

About 1 teaspoon salt, or to taste

For the seasoning

3 tablespoons peanut or canola oil

1 small onion (2 ounces), very finely chopped

1 ripe medium tomato (6 ounces), finely
 chopped (out of season use a canned
 tomato)

½ to 1 teaspoon ground cumin

Extra pats of butter, as required

Combine the split mung beans, rice, turmeric, ginger, and stock or water in a heavy, preferably nonstick pan and bring to a boil. Cover, lower the heat, and simmer very gently for 1½ hours, stirring every 6 to 7 minutes during the last half hour. Do not allow it to scorch or stick at the bottom. Uncover, add 1 teaspoon of salt. (If the stock was salted, taste before adding any salt at all.) Stir and taste. Add more salt, if needed. Remove the ginger slices and mix well; it should have a thick porridgelike consistency. Turn off the heat when done and keep covered.

Prepare the seasoning (this may be done while the "risotto" is cooking). Put the oil in a medium frying pan and set over medium-high heat. When hot, put in the onion. Stir and sauté until the onion turns brown at the edges. Put in the tomato, cumin, and ¼ cup of water, and bring to a simmer. Turn the heat down to medium and cook, uncovered, for 2 to 3 minutes, or until the tomato pieces have softened. Empty the contents of the frying pan into the pot with the risotto. Check the salt; add more if needed. Heat the "risotto" gently over a low flame, stirring as you do so.

To serve, ladle a portion of the "risotto" into an old-fashioned soup plate. Top with a pat of butter, if desired, and serve hot.

SERVES 6

Marjorie Williams'
Black-Eyed Peas and Rice with Pumpkin

TRINIDAD

Although I first learned to cook this in Trinidad, this Creole dish is prepared on most of the Caribbean islands and, in slightly different versions, in much of the American South. It is almost a meal in itself and may be eaten with a green salad and perhaps the Eggplant and Tomato Choka (page 186), and, if you want another vegetable, the Curried Long Beans (page 210).

In most countries, pumpkins are commonly available all year round, but American supermarkets do not, for some reason, carry them nor do most greengrocers. However, they may be found in Chinese and West Indian markets, cut into reasonable portions. Both butternut and Hubbard squashes make a most adequate substitute, though the butternut is easier to peel.

Instead of water, you may use fresh coconut milk (page 719) or a combination of half water and half coconut milk from a well-stirred can.

1 cup dried black-eyed peas, picked over, washed, and drained

¼ cup peanut or canola oil

1 medium onion (5 ounces), peeled and finely chopped

½ to 2 fresh hot green or red chiles, chopped (if using habanero-type West Indian hot peppers, use only about ¼ of a pepper)

2 garlic cloves, peeled and finely chopped

1 cup (4 ounces) pumpkin or butternut squash, peeled and cut into ⅓-inch dice (about 4 ounces)

2 cups long-grain rice (I like to use jasmine rice)

1½ teaspoons salt

Pick over the black-eyed peas and wash them. Drain. Soak the beans overnight in water to cover by at least 5 inches. Drain.

In a large pot, bring the peas and 4 cups of water to a boil. Cover, turn the heat down to low, and simmer gently for 25 minutes, or until the peas are almost tender. Drain but save the cooking liquid. Set the peas and cooking liquid aside.

Put the oil in a good-sized, heavy pot and set over medium-high heat. When hot, put in the onion. Stir and fry until the onion pieces begin to turn brown at the edges, 3 to 4 minutes. Now put in the chiles and chopped garlic. Stir and fry for a minute, then put in the pumpkin. Stir and fry for another minute. Put in the rice and stir and sauté it for a minute. Now add the beans, 3 cups of the bean liquid (if there is not enough, add more water), and the salt. Stir to mix and bring to a boil. Cover, turn the heat down to very low, and cook gently for 25 minutes. Let the pot rest, covered, for another 15 minutes. Stir gently to mix before serving.

SERVES 6

From Victor Matiya's Jerusalem Restaurant in Toronto

Palestinian Rice with Lentils and Browned Onions

PALESTINE

M'Jaddara

This is good for both parties and everyday eating. The first time I had this, it was served with Sliced Tomatoes in a Tomato Sauce (page 303), Buttery Soft Slices of Deep-Fried Eggplant with Garlic (page 191), and Simple Palestinian Salad (page 638). Nothing else was needed.

This recipe may be decreased by halving all the ingredients. The soaking and cooking times will remain the same, though the onion may brown faster.

1 cup (6 ounces) lentils, picked over, washed, and drained

2 cups basmati rice, washed in several changes of water and drained

½ cup olive oil

2 medium onions (8 ounces), peeled, halved lengthwise, and then thinly sliced crosswise

1 teaspoon ground cumin

Freshly ground black pepper

2 teaspoons salt

Soak the lentils in water to cover by 3 inches for 3 to 4 hours. Drain.

Soak the rice in water to cover by 3 inches for 30 minutes. Drain.

Put the oil in a wide, heavy, medium pan and set over medium-high heat. When hot, put in the onions. Stir and fry for about 12 minutes, or until the onion slices are dark brown and crisp. You will need to lower the heat by degrees as the onions darken. Remove the onions with a slotted spoon and spread out on a plate lined with paper towels. Turn the heat to medium and put the drained lentils and rice into the remaining onion-flavored oil left in the pan. Add the cumin, a generous amount of black pepper, and the salt. Very gently, sauté the rice and lentils for 5 minutes, being careful not to break the rice grains. Add 4 cups of water and bring to a boil. Cover very tightly (you may use a piece of foil between the lid and the pot to ensure a tight seal), turn the heat down to very low, and cook gently for 25 minutes.

Fluff up the rice and lentils and spread out on a warm serving plate. Sprinkle the browned, crisp onions over the top.

SERVES 6 TO 8

RISOTTO

A risotto is a creamy, almost flowing pilaf made by the slow addition of hot liquid—water or broth—to starchy, medium-grain rice that is traditionally cooked in an uncovered pan. Some of the flavor comes from the rice itself, some from the ingredients sautéed with the rice (vegetables, seafood, fungi, and so on), some from the broth and its origins, and some from the grated Parmigiano-Reggiano cheese that is generally mixed in at the end. Its magic comes from its texture, which always has the soothing, satisfying qualities of well-made pasta as well as the melting qualities associated with everybody's favorite nursery foods. However, it does have an assertive density, making it adult "nursery food."

Like pasta, a risotto in Italy is frequently eaten as a first or second course, both of which precede the main course. However, in a more informal way of eating, a risotto could, when accompanied by a green salad, be the main meal itself.

One of the characteristics of risotto is that the rice has a decided bite to it. It should not be white in the center—rice that is white in the center is uncooked rice. But it should be firm in the center, just like well-cooked pasta.

To achieve this, the cooking method, the timing, and the amount of liquid are important.

The pan: I like to use a large, heavy nonstick frying pan or sauté pan. Any heavy, shallow pan will do.

The stock and timing: The stock should not be too bland or salty. Bland vegetable stocks do not help a risotto and well-salted ones get saltier as they cook down. Out of all the liquids I have tried, I find that a good cube of dehydrated vegetable stock diluted well with water so it is very light works well. So does the liquid left over after soaking dried mushrooms, which is ideal for a mushroom risotto. The amount of liquid can vary from $2\frac{1}{2}$ times the volume of rice to 6 times the volume, depending upon the density desired. Some risottos are like thick soups. Once I add the liquid, I turn the heat to medium and cook for 22 to 25 minutes, stirring all the time.

The right rice: Risotto rice is a fat, starchy, medium-grain rice. Ask for Arborio, Vialone Nano, or Carnaroli. All are good and slightly different. My own favorite happens to be Vialone Nano. Risotto rice should not be washed before cooking as you need all the starch that clings to the grains—quite a different philosophy from the pilafs of North India!

Using salt: The stock should be lightly seasoned with salt. You should not need much more, as the stock reduces quite a bit. Remember that the cheese is salty as well.

Using a pressure cooker for risotto: Italians insist that the only way to cook a true risotto is in an open pan. I can say with confidence that very good results can be achieved in a pressure cooker as well. Pressure cookers have come a long way from the hissing, steaming dinosaurs they once were. What I have used for my risotto with great success is a virtually nonstick, frying pan–shaped Duromatic pressure cooker made by the Kuhn-Rikon Corp., P.O. Box 1184, Enfield, CT 06083-1184; telephone (203)244-2300; fax (203)246-2217.

In this section, I will provide both methods of cooking risottos. The pressure cooker method requires half the volume of liquid.

Almost all vegetables and beans may be used to make risottos. The recipes here are some of my favorites. I hope they can serve as a guide to your own inventiveness.

Risotto with Peas   ITALY
Risi e Bisi

In the odd years when El Niño plays havoc with our weather, I have found fresh peas as far out of season as February. Whenever I find fresh, tender peas, one of my favorite things to do is make a pea risotto, risi e bisi. I first ate this in Venice a few decades ago and it immediately joined the list of foods I could not live without.

I make this only when I have fresh peas, perhaps because of my earlier associations. You could, however, make it with frozen petits pois. Just defrost them thoroughly, drain them, and add them to the risotto 5 minutes before the rice is fully cooked.

To make this dish, I bought 1¼ pounds of very evenly filled-out pea pods, heavy with peas. From this I got 1¾ cups shelled peas. Your pea pods may be less well endowed, so it is best to get extra peas. Any leftovers may be eaten raw!

Dry the parsley well before chopping it finely.

4 cups light vegetable stock, seasoned (for details, see page 405)

3 tablespoons olive oil

½ smallish onion (about 1 ounce), peeled and finely chopped

1¾ cups fresh tender peas

1 cup unwashed risotto rice

½ cup grated Parmigiano-Reggiano cheese

1 tablespoon unsalted butter

1 tablespoon very finely chopped Italian flat-leaf parsley

Heat the stock and keep it hot over very, very low heat.

Put the oil in a large, heavy, preferably nonstick frying pan or sauté pan and set over medium-high heat. When hot, put in the onion and peas. Stir and fry for a minute. Add the rice. Stir and fry it for another minute. Now pour in a generous ladle of the stock. Turn the heat to medium. Keep stirring the risotto. When the stock has been absorbed, add another ladleful. Keep stirring and adding liquid until all the stock has been used up and the rice has cooked for at least 22 minutes. By this time it should be just done. Cook another minute or so to absorb the last of the liquid. Now add the cheese and butter. Stir until the cheese and butter have melted and have disappeared in the rice. Sprinkle the parsley over the top and stir it in. Turn off the heat. Let the risotto rest for a minute or two, then stir and serve.

SERVES 3 TO 4

Risotto with Dried Porcini Mushrooms   ITALY
Risotto con Funghi

You will need at least ¹/₂ ounce of dried porcini mushrooms for the dish, and double that amount would be even better; I am only being conservative because they are expensive. I like to use sliced mushrooms, but sometimes all one can find are packages of what look like coarsely chopped ones.

4 cups light vegetable stock, seasoned
   (for details, see page 405)

¹/₂ to 1 ounce dried porcini mushrooms

3 tablespoons olive oil

¹/₂ smallish onion (about 1 ounce), peeled and
   finely chopped

¹/₂ teaspoon finely chopped fresh rosemary or
   ¹/₄ teaspoon dry, well crushed in a mortar

1 cup unwashed risotto rice

¹/₂ cup dry vermouth or dry white wine

¹/₂ cup grated Parmigiano-Reggiano cheese

1 tablespoon unsalted butter, cut into
   4 pieces

1 tablespoon very finely chopped Italian
   flat-leaf parsley

Heat the stock and add the mushrooms to it. Let them soak for 2 hours. Lift the mushrooms out of the liquid, squeeze out all their juices into the soaking liquid, and set aside. Line a sieve with a clean cloth and strain the soaking liquid. Put this liquid in a pan, heat it, and keep it hot over very, very low heat.

Put the oil in a large, heavy, preferably nonstick frying pan or sauté pan and set over medium-high heat. When hot, add the onion. Stir and fry for a minute. Add

(recipe continues)

the mushrooms and rosemary. Stir and fry for another minute. Add the rice. Stir and fry it for a minute. Now pour in the vermouth, stirring gently. When the liquid bubbles up, turn the heat to medium. Keep stirring the risotto until the vermouth has been absorbed, then add a ladleful of the stock. Stir until it too is absorbed. Keep adding stock, a ladleful at a time, stirring gently until it is absorbed, until all the stock has been used up and the rice has cooked for at least 22 minutes. By this time it should be just done. Cook another minute or so to absorb the last of the liquid. Now add the cheese and butter. Stir until the cheese and butter have melted and have disappeared in the rice. Sprinkle the parsley over the top and stir it in. Turn off the heat. Let the risotto rest for a minute or two, then stir and serve.

SERVES 3 TO 4

Risotto with Tomato and Eggplant

Here is something that I cook frequently for my family, who love it. It is really a meal in itself and needs only a crisp green salad as an accompaniment.

1 medium eggplant (about ¾ pound)

¼ cup olive oil

Salt

Freshly ground black pepper

4 cups light vegetable stock, seasoned (for details, see page 405)

1 small onion (2 ounces), peeled and finely chopped

2 medium tomatoes (10 ounces), peeled, seeded, and finely chopped (page 300)

5 to 6 fresh basil leaves, torn up

1 cup unwashed risotto rice

⅔ cup grated Parmigiano-Reggiano cheese

1 tablespoon good-quality extra-virgin olive oil

1 tablespoon very finely chopped Italian flat-leaf parsley

Preheat the broiler.

Peel the eggplant and cut it lengthwise into 1-inch-thick slabs. Brush the slabs lightly on both sides with about 1 tablespoon of the oil and then dust them lightly with salt and pepper. Lay the slices on a broiling tray and broil about 4 inches from the heat source until both sides are lightly browned. Cut the slices into 1-inch dice.

Heat the stock and keep it hot over very, very low heat.

Put the remaining 3 tablespoons of olive oil in a large, heavy, preferably nonstick frying pan or sauté pan and set over medium-high heat. When hot, put in the onion. Stir and fry for a minute. Add the tomatoes and basil, and stir and fry for a minute. Add the eggplant. Stir and fry another minute, then add the rice and stir and fry for 1 minute longer. Pour in a generous ladleful of the stock and turn the heat to medium. Stir the risotto until the stock has been absorbed, then add another ladleful. Keep stirring and adding stock until all the stock has been used up and the rice has cooked for at least 22 minutes. By this time it should be just done. Cook another minute or so to absorb the last of the liquid. Now add the cheese. Stir until the cheese has melted and disappeared in the rice. Sprinkle the extra-virgin olive oil and parsley over the top and stir them in. Turn off the heat. Let the risotto rest for a minute or two, then stir and serve.

SERVES 3 TO 4

Variation
Risotto with Tomato, Roasted Eggplant, and Mint

Instead of broiling the eggplant, roast it whole according to directions on page 178. Peel it and mash the flesh coarsely. Cook this for a few minutes with the onion and tomatoes, salting and peppering it lightly. Then add the rice and continue with the recipe. Add a few chopped fresh mint leaves instead of the parsley toward the end.

Risotto with Spinach, Golden Raisins, and Pine Nuts

I love the gentle sweetness of raisins with spinach.
If you wish to use frozen spinach, defrost and drain it first.

4 cups light vegetable stock, seasoned
    (for details, see page 405)

3 tablespoons olive oil

2 tablespoons pine nuts

½ smallish onion (about 1 ounce), peeled and
    finely chopped

1 tablespoon golden raisins

10 ounces fresh spinach, trimmed, well
    washed, patted dry, and cut into fine
    ribbons

1 cup unwashed risotto rice

¼ teaspoon ground cinnamon

½ cup grated Parmigiano-Reggiano cheese

1 tablespoon unsalted butter, cut into small
    pieces

(recipe continues)

Heat the stock and keep it hot over very, very low heat.

Put the oil in a large, heavy, preferably nonstick frying pan or sauté pan and set over medium-high heat. When hot, add the pine nuts. Stir and fry them until they are golden brown. Remove with a slotted spoon and set aside. Now add the onion. Stir and fry it for a minute, then add the raisins. Stir a few times and then add the spinach. Stir and fry the spinach for 3 to 4 minutes. Add the rice and cinnamon. Stir and fry for another minute. Now pour in a generous ladleful of the stock. Turn the heat to medium. Keep stirring the risotto. When the stock has been absorbed, add another ladleful. Keep doing this until all the stock has been used up and the rice has cooked for at least 22 minutes. By this time it should be just done. Cook another minute or so to absorb the last of the liquid. Now add the cheese and butter. Stir until the cheese and butter have melted and have disappeared in the rice. Turn off the heat. Let the risotto rest for a minute or two, then stir and serve, sprinkling the pine nuts over the top.

SERVES 3 TO 4

Vali Manuelides'

Greek Pumpkin Risotto Made in a Pressure Cooker

GREECE

Vali Manuelides is a superb cook and her risotto is made in a pressure cooker using Greek flavorings. It cannot be improved upon. It may be served as a starter course or as the main meal, accompanied by a green salad.

For this dish, I used a section of pumpkin that weighed 1 pound 10 ounces. After removing the seeds and peeling it, I was left with 1¼ pounds of flesh. Any orange-fleshed squash, such as Hubbard or butternut, may be used in place of the pumpkin.

If you do not wish to use a pressure cooker, increase the vegetable stock to 6 cups and follow the general method in the recipe for Risotto with Peas (page 406).

3 tablespoons olive oil

1 medium onion (3½ ounces), peeled and finely chopped

1¼ pounds pumpkin flesh, cut into ½-inch dice

2 teaspoons sugar

1½ cups unwashed risotto rice

2 tablespoons finely chopped fresh dill

1 teaspoon salt, or more if needed

3 cups heated light vegetable stock (for details, see page 405)

Freshly ground black pepper

⅔ cup freshly grated Parmigiano-Reggiano cheese

Put the oil in a pressure cooker and set over medium-high heat. When hot, put in the onion and stir and fry for 2 to 3 minutes, or until the onion bits just begin to brown at the edges. Add the pumpkin and sauté it for 5 minutes. Add the sugar and stir once or twice. Put in the rice, dill, and salt. Sauté the rice gently for 2 minutes. Now put in the stock and cover. Bring the pan up to pressure. Lower the heat a bit to maintain gentle pressure and cook for 5 minutes. Take the pan off the heat and let the pressure drop by itself. This takes 10 to 12 minutes. Uncover and while the risotto is still very hot, stir in a good amount of black pepper and the cheese. Mix well and serve, spreading the risotto out on individual plates.

SERVES 4 TO 6

Variation
Risotto with Pumpkin and Sage

Substitute 6 to 9 fresh sage leaves, very finely chopped, for the dill.

RICE FLOUR

Savory Korean Pancakes with Peppers and Mushrooms   KOREA
Pa'chon

I first had these at a big Korean fair just outside of Seoul where all kinds of foodstuffs were being sold.

The peppers used are mildly hot. I notice that Korean restaurants in New York use a combination of red and green bell peppers as well as a few slices of hot chiles as I have done here. If you wish to use plain mushrooms instead of the fresh shiitakes, stir-fry them first so they lose most of their liquid. Then add the peppers and scallions.

These pancakes are best eaten as soon as they are made with a simple dipping sauce. If you wish to make them in advance, cover them with foil. The entire foil bundle may then be heated in a 350°F. oven or the pancakes may be reheated, one at a time, in a microwave oven for 1 minute.

(recipe continues)

¾ cup unbleached all-purpose white flour

¾ cup rice flour

Salt

1 egg, beaten

1 tablespoon oriental sesame oil

6 tablespoons peanut or canola oil

4 to 5 fresh shiitake mushrooms, stems
removed and caps cut into fine slices

⅓ large red pepper (about 2 ounces in all),
cut into fine long slivers and then halved
lengthwise

⅓ large green pepper (about 2 ounces in all),
cut into fine long slivers and then halved
lengthwise

1 fresh hot red or green chile, cut into fine
long slivers (optional)

2 scallions, quartered lengthwise and then cut
into 2-inch segments

1½ teaspoons sesame seeds

For the dipping sauce

6 tablespoons soy sauce

2 tablespoons red wine vinegar

1 tablespoon oriental sesame oil

Put the 2 flours in a bowl. Slowly add up to 1½ cups of water (you will probably need less) to make a batter that is like flowing cream. Add ¾ teaspoon salt, the egg, and sesame oil. Beat to mix and set aside for 30 minutes (or longer in the refrigerator).

To make the pancakes, put 3 tablespoons of the vegetable oil in a large nonstick frying pan and set over medium heat. When hot, put in the sliced mushrooms, red and green peppers, chile, and scallions. Stir and fry for 1 minute, or until just slightly wilted. Sprinkle very lightly with salt and mix quickly. Now remove the vegetable mixture and turn the heat to medium-low. Put in another tablespoon of oil and spread ½ teaspoon sesame seeds in the center of the pan in an 8-inch circle. Arrange ⅓ of the vegetable mixture over the sesame seeds. Stir the batter and pour ⅓ of it over the vegetables to form an 8-inch pancake. Cover and cook on medium-low heat for 5 to 6 minutes, or until the bottom is somewhat golden.

Using a big spatula, turn the pancake over and cook the second side, covered, for another 4 minutes. Uncover, turn the pancake over, and cook 2 minutes. Turn again and cook, uncovered, another minute or so. Remove the pancake. Cut it into wedges or squares and serve hot with the dipping sauce. (To make the sauce, combine all the ingredients.) Make the second and third pancakes the same way, adding a tablespoon of oil to the pan for each.

MAKES 3 LARGE PANCAKES; SERVES 2 TO 6

Vietnamese Pancakes

Banh Xeo

These pancakes are very similar to the preceding Korean pancakes; it is the trimmings that make the difference.

For the dipping sauce

6 tablespoons soy sauce

2 tablespoons fresh lime juice

2 teaspoons sugar

1 garlic clove, peeled and crushed to a pulp

1 teaspoon finely chopped fresh hot green or
   red chile

2 tablespoons finely chopped roasted peanuts

For the pancakes

¾ cup unbleached all-purpose white flour

¾ cup rice flour

Salt

1 egg, beaten

1 tablespoon butter, melted, or canola oil

6 tablespoons peanut or canola oil

4 to 5 fresh shiitake mushrooms, stems
   removed and caps cut into fine slices

1 fresh hot red or green chile, cut into fine
   rounds

4 scallions, thinly sliced (both white and
   green sections)

For scattering over the top

Generous handful of fresh bean sprouts

Generous handful of small mint leaves

Generous handful of torn basil leaves

Combine all the ingredients for the dipping sauce except the peanuts. Mix well and set aside. (Add the peanuts just before you serve.)

Put the 2 flours in a bowl. Slowly add up to 1½ cups of water (you will probably need less) to make a batter that is like flowing cream. Add ¾ teaspoon salt, the egg, and the melted butter or oil. Beat to mix and set aside for 30 minutes (or longer in the refrigerator).

To make the pancakes, put 3 tablespoons of the peanut or canola oil in a large, nonstick frying pan and set over medium heat. When hot, put in the sliced mushrooms, chile, and scallions. Stir and fry for 1 minute, or until just wilted slightly. Sprinkle very lightly with salt and mix quickly. Now remove the vegetable mixture and turn the heat to medium-low. Put in another tablespoon of oil and lay ⅓ of the vegetable mixture in the center of the pan in a diameter of 8 inches. Stir the batter and pour ⅓ of it over the vegetables to form an 8-inch pancake. Cover and cook on medium-low heat for 5 to 6 minutes, or until the bottom is somewhat golden. Using a big spatula, turn the pancake over and cook the second side,

(recipe continues)

covered, for another 4 minutes. Uncover, turn the pancake over, and cook 2 minutes. Turn again and cook, uncovered, another minute or so. Remove the pancake. Cut it into wedges or squares, scatter the bean sprouts, mint, and basil over the top, and serve hot with the dipping sauce. Make the second and third pancakes the same way, adding a tablespoon of oil to the pan for each.

MAKES 3 LARGE PANCAKES; SERVES 2 TO 6

Indian Rice Flour Pancakes INDIA
Dosa

Serve these spicy pancakes with a cup of tea for breakfast or as a snack. Freshly made or preserved chutneys may be served on the side. These pancakes are almost like breads and may be eaten with a meal as well.

1 cup unbleached all-purpose white flour

1 cup rice flour

1¼ teaspoons salt

1 cup plain yogurt

2 tablespoons finely chopped fresh cilantro

2 teaspoons very finely chopped peeled fresh ginger

2 teaspoons finely chopped fresh hot green chiles

5 to 6 tablespoons peanut or canola oil

Combine the 2 flours, salt, and yogurt in a food processor or blender. Add ¾ cup of water and blend until you have a smooth batter. Pour into a bowl. Add the cilantro, ginger, and chiles. Stir to mix. (You may set this batter aside for several hours, refrigerating it if necessary.)

Put ½ teaspoon of oil in a nonstick frying pan and set over medium-low heat. When it is hot, remove about ⅓ cup of the batter and drop it in the center of the pan. Put the bottom of a rounded ladle or rounded soup spoon on the blob of batter and, using a continuous spiral motion, move it outward in concentric circles. You should end up with a 7-inch pancake. Dribble another ½ teaspoon of oil over the pancake and 1 teaspoon around the edges. Cover and cook the pancake for 4 to 5 minutes, or until it is reddish-brown on the bottom. Turn the pancake over and cook the second side, uncovered, for about 4 minutes, or until it too has reddish spots. Put the pancake on a plate and cover with foil or an upturned plate. Make all the pancakes this way.

You may reheat all the pancakes, wrapped in foil, in a medium oven for 15 minutes. You may also heat them, one at a time, in microwave for 40 to 60 seconds.

MAKES 8

Rice Noodles with Cauliflower

Here, I have cooked dried, flat rice noodles, banh pho, *the way South Indians prepare* idi-appam, *thin, fresh rice noodles. Traditionally, they are seasoned just with oil and spices (rather like Italians serve pasta with nothing more than olive oil and garlic) and are a southern Indian classic. I have tossed in some cauliflower for added interest.*

12 ounces dried rice noodles *(banh pho)*

1 teaspoon plus 6 tablespoons peanut or canola oil

1 (1½-pound) head of cauliflower, cut into small, delicate florets according to directions on page 161

Salt

Freshly ground black pepper

½ teaspoon whole brown mustard seeds

½ teaspoon *urad dal* or yellow split peas

2 whole hot dried red chiles

15 fresh curry leaves (use small, fresh basil leaves as an interesting alternative)

Soak the noodles in water to cover generously for 30 minutes. Bring a large pot of water to a rolling boil. Drain the noodles and cook in the boiling water for 1 minute or less until just done. Drain and quickly rinse under cold running water, washing away as much starch as possible. Put in a bowl, toss with the 1 teaspoon of oil, and set aside.

Put the remaining 6 tablespoons of oil in a large, preferably nonstick frying pan or sauté pan and set over medium-high heat. When hot, put in the cauliflower. Stir and fry for 3 to 4 minutes, or until the cauliflower has browned a bit and is tender-crisp. Use a slotted spoon to transfer to a bowl. Sprinkle about ½ teaspoon salt (or to taste) over the top as well as some black pepper. Toss to mix. Strain the oil remaining in the pan and then return it to the pan.

Just before serving, turn the heat under the pan to medium-high. When very hot, put in the mustard seeds. As soon as the mustard seeds begin to pop, a matter of seconds, put in the *urad dal*. Stir until the *dal* turns red. Quickly put in the chiles. As soon as they darken, a matter of seconds, put in the curry leaves. Stir them once or twice and turn the heat to medium. Now put in the noodles and about ¼ teaspoon salt. Toss the noodles until they are heated through. Check to see if they are properly salted, adding more if needed. Put in the cauliflower and toss a few times. Serve immediately.

SERVES 4

Wheat (and Spelt Wheat)

The population of India is divided between rice eaters and wheat eaters. My North Indian family belonged firmly to the wheat-eating camp. At the spring festival of Holi, when an offering of the new harvest is thrown into a sacred bonfire, we took great delight in heaving big sheaves of still-green wheat and whole plants of green chickpeas into the raging flames. The flames did not last long, but they did manage to singe and roast the grains. The fun part came later as we went on all fours through the smoldering ashes, collecting the cooked grains with greedy hands and putting them into little bowls. What was probably a pagan celebration two thousand or more years earlier had been reworked by Hindus to include Lord Krishna. So as we devoured the fruit of our foraging, we were obviously being blessed by The One Who Mattered. I liked that. I also liked the green wheat, which tasted sweet and of the earth.

According to the *Encyclopedia Britannica,* "there are more pounds of wheat produced than of rice but more people use rice as their chief food." Wheat has been cultivated since 7000 B.C., wild wheat since 9000 B.C. As long ago as 3100 B.C., Sumerians were using wheat to brew beer and make bread. Egyptians probably made the first raised bread of the sourdough variety. Leavened bread was obviously known at the time of the exodus as Hebrews ate *un*leavened bread.

All wheat is not the same. There is hard red winter wheat and hard red spring wheat with 11 to 15 percent protein. Hard red wheat is generally used for bread flours. Soft wheat with 5 to 9 percent protein is used mostly for cakes, crackers, cookies, and pastries. Durum wheat, which is a hard wheat, is ground into semolina and used mainly for making spaghetti and macaroni and other pasta products, including couscous.

The hulled grain has bran on the outside, which is rich in niacin and the B-complex vitamins. Within the bran is the endosperm, which contains cells filled with starch embedded in a protein called gluten. Gluten's elasticity is what enables bread not just to rise but rise and stay there, to retain the gas created by leavening. Kneading encourages the gluten to go to work. At the bottom of the grain is the all-important germ, or embryo, full of fat, concentrated nutritional goodness, and promise. Eating whole wheat is like eating an egg. It is high-energy food as it not only contains the embryo (or germ) that will become the next plant but the food needed to nourish it. Its high fat content, however, makes it perishable, so whole wheat and wheat germ is best stored in the refrigerator to prevent them from becoming rancid.

Today wheat is sold in so many forms for our cooking pleasure, and even our corner health food shops carry many varieties. Here are some varieties I have used in this book:

Whole wheat berries, from both hard and soft wheat: Whole grains that have been hulled but still have all the bran on them are sold in health food stores as winter (planted in the autumn) and spring (planted in the spring) wheat berries. It is best to ask if the wheat is hard or soft (both are grown in each growing season), as the hard wheat takes a bit longer to cook. I love to use these berries in soups. They are also excellent as stuffing, especially in vegetables such as tomatoes (page 420). You may also sprout them to use in breads and salads.

To cook whole wheat berries Take ½ cup (3 ounces) wheat berries, rinse them, then cover them with 4 cups of water. Leave to soak for 12 hours. You may now cook them, covered, in the same water for 1½ hours or in a pressure cooker for 30 minutes, allowing the pressure to drop by itself. Use the berries plus their liquid in soups and stews or drain the berries (save the liquid for stocks) and use them in stuffings and soups. Once drained, ½ cup wheat berries will yield a scant 2 cups cooked berries. Cooked whole wheat berries should be stored with their liquid in a covered container in the refrigerator, where they will last for 4 to 5 days.

Sprouting whole wheat berries Take ½ cup (3 ounces) whole wheat berries and rinse well. Soak them in water to cover them generously for 24 hours, changing the water 2 to 3 times during this period. Drain. Line a large baking tray with a double layer of well-dampened paper towels. Spread the wheat evenly over the paper towels. Cover with more dampened paper towels. Place the baking tray in a dark place, such as an unused oven. Leave for 24 hours, or until small sprouts appear. If the paper towels start to dry out during this period, sprinkle them with a little water. Sprouted berries may be put in a plastic container and stored in the refrigerator for a week. This amount of berries will yield 2 cups sprouts with a lovely, sweet, earthy taste.

Wheat berries, skinned: These cook much faster. However, because they do not retain their shape as well as whole wheat berries, they are best used in soups and stews. These are generally sold in Middle Eastern groceries.

To cook skinned wheat berries Cover ½ cup (3 ounces) berries with 4 cups of water and soak for 12 hours. Bring to a boil in the soaking water. Cover, turn the heat down to low, and cook 30 minutes for a crisp-soft texture and 45 minutes for a fluffy softness like that of cooked barley. Cooked skinned wheat berries may be stored (with their liquid or drained) in a covered container in the refrigerator for 4 to 5 days.

Storing uncooked whole or skinned wheat berries and wheat germ: These are best stored in the refrigerator, as the oily wheat germ can get rancid.

Spelt wheat: This variety of wheat, found mostly in Europe and now in our health food stores, is not so much an early grain as a grain that has not been tampered with or made to pass through genetic hoops through the centuries. This benign neglect has proved a blessing for us, as we now have wheat in one of its original forms. The whole grains cook exactly like whole wheat berries and are now proving very popular both with our star-chefs and all of us commoners who shop in health food shops. Many people who are allergic to wheat—such as my little granddaughter—can eat spelt wheat without any ill effect. When sprouting spelt, the soaking times remain the same, but I find that the sprouting itself can take up to 36 hours.

Bulgur wheat: An ancient West Asian way of preparing wheat, not all that different in philosophy to the way ancient Indians parboiled rice. Here the husk is removed from the wheat and the berries are steamed briefly. After this they are dried and then crushed coarsely or finely as desired.

The coarser bulgur is used for pilafs and salads and the finer one for making "meatballs" and patties.

Because of the precooking of the grain, bulgur wheat can be eaten after it has been thoroughly soaked—which rehydrates it—and then squeezed out. Cooking is not essential. This is the way it is used in many salads, such as the Lebanese tabbouleh (page 423). Soaked bulgur may be mashed and formed into a variety of Syrian-style patties known as kibbee, which are then fried, baked, or poached.

Soaking bulgur If you are in a rush, soak the coarser bulgur in boiling water for about 2 hours, or until it has softened all the way down to its inner core. If you are not in a rush, soak the coarser bulgur in cold water for 4 to 5 hours, or until completely softened. Once the soaking is done, line a colander with a clean cloth, drop the soaked bulgur in it, and twist the top of the cloth bundle to squeeze out all the extra moisture. You could also squeeze out the grains, a handful at a time, between the palms of your hands. The cold water method results in a slightly firmer texture, but both methods work. Fine bulgur need only be rinsed and allowed to stand until it plumps up.

Bulgur wheat may also be cooked like rice. Generally speaking, the proportion of water to bulgur in volume is 1½:1. Sautéed vegetables and legumes may be added, as may seasonings, nuts, and dried fruit. Once the cooking is done, I like to put a towel between the pan and its lid for a little while to absorb extra moisture.

Semolina: Semolina is a flour made out of hard durum wheat with a texture that tends to vary from slightly to very granular. For making pastas and breads, you need fine semolina, which is sold by specialty stores (Middle Eastern stores always have it, labeled "fine semolina," as do stores carrying multi grains). For making desserts and the wonderful "risottos" of southern India known as *uppamas*, the coarser semolina is generally required. This is often just sold as "semolina" *sooji* in Indian shops and Cream of Wheat in the supermarkets. Couscous is made from a mixture of fine and coarse semolina, the finer flour binding itself around the coarser to form the couscous granules.

A 1-cup measure of semolina weighs much more than a 1-cup measure of white or whole wheat flour, so care must be taken when making substitutions in the recipes.

Other wheat flours: There are many other wheat flours in our markets. Whole wheat flour is made from the whole grain and includes the germ and the bran. White flour has no bran and no germ. All-purpose white flour is a combination of hard and soft wheat, so it can be used for both cakes and breads. Cake flour is made from soft wheat and is most suited to cakes and pastries. Bread flour is made from hard wheats and is most suited to bread making. Unbleached flour is flour that has been naturally bleached. (Most flours are bleached with food additives.) Unbleached flour has a more natural taste, though some of the bleached flours are lighter and finer grained. Self-rising flour includes salt and leavening agents such as baking soda. This flour is used for pancakes and cakes but not bread. All flours need to be stored in tightly closed containers. Whole wheat flours are best kept in the refrigerator.

Chapati flour A very finely ground whole wheat flour sold by Indian grocers. If you cannot get it, use a half-and-half mixture of sifted whole wheat and all-purpose flour.

Wheat gluten/seitan: Wheat gluten/seitan has come to us via Asia where it is used commonly by Buddhists and other vegetarians. To extract gluten, you need to buy high-gluten flour, make a dough with it, and then literally wash it again and again until all that is left is a gelatinous mass—gluten. Ready-made gluten may be bought fresh, frozen, or fried in balls at Chinese stores. Since it is completely bland and unseasoned, it needs to be cooked with other ingredients and flavorings. Health food stores also sell wheat gluten in the form of seitan, gluten that has already been boiled for at least an hour in a stock with seasonings, mainly tamari (soy sauce) and *konbu* (a seaweed or laver), the minerals in the seasonings helping to make the gluten much more digestible. It may be added to soups and stews and cooked rather like meat in stir-fries, meat loafs, stews, lasagna, stuffing for eggplants, and so on. It needs beans or dairy dishes to complement it nutritionally.

Wheat pastas and noodles: There is a world of them, from the plump udon of Japan to the wire-thin *seviyan* of India and the curly twists—fusilli—of Italy. I will not even speculate on the origins of pasta but just say (rather generously) that early pastas probably existed simultaneously in East, West, and South Asia, and soon thereafter in parts of Europe, wherever there was wheat. Couscous, or some similar grainy bead, made by hand rolling, the way it is still done today in Morocco, was probably one of the very first pastas.

Cooking pastas and noodles Most fresh or dried pastas need to cook in lots of boiling water, anywhere from 4 quarts or more for a pound of pasta. Generally the water is generously salted—1½ tablespoons for the above amount—and the pasta cooked until it is just tender. I loathe undercooked pasta that has a telltale white core. Pasta should be fully cooked but very firm. I realize that there is a very fine line between undercooked and overcooked pasta. You just need to keep testing it and pour out the boiling water the second it is ready. Couscous is generally steamed over the dish it is to be served with in a special couscousière.

WHEAT AND SPELT BERRIES

George Nikolaides'
Tomatoes Stuffed with Wheat Berries

GREECE

Domato Yemisti Me Sitara

This is a Macedonian specialty. The tomatoes came to our table in Porto Carras on a large platter, surrounded by delicate sprigs of fresh rosemary. I found them utterly delicious and insisted on going into the kitchen and watching their preparation.

The wheat berries may be boiled up to 2 days in advance and kept, with their liquid, in the refrigerator. Drain them just before cooking. You will need to start with ½ cup dried wheat berries.

The stuffing may be made up to 24 hours in advance and can be served all by itself as a salad. See page 640 for details.

I like to serve the tomatoes with some greens.

For the stuffing

2 tablespoons olive oil

1 smallish onion (3 ounces), peeled and finely chopped

1 large or 2 medium garlic cloves, peeled and finely chopped

1 cup finely chopped tomato

1 fresh green chile, finely chopped

2 scant cups drained cooked whole wheat berries (page 417)

½ cup finely chopped parsley

½ teaspoon dried thyme

¼ teaspoon finely chopped fresh rosemary or the same amount dried, well crumbled

¾ teaspoon salt

Freshly ground black pepper

7 medium tomatoes with stable bottoms

Salt

Freshly ground black pepper

2½ tablespoons extra-virgin olive oil

1 cup canned tomato juice

Make the stuffing. Put the oil in a nonstick frying pan and set over medium heat. When hot, put in the onion and garlic. Stir and fry for 2 to 3 minutes, or until the onion has just browned a little. Now put in the tomato and green chile. Stir and fry another 3 minutes. Add the drained wheat berries and stir a few times to mix, then put in the parsley, thyme, rosemary, salt, and pepper to taste. Stir for a minute and turn off the heat.

Preheat the oven to 325°F.

Cut a cap off the top of each of the whole tomatoes and set aside. Scoop out the insides with a spoon, being careful not to pierce the shell. (Save the insides for another use.) Sprinkle a little salt and pepper in each shell and then stuff them loosely with the wheat mixture. Put the tomatoes on a small baking tray. Cover with the reserved caps. Dribble the extra-virgin olive oil over the tomatoes and then pour the tomato juice evenly over the tomatoes as well. Put into the oven and bake for 25 to 30 minutes, basting with the juices now and then. Serve hot.

MAKES 6 TO 7 STUFFED TOMATOES

Spelt Berries with Walnuts and Currants

Slightly sweet and savory at the same time, this dish was inspired by my trip to Turkey. You may serve it with greens and something made with pumpkins or use it to stuff vegetables (page 422).

When the spelt berries have finished their basic cooking, you should have about ½ cup of liquid in the pan. This will happen automatically if you just boil the berries. However, if you choose the pressure cooker method, you may have more liquid than you need. Just discard the extra.

Make sure that the walnuts are of good quality and do not have a rancid aftertaste. I grew up with walnuts (we got them fresh every season from Kashmir and ate them only in the winter) and get unreasonably upset when one of the finest chefs serves a perfectly wonderful dish only to scatter rancid nuts over the top. Always taste nuts before you use them.

½ cup (3 ounces) spelt berries, cooked according to directions on page 417, with about ½ cup of their cooking liquid

2 tablespoons dried currants

2 tablespoons very coarsely chopped walnuts

¾ teaspoon salt

1 tablespoon sugar

⅛ teaspoon cayenne

1 tablespoon olive oil

2 scallions, cut crosswise into very fine rounds (both white and green sections)

(recipe continues)

Heat the spelt berries in their liquid. As soon as they are hot, add the currants, walnuts, salt, sugar, and cayenne. Stir to mix, cover, and turn off the heat. Let the pan sit for 15 minutes to allow the currants to plump.

Heat the oil in a medium frying pan over medium heat. When hot, put in the scallions. Stir and fry for about 2 minutes, or until the scallions are lightly browned. Put in the spelt, turn the heat to high, and stir and cook for 3 to 4 minutes, or until you have just a thick sauce at the bottom of the pan.

SERVES 2 TO 4

Winter Squash Stuffed with Spelt Berries

Here is a superb main dish that may be served with the greens of your choice.

2 good-sized acorn or butternut squashes

Salt

Freshly ground black pepper

2 tablespoons unsalted butter

¼ cup sugar

1 recipe Spelt Berries with Walnuts and Currants (page 420)

2 tablespoons very finely chopped fresh parsley

Preheat the oven to 400°F.

Cut the squashes in half lengthwise and remove the seeds. Lightly salt and pepper them. Score the flesh lightly with the tip of a sharp knife and then put the halves, cut sides down, in a baking tray. Bake for 45 minutes, or until the flesh is soft. Turn the halves over. Dot with the butter and sugar and bake another 5 minutes.

Heat the spelt berry mixture and spoon some into the cavity of each squash. Sprinkle with the parsley and serve immediately.

SERVES 4

Tabbouleh, a Salad of Bulgur and Parsley

There are so many versions of this Middle Eastern salad but my favorite, without a doubt, is the one that uses almost as much finely chopped parsley as bulgur. Buy a lot of parsley, about 9 to 10 ounces; once the stems have been trimmed, you should be left with the right amount. Dry off the parsley sprigs well to facilitate chopping. I have been assured by a friend that well-dried parsley may be chopped in the food processor if you have a new blade. I have yet to try this. As bulgur is basically precooked, this salad requires only soaking and no real cooking.

Serve on a plate with other salads (such as bean salads and yogurt salads) or with whole eggplants (such as Sweet-and-Sour Eggplants, page 194) and a yogurt relish. In Lebanon, they like to pick up this salad with the crisp inner leaves of romaine lettuce.

1 cup bulgur wheat (get the fine grain, if possible)

½ cup finely chopped onion

2½ cups finely chopped fresh parsley (see recipe introduction)

3 tablespoons olive oil (a good virgin oil is best)

¼ cup fresh lemon juice

1¼ teaspoons salt

Bring 4 cups of water to a boil in a medium pan. Remove from the heat and drop in the bulgur. Cover and set aside for 2 hours. (The bulgur will swell and soften.)

Set up a colander in the sink and line it with a clean dish towel. Empty the bulgur into the colander. Gather up the ends of the dish towel and twist, squeezing out as much water as possible. Put the bulgur in a large bowl and fluff it out. Add the onion, parsley, olive oil, lemon juice, and salt, mix thoroughly, and serve at room temperature or chilled.

SERVES 6

Claire Seraphim's

Tabbouleh, a Salad Made with Bulgur and Arugula

LEBANON

I acquired the recipe for this second version of tabbouleh strangely. I was in Nicosia, Cyprus, at the home of Claire Seraphim, when she told me about an Arab visitor from Lebanon who had given her a recipe for a Lebanese tabbouleh in which the main flavoring was not parsley but arugula. Of course, I had to have the recipe. Here it is. The bulgur is soaked in cold water this time and therefore requires a longer soaking period. If you are in a rush, soak the bulgur in the same amount of boiling water for just 2 hours. The cold water method gives the bulgur a firmer texture.

Make sure you wash and dry both the parsley and arugula thoroughly before chopping very finely. I use a salad spinner for drying.

I love to serve this with a few dollops of Classic or Simple Romesco Sauce (pages 669 to 670) on the side.

Salt

1 cup bulgur wheat (get the fine grain, if possible)

2 medium tomatoes (10 ounces), peeled, seeded, and very finely chopped (page 300), then left to drain for 30 minutes or longer

2 well-packed cups finely chopped fresh parsley

1 well-packed cup very finely chopped arugula

8 scallions, thinly sliced crosswise (starting with the white section and going ¾ of the way up the green section) and then very finely chopped

¼ cup olive oil (a good virgin olive oil is best)

¼ cup fresh lemon juice

Freshly ground black pepper

⅛ teaspoon cayenne (optional)

In a bowl, combine 2 cups of water, 1 teaspoon salt, and the bulgur. Set aside to soak for 4 hours.

Set a colander in the sink and line it with a clean dish towel. Empty the bulgur into the colander. Gather up the ends of the dish towel and twist, squeezing out as much water as possible. Put the bulgur in a large bowl and fluff it out. Add the remaining ingredients plus another ½ teaspoon salt. Mix thoroughly and serve at room temperature or chilled.

SERVES 6

Sara Abufares'

Bulgur Wheat with Lentils

SYRIA

M'Jaddarat Burgul

A slightly soft, risotto-like dish of bulgur and lentils, this is always topped in the Middle East with crisply fried onions and served with lemon wedges to squeeze over the top. Yogurt relishes or cheese dishes as well as salads, such as the Simple Syrian Salad (page 637), should be served on the side.

5 tablespoons olive oil

1 medium onion, peeled and cut into fine half rings

1 cup lentils, picked over, washed, and drained

1 cup coarse bulgur wheat

1 teaspoon salt

Lemon wedges

Put the oil in a wide, medium frying pan and set over medium-high heat. When hot, put in the onion. Stir and fry until the onion slices are dark brown and crisp. You will need to lower the heat by degrees as the onions darken. Remove the onions with a slotted spoon and spread out on a plate lined with paper towels. Save the oil.

Combine the lentils and 3½ cups of water in a medium pan and bring to a boil. Cover, turn the heat down to low, and simmer gently for 30 minutes. Put in the bulgur and salt. Stir to mix. Boil rapidly for 10 minutes, stirring as you do so. Cover, turn the heat down to low, and cook another 10 minutes. Lift the cover and pour the reserved oil over the bulgur and lentils. Stir gently to mix. Cover and cook 5 minutes more. Serve with crisp onions scattered over the top and lemon wedges on the side.

SERVES 4 TO 6

Azat Tasci's

Bulgur Wheat with Red Pepper Paste   TURKEY
Kisir

I was offered several versions of this bulgur dish in Turkey. It was always served at room temperature or chilled and eaten either just with a spoon or fork or with scoops of lettuce leaves. Sometimes it had hot peppers and cucumbers in it and sometimes it did not. Often it was mounded up in the shape of a hillock.

The unusual ingredient in it, at least for me, was red pepper paste, which provided a warm, mellow, almost sweet tartness. I had never come across this paste before and now, of course, there is no way I can live without it. Rather like tomato paste, which it resembles in every way except taste, it has become a permanent part of my pantry. (You may buy it ready made from any Middle Eastern store—mine is labeled both "Ates Sos" and "Hot Pepper Sauce." I do not find it hot at all, just pleasingly pungent. You can also make the "sauce" or paste yourself. For more on Red Pepper Paste, see page 673.)

I love to serve this both as a first course and as the main course; I just increase the quantities for the latter. Here is how I do it: For each plate, I make a mound of the bulgur on one side of the plate. Next to it, I put several slices of roasted red bell peppers (these peppers are sectioned, then roasted and peeled according to the method on page 262). I dress the peppers with nothing more than a tiny bit of salt and some good olive oil. Next to the peppers I put a generous dollop of either Classic or Simple Romesco Sauce (pages 669 to 670). Even though the bulgur dish comes from the Eastern Mediterranean and the Romesco Sauce from the Western Mediterranean, I find that all the elements on the plate combine beautifully together.

All the vegetables should be very finely chopped—each piece being about the same size as a cooked bulgur grain. When shopping, remember that you will need about half of a large green bell pepper, 2 good-sized bunches of parsley, a small bunch of mint, and one 6-inch cucumber.

4 teaspoons Red Pepper Paste (see recipe introduction)

2 teaspoons tomato paste

2 tablespoons olive oil

Salt

1 cup bulgur wheat (get the fine grain, if possible)

6 tablespoons very finely chopped green bell pepper (shell only, no seeds or soft veins)

1 small onion (1 ounce), peeled and very finely chopped

2½ well-packed cups (2 ounces) finely chopped parsley

2 to 3 tablespoons finely chopped fresh mint (optional)

6 tablespoons finely chopped peeled seeded cucumber

¼ to ½ teaspoon cayenne, or to taste

1½ tablespoons fresh lemon juice, or to taste

Combine the Red Pepper Paste, tomato paste, olive oil, ½ teaspoon salt, and 2 cups of water in a medium pan. Stir well to mix and bring to a boil. Put in the bulgur wheat. Stir and boil rapidly for 30 to 40 seconds. Cover immediately and take the pan off the heat. Allow to sit, covered and undisturbed, for 1 hour. During this period, the grains will swell and the bulgur will cool off. When cool, add all the remaining ingredients as well as another ½ teaspoon salt. Stir to mix. Taste and adjust the seasonings, if needed.

SERVES 4

Promila Kapoor's

Bulgur Pilaf with Peas and Carrots INDIA

Daliya Namkeen

Northern India has many versions of cracked wheat. One, known as daliya *and very similar to* bulgur, *is used to make this dish called* daliya namkeen *or "savory porridge" in the Punjab.*

If you have a choice, look for the larger (sometimes called "coarser") grains to make this spicy pilaf.

2 tablespoons peanut or canola oil

½ teaspoon whole cumin seeds

1 cup coarse bulgur wheat

1 teaspoon finely chopped ginger

½ fresh hot green chile, finely chopped

½ cup (3 ounces) shelled peas (defrosted frozen peas may be used)

½ cup (2 ounces) peeled diced carrots (dice to size of peas)

¼ teaspoon cayenne

½ teaspoon salt

Put the oil in a medium pan and set over medium-high heat. When it is hot, put in the cumin seeds. Let them sizzle for a few seconds. Turn the heat down to medium and put in the bulgur. Stir constantly for 2 minutes, letting the bulgur brown lightly. Put in the ginger, green chile, peas, carrots, cayenne, and salt. Stir for 30 seconds. Now add 1½ cups of water to the pan. Bring to a boil and cover tightly. Then turn the heat down to very low and cook for 35 minutes. Turn off the heat. Lift the lid and quickly cover the pot with a clean dish towel. Put the lid back on and let the dish towel absorb the moisture for another 20 minutes. Fluff gently and serve hot.

SERVES 4 TO 6

Tassoula David's
Bulgur Risotto with Pumpkin CYPRUS

This dish has a very North African, Arab flavor to it even though it comes from the Greeks of Cyprus. You might serve it as is or with a light sprinkling of confectioners' sugar. I can eat it all by itself, with a green salad or else with Zucchini and Feta Cheese Salad (page 640).

You will need a ¾-pound section of orange pumpkin or hard-shelled squash such as Hubbard or butternut—perhaps a bit more—in order to have the required amount of flesh.

3 tablespoons olive oil

1½-inch cinnamon stick

1 medium onion, peeled and chopped

½ pound pumpkin or other hard-shelled
    winter squash flesh, cut into ½-inch dice

½ cup coarse bulgur wheat

½ teaspoon salt

Put the oil in a heavy, medium pot and set over medium-high heat. When very hot, put in the cinnamon. Stir for 10 seconds. Add the onion. Stir and fry for about 2 minutes, or until the onion pieces brown at the edges. Now put in the pumpkin, bulgur, and salt. Stir and fry for 3 minutes. Add ¾ cup of water, stir, and bring to a boil. Cover tightly, turn the heat down to very low, and cook 30 minutes. Lift the lid, quickly cover the pot with a dish towel, replace the lid, and set aside for 15 minutes. Stir gently before serving.

SERVES 4 TO 6

WHEAT FLATBREADS

Sakina El Alaoui's
Moroccan Flatbread with Yeast MOROCCO
Batbout M'Khamer

These are wonderful, pitalike, pliable breads that are about 6 inches across and ½ inch high.

1 teaspoon active dry yeast

½ teaspoon sugar

1¾ cups (8 ounces) unbleached all-purpose
    white flour

1½ cups (8 ounces) fine semolina

1½ teaspoons salt

Peanut or canola oil

Combine the yeast, sugar, and 2 tablespoons of warm water (105°F. to 115°F.) in a small bowl. Stir to dissolve the yeast completely. Set aside for 5 minutes, or until the yeast begins to bubble.

Meanwhile, mound up the white flour and semolina flour in a large bowl in the shape of a little hill. Make a crater on the hilltop and put the salt and the yeast mixture into it. Now slowly pour warm water (105°F. to 115°F.) into the crater— you will need about 1 cup or slightly more. As you add water, slowly gather the flour together into a ball. Keep adding the water, a little at a time, and gathering the dough, until it begins to form a soft, smooth ball. Once you can form a ball, start to knead. Knead the dough well for about 10 minutes, or until it is smooth and elastic. Form a ball.

Lightly grease a large flat platter and set aside. Coat your hands slightly with oil. Break the dough into 5 equal, smooth balls. Place the balls on the oiled plate at a good distance from each other. Cover with a clean dishcloth and set aside in a warm place for 5 to 10 minutes.

Grease a large work surface, such as a countertop. Take 1 ball and with the flat part of your fingers, flatten it out until it is ¼ inch thick and 6 inches in diameter. Do this with all the balls. Cover the flatbreads with a clean dishcloth and set aside for 1 hour.

Set a large cast-iron frying pan over a medium flame. Let it get very hot. Now pick up 1 flatbread and lay it in the center of the frying pan. Cook for 1 minute. Turn the bread over and cook for another minute. Turn the bread over 4 more times, cooking each side this time for just 30 seconds. Now stand the bread in the pan as if it were a wheel, holding it with 2 oven mitts. Slowly rotate the bread, just like a wheel, and lightly cook the edges for about 1 minute. Lift the bread up with a spatula and place on a dishcloth. Fold the 4 corners of the cloth over the bread and keep it covered. Make all the breads this way, stacking them on top of each other and covering them each time. You can hold the bread this way for about 30 minutes.

MAKES 5

Whole Wheat Tandoori Breads

INDIA

Tandoori Roti

These are the daily flatbreads eaten in most Punjabi villages, baked in free-standing vat-shaped clay ovens, tandoors, *that most families own. The* tandoors *generally sit out in the courtyard, in the open kitchen, which is never too far from where the cows and buffaloes are tethered. There is always an inside kitchen as well that can be used when it rains and to cook dishes like split peas and sweets.*

The breads, always made with nutritious, finely ground whole wheat flour, are slapped onto the inside walls of the hot oven. Very high heat cooks them quite fast. They are retrieved with long hooks before they can loosen and fall to the bottom.

Tandoors are slowly making their way into the Western world but are still not a luxury we can easily install in our homes. My tandoor-*less way to cook these breads is so start off on a well-heated cast-iron frying pan (or griddle or Indian* tava*) and then, once the bread is cooked on one side, place the pan under a hot broiler. The entire process takes about 2 minutes. I like using 7- to 8-inch cast-iron frying pans best for these breads as they have cast-iron handles I can hold easily and that do not get singed in the oven.*

In the Punjab, most people request that their breads be made karak, *or crisp on the outside. My method does this naturally. If you want them softer, cover them as soon as they are made. Their own steam will soften them. If not eating the breads immediately, you should do this anyway.*

If you cannot get chapati flour use a half-and-half mixture of whole wheat flour and all-purpose white flour.

2 cups (10½ ounces) chapati flour, plus extra
    for dusting
½ teaspoon salt, if desired
About 1 cup club soda (make sure it is fizzy)

1 tablespoon peanut or canola oil
About 1 tablespoon unsalted butter for
    buttering the breads (optional)

Put the chapati flour in a bowl. Add the salt, if you are using it. Slowly add the club soda, gathering the flour together to make a dough. Aim for a dough that is soft but not sticky. Knead the dough for 10 minutes and form a smooth ball. Put the ball in a bowl. Cover with a damp cloth and set aside for 15 minutes.

Knead the dough again, using a little flour as needed, and form 6 balls. Dust the balls with flour and set to one side. Dust a work surface lightly with flour. Take 1 ball and roll it out until it is 5 inches in diameter. Smear ½ teaspoon of oil on it. Take a sharp knife and make a cut that goes from the center to any point on the edge, preferably one nearest you. Now make a tight cone by rolling the cut edge over and over itself in a circular manner. The very center, like the point of the compass we used in school, will not move much, but the outside edge will. Once the cone is formed, stand it up, wider side down. Give the tip of the cone 2 little twists in the same direction as you rolled. Now put your palm on top of the tip and flatten the cone so it becomes a patty, about 3 inches in diameter. Make all the patties this way. These patties may either be made into breads right away or, lightly oiled, put on a tray or plate in a single layer, covered with plastic, and refrigerated for up to 24 hours.

When you are ready to cook, light a broiler, arranging a shelf about 6 inches from the source of heat. Also, set a cast-iron frying pan (or griddle or Indian *tava*) over medium-high heat. Give them time to heat up. Put a bowl of water near you as well as a piece of paper towel or a small cloth. Take 1 patty and roll it out until it is about 6¼ inches in diameter. Lift it up carefully on the palm of one hand and slap it onto the heated frying pan. Let it cook for 1 minute. Dip the paper towel or cloth in the bowl of water, squeeze it out lightly, and then dab it gently on top of the bread—the uncooked side. Place the cast-iron frying pan with the bread on it under the broiler for 40 to 60 seconds, rotating the bread if the heat is uneven. The bread should puff up and end up with brown spots all over. Do not worry if it does not puff up fully. Remove it and butter it lightly. If not eating right away, keep the bread in a plate and cover with another upturned plate or keep the bread in a heavy zip-lock plastic bag. Make all the breads this way, stacking them on top of or beside each other. Eat the breads while they are still warm.

MAKES 6

Mohammad Sharif's

Naan

The world of naans or naanlike flatbreads traditionally baked in clay ovens is vast and extends from Turkey all the way through central Asia to India. Actually, pizza too is a kind of naan with a topping.

To simplify matters, I have come up with a basic dough that can be used to make the Indian/Pakistani plain naan, the Afghani sweet naan stuffed with dried fruit, the Turkish ridged bread, and even a cheese-topped pizza. Sometimes I use the basic naan dough to make different breads at the same dinner so people can take a slice of each. Once the basic dough has been made and refrigerated, you may remove just 1 patty to make a pizza or a Turkish pita, if you like.

As with many breads, you need to get the gluten in a small portion of the flour really going well before you add all of the flour. Also, you should end up with a soft dough. This soft dough can be somewhat tricky to work with, but having watched our tandoori chef at Dawat, I have learned a few simple tricks that make it very easy.

To make naans of a decent size without a traditional clay oven or tandoor, *you will need a large cast-iron frying pan. I like to use my 14-inch pan, but a 12-inch one will do.*

For the basic naan dough

About 5 cups unbleached all-purpose white
    flour, plus more for dusting

1½ teaspoons baking powder

1 teaspoon baking soda

½ teaspoon salt

1½ teaspoons sugar

2 tablespoons plain yogurt

1 cup milk

1 egg

1 tablespoon unsalted butter, melted, plus 1
    cup (2 sticks) unsalted butter, melted, for
    assorted other uses (if you are really
    concerned, use peanut or canola oil)

2 tablespoons peanut or canola oil

About ½ teaspoon nigella *(kalonji)* (page 728)

About 2 teaspoons beige sesame seeds

Make the basic naan dough. Sift together the flour, baking powder, baking soda, and salt.

Put the sugar and yogurt into a large mixing bowl. Beat with an electric whisk, which is much easier, or with a wooden spoon. Add the milk and 1 cup of water. Keep beating. Now beat in, a little at a time, about 2 cups or a little more of the flour mixture. Beat very well to encourage the gluten to go to work (100 strokes if you are using a wooden spoon). The batter should look a little pasty. Add the egg and the 1 tablespoon melted butter and keep up the beating. Now slowly add another 2 cups of the flour mixture and keep beating. By the end of this, the whisk will hardly move and you will have a very elastic dough batter. Remove the whisk. Use a wooden spoon and add enough flour (about 1 cup) to make a soft, sticky dough. Empty the dough onto a floured board and knead briefly with oiled hands. Divide the slightly sticky dough into 8 balls with oiled hands. Dust a baking tray rather generously with flour and put the 8 balls on it at a distance from each other. Press on each with a hand dipped in oil to flatten it. Cover with plastic wrap and set aside for 30 minutes or longer. You may even refrigerate the covered tray for up to 48 hours.

This is the basic naan dough.

To make the naan, put a very large cast-iron frying pan on medium-high heat. Light the broiler, keeping a shelf 5 inches from the heat.

Remove a patty. Dip the bottom in fresh flour. Dip both of your hands in melted butter and press down on the patty, enlarging it with your fingers until it has the traditional tear shape and is about 9 inches at its longest and 5 inches at its widest. Dab more melted butter on top with your fingers. Now scatter about ⅛ teaspoon of the nigella and ¼ teaspoon of the sesame seeds over the top. Lift up the naan with both hands and stretch it a bit so it is 12 inches long and about 7 inches wide. Now slap it onto the hot pan, seed side up. Cook for 1 minute and 15 seconds on the first side, moving the naan around after the first 30 seconds so it browns on the bottom evenly. Dab with a little butter and put the whole pan under the broiler for a minute. The naan should develop a few reddish spots. Remove the pan from the broiler. Dab the naan with more melted butter and serve. Make all the naans this way. If not eating immediately, put the naans on a heavy towel and fold the towel over them. They will stay warm for a while. To store, wrap the naans in foil and refrigerate. To reheat, the whole foil bundle may be put in a medium oven for 15 minutes. To heat just 1 naan, you can sprinkle it lightly with water and microwave it for a minute or so.

MAKES 8

Mohammad Sharif's

Kandahari Naan

AFGHANISTAN

I have used just one of the eight patties from the basic naan dough in the preceding recipe to make this slightly sweet, nut-filled naan. It is thicker than plain naan and cooks just a bit longer.

For the filling

2 tablespoons blanched slivered almonds

1 tablespoon golden raisins

1 teaspoon shelled pistachios

Seeds from 2 cardamom pods

1½ teaspoons sugar

1½ teaspoons heavy cream

You also need

1 patty of the basic naan dough (page 432), plus extra flour for dusting

About 2 tablespoons unsalted butter, melted

½ teaspoon beige sesame seeds or a mixture of beige and black

Combine the almonds, raisins, and pistachios and chop coarsely. Add the cardamom and sugar. Moisten with the cream, mix, and set aside.

To make the naan, put a large cast-iron frying pan on medium heat. Give it 6 to 7 minutes to heat up. Light the broiler, keeping a shelf 5 inches from the heat.

Dip the bottom of the dough patty in fresh flour and put it on the work surface. Dip both of your hands in melted butter and press down on the patty, enlarging it with your fingers until it is about 3½ inches in diameter. Put the stuffing right in the center. Bring the edges of the patty over the stuffing, pleating them slightly as you do so. Twist the pleats a bit to enclose the stuffing securely. Now press down on the stuffed ball to flatten it. Using buttered fingers, enlarge the patty until it is about 6½ inches in diameter. Dab a little melted butter on top and then sprinkle the sesame seeds over it.

Lift up the naan and place it on the heated pan, seed side up. Let it cook for 1½ to 2 minutes. Now place the whole pan under the broiler for 1 minute and 15 seconds. Dab the naan lightly with melted butter and serve.

MAKES 1

Cheese Pizza

*I have used just one of the eight patties from the basic naan dough to make this simple pizza.
Fresh mozzarella cheese may be bought both lightly salted and unsalted; here I have used the
salted kind. Serve with a green salad, such as a salad of arugula and lettuce.*

1 patty of the basic naan dough (page 432),
   plus extra flour for dusting

1 tablespoon olive oil

Salt

Freshly ground black pepper

½ cup (3 ounces) coarsely grated salted fresh
   mozzarella cheese (or a combination of
   grated mozzarella and grated fontina
   cheese)

2 teaspoons extra-virgin olive oil

¼ teaspoon dried oregano

To make the pizza, preheat the oven to 425°F. and put a medium cast-iron frying
pan on the oven floor. Make sure there is a shelf at the very top of the oven.

Dip the bottom of the dough patty in fresh flour and put it on the work surface.
Dip both sets of fingertips in the olive oil and press down on the patty, enlarging it
with your fingers until it is about 7 to 7½ inches in diameter. Let a ridge form all
around the edges to hold in the filling. Dust salt and pepper very lightly on top of
the shell. Now spread the cheese (or cheeses) evenly over the top. Sprinkle on a
tiny bit more salt and pepper and then dribble the extra-virgin olive oil over the
cheese. Dust the oregano on top.

Pull out the heated pan and put the pizza on it, cheese side up. Put the pan back on
the oven floor and bake for 15 minutes. Now move the pan to the top shelf of the
oven and bake another 5 minutes, or until the cheese has browned a bit. Serve hot.

MAKES 1; SERVES 1 TO 2

Pizza with Oven-Dried Tomatoes, Cheese, and Rosemary

*I have used just one of the eight patties from the basic naan dough to make this simple pizza.
Oven-dried tomatoes from Australia are beginning to find their way into our specialty markets now so you can actually go out and buy them. However, you may use my recipe, which, oddly
enough, I got from an Australian friend in Melbourne many years ago. They are very simple to
make—and very rewarding. Serve with a green salad.*

(recipe continues)

1 patty of the basic naan dough (page 432),
plus extra flour for dusting

1 tablespoon olive oil

Salt

½ cup (3 ounces) coarsely grated mixture of
fontina, Gruyère, and Bel Paese cheeses

½ teaspoon coarsely ground black pepper

½ teaspoon finely chopped fresh rosemary

About ¾ cup (a rough ¾ teacup measure)
chopped Oven-Dried Plum Tomatoes
(page 305)

2 teaspoons extra-virgin olive oil

Preheat the oven to 425°F. and put a medium cast-iron frying pan on the oven floor. Make sure there is a shelf at the very top of the oven.

Dip the bottom of the dough patty in fresh flour and put it on the work surface. Dip both sets of fingertips in the olive oil and press down on the patty, enlarging it with your fingers until it is about 7 to 7½ inches in diameter. Let a ridge form all around the edges to hold in the filling. Dust salt very lightly on top of the shell. Now toss the cheeses with the black pepper and rosemary and spread evenly over the top.

Pull out the heated pan and put the pizza on it, cheese side up. Put the pan back on the oven floor and bake for 15 minutes. Now move the pan to the top shelf of the oven and bake another 4 minutes, or until the cheese has browned a bit. Scatter the tomatoes over the cheese, dribble the extra-virgin olive oil over the top of the pizza, and continue browning for another minute. Serve hot.

MAKES 1; SERVES 1 TO 2

Turkish Ridged Bread   TURKEY

Ternak Pides

To make this ridged bread, I have used just one of the eight patties from the basic naan dough. It is brushed with an egg yolk–yogurt mixture, sprinkled with both sesame seeds and nigella (kalonji), *and then baked. It is thicker than the plain naan and cooks just a bit longer. Serve it with almost any meal.*

1 patty of the basic naan dough (page 432),
plus extra flour for dusting

About 1 tablespoon olive oil

1 egg yolk

1½ teaspoons plain yogurt

½ teaspoon beige sesame seeds

⅛ teaspoon nigella *(kalonji)* (page 728)

To make the bread, light the oven (assuming the heat source is at the bottom) at the highest temperature and put a medium cast-iron frying pan on the oven floor.

Dip the bottom of the dough patty in fresh flour and put it on the work surface. Dip both sets of fingertips in oil and press down on the patty, enlarging it with your fingers until it is about 5 inches in diameter. Now you have to make the ridges and enlarge the patty simultaneously until you have a 7-inch or larger round. Here is how you do this: Think that you are typing with both hands and that the bread is your keyboard. Put your 8 fingertips down in a row on the extreme left of the top line where the numbers are. Push down and then away from you. (Do not go through the bread.) Lift your fingers just a bit and move one key to the right. Push down and away from you. Keep doing this and moving to the right until you have a whole row of ridges or waves. Make a second row just below the first and then a third and fourth until you have gone down the bread. Now give the bread a quarter turn so the rows you made are vertical. Repeat what you did before, this time making rows at right angles to the first set in a cross-hatch pattern. You should end up with a 7- to 7½-inch round.

Combine the egg yolk with the yogurt and brush just some of it lightly all over the top of the bread. (The rest will be wasted, alas, or may be used for other breads.) Sprinkle the sesame seeds and *kalonji* over the top.

Pull out the heated pan and put the bread on it, seed side up. Put the pan back on the oven floor and bake 7 to 8 minutes. Now light the broiler and place the pan under it for a minute.

MAKES 1

Punjabi Village-Style Flat Whole Wheat Flaky Breads INDIA
Parathas

These very simple everyday flatbreads are eaten daily by village farmers and farmhands in the Punjabi villages of northwestern India. They are accompanied by simple vegetable or bean dishes and either tall glasses of yogurt drinks or plain yogurt. Salads, sometimes just a small onion smashed with a fist, are served on the side.

If you cannot get chapati flour, use an equal mixture of sifted whole wheat flour and all-purpose white flour.

(recipe continues)

2 cups (10½ ounces) chapati flour, plus extra
    for dusting
½ teaspoon salt

2 tablespoons peanut or canola oil
4 to 5 tablespoons unsalted butter, melted, or
    ghee (page 723)

Put the chapati flour and salt into a large bowl. Add the vegetable oil and rub it in. Slowly add about ¾ to 1 cup of water, mixing and kneading as you do so. Aim for a soft but manageable dough. Form a ball and knead it for 10 minutes, or until it is smooth and elastic. Put the dough in a bowl. Cover it with plastic wrap or a dampened cloth and let sit for 30 minutes.

Knead the dough again for 5 minutes. Divide the dough into 8 even balls. You might need to dip your hands in flour to do this.

Set a cast-iron frying pan, griddle, or Indian *tava* on medium-high heat.

Dust the rolling surface and rolling pin with flour. Roll out a ball into a flat, round sphere about 6 inches in diameter. Dribble 1 teaspoon of melted butter or *ghee* on the surface and spread it out evenly with the back of a spoon. Pick up one end of the round and fold it over itself in such a way so as to leave ⅓ of the round uncovered. Now fold this uncovered ⅓ over the rest to form a long rectangle. Dribble ½ teaspoon of melted *ghee* or butter on the surface of this long rectangle and spread it out evenly with the back of the spoon. Fold this rectangle over itself, from the top down, in such a way that ⅓ is left exposed. Now fold the exposed ⅓ over the rest to get a small square. Sprinkle the rolling surface with additional flour as needed. Now roll the small square into a larger one, about 5½ to 6 inches on all sides.

Gently lift the *paratha* from the rolling surface and place it in the center of the heated cast-iron pan. Cook for 30 seconds, or until the dough turns white on top and light brown spots appear on the bottom. Turn the *paratha* over. Spread 1 teaspoon of *ghee* or butter on top of the *paratha*. Cook for 30 seconds. Turn the *paratha* over. Spread 1 teaspoon of *ghee* or butter on the second side of the *paratha*. Cook the *paratha* for another 15 seconds. Keep cooking and turning every 15 seconds for 4 additional times. (Do not add more *ghee* or butter.) The *paratha* is done when it is has light brown spots, and is slightly crisp on the outside and soft but cooked through on the inside.

Make all the *parathas* this way, making sure to wipe the pan with a clean, dry paper towel after each *paratha* is cooked. Turn the heat under the pan down to low while you are rolling out the next *paratha* and then push it back up to medium-high before you slap the *paratha* on. Stack the *parathas* on a plate and cover with aluminum foil or an upturned plate. Serve hot. A bundle of *parathas*, wrapped tightly in foil, may be heated in a moderate oven for 15 minutes. You may also zap a single *paratha* in a microwave for 40 to 60 seconds.

MAKES 8 BREADS

Flaky Flatbreads Stuffed with Cauliflower

INDIA

Gobi Ka Paratha

These parathas *may be eaten by themselves, with a little plain yogurt or chutney for breakfast or with other vegetable and bean dishes at lunch or dinner. They are excellent to take out on picnics.*

If you cannot get chapati flour, use an equal mixture of sifted whole wheat flour and all-purpose white flour.

To grate cauliflower, break off 4 to 5 big florets and grate them on the coarse blade of a grater. If small pieces break off during the grating, just chop them finely.

For the dough

2 cups (10½ ounces) chapati flour, plus extra
 for dusting

½ teaspoon salt

1 tablespoon peanut or olive oil, plus a little
 extra

For the stuffing

1 tablespoon peanut or olive oil

2 teaspoons very finely chopped peeled fresh
 ginger

½ to 1 fresh hot green chile, finely
 chopped

2 cups (6 ounces) grated raw cauliflower

4 tablespoons finely chopped fresh cilantro

About ½ teaspoon salt

Freshly ground black pepper

⅛ teaspoon cayenne

For cooking the parathas

About 4 tablespoons unsalted butter, melted,
 or *ghee,* page 723 (you could also use olive
 oil)

Put the chapati flour and salt into a large bowl. Add the oil and rub it in. Slowly add about 1 cup of water or a bit more, mixing and kneading as you do so. Aim for a soft but manageable dough. Form a ball and knead it for 10 minutes, or until it is smooth and elastic. Form a smooth ball. Rub it with a little oil and put it in a bowl. Cover it with plastic wrap or a dampened cloth and let sit for 30 minutes.

Heat the oil for the stuffing in a small frying pan over medium heat. When hot, put in the ginger. Stir once and put in the green chile and cauliflower. Stir and fry for 30 seconds. Add the cilantro, salt, pepper to taste, and cayenne. Toss for 30 seconds. Turn the heat down to low and cook for 3 to 4 minutes, or until the cauliflower is almost cooked and fairly dry. Leave to cool.

(recipe continues)

Knead the dough again for 5 minutes. Divide the dough into 5 even balls. You might need to dip your hands in flour to do this. Divide the stuffing into 5 portions.

Set a cast-iron frying pan, griddle, or Indian *tava* over medium heat.

Dust the rolling surface and rolling pin with flour. Flatten 1 ball and then roll it into a flat, round sphere about 5 inches in diameter. Take one portion of the stuffing and place it in the center. Bring the edges of the sphere around, pleating them as you do so, until you have enclosed the stuffing in a kind of round dumpling. Give the pleated portion a twist so it will not open up. Flatten the dumpling slightly so it looks like a patty. Flour the work surface again and put the patty on it, pleated side down. Roll out the patty, dusting with flour when needed, until you have a 7-inch round. This is the raw *paratha*.

Gently place the *paratha* on the palm of one hand with all the fingers stretched out and then overturn it with a slap onto the well-heated cast-iron pan. Cook for 45 seconds, or until the dough turns white on top and light brown spots appear on the bottom. Turn the *paratha* over. Cook another 30 seconds. Turn the *paratha* over. Dribble 2 teaspoons melted butter or *ghee* around the edges of the *paratha*. Cook for 15 seconds. Turn the *paratha* over. Cook for 10 seconds and turn the *paratha* over. Now turn the *paratha* every 5 seconds, until it has cooked for about 3½ minutes in all. The *paratha* is done when it has light brown spots all over, and is slightly crisp on the outside and soft but cooked through on the inside.

Make all the *parathas* this way, making sure to wipe the cast-iron pan with a clean, dry paper towel after each *paratha* is cooked. Turn the heat down to low as you stuff your next *paratha* and turn it back to medium in the last stages of rolling it out. Soon you will develop your own rhythm. Stack the *parathas* on a plate and cover with aluminum foil or an upturned plate. Serve hot. A whole bundle of *parathas*, wrapped tightly in foil, may be heated in a moderate oven for 15 minutes. You may also zap a single *paratha* in a microwave oven for 40 seconds to 1 minute.

MAKES 5

Flaky Potato Flatbreads

Aloo Ka Paratha

These very special breads are made with a mixture of mashed potatoes and chapati flour.

    If you cannot get chapati flour, use an equal mixture of sifted whole wheat flour and all-purpose white flour.

    Although these are traditionally eaten with pickles and plain yogurt or meals of vegetables, beans, and yogurt relishes, you may also use them as "wraps" for grated cheese and mango chutney!

For the dough

1 potato with skin (5 ounces)

2 cups (10½ ounces) chapati flour, plus extra for dusting

½ teaspoon salt

1 tablespoon softened unsalted butter, plus a little extra

½ teaspoon peeled ginger, grated to a pulp

1 fresh hot green chile, finely chopped

¼ teaspoon cayenne

1 tablespoon finely chopped fresh mint

2 tablespoons finely chopped fresh cilantro

For cooking the parathas

About 4 tablespoons unsalted butter, melted, or *ghee*, page 723 (you may use olive oil, if you like)

Set the potato to boil without peeling or cutting it.

Put the chapati flour and salt into a large bowl. Add the softened butter and rub it in. Add the ginger, chile, cayenne, mint, and cilantro and rub them in as well.

Test the potato with the point of a knife and when it is tender, hold it with a fork and peel it while it is still hot. Now put it through a ricer or grate it. Add this to the flour mixture in the bowl and rub it in. Slowly add about ¾ cup of water, mixing and kneading as you do so. Aim for a soft but manageable dough. Form a ball and knead it for 10 minutes, or until it is smooth and elastic. Rub it with a little butter and then put it in a bowl. Cover the bowl with plastic wrap or a dampened cloth and let sit for 30 minutes.

Knead the dough lightly on a floured surface. Divide the dough into 5 even balls. The dough will be quite soft. You will need to dip your hands in flour frequently. Flour one area of the work surface well (not where you will be rolling out the breads) and lay the dough balls on it.

Set a cast-iron frying pan, griddle, or Indian *tava* over medium heat.

(recipe continues)

Flour the work surface well and put a ball of dough on it. Flatten the ball into a patty. Roll out the patty, dusting with flour when needed, until you have a 7-inch round. This is the raw *paratha*.

Gently place the *paratha* on the palm of one hand with all the fingers stretched out and then overturn it with a slap onto the well-heated cast-iron pan. Cook for 45 seconds, or until the dough turns white on top and light brown spots appear on the bottom. Turn the *paratha* over. Cook another 30 seconds. Turn the *paratha* over. Dribble 2 teaspoons melted butter or *ghee* around the edges of the *paratha*. Cook for 15 seconds. Turn the *paratha* over. Cook for 10 seconds and turn the *paratha* over. Now turn the *paratha* every 5 seconds, until it has cooked for about 3½ minutes in all. The *paratha* is done when it has light brown spots all over, and is slightly crisp on the outside and soft but cooked through on the inside.

Make all the *parathas* this way, making sure to wipe the cast-iron pan with a clean, dry paper towel after each *paratha* is cooked. Turn the heat down to low while you are rolling out the next *paratha* and then push it back up to medium a little before you slap the *paratha* on. Stack the *parathas* on a plate and cover with aluminum foil or an upturned plate. Serve hot. A whole bundle of *parathas*, wrapped tightly in foil, may be heated in a moderate oven for 15 minutes. You may also zap a single *paratha* in a microwave oven for 40 seconds to 1 minute.

MAKES 5

Melle Derko Samira's

Moroccan Layered Bread   MOROCCO

R'ghaif

I first had this exquisite, satiny bread in Fez. It was served to us as a snack in a break at a food symposium. I found it so similar to the Indian paratha *that I immediately wanted to learn how to make it. It was Samira, a professional chef in Marrakech, who eventually showed me the way to do it.*

The technique seems complicated but is easy to master. Because the dough is very soft, it is essential to keep it and one's hand oiled generously as one is working. If you follow my directions carefully, I am sure you will not have a problem. It is best to eat these breads as soon as they are made.

Serve at breakfast in its more common sweet version, given below, or at a meal, in its basic savory version with bean and vegetable dishes. The savory version could also have a filling in it. Once you've rolled it into a round, you could, if you like, rub each bread with about ½ teaspoon of Moroccan Chile-Garlic Paste (page 672) and a pinch of salt before you fold it.

For the breads

2¼ cups unbleached all-purpose white flour,
  plus extra for dusting

1 teaspoon salt

About ½ cup peanut or canola oil

For the topping

⅔ cup honey

3 tablespoons roasted sesame seeds (page
  734)

Put the flour in a large tray in the shape of a little hill. Make a crater on the hill-top and put the salt in it. Now slowly pour 1 cup of warm water (105°F. to 115°F.) into the crater, working the dough with the flat part of your fingers and palms only, pushing them against the tray and working with a circular motion. Keep adding the water, a little at a time, and working the dough as suggested, until it begins to form a sticky ball. Don't be worried if the dough seems unmanageably sticky. Now wash your hands and dry them off. Coat your hands generously with oil. Grease the working surface (a flat metal tray or an Indian *thali*) with oil as well. Knead the dough for 6 to 10 minutes. Form the dough into a ball, spread oil over it, and set it aside in a bowl, covered with a cloth, for 30 minutes to 1 hour.

Oil your hands well again. Again oil the working surface. Knead the dough for 1 to 2 minutes in the tray.

Now you need to make 10 smooth balls. This is how the Moroccans do it: Smooth out one section of the ball of dough, making sure there are no creases in it. Using the thumb and index finger of one hand and forming a loose fist, grasp the smooth section of the dough and squeeze your fist shut, allowing a ball of dough to squirt out from between your thumb and index finger like a rounded mush-room top. To break off the ball, twist it as near your hand as possible and pull it off. Rub this ball with oil and set it on a large oiled plate. Make all the balls this way. Rub each ball well with oil and lay it on a large tray well separated from the one next to it. Cover loosely with wax paper and let rest for 10 to 15 minutes.

Set a large cast-iron frying pan on medium-high heat. While it gets hot, oil your hands as well as the working surface (the same metal tray). Working with the flat part of your fingers and palms, press out a ball into a flat, round sphere about 5 inches in diameter. You may need to actually stretch it. Sprinkle ⅛ teaspoon flour over the surface. Pick up the dough on one side and fold it over so that ⅓ of the round is left uncovered. Fold this ⅓ over so you have a longish rectangle. Sprinkle another ⅛ teaspoon flour over this rectangle. Now pick up one of the shorter ends and fold it over again so that ⅓ is left uncovered. Fold that ⅓ over to make a small square. Again, using oiled hands, spread the square out, using the flat part of your fingers and palms, so it is roughly a 5-inch square.

(recipe continues)

443

Turn the heat to medium. Carefully lift the bread from the working surface and lay it in the center of the frying pan. Cook for 1½ to 2 minutes, or until the top side has turned almost white and the bottom has light brown spots on it. Dribble about ½ teaspoon oil on the top of the bread, spreading it lightly with the back of the teaspoon. Now turn the bread over. Cook for 1 minute. The bread is done when it is light brown in color, lightly crispy on the outside, and soft but cooked through on the inside. This is the basic savory version of the bread. Put the bread in a plate and cover, either with a piece of foil or another upturned plate. Make all the breads this way, stacking them on top of each other and making sure to wipe the skillet clean with a dry paper towel after each bread is cooked. Ideally, you should serve each bread as soon as it is made.

For the honey-sesame topping, melt the honey in a small pot. Put 1 bread on a plate. Dribble 2 to 3 teaspoons of honey over it, spreading it out with the back of a teaspoon. Sprinkle about 1 teaspoon of roasted sesame seeds over the top and serve immediately.

MAKES 10

Indian Griddle Flatbreads INDIA
Chapatis

Chapatis come in all sizes and in our home, we prefer them quite small. You may serve these with all manner of beans and vegetables. You may also roll foods inside them as you would with a tortilla.

> *The best flour to use here is chapati flour.*
> *Chapatis are generally made without salt. If you wish to add some, put about ½ teaspoon into the dry flour.*

2 cups chapati flour (page 418)

Put the flour in a bowl. Slowly add about ¾ cup plus 2 tablespoons water, just enough to gather the dough together and make a ball. Knead the dough well for 10 minutes. Make a smooth ball and put it in a bowl. Cover with a damp cloth and set aside for 30 minutes. It will turn quite soft. Divide into 12 balls. Keep covered while you work with the twelfth.

Set a cast-iron frying pan or griddle on medium-high heat. Allow it to heat up. Make a small wad with a cloth or paper towel.

Take a ball of dough and dust it well with flour. Now roll it out into a 5½-inch round on a floured surface. Lift it up and slap it back and forth between your palms to shake off the extra flour. Slap the chapati onto the hot griddle. Let it cook for 45 seconds. Turn it over and cook the second side for another 35 to 45 seconds. Turn it over again and cook another 5 to 6 seconds, pushing down on it with the wad and rotating it a little with each push. Do this fast. This helps it to puff up. Put the cooked chapati on a plate and cover it with a towel or another upturned plate. Make all the chapatis this way, making sure to wipe off the cast-iron pan with a paper towel after each one is made. If it takes you a while to roll out the next chapati, turn the heat under the cast-iron pan down to low while you roll it and then turn it up again.

These chapatis are best as soon as they are made, but they can be made ahead and kept in a plastic bag in the refrigerator or freezer. To reheat them, wrap a whole bundle of them in foil and put them in a medium oven for 15 minutes. You can also sprinkle a little water on an individual chapati and then either heat it in a microwave oven for 30 to 45 seconds or slap it onto a hot, lightly greased griddle for a few seconds on each side.

MAKES 12

Wheat Tortillas MEXICO

Tortillas de Harina

As I write this, the latest craze for quick food in America is "wraps," any food that can be wrapped in a flatbread. Because of America's historic connection to Mexico, the flatbread of choice is the larger wheat tortilla, which, for an Indian like me, is just a chapati made with white flour instead of whole wheat flour. It happens to be very easy to make.

When we were little, my mother used to prepare buttas *for us on our return from school or when we needed a snack. Leftover warmed chapatis (page 444) were rolled around just about any leftover cooked food, which, of course, had also been heated. We added pickles and chutneys and had, what for the western world would be the equivalent of a sandwich with ketchup and mustard. "Wraps" are not new, just an old way to do newish things.*

Use these tortillas to wrap around any food of your choice. Add salsas, pickles, chutneys, relishes, and shredded lettuce for more excitement. With these tortillas you can also make Quesadilla with Mushrooms (page 353) and Quesadilla with Cheese (page 352).

(recipe continues)

2 cups all-purpose flour, plus extra for dusting   2 tablespoons vegetable oil (I use olive oil)

1/2 teaspoon salt

Sift the flour and salt into a bowl. Add the oil and rub it into the flour as evenly as possible. Begin to add very warm water slowly, gathering the dough into a ball. You will need about 1/2 cup or a bit more. Knead the ball for about 10 minutes. Now divide it into 8 even portions and make 8 balls from them. Flatten the balls into patties. Put the patties on a large platter or baking tray and cover with a dampened towel or plastic wrap. Set aside for 30 minutes or more.

Set a cast-iron frying pan or griddle on medium-high heat. Allow it to heat up.

Take a ball of dough and dust it lightly in flour. Now roll it out into a 7-inch round on a floured surface. Lift up the tortilla and slap it back and forth between your palms to shake off the extra flour. Slap the tortilla onto the hot griddle. Let it cook for 45 seconds. It will puff up. Turn it over and cook the second side for another 35 to 45 seconds. Put the cooked tortilla on a plate and cover it with a towel or another upturned plate. Make all the tortillas this way, making sure to wipe off the cast-iron pan with a paper towel after each tortilla is made. If it takes you a while to roll out the next tortilla, turn the heat under the cast-iron pan down to low while you roll it and then turn it up again.

These tortillas are best as soon as they are made. To reheat them, wrap a whole bundle of them in foil and heat them in a medium oven for 15 minutes. You can also sprinkle a little water on an individual tortilla and then heat it in a microwave oven for 30 to 45 seconds.

MAKES 8

Cheryl Rathkopf's

Sri Lankan Flatbreads with Coconut

SRI LANKA

Roti

In Sri Lanka, these breads are eaten with local curries. They may also be sprinkled with cheese (grated Cheddar or Parmesan) and grilled briefly. I love to serve them at breakfast with toppings of jam or maple syrup.

It is best to use fresh coconut here. Not only does the freshly grated coconut give the bread a delicate, sweet flavor, but the coconut water—what gushes out when you break the coconut—is the preferred "water" to knead the bread with. So save it when you break the coconut. Strain it well before using. If you wish to use desiccated unsweetened coconut, take 1½ cups (3 ounces) of the finely grated kind and soak it in ¾ cup of water for an hour.

You may also add 2 to 3 very finely chopped fresh green chiles and 2 tablespoons very finely chopped onion to the flour when you are kneading it.

The dough should be made shortly before you make the breads.

1¾ cups unbleached all-purpose white flour

1 teaspoon salt

2½ cups (6 ounces) freshly grated coconut (save the coconut water—see recipe introduction)

2 tablespoons (¼ stick) softened unsalted butter

4 teaspoons peanut or canola oil

Put the flour into a large bowl. Add the salt and coconut and mix well. Add just enough coconut water (or water) to make a medium-soft dough. (The amount of water will vary greatly according to the moisture in the coconut.) Once you have a rough ball, work the softened butter into it and knead briefly. Set aside for 20 minutes.

Divide the dough into 8 equal parts and make 8 balls. At the same time, put a medium cast-iron frying pan over medium-high heat. Let it get very hot.

Tear out a 10-inch sheet of wax paper. Put one ball of dough down on it in the center and flatten it a bit. Now, using your fingers, spread out the patty until it is about 5 inches in diameter.

Put ½ teaspoon of oil into the well-heated frying pan. Lift up the flatbread carefully and slap it down into the center of the frying pan. Let it cook for 40 to 60 seconds on the first side, or until it has browned in spots. Turn the flatbread over with a spatula and cook the second side for 1 minute, or until it too has browned in spots. Remove and put on a plate. Upturn another plate over it to keep it warm. Make all the flatbreads this way.

If you wish to make the flatbreads ahead of time, stack them together and wrap them in foil. To reheat, put the wrapped stack in a medium oven for 15 minutes. You may also heat 1 bread at a time in the microwave oven for about 1 minute.

MAKES 8

From the Advani household

Trinidadian "Roti" or Flatbread

Sada Roti

TRINIDAD

The Indians who were brought to Trinidad as indentured laborers carried a culinary world with them on the ships that transported them to an unknown island. But this world was mostly in their heads. The realities of a very harsh life led to constant adaptations and changes. Their daily bread, the whole wheat "roti," could not be made without the very finely ground ata *they were used to, so they picked up white flour instead. All around them breads were made with fermenting agents, so they too slowly began to use baking powder, insisting still on rolling out their flatbreads the old-fashioned way and cooking them on a cast-iron* tava *or griddle.*

This is the basic bread, thick and pitalike, that is generally eaten by the Indians in Trinidad at breakfast, especially in the small towns and villages, with dishes like Eggplant and Tomato Choka *(page 186). You may also eat it with beans and chickpeas at lunch or dinner or quite simply with cheeses and salads or with butter and jam.*

3½ cups unbleached all-purpose white flour, plus a little extra for rolling out

2½ teaspoons baking powder

½ teaspoon salt

Sift the flour, baking powder, and salt into a bowl. Add about 1¼ cups or a few tablespoons more water—enough to form a soft but not sticky dough. Knead well for 10 minutes. Form a ball of dough and then break it into 8 even parts. Form 8 smooth balls with these parts. Put them in a bowl and cover them with a damp cloth. Set them aside for 30 to 60 minutes (or even longer, refrigerating in a plastic bag if needed and then allowing the dough to come to room temperature).

Set an Indian cast-iron *tava*, a cast-iron frying pan, or a cast-iron griddle over medium-high heat. Allow it to heat up. Make a small wad with a piece of paper towel or a cloth.

Now dip the dough ball lightly in flour and then roll it out until you have a 7- to 8-inch round. Slap it onto the heated *tava*, pan, or griddle. Cook for 45 to 55 seconds, or until one side has reddish-brown spots. Turn it over and cook another 45 seconds, or until the second side too has reddish spots. Turn again and cook for 30 seconds, pressing down on the bread with the wad in quick strokes. Turn and cook another 30 seconds, again pressing down with the wad. Now turn and cook 20 seconds. Turn again and cook 20 seconds. Turn and cook 10 seconds. Turn again and cook another 10 seconds. Remove the bread and keep it between 2 plates, the top one upturned over the bottom one. Make all the breads this way, turning the heat down to low when you have to stop to roll out the next bread. Turn the heat up just before slapping the next bread onto the pan.

The breads will stay hot stacked this way for a good 20 to 30 minutes. If you wish to prepare the breads well in advance, let the breads cool off between the plates and then store them in a plastic bag in the refrigerator. The breads may be reheated one at a time for about a minute in a microwave oven, or they may be stacked, wrapped in foil, and heated in a medium oven for 20 minutes.

These breads can also be frozen and then reheated as suggested above.

MAKES 8

From the Advani household

Trinidadian Roti Stuffed with Split Peas

TRINIDAD

Dal Poori

This superb flatbread is one of the glories of Trinidad. It is a Trinidadian version of the Indian paratha, *only the locals call it a poori and make it with white flour (Indian pooris and* parathas *are made with whole wheat flour). Like the famous rotis of this island, it does contain leavening in the form of baking powder. It remains a flatbread, but a slightly puffy one.*

You may serve these breads at breakfast or as a snack with a chutney such as the fresh Delhi-Style Cilantro and Mint Chutney (page 660), or a sweet preserved chutney, such as Mango Chutney (pages 695 to 698), or with yogurt, or with all of the above. You may also serve them as part of a meal.

For the stuffing

1 cup (6½ ounces) yellow split peas

¼ teaspoon ground turmeric

3 tablespoons peanut or canola oil

1 small onion (3 ounces), peeled and finely chopped

3 garlic cloves, peeled and finely chopped

1 to 2 fresh hot green chiles, finely chopped

1 tablespoon ground cumin

¾ teaspoon salt

Freshly ground black pepper

For the dough

3½ cups unbleached all-purpose white flour, plus a little extra for rolling out

3¾ teaspoons baking powder

½ teaspoon salt

4 tablespoons (½ stick) unsalted butter, cut into small pieces

For making the breads

About ¾ cup peanut or canola oil (some people prefer clarified butter or *ghee*, page 723)

(recipe continues)

449

Soak the split peas overnight in 4 cups of water. Drain them the next day. Put them in a medium pan along with 3 cups of water and the turmeric. Bring to a boil. Cover partially, turn the heat down to low, and cook for 15 minutes, or until the peas are just barely tender without turning at all mushy. Drain. (The liquid may be served for soups.) Now mash the peas coarsely either with a wooden potato masher, in a mortar, or put through a mincing gadget.

Heat the 3 tablespoons of oil in a large nonstick frying pan over medium-high heat. When hot, put in the onion, garlic, and chiles. Stir and fry for 2 minutes, or until the onions are golden. Now put in the mashed split peas and turn the heat to medium. Also put in the cumin, salt, and lots of black pepper. Stir and cook for 2 minutes. Turn off the heat and let the mixture cool off.

Sift the flour, baking powder, and salt into a bowl. Add the butter and rub it in so the mixture resembles coarse bread crumbs. Now add about ¾ cup of warm water, or enough to form a soft but not sticky dough. Knead well for 10 minutes. Form a ball of dough and then break it into 8 even parts. Form 8 smooth balls with these parts. Put them in a bowl and cover them with a damp cloth. Set them aside for 30 minutes to 1 hour (or even longer, refrigerating in a plastic bag if needed and then allowing the dough to come to room temperature).

Divide the stuffing into 8 parts. Make 8 balls by pressing firmly into shape.

Set an Indian cast-iron *tava*, a cast-iron frying pan, or a cast-iron griddle over medium-high heat.

At the same time, pick up a ball and flatten it with your hands into a 4-inch round. Put the ball of stuffing in the center and bring the edges of the dough together to enclose it. Now dip the dough ball lightly in flour and then roll it out until you have a 7- to 8-inch round.

Put 1 teaspoon of oil in the center of the heated cast-iron pan and then slap the flatbread on top of it. Cook for 45 to 55 seconds, or until one side has reddish brown spots. Turn it over, put another teaspoon of oil around the circumference of the bread, and cook it another 45 seconds, or until the second side also has reddish spots. Turn again and cook for 30 seconds. Turn and cook another 30 seconds. Now turn and cook 20 seconds. Turn again and cook 20 seconds. Turn and cook 10 seconds. Turn again and cook another 10 seconds. Remove the bread and keep it between 2 plates, the top one upturned over the bottom one. Make all the breads this way, turning the heat down to low when you have to stop to roll out the next bread. Turn the heat up just before slapping the next bread onto the pan.

The breads will stay hot stacked this way for a good 20 to 30 minutes. If you wish to prepare the breads well in advance, let the breads cool off between the plates and then store them in a plastic bag in the refrigerator. The breads may be reheated one at a time for about a minute in a microwave oven, or they may be stacked, wrapped in foil, and heated in a medium oven for 20 minutes.

These breads can also be frozen and then reheated as suggested above.

MAKES 8

SINDHI FLATBREADS AND BAKES (LOLI)

These whole wheat flatbreads, made in just the same way as they were probably a thousand years ago, are from Sindh, once in western India and now in Pakistan. Their texture seems to keep its feet in two worlds—the slightly crumbly world of cookies and the more sober world of traditional flatbreads. I love their simplicity and honesty.

They are sometimes flavored with black pepper, sometimes sweetened slightly with sugar syrup, and in the last few hundred years, also seasoned with ingredients from the New World such as chiles and tomatoes.

The ideal flour to use here is chapati flour (page 419), sold only by Indian grocers. If you cannot find it, use a well-sifted, fine whole wheat flour or a mixture of whole wheat and white flour.

I like to roll my lolis out with a rolling pin, though some people can pat them out with their hands. You may also use a tortilla/chapati press if you like, lining the two sides with thick plastic as suggested in the recipe for tortillas (page 348).

Lolis may be partially cooked (for about 3 minutes) and then wrapped and frozen. Do not use extra oil in the cooking. Reheat them by taking them from the freezer and then putting them directly on a hot, lightly oiled cast-iron griddle, frying pan, or Indian tava. Cook for 2 minutes, turning every 30 seconds or so.

While the dough in the following three recipes varies, the method of cooking the lolis is the same.

Durupadi Jagtiani's
Sindhi Flatbreads with Black Pepper   INDIA
Kali Mirch Ki Loli

The pepper here should not be too fine or too coarse, but somewhere in the middle.
    Serve these with any meal. They are also excellent with scrambled eggs and, when eaten plain, with a little honey, jam, chutney, or hot pickle on them. I love them this way with a cup of steaming tea!

1½ cups chapati flour (page 419)

1 teaspoon salt

½ teaspoon coarsely ground black pepper

4 tablespoons vegetable oil, plus a little extra

Combine the flour, salt, and pepper in a large, wide bowl. Slowly add the 4 tablespoons of oil, rubbing it into the flour. Now, slowly add about ½ cup of water or enough to form a firm dough. Knead well until the dough is smooth and forms a ball. Cover the dough ball with plastic wrap and set aside for 30 minutes.

Set a cast-iron griddle, cast-iron frying pan, or Indian *tava* over medium-high heat.

Divide the dough into 4 parts. Oil your hands lightly and make 4 balls. Flatten the balls to make 4 patties. Keep 3 balls covered while you work with the fourth.

On a lightly oiled surface, roll out the patty into a 5¼-inch round. (The edges might be slightly rough but that is as it should be.) Prick a few holes on the bread with a fork. Slap the bread onto the hot griddle. Cook for about 1 minute on the first side. Turn the bread over and cook the second side for a minute. Turn it over again. Reduce the heat to medium. Now dribble about ½ teaspoon oil on the griddle very near the circumference of the bread. Cook 30 seconds, pressing down on the bread with a spatula. Turn the bread again, dribbling another ½ teaspoon of oil near its circumference. Cook another 30 seconds, pressing down on the bread again. Keep turning every 30 seconds or so until the bread has a few brown spots and is cooked through, 4 to 5 minutes in all. Remove and keep covered. Turn the heat up to medium-high again and make the second bread. Make all the breads this way.

MAKES 4

Durupadi Jagtiani's
Sweet Sindhi Flatbreads
Masala Loli

INDIA/PAKISTAN

Here the lolis *are flavored with finely chopped onion, garlic, ginger, fresh cilantro, chiles, and tomatoes. Since these seasonings all give off liquid, it is best to limit the amount of water in the dough, even though it might initially seem to be too dry. If the dough is allowed to sit for a few hours, the moisture spreads.*

Serve these lolis *with a meal or with tea.*

1½ cups chapati flour (page 419)

1 teaspoon salt

1 to 2 fresh hot green chiles, finely chopped

3 tablespoons finely chopped tomato

2 tablespoons finely chopped red onion

2 tablespoons finely chopped fresh cilantro

1 teaspoon garlic, peeled and crushed to a
 pulp

1 teaspoon peeled fresh ginger, grated to a
 pulp

4 tablespoons hot peanut or canola oil, plus a
 little extra

Combine the flour, salt, green chiles, tomato, onion, cilantro, garlic, and ginger. Slowly add the 4 tablespoons of hot oil, rubbing it into the flour. Rub the flour and seasonings well for 10 minutes, extracting as much liquid from the seasonings as possible. See if you can form a ball of dough. If you cannot, slowly add 2 to 4 tablespoons water, or enough to form a very firm dough. Knead well and form a ball. Cover the dough ball with plastic wrap and set aside for 2 to 4 hours.

Knead the dough again. If it has gotten too wet, add a little flour. If it is too dry, add a few drops of water.

Set a cast-iron griddle, cast-iron frying pan, or Indian *tava* over medium-high heat.

Divide the dough into 4 parts. Oil your hands lightly and make 4 balls. Flatten the balls to make 4 patties. Keep 3 balls covered while you work with the fourth.

Now follow the directions for making the *lolis* in the master recipe for Sindhi Flatbreads with Black Pepper (page 452).

MAKES 4

Durupadi Jagtiani's

Seasoned Sindhi Flatbreads   INDIA/PAKISTAN

Meethi Loli

It is traditional to eat these with slightly sweet, cardamom-flavored flatbreads with a slightly sour spinach dish, Spinach with Sorrel (page 226), on cold winter days. You may, however, eat them anytime, with tea, coffee, or a meal.

1½ cups chapati flour (page 419)

4 tablespoons peanut or canola oil, plus a
    little extra

3 tablespoons sugar

½ teaspoon crushed or powdered cardamom
    seeds

Put the flour in a large, wide bowl. Slowly add the 4 tablespoons oil, rubbing it into the flour.

Combine the sugar, 5 tablespoons of water, and the cardamom in a small pan. Bring to a simmer over medium-low heat. Stir until the sugar has melted. Take off the heat and allow to get lukewarm. Now, slowly add enough of the syrup to the flour to form a firm dough. Knead well until the dough is smooth and then form a ball. Cover the dough ball with plastic wrap and set aside for 30 minutes.

Set a cast-iron griddle, or cast-iron frying pan, or Indian *tava* over medium-high heat.

Divide the dough into 4 parts. Oil your hands lightly and make 4 balls. Flatten the balls to make 4 patties. Keep 3 balls covered while you work with the fourth.

Now follow the directions for making the *lolis* in the master recipe for Sindhi Flatbreads with Black Pepper (page 452).

MAKES 4

Sweet Puffed Breads   INDIA

Meethi Poori

These superb fried breads are light, crisp, and just a little sweet. Eat them by themselves with tea (Indians nibble on them with sweet halvahs and sweet milk confections) or serve them with a meal. Their slight sweetness is the perfect complement to pumpkin dishes (serve it on the side with a pumpkin soup), yogurt dishes, and all manner of bean stews.

    I do not use ghe, Indian clarified butter, too much in my cooking but I like to put a table-spoon of it in the dough here. It is best to buy it from an Indian or Middle Eastern grocer. You could also substitute slightly softened butter.

It takes less than a minute to make each poori. *Because they are best hot, they should be made just as you sit down to eat.*

2 cups chapati flour (page 419)

1 tablespoon *ghee* (page 723)

2 tablespoons sugar

About 1 cup milk

Peanut oil for deep-frying, plus a little more
for rolling

Put the flour in a bowl. Add the *ghee* and rub it into the flour as evenly as possible. Add the sugar and mix it in. Slowly add the milk, just as much as you need to gather all the flour together, and make a ball that holds together. Knead the dough well for 10 minutes, form a smooth ball, and put it in a bowl. Cover with a damp cloth and set aside for 30 minutes or longer.

Set an Indian *karhai,* wok, or small, deep frying pan over medium-low heat and give it 7 to 8 minutes to heat up. Pour in 2 to 3 inches of oil.

Divide the dough into 16 smooth balls. Flatten each ball into a patty. Keep 15 patties covered as you work with the sixteenth. Rub the patty with a little oil and then roll it out into a 5-inch round. Lay the poori over the oil, making sure that it does not double over. It should immediately surround itself in an orgy of bubbles. Using very quick strokes with the back of a slotted spoon, keep pushing the poori slightly under the oil. It will resist by puffing up within seconds. Turn it over and cook the second side for another 10 to 15 seconds, or until it too is golden. Remove with a slotted spoon and lay on a plate lined with paper towels. Make all the pooris this way, keeping them in a single layer. Serve them as soon as they are made, in small batches if necessary.

MAKES 16

BAKES

Bakes are simple Trinidadian Creole breads. In the old days, most people had barrels of white flour, salt, baking powder, butter, and lard in their kitchens. These would be combined to fashion 1-inch-high round loaves, which were then put in a pan, covered, and "baked" by putting a little fire under them and a few coals on the top. Sometimes the dough was not baked but fried, in which case it was called a fry bake.

The next step would be to "hot up the chocolate," which was made with bay leaf–flavored milk, take out the butter and cheese, and sit down to a simple breakfast.

Bakes were also eaten with *buljol*, a salad of salt cod, tomatoes, peppers, cucumbers, and onions (see my vegetarian Salad of White Beans and Peppers, page 614).

Pepper Bake

This bake is a loaf seasoned with onions and tiny bits of the fiery Scotch bonnet chile (of the habanero family) that is commonly used on this island. If you cannot find it, use any hot green chile, such as jalapeño. You may serve this with butter and cheese or offer slices with a meal.

2 cups unbleached all-purpose white flour

2 teaspoons baking powder

1 teaspoon salt

8 tablespoons (1 stick) unsalted butter

1 smallish onion (3 ounces), finely chopped

½ Scotch bonnet or 1 fresh hot green chile, finely chopped

Sift the flour, baking powder, and salt into a bowl. Cut off 1 tablespoon of the butter and set it aside. Slice the remaining butter thinly and add it to the flour. Rub it in so the mixture resembles coarse bread crumbs.

Put the remaining 1 tablespoon butter in a small frying pan and set it over medium heat. When it has melted, put in the onion. Stir and fry for 4 to 5 minutes, or until the pieces are translucent with a few brown spots. Turn off the heat and allow to cool off.

Now add the onion mixture and the chopped chile to the bowl of flour. Mix. Add about 6 tablespoons of warm water, or enough to form a soft but not sticky dough. Knead for about 5 minutes. Form a smooth ball of dough and put it in a bowl. Cover with a lightly dampened cloth and set aside for 30 minutes. Knead again for 5 minutes. Form a smooth ball and then flatten it so you have a cake about 1 inch high. Put the cake in a small, shallow cake pan or on a baking sheet, cover with a lightly dampened cloth, and leave in a warm place for 30 minutes.

Meanwhile, preheat the oven to 375°F.

Put the bread in the oven and bake for 45 minutes. Remove from the oven and cool on a rack.

MAKES 1 LOAF

Danielle Delon's
Fry Bake or Float

In the Caribbean, the names often explain the dish. A "fry bake" is a dough that could be baked but is fried instead. The other name for the dish, "float," suggests a bread that is so airy and light that it floats on top of the oil.

So what exactly is it? It's a Creole bread with a Mediterranean background (some say its origins lie in Marseilles) not unlike a beignet. It looks like a puffed ball. In its sweetened version —which goes together with coffee as a horse with a carriage—it may be had with butter and honey or—and this is how I serve it—with generous sprinklings of finely granulated sugar. While it is sometimes made with yeast, its simpler version is made with baking powder.

If it is left unsweetened, fry bake is traditionally eaten with salads or fritters made with dried cod, but for vegetarians, it may be served with my Salad of White Beans and Peppers (page 614), or with any bean and vegetable dishes. It may also be used to stuff Refried Beans (page 12) and a salsa.

It is best if eaten while still warm. The dough may be made 1 to 2 days in advance, divided into balls, and kept in a plastic bag in the refrigerator. The cold dough, which is even easier to roll out, is like money in the bank. You can withdraw just enough for your needs, rolling out and frying up quick fry bakes for breakfast or any other meal.

2 cups unbleached all-purpose white flour

2 teaspoons baking powder

½ teaspoon salt

2 tablespoons (¼ stick) unsalted butter,
    broken up into small pats

2 tablespoons vegetable shortening

Peanut or canola oil for deep-frying

Finely granulated sugar

Sift the flour, baking powder, and salt into a bowl. Add the butter and shortening. Rub them into the dry ingredients so the mixture resembles coarse bread crumbs. Now add about ¾ cup or a bit less water, enough to form a soft but not sticky dough. Knead well for 10 minutes. Form a smooth ball of dough and put it in a bowl. Cover with a lightly dampened cloth and set aside for 30 minutes to 1 hour or even longer, refrigerating the ball of dough in a plastic bag if needed.

Divide the dough into 12 smooth balls. Roll each ball out into a 5-inch round. Keep the rounds in a single layer on a work surface. (If they shrink slightly, you may need to roll them out quickly again.)

Pour the oil to a depth of 3 inches in a wok or 1½ inches in a deep frying pan and set over medium-high heat. Wait for the oil to get really hot; this takes about 5 minutes. As soon as the oil is ready, slide in a bread. It will sink to the bottom. Within seconds, it will rise up. Now start tapping it lightly with the back of a slotted spoon, pushing it slightly under the oil each time. Do this for about 10 seconds, or until the bread puffs up. Even if it does not puff up, turn it over. Cook the second side for 10 seconds, or until it is golden. Turn the bread again and cook 5 seconds. Turn the bread and cook 5 seconds. Turn the bread and cook 5 seconds. Turn the bread and cook 5 seconds. Remove with a slotted spoon and keep it in a

(recipe continues)

plate lined with paper towels. Make all the breads this way, rolling the rounds of dough quickly for a second time if they have shrunk a bit while waiting. Remember that each bread takes only about 40 seconds to cook. While the breads are still warm, lift them off the paper towel and put them on a fresh plate. Dust them on all sides generously with the sugar, rubbing some of it over the surface gently, and serve.

MAKES 12

Khadija Ali's
Doubles

TRINIDAD

What are doubles? Once, long ago, I was sitting in a friend's office in Port of Spain when he suggested sending out for some lunch. "How about doubles?" my friend Raju asked. I wondered what they were and he explained that they consisted of bread and chickpeas. That sounded good to me, but I was unprepared for what came.

I was handed a greaseproof paper package, tied up with a rubber band. I discarded the band, opened the package, and found what could be best described as a scrumptious vegetarian "hamburger." Sandwiched between two soft, spongy, fried flatbreads were some delicious chickpeas to which the restaurant had added hot sauce and chutney, their version of mustard and ketchup. I ate this with swigs of fresh coconut water, thoroughly enjoying every last bite.

Doubles, an obvious East-West creation, were evidently popularized by a milkman, San Fernando Ali, who used to sell them from his bicycle and, according to legend at least, eventually retired as a millionaire.

What follows is first a recipe for the chickpeas (I have added some tomatoes to them, which is not commonly done), then a recipe for the breads used in doubles, and finally, how the whole thing is put together.

These breads, which may also be eaten by themselves with any meal, are best when they are hot. They are very easy to reheat, especially if you have a microwave oven.

For the chickpeas

3 (19-ounce) cans chickpeas

3 tablespoons peanut or canola oil

2 medium onions, peeled and finely chopped

6 garlic cloves, peeled and crushed to a pulp

1 tablespoon ground cumin

1 tablespoon ground coriander

¼ teaspoon ground turmeric

1 tablespoon curry powder

1 teaspoon ground ginger

½ to 1 fresh hot green or red chile, finely chopped

1½ cups tomatoes with tomato puree (use 4 tomatoes, well chopped, and some of the puree to make up the correct amount)

1 teaspoon salt

For the breads

3½ cups unbleached all-purpose white flour,
plus a little extra for rolling out

1 tablespoon baking powder

½ teaspoon salt

¼ teaspoon ground turmeric

Peanut or canola oil for deep-frying

For making up the doubles

Any hot sauce (such as the Trinidadian
Pepper Sauce, page 717)

Any mango chutney (such as the Mango
Chutney, page 695)

Make the chickpeas. Drain the chickpeas, discarding the liquid. Rinse the chickpeas well and leave in a strainer.

Put the oil in a medium pan and set over medium-high heat. When hot, put in the onions. Stir and fry them for 4 to 5 minutes, or until they are lightly browned. Add the garlic and stir for 30 seconds. Turn the heat to medium. Add the cumin, coriander, turmeric, curry powder, and ginger. Stir for 30 seconds. Put in the chile as well as the chopped tomatoes and their puree. Stir for a minute. Now put in 2½ cups of water, the salt, and the chickpeas. Stir and bring to a boil. Cover, turn the heat down to low, and simmer gently for 10 minutes.

Make the breads. Sift the flour, baking powder, salt, and turmeric into a bowl. Add about 1¼ cups or a few tablespoons more water, enough to form a soft but not sticky dough. Knead well for 10 minutes. Form a smooth ball of dough and put it in a bowl. Cover the bowl with a damp cloth and set aside for 30 minutes to 1 hour (or even longer, refrigerating in a plastic bag if needed and then allowing the dough to come to room temperature).

Divide the dough into 16 even parts. Form 16 smooth balls with these parts. Keep 15 covered as you work with the last one. Dust the ball lightly in flour and then roll it out into a 5-inch round. In the same way, roll out as many balls as you want to eat and keep them in a single layer on the counter, covered by a cloth.

Pour the oil to a depth of 3 inches in a wok or 1½ inches in a deep frying pan and set over medium heat. Allow it to heat up. It will take 4 to 5 minutes.

The rolled-out breads may have shrunk slightly. Roll 3 to 4 out again quickly.

As soon as the oil is hot, slide in a bread. It will sink to the bottom. Within seconds, it will rise up. Now start tapping it lightly with the back of a slotted spoon, pushing it slightly under the oil each time. Do this for about 10 seconds, or until the bread puffs up. Even if it does not puff up, turn it over. Cook the second side for 6 to 7 seconds, or until it is golden. Remove with a slotted spoon and keep it on a plate lined with a paper towel. Put another paper towel on top of the bread and

(recipe continues)

then cover the whole with an upturned plate. Make all the breads this way, rolling the breads for a second time if they have shrunk a bit. Remember that each bread takes only about 30 seconds to cook. Stack them all on the plate with a layer of paper towels in between to absorb the oil. Either eat the breads while they are still hot, or, if you wish to eat them later, leave the stack covered until cool and then reheat each bread individually in a microwave oven for 40 seconds or so, where it may even puff up again briefly. You may also wrap all the breads in a piece of foil and heat them in a medium oven for 20 minutes.

To make a double, lay down a heated bread. Lift up some chickpeas with a slotted spoon, leaving any sauce behind, and place on top of the bread. Sprinkle liberally with hot sauce and, if you like, dot with a little mango chutney. Cover with a second bread and eat the whole like a sandwich.

MAKES 16 BREADS AND 8 DOUBLES

WHEAT AND SEMOLINA FLOUR BREADS

Melle Derko Samira's

Everyday Moroccan Bread   MOROCCO

Pan de Morocco

This is the bread that the Moroccans eat with most of their everyday meals. It is commonly sold as pan de Morocco. *Every Arab woman must know how to bake bread. Little girls start learning at the age of six or seven. Twice a day, Moroccan women and children can be seen in the narrow streets of the inner cities carrying the family loaves, kneaded and formed at home, on flat boards or trays, often held over their heads. They take them to the local bakery with their own family markings carefully imprinted on each loaf so as not to allow it to be mixed with anyone else's. It is baked in a common bakery and then picked up by the family, all fresh and hot, ready to be cut into wedges and eaten with a puree of split peas or with stews and salads of various sorts.*

This bread may also be made with a mixture of white and semolina flour. If you wish to do this, combine 1³⁄₄ cups unbleached all-purpose flour with 1¹⁄₂ cups fine semolina flour and then proceed with the recipe.

2 teaspoons active dry yeast

1 teaspoon sugar

3¹⁄₂ cups unbleached all-purpose white flour

1¹⁄₂ teaspoons salt

2 teaspoons sesame seeds

1 teaspoon anise seeds

Peanut or canola oil

Cornmeal for dusting

Combine the yeast, sugar, and ¼ cup warm water (105°F. to 115°F.) in a small bowl. Stir to dissolve the yeast completely. Set aside for 5 minutes, or until the yeast begins to bubble.

Meanwhile, put the flour in a large bowl and mound it into the shape of a hill. Make a crater on the hilltop and put the salt, sesame seeds, anise seeds, and yeast mixture into it. Now slowly pour warm water (105°F. to 115°F.) into the crater— about 1 cup or slightly less will be needed to make the dough. As you add water, slowly gather the flour together into a ball. Keep adding the water, a little at a time, and gathering the dough, until it begins to form a soft, smooth ball. Once you can form a ball, start to knead. Knead the dough well for about 10 minutes, or until it is smooth and elastic. Form a ball.

Lightly oil a large baking tray and sprinkle some cornmeal over it. Set aside.

Grease a large work surface, such as a countertop. Put the dough ball on the greased surface and flatten it out to form a round disc, about ½ inch high.

Using both palms and outstretched fingers, carefully lift the disc and place it on the baking tray. With a sharp knife, score the top of the loaf very lightly in a diamond pattern with lines that are about ½ inch apart. Cover with a clean dishcloth (in Morocco, they use a sheepskin) and leave in a warm place to rise for about 1 hour, or until the loaf has doubled in height.

Preheat the oven to 400°F. Adjust the oven rack to the lowest possible shelf.

When the loaf has doubled in height, prick it twice on the sides with a fork. Now put the baking tray on the rack and bake for 25 to 30 minutes, or until the loaf is golden brown on top and sounds hollow when you tap on it. Remove to a cooling rack. Cut into wedges and serve warm or at room temperature.

MAKES 1 LOAF

Semolina Bread with Coconut and Pistachios

INDIAN-AMERICAN

My mother used to make deep-fried turnovers for the autumn festival of lights, Divali, which many consider to be India's New Year's Day as well. These turnovers were filled with a sweet filling of coconut, raisins, pistachios, and a tiny nut called charoli *or* chironji, *which is rather like hazelnuts in taste but not in size. (I am happy to note that these nuts have suddenly begun to find favor with Western chefs. At the moment, they are only sold by Indian grocers.) The spice flavoring was—no surprise here—cardamom, which is the vanilla of India. (Whenever I say this, I cannot help but recall former* Vogue *editor Diana Vreeland's comment that "shocking pink is the navy blue of India!")*

I do not make my mother's turnovers anymore, but I have adapted her recipe so I can use her basic stuffing with my favorite semolina bread.

I use fresh coconut in this recipe but must point out that my mother only used dried coconut, copra, which she grated herself. We do not belong to a tropical, coconut-growing region of India. We were inland northerners. Fresh coconuts were as foreign to us as to New Yorkers.

2 cups warm milk

2 cups golden raisins

2 (¼-ounce) packages active dry yeast

¼ cup honey

8 tablespoons (1 stick) unsalted butter or vegetable shortening, plus extra for greasing

1¾ cups milk, plus a little extra for brushing

1 tablespoon salt

4 teaspoons ground cardamom

About 3½ cups unbleached all-purpose white bread flour

2 eggs, at room temperature

3 cups fine semolina flour

4 tablespoons sugar

2 cups (5½ ounces) freshly grated coconut (see page 722 for details and substitutions), patted dry on paper towels

8 tablespoons coarsely chopped pistachios (or a half-and-half mixture of coarsely chopped pistachios and *chironji* nuts)

Put the 2 cups of warm milk in a bowl. Add the golden raisins and leave to soak for the several hours it takes for the dough to rise.

Combine the yeast and ½ cup of warm water (105°F. to 115°F.) in a cup or small bowl. Mix and set aside to proof (bubble up).

Combine the honey, butter, 1¾ cups of milk, the salt, and 1 teaspoon of ground cardamom in a small pan (or bowl if you are using a microwave oven). Stir and heat until warm. Pour into a large bowl. Slowly add 2 cups of the white bread flour, beating it well with an electric whisk (or 100 times with a wooden spoon) to encourage the gluten in the flour to get moving. Add the eggs and the yeast, beating as you go. Slowly add another cup of white bread flour and then the semolina, little by little. You will now have to shift to a wooden spoon if you had previously been using a whisk. Soon, instead of a batter, you will begin to have a ball of dough. When it becomes too hard to move around with a spoon, empty the dough out onto a floured work surface and begin to knead the dough, incorporating the remaining ½ cup of white bread flour or more, if you require it. The dough should be smooth, but try to keep it as soft as you can handle. Knead well for 10 minutes and form a ball.

Put the ball of dough into a well-greased bowl, turning it around until it is well coated. Cover with a towel or plastic wrap and set aside in a warm place for 1½ hours, or until doubled in bulk. Punch the dough down so it deflates, knead for 2 to 3 minutes, cover again, and leave for another 30 minutes.

Empty the dough onto a floured work surface and knead for a minute. Divide it into 2 balls and let the balls sit, covered loosely with a towel or plastic wrap, for 10 minutes. On a lightly floured surface, roll out the first ball of dough until it is a rectangle of about 15 × 11 inches. Do the same with the second ball. Put the shorter sides nearest you. Brush the tops lightly with milk. Sprinkle ¾ teaspoon ground cardamom over the top of each rectangle. Cover this with 1 tablespoon of sugar for each rectangle. Remove the golden raisins from the milk and squeeze out all the liquid from them. Now pat them dry on paper towels and then scatter them over the sugar. Top the golden raisins with half of the coconut, half of the pistachios, another tablespoon of sugar, and another ¾ teaspoon of ground cardamom for each rectangle. Roll up each rectangle away from you, like a jelly roll. Pinch the ends shut and then tuck them under on the same side as the seam.

Put these loaves into 2 well-greased 9 × 5 × 3-inch loaf pans, seam side down. Cover with a towel or plastic wrap and leave in a warm place for 1 hour.

Preheat the oven to 375°F.

The dough will now have filled the pans and risen above them. Put the loaf pans in the oven and bake for 35 to 40 minutes, or until golden brown and hollow sounding when tapped. Remove the loaves from the pans immediately (go around them with a knife if they resist) and cool on a rack.

Once thoroughly cooled, the breads may be wrapped and either kept in a bread box or frozen for future meals.

MAKES 2 LOAVES

Whole Wheat Bread with Sprouted Wheat, Sunflower Seeds, and Rolled Oats

Some years ago, when I was in London filming a television series over several months, my producers had rented a small apartment for me with a kitchen. Most of my groceries came from a health food shop, the only place within walking distance that seemed to carry any edibles. They carried this bread—and whenever they ran out of it, I was devastated. When I came back to New York, I decided to make it myself. I just love the chewy, crunchy texture of the sprouted wheat and its sweet earthy taste. You will find a method for sprouting whole wheat on page 417. Health food shops carry both the roasted and unroasted sunflower seeds; you need the unroasted kind.

2 (¼-ounce) packages active dry yeast

¼ cup honey

4 tablespoons (½ stick) unsalted butter or vegetable shortening, plus extra for greasing

1¾ cups milk

1 tablespoon salt

About 3 cups or less unbleached all-purpose white bread flour

2 eggs, at room temperature

1 cup sprouted whole wheat

½ cup sunflower seeds

½ cup rolled oats

About 4 cups whole wheat flour

Combine the yeast and ½ cup of warm water (105°F. to 115°F.) in a cup or small bowl. Mix and set aside to proof (bubble up).

Combine the honey, butter, milk, and salt in a small pan (or bowl if you are using a microwave oven) and heat until warm. Pour into a large bowl. Add 2 cups of the white bread flour, beating it in with an electric whisk (or 100 times with a wooden spoon) to encourage the gluten's elasticity. Add the eggs and the yeast, beating as you go. Shift to a wooden spoon if you were not using it before and fold in the sprouted wheat, sunflower seeds, and rolled oats. Slowly add the whole wheat flour and then some of the remaining white bread flour, little by little. Soon, instead of a batter, you will begin to have a ball of dough. When it becomes too hard to move around with a spoon, empty the dough out onto a floured work surface and begin to knead the dough, incorporating more white flour if you require it. The dough should be smooth, but try to keep it as soft as you can manage. Knead well for 10 minutes and form a ball.

Put the ball of dough into a well-greased bowl, turning it around until it is well coated. Cover with a towel or plastic wrap and set aside in a warm place for 1½ hours, or until doubled in bulk. Punch the dough down so it deflates, knead for 2 to 3 minutes, cover again, and leave for another 30 minutes.

Empty the dough onto a floured work surface and knead for a minute. Divide it into 2 balls and let the balls sit, covered loosely with a towel or plastic wrap, for 10 minutes. Now form the balls into loaf shapes and put them into 2 well-greased 9×5×3-inch loaf pans. Cover with a towel or plastic wrap and leave in a warm place for 1 hour.

Preheat the oven to 375°F.

The dough will now have filled the pans and risen above them. Remove the covering and put the loaf pans in the oven to bake for 35 to 40 minutes, or until golden brown and hollow sounding when tapped. Remove the loaves from the pans immediately (go around them with a knife if they resist) and cool on a rack.

Once thoroughly cooled, the breads may be wrapped and either kept in a bread box or frozen for future meals.

MAKES 2 LOAVES

Whole Wheat Bread with Walnuts and Mint

After my last trip to Turkey, I found myself cooking a lot with two ingredients much used in this general region, walnuts and dried mint, even putting them into my daily breads.

I love to eat slices of this bread first lathered with a thick layer of yogurt cheese (pages 556 to 560) and then sprinkled with a little coarse salt and some of the Middle Eastern spice mixture Zahtar (page 705), which contains roasted sesame seeds, thyme, and sumac. You can sprinkle these spices individually over the top, if you like. As a final blessing, I dribble my finest olive oil over the spices! It is quite a treat.

1 (¼-ounce) package active dry yeast

3 tablespoons honey

2 tablespoons (¼ stick) unsalted butter or vegetable shortening, plus extra for greasing

1 cup milk

1½ teaspoons salt

1 cup unbleached all-purpose white bread flour, plus more for dusting

1 egg, at room temperature

1 cup (3 ounces) coarsely chopped walnuts

1 tablespoon dried mint, crumbled

2 tablespoons wheat germ

About 3 cups whole wheat flour, as needed

Combine the yeast and ¼ cup of warm water (105°F. to 115°F.) in a cup or small bowl. Mix and set aside to proof (bubble up).

Combine the honey, butter, milk, and salt in a small pan (or bowl if you are using

(recipe continues)

a microwave oven) and heat until warm. Pour into a large bowl. Slowly add the 1 cup of white bread flour and beat it in with an electric whisk (or 100 times with a wooden spoon). Add the egg and the yeast, beating as you go. Change the whisk, if you were using it, to a wooden spoon. Add the walnuts, mint, and wheat germ. Mix them in. Slowly begin to add the whole wheat flour, little by little. Soon, instead of a batter, you will begin to have a ball of dough. When it becomes too hard to move around with a spoon, empty the dough out onto a floured work surface and begin to knead the dough, incorporating extra whole wheat flour if you require it. The dough should be smooth, but try to keep it as soft as you can manage. Knead well for 10 minutes and make a ball.

Put the ball of dough into a well-greased bowl, turning it around until it is well coated. Cover with a towel or plastic wrap and set aside in a warm place for 1½ hours, or until doubled in bulk. Punch the dough down so it deflates, knead for 2 to 3 minutes, cover again, and leave for another 30 minutes.

Empty the dough onto a floured work surface and knead for a minute. Form a ball and let it sit, covered loosely with a towel or plastic wrap, for 10 minutes. Now form the ball into a loaf shape and put it into a well-greased 9×5×3-inch loaf pan. Cover with a towel or plastic wrap and leave in a warm place for 1 hour.

Preheat the oven to 375°F.

The dough will now have filled the pan and risen above it. Remove the covering and put the loaf pan in the oven to bake for 35 to 40 minutes, or until golden brown and hollow sounding when tapped. Remove the loaf from the pan immediately (go around it with a knife if needed) and cool on a rack.

Once thoroughly cooled, the bread may be wrapped and either kept in a bread box or frozen for future meals.

MAKES 1 LOAF

PANCAKES

Shiu-Min Block's

Scallion Cakes   CHINA

Chung Yo Bin

According to my friend Shiu-Min, when working with dough a good chef must have three "shines." The dough ball must shine, the mixing bowl must shine, and the hands must shine. No messy dough-stuck-all-over-the-fingernails here!

Whether you can manage this or not, here is a relatively easy way to make these "cakes," which are really breads. Serve them with a soy-based dipping sauce (such as the one on page 676), any yogurt-based dip, or any fresh chutney. You may also serve them with a meal as a bread.

Ideally, these cakes should be made just before they are eaten. This way they are nice and crisp. You may cook them fully, wrap them in foil, and keep them for a while, though they will lose their crispness. The whole bundle can be reheated in a medium oven for 15 minutes. The cakes can also be reheated, one at a time, in a microwave oven, for about a minute each.

3½ cups unbleached all-purpose white flour, plus extra for dusting

10 to 12 tablespoons peanut oil, as needed

10 good-sized scallions, cut crosswise into fine rounds (both green and white sections)

1 teaspoon salt

1 teaspoon freshly ground black pepper

Put the flour in a bowl. Add about 1¼ cups of warm water, mixing as you go to make a soft dough. Collect all the dough together and make a ball. Knead briefly and make a ball again. Cover with a damp cloth and set aside for 15 to 20 minutes. Knead again.

Flour a large work surface thoroughly. Put the dough ball in the center. Put some flour on top of the dough ball and roll out a 20-inch round. (Dust with flour whenever you need to.) First spread 5 tablespoons of oil on the round and then spread the scallions over the surface. Sprinkle the salt and pepper over the top. Now roll up the round tightly into a long fat snake. Pinch off the "snake" into 4 equal parts. Take 1 of the 4 "logs" and put it in front of you. Put your hands on either edge of the "log." Twist one end away from you and the other toward you in order to close the ends tightly shut. You will be twisting the entire log slightly, but that is as it should be. Now stand the log on one end and push down to get a patty. Make all the patties this way and keep them well floured.

Flour the work surface again. Roll out one of the patties, always going outward from the center and dusting with flour whenever you need to, until you have a 7-inch round. Roll out all the cakes this way, making sure you keep them in a cool spot well dusted with flour.

Put 3 tablespoons of oil in a nonstick frying pan and set over medium-high heat. When hot, put in a cake. Cook for 3 to 4 minutes, or until golden-red on one side. Turn and cook the second side for about 3 minutes, or until it too is golden-red. Put on a paper towel and cut into wedges.

Serve immediately. Make all the other cakes this way, putting only 1 tablespoon of oil into the frying pan each time.

MAKES 4

Shiu-Min Block's

Stuffed Chinese Pancakes

Moo Shu Row

Rather like the traditional way of eating Peking duck, here thin white flour pancakes are lightly smeared with a little sweet hoisin sauce and used as a covering to roll around stir-fried vegetables. The trick to making these thin pancakes is to stick three well-oiled balls of dough together and roll them out at the same time.

For a party or for the family, these are fun to eat, as everybody has to roll up the pancakes for themselves.

For those who like hot food, any hot sauce, such as chile paste with soybean or chile paste with garlic (page 717), or even Tabasco, may be added to the hoisin sauce.

Even though I have listed the ingredients for the pancakes and stuffing separately, I tend to prepare all the ingredients for the stuffing first, then make the pancakes, and finally stir-fry the stuffing, which only takes a few minutes. The ingredients needed for serving the pancakes may be prepared while the dough is resting.

For the stuffing

1 loosely packed cup dried day lily buds

8 dried Chinese black mushrooms

½ loosely packed cup dried small black tree
ear fungus (also called cloud ears and
mo-er mushrooms)

3 tablespoons peanut or canola oil

2 eggs, beaten

2 scallions, each cut crosswise into 2-inch
sections and the white part cut
lengthwise in quarters

6 thin slices of fresh ginger, cut into fine
strips

1 (8-ounce) can sliced bamboo shoots, drained
and the slices cut lengthwise into fine strips

½ small green cabbage (about ½ pound in
all), cut into fine, long strips (this is best
done if the cabbage head is quartered,
cored, and then cut lengthwise into strips)

3 tablespoons Chinese light soy sauce

1 garlic clove, lightly crushed and peeled but
left whole

1 teaspoon salt

½ teaspoon sugar

1 teaspoon oriental sesame oil

For the pancakes

4 cups unbleached all-purpose white flour,
plus extra for dusting

3 tablespoons oriental sesame oil

4 tablespoons peanut or canola oil

For serving

5 tablespoons hoisin sauce thinned out with
2½ tablespoons water

5 scallions, the bottom 3 inches only, cut
lengthwise into fine, long slivers

Soak the dried day lily buds in water to cover them generously for 30 minutes.

Soak the black mushrooms in hot water to cover them generously for 30 minutes.

Soak the tree ear fungus in water to cover them generously for 30 minutes. Use plenty of water, as they expand considerably.

Drain the day lily buds and rinse well. Snip off the slightly knotted tops and then pull the buds into long shreds.

Lift the mushrooms out of their soaking liquid (the liquid may be strained through a cloth and saved for stock). Cut off and discard the coarse stems. Cut the caps into fine, long shreds.

Lift the tree ear fungus out of its soaking liquid. Feel each piece carefully and snip off any hard, knotted areas. Rinse well and set aside.

Prepare or measure out all the other ingredients for the stuffing and set aside.

Make the pancakes. Put the flour in a large bowl. Put 2¼ cups of water in a jug. Start to pour the water over the flour as you stir with a pair of chopsticks or a wooden spoon. When the loose flour is all gone and you have lumps of dough (you will probably use up all the water), empty the contents of the bowl onto the counter (or other kneading surface) that has been lightly sprinkled with flour. Knead for 1 minute, dusting every now and then with flour. Form a ball and cover with an upturned bowl. Set aside for 20 minutes. (This is a good time to prepare the ingredients needed for serving the pancakes.) Knead the dough again for 2 to 3 minutes, dusting it now and then with flour. It should no longer stick to your hands.

Make a long roll with the dough, about 1¼ inches in diameter. Break this off into 18 pieces. Roll each piece in flour and then form balls with a light hand. Press each ball down with a light hand to make 2½- to 3-inch patties.

Combine 3 tablespoons each of the sesame and vegetable oils in a wide, shallow bowl-like dish.

On a lightly floured surface, roll each patty out into a 4½-inch round. The Chinese way of doing this is to roll from the center out and turn the patty slightly after each roll. Roll out each patty this way.

Dip the bottom of 2 patties in the mixed oil and then stick them to each other as if the oil were some kind of glue. Use this "glue" generously. Dip the bottom of a third patty in the mixed oil and stick it to the other 2. You should now have a small 3-layered "cake" of dough patties. Make 5 more "cakes" the same way.

(recipe continues)

Dust the work surface again with a little flour. Put down 1 "cake" and roll it out, again going from the center out and turning a little after each roll, until you have a 9-inch round. Put it between 2 sheets of wax paper. Make 5 other pancakes exactly the same way, layering each pancake between sheets of wax paper and putting one on top of the other.

Heat ½ teaspoon oil in a large, heavy, nonstick frying pan over medium-high heat. When hot, put in 1 pancake. Let it cook for about 1½ minutes, or until it is translucent. Turn it over and cook the second side for about 20 seconds. Now turn it over again, slapping the pancake down hard into the pan. Cook for 5 seconds. Turn again, slapping the pancake down hard. (This begins to separate the layers.) Turn quickly 2 more times, each time slapping down hard. Remove the pancake and separate the 3 layers. Put the 3 pancakes on a large plate and cover with foil or an upturned plate. Keep covered in a warm place. Make all pancakes this way, separating the layers and keeping them warm with the others.

Quickly stir-fry the stuffing. Put 2 tablespoons of oil in a nonstick wok or large nonstick frying pan and set over high heat. When hot, add the eggs. Scramble them quickly and remove them as soon as they are cooked. Break up the scrambled egg into smaller pieces. Add another tablespoon of oil to the wok or frying pan and put in the mushrooms, scallions, and ginger. Stir twice and add the day lily buds, tree ears, and bamboo shoots. Stir twice and add the cabbage. Stir briefly and add the egg and the light soy sauce. Stir for a minute. Now add ½ cup of water, the garlic, salt, and sugar. Stir for a minute. Add the sesame oil. Stir to mix and turn off the heat. The garlic may be removed.

To eat, each diner should put about 1 teaspoon of the hoisin mixture down the center of the pancake, then scatter a few shreds of raw scallion if desired on top of the hoisin, and finally put some of the stuffing on top of the scallion. Now the pancake can be rolled up and eaten.

MAKES 18 LARGE PANCAKES

Greek Semolina Pancakes

Simigdali Crepa

These are muffinlike pancakes made with a yeast batter, a little stretchy, chewy, and wonderful. They may be eaten with savory dishes, such as Mock Minced Chicken (page 506), or with butter, sugar, and lemon juice or butter and jam. I have made them thick, but you could thin them out.

1 (¼-ounce) package active dry yeast

1 teaspoon sugar

1 cup unbleached all-purpose white flour

1 cup fine semolina flour

1 teaspoon salt

2 to 3 tablespoons unsalted butter, softened

Put ¼ cup of very warm water in a cup. Sprinkle in the yeast and the sugar. Stir and set aside for 10 to 15 minutes. The yeast should bubble up. Meanwhile, warm up another 2 cups of water.

Combine the 2 flours and salt in a bowl. Make a well in the center and pour in the yeast mixture. Stir it in with a wooden spoon. Slowly add the remaining warm water, stirring it in as you do so. Cover the bowl loosely and leave it in a warm place for 1½ hours. Stir thoroughly from the bottom and let the batter rest again, covered, in a warm place for another 30 minutes.

Just before you sit down to eat, set a cast-iron griddle, large cast-iron frying pan, or large, heavy nonstick frying pan over medium heat. Brush with the butter. Using a ladle, lift up about ⅓ cup of the batter at a time and drop as many pancakes as the pan can hold easily. Cook one side for 2 minutes, or until a nice reddish-brown. Turn and cook the second side the same way for another 2 minutes. Remove the pancakes to a plate and, if possible, serve them right away. Make all the pancakes this way. Leftover pancakes may be stored in a plastic bag and kept in the refrigerator. To reheat them, I drop them into the toaster just long enough to get them nice and hot.

MAKES ABOUT 10

South Indian Pancakes with Onion and Tomato

INDIAN-AMERICAN

Unorthodox Utthappam

I love the South Indian utthappam, *a kind of vegetarian, eggless, flat omelet. But it requires a complicated batter that not only has one soaking and grinding rice and split peas but requires a wait of 48 hours for the proper fermentation to take place naturally. When I am in a rush, I use the yeast semolina batter in the preceding recipe; the results are surprisingly good. Eat these pancakes like bread with a meal or as a savory pancake with chutneys and relishes on the side.*

Leftover pancakes may be reheated briefly in a microwave oven.

1 (¼-ounce) package active dry yeast

½ teaspoon sugar

1 cup unbleached all-purpose white flour

1 cup fine semolina flour

1½ teaspoons salt

1 small onion (about 2 ounces), peeled and cut into very fine slivers

1 to 2 fresh hot green chiles, cut into fine slivers (with the seeds)

6 tablespoons peeled, seeded, and chopped tomato (page 300), left in a strainer set over a bowl

Freshly ground black pepper

5 to 6 tablespoons peanut oil

Put ¼ cup of very warm water in a cup. Sprinkle in the yeast and sugar. Stir and set aside for 10 to 15 minutes. The yeast should bubble up.

Combine the 2 flours and salt in a bowl. Make a well in the center and pour in the yeast mixture. Stir it in with a wooden spoon. Slowly add 2 more cups of very warm water, stirring it in as you do so. Cover the bowl loosely and leave it in a warm place for 1½ hours. Stir thoroughly from the bottom and let the batter rest again, covered, in a warm place for another 30 minutes. Just before cooking, add the onion, chile, tomato and some pepper. Stir with a very light hand and leave for 5 minutes as you heat the pan for pancake making.

Set a heavy nonstick frying pan over medium heat. Brush with oil. Let the pan heat up. Using a ladle, lift up about ⅓ cup of the batter and drop it in the center of the pan. Put the rounded bottom of a ladle or soup spoon directly on the blob of batter and, using a continuous spiral motion, spread it outward in concentric circles. You should end up with a 7-inch pancake. Dribble another ½ teaspoon oil over the pancake and 1 teaspoon just outside its edges. Cook one side for 1½ to 2 minutes, or until a nice reddish-brown. Turn and cook the second side the same way for another 1½ to 2 minutes, or until it too is reddish-brown. Remove the pancake to a plate and serve immediately. Repeat with remaining batter.

MAKES ABOUT 10

Soft Spongy Pancakes

MOROCCO

GRAINS

Baghrir

These soft, spongy Moroccan pancakes have the airy holes of a muffin but a texture that is much more satiny and pliable. They are perfect for absorbing butter and honey at breakfast, when they are eaten as sweet pancakes, and equally good at lunchtime when they can be wrapped around beans, vegetables, and cheeses and eaten as a bread.

In Morocco, the pancake batter is prepared by first putting the flour on a large tray in the shape of a hill. A crater is scooped out on the hilltop and filled with the egg, yeast, and salt. Next, the Moroccans slowly add the water, working the dough with the flat part of their palms and fingers until it has transformed itself into a smooth batter.

I find it easier to put the flour, egg, yeast, and salt in a blender. I then add about ¾ of the measured water and blend. After scraping down the contents with a spatula as necessary, I add the remaining water and blend again.

Moroccans cook these pancakes without covering the frying pan. I've not achieved my best results that way. I find covering the pan gives the pancakes a better consistency. You might find that the first pancake or two will not have the perfect airy texture, but the rest will.

These pancakes can be made 1 to 2 hours ahead of time and kept wrapped in a clean dish towel. They can be reheated with a little butter and then served with a honey-butter mixture. As a variation, these pancakes may be eaten with butter and maple syrup.

1½ teaspoons active dry yeast

½ teaspoon sugar

1¼ cups semolina flour

1¾ cups unbleached all-purpose white flour

½ teaspoon salt

1 egg, beaten

1 teaspoon peanut or canola oil

1 cup honey plus 4 tablespoons (½ stick) unsalted butter

9 to 10 tablespoons unsalted butter

Combine the yeast, sugar, and 2 tablespoons of warm water (105°F. to 115°F.) in a small bowl. Stir to dissolve the yeast completely. Set aside for 5 minutes, or until the yeast begins to bubble.

Meanwhile, put the 2 flours, salt, egg, and yeast mixture in a blender. Add 2½ cups of warm water (105°F. to 115°F.) and blend until smooth and free of lumps. You may need to push down with a rubber spatula several times. Empty into a bowl, cover, and set aside in a warm place for 2½ to 3 hours.

Get everything ready to make the pancakes. You need a medium nonstick frying pan to cook the pancakes, a plate with a large, opened-up dishcloth on it to hold the pancakes as they get cooked, a ladle with a round bottom in which you have

(recipe continues)

473

measured about ⅓ cup so you know how much batter to pick up each time, and a spatula to pick up the pancakes.

Set the frying pan on medium heat. Grease the pan lightly with the oil (you will only need to grease the pan once) and let the pan get very hot. Ladle in about ⅓ cup of the batter into the pan. Using the rounded underside of the ladle and a very light touch, quickly spread the batter into a 6-inch round. Cover and cook on medium heat for 1 minute. Uncover and continue cooking for another minute, or until the bottom has turned golden and the top is not only filled with airy holes, but is also cooked through (you might find that the pancakes take less time to cook during the uncovered period as the pan gets hotter). Lift it up with a spatula and place on the dishcloth. Fold the 4 corners of the cloth over the pancake and keep it covered. Make all the pancakes this way, stacking them on top of each other and covering them each time. You can hold the pancakes this way for a couple of hours.

To serve, heat the combined honey-butter mixture in a small pot until both the honey and butter have liquefied and mixed. Stir once or twice. Keep warm.

For each pancake, melt about 2 teaspoons of butter into a nonstick pan on medium-low heat. Gently place 1 pancake, bubbly surface side down, into the pan. Heat for 15 to 20 seconds. Put onto a plate, bubbly side up. Pour some of the honey-butter mixture over the top and serve hot.

MAKES 12 TO 13

NOODLES AND PASTA

Neeru Row Kavi's

Pasta in a Split Pea Sauce INDIA

Dal Dhokli

This is a very ancient, traditional dish from Gujarat in western India. You can even find it in some of the most remote villages of this state, where it is a desert staple. It consists of a spicy, thick split pea soup with wide noodles that is more main dish than soup. It makes a perfect lunch or supper, served with a simple green salad.

The Indus valley civilization flourished nearby more than four thousand years ago and was known for its cultivation of wheat and split peas. This dish uses both. The split peas should be toovar dal, *which go back to India's prehistory. (You may substitute yellow split peas, but they lack the dark earthiness of* toovar dal.) *The noodles here, traditionally homemade, are cut from large rounds of rolled-out whole wheat dough, the same as used for chapatis (Indian Griddle Flatbreads, page 444). These rounds are then cut into noodles, left to dry off briefly, and then dropped into the soup. I have simplified the dish by using store-bought pasta (fettuccine or egg noodles). I have also changed it somewhat by serving a mound of pasta half in and half out of the soup.*

The tomatoes in this dish must have been added to the recipe after the sixteenth century! I peel the tomatoes with a sharp paring knife as if they were apples.

You may substitute a peeled and finely chopped garlic clove for the asafetida, but put it in after the cumin seeds and stir it once or twice before adding the tomatoes.

The soup/sauce part of the recipe may be prepared ahead of time. It may even be left in the refrigerator for 24 hours.

For the soup/sauce

1 cup *toovar dal* (page 85), picked over, washed, and drained

2 tablespoons peanut or canola oil

Generous pinch of ground asafetida

½ teaspoon whole cumin seeds

1¼ pounds ripe tomatoes, peeled and finely chopped

¼ teaspoon ground turmeric

1 to 2 fresh hot green chiles, finely chopped (do not remove seeds)

4 tablespoons chopped fresh cilantro

About 1¼ teaspoons salt

1 tablespoon fresh lemon juice

For the pasta

Salt

¾ pound fettuccine

3 tablespoons peanut or canola oil

½ teaspoon whole brown or yellow mustard seeds

1 whole hot red chile, crumbled

Put the *toovar dal* and 3 cups of water in a heavy pan and bring to a boil. Cover partially, turn the heat down to low, and simmer very gently for 1 hour. You should close the lid for the last 15 minutes. Mash the *dal* against the sides of the pan and set aside.

Put the 2 tablespoons oil in a large frying pan or sauté pan and set over medium-high heat. When hot, put in the asafetida. Five seconds later, put in the cumin seeds. Wait another 5 seconds and put in the tomatoes. Stir the tomatoes for a minute. Now add the turmeric and mix it in. Add the green chile, cilantro, salt, and ¾ cup of water and bring to a boil. Cover, turn the heat down to low, and simmer for 7 to 8 minutes, or until the tomatoes are soft. Now add the tomatoes to the cooked *dal*. Add another 1½ cups of water and the lemon juice. Stir and bring to a boil. Cover, turn the heat down to low, and simmer 15 minutes. This much can be done ahead of time and the soup reheated when needed.

Just before you sit down to eat, bring 4 quarts of water to a rolling boil in a large pot. Add 1½ tablespoons salt and stir. Drop in the fettuccine and stir. While the

(recipe continues)

pasta cooks, put the 3 tablespoons of oil in a small pan and set over medium-high heat. When hot, put in the mustard seeds. As soon as the mustard seeds pop, a matter of seconds, put in the chile. Stir once or twice, or until the chile darkens, and pour the oil and seasonings into a large bowl. Add about ½ teaspoon salt and mix. As soon as the pasta is ready, drain it and put it into the bowl with the oil. Toss thoroughly.

To serve, stir the soup from the bottom and put about ¾ cup in each of 6 soup plates. Divide the pasta into 6 portions and put a mound in the center of each plate. Serve immediately.

SERVES 6

Shiu-Min Block's
Pan-Fried Noodles CHINA

I have always loved pan-fried noodles ever since I first had them over thirty years ago. These are really like a nest of tangled noodles, except that the "nest" is flat. As the noodles are shallow-fried, the "nest" is crisp on the outside and soft on the inside. The "nest" can be covered with almost any topping of your choice, as long as the topping is either saucelike or has at least some sauce in it. At its simplest, you could use an Italian tomato sauce, such as the Simple Tomato Sauce (page 679). If you want to be authentically Chinese, use my friend Shiu-Min's Three Kinds of Mushrooms (page 244) as a topping or else try the Green Beans with Cumin and Fennel (page 202).

These noodles should be served as soon as they have been fried, so have the topping ready beforehand. The boiling of the noodles may be done up to 2 hours in advance.

½ pound fresh Chinese lo mein egg noodles

7 tablespoons peanut oil

Bring a large pot of water (about 13 cups) to a rolling boil in a large pot. Gently separate the noodle strands and drop them into the water. When the water comes to a second boil, pour in a cup of cold tap water. When the water comes to a third boil, pour in another cup of tap water. When the water comes to a fourth boil, empty the contents of the pot into a colander set in the sink. Rinse the noodles under cold running water to cool them off and to wash off the starch. Drain thoroughly and put into a bowl. Toss with 2 tablespoons of the oil and set aside until ready to use.

Just before eating, put the remaining 5 tablespoons of oil in an 8- to 9-inch non-stick frying pan and set over medium-high heat. When hot, put in the noodles, carefully spreading them out evenly so they cover the entire bottom of the pan.

Fry without stirring for about 4 minutes, or until the bottom of the noodle "nest" has browned. Now, slip one spatula under the noodle "nest" and hold the top with another spatula. Carefully turn the "nest" over and brown the other side. When done, carefully lift the "nest" out and put it on a large platter that has a little depth to it. Pour whatever topping you are using over it and serve immediately while the "nest" is still crisp.

SERVES 2 TO 4

"Javanese" Noodles   INDONESIA/MALAYSIA
Mee Java

I had this noodle dish in Malaysia, not in Indonesia, but its name suggests Javanese origins. As I ate the soup on a balmy day in a small coastal town, it struck me that the true origins of the soup lay not in Java at all but in India. It probably originated with Tamil immigrants from South India who made their daily sambar, *a tamarind-soured soup of* toovar dal *and vegetables and then, with Malaysian abandon, added local noodles to it as well as Southeast Asian flourishes such as bean sprouts, crisply fried shallots, chile slivers, and hard-boiled eggs. It became a full meal, just as their* sambar *and rice had been.*

The soup/sauce part of the recipe may be prepared ahead of time. It may even be left in the refrigerator for 24 hours.

The noodles used here were the fresh yellow noodles sold by Chinese grocers. I have used fettuccine, though fresh Chinese lo mein noodles would work as well.

For the soup/sauce

1 cup *toovar dal* (page 85), picked over, washed, and drained

2 tablespoons peanut or canola oil

Generous pinch of ground asafetida

1 teaspoon whole brown or yellow mustard seeds

15 fresh curry leaves, if available

1 medium shallot, peeled and cut into fine slivers

1 to 2 fresh hot green chiles, cut into fine slivers (do not remove seeds)

2 teaspoons curry powder (you may use My Curry Powder, page 707, or any commercial curry powder or commercial sambar powder sold by Indian grocers)

1¼ pounds ripe tomatoes, peeled and finely chopped

4 tablespoons chopped fresh cilantro

About 1¼ teaspoons salt

1 tablespoon thick tamarind paste (page 737) or fresh lemon juice

(recipe continues)

477

For the garnishes

4 tablespoons peanut or canola oil

2 shallots (2 ounces), peeled and cut into fine
    slivers

1 cup fresh bean sprouts

2 fresh hot red or green chiles

2 hard-boiled eggs (optional)

For the pasta

Salt

¾ pound fettuccine

½ teaspoon whole brown or yellow mustard
    seeds

1 whole hot red chile, crumbled

Make the soup/sauce. Put the *toovar dal* and 3 cups of water in a heavy pan and bring to a boil. Cover partially, turn the heat down to low, and simmer very gently for 1 hour. You should close the lid for the last 15 minutes. Mash the *dal* against the sides of the pan and set aside.

Put the oil in a large frying pan or sauté pan and set over medium-high heat. When hot, put in the asafetida. Five seconds later, put in the mustard seeds. Wait another 5 seconds and put in the curry leaves, shallot, and green chile. Stir and cook them for 2 minutes, or until the shallot browns lightly. Add the curry powder and stir twice. Add the tomatoes and stir for a minute. Add the cilantro, salt, and ¾ cup of water. Bring to a boil. Cover, turn the heat down to low, and simmer for 7 to 8 minutes, or until the tomatoes are soft. Now add the tomatoes to the cooked *dal*. Add another 1½ cups of water and the tamarind paste or lemon juice. Stir and bring to a boil. Cover, turn the heat down to low, and simmer 15 minutes. This much can be done ahead of time and the soup reheated when needed.

Prepare the garnishes. Put the oil in a small frying pan and set over medium-high heat. When hot, put in the shallots. Stir and fry, turning the heat down as you proceed, until the slivers are reddish-brown and crisp. Remove with a slotted spoon and spread out on paper towels. Save the oil in the small frying pan. Wash the bean sprouts well and put them in a bowl. Pour boiling water over them to cover and then drain them immediately. Leave in a sieve or colander. Cut the green chiles into fine slivers. Peel and quarter the hard-boiled eggs, if using.

Prepare the pasta. Just before you sit down to eat, bring 4 quarts of water to a rolling boil in a large pot. Add 1½ tablespoons salt. Stir. Drop in the fettuccine and stir. While the pasta cooks, put the frying pan with the reserved oil on medium-high heat. When hot, put in the mustard seeds. As soon as the mustard seeds pop, a matter of seconds, put in the red chile. Stir once or twice, or until the chile darkens, and pour the oil and seasonings into a large bowl. Add about ½ teaspoon salt and mix. As soon as the pasta is ready, drain it and put it into the bowl with the oil. Toss thoroughly.

To serve, stir the soup from the bottom and put about ¾ cup in each of 6 soup plates. Divide the pasta into 6 portions and put a mound in the center of each plate. Scatter the garnishes evenly over the top. Serve immediately.

SERVES 6

Shiu-Min Block's

Chinese Noodles Sautéed with Vegetables

CHINA

Su Chow Mein

Here the noodles themselves may be cooked several hours ahead of time, rinsed well, rubbed with a little oil, and set aside—even refrigerated. They should, however, be stir-fried at the last minute.

The vegetables, too, can be soaked, cut, and sliced as needed well ahead of time. Cover with plastic wrap and set aside.

The bamboo shoots used here were canned. I used half of an 8-ounce can of sliced bamboo shoots in water. I drained the amount needed and then cut each slice into long slivers.

8 Chinese dried black mushrooms

½ pound fresh Chinese egg lo mein noodles

3½ tablespoons peanut oil

2 scallions, first cut into 2-inch lengths (both white and green sections) and then each segment quartered lengthwise

1 tablespoon peeled fresh ginger, thinly sliced first and then cut into fine slivers

½ well-packed cup (2 ounces) slivered bamboo shoots (see recipe introduction)

6 fresh water chestnuts, peeled, sliced, and then cut into long slivers (use canned water chestnuts as a substitute)

½ cup (1½ ounces) julienned carrot (peel carrot and cut into 2-inch segments— slice lengthwise and then cut lengthwise into strips)

4 teaspoons soy sauce

Soak the mushrooms in hot water that covers them well for 30 minutes, or until softened. Lift them out of the water. (Save the soaking water for future stocks.) Cut off and discard the stems. Cut the caps into very fine slices.

Bring a large pot of water to a rolling boil. Drop in the noodles. Bring to a boil again and boil about 2 minutes, or until the noodles are ¾ done. Drain, rinse under cold water, and drain again. Put the noodles in a bowl. Rub with ½ tablespoon of the oil, cover, and set aside.

(recipe continues)

479

Just before eating, put the remaining 3 tablespoons oil in a large nonstick wok, large nonstick frying pan, or sauté pan and set over medium-high heat. When hot, put in the scallions and ginger. Stir for 30 seconds and add the mushrooms, bamboo shoots, water chestnuts, and carrot. Stir and fry for 1 minute. Now add the noodles and the soy sauce. Stir and fry for 2 minutes, or until heated through.

SERVES 2 TO 4

Newel Jenkin's

Spaghetti with Fresh Tomatoes and Lemon Peel

ITALY

Pasta al Pipo

This recipe comes from an American conductor friend who spent much of his life in Italy. He, in turn, got it from a friend, Pipo, on the island of Giglio.

This should be made only in the height of summer when red-ripe tomatoes are abundant. The better the quality of the tomatoes, the better this dish will taste.

Use the peel of an organic or other unsprayed lemon.

Peel from half a lemon (be careful to avoid any white pith), cut into very fine, ¾-inch-long slivers

4 good-sized, red-ripe tomatoes (1½ pounds), peeled, seeded, and coarsely chopped (if you need directions, see page 300)

1 cup chopped fresh basil leaves

½ cup coarsely chopped fresh Italian parsley leaves (discard the stems)

½ cup extra-virgin olive oil

Salt

Freshly ground black pepper

1 pound spaghetti

Bring a small pot of water to a rolling boil. Drop in the lemon peel slivers and boil for 5 seconds. Drain.

Combine the peel, tomatoes, basil, parsley, oil, about ¼ to ½ teaspoon salt (taste as you go), and the pepper in a bowl. Toss to mix and set aside, unrefrigerated, for 1 to 4 hours. Toss every now and then.

Bring 4 quarts of water to a rolling boil in a large pot. Add 1½ tablespoons salt, then drop in the spaghetti and stir. Boil until the pasta is just done; drain the pasta well, then transfer to a big bowl. Add the tomato mixture and toss well. Serve as soon as possible.

SERVES 4

Penne or Fusilli with Fresh Tomatoes

ITALIAN-AMERICAN

I had this dish for the first time at a Fourth of July picnic in Connecticut. All the guests had been asked to bring a salad. An Italian-American friend brought this. His salad had been only partially prepared beforehand. The "dressing" part, which consisted of chopped fresh tomatoes marinated with fresh basil, garlic, and olive oil, was sitting in a large plastic container. He still had to boil the pasta. He had chosen penne, but fusilli works equally well. As soon as it was drained, he tossed it while it was still very hot with lots of freshly grated Parmesan cheese. The cheese promptly melted and clung to the pasta in a most delicious way. Then he added the tomato mixture and tossed again. We ate the salad while the pasta was still a little warm. It was utterly delicious.

Make this dish only when you have access to red-ripe tomatoes. The better the quality of the tomatoes, the better this dish will taste. Also, it is a good idea to peel the tomatoes, but not by dropping them into boiling water. Peel them by hand with a paring knife, as if they were apples.

3 to 4 good-sized red-ripe tomatoes
(1¼ pounds)

15 large basil leaves

½ cup olive oil

3 to 4 large garlic cloves, very lightly crushed
and peeled but left whole

Salt

1 pound penne or fusilli

Freshly ground black pepper

½ cup freshly grated Parmigiano-Reggiano
cheese (you may add a bit more, if you
wish)

Peel the tomatoes with a paring knife (see recipe introduction) and cut into ⅓-inch dice. Tear up the basil leaves and add them to the tomatoes. Put the oil in a medium frying pan along with the garlic and set over medium heat. When the oil begins to bubble, allow to "simmer" for 1½ minutes. Turn off the heat and let the oil cool off. Then pour it over the tomatoes, garlic cloves and all. Toss to mix and set aside, unrefrigerated, for 4 to 6 hours. Toss every now and then.

Bring 4 quarts of water to a rolling boil in a large pot. Add 1½ tablespoons salt. Drop in the pasta and stir. Meanwhile, season the tomato mixture with salt to taste (anywhere from ¼ to ½ teaspoon) and black pepper. Boil the pasta until it is just done and then drain it. Put the pasta in a big bowl. Add the cheese and toss well. Now add the tomato mixture to it and toss again. Serve as soon as possible. (Though this pasta will hold for the next half hour, it is best if it is served immediately.) The garlic cloves may be removed before serving, if you wish.

SERVES 4

From the Antinori home and vineyards in Chianti

Penne with Zucchini and Basil

Penne alle Zucchine

A simple but exquisite dish from the heart of the Chianti area in Tuscany, this first course was created by Allegra Antinori and served at her home in the Chianti vineyards. Here is Tuscan home cooking at its best: the freshest of ingredients, cooked simply—but to perfection.

The pasta, a penne in this case, is enfolded in a sautéed mixture of zucchini and onions that have been cooked until soft. (Barely cooked zucchini, a darling of many restaurants, is currently the bane of our lives.) Fresh basil and mint (mentuccia) *are added at the end, making for an unusual dish. As it was late May, the young zucchini still had flowers attached to them. The flowers had almost melted into a sauce, along with the onions and the sliced zucchini.*

If you have access to zucchini with attached flowers, just leave them attached as you slice the vegetable.

3 to 4 small-medium zucchini (about 14 ounces)

Salt

5 tablespoons extra-virgin olive oil

1 good-sized onion (5 to 6 ounces), peeled and cut into fine half rings

¼ cup vegetable stock

About 30 fresh basil leaves, torn in pieces

½ cup of fresh mint leaves, coarsely chopped or torn

1 pound penne or penne rigate

Freshly ground black pepper

4 to 6 tablespoons freshly grated Parmigiano-Reggiano cheese (optional)

Halve the zucchini lengthwise, then cut crosswise into ¼-inch-thick slices. Place in a bowl, add 1 teaspoon salt, toss, and set aside for 30 minutes. Drain thoroughly and pat dry.

Put the oil in a large frying pan or sauté pan and set over medium heat. Add the onion and cook about 5 minutes without browning, stirring occasionally. Add the zucchini and stir and cook for another 5 minutes or until soft. Taste for salt, adding more only if it is needed. Add the stock, stir once or twice, and turn off the heat. Add the basil and mint leaves and toss. (Leave in a warm spot or reheat while the pasta is cooking.)

Bring 4 quarts of water to a rolling boil in a large pot. Add 1½ tablespoons salt. Drop in the penne and stir. Boil the pasta until it is just done and then drain it. Put the hot pasta into a big bowl. Add the zucchini mixture, black pepper, and cheese, if desired. Toss to mix and serve immediately.

SERVES 4

Fettuccine (or Tagliatelle) with Ricotta, Spinach, and Pine Nuts

ITALY

Fettuccine con Ricotta e Spinaci

This is rich and utterly delicious. I bought 2½ pounds of fresh spinach and, after trimming, was left with the 1½ pounds I needed.

¾ cup (2¼ ounces) fresh ricotta cheese

Salt

Freshly ground black pepper

4 tablespoons (½ stick) unsalted butter

¾ cup (2 ounces) grated Parmigiano-Reggiano cheese

2 tablespoons olive oil

2 tablespoons pine nuts

3 garlic cloves, lightly crushed and peeled but left whole

1½ pounds trimmed, well-washed, and drained spinach

A little freshly grated nutmeg

1 pound dried fettuccine or 1¼ pounds fresh tagliatelle

Put 4 quarts of water in a large pot and bring to a boil.

Turn the oven to "warm." Put the ricotta in an ovenproof serving bowl. Add a light sprinkling of salt and some pepper. Toss, breaking up lumps as you do so. Add half the butter and all the Parmigiano-Reggiano. Toss again and place in the oven.

Put the olive oil in a large, wide sauté pan and set over medium heat. When hot, put in the pine nuts. Stir them until they are golden and then remove with a slotted spoon. Set aside. Add the garlic and stir until the garlic is golden brown. Put in the remaining butter, stir once, and then turn the heat up to high. Quickly put in all the spinach. Cover and cook until the spinach has wilted. Uncover, add about ¾ teaspoon salt, and cook on high heat, stirring, until there is very little liquid left. Add some pepper and nutmeg. Toss, taste for seasoning, and turn off the heat.

Put about 1½ tablespoons of salt in the pot of water and then put in the pasta. Cook until just done and drain, saving 2 tablespoons of the liquid. Working fast, empty the pasta over the cheeses in the serving bowl. Toss. Add the reserved cooking water, spinach, and pine nuts. Toss well, distributing the spinach, and serve hot.

SERVES 4 TO 5

Penne with Artichokes and Peas

ITALY

Penne con Carciofi e Piselli

This is one of my favorite pasta dishes.

Salt

1 pound penne or penne rigate

1 to 2 tablespoons unsalted butter

Freshly ground black pepper

A freshly prepared, still hot recipe of
    Artichokes with Peas (page 131)

Bring a large pot of water (about 4 quarts) to a rolling boil. Put in about 1½ table-spoons salt. When the water comes to a boil again, put in the pasta. Stir once or twice, cover partially, and bring to a boil again. Boil rapidly until the pasta is just done. Drain it in a colander. Put the butter into the pasta pot and then put the drained pasta back in. Add a little salt and pepper. Toss. Add the Artichokes with Peas, toss gently to mix well, and serve immediately.

SERVES 4

Fettuccine with a Mushroom Ragout

ITALY

Fettuccine con Funghi

The mushroom ragout here has both dried porcini mushrooms for flavor and aroma (and for their lovely juices) and plain white mushrooms for texture and bulk. You may also throw in 6 to 7 fresh shiitake mushroom caps (discard their stems) that have been thinly sliced. They have a wonderful silken texture. I use dried fettuccine as my pasta here but pappardelle would also work well.

The mushroom ragout may be made ahead of time and reheated.

You may toss all the pasta with all the sauce in a large bowl as I have done here or you may toss the pasta with a few tablespoons of butter in a warm bowl and then put it into individual soup plates. Spoon some of the ragout over the top. Garnish with a little extra finely chopped parsley and serve.

½ ounce dried, sliced porcini mushrooms

1 cup vegetable stock

¼ cup dry vermouth

6 tablespoons olive oil

1 shallot (1 ounce), peeled and very finely chopped

2 garlic cloves, peeled and very finely chopped

2 tablespoons unbleached all-purpose white flour

10 ounces white mushrooms, thinly sliced

Salt

Freshly ground black pepper

2 to 3 teaspoons fresh lemon juice

3 tablespoons finely chopped fresh parsley

1 pound fettuccine

Put the porcini mushrooms in a small bowl. Add ¾ cup of boiling water and leave to soak 1 hour or longer until very soft. Remove the mushrooms, squeezing all their juice back into the bowl. Add the stock and vermouth to the liquid in the bowl. Set the mushrooms aside. Heat the mushroom liquid until it is very hot.

Put 2 tablespoons of the oil, the shallot, and garlic in a small, heavy saucepan and set over medium heat. When the contents of the pot start sizzling, begin to watch carefully. As soon as the garlic is golden, put in the flour. Stir the flour for a minute. Now add the hot mushroom liquid, a little at a time, mixing it in with a wooden spoon. When all the liquid has been added, mix again to make sure there are no lumps. Simmer the sauce very gently on low heat for 2 to 3 minutes, stirring now and then. Turn off the heat.

Put the remaining 4 tablespoons of oil in a large frying pan or sauté pan and set over high heat. When hot, put in both dried and fresh mushrooms. Stir and sauté them for about 2 minutes, or until they are satiny. Now pour in the sauce and bring to a simmer. Turn the heat down to low and simmer very gently for 10 minutes. Add about ½ teaspoon salt, pepper to taste, and the lemon juice. Stir to mix and taste again. Add the parsley to the ragout just before serving. (If you have made the ragout ahead of time, you will need to reheat it.)

Put 4 quarts of water in a large pot and bring to a boil. Add 1½ tablespoons salt. Put the pasta into the water and as soon as it is done, drain it and put it in a warm bowl. Add the sauce and toss. Serve immediately.

SERVES 4 TO 5

Shiu-Min Block's
Boiled Vegetable Dumplings
Su Jao Ze

This recipe includes a recipe for dumpling skins, but if you wish to buy them ready-made, you can find them in a Chinese grocery in one of the refrigerated compartments. They come in stacks and are called just what they are, dumpling skins.

Serve these dumplings for brunch, lunch, or dinner with a small bowl of dipping sauce for each diner made up of 2 teaspoons Chinese light soy sauce mixed with 1 teaspoon distilled white vinegar per person. Actually wine vinegar or cider vinegar would also do. Some very finely shredded peeled fresh ginger may also be offered for nibbling to those who like it.

The green vegetable used here is bok choy but of the variety where the stalklike section is green instead of white. Any greens, such as plain bok choy, celery cabbage, or Swiss chard, may be substituted.

To roll out the dumplings you need a slim rolling pin. A simple dowel, about ¾ inch in diameter and about 8 inches long, works perfectly.

For the stuffing

5 large Chinese black mushrooms

1.8 ounces cellophane noodles

2¾ lightly packed cups (½ pound) fresh bean
    sprouts

10 ounces green bok choy (see recipe
    introduction)

15 medium white mushrooms

7 tablespoons peanut or canola oil

2 eggs, beaten

3 slices of fresh ginger, peeled and finely
    chopped

4 scallions, cut into very fine rounds all the
    way up their green sections

2 teaspoons oriental sesame oil

For the dumpling skins

3 cups unbleached all-purpose white flour,
    plus extra for dusting

Soak the Chinese black mushrooms in warm water for 30 minutes to 1 hour, or until very soft. Lift out of the water (strain the water and save for stocks or other dishes) and cut off the hard stems. Squeeze out the caps and chop them finely.

Put the cellophane noodles in a bowl. Pour boiling water over them to cover them well. Spread them out a bit and let them soak for 10 minutes. Drain thoroughly and then chop them finely.

Put the bean sprouts in a bowl. Pour boiling water over them. Drain them well and chop them finely.

Remove the root end of the bok choy. Separate the stalks and cut each into 3- to 4-inch segments. Bring a large pot of water to a boil. Drop in the bok choy and let it cook for a minute. Drain and squeeze out all the liquid. Chop very finely.

Mince the white mushrooms very finely by hand or in a food processor. Once minced, squeeze out as much moisture as possible from them.

Put 3 tablespoons of the oil in a large, nonstick frying pan and set over high heat. When hot, put in the eggs and scramble them. Remove the eggs and chop them finely.

Clean and dry the frying pan. Put in the remaining 4 tablespoons of oil and set over high heat. When hot, put in the ginger and scallions. Stir and fry for 10 seconds. Now add the dried mushrooms, cellophane noodles, bean sprouts, bok choy, and plain mushrooms. Stir once and add the eggs and sesame oil. Stir for a minute and then let the mixture cool.

To make the dumpling skins, put the 3 cups of flour in a bowl. Add 1 cup plus 1 tablespoon lukewarm water and stir with a wooden spoon or a pair of chopsticks until you have lumpy bits of dough. Form a smooth ball with minimum kneading. Put the dough ball in a bowl, cover the bowl with a damp cloth, and let it rest for 30 minutes.

Divide the dough into 2 parts. Keep one part covered with a damp cloth while you work with the other.

Make a long snake with one of the dough parts, about ¾ inch in width. Dust with flour as you do this. Break the snake off into ¾-inch pieces.

To prepare each dumpling skin, do the following: (These directions are for a right-handed person. Reverse the directions if you are left-handed.) Roll a piece of dough into a ball and then flatten it. Dust it with flour. Now, holding the dowel in your right hand and manipulating the dough with your left hand, roll the dowel from the outside in, going only as far as the center of the dough, pressing and flattening it out, and then rolling outward again. Rotate the dough very slightly in a counter-clockwise direction and repeat what you did before. This can all be done with great briskness. Go all the way around until you have a disc about 3 inches in diameter and somewhat thicker in the center than at the edges. Make all the skins this way with the first half of the dough. Keep them well dusted with flour so they do not stick to each other, and covered with a damp cloth so they do not dry out.

To fill the skins, put 1 teaspoon of the filling in the center of a dumpling skin. Bring 2 opposite points of the circle together and press them shut only at that central point. Now you need to put 4 pleats on the upper edge of the dumpling

(recipe continues)

that is nearest to you, 2 on either side of where you pressed it shut. Each pleat must go toward the center, the second one on each side overlapping the first one slightly. As you make each pleat, press it tightly against the back edge to seal the opening. The most important thing is to have the dumpling well sealed. If pleating is difficult, just close up the circle to make a half moon (like a turnover) and press shut.

Make as many dumplings as is possible with the first part of the dough, putting them in a single layer on a lightly floured plate or tray. Do not let them touch each other or else they might stick together. Cover the dumplings with a lightly dampened cloth. Do the same thing all over again with the second half of the dough and keep covered. If the dumpling skins dry out too much, you might need to moisten the edges with water to get them to close properly. This seal is important.

To cook the dumplings, bring a large pot of water to a rolling boil. Put in only as many dumplings as will fit in easily, allowing for plenty of "swimming room." As soon as the water comes to a boil again, put in 1 cup of fresh cold water. When the pot comes to a boil again, put in another cup of water. Do this a third time and when the water comes to a boil again, remove the dumplings with a slotted spoon or skimmer and put a fresh lot of dumplings in. Cook all the dumplings this way, eating them as soon as they are made. Serve with the dipping sauce and ginger shreds as suggested in the recipe introduction.

MAKES ABOUT 50 TO 60

SEMOLINA "RISOTTOS"

Uppama

Uppamas belong to South India, more specifically to Kerala, a state on India's southwestern coast. Just like Italian risottos, they are made by adding boiling liquid, a little at a time, to a grain. The grain happens to be not rice, as in Italy, but delicate granules of semolina—so the result is fluffy and light, not flowing and dense. You might describe an *uppama* as a cross between a pilaf and a risotto, only made with semolina.

As in risottos, almost any vegetable, seasonings, even nuts, may be incorporated into the dish and used as flavorings and accents. The liquid added is generally water, but you could also use vegetable stock. No cheese is used traditionally (though I have been known to grate a little Parmigiano-Reggiano and mix it in), but the "dairy" needs of the meal are well taken care of in southern India as an *uppama* is generally served with a yogurt relish. *Uppamas* are really one of the glories of Kerala, just waiting to be discovered by the rest of the world.

You may either buy the very granular semolina needed here from Indian grocers, who sell it as *sooji* or *rava,* or you may very conveniently use Cream of Wheat, the kind that takes 10 minutes to cook and is sold in every supermarket. (The kind that takes 2½ minutes to cook works equally well, but I tend to stay away from it because of the additives used to speed cooking.)

I like to start the cooking in a heavy, large, nonstick frying pan or wok. Seasonings and vegetables are generally put in first, followed by the semolina, which is sautéed until the granules are golden. (The semolina may be sautéed first, all by itself, if you like.) Now begin to add boiling water, a little at a time, taking about 5 minutes to do so. The proportion of water to semolina or Cream of Wheat—in volume—varies between 1¾:1 and 2:1 depending upon the variety of semolina you use, the vegetables that are mixed in, and the texture you like. I tend to like my *uppamas* on the dry side. Once all the water has been added, you have a slightly lumpy consistency that is a bit like bread stuffing. But the cooking is not done yet. The heat is now turned down to very low and you continue to stir for about 10 minutes, mashing down all lumps with the back of a wooden spoon, until all the semolina granules swell up and turn very fluffy, as in a pilaf.

Among the traditional seasonings used for an *uppama* are mustard seeds and, strangely enough, split peas. This is very common in South India where small amounts of split peas, such as *chana dal* (the best substitute here is yellow split peas) and *urad dal,* are used almost as a seasoning. They are lightly browned to add a unique, nutty flavor and a bit of crunch. You may use such nuts as blanched almonds or even raw peanuts instead.

What follow are four recipes for *uppamas*, three of them very traditionally Indian, the other two using ingredients from other parts of the world. Once you learn the method, you can concoct your own *uppamas*. If you like, you may serve the *uppama* with a squeeze of lemon juice over the top, or, if you are serving it hot, with a pat of sweet butter.

Uppamas may be served at breakfast with a yogurt relish, at lunch with a salad, or at dinner with other vegetable and bean dishes. They may also be used as stuffings for vegetables.

Semolina "Risotto" (Uppama) with Cabbage and Peas

INDIA

Here is a classical uppama—*light, fluffy, and spicy. Serve it with a salad or a yogurt relish. Pickles may be offered on the side. I often make large platters of it and serve it with scrambled eggs for brunches. If you wish to be untraditional, mix in very finely grated Parmigiano-Reggiano cheese at the very end and serve it as a first course at a grand, international meal.*

¼ cup peanut or canola oil

Generous pinch of ground asafetida

1 teaspoon whole brown mustard seeds

1 to 2 whole hot dried red chiles

2 teaspoons *chana dal* or yellow split peas

15 to 20 fresh curry leaves (optional)

3 tablespoons shallots or red onion, very finely chopped

1 teaspoon finely grated peeled fresh ginger

1 to 2 teaspoons finely chopped fresh hot green chiles

1 well-packed cup (2½ ounces) finely shredded green cabbage

3 tablespoons peas (if frozen, defrost them)

1 cup (6 ounces) semolina *(sooji)* or Cream of Wheat (the kind that takes 10 minutes to cook)

¾ teaspoon salt

2 tablespoons finely chopped fresh cilantro

Put about 1¾ cups or a few tablespoons more water in a kettle and bring to a boil.

Put the oil in a large, heavy, nonstick frying pan and set over medium heat. When hot, add the asafetida. A second later, add the mustard seeds. As soon as the mustard seeds begin to pop, a matter of seconds, add the red chile and *chana dal*. Stir and fry until the *chana dal* turns reddish in color. Add the curry leaves and stir once. Now add the shallots or onion. Stir and fry until the pieces turn brown at the edges. Now put in the ginger and green chiles. Give 1 or 2 good stirs and add the cabbage and peas. Stir and fry for 2 minutes. Add 3 tablespoons of water, cover, and turn the heat down to low. Cook for 3 to 4 minutes. Uncover, turn the heat up to medium again, and add the semolina or Cream of Wheat. Stir and fry it for 4 to 5 minutes, or until the granules are golden. Now turn the heat down to low and add the salt. Slowly add boiling water, a little at a time, stirring it until it is absorbed before adding more. Keep doing this until you have used up the 1¾ cups of water. Take about 5 minutes to do this. If all the granules are not moistened, add another tablespoon or two of boiling water. Now, keep stirring and cooking over low heat, breaking up lumps with the back of a wooden spoon, for another 10 minutes, or until each grain is light and fluffy. Add the cilantro and stir for another minute. Serve hot or at room temperature.

SERVES 3 TO 4

Semolina "Risotto" (*Uppama*) with Cashews and Green Beans   INDIA

Here the semolina is lightly roasted first and then cooked along with nuts and vegetables in the traditional manner. This is a very useful technique when the vegetables need to be tenderized with a little water first.

¼ cup peanut or canola oil

1 cup semolina *(sooji)* or Cream of Wheat (the kind that cooks in 10 minutes)

½ teaspoon whole brown mustard seeds

1 teaspoon *chana dal* (or yellow split peas)

5 raw cashew nuts, split into halves lengthwise

1 to 2 whole dried hot red chiles

10 to 15 fresh curry leaves, if available

3 tablespoons finely chopped shallots or red onion

1 small carrot, peeled and cut into ¼-inch dice

10 green beans, cut crosswise into ¼-inch segments

6 tablespoons finely chopped tomato

¾ teaspoon salt

Put 2 tablespoons of the oil in a large, heavy, nonstick frying pan and set over medium heat. When hot, put in the semolina or Cream of Wheat. Stir and fry it for 4 to 5 minutes, or until it is golden. Remove it and set aside. Wipe out the pan.

Put 1¾ cups or a few tablespoons more water in a kettle and bring to a boil.

Put the remaining 2 tablespoons oil in the same frying pan that you used earlier and set over medium heat. When hot, add the mustard seeds. As soon as the mustard seeds begin to pop, a matter of seconds, add the *chana dal*. Stir and fry until the *chana dal* turns light brown in color. Add the cashews and red chile. Continue to stir and fry until the *chana dal* is reddish and the cashews are golden. Add the curry leaves and stir once. Now add the shallots or onion. Stir and fry until the pieces turn brown at the edges. Now add the carrot and green beans. Stir for 30 seconds. Add in the tomato. Stir another few seconds. Now add 6 tablespoons of water and bring to a simmer. Cover and turn the heat down to low. Simmer gently for 3 to 4 minutes, or until the carrots and beans are just tender.

Uncover, add the semolina or Cream of Wheat and salt, and stir well. Now turn the heat down to low. Slowly add boiling water, a little at a time, stirring it until it is absorbed before adding more. Keep doing this until you have used up the 1¾ cups of water. Take about 5 minutes to do this. If all the granules are not moistened, add another tablespoon or two of boiling water. Now, keep stirring and

(recipe continues)

cooking on low heat, breaking up lumps with the back of a wooden spoon, for another 10 minutes, or until each grain is light and fluffy. Serve hot. In the summer, this dish may be served at room temperature.

SERVES 3 TO 4

Semolina "Risotto" (*Uppama*) with Peanuts and Cilantro

INDIA

Curry leaves give this dish a wonderful flavor, but if you cannot get them, just leave them out.

¼ cup peanut or canola oil

Generous pinch of ground asafetida (optional)

1 teaspoon whole brown mustard seeds

1 to 2 whole dried hot red chiles

4 tablespoons raw, skinned peanuts

15 to 20 fresh curry leaves

3 tablespoons very finely chopped shallots or red onion

1 teaspoon finely grated peeled fresh ginger

1 to 2 teaspoons finely chopped fresh hot red or green chiles

4 tablespoons peas, defrosted if frozen

¼ teaspoon ground turmeric

1 cup semolina (*sooji*) or Cream of Wheat (the kind that takes 10 minutes to cook)

¾ teaspoon salt

2 tablespoons finely chopped fresh cilantro

Put about 1¾ cups or a few tablespoons more water in a kettle and bring to a boil.

Put the oil in a large, heavy, nonstick frying pan and set over medium heat. When hot, put in the asafetida. A second later, add the mustard seeds. As soon as the mustard seeds begin to pop, a matter of seconds, add the dried red chile and peanuts. Stir and fry until the peanuts are golden in color. Add the curry leaves and stir once. Now add the shallots or onion. Stir and fry until the pieces turn brown at the edges. Now add the ginger and fresh chiles. Give 1 or 2 good stirs and add the peas and turmeric. Stir and fry for 2 minutes. Add 4 tablespoons of water. Cover, turn the heat down to low, and cook for 4 to 5 minutes. Uncover, turn the heat to medium again, and add the semolina or Cream of Wheat. Stir and fry it for 4 to 5 minutes, or until the granules are golden. Now turn the heat down to low and add the salt. Slowly add boiling water, a little at a time, stirring it until it is absorbed before adding more. Keep doing this until you have used up the 1¾ cups of water. Take about 5 minutes to do this. If all the granules are not moistened, add another tablespoon or two of boiling water. Keep stirring and cooking on low heat, breaking up lumps with the back of a wooden spoon, for another 10 minutes, or until each grain is light and fluffy. Add the cilantro and stir for another minute. Serve hot. In the summer, this dish may be served at room temperature.

SERVES 3 TO 4

Semolina "Risotto" *(Uppama)* with Potato and Rosemary

We have a rosemary bush growing outside our door and I concocted this dish one day when I had a waxy boiled potato sitting in the refrigerator. Fresh rosemary is ideal here, but if you wish to use the dried kind, crush it well in a mortar.

3 tablespoons olive oil

½ teaspoon whole brown or yellow mustard seeds

2 teaspoons blanched almond slivers

1 medium boiled potato (4 to 5 ounces), cooled, then cut into ½-inch dice

½ teaspoon finely chopped fresh rosemary or ¼ teaspoon dried, crushed

Lots of freshly ground black pepper

1 cup (6 ounces) semolina *(sooji)* or Cream of Wheat (the kind that takes 10 minutes to cook)

¾ to 1 teaspoon salt

Put about 1¾ cups or a few tablespoons more water in a kettle and bring to a boil.

Put the oil in a large, heavy, nonstick frying pan and set over medium heat. When hot, put in the mustard seeds. As soon as the mustard seeds begin to pop, a matter of seconds, add the almonds. Stir and fry until the almonds barely turn golden. Now add the potato. Stir and fry until the pieces have browned on all sides. Add the rosemary and black pepper and stir once. Now add the semolina or Cream of Wheat and salt. Stir and fry it for 4 to 5 minutes, or until the granules are golden. Turn the heat down to low. Slowly add boiling water, a little at a time, stirring it until it is absorbed before adding more. Keep doing this until you have used up the 1¾ cups of water. Take about 5 minutes to do this. If all the granules are not moistened, add another tablespoon or two of boiling water. Now keep stirring and cooking on low heat for another 10 minutes, or until each grain is light and fluffy.

Serve hot. In the summer, this dish may be served at room temperature.

SERVES 3 TO 4

COUSCOUS

Couscous, a food that seems native to the Berbers of North Africa, is really a kind of pasta—little grains formed generally with semolina but sometimes with corn, crushed wheat, or barley as well. It may be eaten very simply with milk (sweetened with sugar and flavored with cinnamon) or with buttermilk, sometimes with the addition of steamed young fava beans and chunks of pumpkin and sometimes the spice mixture Zahtar (page 705).

In Algeria, couscous is combined with fennel shoots and young carrot tops and then eaten with a fiery tomato and potato sauce. At a Moroccan breakfast I have had a kind of porridge couscous made with crushed wheat and milk that had been accented delicately with orange flower water. In the Sahara desert, sweet dates might be mixed in with the couscous. Of course, there is also the couscous that we are all more familiar with, which is served with a variety of stews and hot sauces.

In Morocco, the best you can do for favored guests is to offer them couscous that you have made yourself—from scratch. Like any fresh pasta, it requires some practice. First of all, you need two kinds of semolina, a coarse-grained one and a very fine one. Here is how my teacher in Marrakech, a professional chef named Melle Derko Samira, went about it: She spread some coarse semolina in a large, round tray. Then she sprinkled some cold water over it. Next she put the flat of her right hand (palm down), on top of the semolina and began rotating it lightly to form tiny, bread crumb–like pellets. Now the fine semolina was sprinkled on the pellets and some more cold water as well. There was more rotating of the hand to firm up the pellets, which were then passed through a coarse sieve to ensure an even size. There was a final sifting in a fine sieve to get rid of any loose flour. The couscous was now ready to be steamed.

Steaming the couscous in the traditional manner not only requires a special, tall steamer with two sections, called a couscoussière, which is a ritual unto itself that takes about one and a half hours. When I wondered how working people had time to do this on a daily basis I was told that families generally had couscous on Fridays or at banquets—unless, of course, there was a housewife at home who did little else.

I have never seen a couscoussière for one person, or even for two; couscous is generally steamed in bulk. The bottom part of the utensil contains the soupy stew (or water) and the top, perforated section holds the couscous. Quite magically, the couscous never falls through the holes into the liquid below because of the pressure of the steam. In order to keep the pressure up and directed firmly toward the couscous, the two parts of the couscoussière are literally bandaged together with a damp cloth dusted with flour. There are three stages of steaming, with the bandage going on and off and on and off. (There is a threatening Arab proverb that warns you will never succeed if you do not put the bandage back on!) If properly done, each grain of couscous comes out separate and independent. It is quite a triumph.

My Moroccan notes on preparing couscous begin almost like a latter-day haiku—or a recipe from Macbeth's witches:

Sprinkle water twice and mix
Sprinkle water twice and mix
Sprinkle water twice and mix
Rub between the hands
No lumps
Steam . . .

The cooked couscous is mounded onto a large round tray in the shape of a hill. A crater is made in the center and the solids from the stew are placed in it. A few solids are also used to decorate the slopes of the "hill." Some liquid from the stew is ladled over the surrounding couscous. Diners sit around the large tray and share the meal, eating with their fingers; a fiery chili sauce is passed. At banquets, couscous is one of the last courses, coming well after the salads, dips, savory pies, roasts, and *tajines*.

There are several types of couscous. Here is what is available in our markets:

Instant or quick-cooking couscous: This is generally what most of us can manage to buy and to prepare. Sold in many supermarkets and most health food shops, it requires no actual cooking. Water is brought to a boil, 1¼ cups of water to every 1 cup of couscous, then the couscous dropped in along with some salt and oil. The pot is covered, left off the heat, and the couscous, rather like bulgur, is allowed to swell up inside. I like to let the pan sit for a good 15 minutes before I fluff up the couscous very thoroughly with a fork. It is greatly helped by the fluffing, increasing in volume with each stroke.

Whole wheat couscous: Sold now in most health food stores, this is rather dense and tastes of wheat. I use organic whole wheat couscous. The required ratio of boiling water to couscous, in volume, is 1:1. It cooks for about 5 minutes but does need to sit off the heat for 5 to 15 minutes and requires thorough fluffing with a fork to increase its volume.

I thought I could improve the texture of this couscous by trying to cook it by the long Moroccan method, but after 2 hours of sprinkling water, raking, and double steaming, I found no great improvement. What does improve the texture, and this I discovered almost by accident, was browning the grains in a little bit of oil before cooking them for 5 minutes.

Moroccan (semolina) couscous: This is available only in specialty stores that carry Middle Eastern and North African ingredients (see mail-order sources for details). It is this couscous that deserves to be cooked in a traditional couscoussière, using the traditional Moroccan method. I have tried improvising other utensils for the steaming but find that, for one reason or another, none are really adequate; a couscoussière has just the right shape to do the job properly. A detailed recipe can be found on page 499.

Israeli couscous: This is relatively new on the market and consists of small balls about the size of peppercorns. It is sold by Middle Eastern grocers where it is sometimes labeled Israeli Toasted Pasta, as the balls are very lightly toasted. I like to cook this couscous like most pastas, in lots of boiling, salted water. It cooks in 8 to 10 minutes, but you should check by removing one ball and biting into it.

If you like, you can undercook this couscous slightly (cooking it for just 7 minutes or so) and then add it to other vegetables that are in the process of being sautéed, where it will finish cooking and pick up exciting new flavors. I like this couscous very much.

Lebanese couscous: This also consists of small balls that have been toasted, but they are slightly larger in size than Israeli couscous. Lebanese couscous is sold by Middle Eastern grocers, often under the name *maghrebia* or *mograbeyeh*. *Maghreb* means "west" in Arabic, so to the Lebanese this is the pasta of the "western" nations, Algeria, Tunisia, and Morocco. It cooks slowly (taking about 25 minutes) and unevenly and is therefore, in my opinion, best for soups or stews where it turns into pea-sized dumplings. I have not used it in this chapter, but I mention it because you should not confuse it with Israeli couscous.

Instant (or Quick-Cooking) Couscous

Instant couscous, sometimes labeled "quick-cooking" couscous, is quite painless to prepare. It could be served with the Moroccan Casserole of Vegetables (page 309) or with Chickpeas, Pumpkin, and Raisins with Couscous (page 501). It may also be used to make a variety of salads.

You may use vegetable stock instead of water in this recipe.

1½ teaspoons salt

1 tablespoon olive oil

2 cups instant or quick-cooking couscous

Bring 2½ cups of water to a boil. Add the salt, oil, and couscous, stir once, and cover. Remove from the heat. Let the pot sit in a warm place for 5 minutes or longer. Fluff thoroughly with a fork and serve.

SERVES 4

Plain Whole Wheat Couscous

Sold now in health food and specialty shops, this is another quick-cooking variety. I only use the organic kind, which has a lovely wheat taste and a much denser texture than traditional semolina couscous.

1½ teaspoons salt

1 tablespoon olive oil

2 cups whole wheat couscous (preferably organic)

Bring 2 cups of water to a boil. Add the salt, oil, and couscous, stir once, cover tightly, and turn the heat to very, very low. Cook gently for 5 minutes. Remove from the heat and let the pot sit in a warm place for 5 minutes or longer (15 minutes is better). Fluff thoroughly with a fork and serve.

SERVES 4

Plain Toasted Whole Wheat Couscous

Lightly browning whole wheat couscous helps keep the grains separated and provides a delicious toasted taste.

Have boiling water at the ready before you start to cook.

1 tablespoon olive oil

2 cups whole wheat couscous (preferably organic)

1½ teaspoons salt

Put the oil in a heavy pan and set over medium heat. When hot, put in the couscous. Stir and fry for 2 to 3 minutes or until lightly browned. Add 2 cups of boiling water and the salt. Stir once, cover tightly, and turn the heat down to very, very low. Cook gently for 5 minutes. Remove from the heat and let the pot sit in a warm place for 15 minutes. Fluff thoroughly with a fork and serve.

SERVES 4

Whole Wheat Couscous with Sesame Seeds and Raisins

I love this earthy combination, which uses very Indian Gujarati seasonings.

2 tablespoons olive oil

½ teaspoon whole brown or yellow mustard seeds

2 teaspoons sesame seeds (I sometimes mix the black and beige kinds)

2 tablespoons coarsely chopped raw cashews

2 tablespoons raisins

2 cups whole wheat couscous (preferably organic)

1 to 2 teaspoons very finely chopped fresh green chile (optional)

1½ teaspoons salt

Put the oil in a small, heavy pan and set over medium heat. When the oil is very hot, put in the mustard and sesame seeds. As soon as they start to pop, a matter of seconds, put in the cashews. Stir once or twice and put in the raisins. Stir once and put in the couscous, chile, and salt. Stir for 1 to 2 minutes, or until the couscous is lightly toasted. Add 2 cups of water and bring to a boil. Stir once, cover tightly, and turn the heat down to very, very low. Cook gently for 5 minutes. Remove from the heat and let the pot sit in a warm place for 15 minutes or longer. Fluff thoroughly with a fork and serve.

SERVES 4

Whole Wheat Couscous with Cumin and Cauliflower

Here is a delicious way I have devised for serving this nutritious couscous to my family. It is very easy to prepare. Put some water to boil before you start to cook.

2 tablespoons olive oil

½ teaspoon whole cumin seeds

1 teaspoon peeled and very finely chopped fresh ginger

2 cups small cauliflower florets

1 teaspoon very finely chopped fresh hot green chile (with seeds)

2 cups whole wheat couscous (preferably organic)

1 tablespoon fresh lemon juice

1½ teaspoons salt

2 tablespoons finely chopped fresh cilantro

Put the oil in a heavy pan and set over medium-high heat. When hot, put in the cumin seeds. Let the cumin seeds sizzle for 10 seconds. Now put in the ginger and cauliflower. Stir and fry until the cauliflower has browned in spots. Add the chile and couscous. Stir and fry for 1 to 2 minutes, or until the couscous is lightly browned. Add 2 cups of boiling water, the lemon juice, and the salt. Stir once, cover tightly, and turn the heat down to very, very low. Cook gently for 5 minutes. Remove from the heat and let the pot sit in a warm place for 15 minutes. Add the cilantro. Fluff thoroughly with a fork and serve.

SERVES 4

Melle Derko Samira's

Traditional Moroccan Couscous MOROCCO
Sesku

Even though making this couscous takes time, it produces perfect results: light, delicate grains that do not lump together and are perfectly cooked in steam.

To be successful, you need two things—a coussoussière and Moroccan couscous. The first is a tall steaming contraption that has two parts. The bottom is a tall pot with a somewhat narrow neck. On this neck sits a basin with holes to allow steam to enter. There is usually a cover but this is not needed. Moroccan couscous is sold by Middle Eastern grocers.

You also should have on hand a large basin, high-sided baking tray, or a shallow but wide pan in which to aerate the couscous, and a long piece of muslin or cheesecloth. This is wetted, dipped in flour, and then wound around the neck of the coussoussière to keep the two parts of the utensil firmly "joined at the hip" as it were, so no steam can escape.

This couscous may be used in the dish Chickpeas, Pumpkin, and Raisins with Couscous (page 501), or served with the Potato Sauce in Speckled Green Couscous with Red Potato Sauce (page 502), the Moroccan Casserole of Vegetables (page 309), or any other bean or vegetable stew in this book.

Couscous is generally steamed over the soupy stews with which it is frequently served but, since no long-simmering meats and bones are called for in these recipes, I find it much easier to steam over water and cook my stews not in the bottom half of the coussoussière but in a separate pan on the side.

2 cups Moroccan couscous

½ teaspoon salt

2 teaspoons olive oil

(recipe continues)

Put the couscous in a large bowl. Cover with 6 cups of water. Quickly swish your hands around in the water, moving the couscous around, then pour most of the water out. Do this a few times and then drain the couscous in a fine sieve (or a coarser sieve lined with a cloth).

Fill the bottom of the couscoussière with water (make sure the water does not remotely touch the upper half). Take your dampened cloth dipped in flour and wrap it firmly where the two parts of the couscoussière meet so no steam can escape. Now set the water to boil over high heat.

Spread out the couscous in a large basin or other wide utensil in as thin a layer as possible and allow it to sit for 10 minutes to absorb the water and dry out a little. For the next 10 minutes, you need to aerate the couscous. Do this by picking up a small handful of couscous and rubbing it lightly between your two palms and then letting it cascade down from a little height. Stop every now and then to rake the couscous with your fingers and then pick some more up, rub it between your palms, and allow it to cascade down. By the end of this period all the grains will appear separated.

Put the couscous in the top half of the couscoussière (do not cover) and steam for 20 minutes. This is the first steaming.

Undo your cloth "bandage," lift up the top of the couscoussière by its handles, and empty the couscous into your basin again. Spread it out with a spoon. It will appear slightly lumpy and you might well think, "What was all that work for?" Wait. Sprinkle about ¼ cup of cold water on the couscous, a little at a time, as well as ½ teaspoon salt and the oil. Once again begin picking up some of the couscous, rubbing it between your palms and letting it cascade down and alternate this with finger-raking. Do this for 10 minutes. Stop if the couscous appears to have dried out but continue for another 5 to 10 minutes if it has not. Cover with a damp cloth and set aside.

Just before eating, make sure that there is water in the lower half of the couscoussière and attach the top firmly once more with the "bandage." Once the water is boiling, rake the couscous again, give it a final rub between the palms, and put it into the steamer. Steam for 20 minutes, uncovered. After the second steaming serve right away.

SERVES 4

Chickpeas, Pumpkin, and Raisins with Couscous

This superb dish consists of two parts—the couscous and the chickpea stew. I serve it with a simple green salad.

When I ate it in Morocco, the stew contained some fresh green shelled and peeled fava beans. These are not always easy to find so I have used zucchini instead, which cooks in as short a time as the fava. If you can find the fresh fava, do use them.

You may use canned chickpeas if you like; just rinse them out well and then use all the stock in the recipe. If you boil your own chickpeas, use the cooking liquid and enough vegetable stock to make up the required 3½ cups.

Even though there are quite a few ingredients here, the stew cooks very easily, is easily doubled, and is perfect for entertaining.

Ideally, you should serve the couscous-stew combination with harissa (Moroccan Chile-Garlic Paste, page 672), which is added at the table as needed. You may use any store-bought chile paste, such as a Caribbean pepper sauce or an Indonesian sambal oelek, *if you find that easier. Any chile paste should be thinned out with a little liquid from the stew.*

For the stew

1 teaspoon ground ginger

1 teaspoon ground cumin

1 teaspoon ground paprika

¼ teaspoon ground turmeric

¼ teaspoon cayenne

3 tablespoons olive oil

1 cinnamon stick, about 2 inches

1 medium onion, peeled and cut into fine half rings

3 medium tomatoes (12 ounces), peeled and finely chopped

2 cups cooked, drained chickpeas

2 heaped cups peeled, seeded pumpkin or butternut squash that has been cut into 1-inch dice (see page 287 if you need help)

2 tablespoons raisins

3½ cups vegetable stock

Salt to taste (this will depend upon the saltiness of your stock)

1 cup zucchini that has been cut into ½-inch dice

1 tablespoon finely chopped cilantro

1 tablespoon finely chopped fresh parsley

You also need

Instant Couscous (page 496) *or* Plain Whole Wheat Couscous (page 497) *or* Plain Toasted Whole Wheat Couscous (page 497) *or* Traditional Moroccan Couscous (page 499)

Moroccan Chile-Garlic Paste (page 672) or any hot sauce, thinned out with a little liquid from the stew

(recipe continues)

Combine the ginger, cumin, paprika, turmeric, and cayenne in a small cup and set aside.

Put the oil in a good-sized pan and set over medium-high heat. When hot, put in the cinnamon stick. Stir for a few seconds and put in the onion. Stir and fry the onion about 3 minutes, or until it is medium brown. Now, put the reserved mixed spices in the cup. Stir once and quickly put in the tomatoes. Stir and cook for 3 to 4 minutes, or until the tomatoes have softened. Add the chickpeas, pumpkin or squash, raisins, stock, and salt and bring to a simmer. Cover, turn the heat down to low, and cook for 13 to 15 minutes, or until the pumpkin is just tender when pierced with the point of a knife. Add the zucchini and simmer uncovered for another 5 minutes, stirring gently now and then. Add the cilantro and parsley just before serving.

To serve: Put a mound of couscous on each plate. Make a well in the center and, using a slotted spoon, put some of the solids from the stew in the well. Dampen the couscous generously with some of the sauce. Pass the hot sauce on the side.

SERVES 4

Speckled Green Couscous with Red Potato Sauce   TUNISIA

This is an amazing dish where the finely chopped greens are steamed first in the couscoussière, then partially cooked couscous is spread over them and steamed until it, too, is ready. The somewhat verdant couscous is served with a fiery red sauce containing potatoes and onions.

The greens are unusual. Tunisians use the fine, feathery shoots that grow from the sides of fennel stalks and very young carrot tops as well as onion stalks and cilantro. Not being able to get some of these items, I have improvised with dill and finely chopped arugula.

As far as the couscous is concerned, you may cook it according to the recipe for Traditional Moroccan Couscous (page 499). If you wish to do this, go through with the first steaming of your couscous. Empty it into your basin and go through with its salting, oiling, and aerating. While it is drying, spread the mixture of chopped parsley, cilantro, dill, scallions, and arugula in the steamer section of the couscoussière and steam for 10 minutes. Now put in the couscous and steam for 20 minutes. Once done, you can upturn the steamer onto a serving platter so the greens are on top or you can toss the greens and couscous together.

I have used instant couscous here, but you must make sure that you separate all the grains with a fork when done.

You can add green beans and carrots to the potato sauce if you like. This sauce, in Tunisia, is very hot. They even put some harissa (Moroccan Chile-Garlic Paste, page 672) into it. However, what I often do is keep the sauce mild and ladle some of the liquid from it into a small bowl to which I add lots of extra cayenne (or better still, if you can find it, coarsely crushed Aleppo pepper, sold by Middle Eastern grocers or the very red, coarsely crushed chiles sold by Korean grocers). This I pass on the side.

For the potato sauce

3 tablespoons olive oil

1 medium onion, peeled and coarsely chopped

5 garlic cloves, peeled and crushed

2 tablespoons tomato paste

1 teaspoon ground cumin

1 teaspoon ground coriander

1 teaspoon paprika (make sure it is nice and red)

¼ teaspoon cayenne

12 ounces boiling potatoes, peeled and cut into 1 × ½ × ½-inch pieces

1½ teaspoons salt, or to taste

For the couscous

1½ teaspoons salt

1 tablespoon olive oil or unsalted butter

8 tablespoons finely chopped parsley

4 tablespoons finely chopped cilantro

4 tablespoons finely chopped dill

4 scallions (green sections only), cut crosswise into very fine rings

½ cup finely chopped arugula

2 cups instant or quick-cooking couscous

For the extra-hot sauce

1 to 2 teaspoons cayenne or as suggested above

Make the potato sauce. Put the oil in a medium pan and set over medium-high heat. When hot, put in the onion and stir and fry for a minute. Put in the garlic, stir and fry for 30 seconds, then put in the tomato paste. Stir it for a minute, then add the cumin, coriander, paprika, and cayenne. Stir once and put in 4 cups of water, the potatoes, and salt. Stir and bring to a boil, then cover and cook about 30 minutes, or until the potatoes are tender. Taste for salt.

Make the couscous. Bring 2½ cups of water to a boil. Add the salt, oil, parsley, cilantro, dill, scallions, and arugula. Cover, turn the heat down to low, and simmer gently for 10 minutes. Add the couscous. Stir once and cover. Remove from the heat and let the pot sit in a warm place for 5 minutes or longer. Fluff thoroughly with a fork.

Make the hot sauce. Put the cayenne in a small bowl. Ladle in about ¼ cup of the liquid from the potato sauce and mix.

SERVES 4

Israeli Couscous with Asparagus and Fresh Mushrooms

I make a very elegant dish using a mixture of fresh morel mushrooms (you only need 2 or 3 so this will not break the bank!), fresh shiitake mushrooms, and plain mushrooms. Any combination of mushrooms will do; you may even use all plain ones.

Serve this dish by itself, with a salad on the side. It may also be served as a first course and should feed 5 to 6 people.

Salt

2 cups Israeli couscous

3 tablespoons olive oil

1 medium shallot (½ ounce), peeled and finely chopped

1 small garlic clove, peeled and finely chopped

2 large white mushrooms (2 ounces), sliced thinly lengthwise

4 to 5 fresh shiitake mushrooms (2 ounces), stems removed and the caps thinly sliced

2 or 3 fresh morel mushrooms (1 ounce), halved lengthwise, then cut crosswise into ¼-inch slices

½ pound asparagus (of medium thickness), trimmed, peeled, and cut into 1-inch sections

½ cup vegetable stock

¼ cup dry white vermouth

Freshly ground black pepper

3 tablespoons grated Parmigiano-Reggiano cheese

2 tablespoons finely chopped fresh parsley

Bring 4 quarts of water to a rolling boil. Add 1½ tablespoons of salt and stir, then add the couscous. Let it boil rapidly for about 7 minutes, or until it is almost but not quite ready; it should have a hard core in its very center. Drain the couscous quickly and then rinse it thoroughly under cold running water, turning it over several times. Leave in a sieve or colander.

Put the oil in a large sauté pan or large frying pan (preferably nonstick) and set over high heat. When hot, put in the shallot and garlic. Stir for 20 seconds and put in all the mushrooms. Stir rapidly for about 1 minute, or until the mushrooms look satiny. Now put in the asparagus. Stir for 30 seconds, then add the stock, vermouth, and about ⅛ teaspoon salt. Bring to a boil, cover, and keep cooking on high heat for 2½ minutes. Put in the partially cooked couscous and cook, uncovered, for another 2½ minutes on high heat, stirring frequently. Turn off the heat. Check the salt. You will probably need about ¼ teaspoon more. Add the salt, pepper, cheese, and parsley. Stir to mix and serve immediately.

SERVES 3 TO 4

Mock Lamb Curry

Seitan may be made into almost anything. How about a lamb curry? Serve it with rice, dal *dishes, and a full complement of chutneys,* poppadums, *and relishes!*

Prepare all your ingredients first. Measure out all the spices you require and keep them near you. They will go into the pan at a fast clip.

You may add boiled potatoes to this dish, if you like.

3 tablespoons peanut or canola oil

3 whole cardamom pods

1 cinnamon stick (about 2 inches)

1 smallish onion (3 ounces), peeled and very finely chopped

3 garlic cloves, peeled and crushed to a pulp

1 (2-inch) piece of fresh ginger, peeled and grated to a pulp

1 teaspoon ground coriander

1 teaspoon ground cumin seeds

¼ teaspoon cayenne

¼ teaspoon ground turmeric

4 tablespoons plain yogurt

1 medium tomato, peeled and finely chopped

8 ounces seitan, drained

About 1½ cups vegetable stock

Salt

½ teaspoon commercial garam masala

4 tablespoons heavy cream

2 tablespoons cilantro, for garnishing

Put the oil in a medium pan and set over medium-high heat. When hot, put in the cardamom and cinnamon. Stir once and put in the onion. Stir and fry until the onion starts to brown. Put in the garlic and ginger and stir for 30 seconds. Now put in the coriander, cumin, cayenne, and turmeric. Stir a few times. Put in 1 tablespoon of the yogurt and stir until it disappears. Put in the rest of the yogurt the same way, a tablespoon at a time. Now put in the tomato and stir until it softens and thickens. Add the seitan, stock, and, after tasting, some salt as needed. Bring to a boil. Cover, turn the heat to low, and simmer 15 minutes. Add the garam masala and cream and stir them in. Garnish with the cilantro before serving.

SERVES 2

Mock Minced Chicken

Here I have used seitan—the prepared wheat gluten found in the refrigerated section of health food shops—to attempt a quick sauced dish that may be had with pasta or bread. A Mediterranean bean dish could be served on the side.

3 tablespoons canola or peanut oil

2 garlic cloves, peeled and very finely chopped

1 smallish onion (3 ounces), peeled and very finely chopped

2 medium tomatoes, very finely chopped

1/2 teaspoon dried oregano

1/2 teaspoon dried thyme

1/8 teaspoon cayenne

8 ounces seitan, drained and cut into 1/4-inch pieces

1 cup vegetable stock

1/2 teaspoon salt, or to taste

Put the oil in a medium pan and set over medium-high heat. When hot, put in the garlic and onion and stir until just beginning to brown. Put in the tomatoes and stir for 1 to 2 minutes, or until they are soft. Add the oregano, thyme, cayenne, seitan, stock, and salt. Bring to a boil. Cover and simmer very gently for 15 minutes.

SERVES 2

Wild Rice

Also known as Indian rice or water oats, wild rice is not a rice at all but, according to the *Encyclopedia Britannica,* "a coarse, annual grass, the grain of which has long been used as an important food by various Indian tribes and early settlers in North America. It is commonly found on the muddy bottom in fresh to brackish water along shores, streams, or in lakes and swampy places from the Atlantic Coast west to the Mississippi Valley."

Nutty and crunchy, wild rice is expensive. Once hulled, the long black grains look like dark pine needles. Native Americans used to gather them by paddling in their boats until they were well under the tall grasses, then bending the ripe stalks over the boats and beating the seed-filled tops until they yielded their bounty. Much of the bounty fell into the water (thus ensuring the next year's supply) but enough was gathered for home use and sale. Today, even though mechanical harvesters manage to catch more of the yield, old methods of harvesting still yield the best results, keeping the cost of wild rice high. Perhaps because of this, it is sometimes mixed with brown rice or other grains and packaged before being sold to consumers.

Wild rice is simple enough to cook. I soak it in double the volume of water for 1 hour and then cook it in the same water for 1 hour. Some of the grains split open as they cook but the rice remains crunchy and fairly firm.

Once cooked, wild rice may be combined quickly with any lightly sautéed vegetables such as mushrooms, carrots, peas, asparagus, green beans, or peppers.

It is good to remember that wild rice not only has more protein than ordinary rice but that its proteins are more complete.

Plain Wild Rice

I find that presoaking wild rice helps to cook it faster and give it a better texture. You may make salads with this cooked wild rice (add diced peppers, scallions, lots of parsley, and a dressing); you could use it to stuff vegetables (sauté shallots with mushrooms, then add some wild rice) or use it in a casserole (combine it first with sautéed corn and tomatoes, mix in some cheese, and bake as a casserole).

1 cup wild rice, washed and drained

½ teaspoon salt

1 teaspoon olive oil

Put the rice in a bowl. Add 2 cups of water and leave it to soak for 1 hour. Put the rice and its soaking liquid in a heavy pan. Add the salt and oil. Mix and bring to a boil. Cover, turn the heat to very low, and cook for 1 hour. If any liquid is left at the bottom of the pan, remove the lid and boil it away.

SERVES 2 TO 3

Wild Rice with Brown Rice

A simple combination that may be served with all manner of beans, vegetables, and salads.

½ cup long-grain brown rice, washed and drained

½ cup wild rice, washed and drained

2 teaspoons olive oil

2 scallions, cut into fine rounds (use both green and white sections)

2 tablespoons finely chopped flat-leaf parsley

½ teaspoon salt

(recipe continues)

Put the 2 rices in a bowl. Cover with 2 cups of water and leave to soak for 1 hour.

Put the oil in a small, heavy pan and set over medium heat. When hot, put in the scallions. Stir it around for 30 seconds. Put in the parsley and stir once. Now put in the 2 rices and their soaking liquid as well as the salt and bring to a boil. Cover tightly, turn the heat to very low, and cook gently for 1 hour.

SERVES 2 TO 4

Wild Rice Sautéed with Corn, Mushrooms, and Asparagus

This elegant dish can easily be doubled in quantity. Serve with a salad. In it I have combined thyme and oriental sesame oil, which go together well.

If you have access to fresh wild mushrooms, use them instead of the cultivated ones. The corn kernels needed here may be taken off the cob in season; otherwise frozen, defrosted corn may be used. If asparagus is not available, use tender green beans, cut into 1-inch lengths.

2 tablespoons olive oil

1 small garlic clove, peeled and finely chopped

1 medium shallot (½ ounce), peeled and finely chopped

3 large mushrooms, thinly sliced

½ pound asparagus (of medium thickness), trimmed, peeled, and cut into 1-inch sections

1 cup corn kernels

¼ cup vegetable stock

¼ teaspoon or more salt

Freshly ground black pepper

½ teaspoon dried thyme

Plain Wild Rice, cooked according to the recipe on page 507

1 teaspoon oriental sesame oil

2 teaspoons roasted sesame seeds (page 734), optional

Put the oil in a large sauté pan or large frying pan and set over medium-high heat. When hot, put in the garlic and shallot. Stir and cook for 10 seconds. Put in the mushrooms and stir and cook for about 30 seconds, or until silken. Add the asparagus. Stir and cook for 30 seconds. Add the corn, stir once, then pour in the stock and bring to a simmer. Cover, turn the heat to medium, and cook for 3 minutes. Uncover, add the salt, pepper, and thyme. If there is a lot of liquid left, boil most of it away by turning up the heat a bit. Stir in the wild rice. Drizzle the sesame oil over the top and stir to mix. Serve sprinkled with the roasted sesame seeds, if you like.

SERVES 3 AS A MAIN DISH; 4 AS A SIDE DISH

Wild Rice Stew with Pearl Onions, Lentils, and Green Beans

A simple, light stew that may be served all by itself with some good bread and butter.

Mushrooms, wild or cultivated, may be added to the stew at the same time as the vegetables. In the spring, I love to put in four fresh morels that have been halved lengthwise.

When adding the cooked rice, put in only half of it to start, then add more according to the density you prefer.

2 tablespoons olive oil

12 to 16 small pearl onions, peeled and left whole

½ cup green lentils

4 cups vegetable stock

2 medium carrots (5 ounces in all), peeled and cut into ¾-inch-thick slices

2 smallish zucchini (½ pound in all), cut into ¾-inch rounds

20 green beans, cut into 1-inch lengths

Salt

Freshly ground black pepper

Plain Wild Rice, cooked according to the recipe on page 507

2 medium tomatoes, peeled, seeded, and cut into ¼-inch dice

2 tablespoons finely chopped parsley

Put the oil in a wide pan and set over medium-high heat. When hot, put in the onions. Stir and fry them until they are reddish-brown. Add the lentils and the stock and bring to a boil. Cover, turn the heat to low, and simmer for 35 minutes, or until the lentils are tender. Add the carrots, zucchini, and green beans as well as some salt (this will depend upon the saltiness of your stock) and pepper and bring to a simmer. Simmer uncovered about 5 minutes, or until the vegetables are just tender. Add as much of the rice as you like as well as the tomatoes and just heat through. Sprinkle the parsley over the top when serving.

SERVES 4

Dairy

Eggs   *512*
   Soft- and Hard-boiled Eggs   513
   Poached Eggs   519
   Fried Eggs   524
   Scrambled Eggs and Omelets   525
   Frittatas and Egg Pies   536

Yogurt   *544*

Yogurt Cheeses   *556*

Homemade Cheeses   *560*

Our associations with the word *dairy* help place us in this world. In much of the West, dairy conjures up a past and present of pastoral idylls, with farmhouse and cow, brown eggs, and, in the golden "olden" days, saucy or blushing milkmaids. Even when we have a room painted a "cream" color, those pleasant associations remain because words like *creamery* and *buttery* are embedded in our hearts even as we try to push them away from our thoughts.

In India, dairy begins to have religious, even sensuous and musical reverberations, as Hindus picture Lord Krishna, the cowherd, who loved—indeed, stole—butter as a child and, as an adult, dallied with the milkmaidens while playing his flute (sometimes) in the North Indian countryside. (Have we not seen this in hundreds of paintings, sculptures, and dance performances? Every Indian can sing at least one hymn in medieval Hindi about Krishna eating butter.) Eggs are never part of this picture even though they are very much a part of the Indian culinary scene. Somehow, in the Indian view of "dairy," eggs have been removed and placed elsewhere. Many Indian vegetarians do not eat eggs at all.

The Jewish dietary world also separates milk products from eggs. Eggs are *parve* or neutral and may be eaten with all meals. Milk products (*milchig* or dairy), on the other hand, may be eaten with all neutral foods but may not be combined with meat products *(fleischig)* as that violates a Torah admonition not to "boil a kid in its mother's milk" (Exod. 23:19; Exod. 34:26; Deut. 14:21).

In much of East Asia, where lactose intolerance is a fact of life and soy milk products have more than filled in for milk products, the concept of dairy does not even exist. Eggs are still loved and transformed into savory custards with stocks, savory omelets, and into dozens of toppings for rice, but milk is rarely used in traditional cooking. That does seem to be changing. Japan, for example, has, in the last thirty years, increased its consumption of milk products dramatically.

Mexico had no milk products until the arrival of the Spaniards. Local cuisines since then often seem to be making up for the lost centuries with heavy doses of sour cream and cheeses in both everyday and party foods.

Dairy dishes—and here the word is used in its loosest Western sense—are scattered throughout this book. You will find some in the Drinks section, for example. What you will find in the chapter here are egg recipes from around the world as well as some of my favorite dishes prepared with homemade cheeses and yogurt.

Eggs

When looking for a quick, easy meal, how many of us turn without thought to eggs: an omelet, perhaps with herbs, served with a salad, or a pair of eggs, scrambled quickly and served on toast.

I have always found great satisfaction in a single boiled egg, done just to my taste with the white set but the yolk still flowing thick and molten. I serve myself in an old egg cup, slicing off the top of the egg and sprinkling some salt and pepper over the opening. I wait, each time with equal excitement, for my first mouthful, which must include a bit of the white, a bit of the yolk, and a touch of the salt and pepper; a bite of toast has to follow. My mother always kept a special salt on the table that included some ground and roasted cumin seeds. This went well with most things but on eggs, it was heaven. I do the same. You will always find my mother's salt mixture on my table, especially at breakfast (page 705, An Indian Salt Mixture).

While I have always been partial to boiled or scrambled eggs, my father was strictly a fried egg man, and he ate them strangely. He would work all around the egg yolks, eating first one white, then the second. When only the yolks were left, glistening yellow orbs dotted with my mother's salt, he would ease his fork under one, pick it up whole, and deposit it in his mouth. He chewed slowly and long. The fork would go next to the second yolk, which would also be picked up whole, shaking like Jell-O, and it too would disappear. My five brothers and sisters and I were mesmerized. More chewing would follow, with the veins near my father's temples throbbing all the time. My father loved his fried eggs. He ate them in total silence. If you asked him a question before he started on his eggs, he would answer only when he had finished. If he himself were in midstory at the start, we would all have to wait until he had finished his egg ritual to hear its conclusion.

Eggs may be quick and easy to cook, but they require care and timing.

For poached, boiled, and fried eggs, use the freshest eggs you can find or the top-grade ones. They fill their shells if they are boiled and so have a perfect "egg" shape with no depression at the top. Because the white and yolks are well bound together at this stage, they hold their shapes when broken into a pan for frying and poaching. However, all upsides have a downside and very fresh hard-boiled eggs are sometimes hard to peel, as the shell can stick to the whites.

Eggs may be poached and covered with all manner of sauces or served over cooked vegetables, or they may be poached in the sauce itself as is common in Irani villages. They may be scrambled with a variety of spicy seasonings (coconut, chiles, ginger, mustard seeds) as is common in India or with cooked vegetables such as cauliflower, asparagus, and the best of wild mushrooms.

In many parts of the world they are made into pancakes or cakelike pies. Known variously as *kookoo* (Iran), *tortilla* (Spain), *torta, tortina,* and *frittata* (Italy), and *eggah* (Middle East), these pies sometimes have a little flour in them and sometimes not. They may be flavored with herbs, or with tomatoes, zucchini, mushrooms, potatoes, asparagus, or even sliced and fried artichoke hearts. In India, they are frequently flavored with fresh coconut and fresh curry leaves.

Because their own flavor is mild, the fat used in the preparation of eggs makes a great difference. Tuscan fried eggs cooked in generous amounts of excellent virgin olive oil (sometimes with a clove of garlic slipped into the oil) have one flavor whereas a French-style omelet cooked in butter has another. French toast in America is all buttery, cinnamony, and sweet whereas the French toast of Bengal with its strong taste of onion, green chiles, and mustard oil is a world apart. The Far East, where eggs are sometimes seasoned with drops of oriental sesame oil, soy sauce, and even scallions, offers yet another group of flavorings.

What you serve with eggs also affects their final taste. In the Mediterranean, eggs are generally eaten with crusty bread: The last mouthful is invariably part egg and part olive oil, cleaned off the plate with a bit of bread. Middle Eastern egg pies are often served with yogurt and naanlike flatbreads. In India, hard-boiled eggs are thrown into curry sauces and served with rice, while scrambled eggs may be served with a range of flatbreads. In Japan, eggs (poached or made into omelets) are often placed decorously over a bowl of rice or noodles to make meals-in-a-bowl. There is always a little lubrication for the rice in the form of a sweet-salty sauce or a stock. In Indonesia, Thailand, and even Korea, flat omelets are cut into fine strips and used to both garnish and flavor all manner of foods from soups to fried rice. The eggs leave just a hint of taste and texture, while adding immensely to the nutritional value.

For reasons of safety, buy eggs from a reliable source and keep them refrigerated until you are ready to use them. Leaving eggs decorative in a bowl in the kitchen, in loving memory of lives in old farmhouses, is no longer a sound idea.

SOFT- AND HARD-BOILED EGGS

Use only fresh, top-grade eggs for boiling.

Soft-boiled eggs: Fill a pan with enough water to cover all the eggs you wish to cook. Bring to a boil, then turn the heat down to low so that there are just a few gentle bubbles rising to the surface. Now lower as many eggs as you wish to boil, one at a time, into the water with the help of a spoon. Set your timer for 4 minutes if you want the whites soft and semiclear, 5 to 5½ minutes if you want the whites almost but not quite set, and 6 minutes if you want the whites fully set. (I like the 5½-minute egg.) The yolks get consistently thicker with each passing minute but they remain runny even at 6 minutes. Remove the eggs with a spoon and serve immediately, either in egg cups or remove the eggs from their shells and serve them in a cup. These eggs are generally eaten with just salt and pepper, though some people, like my husband, throw in a pat of butter as well. In Eastern Asia, soft-boiled eggs are served in a cup mixed with a few drops of soy sauce and oriental sesame oil. At my home in India, we served them with a cumin-flavored salt mixture (see An Indian Salt Mixture, page 705).

Hard-boiled (hard-cooked) eggs: These eggs have firm, opaque whites and firm yolks that set into balls. To make them, fill a pan with enough water to cover all the eggs you wish to cook. Bring to a boil. Turn the heat down to low so that there are just a few gentle bubbles rising to the surface. Now lower as many eggs as you wish to boil, one at a time, into the water with the help of a spoon. Set your timer for 12 minutes. Once the eggs are done, remove them immediately with a spoon and run them very briefly under cold water if you wish to eat them hot or you may run them under cold water long enough to cool them off thoroughly if you wish to eat them cold. They may now be cracked and peeled or left in their shells and refrigerated if you wish to take them on a picnic.

Hard-boiled eggs may be put into curry sauces; they may be deviled, their yolks creamed with mustard and then mounded back into the halved whites; they may be fried in a Southeast Asian style and put into fragrant chile sauces; or the shells may be cracked and eggs cooked in tea or soy sauce in a Chinese manner that leaves the whites quite marbled.

Soy Sauce Eggs with Rosemary

The Chinese have a wonderful way with hard-boiled eggs. Once the whites are set, they remove them from the hot water and lightly crack the shells all over with a spoon. They are then put back into a pan with a braising liquid and allowed to cook slowly for about 1½ hours. When the shells are removed, beautifully marbled eggs are revealed. The flavor penetrates as well, making eggs that are as delicious as they are pretty—perfect for picnics and buffets.

I have been making these soy sauce eggs for decades but one year, having a rather healthy rosemary bush on the patio, I decided to throw a small sprig of rosemary into the braising liquid. I loved the result.

8 eggs

3 cups vegetable stock

¾ cup soy sauce

3 thin slices of fresh ginger

2 scallions, cut crosswise into about 4 pieces, both green and white sections

1 whole star anise

A small sprig of fresh rosemary

¼ cup Chinese Shao Hsing wine or dry sherry

4 tablespoons sugar

Salt, if needed

Wash the eggs gently so they are clean and shiny. Fill a small pan with enough water to cover the 8 eggs and bring to a boil. Turn the heat down to low so that there are just a few gentle bubbles rising to the surface. Now lower the eggs, one at a time, into the water with the help of a spoon. Set a timer for 6 minutes.

Once the eggs have cooked for 6 minutes, drain them and cover with cold water for a minute. Now drain the eggs again and tap each of them gently to create a network of small, connected cracks all over.

In the same pan that you used before, combine the stock, soy sauce, ginger, scallions, star anise, rosemary, wine, sugar, and about ¾ teaspoon salt if the stock was unsalted. Bring to a gentle simmer. Add the eggs, cover, and simmer gently for 1½ hours, turning the eggs now and then.

If you wish to eat the eggs hot and immediately, remove them from the braising liquid. Strain the liquid and peel the eggs while they are still hot. Halve the eggs and serve the braising liquid as a dipping sauce. (You may also refrigerate the eggs and reheat them in their braising liquid the next day.)

If you wish to eat the eggs cold, leave them in the braising liquid and refrigerate overnight in the shells. Shell and serve, either with the cold braising liquid as a dip or, on a picnic, simply with a little salt.

MAKES 8 EGGS

Cheryl Rathkopf's

Sri Lankan White Egg Curry SRI LANKA

Biththara Kiri Hodi

For this dish, you need to make the coconut milk sauce on page 661 and then slip hard-boiled eggs into it. Serve with rice and condiments.

4 freshly prepared hard-boiled eggs   Coconut Milk Sauce (page 661)

Put the eggs in cold water as soon as they are done and then peel them. Set the coconut milk sauce over low heat in a shallow saucepan. Make 3 to 4 long lengthwise slits in the eggs without going to the very tip or the very bottom and making sure you cut all the way to the yolk but no further. Slip the eggs into the sauce and simmer gently for 3 to 4 minutes, spooning the sauce over them and turning the eggs in the sauce every now and then. Serve hot.

SERVES 2 TO 4

Tea Eggs

Cha Yeh Dan

Here the eggs are cooked in black tea and seasonings rather than soy sauce. These eggs, too, may be served hot or cold and are perfect for picnics.

8 eggs

3 tablespoons soy sauce

1 tablespoon salt

3 thin slices of fresh ginger

3 tea bags (any black tea)

1 whole star anise

1 tablespoon sugar

Wash the eggs gently so they are clean and shiny. Fill a small pan with enough water to cover the 8 eggs and bring to a boil. Turn the heat down to low so that there are just a few gentle bubbles rising to the surface. Now lower the eggs, one at a time, into the water with the help of a spoon. Set a timer for 6 minutes.

Once the eggs have cooked for 6 minutes, drain them and cover with cold water for a minute. Now drain the eggs again and tap each of them gently to create a network of small, connected cracks all over.

In the same pan that you used before, combine the soy sauce, salt, ginger, tea bags, star anise, sugar, and 3¾ cups of water. Bring to a gentle simmer. Add the eggs, cover and simmer gently for 1½ hours, turning the eggs now and then.

If you wish to eat the eggs hot and immediately, remove them from the braising liquid. Strain the liquid and peel the eggs while they are still hot. Halve the eggs and serve the braising liquid as a dipping sauce.

If you wish to eat the eggs cold, leave them in the braising liquid and refrigerate overnight in the shells. Shell and serve, either with the cold braising liquid as a dip or, on a picnic, simply with a little salt.

The eggs may also be eaten hot the next day. Just heat them gently in their braising liquid. Then peel them and strain the braising liquid to use as a dip.

MAKES 8 EGGS

Hard-Boiled Eggs in a Tomato-Cream Sauce

INDIAN STYLE

Perfect for brunch or a late supper, this creamy dish is fine with toast, thick slices of grilled Tuscan-type bread, or French bread. You may also serve this with Indian breads such as naan or store-bought pita bread.

If you cannot get fresh curry leaves, just leave them out and go on to the next step. This makes a generous amount of sauce, so you can vary the number of eggs from 8 to 12, depending on your appetite.

2 tablespoons peanut or canola oil

½ teaspoon whole cumin seeds

10 fresh curry leaves, if available

1 medium shallot, peeled and finely chopped

1 teaspoon very finely grated fresh ginger

1 garlic clove, peeled and crushed to a pulp

2 cups peeled, seeded, and finely chopped tomatoes (if you need information on how to do this, see page 300)

1 fresh hot green chile, finely chopped (use more or less, as desired)

¼ teaspoon cayenne, or to taste

1 teaspoon ground roasted cumin seeds (page 724)

1 teaspoon garam masala (store-bought is fine)

1 cup heavy cream

2 tablespoons finely chopped fresh cilantro

¾ teaspoon salt, or to taste

Freshly ground black pepper

8 to 12 hard-boiled eggs, peeled

Put the oil in a large, preferably nonstick frying pan or sauté pan and set over medium-high heat. When hot, put in the whole cumin seeds. Let them sizzle for 10 seconds, then put in the curry leaves. Stir once and add the shallot. Stir for 30 seconds and then add the ginger and garlic. Stir for 10 seconds and add the tomatoes, chile, cayenne, roasted cumin, and garam masala. Stir and cook the tomatoes for a minute. Cover, turn the heat down to low, and simmer gently for 10 minutes. Now add the cream, cilantro, and salt and pepper to taste. Bring to a simmer. Simmer gently, uncovered, for 2 minutes. Taste for the balance of flavors. Add the eggs and cook gently another minute, turning them now and then. When serving, spoon some of the sauce over the eggs.

SERVES 4

Egg Curry, Goan Style

Unday Ki Kari

This wonderfully spicy egg curry can be served with rice or crusty bread.

Instead of cutting the eggs in halves, as I have done here, you could also leave them whole. Just cut 3 or 4 long slits in the whites, going all the way to the yolk, to allow the sauce to penetrate. The slits should stop short of the very top and bottom of the eggs.

3 tablespoons peanut or canola oil

1 medium red onion (4 ounces), coarsely chopped

3 to 6 fresh hot green chiles, coarsely chopped

2 teaspoons peeled and coarsely chopped garlic

1 tablespoon peeled and very finely chopped fresh ginger

1 teaspoon ground cumin seeds

1 teaspoon ground coriander seeds

1 teaspoon cayenne

¼ teaspoon ground turmeric

2 medium tomatoes (about 10 ounces), chopped

2 teaspoons tomato paste

½ teaspoon whole brown mustard seeds

About 30 fresh curry leaves, if available

1½ cups coconut milk from a well-shaken can

1¼ teaspoons salt, or to taste

8 to 12 hard-boiled eggs, peeled and cut into halves lengthwise

1 lightly packed cup coarsely chopped fresh cilantro

Put 2 tablespoons of the oil in a large skillet and set over medium-high heat. When hot, add the red onion and stir and fry until lightly browned. Add the green chiles, stir and fry for another minute, then put in the garlic and ginger. Continue to stir and fry for 2 minutes. Add the cumin, coriander, cayenne, and turmeric, stir for 1 minute, then add the tomatoes and tomato paste and cook, stirring often, until the tomatoes have softened. Add ¾ cup of water and bring to a simmer. Cover and simmer gently for 5 minutes.

Empty the contents of the pan into a blender or food processor. Puree, pushing down with a rubber spatula if needed, until you have a paste.

Clean out the skillet you used earlier and heat the remaining 1 tablespoon oil over medium-high heat. When hot, put in the mustard seeds. As soon as they pop, a matter of seconds, put in the curry leaves. Five seconds later, add the paste from the blender, the coconut milk, and the salt. Stir again and bring to a simmer. Simmer gently for 5 minutes. Gently slip the hard-boiled eggs, cut sides up, into the sauce and simmer gently for 5 minutes, spooning the sauce over the eggs if needed. Scatter cilantro over the top before serving.

SERVES 6

Eggs in a Mulligatawny Sauce

Hard-boiled eggs in an interesting, flavorful sauce make a quick, easy meal. Then all you need is rice and a vegetable or salad. Here the eggs are served in a soup—mulligatawny soup—which kept thick (not thinned as suggested in the soup recipe) complements the eggs perfectly. You will need only about ½ recipe of Vegetarian Mulligatawny Soup, but you can freeze what you do not use or make just half the recipe.

1 tablespoon peanut or canola oil

½ teaspoon whole brown mustard seeds

3 cups Vegetarian Mulligatawny Soup
   (page 592)

8 hard-boiled eggs, peeled and halved
   lengthwise

Salt

Freshly ground black pepper

Squeeze of lime or lemon juice

Put the oil in a medium saucepan and set over medium-high heat. When hot, put in the mustard seeds. As soon as the mustard seeds begin to pop, a matter of seconds, put in the soup. Stir and bring to a simmer.

Pour the sauce into a shallow serving dish. Arrange the eggs in the sauce in a single layer, cut sides up, so that the tops are quite visible and uncovered by sauce. Sprinkle the eggs with a little salt and pepper. Sprinkle lime juice over the entire dish and serve.

SERVES 4

POACHED EGGS

I hate to say this, but fussy French culinary technique has made home cooks wary of poaching eggs. I love poached eggs and I do not care to have them served to me in neat oval shapes. In fact, the oval shape seems unnatural and unnecessary. I certainly do not like the taste of vinegar in the poaching water, a commonly suggested trick for coagulating the whites.

So how do I poach my eggs? This is a method I learned some decades ago in Japan. My eggs turn out looking like fried eggs, only instead of oil, I use water.

I use a nonstick frying pan, preferably with a lid. It is important that the pan be of a size that just accommodates the number of eggs being cooked with ease; it should not be too large or too small. For a single egg, you need a 5-inch frying pan. For 4 eggs, a 9-inch pan is best, although one that is a bit larger or smaller would also work.

Ideally, poached eggs should be served as soon as they are made. However, if you wish to hold them for a while, place them side by side on a lightly greased plate, which may be covered with an upturned plate and even refrigerated. When ready to eat, slip the eggs back into a frying pan filled with hot but not boiling water, keeping them in a single layer. As soon as they are warmed through, they may be removed with a slotted spoon and served.

Poached eggs may be served over all manner of cooked vegetables such as artichoke hearts, spinach, asparagus, and even lightly grilled tomato slices.

Put ¾ inch of water in a 9-inch nonstick frying pan and bring it to a low simmer. Break 4 eggs into the water in such a way that they sit side by side. Let the water simmer very gently until the egg whites are almost set. Now turn the heat off and cover very loosely. Allow the eggs to set to the consistency you like. Separate the eggs, lift them out of the water with a slotted spatula, and serve on toast or over vegetables as desired.

Poached Eggs Served in a Korean Manner

Here, I have used a simple soy sauce and sesame oil dressing for poached eggs, the kind I ate every day in Korea. For a meal, you could serve plain rice on the side as well as Green Salad with a Korean Dressing (page 631).

1 scallion, thinly sliced (use both green and
    white sections)

2 tablespoons soy sauce

2 tablespoons oriental sesame oil

½ teaspoon sugar

4 eggs, freshly poached according to
    directions above

Put the scallion rings in a bowl of cold water and refrigerate for 30 to 60 minutes. Drain and place on a dish towel. Wring out by bringing the ends of the cloth together and twisting. Put the scallion rings in a small serving bowl and toss to separate them.

Combine the soy sauce, sesame oil, and sugar in another small bowl. Beat well to mix. (Remember to mix again just before serving; all this can be done ahead of time.)

To serve, arrange the poached eggs on plates. Pass along the soy sauce mixture and scallion. Diners should dot their eggs with some of the sauce (as if it were salt) and some scallion.

SERVES 2 TO 4

Shamsi Davis'

Persian Eggs Poached
in a Tomato Sauce

IRAN

Omlette Gojay Farangi

The Persian gojay farangi, *or "foreign plums," are tomatoes and this simple peasant dish consists of eggs broken into a frying pan that is lined with a freshly made tomato sauce. It is generally eaten with flatbreads (such as naans or pita breads) as lunch or as a light supper.*

3 tablespoons olive oil, *ghee* (page 723), or
    unsalted butter

1 small onion (2 ounces), peeled and finely
    chopped

1 garlic clove, peeled and finely chopped

4 to 5 ripe medium tomatoes (about 2 pounds),
    peeled, seeded, and chopped (page 300)

Salt

Freshly ground black pepper

4 eggs

2 teaspoons very finely chopped chives

Put the oil in a 10-inch nonstick frying pan and set over medium-high heat. When hot, put in the onion and garlic. Stir and fry for a minute, then turn the heat to medium-low and continue to stir and cook another 3 to 4 minutes, or until the onion is golden. Add the tomatoes and bring to a simmer. Cook, uncovered, for 8 to 10 minutes, or until the sauce has thickened. Add about ¼ teaspoon salt or to taste and some black pepper and stir to mix. Now break an egg carefully into each "corner" of the pan, first pushing aside the tomato sauce in the area where the egg will land. Partially cover the pan and cook on medium-low heat until the eggs are done the way you desire them. Remove carefully to serving plates and serve garnished with the chives.

SERVES 2 TO 4

Variation

For a slightly spicier dish, omit the onions and instead add 1 dried hot red chile to the oil and stir once before cooking the garlic. Cook the sauce as above, then cook and serve the eggs, omitting the chives.

Poached Eggs over Artichoke Hearts with a White Sauce

A much-loved brunch dish in our house, this really consists of three parts. There are the artichoke hearts, which need to be prepared ahead of time and then just reheated. The eggs may be poached just before eating (which is what I prefer) or prepared ahead and reheated in hot water, as suggested on page 519. The sauce may also be made in advance (which is what I do) and then reheated. A film will form on the sauce as it waits, but do not worry; you can whisk it in.

For the sauce

3 tablespoons unsalted butter

1 tablespoon olive oil

1 tablespoon finely chopped shallots

¾ cup dry white vermouth

2 teaspoons fresh lemon juice

2 teaspoons cornstarch

1 cup heavy cream

½ cup vegetable stock

Scant ½ teaspoon salt

Freshly ground black pepper

Generous pinch of cayenne

1 tablespoon finely chopped fresh parsley

You also need

4 large artichoke hearts, precooked according to directions on pages 128 to 129

4 eggs, freshly poached according to directions on page 519

To make the sauce, put 1 tablespoon of the butter and the olive oil in a heavy saucepan and set over medium heat. When the butter has melted, put in the shallots and stir and fry for a minute; do not allow the shallots to brown. Add the vermouth and lemon juice, turn the heat up a bit, and boil the liquid down until you have about 4 tablespoons. Turn off the heat.

Put the cornstarch in a small bowl. Slowly add the cream and vegetable stock, stirring with a whisk as you go. Add this mixture to the saucepan with the shallots and vermouth. Bring to a simmer as you stir with a whisk. Simmer gently over medium-low heat for 2 minutes, or until slightly thickened, stirring as you go. Add the salt, pepper to taste, cayenne, and parsley. Stir to mix and remove from the heat. (You can hold the sauce at this stage. When you are ready to eat, heat it gently over medium heat, stirring in any film that has formed with a whisk.)

Heat the artichokes gently in their cooking liquid until well warmed. Rinse off under hot water to remove extra starch and place on serving plates. Lay warm poached eggs over the top of each heart. Whisk the remaining 2 tablespoons of butter into the warm sauce off the heat. Now pour as much of the sauce as you like over the top and serve immediately.

SERVES 4

Poached Eggs on
Japanese Noodles

JAPANESE STYLE

I refer to this easy lunch as "Japanese style" because the broth is not particularly Japanese but rather a light vegetable stock (light in salt and color), which lends itself to further flavoring with sake, soy sauce, and sugar. The exact quantities of the last two ingredients will depend upon the taste and the saltiness of your particular stock. Dried Mushroom Stock (page 577) may be used here. You will need about 1½ times the recipe.

Japanese udon noodles are used in this recipe. These thick wheat noodles are sold by Japanese and other oriental grocers. If you cannot get them, use Italian linguine, cooking them just when needed in a large pot of unsalted water until done.

The Japanese poach their vegetables one at a time. I do indeed prepare my mushrooms separately but then cook all the remaining vegetables together in the stock. If asparagus is unavailable, double the quantity of beans.

12 medium white mushrooms

2 tablespoons peanut or canola oil

8 cups vegetable stock

Up to 6 tablespoons soy sauce

Up to 3 tablespoons sugar

½ teaspoon oriental sesame oil

¼ cup sake

14 ounces Japanese udon noodles

8 tender green beans, cut into 2-inch lengths

8 asparagus spears, partially peeled (see page 133 for directions) and cut into 2-inch pieces

1 medium carrot, peeled and cut on a slight diagonal into thin ovals

1 scallion, thinly sliced (use both white and green sections)

4 freshly poached eggs (page 519)

Few dashes of Japanese 7-spice seasoning

Wipe off the mushrooms with a damp cloth. Halve them lengthwise through the stem.

Put the oil in a medium pan and set over high heat. When hot, put in the mushrooms and stir for 1 minute. Turn off the heat, add 2 tablespoons of the stock, 1 teaspoon of the soy sauce, 1 teaspoon of the sugar, and ½ teaspoon of the oriental sesame oil to the pan, and bring to a simmer. Cover and simmer very gently for 5 minutes. Turn off the heat. Using a slotted spoon, remove the mushrooms from the liquid.

To the remaining stock add the sake, 2 tablespoons of the soy sauce, and 2 tablespoons of the sugar. Bring to a simmer and cook gently for 1 minute. Taste the stock, adding more soy sauce or sugar as needed to make a slightly sweet, delicious stock. Simmer 3 more minutes. Turn off the heat.

(recipe continues)

To cook the udon, bring a large pot of water to a rolling boil. Drop in the udon. When the water comes to a boil again, put in an extra cup of water. Repeat this 3 to 4 times, each time waiting for the water to come to a boil and then adding fresh water to stop the boiling. Keep testing the noodles until you feel that they are just done. Now drain the noodles and rinse them under running water, rubbing them to remove the starch. Set aside in a colander. When you are ready to eat, reheat by dropping the noodles into boiling water for a few seconds and then draining.

Just before you sit down to eat, bring the stock to a boil. Add the beans, asparagus, and carrot and bring to a boil again. Turn the heat down to low and simmer gently for 3 to 4 minutes, or until the vegetables are just tender. Add the scallion and turn off the heat.

Divide the hot udon noodles among 4 large bowls. Cover evenly with the heated stock, dividing the vegetables (beans, asparagus, carrot, and mushrooms) among the bowls. Lay a freshly poached egg over the top of each serving. Dust with the 7-spice seasoning and serve immediately. (Eat with chopsticks and a Chinese spoon or a spoon and fork.)

SERVES 4

FRIED EGGS

Our cooks in India always fried our eggs over high heat in lots of oil so that the edges of the whites turned crisp and brown. I never developed a taste for these eggs, but my children succumbed on their very first visit when they were tiny mites. (Perhaps it was India that they really succumbed to!) Even today when my children, now with children of their own, come to visit, I have to cook their fried eggs karara, or "crisp."

Fried eggs taste best with toast, though I have seen them fried in green olive oil in Italy and then eaten with crusty bread. They may be accompanied, if you like, with grilled tomato halves and sautéed mushrooms.

Western Fried Eggs

Here is a recipe for the more common fried eggs. The secret to their success is in keeping the heat low and basting the eggs with the hot fat. The frying pan you choose should just about hold the eggs with ease, being neither too big nor too small. For 2 eggs, a 7-inch pan is perfect. The eggs should be fresh and of top quality.

1 tablespoon olive or canola oil   2 eggs

Put the oil in a medium, nonstick frying pan and set it over medium-low heat. When hot, break the eggs into it, side by side. Let the bottoms set. Now baste the top of the eggs with the hot oil, tilting the pan to get at the oil, if needed, until the whites set completely. You could also partially cover the pan for a brief period, especially if you want to set or partially set the yolks. Lift the eggs out with a slotted spatula and serve immediately. (If you wish to turn the eggs over, slide the spatula carefully under them and turn them over. Cook for 20 seconds, then turn them over again and serve.)

SERVES 1 TO 2

Mexican Fried Eggs MEXICO
Huevos Rancheros

This was my most loved breakfast in Mexico City—two fried eggs topped with hot tomato sauce and Refried Beans (page 12) on the side. I serve plain, freshly heated tortillas (or pita bread!) with the eggs, even though in Mexico the tortillas were generally lightly fried. Of course, you could serve the eggs with just the sauce and buttered toast. They are very good that way too.

Have the sauce heated and ready before you fry the eggs.

4 fried eggs, freshly made according to the recipe on page 524

About 1 cup Cooked Tomato Salsa (page 683)

Put 2 eggs on each plate and pour half of the sauce over each pair of eggs. Serve immediately.

SERVES 2

SCRAMBLED EGGS AND OMELETS

Scrambled eggs mean different things to different peoples. In China, eggs are lightly cooked in a wok with scallions, Chinese chives, or tomatoes and then seasoned with salt or a few drops of soy sauce and sesame oil. They are generally eaten with rice. In North India, the eggs may be cooked with anything from tomatoes and onions to mushrooms and cauliflower but they are nearly always cooked until they are fairly firm so they can be easily eaten with flatbreads. They tend to be very spicy (and so good!). In the West, eggs are often scrambled with the addition of just a little cream, milk, or water. They are very lightly cooked and remain creamy. Indeed, the cooking is often stopped with the addition of a little cold butter.

Scrambled eggs are best made in a nonstick frying pan.

Scrambled Eggs, the Western Way

These may be served with toast or on toast.

4 eggs, lightly beaten

2 tablespoons milk

Salt

Freshly ground black pepper

3 tablespoons unsalted butter

Combine the eggs, milk, and salt and pepper to taste in a bowl.

Put 2 tablespoons of the butter in a nonstick frying pan and set over low heat. When the butter has melted completely, pour in the egg mixture. Stir the eggs gently to form soft curds, lifting up the bottom section as soon as it sets and letting the still-liquid parts flow into its place. As soon as the eggs are done to your taste, or even a few seconds before, put in the remaining tablespoon of butter and turn off the heat. Mix gently and serve immediately.

SERVES 2

Variation
Scrambled Eggs with Fresh Herbs

Make the eggs in exactly the same way as above, but when you combine the eggs, milk, salt, and pepper, also add ¼ teaspoon finely chopped fresh thyme, ¼ teaspoon finely chopped fresh tarragon, and 1 teaspoon finely chopped fresh parsley. Other fresh herbs of your choice may be substituted.

Indian Scrambled Eggs with Onion and Tomatoes   INDIA
Khichri Unda

This is one of the simplest preparations for scrambled eggs in India. It is generally eaten with buttered toast.

3 tablespoons peanut or canola oil (you may also use olive oil)

2 tablespoons finely chopped onion

1 fresh hot green chile, finely chopped

1 small tomato, finely chopped

2 tablespoons finely chopped fresh cilantro

8 eggs, lightly beaten

Salt

Freshly ground black pepper

Put the oil in a large nonstick frying pan and set over medium heat. When hot, put in the onion and stir for 20 seconds. Add the green chile and tomato, and stir until the onion and tomato are soft, 2 to 3 minutes. Now add the cilantro, eggs, and salt and pepper to taste. Stir the eggs gently until they form thick, soft curds or are done to your taste. Remove from the heat and serve immediately.

SERVES 4

Scrambled Eggs with Scallions and Mushrooms INDIA

Khumbi Wala Khichri Unda

Serve this with toast or any flatbread.

3 tablespoons peanut or canola oil (you may also use olive oil)

4 medium white mushrooms, trimmed and cut into ¼-inch dice

2 scallions, thinly sliced (use both white and green sections)

½ to 1 fresh hot green chile, finely chopped

1 small tomato, finely chopped

1 tablespoon finely chopped fresh cilantro

8 eggs, lightly beaten

Salt

Freshly ground black pepper

Put the oil in a large nonstick frying pan and set over high heat. When hot, put in the mushrooms. Stir and fry until the mushrooms appear silken. Add the scallions, green chile, and tomato. Turn the heat to medium and stir until the tomato softens. Add the cilantro, eggs, and salt and pepper to taste. Stir the eggs gently until they form thick, soft curds or are done to your taste. Remove from the heat and serve immediately.

SERVES 4

Indian-Style Stir-Fried Eggs

INDIA

Unday Ki Bhurji

Here is the way eggs are scrambled in the Indian state of Punjab. This is generally prepared in a well-seasoned karhai *(wok). Serve these eggs—which in India are cooked until they are quite firm—with sliced bread or with any flatbread such as pita or naan.*

8 eggs, lightly beaten

1/8 teaspoon ground turmeric

1/8 teaspoon cayenne

2 tablespoons peanut or canola oil

1/3 teaspoon whole cumin seeds

2 tablespoons finely chopped onions

1/2 × 1-inch piece of fresh ginger, peeled and
   very finely chopped

1/2 cup finely chopped tomato

1 to 3 teaspoons finely chopped fresh hot
   green chile (optional)

Salt

1/4 teaspoon store-bought garam masala

Combine the beaten eggs, turmeric, and cayenne. Mix and set aside.

Put the oil in a nonstick frying pan or well-seasoned wok and set over medium-high heat. When it is hot, add the cumin seeds. Let them sizzle for a few seconds, then add the onions. Stir and fry until the onions are light brown at the edges. Put in the ginger and stir once, then add the tomato and cook for a few seconds. Stir in the green chile, if using. Now turn the flame down to medium, add the eggs, salt to taste, and garam masala. Stir the eggs gently until they form thick, soft curds or are done to your taste. Remove from the heat and serve immediately.

SERVES 4

Scrambled Eggs with Cauliflower

INDIA

Gobi-Vala Khichri Unda

This quick dish is equally good for supper or brunch, accompanied by a green salad and bread.

2 tablespoons olive oil

1/2 teaspoon cumin seeds

1 large cauliflower, cut into delicate florets

2 scallions, thinly sliced

1/2 teaspoon very finely chopped fresh ginger

1 fresh hot green chile, finely chopped

5 eggs, lightly beaten

2 teaspoons finely chopped fresh oregano

1 tablespoon finely chopped fresh parsley or
    fresh cilantro leaves

Salt

Freshly ground black pepper

Put the oil in a frying pan and set over medium-high heat. Add the cumin seeds and stir once or twice. When the seeds begin to sizzle, add the cauliflower. Turn the heat down to medium-low and stir for 2 minutes. Add the scallions and cook 1 minute. Put in the ginger and green chile and cook another minute, stirring frequently. Now quickly add the eggs, oregano, parsley, and salt and pepper to taste. Stir rapidly with a spatula. Cook until the eggs are done to your taste. Serve hot.

SERVES 3 TO 4

Japanese/Korean-Style Scrambled Eggs with Bean Curd

Such egg dishes exist all over East Asia and are nearly always eaten with plain rice. This recipe may easily be doubled by doubling all ingredients and using a larger frying pan. The cooking times will remain about the same. If you like, you may make this with 4 lightly beaten egg whites. The color will be a bit brownish but the taste will still be wonderful.

3 ounces firm bean curd

2 teaspoons peanut or canola oil

1 scallion, finely chopped (both white and
    green sections)

1 tablespoon peeled and very finely diced
    carrot

1 tablespoon very finely diced green pepper

1½ teaspoons soy sauce

½ teaspoon sugar

2 eggs, lightly beaten

Put the bean curd on a plate and mash well with a fork. Scrape the mashed bean curd onto the center of a clean dishcloth. Bring the ends of the cloth together and squeeze out as much moisture as you can. Set the bean curd aside.

Put the oil in a small (6-inch) nonstick frying pan and set over medium heat. When hot, put in the scallion, carrot, and pepper and stir and fry for 1½ to 2 minutes. Add the bean curd. Stir and cook for another minute. Add the soy sauce and sugar. Stir and cook for 1 minute. Now put in the beaten eggs. Stir gently and cook until the eggs are done to your liking.

SERVES 1 TO 2

(recipe continues)

Variation I

Japanese/Korean-Style Scrambled Eggs with Sesame Seeds and Bean Curd

Prepare as on page 529 but after the oil is hot, add 1½ teaspoons sesame seeds. Stir until they turn a shade darker or start to pop. Now put in the vegetables and proceed with the recipe.

Variation II

Chinese-Style Scrambled Eggs with Ginger and Bean Curd

Prepare as on page 529 but when putting the vegetables into the frying pan, add ¼ teaspoon very finely grated fresh ginger and ¼ teaspoon very finely chopped fresh hot green or red chile. Proceed with the recipe.

Shiu-Min Block's

Egg Whites with Peas   CHINA

Ching Do Chow Tan Bai

Known as "Jade Green with Snow Drops," this easy, mild dish may be eaten at breakfast or as part of a meal. The Chinese would have rice with it, but you may also serve it with bread.

Salt

2 cups (10 ounces) fresh or frozen peas

3 tablespoons peanut or canola oil

2 scallions, thinly sliced (white and green sections)

4 egg whites, beaten lightly

A little white pepper

1 teaspoon cornstarch mixed well with 2 teaspoons water in a small bowl

1 teaspoon oriental sesame oil

Bring 4 cups of water to boil in a medium pot. Add ½ teaspoon salt and stir. Add the peas and cook until they are just tender, about 5 minutes. Drain and rinse under cold water to preserve their color. Drain again and set aside.

Put the oil in a nonstick frying pan and set over medium-high heat. When hot, put in the scallions and stir for 5 seconds. Put in the egg whites and stir for a second, then put in the peas, 1 teaspoon salt, and the pepper. Stir for 3 to 4 minutes. Turn the heat down to low and slowly stir in the cornstarch mixture. Stir and cook for a minute. Turn off the heat and pour in the sesame oil. Stir and serve at once.

SERVES 3 TO 4

French Omelet

Omelette

The traditional French omelet is a work of art, a light, puffy cocoon-shaped creation, just about firm on the outside but vulnerably soft and creamy inside, born in a very brief burst of activity over fairly high heat. This is the omelet many of us aspire to but make with varying degrees of success.

When I first started teaching cooking, I began with Indian food—naturally. This is what I really knew best or, I should say, better than most people around me. I was teaching in James Beard's house, with him not only watching over me in an avuncular manner, but as he grew old and infirm, sending down for a taste of everything I was preparing on the ground floor of his four-storied brownstone home. At first, he kept up with his own classes at least a few times a year, but later he would ask me to teach the actual class while he sat in a high director's chair, watching and giving advice.

The first class he asked me to teach was Sauces, Crepes, Soufflés, and Omelets—all very French, of course. It was not that I hadn't cooked these things at home many times. But teach them? Not one to say no, I agreed and then rushed home in an absolute panic and fell on my already well-worn copy of Mastering the Art of French Cooking *by Julia Child et al.*

I made hollandaises again and again, crepes by the dozen were swirled into pans (the wrist, the wrist), soufflés were rising (and falling), and omelets were dissected for proper creaminess within. I realized then that tossing omelets into the air and catching them again was an iffy matter for me. I needed to keep matters in hand with forks and spatulas.

Over the years, I have developed my own approach to the cooking of an omelet based on what I know I can do with ease. All egg cooking requires timing and practice, and omelets are no different. But first we need to relax. This is my simplified way of going about it.

For a 2-egg omelet, I use a nonstick pan that is about 6 inches at the bottom and 8 inches at the top. It is best to use a wooden fork so it does not scratch the pan as well as a wooden or plastic spatula. The omelet cooks in less than a minute, so read the recipe thoroughly before you begin.

French omelets are traditionally cooked in butter. You may certainly do so. I use olive oil.

---

2 eggs

Generous pinch of salt

Freshly ground black pepper

2 teaspoons olive oil

Beat the eggs until the whites and yolks are well blended. Add the salt and pepper to taste and mix well.

Put the oil in a nonstick omelet pan and set over medium-high heat. As soon as the oil is hot, pour in the beaten eggs. Allow them to set at the bottom for just a few seconds, then scramble the eggs lightly with the back of your fork, allowing them to stay spread out at the bottom of the pan.

(recipe continues)

Holding the handle of the pan, tilt it very slightly away from you and begin to jerk the omelet toward you. The omelet will begin to fold up on itself but stay at the far end of the pan. Keep doing this until a cocoon has formed at the far end. If you cannot manage this, use your spatula, and while the top of the omelet is still quite wet, fold it in thirds and then quickly turn it over. Roll the omelet onto a warm plate and serve immediately.

MAKES 1

Variation
French Omelet with Herbs
Omelette Aux Fines Herbes

Follow the preceding recipe but once the eggs have been beaten, add to them a tablespoon of finely chopped fresh herbs, such as thyme, tarragon, parsley, and chives. Proceed as above.

French Omelets with Fillings

Once you have mastered the preceding recipe you are ready to attempt further embellishments. Fillings go in just after the eggs have been scrambled lightly and are still very wet at the top. The filling should be spread in a line across the center of the omelet, which is then folded in thirds over it and either rolled over or turned over briefly before serving.

You will find two of my family's favorite fillings below. Remember, almost anything may be used: chopped, lightly cooked tomatoes, goat cheese and herbs, leftover vegetables, sautéed peppers of different colors, and sautéed mushrooms.

Omelet Filled with Cheese and Chives
Use 2 tablespoons grated sharp Cheddar cheese and 1 tablespoon finely sliced fresh chives, or very finely sliced scallion greens.

Omelet with Asparagus
Prepare Basic Asparagus, My Way (page 134), and keep warm. You will only need 5 to 6 spears for an omelet. Lay them in the center of the still-wet eggs and fold over the spears.

MAKES 1

Japanese/Korean-Style Omelet with Sesame Seeds and Bean Curd

Serve with Plain Japanese Rice (page 378) and a dipping sauce, such as Japanese Dipping Sauce (page 680) or Korean Dipping Sauce (page 680).

If you buy a 1-pound cake of bean curd, cut it in half horizontally; a flatter piece is always easier to press. The rest of the bean curd may be refrigerated in a bowl of water for future use.

5 Chinese dried black mushrooms

½ pound firm bean curd

3 tablespoons peanut or canola oil

2 tablespoons sesame seeds

4 scallions, thinly sliced (white and green sections)

½ teaspoon sugar

2 tablespoons soy sauce

6 eggs, lightly beaten

Soak the dried mushrooms in hot water to cover for 30 minutes, or until completely softened. Lift out of the liquid. (Strain the liquid and save for another use.) Cut off the hard stems, then cut the caps into ¼-inch dice.

Put the bean curd on a double layer of paper towels. Cover with another double layer of paper towels. Put a board or a large plate on top and put a 5-pound weight on top of that. Set aside for 30 minutes. Remove the weight and paper towels. Pat dry and cut into ½- to ¾-inch squares.

Put the oil in a nonstick frying pan with a metal handle (mine is about 10 inches at the top and about 7 inches at the bottom) and set over medium heat. When hot, put in the sesame seeds. As soon as they turn a shade darker or start to pop, put in the mushrooms and scallions. Stir for a minute, then add the bean curd, sugar, and soy sauce and stir gently for another minute. Pour in the beaten eggs, allowing them to spread evenly in the pan. Cover and let the omelet cook for 5 minutes.

Meanwhile, preheat the broiler.

When the eggs have cooked for 5 minutes, turn the heat down to low and cook another 5 minutes. Uncover the frying pan and put it under the broiler for 1 to 2 minutes, or until the top has just set. Slide the "pie" onto a serving plate and serve hot, cut into 1-inch squares or diamond shapes.

SERVES 3 TO 4

Soft Japanese Omelet and Bean Curd over Rice

Tofu Donburi

Donburis are among Japan's many fast foods of relatively recent origin. Whole restaurants are devoted to them. I quote here from Professor Shizuo Tsuji's excellent book, Japanese Cooking: *"A* donburi *is a deep-footed bowl, usually of porcelain, about 6 inches in diameter at the lip, about twice as large—to hold twice as much—as a standard rice bowl." In Japan, both this lidded bowl and the rice-based, meal-in-a-bowl served in it are known as* donburi.

In many small towns and villages, they often account for everyday lunches and dinners because of the simplicity of their preparation.

The basis of every donburi *is 1½ to 2 cups of hot rice. (Reheated leftover rice could be used here.) This is topped with leftover or freshly cooked foods, which for vegetarians might include fried bean curd or batter-fried vegetables heated in a slightly sweet broth made with stock and soy sauce. Eggs and scallions or the slightly larger* naganegi, *which look like very young, slim leeks, are often added as well. The broth lubricates the rice and the other ingredients provide nutritional value.*

In this particular dish, which was served to me by a farmer-carpenter with a small rice holding just outside Kyoto, the rice is topped with bean curd (the farmer used fried bean curd, which is sold everywhere in Japan) and a soft omelet poached in broth. It requires little else. Serve it in bowls, Japanese style.

The vegetable stock used here should be fairly light both in flavor and saltiness.

8 ounces firm bean curd

Peanut or canola oil

2 cups vegetable stock

¼ cup soy sauce

2 tablespoons sake

3 tablespoons sugar

6 eggs, lightly beaten

2 scallions, thinly sliced (both white and green sections)

½ cup peas (defrosted if frozen, parboiled if fresh)

2 cups Japanese short-grain rice, cooked according to the recipe on page 378

Put the bean curd on a double layer of paper towels. Cover with another double layer of paper towels. Put a board or a large plate on top and put a 5-pound weight on top of that. Set aside for 30 minutes. Remove the weight and paper towels. Pat dry and cut into ¾-inch squares.

Put ⅛ inch of oil in a 7- to 8-inch frying pan and set over medium heat. When hot, put in the bean curd pieces. Stir and fry until the pieces are golden red. Remove with a slotted spoon and drain thoroughly on paper towels.

Empty the frying pan (save the oil for another use) and wipe it out well. Combine the stock, soy sauce, sake, and sugar in the pan and bring to a boil. Turn the heat down to low and simmer for a minute. Now put in the bean curd, bring to a simmer, and cook gently for 5 minutes. Add the beaten eggs all at once, as well as the scallions and peas. Continue heating until the mixture begins to bubble around the edges. Cover, turn the heat down to low, and cook about 3 minutes, or until the eggs are just set. Uncover and remove from the heat.

Divide the cooked rice among the serving bowls. Use a large spoon to divide and lift up the solids—and some of the liquid—from the pan and lay on top of the rice. Moisten the rice with as much more of the liquid as you like and serve immediately.

SERVES 3 TO 4

Masala Omelet   INDIA

Masala Omlate

This is the most common omelet in India. Most cafés and coffee shops serve it, generally with just a slice of bread or toast. It is not at all creamy inside but fully cooked through. You can make a wonderful sandwich with this omelet as well.

2 eggs, lightly beaten

1 tablespoon very finely chopped onion

2 tablespoons chopped fresh cilantro

1/2 teaspoon finely chopped fresh hot green
  chile, or to taste

2 tablespoons finely chopped tomato

Dash of salt

Freshly ground black pepper

1 tablespoon peanut or canola oil

Combine the eggs, onion, cilantro, chile, tomato, salt, and pepper to taste in a bowl and mix.

Put the oil in a medium nonstick frying pan and set over medium heat. When hot, pour in the egg mixture. As the bottom sets, push the egg a little to one side, tilt the pan a bit, and let the uncooked egg mixture flow into the area just vacated. Keep doing this until the egg is almost set. Now fold the egg into thirds and press down on it with a spatula. Turn the omelet over and press down again. When the omelet is cooked through, serve immediately.

SERVES 1

FRITTATAS AND EGG PIES

Rosario Guillermo's

Spanish Egg and Potato Cake   SPAIN/MEXICO

Tortilla de Patata

Spaniards of all classes are fond of this sturdy cake, which is served in bars as tapas. It is also a meal in itself and may be served with a salad.

1¼ pounds Idaho or other baking potatoes, peeled and cut into ¹⁄₁₆-inch slices

½ medium onion (3 ounces), peeled and thinly sliced

1¼ teaspoons salt

1 cup olive oil

Black pepper

Generous pinch of dried oregano

4 eggs, beaten

Arrange the potato and onion slices evenly in the bottom of a 10-inch frying pan. Sprinkle 1 teaspoon salt over the top. Pour all the oil into the pan, turn the heat to medium, and bring to a simmer. Cover the pan, turn the heat down to low, and simmer gently for about 12 minutes, or until the potatoes are tender. Pour out all the oil (it can be used later in salads and other cooking).

Add ¼ cup of water, ¼ teaspoon salt, pepper to taste, and the oregano to the beaten eggs. Stir to mix.

Put 3 tablespoons of the used olive oil in an 8-inch nonstick frying pan and set over medium-high heat. When hot, pour in the egg mixture and stir gently once or twice. Turn the heat down to low. Arrange the potato and onion slices evenly in the pan, cover, and cook for about 7 minutes, or until the top has just set. Remove from the heat.

Put a large plate over the frying pan and invert the cake onto the plate. Slide the cake back into the pan, set it over low heat, and cook, uncovered, for another 2 minutes, or until it is all set on the bottom but still slightly creamy on the inside. Slide onto a serving dish and serve hot or at room temperature.

SERVES 4 TO 6

Shamsi Davis'
Persian Egg Pie with Herbs   IRAN
Kookoo Sabzi

Serve this versatile egg dish hot or chilled. It may be eaten with toast for breakfast, with crusty bread and salad for lunch, and even taken on picnics for the whole family to enjoy. My little grandson adores it. The Persians garnish it with fresh watercress, which is eaten, and serve yogurt and flatbreads such as naans as accompaniments.

Be sure to dry the herbs thoroughly before you chop them.

6 eggs

¼ teaspoon salt

Freshly ground black pepper

1 garlic clove, peeled and crushed to a pulp

½ well-packed cup finely chopped fresh parsley

¼ well-packed cup finely chopped fresh cilantro

½ well-packed cup finely chopped fresh chives or scallions

¼ well-packed cup fresh or 1 tablespoon dried and crumbled fenugreek greens *(methi)*, page 722 (optional)

2 tablespoons chopped walnuts

1 tablespoon dried currants, rinsed and patted dry

3 tablespoons *ghee* (page 723) or peanut oil

In a mixing bowl, beat the eggs well. Add the salt, pepper to taste, garlic, parsley, cilantro, chives, fenugreek greens if you wish to use them, walnuts, and currants. Beat again to mix.

Put the *ghee* or oil in a nonstick, omelet-type frying pan with a metal handle (mine is about 10 inches at the top and about 7 inches at the bottom) and set over medium-low heat. Stir the egg mixture in the bowl and pour it in, swirling the pan to spread it evenly. Cover and cook for 5 minutes.

Meanwhile, preheat the broiler.

When the egg has cooked for 5 minutes, turn the heat down to low and cook another 5 minutes. Uncover the frying pan and put it under the broiler for about 2 minutes, or until the top has set. Slide the "pie" onto a serving plate and serve hot or as suggested above.

SERVES 3 TO 4

(recipe continues)

537

Variation I

Persian-Style Egg Pie with Herbs and Cheese

Make in exactly the same way as the preceding recipe but place the frying pan under the grill for just 1 minute. Remove and sprinkle 6 tablespoons grated Cheddar cheese evenly over the top before placing under the grill for another minute or so. Wait for the cheese to develop a few brown spots before removing. Eat this one hot!

Variation II

Persian-Style Egg Pie with Tomato and Herbs

Here I have Indianized the eggs somewhat. Put the *ghee* or oil in the pan and set over medium heat. When hot, put in about 4 tablespoons peeled, seeded, and chopped tomato and 1 teaspoon finely chopped fresh hot green chile. Stir them for about a minute. Stir the egg mixture and pour it in. Cover, turn the heat down to medium-low, and proceed as above.

Shamsi Davis'

Persian Egg and Potato Cake   IRAN

Kookoo Seeb Zameeni

I often serve this delicate, savory cake with a green salad and some asparagus if it is in season. Roasted red peppers may also be added to the plate. I have also served it with Black-Eyed Peas with Swiss Chard (page 20) and a salad of sliced tomatoes, but it would go well with grilled mixed vegetables too. If you like, once the cake is made, you can spread a topping of Simple Tomato Sauce (page 679) over it, then sprinkle the grated cheese of your choice on top and slide it briefly under the broiler until the cheese melts.

For best results, use a nonstick frying pan with a metal handle. The size of the pan can vary slightly, making a slightly thinner or thicker cake. A 7-inch size, however, is ideal. Persians tend to use clarified butter to make this—and a generous amount too. I prefer olive oil or a mixture of olive oil and butter.

2 large boiling potatoes (13 to 14 ounces)

For the onion-garlic mixture
2 tablespoons olive oil or a mixture of olive oil
    and butter

1 medium onion (4 ounces), peeled and very
    finely chopped

1 garlic clove, peeled and very finely chopped

You also need

¾ teaspoon salt, or to taste

Freshly ground black pepper

4 large eggs, lightly beaten

½ cup very finely chopped fresh chives

3 tablespoons olive oil or a mixture of olive oil and butter

Cover the potatoes with water and boil them until they are soft.

While they boil, put the 2 tablespoons of olive oil in a medium frying pan and set over medium-high heat. Add the onion and garlic and stir and fry, turning the heat down after 3 to 4 minutes, until the onion and garlic are golden. Set aside.

Peel the potatoes while they are still hot (hold each with a fork to do this). Now, either put them through a ricer or mash them well with a fork. Add the salt and pepper to the potatoes and mix. Add the beaten eggs and all but 1 tablespoon of the chives. Mix again.

Put the remaining 3 tablespoons of olive oil in a 7-inch nonstick frying pan and set over medium heat. Pour in the egg-potato mixture. Turn the heat down to low and cook, uncovered, for 15 minutes.

Preheat the broiler.

When the egg-potato mixture has cooked for 15 minutes, put the frying pan under the broiler very briefly, about 1½ minutes, or until the top has just set. Now flip the cake over (if it helps, invert it onto a plate and then slide it back into the pan) and cook on low heat for another 5 minutes. Slip into a serving dish, sprinkle with the remaining chives, and serve hot.

Note: You may also serve this at room temperature or chilled.

SERVES 2 TO 4

Variation

Indian Egg and Potato Cake INDIA

Aloo Omlate

Make this just like the preceding recipe but when making the onion-garlic mixture, heat the 2 tablespoons olive oil. When very hot, put in 1 teaspoon whole brown mustard seeds. As soon as they pop, a matter of seconds, put in the onion, garlic, 1 finely chopped fresh hot green chile, and 2 teaspoons very finely ground fresh ginger. Stir and fry as in the basic recipe. When adding the chives, also put in 4 tablespoons chopped fresh cilantro.

Frittata with Swiss Chard

ITALY

Frittata di Beitole

Served with a salad of tomatoes and some crusty bread, this makes a delightful meal. It may also be served cold and makes an excellent picnic food.

For the Swiss chard

¾ pound Swiss chard, coarsely chopped (use both stems and leaves)

2 tablespoons olive oil

1 garlic clove, peeled and finely chopped

About ¼ teaspoon salt

For the eggs

6 eggs

¼ teaspoon salt

Freshly ground black pepper

3 tablespoons extra-virgin olive oil

To prepare the chard, bring a large pot of water to a rolling boil, as if you were boiling pasta. Drop in the chard and boil for 3 to 4 minutes, or until it is tender. Drain. Rinse under cold water and then squeeze out as much moisture as you can.

Put the 2 tablespoons olive oil and garlic in a nonstick frying pan or sauté pan and set over medium-high heat. When the garlic starts to sizzle, add the greens and about ¼ teaspoon salt (taste as you go) and mix well. Stir and cook for about 1 minute. Turn off the heat.

Put the eggs into a medium bowl and beat them well. Add the salt, pepper to taste, and chard. Mix well, separating the chard pieces.

Put the 3 tablespoons olive oil in a nonstick, omelet-type frying pan with a metal handle (mine is about 10 inches at the top and about 7 inches at the bottom) and set over medium-low heat. Stir the egg mixture in the bowl and pour it in, swirling the pan to spread it evenly. Cover and cook for 5 minutes.

Meanwhile, preheat the broiler.

When the eggs have cooked for 5 minutes, turn the heat down to low and cook another 5 minutes. Uncover the frying pan and put it under the broiler for about 2 minutes, or until the top has set. Slide the frittata onto a serving plate and serve hot.

SERVES 3 TO 4

Allegra Antinori's

Tuscan Zucchini Pie   **ITALY**

Tortina di Zucchine

This recipe, from the heart of Chianti country, makes 2 thin 8-inch "pies" that are like delicate, light quiches without crusts. They may be served by themselves or with a salad of tomatoes and basil or a green salad. Four tablespoons of grated cheese, such as Parmigiano-Reggiano or pecorino, may be added to the egg batter, if you like.

2 medium zucchini (about 12 ounces in all)

Salt

2 eggs

¼ cup unbleached all-purpose flour

¼ cup milk mixed with ¼ cup water

¼ teaspoon very finely chopped garlic

3 scallions, thinly sliced (use both white and green sections)

Freshly ground black pepper

Dash of freshly grated nutmeg

3 tablespoons extra-virgin olive oil (use the best quality here)

Trim the zucchini ends and then cut them crosswise into ⅛-inch-thick rounds. Put in a bowl, sprinkle about ⅓ teaspoon salt over the top, toss, and set aside for 30 minutes. Drain and pat dry.

Preheat the oven to 425°F.

Put the eggs in a bowl and beat them well. Add the flour and beat it in. Add the milk and water mixture and beat it in as well. (This much of the batter can be made in a blender, if you like.) Now add the garlic, scallions, about ⅓ teaspoon salt, pepper to taste, and nutmeg. Mix well.

Arrange the zucchini slices without overlapping in the bottom of two 8-inch non-stick cake or pie tins. (You will probably be able to make 2 layers in each of the tins.) Stir the egg mixture well and pour it evenly over the 2 pans. Drizzle 1 tablespoon oil over each pie, put the pies in the oven, and bake for 30 minutes. Serve hot, with another ½ tablespoon of oil drizzled over each pie.

SERVES 4 AS A MAIN COURSE, 6 AS AN APPETIZER

Indian "French" Toast

Unday Ka Toast

Various interpretations of "French" toast are enjoyed around the world, two of which I provide here. This one is for a savory and hot Indian version. Actually, there are as many versions in India as there are Indian families. A Bengali family might cook theirs in mustard oil (unique and delicious) while a Gujarati family might serve theirs with a sweet mango chutney. I serve it with any fresh or preserved chutney—whatever happens to be on hand—or no chutney at all.

The best French toast is made with slightly stale, hard bread, as it holds together best.

When you beat the eggs, put them into a fairly shallow, gratin-type dish or pie tin or any other shallow dish in which the 2 slices of bread can fit side by side with ease. If necessary, cut the bread slices into halves.

This recipe may easily be doubled by doubling all ingredients and cooking the toasts in 2 batches.

1 egg, well beaten

1 tablespoon milk

Dash of salt

Freshly ground black pepper

1 tablespoon finely chopped scallion (use the
    white and some of the pale green section)

1 to 2 teaspoons very finely chopped fresh hot
    green chiles

2 slices of slightly stale bread

3 tablespoons peanut or canola oil

Put the beaten egg and milk in a shallow dish. Add the salt, pepper to taste, scallion, and chile and stir to mix. Lay the slices of bread in the dish and turn them over quickly a few times. Let them soak about 3 minutes, or until the bread has softened a bit and the egg mixture has been somewhat absorbed, turning the slices occasionally. With a spoon, lift up some of the solids in the egg mixture (chile and scallion) and spread them on top of the slices.

Put the oil in a large, nonstick frying pan and set over medium heat. When hot, put the slices of bread in the pan, scallion-chile side down. Cook for a minute while you spoon the remaining solids over the bread slices. Turn the slices over and cook another minute. Turn the slices over again and cook both sides for another 30 seconds each, or until nicely browned. Serve hot.

MAKES 2 SLICES

American "French" Toast

As in the preceding recipe, stale, somewhat hard bread is best here. I use a crusty peasant loaf, cutting it into ¾-inch-thick slices. It ends up being quite cakelike. My grandsons love it and can be seen many a Sunday with their sweet mouths smeared with confectioners' sugar. You may use maple syrup instead of the confectioners' sugar if you prefer.

When you beat the eggs, put them into a fairly shallow, gratin-type dish or pie tin or any other shallow dish in which the 2 slices of bread can fit side by side with ease. If necessary, cut the bread slices into halves.

This recipe may easily be doubled by doubling all ingredients and cooking the toasts in 2 batches.

1 egg, well beaten	2 slices of slightly stale bread
¼ cup milk	3 tablespoons peanut oil or unsalted butter or
Dash of salt	a mixture of the two
1 teaspoon sugar	Confectioners' sugar for dusting

Put the beaten egg and milk in a shallow dish. Add the salt and sugar and stir to mix. Lay the slices of bread in the dish and turn them over quickly a few times. Let them soak about 3 minutes, or until the bread has softened a bit and the egg mixture has been somewhat absorbed. Turn the slices over a few times during this period.

Put the oil in a large, nonstick frying pan and set over medium heat. When hot, add the slices of bread in a single layer and cook for a minute. Turn the slices over and cook another minute. Turn the slices over again and cook both sides for another 30 seconds each, or until nicely browned. Serve hot, sprinkled generously on one side with confectioners' sugar.

MAKES 2 SLICES

Yogurt

Among dairy foods, yogurt reigns supreme in the region bounded by Greece and India. It is stuffed into small triangular pies in Syria, swirled with fresh mango pulp in India, thickened into cheeses in Turkey, put into cold soups of chickpeas and wheat in Armenia, combined with feta cheese and cucumbers to make a dip in Greece, and blended with ice and rosewater to make a soothing summer drink in Iran. It can also be thickened and stirred into vegetable dishes, combined with bean flours and made into stews, set with cooked rice in it, used as a sauce for stuffed vegetables, made into fritters, cakes, and halvahs, used as a dressing, a dip, and a relish, and, of course, eaten as is.

At my home in India, my mother set the yogurt herself every night in a rough ceramic bowl. By morning it was firm, ready to appear at our lunch table if we were all eating at home or go into numerous lunch boxes if members of the family were headed out to offices and schools.

In the villages of Punjab in northern India, buffalo milk, with its rich fat content, is first thickened slowly in special clay pots set inside larger clay pots filled with glowing embers. Here it simmers very gently for several hours. Once it has achieved the density of evaporated milk, it is allowed to set up into a creamy, heavenly yogurt. Eaten with a little honey or jaggery (page 724), it is a natural dessert.

There is no vegetable and almost no herb that cannot be mixed into yogurt. It lends itself to being seasoned with a variety of spices as well, from crushed mustard seeds to roasted cumin seeds. Yogurt is also known to settle the stomach, especially when combined with plain rice. Yogurt may be cooked and used as a sauce but since it curdles, it needs to be stabilized first. In India, this is usually done with chickpea flour (see Vegetable Stew with Chickpea Flour Sauce [Karhi], page 36).

There was a time when good yogurt was hard to find in the West. These days many varieties, from full fat to skim milk yogurts, are available. For those who eat yogurt frequently, yogurt-making machines are a worthwhile investment.

Yogurt is also very easy to make at home without machines. After all, that is how it has been made in Eastern Europe and both southern and western Asia for thousands of years. In ancient India, indeed in my own family today, it is still a major ingredient in *Charnamrit* (page 649), a milk and yogurt drink that is offered in prayer and then drunk after it has been blessed. This drink is over five thousand years old. The recipe does not seem to have changed one bit.

The most important part of making yogurt at home is finding a good yogurt culture, which determines the flavor. I know a family who brought their yogurt culture, on ice, from India to America—it was that important to them. If you visit a home or even a restaurant where you like the taste and texture of the yogurt very much, ask for a few tablespoons to bring home, then use this to start your own batch with whole, low-fat, or skim milk, as you please.

Basic Recipe for Homemade Yogurt

You may also halve these quantities to make a smaller batch.

1 quart milk (skim, low-fat, or whole) 2 tablespoons plain yogurt with active cultures

Bring the milk to a boil in a heavy pan. As soon as it starts to rise, turn the heat off and let the milk cool in a pitcher or large measuring cup until it is just warm (100°F. to 110°F.).

Meanwhile, put the yogurt in a large ceramic bowl. Beat it until it is creamy. When the milk has reached the correct "warm" temperature, add it very slowly to the yogurt, a little at a time, stirring as you go. (Any film that has formed at the top may be stirred in.) When all the milk has been added, cover the bowl with plastic wrap and leave it in a place where the temperature hovers around 85°F. to 100°F. You could also wrap the bowl in a blanket and put it inside the oven if there is a pilot light to keep it warm. In 6 to 8 hours the yogurt should set up. When refrigerated, it will last 3 to 4 days.

MAKES 1 QUART

Yogurt Made with Thickened Milk

This is creamier and richer than the basic yogurt.

1 quart whole milk 2 tablespoons plain yogurt

Bring the milk to a boil in a heavy pan. As soon as it starts to rise, turn the heat down to medium. Now stir and cook the milk until it has reduced to half its volume. Let the milk cool in a jug until it is just warm (100°F. to 110°F.).

Meanwhile, put the yogurt in a large ceramic bowl. Beat it until it is creamy. When the milk has reached the correct "warm" temperature, add it very slowly to the yogurt, a little at a time, stirring as you go. (Any film that has formed at the top may be stirred in.) When all the milk has been added, cover the bowl with plastic wrap and leave it in a place where the temperature hovers around 85°F. to 100°F. You could also wrap the bowl in a blanket and put it inside the oven if there is a pilot light to keep it warm. In 6 to 8 hours the yogurt should set up. When refrigerated, it will last 3 to 4 days.

MAKES 2 CUPS

"Pickled" Yogurt

Dahi Ka Achar

I am only guessing here but from the original ingredients—yogurt, mustard seeds, cumin seeds, ginger, asafetida, and mustard oil—I would guess that this is a very ancient recipe. There are no chiles from the New World. The dish gets its strange name because all seasonings used in it are also those used in the making of traditional pickles.

India has, for the last six thousand years, been very much a milk culture, with milk in some form or other served at every meal. To the many thousand yogurt dishes that the country probably started off with, more are added daily. But this dish seems to belong to antiquity.

I have seen it being prepared. First the mustard seeds are ground and put into a shallow plate. A little very hot water is mixed in with the flat of the hand. Then a little mustard oil is added the same way. This has the same emulsifying effect as beating oil and vinegar together with a fork.

Over the years I have simplified and modified the dish somewhat, using coarse French Pommery mustard instead of grinding my own. In my New World version I use extra-virgin olive oil instead of the mustard oil! Serve it as a relish with meals that include beans and rice or use it as a dip for vegetables. By adding lightly boiled vegetables, such as potatoes (2 medium potatoes, boiled, cooled, peeled, and diced) or cauliflower florets (about 2 cupfuls parboiled in salted water), you will make a wonderful salad.

1 cup plain yogurt

¼ to ⅓ teaspoon salt

⅛ teaspoon cayenne

Freshly ground black pepper

1 teaspoon very finely grated fresh ginger

½ teaspoon ground roasted cumin seeds (page 734)

2 teaspoons coarse French mustard, such as Pommery

1 tablespoon plus 1 teaspoon extra-virgin olive oil

Generous pinch of asafetida

¼ teaspoon whole cumin seeds

Optional additions

1 peeled and grated carrot

2 tablespoons finely chopped fresh cilantro

6 tablespoons grated daikon

Put the yogurt in a bowl and beat lightly with a fork until smooth and creamy. Add the salt, cayenne, black pepper to taste, ginger, roasted cumin, mustard, and a tablespoon of extra-virgin olive oil. Mix well and taste for the balance of flavors, adjusting to taste.

Put the remaining 1 teaspoon olive oil in a small pan and set over medium heat. When very hot, put in the asafetida and the whole cumin seeds. As soon as the cumin seeds are a shade darker, a matter of seconds, pour the contents of the pan over the yogurt. Stir and mix in.

Add the optional ingredients, if using, and mix well.

SERVES 4 TO 6

Carrot "Raita"   INDIA

Gajar Ka Raita

Gently sweet and saffron-colored (because of the carrots, of course), this yogurt dish is just as good for a simple, light lunch as when it forms a part of a full Indian meal. Its gentle flavor also makes it compatible with virtually any collection of international salads. In the summer, I often serve it with Turkish, Greek, and Moroccan salads, as well as some flatbreads.

You may leave out the asafetida if you wish but it does give the dish a haunting, trufflelike flavor. When making this for my little grandchildren, who love it, I include the asafetida but leave out the cayenne.

2 tablespoons peanut or olive oil

1 teaspoon whole brown or yellow mustard
    seeds

Pinch of ground asafetida

4 medium carrots (8 ounces), peeled and
    coarsely grated

Salt

2 cups plain yogurt, fat-free, low-fat, or rich,
    according to taste

Freshly ground black pepper

⅛ to ¼ teaspoon cayenne (optional)

Put the oil in a medium frying pan and set over medium-high heat. When hot, put in the mustard seeds. As soon as the mustard seeds begin to pop, a matter of seconds, put in the asafetida. Stir once and add the grated carrots. Stir and mix for 15 seconds, then turn off the heat. Add ¼ teaspoon salt and mix again. Let the carrots cool to room temperature.

Meanwhile, put the yogurt in a bowl and mix lightly with a fork or whisk until smooth and creamy. Add ¼ teaspoon salt, some black pepper, and the cayenne, if you wish to use it, and mix. When the carrots have cooled, mix them in. Serve at room temperature or chilled.

SERVES 2 TO 6

Yogurt with Herbs

INDIA

Hara Dahi

This makes a very refreshing relish at a meal. Try a dollop on a baked potato or baked eggplant.

1 cup plain yogurt

⅓ teaspoon salt

Freshly ground black pepper to taste

½ to 1 fresh hot green chile, finely chopped

1 tablespoon finely chopped fresh mint

2 tablespoons finely chopped fresh cilantro

1 tablespoon finely chopped chives

Put the yogurt in a bowl and beat lightly with a fork until smooth and creamy. Add the remaining ingredients and mix. Taste for the balance of flavors.

SERVES 4 TO 6

Onion and Mint "Raita"

INDIA

Pyaz Aur Pudina Ka Raita

This complements most bean dishes beautifully.

4 scallions

1 cup plain yogurt (a little less or more does
   not make any difference)

⅓ teaspoon salt, or to taste

Freshly ground black pepper

1 teaspoon ground roasted cumin seeds
   (page 724)

⅛ teaspoon cayenne

2 to 3 tablespoons finely chopped fresh mint

Cut the scallions into very thin rounds starting at the white section and going halfway up the pale green section (do not use the green parts). Put them into a small bowl filled with ice-cold water. Cover and refrigerate for 1 to 2 hours. Drain. Put the sliced scallions in a dish towel. Bring the 4 ends of the towel together and squeeze out as much moisture as possible from the scallions. Set aside.

Put the yogurt in a bowl and whisk lightly with a fork until smooth and creamy. Add the salt, pepper to taste, ground roasted cumin, and cayenne and mix well, then add the scallions and mint. Stir to mix. Serve chilled.

SERVES 4

Variation
Yogurt with Onion, Mint, and Chickpeas
Pyaz, Pudinay Aur Chholay Ka Raita

This is made exactly like the preceding recipe except that 1 cup (6 ounces) of drained cooked chickpeas is added at the end and mixed in. A little extra salt may be required. Sometimes I like to swirl a tablespoon of Tamarind Chutney (page 677) over the top. Serve with an Indian meal or eat by itself as a snack.

Yogurt with Spinach and Cloves   INDIA
Saag Ka Dahi

In this unusual Hyderabadi dish, which I discovered very recently, a little roasted rice powder is added to the yogurt and the flavorings come from cinnamon, cloves, and cardamom.

I call for 1 tablespoon of rice here even though much less is actually needed. It is just that very small amounts are hard to grind in electric machines.

Serve with a meal of rice or flatbreads and beans. It is amazingly good.

2 tablespoons plus 1 teaspoon peanut, canola, or olive oil

4 whole cardamom pods

1 small cinnamon stick (about 1 inch)

8 cloves

1 small onion (2 ounces), peeled, halved, and thinly sliced

1 teaspoon very finely grated fresh ginger

1 garlic clove, peeled and crushed to a pulp

10 ounces spinach, trimmed, washed, drained, and coarsely chopped

Salt

2 cups plain yogurt

Freshly ground black pepper

⅛ teaspoon cayenne, or to taste

1 tablespoon raw long-grain rice

Put 2 tablespoons of the oil in a large, wide, preferably nonstick frying pan or sauté pan and set over medium-high heat. When very hot, put in the cardamom, cinnamon, and 4 of the cloves. The spices will sizzle and expand in seconds. Quickly add the onion and stir and fry until the onion pieces begin to brown at the edges, about 3 minutes. Put in the ginger and garlic and stir once or twice. Add the spinach and ¼ teaspoon salt. Stir and cook the spinach for 3 to 4 minutes, or until it has wilted completely and is tender. Once the spinach is done, turn off the heat. Pick out all the whole spices (cardamom, cinnamon, and cloves) and discard them.

(recipe continues)

Put the yogurt in a bowl and beat it lightly with a fork until it is smooth and creamy. Add ½ teaspoon salt, pepper to taste, and cayenne. Mix again.

Put the rice into a small, preferably cast-iron frying pan and set over medium-high heat. Stir the rice until it is reddish in color, about 4 minutes. Remove and cool. Now grind the rice to a fine powder in a clean coffee grinder or other spice grinder. Add 1½ teaspoons of this rice powder to the yogurt and mix it in. Stir in the spinach, making sure it is distributed evenly throughout the yogurt.

Put the remaining 1 teaspoon oil in a small pan and set over medium-high heat. When hot, add the remaining 4 cloves; they will sizzle and expand. Pour the oil and cloves evenly over the yogurt but do not stir. Since the yogurt may be served at room temperature or chilled, you may cover and refrigerate it at this point. Just before serving, remove the cloves and mix the clove-scented oil into the yogurt.

SERVES 4 TO 6

Gujarati Cucumber "Raita"   INDIA
Kheera Raita

Serve as a relish or eat as a snack.

1 cup plain yogurt

½ teaspoon salt

½ teaspoon sugar

⅛ teaspoon cayenne

1 medium cucumber (about 5 inches), peeled and grated

1 tablespoon peanut or canola oil

½ teaspoon whole brown mustard seeds

¼ teaspoon whole cumin seeds

Put the yogurt in a bowl and beat lightly with a fork. Add the salt, sugar, and cayenne and mix. Add the cucumber and mix again.

Put the oil in a small frying pan and set over medium-high heat. When hot, put in the mustard and cumin seeds. As soon as the mustard seeds begin to pop, a matter of seconds, pour the contents of the frying pan over the yogurt. Stir to mix. Serve chilled.

SERVES 4

Yogurt with Tomatoes and Basil

This dish came about one year when we had leftovers of a tomato and basil salad from our lunch. I had refrigerated it but by dinnertime it was looking a bit tired, so I added fresh tomatoes and some yogurt and a most pleasing new dish was born. We were going to be doing a big outdoor grill for dinner that day (mixed vegetables, corn, and potatoes) and this turned out to be a perfect accompaniment.

1 cup plain yogurt

½ teaspoon salt

Freshly ground black pepper

2 medium tomatoes, peeled, seeded, and
diced into ¼-inch pieces

2 tablespoons chopped fresh basil

1 tablespoon extra-virgin olive oil

Put the yogurt in a bowl and beat lightly with a fork until smooth and creamy. Add the salt, pepper to taste, tomatoes, and basil. Mix and taste for the balance of flavors. Put in a serving bowl. Dribble the olive oil over the top just before serving.

SERVES 4 TO 6

Shamsi Davis'

Yogurt with Celery and Pistachios

IRAN

Boorani Karas

A medley of fresh, green colors, this boorani *is as soothing in looks as it is in taste. Serve as a starter, with flatbreads or with the main meal.*

2 tablespoons unsalted shelled pistachios

2 tablespoons unsalted butter

3 tablespoons very finely chopped onion

1½ cups very finely sliced celery

Salt

2 cups plain yogurt

Soak the pistachios in hot water for 3 hours. Taking a few out at a time, peel and quarter them lengthwise. Set aside.

Put the butter in a small frying pan and set over medium-high heat. When melted, add the onion and celery. Stir and fry for 3 to 4 minutes, or until slightly softened, turning the heat down if the celery threatens to take on any color. Add a little salt (about ¼ teaspoon or less) and stir to mix. Turn off the heat and allow to cool a bit.

(recipe continues)

Put the yogurt in a bowl and beat lightly with a fork until smooth and creamy. Stir in ½ teaspoon salt. Set aside 1 tablespoon of the celery mixture and add the rest of the contents of the frying pan to the yogurt. Stir all but 2 teaspoons of the pistachios into the yogurt bowl as well. Serve garnished with the reserved celery and pistachios.

SERVES 4 TO 6

Shamsi Davis'

Yogurt with Eggplant and Walnuts IRAN

Boorani Bademjan

Offered with flatbreads at the start of a meal (but also wonderful with it), this dish is served at room temperature or chilled.

The saffron used here is often the ground powder. I, however, feel that if you are to use it at all, it is best to take a generous pinch of saffron threads and then pound them to a powder with a pinch of coarse sugar in a mortar. You could also leave the saffron out altogether.

1 large eggplant (¾ to 1 pound)

2 tablespoons unsalted butter

1 garlic clove, peeled and finely chopped

3 tablespoons finely chopped onion

2 cups plain yogurt

¾ to 1 teaspoon salt

Freshly ground black pepper

3 tablespoons chopped walnuts

Generous pinch of ground saffron (see recipe introduction)

6 to 8 fresh basil leaves

Preheat the oven to 450°F. Prick the eggplant all over with a fork first and lay it in a baking tray lined with foil. Bake, turning every 15 minutes, for about an hour. It should flatten and turn very soft inside. Allow the eggplant to cool somewhat, then peel by hand, chop off the stem end, and mash finely in a bowl.

Put the butter in a small pan and set over medium heat. As soon as it has melted, put in the garlic and onion and stir and sauté until they soften, turning the heat down as needed so they do not brown. Turn off the heat and allow to cool.

Put the yogurt in a bowl and beat lightly with a fork until smooth and creamy. Add the salt, pepper to taste, mashed eggplant, and walnuts and mix well. The yogurt may now be covered and refrigerated until needed. To serve, transfer to a serving bowl and sprinkle saffron over the top. Garnish with the basil leaves.

SERVES 6

Yogurt with Green Mango

INDIA

Mangai Pacchadi

This makes a very pleasant counterpoint to grain and bean dishes.

If you cannot get a sour green mango—which is sold by Indian and Thai grocers—use a rock-hard, semiripe mango. Its flesh will be somewhat sweet but will still taste good.

1 cup plain yogurt

1 small-medium, green unripe sour mango
    (page 315), peeled, the flesh removed
    from the stone and then cut into ¼-inch
    dice

Scant ½ teaspoon salt, or to taste

Freshly ground black pepper

1 garlic clove, peeled and crushed to a pulp

1 teaspoon peanut or canola oil

¼ teaspoon whole cumin seeds

1 dried hot red chile, crumbled

10 fresh curry leaves, if available

Put the yogurt in a bowl and beat lightly with a fork until smooth and creamy. Add the mango, salt, pepper, and garlic. Stir and taste for saltiness.

Put the oil in a small pan and set over medium heat. When very hot, add the cumin seeds. A few seconds later, add the chile and a second later, the curry leaves. Now quickly pick up the pan and pour its contents over the yogurt. Stir to mix.

SERVES 4 TO 6

Chayote with a South Indian Yogurt Sauce

INDIA

Moru Kootu

In South India, yogurt is used as a sauce for boiled, steamed, and stir-fried vegetables. Because no thickening agent is added to stabilize it, the yogurt is added at the last minute and then just gently heated through to prevent curdling. It does not go into the pan alone, but is accompanied by fresh coconut and a few choice roasted spices.

The chayote (also known as sayote *and* chow chow*) is a vegetable I just adore. Shaped like a somewhat flattened pear and light green in color, it has a squashlike taste but a much firmer, crunchier texture. It should be peeled, and the seed inside may be removed or not as you wish—it has a different texture from the vegetable's flesh but is really very good.*

If you cannot find chayotes, you may substitute an equal quantity of zucchini (cook it in

(recipe continues)

DAIRY

half the water for just 5 minutes); potato (boil, peel, dice, and then cook like the zucchini); or peeled pumpkin (cooked like the chayote but for 15 minutes).

Fresh coconut makes the sauce really creamy but if you cannot find it or are pressed for time, use 5 tablespoons of dessicated unsweetened coconut that has been soaked in 3 tablespoons of hot water for an hour.

This is a wonderful dish that you will want to make with great frequency. Serve it with rice and split peas or beans.

3 chayotes (about 1½ pounds in all)

2 tablespoons peanut or canola oil

¼ teaspoon whole brown mustard seeds

10 to 15 fresh curry leaves, if available

⅛ teaspoon ground turmeric

1 teaspoon salt

2 teaspoons whole coriander seeds

1 whole dried hot red chile

¼ teaspoon fenugreek seeds

1 teaspoon *chana dal* or yellow split peas

1 cup plain yogurt

½ cup finely grated fresh coconut (page 718)

½ to 1 fresh hot green chile, very finely chopped

Peel the chayotes and then halve each one lengthwise like an apple. Lay each half on a board, cut side down, and slice it lengthwise into 3 sections. Cut these sections crosswise into ½-inch pieces. Leave the seeds in.

Put the oil into a wide pan or frying pan and set over medium-high heat. When very hot, put in the mustard seeds. As soon as the mustard seeds pop, a matter of seconds, put in the curry leaves. Stir once and add the chayote pieces. Stir for a minute and add the turmeric and ¾ teaspoon of the salt. Stir for another minute and then add ½ cup of water and bring to a boil. Cover, turn the heat down to low, and cook 20 minutes, or until the chayote is tender.

While the chayote cooks, put the coriander seeds, red chile, fenugreek seeds, and *chana dal* in a small cast-iron frying pan over medium heat. Stir and cook until the *chana dal* is reddish in color. Remove and cool, then grind in a clean coffee grinder until powdery.

Put the yogurt in a bowl. Add the remaining ¼ teaspoon salt, the roasted spices, coconut, and chile and combine.

As soon as the chayote is tender, uncover the pan, turn the heat down to very, very low, and add the yogurt mixture. Stir it in. Taste for salt. Heat gently, stirring all the time. Do not let the yogurt come even near a boil. As soon as it is heated through, turn off the heat.

SERVES 4

Yogurt with Banana in the South Indian Style

INDIA

Pacchadi

Pacchadis *are the raitas of South India. Often thickened with very fresh, finely grated coconut, they appear at many vegetarian meals in different guises. Here is a very simple rendition. If you cannot get fresh coconut, just leave it out.*

You may serve this as a relish or eat it as a snack.

1 cup plain yogurt

⅓ teaspoon salt

Freshly ground black pepper

1 teaspoon very finely grated fresh ginger

1 teaspoon sugar

2 tablespoons very finely grated fresh coconut, if available

½ to 1 fresh hot green chile, finely chopped

2 teaspoons peanut or canola oil

½ teaspoon whole brown mustard seeds

1 firm but ripe medium banana

Put the yogurt in a bowl and beat lightly with a fork until smooth and creamy. Add the salt, pepper to taste, ginger, sugar, coconut, and chile. Taste for the balance of flavors. Put the oil in a small pan and set over medium-high heat. When very hot, put in the mustard seeds. They will begin to pop almost immediately. Pour the oil with the mustard seeds over the yogurt and stir the mixture in. Just before you sit down to eat, slice the banana into ⅓-inch-thick rounds and blend into the yogurt mixture. Serve immediately.

SERVES 4

Yogurt with Walnuts and Raisins

INDIA

Akhrote Aur Kishmish Ka Raita

You can add a few tablespoons of diced sour green apple to this if you like.

1 cup plain yogurt

¼ teaspoon salt, or to taste

1 teaspoon sugar

Freshly ground black pepper

1 tablespoon finely chopped fresh mint

¼ cup chopped walnuts

1 tablespoon *ghee* (page 723) or peanut oil

¼ cup golden raisins

(recipe continues)

Put the yogurt in a bowl and beat lightly with a whisk or fork until it is smooth and creamy. Add the salt, sugar, pepper to taste, mint, and walnuts and combine.

Put the *ghee* in a small frying pan and set over medium heat. When hot, put in the raisins. Stir them briefly just until they plump up. Quickly pour the *ghee* and raisins into the bowl with the yogurt. Stir to mix.

SERVES 4 TO 6

YOGURT CHEESES

Yogurt cheeses are eaten all the way from the eastern Mediterranean to the Indian subcontinent. They are simple enough to prepare. Just put yogurt in a cheesecloth or a piece of muslin, tie it into a bundle, and hang it up to allow some of the liquid to drip out. You could also put the yogurt in a coffee filter and set it in a strainer which you then balance over a bowl. During this process, the yogurt consolidates itself enough to become spreadable. If you want a soft cheese, hang it up for 3 hours; if you want a firmer cheese, hang it for up to 8 hours. Now, almost anything may be added to it. In western Greece, it could be grated feta cheese and chopped red bell peppers; in eastern Turkey, it might be chopped olives and gherkins or walnuts and red pepper paste; and in western India, it could be a puree of fresh summer mangoes. Yogurt cheeses may be served as appetizer courses, at breakfast, as parts of the main meal, and even as dessert. Even though rich, whole-milk yogurt makes the richest cheese, low-fat yogurt is also quite acceptable.

Yogurt Cheese

If you intend to eat this cheese plain, sprinkle about ¼ teaspoon salt over the yogurt before you hang it up to drain off the liquid. One of the commonest ways of serving this in the Middle East is to spread it out in a shallow bowl or saucer and sprinkle some paprika and good olive oil over the top. It is eaten with flatbreads.

If you make yogurt cheese often, you could sew yourself a bag of tripled cheesecloth or muslin that ends up being a foot square.

2 cups plain whole milk or nonfat yogurt

Set a strainer over a bowl. Cut out a tripled thickness of cheesecloth about 13 inches square and line the strainer with it. Empty the yogurt into the center of the cheesecloth. Bring the 4 corners of the cheesecloth together and make a loose bundle, tying the top with twine. Hang up the bundle where it can drip for 3 to

8 hours, as your recipe requires (3 hours will make for a creamier cheese and 8 hours for a firmer one). Untie the bundle and remove the cheese from the cloth. It may now be refrigerated in a closed container where it will keep for 48 hours.

MAKES ABOUT 1 CUP

Yogurt Cheese with Zahtar and Olive Oil

Here is a very common way of eating yogurt cheese all over western Asia. Serve it with flatbreads at the start of a meal or with breakfast.

Zahtar may be made at home or bought from a Middle Eastern grocer.

2 cups plain whole milk yogurt

¼ teaspoon salt

1 tablespoon Zahtar (page 705)

1 tablespoon good-quality extra-virgin olive oil

Make the soft yogurt cheese according to directions on page 556, draining the yogurt for 8 hours. Transfer to a bowl, add the salt, and mix. Spread the cheese in a shallow serving plate and sprinkle the Zahtar evenly over the top. Dribble the oil on top of the spice mixture and serve.

MAKES ABOUT 1 CUP

Sweet Yogurt Cheese with Bananas

Kela Shrikhand

This is a slightly sweetened yogurt, which is served with the meal in Gujarat, where it originated, but may be served as dessert or a snack if preferred.

2 cups plain whole milk yogurt

¼ teaspoon ground cardamom seeds

¼ cup packed brown sugar

1 ripe banana, mashed

1 teaspoon *ghee* (page 723) or peanut oil

2 tablespoons chopped pistachios

2 tablespoons chopped blanched almonds

(recipe continues)

Make the soft yogurt cheese according to directions on page 556, draining the yogurt for 3 hours. Transfer the yogurt cheese to a bowl and add the cardamom, sugar, and banana. Mix, push through a coarse strainer, and put in a serving bowl.

Put the ghee in a small frying pan and set over medium heat. When hot, put in the pistachios and almonds and stir them about until they are lightly toasted. Remove them and scatter them evenly over the yogurt. Cover the yogurt bowl and chill in the refrigerator.

MAKES ABOUT 1¾ CUPS

From the Ta Nissia Restaurant in Salonica

Soft Yogurt Cheese with Cucumber   GREECE

Tzatziki

Serve this as a dip with a pita-type bread or with any fritters, such as Crisp Zucchini Fritters (page 298). You may also serve this as part of any meal as a salad.

2 cups plain whole milk yogurt

1 Kirby cucumber or a 5-inch segment of an English (hothouse) cucumber

½ teaspoon salt

1 to 2 tablespoons finely chopped fresh dill

1 garlic clove, peeled and finely crushed

2 tablespoons olive oil

Make the soft yogurt cheese according to directions on page 556, draining the yogurt for 4 to 5 hours.

Peel the cucumber and cut it into ¼-inch dice. Sprinkle with ¼ teaspoon salt, toss, and set aside for 1 hour. Squeeze out as much moisture as possible.

Put the yogurt cheese into a bowl. Add ¼ teaspoon salt, as well as the dill, cucumber, garlic, and oil. Mix well.

MAKES ABOUT 1¼ CUPS

From the Ta Nissia Restaurant in Salonica

Soft Yogurt Cheese with Feta   GREECE

Htipiti

There is nothing quite like sitting at a beach table in Greece, slathering mounds of this dip onto triangles of pita bread and washing it down with beer or milky ouzo. You may also serve this with fritters, such as Crisp Zucchini Fritters (page 298). The dip may be included in any meal as a salad.

As feta cheese can be fairly salty, it is best to taste the dip before adding any salt whatsoever.

2 cups plain whole milk yogurt

⅓ cup (2 ounces) very well crumbled
  imported feta cheese or soft goat cheese

1 tablespoon lightly crushed green
  peppercorns

2 tablespoons very finely chopped red bell
  pepper

½ to 1 very finely chopped hot green chile

1 tablespoon olive oil

Salt (optional)

Make the soft yogurt cheese according to directions on page 556, draining the yogurt for 3 hours. Put the yogurt cheese in a bowl. Add all the other ingredients *except* the salt. Mix well and taste. Add a little salt only if you need it.

MAKES ABOUT 1½ CUPS

Spiced Yogurt Cheese with Olives and Gherkins   TURKEY

Acili Yagur

I was served this around sunset, as I sat sipping a drink on the banks of the Bosphorus in Istanbul. There were some flatbreads on the side. Nothing else was required. (You may also serve this yogurt cheese as a dip for potato chips.)

In order to chop the vegetables finely, you may use a knife or a mezzaluna.

The chile powder from Aleppo that was used for seasoning was coarse, very red in color, and delicious. I find that the coarse Korean chile powder used in the making of kimchi works very well too.

(recipe continues)

2 cups plain whole milk yogurt

1 garlic clove, peeled and finely crushed

¼ to ½ teaspoon coarse chile powder (see
   recipe introduction)

¼ teaspoon salt

12 to 14 green olives stuffed with pimiento,
   very finely chopped

3 to 4 small gherkins, very finely chopped

Make the soft yogurt cheese according to directions on page 556, draining the
yogurt for 8 hours. Transfer the yogurt cheese to a bowl; add all the other ingredients. Mix well and taste for the balance of seasonings. Pile the cheese in the shape
of a rounded hillock on a serving dish and serve with flatbreads.

MAKES ABOUT 1¼ CUPS

Yogurt Cheese with
Red Pepper Paste   TURKEY/WESTERN ASIA

*This makes a wonderful dip for flatbreads, even for potato chips. It may also be used as a spread
for sandwiches.*

   *Make it as spicy as you like. Red pepper pastes come in varying degrees of heat (mine, page
673, is relatively mild). You can increase the heat by adding some coarse chile powder from Aleppo,
if you can get it, or just a generous pinch of cayenne.*

2 cups plain whole milk yogurt

¼ teaspoon salt

¼ teaspoon dried thyme or ½ teaspoon fresh

2 tablespoons chopped walnuts

1 tablespoon Red Pepper Paste (page 673)

⅛ to ¼ teaspoon coarse chile powder (see
   recipe introduction)

3 tablespoons extra-virgin olive oil

Make the soft yogurt cheese according to directions on page 556, draining the
yogurt for 8 hours. Transfer to a bowl and add the salt, thyme, and walnuts. Mix
well and taste for the balance of seasonings. Put the pepper paste in a small cup.
Add the chile powder, if desired, and mix it in. Now add the oil and mix it in as
well, but not thoroughly. Add the red pepper paste mixture to the yogurt cheese.
Stir with a wooden spoon in circular motions, but do not mix thoroughly. The idea
here is to retain streaks of red (the pepper paste) and yellow (the oil) in the white
cheese. Pile the cheese in a mound on a serving dish.

MAKES ABOUT 1 CUP

Homemade Cheeses

Cheese making is generally a complicated craft but there are many simple cheeses and simplified versions of more complicated cheeses that we can all make at home as our ancestors did, using readily available curdling agents such as vinegar, vegetarian rennet, tartaric acid, citric acid, and even lemon juice or buttermilk.

Cheese-making equipment need not be complicated either: A heavy pan, a wooden spoon, a colander, meat thermometer (or cheese thermometer, if you can get one), and cheesecloth are all you need. If weights are called for, use large cans balanced on a board. One useful hint: After you have made your cheese, soak all soiled equipment in tap water at room temperature. They will clean up much more easily this way.

Homemade Indian Cheese INDIA
Paneer

The Indian-style homemade cheese, known almost universally by its Indian name, paneer, *is not at all unlike Italian mozzarella. Indeed, mozzarella in Italy is made from the milk of the descendants of imported Indian water buffaloes! Water buffalo milk is richer than cow's milk and makes for a creamier cheese. Indian* paneer *may be eaten as is with spicy toppings of saladlike vegetables (rather like mozzarella with tomatoes and basil) and it can also be cooked with innumerable sauces and seasonings.*

Paneer is really native to the dairy-rich northern state of Punjab. Here every little dhaba— *the best equivalent to this would be the American coffee shop—makes its own. As one batch is used up, a new one is readied to serve a steady stream of customers, from truck drivers to industrialists. It is also sold ready-made in the markets all over India, as its popularity has spread across the nation in the last fifty years. Paneer is so easy to make at home that I am surprised more people do not do it. Among the advantages of preparing it yourself is that you can press it to the degree you want. One day you might want very soft curds to make into a simple salad—many old people prefer soft curds as they do not require much chewing—and in this form it may also be used in place of ricotta. Another day you may want to make a proper* paneer *and then convert it into crisply fried, spicy slices. I make large, thick patties of cheese if I want to cut slices. When I want cubes, I generally make small patties.*

I used to press the cheese for several hours, making it quite dense. On my last trip to the villages of the Punjab, I realized that this was not at all necessary. The villagers were pressing their cheeses for a mere 3 to 4 minutes! The cheeses were light and delicious.

The quantities below will yield 9 ounces of Soft Cheese Curds *or a small (3½ × ¾-*

(recipe continues)

inch) patty of Homemade Indian Cheese. *For a large (5½ ×1-inch) patty, double the quantities of whole milk and vinegar. The pressing time remains the same.*

2 quarts rich whole milk   3 to 4 tablespoons distilled white vinegar

Put the milk in a large, heavy pan and set over medium-high heat.

Meanwhile, place a colander in the sink and line it with a clean dish towel or 3 to 4 layers of cheesecloth at least 24 inches square.

When the milk begins to boil, turn the heat down to low. Quickly add 3 table-spoons of the vinegar and stir. The mixture will curdle at this point, the thin, greenish whey completely separating from the white fluffy curds. If this does not happen, add the remaining tablespoon of vinegar and repeat the process. Empty the mixture into the lined colander. Most of the whey will drain out.

To prepare soft Homemade Indian Cheese curds: Let the cheese sit in the colander for 6 to 10 minutes. The curds are now ready to be eaten.

To prepare firm Homemade Indian Cheese *patties* **large and small for frying, slicing, or cubing:** Allow most of the whey to drain out of the colander. As soon as the curds have drained, gather up the ends of the cheesecloth and twist to squeeze out as much water as possible. You will now have a round bundle and a well-twisted section of cloth just above it, which you can tie firmly with string or just leave tightly twisted. Lay the cloth and its contents on a flat board set in the sink. Flatten the bundle into a patty shape, making sure that the twisted section or knot holds the cheese in place. This section can be folded over to one side. Put another board on top of the patty. Now put a 5-pound weight on the patty and press for 3 to 4 minutes. The cheese is now ready. It may be unwrapped, covered with a clean, damp cloth, and kept in the refrigerator for 24 hours but is best if used immediately.

Variations

You can also flavor the cheese, if you like. As soon as most of the whey has drained out of the colander, add any spices or herbs of your choice to the cheese and mix them in gently. Then proceed to tie up the cheesecloth bundle and weight it. The seasonings do not have to be Indian. Here are two examples of flavored home-made cheese *(paneer)*:

Homemade Indian Cheese Flavored with Black Pepper, Roasted Cumin Seeds, and Roasted *Ajwain* Seeds

Try marinating this along with the vegetables in Mixed Grilled Vegetables, Indian Style (page 314), then broiling quickly on both sides, or until it has a few brown spots. It can also be charcoal grilled along with the vegetables.

For a large patty, combine 1 teaspoon black peppercorns, ½ teaspoon whole cumin seeds, and ½ teaspoon *ajwain* seeds. (For a smaller patty, halve these quantities.)

Put a small cast-iron frying pan to heat over a medium flame. When hot, put in the spices. Stir them around for a minute until very lightly roasted. Remove and let them cool. Grind very coarsely. Now add these to the curds once most of the whey has drained out of the colander. Stir gently to mix and then proceed to tie up the curds and put a weight on them to complete making the cheese.

Homemade Indian Cheese Flavored with Rosemary, Thyme, and Oregano

This is excellent when marinated in a simple dressing (such as a vinaigrette) for 2 to 3 hours and broiled quickly on both sides or until it has a few brown spots. It can also be charcoal grilled.

For a large patty, add 1 teaspoon finely chopped fresh rosemary or ½ teaspoon dried crumbled rosemary, 1 teaspoon finely chopped fresh thyme or ½ teaspoon dried thyme, and 1 teaspoon finely chopped fresh oregano or ½ teaspoon dried oregano to the curds once most of the whey has drained out. (For a small patty, just halve the seasonings.) Stir gently to mix and then proceed to tie up the curds and put a weight on them to complete making the cheese.

With the assistance of Ricki Carroll of The New England Cheesemaking Supply Company

Homemade White Latin American Cheese

LATIN AMERICA

Queso Blanco

Although almost identical to Indian paneer, queso blanco is made from milk that has not been allowed to come to a boil. Once the curds and whey have separated, it is drained for 1 hour, or until it stops dripping. It may be used in stir-fried dishes just like bean curd or added to soups and pasta dishes. It may also be used in any of the paneer recipes.

1 gallon rich whole milk   6 to 8 tablespoons white vinegar

Put the milk in a large heavy pan and set over medium heat.

Meanwhile, place a colander in the sink and line it with a clean dish towel or 3 to 4 layers of cheesecloth at least 24 inches square.

When the milk reaches 185°F., slowly add the vinegar as you stir. The mixture will curdle at this point, the thin, greenish whey completely separating from the white fluffy curds. (The temperature may continue to rise. Try to maintain an even temperature until curdling takes place, but do not let the milk boil.) Empty the curdled mixture into the lined colander. Most of the whey will drain out. Gather up the ends of the cloth, twist the cloth, and squeeze out as much water as possible. You will now have a round bundle and a well-twisted section of cloth just above it, which you can tie firmly with string or leave tightly twisted. Hang up this bundle for 1 to 3 hours (I hang it on the kitchen faucet so it drips into the sink), or until it stops dripping. The cheese is now ready. Unwrap it, cover it with plastic wrap, and refrigerate it. It should last 3 to 4 days, though it is best used within 24 hours.

MAKES ABOUT 1½ POUNDS

With the assistance of Ricki Carroll of The New England Cheesemaking Supply Company

Homemade Italian Mascarpone ITALY

This soft, sweet, buttery Italian cheese is now available in most specialty shops. But if for some reason you are stuck somewhere where you cannot lay your hands on it or simply find it too expensive, I offer a very simple recipe. All you really need are light cream and tartaric acid. Tartaric acid is easy enough to get but for some reason I often have great difficulty finding light cream with 25 percent butterfat, once a common item in all our supermarkets. My cheese coach suggested I experiment with 1/3 heavy cream and 2/3 skim milk, and this worked perfectly.

Serve a little of this cheese on toast with jam or with fresh fruit.

2 cups heavy cream

6 cups skim milk

1/2 teaspoon tartaric acid (I use cream of tartar, which works perfectly)

Place a large colander in the sink and line it with a clean dish towel or 3 to 4 layers of cheesecloth at least 24 inches square.

Combine the cream and milk in the top half of a double boiler and set it over high heat. Stir frequently with a wooden spoon and keep a thermometer nearby. When the temperature begins to near 175°F., turn the heat down to low. You are aiming for a temperature of 185°F., but you do not want to shoot past it. As soon as you hit the correct temperature, turn the heat down to very, very low and scatter the cream of tartar over the top of the cream. Mix it in thoroughly, turn off the heat, but leave the double boiler in place. Within a minute, the cream should begin to thicken and set. You should also begin to see a thin line of greenish whey forming around the edges. If that does not happen, add just another pinch of the tartar, no more. Stir this in as well. Within 2 to 3 minutes, the cream should have coagulated. Pour the contents of the pan into the lined colander in the sink.

If the draining is held up by the thick curds, lift up the cloth by its 4 ends, forming a loose bundle. If the flow of whey slows down, encourage it by sloshing the cheese from side to side or pushing the bundle against the sides of the colander and pressing with a big spoon. When you feel you have got out as much whey as you can easily, put the cheese bundle in a small sieve, set the sieve on a small bowl, and put the whole thing in the refrigerator. The cheese is full of butterfat and will spoil easily, so let it drain in cool comfort. When it stops dripping, 2 to 4 hours, remove the cheese from the cloth and put it in a tightly covered container before you refrigerate it again.

MAKES ABOUT 2 CUPS/1 POUND

With the assistance of Ricki Carroll of The New England Cheesemaking Supply Company

Homemade Syrian Cheese SYRIA

Joban

Another mozzarella-type cheese, but softer and more delicate, this Syrian creation is almost always a part of the maza *or appetizer course in that country, along with flatbreads, bulgur and chickpea salads, and olives. I remember being offered breads, cheeses, and olives for breakfast as well—this is still very much a Mediterranean country.*

You can also serve this cheese as you would Italian mozzarella, with sliced tomatoes and olive oil.

To make this cheese you need rennet—vegetarian rennet. Vegetarian coagulating agents have existed since Roman times, when an extract made from the bark of a fig tree was used. Today, the flower of the thistle (Cynara cardunaculus) *is commonly used in Spain and Portugal. Extracts from weeds such as lady's bedstraw* (Galium verum) *and the stinging nettle* (Urtica dioca) *have been known to serve the same purpose. For our home use, we can buy commercial vegetarian rennet derived from mold, which is sold in liquid form. Look for it in specialty food shops and health food stores. If all else fails, you can get it from my source, The New England Cheesemaking Supply Company, 85 Main Street, Ashfield, MA 01330, Fax (413) 628-4061, Phone (413) 628-3808. Once opened, it should be refrigerated.*

1 gallon rich whole milk

¼ teaspoon liquid vegetarian rennet diluted
    in 1½ tablespoons water

Good sea salt or kosher salt

Put the milk in a large heavy pan over low heat. Stir occasionally until the milk is lukewarm and registers around 100°F. on a thermometer. Sprinkle the rennet mixture over the surface of the milk and stir very thoroughly with a wooden spoon to mix. Turn off the heat, cover, and let the pan sit for 15 minutes. Uncover and stir gently, letting your spoon go all the way to the bottom, and cover again. Let the pan sit for 45 minutes, or until the milk looks set.

In the meantime, place a large colander in the sink and line it with a clean dish towel or 3 to 4 layers of cheesecloth at least 24 inches square. Empty the cheese into the lined colander. The whey should run out. If it does not—sometimes the thick curds block the flow—gather the 4 ends of the cloth together and pick up the cheese bundle; the liquid should flow out more easily. Press the bundle a bit to help get rid of the whey. When most, but not all, of the liquid has been removed, put the bundle back in the colander and open it up. Now pick up a handful of the curds and put them on one palm. Press down with a slightly cupped second palm.

The dual aim here is to form a patty about 1½ inches thick and at the same time squeeze out the remaining moisture. (The last bit of liquid must be removed this way or you will not be able to form soft, whole patties.) Form 5 patties, making a dimple on top of each one.

Lay the patties in a single layer. Sprinkle coarse salt over the top. Either eat immediately or cover with plastic wrap and refrigerate.

MAKES 5 THICK 3½-INCH CAKES

Delicate Stir-Fry of Soft Cheese Curds and Vegetables

You may use 9 ounces of any mixed vegetables here. Just cut them to a uniform small size. This is a delicate dish that I made up when some friends were coming for lunch and wanted something very light. I served it with plain rice and a salad.

20 fresh asparagus spears

1 recipe Homemade Indian Cheese, prepared in the Soft Curds style (page 561)

1 tablespoon olive oil

1 carrot, peeled and diced into ⅓-inch pieces

½ cup shelled peas (defrosted frozen peas may be used)

1 scallion, cut into ⅓-inch lengths (use both white and green sections)

1½ tablespoons oriental sesame oil

4 teaspoons soy sauce

½ teaspoon sugar

Cut the tough ends off the asparagus spears and discard. Peel the lower half of the asparagus. Stacking several spears together, cut into ⅓-inch-long segments, leaving the heads whole.

In a bowl, crumble the cheese into small pieces. Set aside.

Put the olive oil in a medium nonstick frying pan or sauté pan and set over medium-high heat. When it is hot, put in the asparagus, carrot, peas, and scallion. Stir for 1 minute, or until they brighten in color. Add ¼ cup of water and bring to a simmer. Cover the pan, turn the heat to medium-low, and cook for 3 minutes, or until the asparagus is just tender. Uncover and add the sesame oil, soy sauce, and sugar. Stir and cook gently, uncovered, for 1 minute. Put in the cheese, stir to mix well, and serve immediately.

SERVES 4 TO 6

Homemade Indian Cheese Served with a "Salsa"

INDIA

Chatpata Paneer

There are hundreds of Indian relishes and fresh chutneys that could be called "salsas." This one is made with a traditional mixture of onions and tomatoes with the addition of avocados, which are now quite widely cultivated in India. It makes a perfect topping for fresh paneer. *The avocado should be cut and folded into the salsa at the last moment.*

1 cup peeled and coarsely chopped ripe
    tomatoes

½ cup very finely diced onion

½ to 1 fresh hot green chile, finely chopped

3 to 4 tablespoons chopped fresh cilantro

½ × 1-inch piece of fresh ginger, peeled and
    finely diced

3 tablespoons fresh lemon juice

¾ to 1 teaspoon salt

¼ teaspoon cayenne

1 teaspoon ground roasted cumin seeds
    (page 720)

½ medium avocado, peeled and coarsely
    chopped

1 small patty Homemade Indian Cheese
    (Paneer) (page 561), cut crosswise into
    ¼- to ½-inch-thick, long oval slices

Combine all the ingredients except the cheese in a bowl and toss well. Divide the cheese slices among 2 to 4 serving plates. Spoon the "salsa" over the cheese slices and serve immediately.

SERVES 2 TO 4

Homemade Indian Cheese with Tomatoes

INDIA

Timatar Paneer

A very simple paneer *dish from the Punjab region of northwestern India, this creation with its gnocchilike taste and texture may be served as an appetizer or a main course. It is a very common winter dish in the villages of the Punjab, where it is served with plain whole wheat breads called* rotis. *Perhaps store-bought pita bread could serve as a convenient alternative. An attractive, substantial green salad would be all that is needed to complete the meal. In Punjab, this "salad" could take the form of sliced white radishes and cucumbers or some delicious pickles.*

2 tablespoons peanut or canola oil

¼ cup finely chopped onion

1¼ cups peeled and finely chopped tomatoes

1 teaspoon ground cumin seeds

½ teaspoon ground turmeric

¼ teaspoon cayenne

⅓ teaspoon salt, or to taste

1 small patty Homemade Indian Cheese *(Paneer)* (page 561), cut into 1 × ¾-inch cubes

Freshly ground black pepper

2 to 3 tablespoons finely chopped fresh cilantro or parsley

Put the oil in a frying pan over medium-high heat. When hot, put in the onion and stir and fry until the onion is light brown at the edges. Add the chopped tomatoes, the cumin, turmeric, cayenne, and salt. Stir and cook over medium heat until slightly reduced, about 5 minutes. Add the *paneer* cubes and stir gently. Cook over low heat for 2 minutes. Stir in black pepper to taste and cilantro. Serve hot.

SERVES 3 TO 4

Homemade Indian Cheese Cooked in the Style of Scrambled Eggs INDIA
Paneer Ki Bhurji

This is one of the most popular dishes served at the truck stops—dhabas—of Punjab. The Grand Trunk Road running across the breadth of India is dotted with such eateries, where most of the cooking is done outdoors, barely protected by a colorful canvas top. The style of cooking is quick stir-frying, with lots of karhais *(Indian woks) working full time over hot wood fires. Orders for* paneer bhurji *come in every few minutes. A little oil is thrown into the* karhai, *in go some cumin seeds, some onions, ginger, tomatoes, and green chile. There is some fast stirring. A few handfuls of grated fresh cheese are strewn in and stirred. Some salt and other dry spices are sprinkled, another stir, and, voilà!, it is ready. It takes about as long to cook as it took me to write this paragraph. This dish, which does indeed resemble scrambled eggs, is generally eaten with Indian* rotis *or* naans *but may be eaten with pita breads or, indeed, any bread. A salad would be good on the side.*

(recipe continues)

2 tablespoons peanut or canola oil

1/3 teaspoon whole cumin seeds

2 tablespoons finely chopped onion

1/2 × 1-inch piece of fresh ginger, peeled and very finely chopped

1/2 cup finely chopped tomato

1 to 3 teaspoons finely chopped fresh hot green chile (optional)

1 small patty Homemade Indian Cheese *(Paneer)* (page 561), grated on the coarsest holes of a grater to get long shreds

1/8 teaspoon ground turmeric

1/8 to 1/4 teaspoon cayenne

Scant 1/2 teaspoon salt

1/8 teaspoon garam masala (page 723)

Put the oil in a frying pan and set over medium-high heat. When it is hot, put in the cumin seeds and let them sizzle for a few seconds. Add the onion and stir and fry until the onion is light brown at the edges. Put in the ginger and stir once. Then add the tomato and cook for a few seconds. Stir in the green chile, if desired. Turn the heat down to medium, add the grated cheese, turmeric, cayenne, salt, and garam masala, and stir gently to mix. Serve hot.

SERVES 4

Homemade Indian Cheese with Spinach

INDIA

Saag Paneer

Here's another Punjabi specialty eaten with whole wheat rotis *(flatbreads) through the winter months when spinach, indeed an enormous variety of greens, is plentiful. The spinach is sometimes cooked by itself and at other times in combination with other greens such as mustard greens* (sarson) *and fenugreek greens* (methi). *A few green chiles are always thrown in, partly for their heat and partly for their vitamins. The mixture is cooked until it is buttery soft and then lightly mashed, almost churned, with a special wooden masher not dissimilar to an implement used in Mexico to froth up milk. A medley of tomatoes, ginger, and onions is then sautéed separately and added to the greens. Pieces of fresh* paneer *are thrown in only for the last 5 minutes of cooking.*

Despite its peasant origins, this dish is loved by even the most sophisticated Punjabis and has, in some mysterious way, become an Indian restaurant staple. Sadly, restaurants seldom make it with fresh greens or with paneer *that has been made just that morning. But you can have it that way at home.*

If you like, fresh or dried fenugreek greens, sold by Indian grocers, may be added for an extra earthy flavor. If using fresh fenugreek, take the leaves off the stalks and wash them well.

1¾ pounds fresh spinach, trimmed, washed, and coarsely chopped

2 tablespoons dried fenugreek leaves (dried *methi*) or 2 to 3 handfuls of fresh fenugreek leaves (fresh *methi*), optional (see recipe introduction)

1 fresh hot green chile, coarsely chopped

1 teaspoon cornmeal

3 tablespoons peanut or canola oil

¼ cup finely chopped onion

1½ × 1-inch piece of fresh ginger, peeled and finely grated to a pulp

1 cup finely chopped tomatoes

1¼ teaspoons salt

1½ to 2 teaspoons ground roasted cumin seeds (page 724)

¼ teaspoon cayenne

¼ teaspoon ground cinnamon

1 small patty Homemade Indian Cheese *(Paneer)* (page 561), cut into 1 × ¾-inch cubes

Bring 1 cup of water to boil in a large pan. Put in the washed spinach, dried or fresh fenugreek leaves, if using, and green chile. Cover the pan and cook gently for 25 minutes. Now mash the spinach with a wooden masher or potato masher until you have a coarse puree. (You can blend the spinach in a blender but that texture is too fine for my taste.) Blend in the cornmeal and cook gently for another 5 minutes, stirring now and then.

In a separate frying pan, heat the oil over medium-high heat. When hot, add the onion and stir and fry until it begins to brown. Add the ginger and stir once or twice, then add the tomatoes and cook over medium-low heat for 10 minutes, or until the texture thickens and the color of the tomatoes intensifies. Stir the tomato mixture into the spinach mixture, then add the salt, roasted cumin, cayenne, and cinnamon and stir to mix. Cook gently for 5 minutes. Finally, add the cubed *paneer*, stir gently, and cook, covered, on low heat for 5 minutes. Serve hot.

SERVES 4 TO 5

Crispy, Spicy Slices of Homemade Indian Cheese

INDIA

Tala Panir

Once Indian-style fresh cheese is made, there is so much you can do with it. The patties of cheese may be sliced crosswise into long ovals or sticks, smothered with spices, and deep-fried. They turn wonderfully crisp on the outside, while staying soft on the inside. Serve them plain or over a salad.

(recipe continues)

¼ to ½ teaspoon cayenne

1½ teaspoons cumin powder

1½ teaspoons dried oregano

2 tablespoons chickpea flour

1 large patty Homemade Indian Cheese
  (Paneer) (page 561), cut crosswise into
  ⅓-inch-thick oval slices

2 lemons, cut in half

Salt

Freshly ground black pepper

Peanut or canola oil for deep-frying

Combine the cayenne, cumin, oregano, and chickpea flour in a small bowl. Lay the cheese slices on a flat surface in a single layer. Lightly score the slices and squeeze the juice of half a lemon onto them. Sprinkle them generously with salt and pepper, then sprinkle with half of the spice mixture. Pat the seasonings in. Turn the slices over and do the same on the other side.

Heat oil for deep-frying to a depth of ¾ inch in a wok or deep-fryer over medium heat. When very hot, gently lower as many cheese slices into the oil as will fit in a single layer. Fry for about 2 minutes, or until light golden brown. Lift the slices out with a slotted spoon and drain on paper towels. Quickly sprinkle some extra salt, black pepper, and generous amounts of lemon juice over the top. Serve immediately.

SERVES 4 FOR A MEAL, 8 AS AN APPETIZER

Syrian Cheese with Olives
Joban

SYRIA

This is an appetizer that needs to be shared at the table. You can set out other appetizers as well, such as a bean salad, a bulgur salad, a tomato salad, and an artichoke salad. All should be eaten with flatbreads (store-bought pita breads will do).

3 patties Homemade Syrian Cheese (page 566)

½ teaspoon finely chopped fresh rosemary
  plus a sprig for garnishing

5 to 6 tablespoons extra-virgin olive oil

About 18 good-quality black olives

Arrange the patties, dimple side up, in the center of a shallow bowl. Scatter the chopped rosemary over the top. Spoon the olive oil over the patties. Place 1 olive each in the dimple of each patty and scatter the others around them. Garnish with the rosemary sprig and serve.

SERVES 3 TO 6

Syrian Cheese with Cucumber and Sesame Seeds

This makes a light, cool salad.

2 (4-inch) cucumbers or 8 inches of a large
    one, peeled and cut into ⅓-inch dice

2 patties Homemade Syrian Cheese (page
    566), cut into ⅓-inch dice

½ teaspoon salt, or to taste

Freshly ground black pepper

1 tablespoon finely chopped fresh mint

⅛ teaspoon cayenne

1½ tablespoons fresh lemon juice

1½ tablespoons olive oil

2 teaspoons roasted sesame seeds (page 734)

Mix all the ingredients in a bowl and toss. Taste for the balance of flavors, adding more salt, if needed.

SERVES 4

Syrian Cheese with Tomatoes   SYRIA
Joban

This makes a delightful first course or light lunch.

2 patties of Homemade Syrian Cheese
    (page 566)

2 medium red-ripe tomatoes (10 to
    12 ounces)

Salt

Freshly ground black pepper

¼ cup extra-virgin olive oil

Cut each cheese patty into ¼-inch-thick slices. Cut the tomatoes into rounds of the same thickness. Layer the cheese and the tomatoes on 2 plates, alternating the slices and overlapping them slightly. Sprinkle salt and pepper over the top. Dribble the olive oil over the top as well and serve.

SERVES 2

Soups, Salads, and Drinks

Stocks   576

Soups   578
   Cold Soups   578
   Nut and Vegetable Soups   585
   Bean Soups   594
   Miso Soups   603
   Sweet Soups   610

Salads and Saladlike Dishes   612

Drinks   643

Thin enough to drink or thick enough to be picked up with a fork,

soups reflect the world's culinary preoccupations. In Korea, students in a bar reach with long-handled spoons for a thin seaweed soup as casually as Americans might reach for peanuts. In Japan, *miso shiru*, a fermented bean paste soup, is sucked directly from the soup bowl at least once a day by much of the population. In China you can spoon up a thin sweetened puree of mung beans as you watch the opera. The Arabs spread the delicious concept of almond soups to Spain as well as to India while in the Caucasus region yogurt was thinned down and combined with chickpeas to make nourishing coolers. Italians combine vegetables and beans in slow-cooked soups that are then ladled over bread to make filling meals and Trinidadians have a complete winner in their kallaloo, a kind of hot gumbo with okra, colocasia (dasheen) leaves, and coconut milk.

Some soups need only water in their cooking but others require the richness of stock. I have provided three stock recipes: a very basic *konbu* (kelp) stock that is very light and used primarily for Japanese soups; a mushroom stock that can be used for Asian and Western soups; and a mixed vegetable stock for universal use.

Supermarkets now carry all manner of stocks for vegetarians as well, both in the form of dried cubes and in cans. Some are quite good—and quite necessary when you are rushed. You should experiment with them. However, there are two things to watch out for: The first is saltiness, as some store-bought stocks can be very salty. You can control this by diluting them. This is especially true when a recipe calls for soy sauce as well. Other stocks, especially those made from cubes, get a great deal of their flavor from fat. This is generally fine except in some cold soups where you do not want bits of fat floating on the top. The way around it is to make the stock ahead of time in the usual way. Let the stock cool and then refrigerate it. Once cold, you can easily lift the fat off with a spoon.

On the pages that follow you will find some of the soups I enjoy most. You'll find they are arranged alphabetically by main ingredient. I start with cold soups, then go alphabetically through nut and vegetable soups, then on, alphabetically, again, to bean and miso soups and end with sweet soups.

Just as with soups, almost any food can be made into a salad, from bread to bean curd. What you will find in this section are the salads that I cannot live without that are part of my weekly repertoire, salads that have come into my orbit only recently but deserve to be better known, "occasional" salads that can only be made in season when the ingredients deign to appear, such as the Artichoke Heart and Fresh Fava Bean Salad, and very simple salads that may not be able to stand up in a ring by themselves but accompany some other dish in this book to perfection.

Here again I have arranged the recipes alphabetically according to basic ingredient, starting with an *a*rtichoke salad and going on to Guacamole (which has *a*vocado in it). Lastly, after a zucchini salad, are two mixed vegetable salads.

Lastly, in this section I offer a small collection of drink recipes. For our summer holidays on Martha's Vineyard, I take at least a dozen jars of fresh fruit syrups that I make in the months before. June and July are perfect for bottling the rhubarb and sour cherry syrups that even our grandchildren love and the lime syrup with which I refresh myself every midday. With these syrups on hand all we have to exert ourselves to do is add ice and water!

While we are on holiday we drink cool *lassis* when we return from the beach and hot flavored teas when the nights get chilly. Sometimes, when we have guests, we make our much loved ginger fruit punch. Grown-ups can add gin or vodka to it if they like. All these recipes and more are to be found in this chapter.

As before, the recipes are arranged alphabetically, according to main ingredient, starting with almond syrup and ending with the yogurt drink, *lassi*.

Stocks

Vegetable Stock

Vegetable stock can come from the water used to steam or boil vegetables (corn water is one such example), from the liquid used to boil various dried beans and peas—even from the water used in boiling grains. Here is a more all-purpose stock that can even be frozen, if desired.

1 tablespoon peanut or canola oil

2 medium carrots, peeled and coarsely sliced into rounds

2 celery stalks (4 ounces), coarsely chopped

1 large onion (8 ounces), coarsely chopped

¾ pound mushrooms, sliced

1 medium potato (7 ounces), coarsely chopped

1-inch piece of fresh ginger, thinly sliced

4 whole scallions

8 parsley sprigs

1¼ cups mung or soybean sprouts

¼ teaspoon salt

Put the oil in a large, deep stockpot and set over medium-low heat. When hot, add the carrots, celery, and onion. Stir and cook slowly for 10 minutes. Add the mushrooms and cook, stirring, for another 10 minutes, or until the vegetables soften. Lower the heat if the vegetables start to brown.

Add the potato, ginger, scallions, parsley, bean sprouts, salt, and 12 cups of water. Bring to a boil. Cover, turn the heat down to low, and simmer gently for 45 minutes. Strain the stock through a sieve, pushing down on the vegetables and extracting as much liquid as possible.

MAKES 2½ QUARTS

Konbu Stock

JAPAN

Konbu Dashi

Rich in calcium and natural flavoring (glutamic acid), this dried kelp consists of long dark green "leaves" that resemble the leaves of the canna plant. Because of their size, they are generally sold folded up or cut into segments. You can cut the larger leaves yourself with a pair of scissors. As the flavor resides very near the surface, konbu *should never be washed but wiped lightly with a damp cloth. For stocks it should also be cooked very briefly.* Konbu *is sold by Japanese grocers, in health food shops, and in many specialty food shops.*

This is a very mild stock that should be used only when specifically called for in a recipe.

1 piece of *konbu,* about 13 × 4 inches, cut into
    2 pieces

Wipe the *konbu* with a lightly dampened cloth and put the pieces in a pan with 6 cups of water. Bring to a boil. As soon as the water comes to a boil, turn off the heat. Let the *konbu* sit in the water for a minute and then remove it.

MAKES 6 CUPS

Dried Mushroom Stock

This is a very good, light stock for all Chinese and Japanese soups, indeed, for all clear or light soups. Leave out the soy sauce and any extra salt if you are using the stock to make a miso soup. If you are making a mixed vegetable soup, 1 or 2 chopped tomatoes may also be added here as can a quartered corncob whose kernels have been removed and a broken celery stalk.

10 to 12 fresh mushrooms, trimmed

18 dried shiitake or Chinese black
    mushrooms

3 thin slices of fresh ginger, very lightly
    crushed

8 scallions, each cut into 3 pieces (both white
    and green portions)

3 medium carrots, peeled and cut into
    3 chunks each

3 good handfuls of fresh bean sprouts

½ teaspoon salt, plus more to taste

1½ tablespoons soy sauce

1 teaspoon sugar

1 teaspoon oriental sesame oil

(recipe continues)

Rinse the fresh mushrooms quickly and put them in a large pot along with the dried mushrooms, ginger, scallions, carrots, bean sprouts, and ½ teaspoon salt. Bring to a boil. Cover and simmer gently for 40 minutes. Strain thoroughly through a sieve lined with muslin, 3 layers of cheesecloth, or a man's handkerchief to catch all the mushroom grit. Add the soy sauce, sugar, and sesame oil and stir to mix. Taste for salt, adding more only if you need it.

MAKES ABOUT 6 CUPS

Soups

COLD SOUPS

Cold Almond Soup

SPAIN

Ajo Blanco

Of Moorish heritage, this elegant, creamy, soothing soup is served with peeled grapes and croutons. I put my almonds into a bowl of milk and leave them to soak overnight in the refrigerator.

1¼ cups (6 ounces) blanched, slivered
　　almonds

2 cups milk

3 slices of white bread (no crusts), soaked in
　　water until soft and then squeezed out

2 tablespoons olive oil

2 tablespoons white wine vinegar

2 cups vegetable stock

¾ to 1 teaspoon salt

For the garnishes

Peanut or canola oil for shallow frying

3 garlic cloves, very lightly crushed and
　　peeled but left whole

2 slices of white bread, crusts removed, cut
　　into ½-inch cubes

About 40 green grapes, peeled and halved,
　　with seeds, if any, removed

In a bowl, combine the almonds with the milk and refrigerate overnight.

Next day, put the almonds, milk, and bread into a blender. Blend thoroughly until you have a smooth paste. Set a fine sieve over a bowl. Pour the thick milk into the sieve and strain it, pushing out every last drop of liquid; discard the solids. Put the strained milk back into the clean blender container and add the olive oil, vinegar, stock, and salt. Blend briefly and taste, adding as much salt as you need. Cover the soup and refrigerate it; it must be served very cold. (The soup thickens slightly as it sits.)

To make the croutons, pour ½ inch of oil into a frying pan. Add the 3 garlic cloves and set over medium heat. Press down on the garlic as the oil heats. When the garlic cloves are golden, press down on them one more time and then discard. The oil should be hot by now. Put in as many cubes of bread as will fit in easily in a single layer. Stir and fry them until they are golden brown, turning them now and then. Remove the croutons with a slotted spoon and spread them out to drain on paper towels. Make all the croutons this way.

To serve the soup, divide the soup among 4 soup plates. Divide the grapes among the plates. Put 5 to 6 croutons in each plate and pass the rest around in a bowl.

SERVES 4

Cold Avocado and Buttermilk Soup

The inspiration for this soup comes from South Indian buttermilk dishes. All I have done is add an avocado, some lemon juice, and tomatoes.

The entire soup is made in a blender and involves no cooking whatsoever, making it a perfect summer soup. The only major requirement here is a really ripe avocado.

2 cups buttermilk

½ teaspoon whole cumin seeds

3 thin slices of peeled ginger, finely chopped

½ to 1 fresh hot green chile, coarsely chopped

4 tablespoons chopped cilantro

4 teaspoons fresh lemon juice

1 ripe avocado

2 cups cold vegetable stock

About 1 teaspoon salt, or to taste

4 tablespoons peeled and seeded tomatoes (page 300), cut into ¼-inch dice

Put the buttermilk, cumin seeds, ginger, green chile, cilantro, and lemon juice into an electric blender. Blend until very smooth. Strain this mixture through a very fine sieve, pushing out all the liquid. Now put it back in the blender. Peel and coarsely dice the avocado and add it to the blender with the stock. Blend. Add the salt and blend again to mix. Chill thoroughly.

When you are ready to eat, ladle out the soup and scatter 1 tablespoon of the tomatoes over each serving.

SERVES 4

Cold Pomegranate Soup

INDIA

Anar Ka Ras

I was intrigued when I found a 3,000-year-old reference to this ancient Indian soup and decided to re-create it. It is not made in India today—at least not as far as I know. According to India's ancient Ayurvedic system of preventive medicine and healing, soups such as this, offered at the start of a meal, get the gastric juices flowing, thus aiding digestion.

*Make this when fresh red pomegranates are in season, and use a proper juicer, not a blender, to extract the juice. If it is too sour, add a little sugar. If it is pale and bland, add both lemon juice and sugar. Middle Eastern shops also sell bottled pomegranate juice (*not *pomegranate molasses), which can be used as a substitute.*

Serve this soup as cold as possible. I serve it in tiny glasses—sherry glass size—at the start of a meal.

2 cups pomegranate juice (see recipe introduction)

½ teaspoon whole black peppercorns

1 teaspoon whole cumin seeds

1-inch piece of fresh ginger, peeled and finely chopped

½ teaspoon salt

Combine all the ingredients in a blender and blend thoroughly. Strain the soup through a fine sieve and chill, covered, in the refrigerator.

SERVES 8

Heawan Stuckenbruck's
Cold Wakame Seaweed Soup

KOREA

Mee Yuk Muchim

This is a cooling, brothy soup with bits of cucumber, peppers, and seaweed lending taste, crunchiness, and minerals. I first had this in a bar in Seoul where I noticed patrons interspersing their consumption of hard liquors and beer with spoonfuls of this soup. I now make it for myself and drink it frequently when working as a pick-me-up. I get a good dose of much-needed minerals besides!

Dried wakame seaweed is sold by all health food shops.

Dried Mushroom Stock (page 577) or Vegetable Stock (page 576) may be used here. If you wish to use stock cubes, keep the broth light and make it ahead of time so you can refrigerate it and remove the fat.

I like to use smaller cucumbers with less developed seeds here, such as Kirbies. I also peel my red pepper while it is still whole—just use a sharp paring knife and peel it like an apple!

¼ cup (¼ ounce) dried wakame seaweed, broken into 1-inch pieces

4 cups vegetable stock

1 small garlic clove, peeled and finely chopped

4 teaspoons soy sauce, or to taste

¼ teaspoon sugar

1 teaspoon oriental sesame oil

2 Kirby cucumbers or 1 regular cucumber (about 8 ounces in all), peeled and cut into ¼-inch dice

4 to 5 tablespoons red bell pepper, peeled and cut into ¼-inch dice

1 teaspoon red wine vinegar

1 teaspoon fresh hot green or red chile, finely chopped, ¼ to ½ teaspoon coarse Korean red pepper, or ⅛ teaspoon cayenne

Put the seaweed in a bowl. Pour very warm water over it to cover generously and let it soak for 5 to 10 minutes, or until it is soft. Lift the seaweed out of the water with your hands and form a ball. Squeeze out as much water as you can between cupped hands and then chop coarsely.

Combine the stock, seaweed, and garlic in a small pan and bring to a simmer. Simmer gently, uncovered, for 5 minutes, then turn off the heat. Add the soy sauce, tasting as you go, then add the sugar and sesame oil. Stir to mix and taste again. Allow to cool completely.

Add the cucumber, red pepper, vinegar, and chile. Stir and taste for the balance of seasonings. Cover and chill thoroughly. Stir well before serving.

SERVES 4

Cold Yogurt Soup with Chickpeas and Celery

This is ideal for a light summer lunch. If you wish to use canned chickpeas, just rinse them thoroughly first. Dried mint has its own taste; do not substitute fresh mint here.

2 cups plain yogurt

1 cup cold vegetable stock

2 tablespoons peanut or canola oil

1 large celery stalk, thinly sliced crosswise

1 cup cooked drained chickpeas (page 26)

½ teaspoon salt, or to taste

1 teaspoon dried mint, plus a little more for garnishing

(recipe continues)

Put the yogurt in a bowl. Beat lightly with a fork until smooth and creamy. Add the stock and combine well.

Put the oil in a medium frying pan and set over medium heat. When hot, put in the celery. Stir and cook until the celery has softened but not browned. Empty the contents of the frying pan into the bowl of yogurt. Add the chickpeas and salt. Crumble in the mint, letting it turn powdery in your fingers first. Mix well.

Chill the soup until needed. Crumble some more mint over the top of each serving.

SERVES 4 TO 6

Cold Yogurt Soup in the South Indian Style

I have based this soup on the many yogurt salads of South India. The rice here needs to be freshly cooked. If you wish to use cold leftovers, heat them thoroughly with generous splashes of water, either in a covered pan or in the microwave. The rice should be soft.

2 cups plain yogurt

1 cup milk

¾ teaspoon salt

Freshly ground black pepper

⅛ teaspoon cayenne

½ cup cooked rice

1 tablespoon peanut or canola oil

¼ teaspoon whole brown mustard seeds

8 fresh curry leaves, if available, or else use small basil leaves

¼ cup finely diced peeled cucumber

¼ cup finely diced, peeled, seeded, and chopped tomato (page 300)

20 seedless green grapes, peeled and halved

Put the yogurt in a bowl and beat lightly with a fork until smooth and creamy. Slowly add the milk, mixing as you go. Add the salt, pepper to taste, cayenne, and rice. Stir to mix.

Put the oil in a small pan and set over medium-high heat. When hot, put in the mustard seeds. As soon as the mustard seeds begin to pop, a matter of seconds, put in the curry leaves. Stir once and then pour the oil with the seasonings over the yogurt mixture. Add the cucumber, tomato, and grapes and mix. Chill until needed.

SERVES 4

Indian Almond and Cashew Nut Soup   INDIA

Badaam Ka Shorva

This is a vegetarian adaptation of a Muslim soup from western India, a soothing, spicy soup made of the milk from white nuts as well as the liquid left from cooking split peas (toovar dal, in this case). It is amazingly similar in philosophy to the very Moorish ajo blanco of Spain, only this is a cooked version.

The leftover toovar dal *may be frozen and thinned out for use in the future.*

1 cup (4 ounces) blanched slivered almonds

1 cup (4 ounces) raw cashews

1 dried hot red chile, broken up

4 to 5 cups vegetable stock

1 cup (6 ounces) *toovar dal*

3 tablespoons peanut or canola oil

½ teaspoon whole cumin seeds

2-inch piece of fresh ginger, peeled and very finely chopped

3 garlic cloves, peeled and very finely chopped

5 to 6 shallots (about 3 ounces), peeled and finely chopped

1 to 2 fresh hot green chiles, finely chopped

1 teaspoon ground cumin

1 teaspoon ground coriander

1 teaspoon store-bought garam masala

¼ teaspoon ground turmeric

¼ cup fresh lemon juice

1¼ teaspoons salt

Chopped fresh cilantro for garnishing

Soak the almonds, cashews, and dried chile in water that covers them generously for 6 to 8 hours. Drain. Put the nuts and chile in a blender. Add 3 cups of the stock and blend thoroughly until you have a smooth paste. Set a fine sieve over a bowl. Strain the paste, getting from it every last bit of nut milk that you can. You should have at least 3 cups of strained milk.

In the meantime, combine the *toovar dal* and 6 cups of water in a heavy pan and bring to a boil. Skim off the froth, then cover partially, turn the heat down to low, and simmer gently for 1 hour. Turn off the heat and let the split peas settle to the bottom. A thin liquid will rise to the top. Remove 2 cups of it as well as ½ cup of the thick split peas.

Put the oil in a heavy pan and set over medium-high heat. When hot, put in the whole cumin seeds. Ten seconds later, add the ginger, garlic, shallots, and green chile. Stir them for 2 to 3 minutes, or until they just start to brown, then turn the heat down to low and add the ground cumin, coriander, garam masala, and

(recipe continues)

turmeric. Stir once or twice and put in the nut milk, the split peas and the measured cooking liquid, the lemon juice, and salt as well as 1 more cup of the stock. Stir and bring to a simmer, then cover partially and simmer gently for 15 minutes. Taste for the balance of seasonings. Strain the soup through a fine sieve, pushing out as much liquid as possible. When you are ready to serve, heat the soup. (If the soup seems too thick, it may be thinned out with more stock.) Garnish with the cilantro.

SERVES 4 TO 6

Indonesian Corn Soup

INDONESIA

Sop Jagung

This is a light, aromatic soup best made when corn is in season.

2 ears of fresh corn

6 cups light vegetable stock

2 fresh lemongrass stalks (use only the bottom 6 inches and crush the bulbous end lightly)

8 to 10 fresh cilantro stems

2 fresh hot green chiles, halved

4 thin slices of fresh ginger

2 medium tomatoes (10 ounces), peeled, seeded, and cut into ¼-inch dice (page 300)

1 (15-ounce) can straw mushrooms, drained

1 teaspoon salt, or to taste

4 to 5 teaspoons fresh lime juice, or to taste

¼ cup finely chopped cilantro, leaves only

Cut the corn off the cobs and set aside. Break the remaining cobs into 2 pieces each and combine in a pan with the stock, lemongrass, cilantro stems, chiles, and ginger. Bring to a boil, cover, turn the heat down to low, and simmer gently for 30 minutes. Strain.

Add the reserved corn, tomatoes, straw mushrooms, salt, lime juice, and chopped cilantro and bring to a simmer. Turn the heat down to low and simmer gently for 4 to 5 minutes.

SERVES 4

Birdie's
Kallaloo

TRINIDAD

One of the glories of Trinidad and fit for kings, this gumbolike Creole dish is a meal in itself. Some people blend all the ingredients; others would die before they did that: Passions seem to run deep. This vegetarian version is best, I think, when it has been blended. The original dish contains crabs and is generally eaten with rice; this is a vegetarian version and may be served as is or with crusty bread or plain rice. I have served it both as a first course at dinner and as the only dish for lunch.

The recipe requires dasheen leaves, the leaves of a colocasia or taro plant. These very large leaves look like elephant ears, and can be found in West Indian and Indian markets. (In Indian shops ask for arvi *leaves.) If all else fails, use the green, leafy section of Swiss chard, cut into fine ribbons. I find that Swiss chard contains fairly tough fibers, so the soup will need to be strained through a coarse sieve before it is served.*

The stems of dasheen leaves should be used as well. Just cut off the stem as close to the leaf as possible and then peel it. This is easy. Just start peeling downward with a sharp paring knife and then pull the skin. It will come off in long strips. After peeling, the stem can be cut crosswise into small rounds.

Okra is essential here as it binds the soup together, rather like a New Orleans gumbo. It should be washed and patted dry before cutting.

As I watched this soup being made in Port of Spain, I noticed that Maggi cubes were added, providing both flavor and salt. These were the large cubes, the equivalent of about 4 of the smaller ½-inch cubes. I have used Maggi cubes in my recipe as well, but you could use vegetable stock instead of the water and add salt to taste.

2 pounds dasheen leaves

¼ cup peanut or canola oil

2 medium onions (10 ounces), peeled and coarsely chopped

5 to 6 garlic cloves, peeled and coarsely chopped

1 medium carrot, peeled and cut into thick rounds

20 green beans, cut into 1-inch pieces

8 to 9 okra pods, trimmed at the ends and cut crosswise into thick slices

2 large or 8 small Maggi bouillon cubes or any other good vegetable stock cubes

1 habañero or Scotch bonnet chile, left whole, or 1 to 3 fresh hot green chiles, coarsely sliced

3 cups coconut milk

Salt (optional)

Freshly ground black pepper

A little butter (optional)

(recipe continues)

585

Wash the dasheen leaves and cut off the stems. Roll up several leaves at a time and cut them crosswise into fine ribbonlike strips. Peel the stems and cut crosswise into ½-inch pieces.

Put the oil in a large pot and set over medium-high heat. When hot, put in the onions, garlic, carrot, green beans, and okra. Stir and sauté for 5 minutes. Now put in the dasheen leaves and stems and sauté for another 5 minutes. Add 6 cups of water and the Maggi cubes, stir, and bring to a boil. Drop the whole habañero or the sliced chiles into the pot. Cover, turn the heat down to low, and simmer gently for 25 to 30 minutes. Remove the habañero chile if using, then put the soup into a food processor or blender and blend coarsely or finely, as desired; you will need to do this in several batches. Put the soup back into the pot, add the coconut milk, salt only if needed, and some black pepper. Stir and bring to a simmer. Swirl in the butter just before serving if you wish.

SERVES 8 TO 10

Red Pepper Soup

This is a lovely, easy-to-make soup with an attractive orange-red color. I serve it plain, drizzled with a little extra-virgin olive oil on top, but you could also take a slice of crusty bread for each person, rub a cut garlic clove over it, and then toast it lightly. Put this at the bottom of a soup plate and pour the hot soup over the top.

Red Pepper Paste gives this soup depth. I have a recipe for this paste on page 673, and you can also buy it ready made from a Middle Eastern grocer. Yet another alternative is to use tomato paste plus ⅛ teaspoon cayenne. As far as the vegetable stock is concerned, it is perfectly acceptable to use good-quality bouillon cubes here.

3 tablespoons olive oil

1 medium onion (4 to 5 ounces), peeled and
    chopped

3 large red bell peppers (about 1¼ pounds),
    cored, seeded, and coarsely chopped

2 garlic cloves, peeled and coarsely chopped

1 medium baking potato (7 ounces), peeled
    and cut into ¼-inch dice

4 cups vegetable stock

1 tablespoon Red Pepper Paste, either
    homemade (page 673) or store-bought, *or*
    tomato paste plus ⅛ teaspoon cayenne

Salt as needed

Freshly ground black pepper

4 teaspoons extra-virgin olive oil for drizzling

Put the olive oil in a large, wide pan and set over medium-high heat. When hot, put in the onion, red peppers, garlic, and potato. Stir and cook for about 12 minutes. At first the vegetables will stew but then you should be able to sauté them and they will begin to brown very slightly. Add the stock and the Red Pepper Paste, stir, and bring to a boil. Cover, turn the heat down to low, and simmer very gently for 20 minutes. Taste the soup for salt, adding more if needed. Add the black pepper.

Set a coarse sieve over a large bowl.

Transfer the soup to a blender in batches and blend until you have a very smooth puree. As each batch is pureed, empty it into the sieve and push it through, extracting the last drops of liquid. The soup can be covered and refrigerated for 24 hours.

Just before serving, heat the soup and pour it into soup plates or bowls. Drizzle a teaspoon of the extra-virgin olive oil over each portion and serve.

SERVES 4

Spanish Potato, Chard, and Bean Soup   SPAIN
Caldo Gallego

Use any medium-small white beans here. This is a pale soup with flecks of dark green. It is served with a little dribble of fruity olive oil. A good crusty bread on the side makes it into a perfect lunch or first course.

This soup may be made in advance and reheated.

1 cup (6 ounces) dried white beans, such as
    cannellini or navy

5 cups vegetable stock

1 garlic clove, peeled

2 teaspoons chopped fresh oregano or
    ½ teaspoon dried

3 tablespoons olive oil

2 smallish onions (7 ounces), peeled and cut
    into ¼-inch dice

1 medium baking potato (8 ounces), peeled
    and cut into ¼-inch dice

4 lightly packed cups (8 ounces) chopped
    chard (both stems and leaves)

2 tablespoons finely chopped fresh parsley

Salt as needed

Extra-virgin olive oil, about 1 teaspoon per
    serving

(recipe continues)

Soak the beans overnight as suggested on page 6, or use the Quick-Soak Method on page 6. Drain, discarding any soaking liquid.

In a medium pot, bring the beans and stock to a boil, skimming off the froth that rises to the top. Add the garlic and oregano. Stir and turn the heat down to low. Cover partially and simmer gently for 40 to 60 minutes, or until the beans are tender. (Older beans will take longer to cook.) Crush the garlic clove against the side of the pot and mix well.

Put the oil in a large pan and set over medium-high heat. When hot, add the onions and potato. Stir and cook for 4 to 5 minutes so there is a little bit of browning. Add the chard and parsley. Stir for about 1½ minutes, or until the chard has wilted. Now add the cooked beans and their liquid and bring to a boil. Cover partially, turn the heat down to low, and simmer gently for 30 minutes, stirring now and then. Mash some of the beans and the potato pieces against the sides of the pan. Taste for salt; you will probably need to add some even if your stock was salted. Mix well.

Ladle into soup plates and dribble a teaspoon of extra-virgin olive oil over each serving.

SERVES 6

Margarita Salinas'
Mexican Potato Soup MEXICO
Caldo de Papa

Sometimes I wonder what the origins of gazpacho, the cold Spanish soup, really are. White gazpacho, made with almonds, is clearly of Moorish origin but the red one that uses tomatoes seems to have Mexican connections. Here is a hot Mexican soup that could well have been the "mother" of Spain's red gazpacho. Instead of bread, a more local ingredient, potatoes, thickens the soup.

You need chipotle chiles for this dish. Chipotles are just dried jalapeños. Jalapeños have a very thick skin that is hard to dry in the sun—a process other chiles take to quite comfortably. So jalapeños are aided by man and smoked dry to become chipotles. This accounts for their smoky flavor. They can generally be found in cans wherever Mexican ingredients are sold. If you cannot get them, use the chipotle peppers in adobo sauce that are more commonly available.

For this recipe, I used one small chile to create a fairly spicy soup; you might want to start with half a chile. If you cannot get any chipotles, use part or all of a fresh hot red chile, chopping it coarsely before putting it into the blender, or ¼ to ½ teaspoon cayenne.

1 pound boiling potatoes, peeled and cut into
  ½-inch dice

3 large red-ripe tomatoes (1¼ pounds) (see
  Note), peeled and coarsely chopped

1 medium onion (4 ounces), coarsely chopped

1 to 2 garlic cloves, peeled and coarsely
  chopped

½ to 1 chipotle chile, chipotle in adobo sauce,
  or fresh hot red chile, coarsely chopped

2 cups vegetable stock

About 1 teaspoon salt, or to taste

5 tablespoons chopped fresh epazote or
  cilantro

¼ cup sour cream or heavy cream (optional)

Put the potatoes in a pan with water to cover by about 3 inches. Bring to a boil, cover, turn the heat to medium-low, and cook until tender but still firm. Drain.

Combine the tomatoes, onion, garlic, and chile in an electric blender and blend until you have a smooth paste. Empty into a medium saucepan. Add the stock and potatoes. Add the salt a little at a time, tasting as you go. Stir to mix and bring to a boil. Simmer gently for 7 to 8 minutes. Mash 2 or 3 pieces of potato against the sides of the pan if you want the soup a little thicker. (I like to do this.) Add the epazote or cilantro and simmer another 2 minutes. Serve with dollops of sour cream or a bit of heavy cream, if you like.

Note: While the potatoes boil, drop the tomatoes into the boiling water for 15 seconds to loosen the skins. Remove with a slotted spoon, peel, and chop.

SERVES 4

Simple Pumpkin Soup

For this dish, I used a section of pumpkin that weighed 1 pound, 10 ounces. After removing the seeds and peeling it, I was left with 1¼ pounds or about 3½ cups of flesh. Any orange-fleshed squash, such as Hubbard or butternut squash, may be used instead of pumpkin.

The stock I used here was very lightly salted, so you may need to adjust the salt accordingly.

3 tablespoons olive oil

1 medium onion (4 ounces), peeled and finely
  chopped

3 thinnish slices of fresh ginger

1 medium potato (4 ounces), peeled and
  coarsely diced

1¼ pounds pumpkin flesh, cut into 1-inch
  cubes

4 cups vegetable stock

2 bay leaves

1¼ teaspoons salt

Freshly ground black pepper

½ cup milk

1 to 2 tablespoons finely sliced fresh chives
  for garnishing (optional)

(recipe continues)

589

Put the oil in a large pot and set over medium-high heat. When hot, put in the onion and ginger. Stir and fry for 2 to 3 minutes, or until the onion bits just begin to turn brown at the edges. Turn the heat to medium and sauté for another 2 minutes, or until the onions are light brown. Put in the potato and pumpkin pieces and stir once or twice. Now put in the stock, bay leaves, salt, and pepper and bring to a boil. Cover, lower the heat, and simmer gently for 45 minutes. Remove the ginger slices and the bay leaves. In several batches, blend the soup to a smooth puree in a blender. Return the soup to the pot in which it had been cooking, add the milk, and stir to mix. Reheat if necessary and garnish with chives, if desired.

SERVES 4 TO 5

Variation I
Pumpkin Soup with Fresh Curry Leaves

After the oil has heated, throw 8 to 10 fresh curry leaves into the oil. Stir once and put in the onion and ginger. After the onion has turned light brown, put in 1 tablespoon curry powder. Stir once or twice and put in the potato and pumpkin. Now proceed with the recipe.

Variation II
Pumpkin Soup with Tomato

When adding the pumpkin, put in 2 to 3 peeled and chopped medium tomatoes as well as ½ teaspoon dried oregano. Now proceed with the recipe. At the end, add heavy cream instead of the milk.

Tomato Soup with Lemongrass

I use lemongrass, fresh curry leaves, and cumin seeds to make a very aromatic soup that may be served hot or cold.

Use only the bottom 6 inches of the lemongrass stalks, mashing the bulbous end lightly.

2 tablespoons olive, canola, or peanut oil

¼ teaspoon whole cumin seeds

1 large baking potato (9 ounces), peeled and
    cut into small dice

2 medium onions (9 ounces in all), peeled and
    cut into small dice

1 celery stalk, cut into small dice

About 30 fresh curry leaves

1 fresh lemongrass stalk (see recipe
    introduction)

2 pounds red-ripe tomatoes, chopped

2 teaspoons tomato paste

⅛ teaspoon cayenne

About 1¾ teaspoons salt, or to taste

Put the oil in a large pan and set over medium-high heat. When hot, put in the cumin seeds and let them sizzle for 10 seconds. Now add the potato, onions, celery, curry leaves, and lemongrass. Turn the heat to medium and sauté for 4 to 5 minutes. Add the tomatoes and stir a few times.

Now put in 4 cups of water, the tomato paste, cayenne, and salt. Stir and bring to a boil. Cover, turn the heat down to low, and simmer gently for 1 hour. Discard the lemongrass and puree the soup in batches, using a blender. Push the soup through a coarse strainer, reheating if necessary.

SERVES 4

Madras Curried Tomato Soup INDIA

The origins of this recipe lie in an old Anglo-Indian cookery book. This is very much a "Raj" period soup and has the old-fashioned taste of hotel soups that I associate with my holidays in distant Himalayan resorts as a child in British India.
  You may use My Curry Powder (page 707) or a standard Madras curry powder here.
  Serve hot or cold, with thin, crisp toast.

2 tablespoons peanut or canola oil

1 medium onion (4 ounces), peeled and
  chopped

2 tablespoons curry powder

2 cups (1 pound) coarsely chopped tomatoes

2 medium carrots, peeled and cut into coarse
  rounds

2 medium potatoes (12 ounces), peeled and
  cut into rough dice

1 cup fresh or frozen and defrosted peas

2¼ teaspoons salt, or to taste

1 cup heavy cream

About 1 cup vegetable stock, as needed

1 tablespoon finely chopped fresh chives for
  garnishing (optional)

Put the oil in a medium-large pan and set over medium-high heat. When hot, put in the onion. Stir and sauté 4 to 5 minutes, or until the onion is golden. Put in the curry powder and stir it around for 10 seconds, then put in the tomatoes, carrots, potatoes, peas, salt, and 4 cups of water. Bring to a boil. Cover, turn the heat down to low, and simmer gently for 45 minutes. Blend the soup in batches in a blender and then strain it back into the saucepan through a coarse sieve, making sure you collect all the pulp under the sieve. Add the cream and stir. Now add enough stock to create a soup of the thickness you desire. Stir to mix. Heat the soup, if you want to serve it hot, or cover and refrigerate if you want to serve it cold. Garnish with the chives, if desired, when serving.

SERVES 4 TO 6

Vegetable Mulligatawny Soup

The Tamil words milagu tannir *mean "pepper-water," so it is not surprising this vegetable soup has a peppery bite. You can add 4 tablespoons of red lentils, if you so desire. The soup is fairly thick but may be thinned out with as much stock as you wish. In its thick version, it makes a very good sauce for hard-boiled eggs (see Eggs in a Mulligatawny Sauce, page 519).*

Serve as a first course or a light meal with crusty bread, fried croutons, or plain rice. Offer lime wedges on the side.

1 teaspoon whole black peppercorns

2 tablespoons whole coriander seeds

1 teaspoon whole cumin seeds

½ teaspoon whole fennel seeds

½ teaspoon ground turmeric

¼ teaspoon cayenne

1½ tablespoons chickpea flour (page 27)

4 to 5 cups vegetable stock (bouillon cubes may be used here)

2 small potatoes (8 ounces), peeled and diced

2 medium carrots, peeled and sliced

2 small turnips (8 ounces), peeled and diced

12 fresh curry leaves or 8 fresh basil leaves

2 garlic cloves, peeled and coarsely chopped

1 medium onion, coarsely chopped

1 tablespoon peeled and finely chopped fresh ginger

1 (14-ounce) can coconut milk

1¼ teaspoons salt, or to taste

Lime wedges for serving

Put the peppercorns, coriander seeds, cumin seeds, and fennel seeds in a small cast-iron frying pan and set over medium-high heat. Stir and roast until the spices emit a roasted aroma and some turn a shade darker. Empty into a plate to cool, then grind in a clean coffee grinder or other spice grinder. (It is a good idea to sift the ground spices through a fine sieve, stirring them about with a spoon as they pass slowly through the mesh. This is not absolutely necessary, but it makes for a finer soup.) Add the turmeric and cayenne to the spice mixture.

Put the chickpea flour in a bowl. Slowly add 2 tablespoons of the stock, mixing as you go. Add another 4 cups of stock and mix.

Combine the chickpea flour mixture, spices, all the vegetables, the curry leaves, garlic, onion, and ginger in a large pan and bring to a boil. Cover, turn the heat down to low, and simmer for about 50 minutes, or until all the vegetables are tender. Blend the soup in a blender in several batches, if necessary, and then press through a coarse sieve. Return the soup to the soup pan, add the coconut milk and salt, and bring to a simmer. Simmer gently for 2 to 3 minutes to blend the flavors; thin out with more stock, as needed. Serve hot with lime wedges.

SERVES 4 TO 6

Sichuan Vegetable Soup and Bean Curd

CHINESE-AMERICAN

A spicy, nourishing soup, filled with vegetables and bean curd, this makes a fine lunch all by itself.

12 Chinese dried black mushrooms

1 heaping tablespoon small black fungus (page 722)

2½ teaspoons cornstarch

3½ cups vegetable stock

1½ teaspoons black bean sauce with chili

2 tablespoons Chinese Shao Hsing wine or dry sherry

1 tablespoon soy sauce

1½ teaspoons red wine vinegar

2 tablespoons peanut or canola oil

1 teaspoon peeled and finely chopped garlic

1 teaspoon finely chopped peeled fresh ginger

2 small carrots (4 ounces), peeled and cut into ¼-inch dice

½ cup plus 2 tablespoons canned drained bamboo shoots, cut into ¼-inch dice

About ¼ teaspoon salt, or to taste

Lots of freshly ground black pepper

1 pound bean curd (soft, medium, or firm), cut into ¾-inch cubes

1 scallion, cut crosswise into fine rounds (use both white and green sections)

½ cup frozen peas, defrosted (if using fresh peas, parboil them for 3 to 4 minutes)

1 teaspoon oriental sesame oil

Soak the dried mushrooms in hot water to cover for 30 minutes, or until completely softened. Lift out of the liquid. (Strain the liquid and use as part of the stock.) Cut off the hard stems, then cut the caps into ¼-inch dice.

While the mushrooms soak, rinse off the black fungus and put it in a bowl of hot water to soak for 30 minutes, or until softened. Lift out of the water and rinse again. Cut off any hard eyes and then chop coarsely into ¼-inch pieces.

Put the cornstarch in a large bowl. Slowly add the vegetable stock, stirring as you go. Now add the black bean sauce, wine, soy sauce, and vinegar. Mix and set aside.

Put the oil in a wide saucepan and set over medium-high heat. When hot, put in the garlic and ginger. Stir for 5 seconds and add the carrots and bamboo shoots. Stir for 30 seconds and add the mushrooms and black fungus. Stir for 30 seconds. Give the stock mixture a stir and pour it into the saucepan. Bring to a boil, stirring, then turn the heat down to low and simmer for 3 minutes. Check the salt, adding what you need, as well as the black pepper. Add the bean curd and simmer gently for 2 minutes. Put in the scallion and peas, simmer for a minute, and turn off the heat. Pour the sesame oil over the top just before serving.

SERVES 4 TO 5

Trinidadian Black-Eyed Pea Soup

TRINIDAD/UNITED STATES

I have used frozen black-eyed peas in this recipe. If you can only get the dried kind, soak ¾ cup overnight, or use the Quick-Soak Method on page 6. This soup can be a meal in itself served with a green salad.

2 tablespoons olive oil

1 green bell pepper, cored, seeded, and cut into ¼-inch dice

1 medium onion (4 ounces), peeled and cut into ¼-inch pieces

2 medium carrots, peeled and cut into ¼-inch dice

4 tablespoons finely chopped culantro or cilantro

1 (10-ounce) package frozen black-eyed peas

6½ cups vegetable stock (bouillon cubes may be used here)

4 tablespoons brown rice

½ teaspoon ground ginger

½ teaspoon ground allspice

½ teaspoon dried thyme

½ teaspoon mustard powder mixed with 1 tablespoon hot water

¼ Scotch bonnet (habañero-type hot chile), chopped, ¼ to ½ teaspoon cayenne, or drops of Trinidadian Pepper Sauce (page 771), as desired

Salt as needed

1 tablespoon finely chopped chives

Lime or lemon wedges for serving

Put the oil in a large pan and set over medium-high heat. Put in the pepper, onion, and carrots. Stir and sauté for 3 minutes, or until the onion turns translucent and slightly brown at the edges. Add the culantro or cilantro and stir once. Now add the peas, stock, rice, ginger, allspice, thyme, mustard, and hot chile. Stir and bring to a boil. Cover, turn the heat down to low, and simmer gently for 1½ hours, stirring now and then. Taste for salt, adding some if needed. The soup should be spicy, so add more pepper sauce or cayenne if you wish. Serve garnished with the chives and offer the lime or lemon wedges on the side.

SERVES 6

Albertina Brenes de Estrada and Ada Bassey's

Costa Rican Black Bean Soup   COSTA RICA

Sopa Negra

This is a delicious soup flavored with peppers and cilantro. I like to serve it with a dollop of sour cream into which I mix a few teaspoons of canned Mexican chipotle peppers. One egg per serving could be poached in it as well. In Costa Rica, it is generally served with a spicy bottled sauce known as Salsa Lizano.

This soup is made with the liquid from a pot of cooked beans plus a few of the beans themselves. A lot of the beans are left over. Traditionally, these leftover beans are sautéed with rice in a dish called Gallo Pinto, or "Spotted Rooster" (page 14), and served at breakfast.

For boiling the beans

2 cups (12 ounces) dried black beans, picked over, washed, and drained

4 to 5 garlic cloves, peeled and coarsely chopped

8 tablespoons finely chopped red or green bell pepper (about half of a large one, seeded)

6 tablespoons finely chopped cilantro

2 teaspoons salt

For finishing the soup

¼ cup olive oil

1 garlic clove, peeled and chopped

2 medium onions (8 ounces), peeled and chopped

1 large red or green bell pepper, seeded and chopped

½ to 1 jalapeño pepper, seeded and chopped (optional)

2 celery stalks, diced

2 well-packed cups (3 ounces) chopped fresh cilantro

1 teaspoon salt

Freshly ground black pepper

¼ teaspoon cayenne (optional)

For serving with the soup (optional)

3 tablespoons heavy cream

3 tablespoons sour cream

1 tablespoon finely chopped fresh cilantro

1 tablespoon canned chipotle peppers, strained (or any bottled hot sauce)

Dash of salt

Soak the beans overnight in water to cover by 5 inches. Alternatively, you could put the beans in a pot with the same amount of water, bring to a boil, and then boil for 2 minutes. Cover and turn off the heat. Let the pot sit, covered, for 1 hour.

Drain the beans and combine in a large pot with 8¾ cups of fresh water. Add the garlic, pepper, and cilantro and bring to a boil. Cover, leaving the lid slightly ajar, and cook for 1½ hours, or until the beans are fairly tender. Add the salt. Stir and

(recipe continues)

cook another 15 minutes, or until the beans are very tender. Strain, reserving all the liquid in the large pot and the beans in a separate bowl.

To finish the soup, put the oil in a large frying pan and set over medium-high heat. When hot, put in the garlic, onions, bell pepper, jalapeño, if using, and celery and sauté for 5 to 6 minutes. Turn the heat down slightly and sauté another 2 to 3 minutes. Add the cilantro and sauté another minute, then turn off the heat. Combine the contents of the frying pan plus 1 cup of the cooked beans and about 3 large ladles of the strained bean liquid in a blender. Blend until you have a smooth puree. Empty this puree into the pot with the remaining strained bean liquid. Add the salt, pepper to taste, and cayenne. Stir to mix and taste for the balance of flavors. Now push this soup through a coarse sieve, making sure you press out every last bit of liquid. Reheat the soup before serving.

Beat the heavy cream until frothy but not stiff. Fold in the sour cream, cilantro, chipotle, and salt and float a dollop of it on top of each serving.

SERVES 4 TO 6

Chickpea and Escarole Soup ITALY

Zuppa di Ceci con Escarole

Even though this soup is Italian, I have had similar soups in other parts of the Mediterranean and in Mexico as well.

I make this soup with dried chickpeas as their broth is all-important to the taste of the finished dish. This is a good dish to make ahead and reheat.

1 cup (6 ounces) dried chickpeas

A little crumbled dried sage or dried thyme

2 cups vegetable stock

Salt

20 to 22 well-washed escarole leaves, cut crosswise into ¼-inch-wide strips

4 teaspoons fruity extra-virgin olive oil

Pick over the chickpeas and wash in several changes of water. Drain. Cover with 5 cups of water and leave overnight to soak. (Alternatively, you could use the Quick-Soak Method described on page 6.)

Drain the chickpeas, then combine with 6 cups of water and the sage or thyme in a medium pot and bring to a boil. Turn the heat down to low, cover, and cook gently for 1 to 3 hours, or until the chickpeas are very tender. (Alternatively, you could put the drained chickpeas and 4 cups of water into a pressure cooker, cover, and bring up to pressure. Cook for 30 to 35 minutes. Reduce the pressure.) Skim off and discard any skins that are loosened or floating around. Add the vegetable stock and salt as needed.

Bring a large pot of lightly salted water to a rolling boil. Drop in the escarole and boil rapidly for 5 minutes. Drain thoroughly and add to the pot with the soup. Bring the soup to a boil. Turn the heat down to low and simmer gently for 8 to 10 minutes, or until the flavors are well blended. Drizzle olive oil over the top when serving.

SERVES 4

Variation I
Chickpea Soup with Escarole and Tomato

You may add 1 medium tomato, peeled, seeded, and finely chopped, to the soup about 2 minutes before the cooking time is over.

Variation II
Mexican-Style Chickpea Soup

For a spicy Mexican flavor, add ½ teaspoon finely chopped fresh hot green chiles (such as jalapeños) to the soup 3 minutes before the cooking time is over. Serve with a light squeeze of lime or lemon juice.

Variation III
Chickpea Soup with Escarole and Dried Porcini Mushrooms
Zuppa di Ceci con Escarole e Porcini Secchi

Soak ½ ounce dried porcini mushrooms in 1 cup of hot water for 1 hour, or until very soft. Lift the mushrooms out of the liquid and then strain the liquid through a fine cloth. (The strained mushroom broth may be used as part of the vegetable stock.) Add the mushrooms to the soup at the same time as you put in the cooked escarole.

Rosemary-Flavored Chickpea and Spinach Soup

ITALY

Zuppa di Ceci con Spinaci

This delicious rosemary-flavored Tuscan soup is almost a meal in itself, especially if you follow it with some fruit and cheese. Instead of spinach, you may use beet greens.

Use a sprig of fresh rosemary here as it is much easier to remove and has a cleaner flavor. If you have access only to the dried herb, thoroughly crush 1 teaspoon in a mortar before adding it.

1 cup (6 ounces) dried chickpeas

Salt

1/2 pound fresh spinach or beet greens, well washed

2 tablespoons olive oil

1 garlic clove, peeled and finely chopped

1 small onion, peeled and finely chopped

1 fresh rosemary sprig or 1 teaspoon dried, pounded to a powder

2 teaspoons tomato paste

2 cups vegetable stock

Freshly ground black pepper

4 (3/4-inch-thick) slices of good crusty bread (Tuscan is ideal)

4 teaspoons fruity extra-virgin olive oil

Pick over the chickpeas and wash in several changes of water. Drain. Cover with 5 cups of water and soak overnight. Drain. (Alternatively, you could use the Quick-Soak Method on page 6.)

Bring a large pot of lightly salted water to a rolling boil. Drop in the spinach or beet greens and boil rapidly for 5 minutes. Drain thoroughly, squeezing out as much liquid as possible, and chop finely.

Put the 2 tablespoons olive oil in a medium pot and set over medium-high heat. When hot, put in the garlic and onion. Stir and sauté until the onion is translucent; turn the heat down, if necessary, to prevent browning. Now add the drained chickpeas and the greens and sauté for another 5 minutes. Add 6 cups of water and the rosemary and bring to a boil. Turn the heat down to low, cover, and cook gently for 1 to 3 hours, or until the chickpeas are very tender. (Alternatively, you could do the sautéing in a pressure cooker, then put in the drained chickpeas, rosemary, and 4 cups of water, cover, and bring up to pressure. Cook for 30 to 35 minutes. Reduce the pressure.) Discard the rosemary sprig.

Skim off the skins of the chickpeas if you see any that are loosened or floating around. Slowly add the tomato paste to the vegetable stock and mix well. Add this mixture to the soup and mix. Taste for salt and add what you need. Add some black pepper as well. Mix again. Bring the soup to a simmer, cover, and simmer gently for 20 minutes to blend all the flavors. (All this may be done in advance.)

Just before serving, heat the soup. Toast the slices of bread and put them at the bottom of 4 soup plates. Ladle the soup over the toast and drizzle a teaspoon of extra-virgin olive oil over the top of each serving.

SERVES 4

Curried Red Lentil Soup   INDIA
Masoor Dal Soup

This is a quick soup that I have devised for family lunches and easy weekend entertaining. It is based on my mother's recipe, which was heavily accented with cloves. I have carried those childhood flavors a step further, adding a little bit of curry powder and a few more vegetables. My mother used to serve her soup with fried croutons or thin slices of bread that had been crisped in the oven; I like to put 2 tablespoons of cooked rice per person right into the hot soup.

If you are using stock that is salted, check your soup before adding any more salt.

2 tablespoons olive oil

3 tablespoons chopped onion

1 garlic clove, peeled and chopped

1 teaspoon freshly grated peeled ginger

2 teaspoons hot or medium curry powder (I like to use Bolsts' curry powder)

¼ teaspoon ground cloves

½ cup diced peeled potato

1 small carrot, peeled and sliced into thin rounds

1 cup (6 ounces) red lentils, rinsed and drained

4 cups vegetable stock or water

1¼ teaspoons salt, or to taste

Freshly ground black pepper

Lemon or lime wedges

Put the olive oil in a medium pot and set over medium-high heat. When hot, put in the onion, garlic, and ginger. Stir and sauté 2 to 3 minutes, or until the onion softens and just starts to brown. Add the curry powder and stir for 10 seconds. Now put in the cloves, potato, and carrot. Stir for a few seconds, then add the lentils and stock. Stir and bring to a boil. Cover partially, leaving the lid slightly ajar, turn the heat down to low, and cook gently for 45 minutes, or until the lentils are completely soft. Add the salt and pepper to taste. Taste again for the balance of flavors.

Empty the soup into a blender and blend briefly; the soup should not be completely smooth. Serve hot with lemon or lime wedges on the side.

SERVES 4

599

Simple Red Lentil Soup

TURKEY

You may serve this soup with a Scandinavian crisp bread, fried croutons (look for a recipe with Cold Almond Soup, page 578), or thin bread slices that have been crisped in the oven. Plain French bread will do as well.

1 cup (6 ounces) red lentils, rinsed and
    drained

4 cups vegetable stock

2 tablespoons chopped onion

½ cup diced peeled potato

1 teaspoon paprika

1¼ teaspoons salt

Freshly ground black pepper

In a medium pot, combine the lentils, stock, onion, potato, and paprika. Bring to a boil, then cover partially, leaving the lid slightly ajar, turn the heat down to low, and cook gently for 45 minutes, or until the lentils are completely soft. Add the salt and pepper to taste.

Empty the soup into a blender and blend briefly. Serve hot.

SERVES 4

Maya's

Red Lentil Soup with Mustard Seeds and Curry Leaves

INDIA

Masoor Dal Soup

This is my sister-in-law's soup. You may serve it with homemade croutons or crusty bread. Sometimes I just scatter some plain cooked rice into the bowl or plate.

3 tablespoons peanut or canola oil

1-inch piece of peeled fresh ginger, grated to
    a pulp

4 garlic cloves, peeled and crushed to a pulp

1 cup (6 ounces) red lentils, rinsed and drained

4 cups vegetable stock or water

10 to 15 fresh curry leaves (use 5 basil leaves
    as a very different substitute)

2 medium tomatoes, chopped

1¼ teaspoons salt

Freshly ground black pepper

¼ teaspoon cayenne

½ teaspoon whole brown mustard seeds

Put 2 tablespoons of the oil in a medium saucepan and set over medium-high heat. When hot, put in the ginger and garlic and stir for a minute. Put in the lentils, stock or water, and curry leaves and bring to a boil. Cover partially, leaving the lid slightly ajar, turn the heat down to low, and cook gently for 40 minutes, or until the lentils are soft. Add the tomatoes, salt, pepper to taste, and cayenne. Stir and bring to a simmer again. Cover partially and simmer gently for another 10 minutes, or until the tomatoes have softened. Press the soup through a sieve; do not forget to collect all the puree at the bottom of the sieve. Return the soup to its saucepan.

Put the remaining tablespoon of oil in a small frying pan or saucepan and set over medium-high heat. When very hot, put in the mustard seeds. As soon as the mustard seeds begin to pop, a matter of seconds, pour the oil and seeds into the soup. Mix well and reheat if necessary. Serve hot.

SERVES 4

Mixed Bean Soup

The ancestry of this soup is just as mixed as its contents. I created it in an effort to find nourishing soups for the family that would serve as one-dish lunches and that could easily be made ahead of time and reheated.

½ cup (3 ounces) dried cannellini beans, picked over and washed

½ cup (3 ounces) dried black-eyed peas, picked over and washed

10 large raw cashews

2 medium red or other boiling potatoes (about 6 ounces in all), peeled and cut into ¼-inch dice

1 medium carrot, peeled and cut into ¼-inch dice

1 large leek, halved lengthwise, well washed, and then cut crosswise into ¼-inch dice (use white and pale green sections)

1 celery stalk, cut into ¼-inch dice

½ teaspoon dried thyme or 2 teaspoons fresh thyme leaves

2 bay leaves

1½ to 1¾ teaspoons salt

1½ cups skim milk

1 tablespoon olive oil

2 garlic cloves, lightly crushed and peeled but left whole

1 good-sized tomato (6 ounces), peeled and finely chopped

Lemon wedges (optional)

(recipe continues)

Combine the cannellini beans, black-eyed peas, and cashews in a bowl. Add enough water to cover by at least 3 inches and leave to soak overnight. Drain.

Put the mixture of beans, peas, and nuts in a large pot. Add 4 cups of water and bring to a boil. Cover partially and simmer gently for 40 minutes, or until almost tender. Now add the potatoes, carrot, leek, celery, thyme, and bay leaves and cook for another 20 to 30 minutes. Add the salt; stir to mix.

Transfer half of the soup to a blender, making sure to include all the cashews. (Discard the bay leaves.) Blend along with the milk, then pour the pureed soup back into the pot.

Put the oil in a small pan or small frying pan and set over medium-high heat. When hot, put in the garlic cloves. Press down on them and when one side is golden, turn them over. Press down on them again. When the second side is golden, remove and discard them. Add the tomato and stir for a minute. Now pour the oil-tomato mixture into the soup pot and stir to mix. Heat again before serving.

Serve with lemon wedges, if desired.

SERVES 4 TO 5

Trinidadian Split Pea Soup   TRINIDAD
Sans Coche

Trinidad is the one place on earth where Africa, the Mediterranean, India, and the New World met in a state of shock and, speaking in culinary terms, reconciled fast in a spirit of mutual survival. This Creole soup speaks of this creative reconciliation.

The origin of the soup's name is anybody's guess. The use of yellow split peas could be Mediterranean or Indian. The seasonings are part Mediterranean and part New World. The heart of the soup—and by this I mean what floats around in it when served in the Breakfast Shed on the wharf in Trinidad—are the "provisions": yams and other roots of both the Old and New World that helped slaves and indentured laborers survive. It is a glorious soup!

Traditionally, the yellow split peas are combined with a stock made with preserved meat parts, but I have adapted the recipe to the needs of a vegetarian. I have also left out the "provisions" as most of us tend to eat more lightly. However, if you wish to add them, about 20 minutes before the cooking is done, put in about a cupful of diced (¾-inch pieces) peeled green plantains or the same amount of pumpkin flesh, peeled eddoes (taro), or yams—or a combination of all.

This soup is generally served with rice on the side (in Trinidad it is a pilaf—pelau—topped with tomato, cucumber, and watercress). Pepper sauce to season the soup is a must (see Trinidadian Pepper Sauce, page 771). If you do not have it, Tabasco sauce is one alternative. The other is a combination of lime juice and cayenne sprinkled over the top.

3 tablespoons peanut or canola oil

1 good-sized onion (5 ounces), peeled and
    finely chopped

1 celery stalk, finely chopped

2 garlic cloves, peeled and finely chopped

1 fresh hot green chile, finely chopped

1 teaspoon chopped fresh thyme or
    $\frac{1}{2}$ teaspoon dried

1 tablespoon finely sliced chives

1 cup coarsely grated peeled carrot

1 cup ($7\frac{1}{2}$ ounces) yellow split peas (picked
    over, rinsed, and drained)

6 cups vegetable stock

Salt

Freshly ground black pepper

Put the oil in a large pan and set over medium-high heat. When hot, put in the onion, celery, garlic, green chile, thyme, and chives. Stir and sauté for 5 minutes; a little browning should be encouraged. Add the carrot and continue to stir and fry for another 3 minutes. Add the split peas and stock and bring to a boil. Cover partially, turn the heat down to low, and simmer gently for $1\frac{1}{4}$ to $1\frac{1}{2}$ hours, or until very tender and a homogeneous mass. Begin to check after 1 hour, stirring now and then. When done, taste for salt, adding as much as needed and add black pepper to taste.

SERVES 4

MISO SOUPS

In Japan, to be considered an acceptable bride, every young woman must know how to make a good miso soup. Breakfasts start with it, banquets end with it, and it is not uncommon to serve it at lunch and dinner as well.

Miso is a fermented paste made with soybeans that have generally been mixed with grains such as rice or barley. It is very rich in protein. Because of the fermentation process this protein is easy to digest, making it doubly valuable to our bodies. Also, for women of a certain age—and this includes me—it is good to know that all soybean products contain natural estrogen. I have a bowl of miso soup—often with bean curd in it—every single day.

The origins of this natural health food lie in ancient China. Fermented soybean pastes can still be found there under the name *chiang,* and are used today mainly as nutrient flavorings (hoisin sauce is a good example). They exist in Korea as well, where they are called *chang* (*kochu chang* and *toen chang* are the most popular), and are used both as flavorings and to make everyday stews. In Japan, of course, they are known as miso and even though used primarily in miso soup, they are also used as flavorings, dressings, and toppings for everything from bean curd rectangles to rice. All versions of bean paste have their own national identities, though they can all be traced back to early Chinese beginnings.

In Japan, to step into a traditional miso shop is to step into the timeless world of the well-ordered yesteryears. There are row upon row of wooden casks, heaped with miso of every earthy color: beiges, tans, brown, reddish-brown, blackish-brown, creamy-white, yellowish-white, and all shades in between. As orders come in, the thick paste is scraped off with wooden scoops and put into small containers. The emperor's order—and his household drinks miso soup just like everyone else—is always taken from deep down in the center of a cask.

For most of us in the West, miso may be bought from Japanese grocers and from health food shops in plastic bags or cartons. There is generally a dark brown miso, a reddish-brown one, a dull yellow one, and sometimes a sweetish white one. In Japanese shops, the names identifying the misos are often in Japanese, so it is best to go by color and, once you have tried the miso, by taste. All are fairly salty, though now new low-salt ones can also be found. Since only about ½ to 1 tablespoon of miso is required to make a cup of soup, this is not really a problem. It is like using a bouillon cube to make a cup of soup, only this "cube" is a protein-rich, all-vegetarian mass of living microorganisms that is very kind to your digestive tract. Different misos may also be mixed to get a more customized taste. Experimenting with what is available locally is your best bet.

The texture of miso is rather like peanut butter, and like peanut butter, some misos are chunky and others are smooth. I tend to use low-salt misos.

To make a miso soup, you need the miso of your choice—or a mixture of misos—some stock, and a few solid ingredients to give the soup texture and added flavor.

The traditional stock for *miso-shiru* is made with *konbu* (page 726), dried shiitake or Chinese black mushrooms (page 728), or the broth that is left when soybeans are boiled. I am easy about this. I use homemade stocks, canned stocks, stock from soaked dried mushrooms or from cooked vegetables, broth from cooking dried beans—whatever is accessible. It is important, though, to use no-salt or low-salt stocks, as miso is salty in itself. You might even mix canned stock with equal parts of water.

As for the solid ingredients in a miso soup, the possibilities are endless. I like to combine spinach, bean curd, and scallions, or white radish (daikon), carrot, and bean sprouts, or shiitake mushrooms and egg, or shredded Chinese cabbage and leeks, or grilled eggplant slices and roasted sesame seeds. Pumpkin cubes, cucumbers, asparagus, fried bean curd, and small turnips are all welcome in combinations of your choice. In Japan, ingredients that symbolize the time of year, sometimes just in shape, are preferred.

Extra seasonings, such as Japanese seven-spice powder, red pepper, lime or ginger juice, or hot mustard, may also be added. Feel free to use whatever spicing your palate desires. The Japanese even put in curry powder, so there are no regional rules here!

As the microorganisms in fermented bean paste are destroyed with overcooking and boiling, it is best to add it at the last minute. There are several ways to dissolve the thick paste and add it to the soup. You could put the miso in a bowl and slowly add ladles of the heated stock to it, stirring as you go. When it is like cream, pour it back into the soup, stirring gently as you do this. Another method, and this is the one I was taught first and have used ever since, is to put the bean paste in a small sieve, then lower the sieve into the almost-cooked soup. Stir the paste with a spoon until all of it goes through. Sometimes, with a coarse paste, bits of fermented beans and grains are left in the sieve. You may add them to the soup or not, as you prefer.

Once miso soup is prepared, it separates—with the thicker parts of the liquid hovering near the bottom. It is always stirred before being served and stirred again before drinking every other mouthful. The Japanese tend to pick up the solids with chopsticks and drink the soup directly from the bowl itself. If you are using Japanese-style soup bowls, you may follow the Japanese example or else use soup spoons and any bowls or plates of your choice.

What follow are several recipes for Japanese-style miso soup. Once you know the general method, I am sure you will begin to improvise your own recipes.

Miso Soup with Bean Curd and Spinach   JAPAN
Miso Shiru

You may use the reddish-brown, brown, or beige-yellow miso here. As the darker misos tend to be more salty, you might want to use a bit less, 2½ to 3 tablespoons instead of the 4. You should taste as you go. You may also mix different misos or try a low-salt one, if available.

Use 4 cups of Konbu Stock (page 577), Dried Mushroom Stock (page 577) (without the soy sauce and extra salt), or Vegetable Stock (page 576). If using canned or powdered vegetable broth/stock, use half stock and half water, as it can be fairly salty.

4 cups vegetable stock

24 well-washed spinach leaves

½ pound soft, medium, or firm bean curd, cut into ¾-inch cubes

2 scallions, cut into very, very fine rings (use both white and green portions)

2½ to 4 tablespoons miso (see recipe introduction)

⅛ teaspoon Japanese Seven-Spice Seasoning (page 725) or a pinch of cayenne (optional)

(recipe continues)

605

Put the stock in a medium pot and bring to a simmer. Add the spinach leaves and bring to a simmer again. As soon as the leaves wilt, 1 to 2 minutes, put in the bean curd and the scallions. Simmer for half a minute. Now turn the heat down to low. Put the miso in a small sieve and lower it into the soup (you may have to move the bean curd pieces aside). Push the miso through with a spoon. Turn off the heat, stir once, and serve with a light sprinkling of the Seven-Spice Seasoning, if desired.

SERVES 2 TO 4

Variation
Miso Soup with Snow Peas and Bean Curd

Substitute 16 trimmed snow peas (remove the stems and the "thread" along the "back bone") for the spinach. Halve each snow pea crosswise, on the extreme diagonal.

Miso Soup with Pumpkin and Onion   JAPAN
Miso Shiru

This is a lovely winter soup. You may use the reddish-brown, brown, or beige-yellow miso here, though you might want to use a bit less, 2½ to 3 tablespoons instead of the 4, of the darker misos, as they tend to be more salty. You should taste as you go. You may also mix different misos or try a low-salt one, if available.

Use 4 cups of Konbu Stock (page 577), Dried Mushroom Stock (page 577) (without the soy sauce and extra salt), or Vegetable Stock (page 576). If using canned or powdered vegetable broth/stock, use half stock and half water as it can be fairly salty.

2 tablespoons peanut or canola oil

1 medium onion, peeled, halved, and thinly sliced

2 cups (about ¾ pound) peeled pumpkin or butternut squash, cut into ¾-inch cubes

4 cups vegetable stock

2½ to 4 tablespoons miso (see recipe introduction)

3 to 4 *shiso* leaves, cut into fine shreds (use 2 tablespoons chopped cilantro as a substitute)

Put the oil in a medium pan and set over medium-high heat. When hot, put in the onion. Stir and fry until translucent, turning the heat down a bit, if necessary, to avoid browning. Put in the pumpkin cubes and stir once or twice. Now put in the stock and bring to a boil. Cover, turn the heat down to low, and simmer gently for

10 to 15 minutes, or until the pumpkin is just tender but retains its shape. Put the miso in a small sieve and lower it into the soup (you may have to move the pumpkin pieces aside). Push the miso through with a spoon. Turn off the heat, stir once, and serve sprinkled with the *shiso* leaves.

SERVES 2 TO 4

Variation
Curried Miso Soup with Pumpkin

Make exactly as above but once the onions have turned translucent, add 2 teaspoons curry powder and sauté an extra 30 seconds. Now add the pumpkin and proceed with the recipe. As a garnish and final flavoring, use cilantro leaves instead of the shredded *shiso*.

Miso Soup with Shiitake Mushrooms and Egg Strands   JAPAN
Miso Shiru

This could make a wonderful, simple meal if you served rice and a salad on the side. It could also be a first course or a light lunch.

You may use the reddish-brown, brown, or beige-yellow miso here. As the darker misos tend to be more salty, you might want to use a bit less, 2½ to 3 tablespoons instead of the 4. You should taste as you go. You may also mix different misos or try a low-salt one, if available.

Use 3 cups of Konbu Stock (page 577), Dried Mushroom Stock (page 577) (without the soy sauce and extra salt), or Vegetable Stock (page 576). If using canned or powdered vegetable broth/stock, use half stock and half water, as it can be fairly salty.

8 large dried shiitake mushrooms (Chinese black mushrooms)

3 cups vegetable stock

2 scallions, cut into very, very fine rings (use both white and green portions)

2½ to 4 tablespoons miso (see recipe introduction)

2 eggs, lightly beaten

⅛ teaspoon Japanese Seven-Spice Seasoning (page 725) or a pinch of cayenne (optional)

Soak the mushrooms in 1 cup of hot water for 30 minutes, or until softened. Lift the mushrooms out of the liquid (save the liquid) and cut off the hard stems. Slice the caps finely. Strain the soaking liquid through a fine cloth.

(recipe continues)

Put the stock and the mushroom soaking liquid into a medium pot and bring to a simmer. Add the mushroom slices and scallions and bring to a simmer again. Simmer for half a minute. Now turn the heat down to low. Put the miso in a small sieve and lower it into the soup, then push the miso through with a spoon. Stir for 10 seconds and take the pan off the heat. Carefully pour in the beaten eggs in a slow, steady, thin stream, covering the entire surface of the soup with a squiggly, netlike pattern. Put the soup on low heat and bring to a simmer, stirring very slowly and gently. As soon as the eggs set into satiny skeins, a matter of seconds, turn off the heat. Stir once and serve with a light sprinkling of Seven-Spice Seasoning, if desired.

SERVES 2 TO 4

Fireman's Soup

This earthy, nourishing soup was created for my little grandson who, like many little boys, plays at being a fireman much of the time. I have managed to convince him that to save lives, he must be strong and that to be strong, he needs a steady dose of Fireman's Soup! He loves it. So do we all.

    If you cannot get hulled and split mung beans, sold in Indian shops as moong dal, *use red lentils* (masoor dal).

2 tablespoons olive or canola oil

2 celery stalks, very finely diced

2 small carrots (5 to 6 ounces), peeled and very finely diced

1 medium onion (4 ounces), peeled and very finely diced

15 to 20 green beans, cut crosswise at ¼-inch intervals

6 cups vegetable stock

5 tablespoons bulgur wheat

5 tablespoons hulled and split mung beans *(moong dal)*

Salt

Put the oil in a medium pan and set over medium-high heat. When hot, put in the celery, carrots, and onion. Stir and sauté until the onion is translucent, turning the heat down if necessary to avoid browning. Put in the green beans and stir for a minute. Now put in the stock, the bulgur wheat, and the mung beans and bring to a boil. Cover, turn the heat down to very low, and simmer gently for 40 minutes. Taste and add salt to taste. If the stock is salted, you will need just a little extra salt.

SERVES 4 TO 6

Skinned Wheat Berry Soup with Ginger and Cilantro

INDIAN-AMERICAN

Here is a soup I make in large batches and keep in the refrigerator, where it lasts for several days. It makes for a perfect lunch, especially in the winter.

Directions for soaking and cooking skinned wheat berries are on page 417. (If you cannot get skinned berries, use whole wheat berries and follow directions for cooking them on page 417.)

2 tablespoons peanut or canola oil

1 medium onion (5 ounces)

1 celery stalk, cut into ¼-inch dice

1 carrot (4 ounces), peeled and cut into ¼-inch dice

½ pound boiling potatoes, peeled and cut into ¼-inch dice

2 teaspoons fresh ginger that has been peeled and grated to a pulp

3 tablespoons finely chopped fresh cilantro

1 teaspoon ground cumin

¼ teaspoon ground turmeric

⅛ to ¼ teaspoon cayenne

1 cup canned tomato sauce

½ cup (3 ounces) skinned wheat berries, soaked and cooked for 45 minutes according to directions on page 417, with their liquid

3 cups vegetable stock or water

Salt

Freshly ground black pepper

Put the oil in a medium pan and set over medium heat. When hot, put in the onion, celery, carrot, and potatoes. Stir and sauté for 5 minutes. Add the ginger and cilantro and stir for 30 seconds. Now put in the cumin, turmeric, and cayenne. Stir once. Put in the tomato sauce, the skinned wheat berries and their liquid, and the stock or water. Stir and bring to a boil. Cover, turn the heat down to low, and cook for 15 minutes. Taste for salt, adding black pepper to taste. Stir, cover, and simmer another 15 minutes.

SERVES 4 TO 6

SWEET SOUPS

Though seldom seen in American kitchens, sweet soups are much favored around the world. Some are served for breakfast, others as snacks, some as first courses at dinners, and some as desserts. They can be made with fruit and served cold in the summer, or made of dried beans, nuts, and seeds and served either hot or cold.

In China, sweet soups are usually sweetened with rock sugar, which has a gentler taste and, when required, provides a smooth glaze. The soups are never too sweet, just very gently so.

Sweet Almond Soup   ALL OF EAST ASIA

Some sweet soups are medicinal. In Hong Kong I visit a shop that serves nothing but medicinal soups. You explain your condition to the man at the counter and he picks out your soup, unless, of course, you know how the system works and can order your own. The almond soup, I have been told, encourages a smooth, pale complexion, rather like the almond itself.

When I was an awkward, bookworm-y, bespectacled thirteen, a most beautiful dancer from the south of India came to stay at our house. Her face was indeed like a blanched almond in shape and color—a pale, Modigliani face. Her name was an exotic "Nina," she could speak French (I did not know any Indian then who spoke French), and her dancing was sensuous, earthy, and a technical marvel. I wanted desperately to be her. So, decades later, in memory of those dreams, I ordered an almond soup. There are so many different versions of this soup in East Asia. This is the simplest one. It requires no thickening other than what comes from the nuts themselves. Serve it hot in the winter and chilled in the summer.

1 cup (4 ounces) blanched slivered almonds   5 to 6 tablespoons sugar

Put the almonds and 3 cups of water into a blender and blend thoroughly until you have a smooth paste. Set a fine sieve over a bowl. Pour the thick milk into the sieve and strain it, pushing out every last drop of liquid; discard the solids. Put the strained milk back into a clean blender container. Line the same sieve you used before with a triple layer of muslin. Pour the milk into the lined sieve. Now pick up the muslin by its 4 corners and squeeze the milk out. The aim is to get rid of all the grainy residue. Put the milk and the sugar into a small pan and slowly bring to a simmer, stirring all the time. Turn the heat down to low and simmer very gently for 10 minutes, stirring frequently. Turn off the heat.

SERVES 3

Shiu-Min Block's

Sweet "Green Pea" Soup   CHINA

Leu Dou Tang

This is a mung bean soup, earthy, basic, and satisfying. It is very nutritious too, full of fiber, protein, and the cholesterol-fighting properties of legumes. In mainland China, it is generally had in its very plain form, hot in the winters and chilled in the summers, poured into bowls and eaten with soup spoons. It is most often eaten as a snack, though it is sometimes served as dessert at the end of a meal. You can even buy a bowl at intermission during a tent performance of the traveling Chinese opera! The boiled beans and their liquid are all served together.

I like it as a snack or a simple lunch.

1 cup (5 ounces) whole dried mung beans, picked over, washed, and drained

½ cup (4 ounces) crushed rock sugar (use 5 to 7 tablespoons sugar as a substitute, tasting as you go)

Soak the beans overnight in water to cover them generously. The following day, drain the beans and combine with 8 cups of water in a heavy pot. Bring to a boil, cover partially, turn the heat down to low, and simmer gently for 1½ hours. Uncover and stir in the rock sugar. Simmer, uncovered, another 15 to 20 minutes. Serve hot or nicely chilled.

SERVES 6

Variation I

Creamy Sweet "Green Pea" Soup   HONG KONG

Leu Dou Hu

Follow the preceding recipe and make the soup. Mix 2 teaspoons cornstarch in 2 tablespoons water and add to the soup. Bring to a boil, turn down the heat, and simmer 2 minutes. Blend the soup in a blender and serve hot.

or

Follow the preceding recipe and make the soup. Blend it in a blender. Add ½ cup heavy cream and mix well. Serve hot.

(recipe continues)

Variation II

Sweet "Green Pea" Soup with Coconut Milk INDONESIA

Bubur Kacang Hijao

Follow the master recipe for Sweet "Green Pea" Soup. When it is ready, crush the beans coarsely with a potato masher. Add ½ cup coconut milk from a well-stirred can, mix well, and just heat through. Serve hot, at room temperature, or chilled.

Variation III

Sweet Red Bean Soup CHINA

Hung Do Tang

This soup is made in exactly the same way as the Sweet "Green Pea" Soup on page 611, except that it uses the same quantity of small Chinese red beans instead of the whole mung beans. These red beans are called *hung do* in Chinese markets and azuki beans in Japanese and many international markets. The red beans may be cooked using all the variations that apply to the mung beans.

Salads and Saladlike Dishes

Artichoke Heart and
Fresh Fava Bean Salad GREECE

Aginares Me Koukia

Here is one of the many wonders of Greece. The yield from fresh fava beans varies quite a bit. I bought a little over 2 pounds of whole fava bean pods. The yield, after shelling, was small and quite varied in size, about 1¾ cups. The fresh artichokes I used in this recipe weighed 8 to 10 ounces; if the artichokes are either larger or smaller, you will need to adjust the cooking time.

2 tablespoons unbleached all-purpose
    white flour
3 tablespoons fresh lemon juice
Salt

3 fresh artichoke hearts (for preparation
    directions, see page 128)
1¾ cups shelled fresh fava beans
2 tablespoons extra-virgin olive oil
1 tablespoon finely chopped fresh dill

Put the flour in a medium bowl. Slowly add 4 cups of water, stirring with a whisk as you do so. Add 2 tablespoons of the lemon juice and 1 teaspoon salt. Transfer to a medium pot and bring to a simmer. Turn the heat down to low and simmer very gently for 5 minutes. Arrange the artichoke hearts in the bottom of the pan in a single layer and simmer gently for 15 to 20 minutes, until tender or the tip of a knife pierces the flesh easily. Let them cool in the liquid.

Put the beans into a medium saucepan with water to cover by 1 inch. Bring to a boil and cover. Lower the heat and simmer gently for 10 to 15 minutes, or until the beans are tender. Remove from the heat, rinse under cool water, and peel off the outer skins.

Remove the artichoke hearts from the cooking liquid and rinse well. Slice the artichoke hearts crosswise into ¼-inch-thick slices. Combine with the fava beans in a shallow bowl. In a small bowl, combine the olive oil, the remaining tablespoon of lemon juice, and ⅓ teaspoon salt. Mix well and pour over the artichokes and beans. Sprinkle the dill over the top and toss gently to mix. Serve at room temperature or chilled.

SERVES 4 AS A SIDE DISH AND 2 AS A MAIN COURSE

Rosario Guillermo's

Guacamole   MEXICO

Salad of Avocado and Tomatillos

If jalapeño or chile serrano peppers are unavailable, any other fresh or canned hot green chile may be used. The amount can be varied according to your taste.
   Serve guacamole as a salad or as a dip with tortilla chips.

4 green tomatillos

1 ripe medium avocado, preferably Haas

3 tablespoons finely chopped onion

½ to 1 fresh or canned jalapeño or serrano
   chile, finely chopped

1 tablespoon finely chopped fresh cilantro

1 garlic clove, peeled and crushed

3 tablespoons fresh lime juice

¾ teaspoon salt

Remove the papery husks of the tomatillos and rinse off. Put the tomatillos in a small pot with just enough water to cover. Bring to a boil over medium-high heat. Turn the heat down to medium and continue to boil for 7 to 10 minutes, or until the tomatillos are soft and tender. Drain. Let the tomatillos cool just enough to handle. Peel away their skins and mash into small pieces. Set aside.

(recipe continues)

Cut the avocado in half lengthwise. Remove the pit and peel the skin away. In a mortar or ceramic bowl, mash the avocado into small but slightly coarse pieces. Add the tomatillos, onion, chile, cilantro, and garlic. Mix well. Add the lime juice and salt and stir once again. Serve chilled or at room temperature.

MAKES 1 CUP

Salad of White Beans and Peppers

1¼ cups (8 ounces) dried white kidney beans or any white beans

4 tablespoons very finely chopped onion

2 to 3 bay leaves

2 garlic cloves, peeled and finely chopped

1¼ teaspoons salt

¼ cup peeled and seeded tomato, cut into ¼-inch dice

¼ cup red pepper, seeded and cut into ¼-inch dice

¼ cup green pepper, seeded and cut into ¼-inch dice

3 tablespoons olive oil

1½ tablespoons fresh lemon juice, or to taste

Freshly ground black pepper

2 tablespoons chopped parsley

Soak the beans overnight as suggested in Cooking White Beans on page 52, or use the Quick-Soak Method on page 6. Drain, discarding any soaking liquid.

In a medium pot, bring the beans, onion, bay leaves, garlic, and 3 cups of water to a boil. Cover the pot in such a way as to leave it slightly ajar. Turn the heat down to low and simmer gently for 40 to 80 minutes, or until the beans are just tender. (Older beans will take longer to cook.) Add 1 teaspoon of the salt. Mix well and let cool. Remove the bay leaves. Drain off extra liquid, if any. Add the tomato, peppers, oil, lemon juice, remaining ¼ teaspoon salt (or to taste), black pepper, and parsley. Toss to mix and taste for the balance of flavors.

SERVES 4

Bean Curd Salad or Spread

The first time I had this was when a fellow actress brought a sandwich to the rehearsal of a play we were doing in New York. She offered me half and I found it utterly delicious. When I asked her where she had bought the spread, which she had layered rather thickly on the bread, she mentioned the local health food shop. I was hooked for a while until I decided that I could have a better, fresher spread if I made it myself. My friend had made her sandwich with walnut bread, but since I didn't always have walnut bread around, I decided to put walnuts in the spread! A scoop with some lettuce makes a perfectly good salad as well.

When cutting off the amount of bean curd you need for this recipe, cut the cake horizontally. The larger surface you have to press down, the easier it will be.

8 ounces firm or extra-firm bean curd

2 tablespoons soybean or olive oil

1 tablespoon very finely chopped red bell pepper (no seeds)

1 tablespoon very finely chopped green bell pepper (no seeds)

1 tablespoon very finely chopped peeled carrot

1 tablespoon very finely chopped scallion

1 tablespoon very finely chopped parsley

1 tablespoon very finely chopped white mushroom

1 tablespoon very finely chopped walnuts

1 teaspoon soy sauce

½ teaspoon sugar

Freshly ground black pepper

¼ teaspoon salt, or to taste

½ teaspoon oriental sesame oil

2 teaspoons roasted sesame seeds (page 734), optional

Spread some paper toweling on a chopping board and lay the bean curd in the center. Top with more paper towels and then another board or a large plate. Put a weight, roughly 4 pounds, on top of the last board, making sure that it is balanced properly and will not topple over. Leave for 30 minutes.

Meanwhile, put the oil in a medium frying pan and set over medium-high heat. When hot, add the red pepper, green pepper, carrot, scallion, parsley, mushroom, and walnuts. Stir and sauté for about 40 seconds. Turn off the heat.

Remove the weight from the bean curd and press it through a coarse sieve into a bowl. Add the stir-fried vegetables as well as the soy sauce, sugar, pepper to taste, salt, sesame oil, and sesame seeds and mix well. Taste for the balance of flavors, cover, and store in the refrigerator.

MAKES ABOUT 1 CUP

Tomato-Flavored Bean Curd Spread or Salad

UNITED STATES

This is a delicious, nutritious spread to use on breads and is very easy to prepare. You can also serve a small scoop of it as a salad.

8 ounces firm or extra-firm bean curd

1 tablespoon tomato paste

2 tablespoons olive oil

1 tablespoon fresh lemon juice

¾ teaspoon salt

¼ teaspoon dried thyme

¼ teaspoon dried oregano

Spread some paper toweling on a chopping board and lay the bean curd in the center. Top with some more paper toweling and then with another board or a large plate. Put a weight, roughly 4 pounds, on top of the second board, making sure that it is balanced properly and will not topple over. Leave for 30 minutes.

Remove the weight from the bean curd and press it through a coarse sieve into a bowl. Add all the remaining ingredients and mix well. Cover and refrigerate.

MAKES 1 CUP

Cabbage Salad with Oregano

EL SALVADOR

Curtido

This is the deliciously spicy and sour salad that is served with papoosa, *the stuffed corn breads of El Salvador. It is so good that it has almost replaced coleslaw in my household.*

I make it at least an hour ahead of time as it needs to sit and "pickle" in its own juices. You can even make it a day in advance; just keep it covered and refrigerated.

Here I used half of a 2-pound green cabbage, cored, with the coarse outer leaves removed.

6 well-packed cups shredded green cabbage

1 cup shredded crisp lettuce, such as iceberg

1 medium carrot, peeled and coarsely grated

1½ teaspoons salt

2 tablespoons red wine vinegar

¼ teaspoon cayenne

1 teaspoon dried oregano

1 tablespoon olive oil

Combine all the ingredients in a large bowl and toss well to mix. Set aside for 1 hour or longer, refrigerating if necessary.

SERVES 6

Cabbage Salad with Mustard Seeds INDIA
Bund Gobi Ka Salaad

This simple salad from the Goan Coast in India is wonderful with bean dishes. Make it as hot as you like, but do allow 1 hour for the salad to sit and "pickle" in its own juices. You can make it a day in advance; just keep it covered and refrigerated.

Here I used half of a 2-pound green cabbage, cored, with the coarse outer leaves removed.

6 well-packed cups (1 pound) shredded green
    cabbage

1 medium carrot, peeled and coarsely grated

1 to 2 fresh hot green chiles, cut into fine
    shreds

1½ teaspoons salt

2 tablespoons red wine vinegar

¼ teaspoon cayenne

2 tablespoons peanut or canola oil

1 teaspoon whole brown mustard seeds

Combine the cabbage, carrot, chiles, salt, vinegar, and cayenne in a large bowl and toss well to mix. Put the oil in a small frying pan and set over medium-high heat. When hot, put in the mustard seeds. As soon as the mustard seeds begin to pop, a matter of seconds, pour the oil and seeds over the salad. Toss well to mix. Set aside for 1 hour or longer, refrigerating if necessary.

SERVES 6

Moroccan Cabbage and Orange Salad MOROCCO

This is a simple, refreshing salad to be had with almost any meal. Make sure you use very young, fresh cabbage.

½ small head green cabbage (12 ounces),
    cored and shredded

3 medium oranges, peeled and cut into skin-
    free segments

5 tablespoons orange juice

3 tablespoons raisins

2 tablespoons fresh lemon juice

2½ teaspoons sugar

1½ teaspoons salt

⅛ teaspoon cinnamon

Combine all the ingredients in a bowl. Refrigerate, covered, for 2 to 3 hours. Drain lightly before serving.

SERVES 6

Carrot and Cilantro Salad

Carotte M'chermel

This simple, delicious salad can be served at room temperature or cold at virtually any meal. In Morocco, it is generally part of a very attractive first course of salads, with Moroccan breads served on the side.

8 medium carrots (16 ounces), peeled and cut into 1½ × ¼ × ¼-inch sticks

4 tablespoons finely chopped fresh cilantro leaves

4 teaspoons fresh lemon juice

4 teaspoons olive oil

1 teaspoon salt

½ teaspoon cayenne

1 teaspoon paprika

Fill a large pot with water and bring it to a rolling boil. Drop the carrots into the boiling water and boil for 10 seconds. Drain immediately. Transfer the carrot sticks to a bowl and add the cilantro, lemon juice, olive oil, salt, cayenne, and paprika. Mix well. Serve at room temperature or chilled.

SERVES 4

South Indian Carrot and Ginger Relish

The recipe for this South Indian salad may easily be doubled. It is particularly good with all manner of rice and bean dishes.

2 smallish carrots (4 ounces), peeled and cut into very fine julienne strips

1-inch piece of fresh ginger, peeled, thinly sliced, and cut into very fine slivers

½ to 1 fresh hot green chile, finely chopped

½ teaspoon salt

¼ teaspoon cayenne

1 tablespoon fresh lemon juice

1 tablespoon peanut or canola oil

Pinch of ground asafetida

¼ teaspoon skinned and split *urad dal, chana dal,* or yellow split peas

½ teaspoon brown mustard seeds

In a bowl, combine the carrots, ginger, green chile, salt, cayenne, and lemon juice. Stir to mix.

Put the oil in a small pan and set over medium-high heat. When hot, put in the asafetida. A second later, put in the *urad dal* and stir it very briefly until it turns reddish. Now put in the mustard seeds. When they start popping, a matter of seconds, pour the oil and seasonings over the carrots. Stir to mix.

Cover and refrigerate until ready to serve.

SERVES 2 TO 4

Thai "Pickled" Carrot Salad   THAILAND

By reducing the large quantity of oil that covered the vegetables in order to preserve them, I have converted what was served to me in Bangkok as a pickle into what may now be called a salad. But the taste remains the same. It is spicy, utterly addictive, and can perk up any meal.

In Bangkok, the red chiles, shallots, and garlic were pounded into a paste in a mortar and the vinegar was added later along with the salt and sugar. You may do the same if you wish, but I find it more convenient to use a blender.

3 tablespoons peanut or canola oil

2 dried hot red chiles

3 large shallots (2 ounces), peeled and slivered

3 garlic cloves, peeled and slivered

2 to 2½ tablespoons rice vinegar

3 large carrots (14 ounces), peeled and cut into 2 × 1⅛ × 1⅛-inch sticks

2 teaspoons sugar

1¼ teaspoons salt

1 tablespoon freshly roasted sesame seeds (page 734)

Put the oil in a medium frying pan and set over medium-high heat. When the oil is very hot, put in the chiles. Stir for a few seconds until the chiles darken and swell, then add the shallots and garlic. Stir and fry for about 3 minutes, or until the shallots and garlic turn reddish-brown. Turn off the heat. Empty the mixture from the frying pan into a blender, including all the oil. Add the vinegar and blend until you have a smooth paste, scraping down the sides of the blender with a spatula as needed.

Put 2 quarts of water in a good-sized pot and bring to a rolling boil. Add the carrots. When the water returns to a boil, drain the carrots in a colander.

Put the carrots into a medium bowl. Add the paste from the blender, making sure to get every last bit. Add the sugar and salt and mix well. Just before serving, add the sesame seeds and toss. Serve at room temperature or chilled.

SERVES 4 TO 6

Moroccan Carrot Salad with Orange Juice

This unusual Moroccan salad gets its sour-sweet citrus flavor from the juice of a good orange. To allow the flavors to blend well, it is a good idea to make the salad a few hours ahead of time, cover it, and let it sit in the refrigerator until you are ready to eat. This salad can stay in the refrigerator for 24 hours. It may be served with almost any meal.

4 medium carrots (8 ounces), peeled and grated

¼ cup golden raisins

1 teaspoon salt

½ cup fresh orange juice

In a bowl, combine all the ingredients and mix well. Cover and refrigerate until ready to eat. Drain lightly just before serving.

SERVES 4

Soft Cheese Salad with Tomato and Basil Topped with Asparagus

Here is a wonderful stir-fry of vegetables with soft cheese curds that can serve as a light meal in itself. It uses Indian-style cheese in a very un-Indian way.

The soft cheese curds are best eaten the day they are made. They do not keep well in the refrigerator, where they tend to harden.

1 scallion

18 fresh asparagus spears

1 recipe Indian Homemade Cheese curds, prepared in the Soft Curds style (page 561)

1 tomato, peeled, seeded, and cut into ⅓-inch dice (see page 300 for directions)

⅓ large green bell pepper, cut into ⅓-inch dice

¼ cup finely chopped parsley

3 tablespoons olive oil

¼ cup fresh lemon juice

¼ teaspoon crushed garlic

1 teaspoon salt

1 tablespoon peanut or canola oil

2 teaspoons oriental sesame oil

½ cup fresh basil, cut into fine strips (chiffonade)

Cut the scallion into 2-inch segments. Stack the segments together and cut into very fine rounds. Put the rounds into a small bowl of ice water, cover, and refrigerate for 30 minutes. Drain. Spread the scallion rounds in a dish towel and wring out.

Cut off the tough ends of the asparagus spears and discard. Peel the lower half of the spears, then cut into ⅓-inch-long segments, leaving the heads whole.

In a bowl, crumble the cheese into small pieces. Add the scallion, tomato, bell pepper, parsley, olive oil, lemon juice, garlic, and ¾ teaspoon salt. Mix well and set aside.

Put the vegetable oil in a nonstick medium frying pan or sauté pan and set over medium-high heat. When it is hot, add the asparagus and stir once or twice. Add the remaining ¼ teaspoon salt and ¼ cup of water to the pan and mix. Cover and cook for 2 to 3 minutes, or until the asparagus is just tender. Uncover and add the sesame oil; stir to mix. Turn the heat up to high and cook until all the liquid is evaporated. Remove from the heat.

Toss the basil with the cheese mixture. Mix well. The asparagus can either be arranged on top of the cheese mixture or mixed into the cheese. Serve warm, at room temperature, or chilled.

SERVES 4

Greek Eggplant Salad GREECE

Melitzanosalata

Here is a Greek version of the popular eggplant "dip," a much-loved first course, eaten with bits of pita bread.

1 large eggplant or 2 smaller ones (1¼ pounds in all)

3 tablespoons mayonnaise

1 tablespoon white wine vinegar

1¼ teaspoons salt

Freshly ground black pepper

2 tablespoons very finely chopped onion

2 tablespoons very finely chopped parsley

2 tablespoons finely chopped red bell pepper (you could use a roasted red pepper—see page 262 for roasting peppers)

Roast the eggplant according to any of the methods suggested on pages 178 to 179 until it is soft. Peel away the skin and mash the pulp finely. Add all the remaining ingredients and mix well.

Serve warm, at room temperature, or chilled.

SERVES 6

Promila Kapoor's

Spicy Corn Salad

INDIA

Corn grows all over the Punjab in northwestern India, which is where this spicy snack originates. The potatoes in this salad taste much better if they have been freshly boiled and have not been refrigerated; use small new, waxy potatoes when available. I have used olive oil here because I like its taste, but any oil will do.

I like to use kernels of corn that have just been taken off fresh ears (you will need 3 to 4 ears, depending upon size), but frozen kernels may also be used. If you cannot get ajwain *seeds, use ½ teaspoon whole cumin seeds in their place and sprinkle ½ teaspoon fresh thyme at the same time you sprinkle the cayenne.*

1 pound waxy red potatoes, peeled

3 tablespoons olive oil

½ teaspoon *ajwain* seeds (page 711)

2½ cups fresh corn kernels (see recipe introduction)

3 tablespoons finely chopped onion

3 tablespoons fresh lemon juice

2 teaspoons ground *amchoor* (page 711)

¼ teaspoon cayenne

1½ teaspoons ground roasted cumin seeds (page 724)

½ teaspoon garam masala (store-bought is fine here)

2 tablespoons coarsely chopped fresh cilantro

1 teaspoon salt

Boil the potatoes in 6 cups of water until tender. Drain. Allow to cool just long enough to handle, then cut into ¾- to 1-inch cubes. Set aside.

Meanwhile, put the oil in a nonstick medium frying pan or sauté pan and set over medium-high heat. When it is hot, put in the *ajwain* seeds. Let them sizzle for a few seconds as you shake the pan, then add the corn. Turn the heat down to medium and stir for 1 minute. Add ¼ cup of water to the pan, mix, and bring to a simmer. Cover the pan and turn the heat down to low. Cook for 4 minutes, or until the corn is just done. If there is liquid left at the bottom of the pan, boil it away over slightly higher heat. Empty the corn into a large bowl. Add the potatoes, onion, lemon juice, *amchoor*, cayenne, ground roasted cumin, garam masala, cilantro, and salt. Stir to mix well. Serve warm or at room temperature.

SERVES 4 TO 6

Fennel and Orange Salad   MOROCCO

This light, cleansing salad comes from a land where oranges have superb flavor and texture and where most salads are served at the start of a meal, almost as appetizers. I, on the other hand, like to serve this salad at the end of the meal, almost in lieu of dessert. It is a great refresher with an unimaginably rejuvenating taste.

This salad can last in the refrigerator for 24 hours. In fact, its flavor improves.

The best ground cinnamon is that which you grind yourself. Use a coffee grinder to do the job.

2 fresh medium fennel bulbs, cut crosswise into paper-thin rounds, enough to fill a 2-cup measure

2 navel oranges, peeled and cut into skinless segments

6 tablespoons fresh orange juice

2 tablespoons fresh lemon juice

1 teaspoon salt

1 teaspoon sugar

⅛ teaspoon ground cinnamon

Put all the ingredients in a bowl, toss well, and refrigerate, covered, for 30 to 60 minutes. Drain lightly before serving.

SERVES 4

Figs with Mustard Seeds and Curry Leaves   INDIAN-AMERICAN

For me, this dish, a kind of warm salad, is heavenly. I have served it both as a first course and as part of a meal. You can eat it hot, warm, or cold. Something amazingly good happens to ripe figs if they are allowed to touch high heat for a moment: They caramelize and concentrate themselves. The mustard seeds and curry leaves just make them more exquisite. If you cannot get curry leaves, use basil leaves, either Thai holy basil or regular Italian basil. For this dish you may use green or purple figs but they must be really ripe and sweet.

8 ripe purple or green figs

1 tablespoon olive oil

¼ teaspoon whole brown or yellow mustard seeds

8 fresh curry leaves

Salt

Cayenne

Half a lemon

(recipe continues)

Cut the figs in halves lengthwise.

Put the oil in a nonstick frying pan and set over medium-high heat. When hot, put in the mustard seeds. As soon as they begin to pop, a matter of seconds, put in the curry leaves. Stir the leaves around for 10 seconds. Now add the figs in a single layer, cut sides down. Move them around gently for a minute, then turn them over. Sprinkle very lightly with salt and cayenne and squeeze a few drops of lemon juice over each fig half. This should take about half a minute. Turn off the heat. Put the figs on a plate, cut sides up. Make sure there are some mustard seeds and 1 curry leaf on top of each fig half. Serve hot, warm, or chilled.

SERVES 4 AS A FIRST COURSE AND 2 AS PART OF A MEAL

M. L. Taw Kritakara's

Thai Fruit and Vegetable Salad THAILAND

The Thais make so many salads with fruit and vegetables. At a fine Bangkok restaurant this one was served most elegantly in little, individual baskets made of crisply fried potato straws. In our own homes, we do not need to go to such elaborate lengths; the salad, by itself, is quite sufficient. All the elements can be prepared ahead of time, but the salad should be tossed at the last minute. You could substitute 2 tablespoons of olive or peanut oil for the coconut milk.

Serve with cottage cheese or all by itself as a light lunch.

1 ounce mung bean threads

Salt

1 medium green apple

1 cup red seedless grapes, halved lengthwise

1 navel orange, peeled, the segments skinned and cut crosswise at ¼-inch intervals

1 cup (4 ounces) fresh green beans, cut into ½-inch pieces

1½ cups (12 ounces) cored and finely shredded red cabbage (green can be used)

Peanut or canola oil for shallow frying

1 garlic clove, peeled and cut into fine slivers

8 shallots (8 ounces), peeled and cut into fine slivers

Generous handful of fresh cilantro leaves

3 tablespoons coconut milk from a well-stirred can

3 tablespoons fresh lemon juice

1½ teaspoons salt

1 tablespoon sugar

¼ teaspoon cayenne

¼ cup dry-roasted peanuts, coarsely chopped

Cut the noodles into 1-inch lengths. Put 2 cups of water in a small pot and bring to a boil over high heat. Turn the heat off and add the noodles. Let the noodles soak for 15 minutes. Drain and set aside.

Combine 1 teaspoon of salt with 2½ cups of cold water in a bowl. Peel and core the apple and cut it into ¼-inch dice. Put the pieces into the salted water and set aside.

Put the grapes in a serving bowl. Arrange the orange segments over the grapes. Cover and set aside.

Bring 2 quarts of water to a boil in a medium pot over high heat. When it reaches a rolling boil, lower the beans in a sieve into the water for 3 minutes. Lift up the sieve and run the beans under cold water. Set aside. Bring the water back to a boil and add the cabbage. When the water returns to a rolling boil, drain the cabbage and run it under cold water. Set aside.

Pour oil to a depth of ¾ inch into a small to medium frying pan over medium-low heat. While you are waiting for the oil to get hot, set a sieve over a small heat-proof bowl and place it near the pan. Spread some paper toweling over a large plate. When the oil is hot, put in the garlic slivers. Stir and fry until they are golden, 30 seconds to 1 minute. Pour the garlic and the oil into the sieve. When the garlic has drained, spread it on the toweling.

Pour the oil back into the pan and set it over medium heat. Put the sieve back on the small bowl. When the oil has reheated, fry the shallots until they are golden and crisp, 6 to 7 minutes. Empty the contents of the frying pan into the sieve. When the shallots have drained, spread them out near the garlic on the paper towel. (Save the oil for cooking other foods or for the dressing, should you require it.)

Just before serving, drain the apple and add to the grape and orange mixture. Separate the mung bean noodles and add to the fruit along with the green beans, cabbage, and a generous handful of cilantro leaves. Toss to mix.

Put the coconut milk (or 3 tablespoons of the oil used to fry the shallots) in a small bowl and stir until smooth. Add the lemon juice, salt, sugar, and cayenne. Mix well and pour over the salad. Toss and add most of the crisply fried shallots and garlic, as well as most of the peanuts. Toss. Garnish with the reserved fried shallots and garlic as well as the reserved peanuts. Serve immediately.

SERVES 6

Malaysian Mixed Fruit and Vegetable Salad with Sweet Soy and Peanut Dressing

MALAYSIA

Rojak

On the beaches of Malaysia, Singapore, and Indonesia, one of the most popular snacks sold from canopied carts is rojak. *Nothing quite like it exists in the West. It is a sweet-and-sour salad made up of fruit and vegetables that can include anything from pineapples to bean sprouts. What binds the ingredients together is the dressing, which can vary. It could be a combination of palm sugar, vinegar, and chiles, or lime juice, sugar, and chiles, or even sweet soy sauce (ketjap manis), lime juice, and hot pepper. The top of the salad is invariably strewn with roasted peanuts or roasted sesame seeds or, in one version I had, both. So it is nutty, sweet, sour, salty, and hot—glorious! My husband thinks it is God's gift to man.*

You can change the salad ingredients a bit if you like (but not the dressing). If you cannot find jicama—the Mexican vegetable now used as far away as India and China—use fresh water chestnuts or a very hard pear. Instead of a green mango, try a crisp, sour apple. Soak the apple and pear in salted water until you are ready to eat or they will brown. Drain and pat dry just before serving. Instead of a green mango, you could also use a half-ripe, hard mango, which will have pale yellow flesh.

1 scant cup (4 ounces) peeled unripe green mango flesh (page 694), cut into ¾-inch dice

1 cup (5 ounces) peeled jicama, cut into ¾-inch dice

1-inch-thick slice of peeled pineapple, cut into ¾-inch segments

1 small cucumber (5 ounces), peeled and cut into ¾-inch dice

1¼ cups (3 ounces) crisp bean sprouts, washed and patted dry

6 tablespoons ketjap manis (page 735)

1½ tablespoons fresh lime juice

⅛ to ¼ teaspoon cayenne

½ cup roasted peanuts, lightly crushed

1½ tablespoons roasted sesame seeds (page 734)

Combine the mango, jicama, pineapple, and cucumber on a large plate or in a shallow bowl. Scatter the bean sprouts over the top. Cover and refrigerate until needed. Combine the ketjap manis, lime juice, and cayenne. Mix and set aside.

Just before serving, pour the dressing evenly over the fruit and vegetables. Scatter first the peanuts and then the sesame seeds evenly over the top.

SERVES 4

Shamsi Davis'

Fresh Herbs with Bread IRAN

Sabzi Khordan Ba Naan

Iranis love fresh herbs as perhaps no one else in the world (barring the Vietnamese!). They show their passion by eating them both raw and cooked—and in abundance. This dish celebrates herbs in their raw state. Chives, tarragon, and basil are rolled into squares of fine, warm flatbreads (such as lavash) along with cheese, fresh walnuts, and dates and then eaten with bites of crunchy radishes. It is a glorious, very Persian, and very timeless mélange of tastes, textures, and aromas. I always feel that I am stepping into a medieval Persian miniature painting with my very first bite!

I have not said how many this serves as I can hardly call this a recipe at all. It is just a collection of ingredients that, in Irani restaurants, are placed on the table as soon as you come in and served as starters and are eaten in homes just after the main dish, almost like the European cheese course before dessert.

A basket of warmed flatbreads, such as lavash, pita, and naan (the thinner the better)

Feta cheese (I find that imported Greek feta cheese is best—refrigerating it in a bowl of water that is changed frequently helps remove some of the salt)

Pitted dates

Freshly shelled walnuts

A bunch of fresh chives

A bunch of fresh basil

A bunch of fresh tarragon

A bunch of radishes

To eat, break off a 2-inch square of bread. Roll some cheese, dates, walnuts, and herbs in the bread and eat, taking bites of radish on the side.

Kohlrabi, Carrot, and Daikon Salad KOREAN-STYLE

I have eaten this salad hundreds of times in Korea and in Korean restaurants in New York. It is generally made with either daikon alone or a combination of daikon and carrot. I have, of my own volition, added kohlrabi, which is used freely in China, Vietnam, and Thailand.

Serve this perky salad with any rice and bean combination. I love to eat it with Refried Beans (page 12), plain rice, and some Instant Korean Cabbage Pickle (page 685).

(recipe continues)

1 large kohlrabi (9 to 10 ounces without leaves), the bottom ⅛ of the head discarded, peeled and cut into julienne strips about 2 × ¹⁄₁₆ × ¹⁄₁₆ inch

1 medium carrot, peeled and cut into julienne strips the same size as the kohlrabi

5-inch chunk of daikon (about 2 inches in diameter), peeled and cut into julienne strips the same size as the kohlrabi

1 teaspoon salt

2 teaspoons soy sauce

1½ to 2 teaspoons distilled white vinegar

½ teaspoon Korean crushed red pepper or ¼ to ½ teaspoon cayenne

1 tablespoon roasted sesame seeds (page 734)

2 teaspoons oriental sesame oil

Put the kohlrabi, carrot, and daikon in a bowl. Add the salt and mix well. Set aside for 30 minutes. Drain and put the vegetables in a clean bowl. Add the soy sauce, vinegar, Korean red pepper, sesame seeds, and sesame oil. Toss and taste, adjusting the seasonings as needed.

SERVES 4

Kohlrabi Salad   VIETNAM/THAILAND

I have eaten salads similar to this one in both Vietnam and Thailand. Ideally, the peanuts, cilantro, and crisply fried shallots should all be mixed into the salad at the last moment, but even if they are not, the salad still tastes quite wonderful; I have eaten leftovers straight from the refrigerator the following day, and it was still superb. The peanuts make this a very nutritious dish. Serve with a selection of salads on a hot summer day or as part of a meal.

2 large kohlrabi (1¼ pounds without leaves)

1¼ teaspoons salt

Peanut or canola oil for shallow frying

3 medium shallots, peeled and cut into fine slivers

5 to 6 teaspoons fresh lemon juice, according to taste

1½ teaspoons sugar

¼ teaspoon cayenne

2½ tablespoons coarsely chopped roasted peanuts

2 tablespoons very finely chopped fresh cilantro

Cut about ⅛ inch off the bottom of each kohlrabi. (This end is fairly coarse.) Peel the rest and cut into ⅛-inch-thick slices. Stack the slices together and cut into fine julienne strips. For greater convenience, you could also shred the kohlrabi, as if for coleslaw. Put into a bowl. Add 1 teaspoon salt and toss. Set aside for 15 minutes. The kohlrabi will give off liquid.

Meanwhile, pour the oil to a depth of ¼ inch into a small frying pan and set over medium-high heat. When hot, put in the shallots. Stir and fry until the shallots just begin to brown, then turn down the heat. Continue to fry until the shallots are reddish-brown and crisp. Remove with a slotted spoon and spread out on paper towels to drain and crisp up.

Once the kohlrabi has wilted, squeeze out as much water as you can and pat it dry. Put in a fresh bowl. Add the remaining ¼ teaspoon salt, the lemon juice, sugar, and cayenne. Toss to mix. Add the peanuts, cilantro, and shallots and toss again.

SERVES 4

From Meskerem
Ethiopian Lentil Salad with Crushed Mustard Seeds

ETHIOPIA

Azefa

In the West, we are used to buying prepared mustard in a bottle. Many of the older civilizations, Ethiopia included, know better. Mustard is very malleable. If you grind it, it is slightly bitter and quite hot. However, if you grind it and then add hot water to it, it turns delightfully, pleasingly, nose-tinglingly pungent. It is this form that the Ethiopians use to dress their lentils. The flavors are haunting.

1 cup (6½ ounces) green lentils

1 teaspoon salt

¼ teaspoon cayenne

2 teaspoons brown mustard seeds

6 to 7 whole black peppercorns

3 tablespoons fresh lemon juice

3 tablespoons olive oil

½ large green pepper (3 ounces), cored, seeded, and cut into ¼-inch dice

Pick over the lentils and wash them in several changes of water. Drain.

Put the lentils and 2½ cups of water in a medium pan and bring to a boil over medium-high heat. Turn the heat down to low, cover the pan, and cook gently for 30 to 35 minutes, or until the lentils are tender. Allow to cool.

(recipe continues)

Put the salt, cayenne, mustard seeds, and peppercorns into a clean coffee grinder or other spice grinder and grind finely. Put into a bowl. Add 2 tablespoons of boiling water and mix. Now add the lemon juice and olive oil. Beat well to mix. Add this mixture as well as the green pepper to the lentils and mix. Taste for the balance of seasonings.

SERVES 4 TO 6

Greek-Style Lentil Salad

Served with crusty bread and some cheese, this could be a whole meal. Cut the tomatoes, pepper, tomato, and cucumber into ¼-inch dice.

1 cup (6½ ounces) green lentils

2 tablespoons finely chopped onion

¼ cup peeled, seeded, and diced tomatoes (page 300)

¼ cup cored, seeded, and diced green pepper

¼ cup peeled and diced cucumber

¼ cup finely chopped parsley

2 teaspoons finely chopped fresh oregano or ½ teaspoon dried

3 tablespoons olive oil

3 tablespoons fresh lemon juice

1¼ teaspoons salt

Freshly ground black pepper to taste

Pick over the lentils and wash them in several changes of water. Drain.

Put the lentils and 2½ cups of water in a medium pan and bring to a boil over medium-high heat. Turn the heat down to low and cover the pan. Cook gently for 30 to 35 minutes, or until the lentils are tender. Allow to cool.

Put the lentils in a bowl. Add all the remaining ingredients and toss to mix. Taste for the balance of seasonings. Cover and refrigerate until needed.

SERVES 4 TO 6

Green Lettuce with a Korean Dressing

KOREAN-AMERICAN

This is a very pleasing salad served by a favorite New York Korean restaurant.

1 head romaine lettuce or any other crisp
    lettuce (about 10 ounces), washed and
    dried

15 to 20 delicate fresh cilantro sprigs, washed
    and patted dry

2 tablespoons soy sauce

1 garlic clove, peeled and crushed to a pulp

1 tablespoon oriental sesame oil

4 teaspoons distilled white vinegar

½ teaspoon sugar

¼ teaspoon cayenne

1 teaspoon roasted sesame seeds (page 734)

Break the lettuce leaves into a large salad bowl. Add the cilantro.

Combine the soy sauce, garlic, sesame oil, vinegar, sugar, cayenne, and sesame seeds in a small bowl. Mix well.

Just before eating, pour the dressing over the salad and toss to mix well.

SERVES 4 TO 6

Green Salad with a Bean Curd "Mayonnaise"

Here I take big chunks of crisp lettuce—generally halves of lettuce hearts—and put a generous dollop of a thick bean curd "mayonnaise" on top. Tackle this with a knife and fork.

The "mayonnaise" has no egg in it, just bean curd, oil, and vinegar; it is thick, creamy, and delicious. You could also use it as a dip for cut vegetables and chips.

3 to 4 hearts of crisp lettuce, such as romaine,
    iceberg, Bibb, or Boston, halved

2 tablespoons red wine vinegar

½ teaspoon salt

¼ cup peanut, canola, or olive oil

1 tablespoon oriental sesame oil

¾ cup (4 ounces) crumbled firm bean curd

Set the lettuce halves or quarters out on individual plates.

Put the vinegar, salt, 1 tablespoon of water, the oil, sesame oil, and crumbled bean curd into a blender in that order. Blend, pushing down when needed, until you have a smooth, creamy, mayonnaise-like blend. Top each lettuce half with a generous dollop of the bean curd "mayonnaise."

SERVES 3 TO 4

Onion Salad

Pyaz

This is a delightful salad of thinly sliced raw onions flavored with sumac, which is sour and acts like lemon juice, and parsley. The chile powder needed here is made from just chiles and is not the Tex-Mex mixture.

1 medium red onion (4 ounces), peeled, halved, and thinly sliced

½ teaspoon salt

2 teaspoons ground sumac (page 736)

¼ teaspoon coarsely ground chile powder (such as some of the Korean chile powders) or cayenne

5 tablespoons very finely chopped parsley (wash and dry the parsley sprigs before chopping)

Combine all the ingredients and mix well. Set aside for at least 30 minutes to mellow before serving.

SERVES 4

Green Pepper and Cucumber Salad

This is a lovely, cooling salad.

1 medium green bell pepper (5 ounces), seeded and cut into ¼-inch dice

2 Kirby cucumbers or 1 medium cucumber (5 ounces in all)

1 very ripe medium tomato (7 ounces), peeled and cut into ¼-inch dice

4 teaspoons fresh lemon juice

2 tablespoons olive oil

¾ teaspoon salt

Freshly ground black pepper to taste

Combine all the ingredients in a bowl and toss well. Serve chilled or at room temperature.

SERVES 4

North African Green and Red Pepper Salad

TUNISIA AND MOROCCO

This salad uses what the entire Mediterranean region has in such abundance, red and green bell peppers. I love to serve this as a first course, though you could, of course, serve it at a summer lunch with other salads.

2 large green bell peppers, quartered and
    seeded

1 large red bell pepper, quartered and seeded

2 tablespoons olive oil

2 tablespoons finely chopped onion

1 small garlic clove, peeled and finely
    chopped

1⅓ cups very ripe tomatoes, peeled, seeded,
    and cut into ¼-inch dice

½ teaspoon salt

1 teaspoon ground cumin

¼ teaspoon cayenne

Dressing for the red pepper

1 tablespoon extra-virgin olive oil

½ teaspoon balsamic vinegar

Small pinch of salt

Freshly ground black pepper to taste

Roast and peel the green and red bell peppers (page 262). Cut the green bell peppers into ¼-inch dice. Leave the red bell pepper quarters as they are.

Put 2 tablespoons olive oil in a nonstick frying pan and set over medium-high heat. Add the onion, stir for 1 minute, then add the garlic and stir for 30 seconds. Put in the green pepper, turn the heat down to medium, and cook for 5 minutes, stirring frequently. Add the tomatoes, salt, cumin, and cayenne and mix well. Cook for 6 minutes, or until the mixture loses some of its moisture. Set aside.

Make the dressing for the red pepper by combining the olive oil, balsamic vinegar, salt, and pepper in a small bowl. Stir well to mix.

When you are ready to serve, arrange the red pepper quarters on 4 individual salad plates or a single larger dish. Mix the dressing again and drizzle it evenly over the red pepper pieces. Spoon the green pepper mixture on top of the red pepper in such a way that it appears to spill over. Serve at room temperature or chilled.

SERVES 4

Moroccan Green Pepper Salad

MOROCCO

Felfla Mechouia

This delicious salad has little bits of the peel from preserved Moroccan lemons. You can follow the recipe for making these lemons on page 689 or use the peel from Simple Lemon Pickle (page 690), which works equally well.

2 large green bell peppers (10 ounces)

½ preserved lemon (see recipe introduction)

2 tablespoons extra-virgin olive oil

2 tablespoons fresh lemon juice

6 tablespoons finely chopped parsley

1 teaspoon salt

Preheat the broiler.

Quarter the green peppers and remove the seeds and stem area. Lay the peppers on a broiler pan in a single layer, seeded side down. Broil according to directions on page 262, until the outside has browned. You may need to move the peppers around to brown evenly. Immediately put the peppers into a paper bag and close tightly. Set aside for about 10 minutes. Peel the peppers by scraping back the skin with dry paper towels. Cut them into ¼-inch dice and place in a bowl.

Discard the flesh of the preserved lemon and wash the peel. Pat it dry and cut it into very small dice.

Combine the green peppers, preserved lemon, olive oil, lemon juice, parsley, and salt. Serve at room temperature or chilled.

SERVES 2

Seasoned Radishes

All those who know me know of my passion for radishes. This is what I often serve with drinks at my dinner parties. They are easy to put together and do not fill everyone up.

12 good-sized radishes, trimmed (about 7 ounces)

4 teaspoons Chinese light soy sauce or any soy sauce

½ teaspoon red wine vinegar

Cut the radishes in half lengthwise and put in a smallish bowl. Add the soy sauce and vinegar. Toss to mix. Set aside for 20 to 30 minutes, tossing now and then. Drain and serve.

SERVES 3 TO 4

Shiu-Min Block's

Radish Salad CHINA

Hong Lowa Baw Liang Tsai

I love radishes in all forms but this is one of my favorites. Here the radishes are left whole. They are just lightly crushed to absorb the sauce. I often serve this with drinks as well, but it would go with any meal.

12 good-sized radishes, trimmed (about 7 ounces)

2 tablespoons plus 1 teaspoon Chinese light soy sauce

1 tablespoon distilled white vinegar

1 teaspoon sugar

½ garlic clove, lightly mashed and peeled but left whole

¾ teaspoon oriental sesame oil

Hit each radish with a potato masher or heavy cleaver or other such object to crush it lightly. A few pieces may fly off but the radishes must stay whole.

Put the soy sauce, vinegar, sugar, garlic, and sesame oil in a bowl and mix well. Add the radishes and mix again. This salad may be served immediately or kept refrigerated in a closed jar for up to 2 weeks.

SERVES 4

From the El Fassi in Fes

Radish Salad with Orange Juice MOROCCO

This is a delightful, citrus-flavored salad that, in Morocco, is served as part of a first course comprising many salads.

1 (10-ounce) piece of daikon, peeled and grated (about 2½ cups)

¼ cup orange juice

1 tablespoon fresh lemon or lime juice

¾ to 1 teaspoon salt

⅛ to ¼ teaspoon cayenne

In a bowl, mix all the ingredients together. Serve at room temperature or chilled.

SERVES 4

Felix Oksengorn's

Ukrainian Radish Salad UKRAINE

Salat Iz Redisky

When I last visited what was then the Soviet Union, olive oil was hardly ever used in salads, though many of those who have migrated to the West have since begun using it instead of the more common sunflower oil.

½ pound radishes, thinly sliced into rounds (about 2 cups)

1 scallion, cut crosswise into very fine rounds (use both the green and white portions)

3 tablespoons finely chopped fresh dill

1 tablespoon olive oil

½ teaspoon salt

¼ teaspoon cayenne

1 cup sour cream

¼ teaspoon bright red paprika

In a bowl, combine the radishes, scallion, dill, olive oil, salt, and cayenne. Mix well. Now add the sour cream and paprika. Mix again. Serve chilled.

SERVES 4

Moroccan Tomato Salad MOROCCO

This salad is best made with red-ripe cherry tomatoes. I used rather large ones, weighing almost 1 ounce each, and cut them into quarters. If yours are small, just halve them. If cherry tomatoes are unavailable, use ordinary tomatoes, cut into smallish dice. The addition of Moroccan Chile-Garlic Paste (Harissa) *will make the salad hot and garlicky; the use of cayenne will just make it hot. Both may be left out or used in smaller quantities.*

Serve with almost any Middle Eastern, North African, Southeast Asian, or Indian meal.

2 tablespoons fresh lemon juice

½ to 1 teaspoon Moroccan Chile-Garlic Paste (page 672) or ⅛ to ¼ teaspoon cayenne

8 to 16 cherry tomatoes (about 8 ounces), cut into halves or quarters, depending upon size

2 tablespoons finely chopped onion

1 tablespoon finely chopped fresh cilantro

½ teaspoon ground roasted cumin seeds (page 724)

½ teaspoon salt

In a small bowl, stir together the lemon juice and Moroccan Chile-Garlic Paste. Set aside.

In a separate bowl, combine the remaining ingredients. Add the lemon juice mixture and mix well. Serve immediately or let sit at room temperature for 30 minutes to marry the flavors. This salad may be kept in the refrigerator, covered, for 24 hours. Serve at room temperature or chilled.

SERVES 4

Sara Abufares'
Simple Syrian Tomato Salad   SYRIA
Salata

This is particularly good served with all manner of bean, lentil, and chickpea dishes. Use only dried mint for this recipe, not fresh. A dash of cayenne may be added, if you like.

2 small onions (4 ounces), peeled, halved, and thinly sliced

2 medium tomatoes (about 11 ounces in all), chopped

About ½ cup chopped parsley

¼ cup fresh lemon juice

1½ tablespoons olive oil

1½ to 2 teaspoons salt

1 teaspoon well-crumbled dried mint

Combine all the ingredients in a bowl and mix well. Serve at room temperature or chilled.

SERVES 4

From Victor Matiya's Jerusalem Restaurant in Toronto

Simple Palestinian Salad

PALESTINE

One of the simplest of Middle Eastern salads.

1 medium cucumber, peeled and cut into
    ¼-inch dice

1 medium tomato, cut into ¼-inch dice

½ cup finely chopped fresh parsley

1 teaspoon salt

Freshly ground black pepper

3 tablespoons olive oil

1 to 1½ tablespoons fresh lemon juice

Combine all the ingredients in a bowl and mix well. Taste and adjust the seasonings, if required.

SERVES 4

Shiu-Min Block's

Green Turnip Salad

CHINA

Lieu Lowa Baw Liang Tsai

Long green turnips are available only in oriental markets. They look a little like large daikon, only they are shorter and plumper and fairly green, especially near the top. If you cannot find them, use daikon. Depending upon the size of the turnip, you may need to use only a portion of it.

10 ounces green turnip, about 2 cups when
    julienned

2 teaspoons salt

2 teaspoons sugar

2 teaspoons distilled white vinegar

2 teaspoons oriental sesame oil

Peel the turnip and then cut it, on the diagonal, into very thin slices. Stacking several slices together, cut them into very fine julienne strips. Put the strips in a bowl. Sprinkle with the salt and toss well. Set aside for 2 to 3 hours.

Rinse the turnip strips and squeeze out as much liquid as possible. Add the sugar, vinegar, and sesame oil and toss again. This salad may now be served or kept in a closed container in the refrigerator for several days.

SERVES 3 TO 4

Melle Derko Samira's

Turnip Salad

MOROCCO

Lift

This is made with long turnips. It can also be made with young white turnips and with daikon. Serve with all Middle Eastern and North African meals, at room temperature or chilled.

Salt

1½ cups (7 ounces) turnips, peeled and diced into ¼ × ¾-inch pieces

1 tablespoon finely chopped fresh parsley

1 small garlic clove, peeled and finely chopped

¼ teaspoon freshly ground black pepper

¼ teaspoon paprika

¼ teaspoon ground cumin

2 tablespoons olive oil

2 tablespoons fresh lemon juice, or to taste

Put ½ cup of water into a small pan and set on medium heat. Add ¼ teaspoon salt and the turnips. Stir once or twice. Poach the turnips for 4 to 6 minutes, or until just tender. Drain and empty the turnip pieces into a bowl.

Add the parsley, garlic, black pepper, paprika, cumin, olive oil, and lemon juice. Mix well and taste, adding a little more salt as needed.

SERVES 2

Spelt Berry Salad with Red Pepper Paste

Serve this delicious salad with yogurt cheese—or even cottage cheese—and perhaps some sliced tomatoes.

½ cup (3 ounces) spelt berries

¾ teaspoon salt

1½ tablespoons Red Pepper Paste (use my recipe, page 673, or the store-bought kind)

5 tablespoons celery (about 1 stalk), cut into ⅛-inch dice

4 tablespoons peeled carrot, cut into ⅛-inch dice

4 arugula leaves, finely chopped

4 tablespoons finely chopped fresh parsley

2 tablespoons extra-virgin olive oil

1 tablespoon fresh lemon juice

Cook the spelt berries according to the directions on page 417 for soaking and cooking whole wheat berries; drain. Combine with the remaining ingredients in a bowl and toss to mix.

SERVES 2 TO 4

Salad of Whole Wheat Berries

Nothing makes a better lunch than a combination of salads on the same plate, such as this salad, a bean salad, and a crisp salad of a variety of greens.

Turn to the recipe Tomatoes Stuffed with Wheat Berries (page 420). Now make *just the stuffing*, but add to it another 2 tablespoons of chopped parsley and 2 table-spoons of lemon juice. Mix well and serve warm, at room temperature, or chilled.

SERVES 3 TO 4

Zucchini and Feta Cheese Salad
Kolokithi Me Feta Salata

I discovered this pleasing, cooling salad in a Greek market in Athens. I like to use young zucchini, each weighing no more than 4 ounces; you should need 6 to 7 of them.
The saltiness of feta cheese can vary, so taste carefully before adding salt.

1½ pounds young zucchini

Salt

2 scallions, cut into fine rounds (use the white and some of the green portions)

¼ pound feta cheese, crumbled coarsely

2 tablespoons chopped fresh dill

¼ cup extra-virgin olive oil

¼ cup fresh lemon juice

Trim away the zucchini ends and then quarter them lengthwise. Cut each long piece roughly into 1¼-inch segments.

Put 4 cups of water into a pan and bring to a boil. Add 1 teaspoon salt and stir to mix. Put in the zucchini and boil rapidly, uncovered, for about 2 minutes, or until the pieces are just tender. Drain and rinse under cold water to cool off completely. Pat dry and put in a bowl. Check for salt. If the zucchini need more salt, add it now and mix. Add all the remaining ingredients. Toss to mix and check the salt one last time. Cover and refrigerate until needed.

SERVES 4

From the Ciragan Hotel in Istanbul

Turkish Vegetable Salad with Red Pepper Dressing

TURKEY

Acili Ezme

A meze or appetizer from southeastern Turkey, this is a mixture of very finely diced tomatoes, cucumbers, peppers, and onion, seasoned not just with olive oil and lemon juice but with chile flakes, Red Pepper Paste, and ground sumac as well. The dicing is so fine that the vegetables appear almost pastelike. Sometimes the Red Pepper Paste is replaced with tomato paste and sometimes pomegranate juice is used instead of the sumac. The salad is well drained and then piled in the center of a plate in the shape of a hill. Decorative markings are put on the pile, as if it were molded butter. It is eaten with pitalike flatbreads.

You will need about 2 medium cucumbers for this salad and about a quarter each of large red and green peppers. Dry the parsley well before chopping it.

¾ cup very, very finely diced peeled, halved, and seeded cucumber

Salt

2 medium tomatoes, peeled, seeded, and very finely diced (page 300)

¼ large red bell pepper (no seeds), very, very finely diced

¼ large green bell pepper (no seeds), very, very finely diced

3 smallish scallions, first cut into very fine rings (both white and green sections) and then finely chopped

6 tablespoons very, very finely chopped parsley

1 garlic clove, peeled and very, very finely chopped

1 tablespoon Red Pepper Paste (page 673)

1½ teaspoons ground sumac, page 736 (use the same quantity of extra lemon juice as a substitute)

1½ tablespoons fresh lemon juice

1 tablespoon extra-virgin olive oil

½ to 1 teaspoon hot red pepper flakes

Put the diced cucumber and ¼ teaspoon salt in a bowl and set aside for 30 minutes. Drain well, squeezing out as much water as possible.

Put the diced tomatoes and ¼ teaspoon salt in a bowl and set aside for 30 minutes. Drain as thoroughly as possible.

Combine the cucumber, tomato, peppers, scallions, parsley, and garlic. Toss to mix.

Combine the Red Pepper Paste, sumac, lemon juice, olive oil, red pepper flakes, and ¼ teaspoon salt. Mix well and set aside to use as the dressing. Just before

(recipe continues)

serving, drain the vegetables again and add the dressing. Mix well. Taste for the balance of flavors, adding more seasoning as desired. Mound the salad in the center of a serving dish and serve with flatbreads, such as pita bread.

SERVES 4 TO 6

Shiu-Min Block's

Chinese Mixed Vegetable Salad

CHINESE-AMERICAN

Hwang Gwa Su Liang Tsai

This is my friend Shiu-Min's signature salad. I have been eating it for more than twenty-five years and I still love it. She cuts each vegetable into the most even julienne strips as only she can. (You can either julienne by hand or else use the wonderful Japanese mandoline, the Benriner, that is sold by Japanese cookware shops—or any other gadget that juliennes.) The prepared vegetables can be refrigerated until serving time. Pour the dressing over at the last minute and then toss. You may serve this with almost any meal.

If you cannot get jicamas, you may increase the kohlrabi or cucumber.

2½ cups (7 to 8 ounces) fresh bean sprouts

About ½ large kohlrabi (you need about 7 to 8 ounces)

½ good-sized jicama (you need about 7 to 8 ounces)

2 large cucumbers (about 1½ pounds)

1 carrot (5 ounces)

6 to 7 tablespoons Chinese Soy Sauce Salad Dressing (page 677)

Bring a large pot of water to a rolling boil. Throw in the bean sprouts. Stir once and empty into a colander. Drain well. Put the sprouts at the bottom of a serving bowl.

Peel the kohlrabi and cut it first crosswise into ⅛-inch slices and then cut the slices lengthwise into ⅛-inch-thick julienne strips. Arrange these strips over the sprouts.

Peel the jicama and first cut it crosswise into ⅛-inch slices and then cut the slices lengthwise into ⅛-inch-thick julienne strips. Layer these strips over the kohlrabi.

Peel the cucumbers and cut them into 3-inch chunks. The best way to julienne the dense flesh (not the seeds) is to start cutting one side of a cucumber chunk from the outside into ⅛-inch slices. Stop when you reach the seeds. Do the same on the opposite side and then cut off the remaining hard flesh the same way. Cut both the cucumbers in this manner and discard the seeds. Now cut the cucumber slices into ⅛-inch-thick julienne strips. Layer these strips over the jicama in the bowl.

Peel the carrot and cut it diagonally into 3-inch ovals that are ⅛ inch thick. Cut these oval slices into ⅛-inch julienne strips. Put the carrots on top of the cucumbers. If not eating immediately, cover with plastic wrap and refrigerate until needed.

Just before eating, pour on the salad dressing, toss, taste, and serve.

SERVES 6 TO 8

Drinks

Almond Milk   MOROCCO

Lait d' Amande

This refreshing drink may be served with a meal (I was served it for breakfast) or at a midday break.

1½ cups whole milk

2 teaspoons honey

3 tablespoons (1½ ounces) slivered blanched almonds

Combine all the ingredients in a blender and blend to a puree. Refrigerate, covered, for 1 to 2 hours. Strain through a fine cloth, pressing out as much liquid as possible. Pour into 2 wineglasses. Serve cold.

SERVES 2

Cooling Cucumber and Mint "Drink"   IRAN

This very refreshing, lightly sweetened dish, eaten at all times of the day, is hardly a drink though it is full of liquid. In Iran it is served in bowls and eaten with a spoon on blisteringly hot summer days; it is remarkably cooling.

It is best to have tender mint leaves for this, but if your leaves are large and coarse, just chop them up very finely. The best cucumber to use here is the crisp, pickling Kirby. If you cannot get these, use any other crisp cucumber with small, undeveloped seeds.

2 good-sized Kirby cucumbers (10 ounces), peeled and very finely chopped

50 young mint leaves, very finely chopped

½ cup Simple Sugar Syrup (page 735)

10 to 12 ice cubes

(recipe continues)

Combine the cucumbers, mint, and sugar syrup in a medium bowl and mix well. Pour into 2 individual bowls, such as ice-cream dishes. Divide the ice cubes between the bowls. Stir each to mix. Serve immediately and eat with spoons.

SERVES 2

An Ancient Indian Drink with Ginger and Cardamom
Panaka

INDIA

Here is an Indian drink that seems to have been popular about three thousand years ago. It does not exist today.

That is probably a dangerous statement to make. There may well be some pocket of India, some community, some temple, that still prepares it according to a time-honored recipe. Perhaps I should say that I have not seen it served, nor have I ever seen a full recipe for it, just a mention in ancient texts.

The base of the drink is jaggery (page 724), a raw, lump sugar that is very similar to palm sugar, except that it is made with sugar cane juice. It was a common ingredient in India in ancient times and is still much loved today, though its use is confined to sweetmeats and desserts, holy offerings, and a few sweet-and-sour dishes. On the whole, it has been replaced by refined sugar for daily use. As it is not always easy to find in the West, I have used dark brown sugar instead.

2-inch piece of fresh ginger, peeled and coarsely chopped

6 tablespoons dark brown sugar

10 cardamom pods, lightly crushed

Combine the ginger, sugar, cardamom pods, and 4 cups of water in a pan and bring to a boil. Turn the heat down to medium-low and simmer, uncovered, for 15 to 20 minutes, or until you have 3 cups. Strain. Serve hot, in small quantities.

SERVES 6

Variation
A Cold Ginger-Cardamom Drink with Lemon and Mint

Make the drink exactly as above, but using 2 cups of water. Simmer on medium-low heat about 15 minutes, or until you have 1½ cups left. Strain and cool. Add 6 tablespoons of fresh lemon juice, mix, and refrigerate. Serve in small quantities with lots of ice and mint sprigs.

Ginger Fruit Punch

INDIA

Phal Ras

You can make this simple but spectacular drink for a large party by doubling or tripling the ingredients.

8-inch piece of fresh ginger (about 3 ounces), peeled and coarsely chopped

1 cup sugar

1 cup fresh lemon juice

1½ cups fresh orange juice

3 cups sparkling water, club soda, or plain cold water

Ice cubes

Combine the ginger, sugar, and 1 cup of water in a heavy pan and bring to a boil. Turn the heat down to low and simmer very gently, uncovered, for 15 minutes, or until you have a syrup. Strain the syrup into a pitcher or large measuring cup and allow it to cool. (The ginger can be discarded.) Add the lemon juice and orange juice and refrigerate until needed. Just before serving, add the sparkling water or plain water (which is just as good) and lots of ice cubes.

SERVES 4 TO 6

Shamsi Davis'

Sour Cherry Syrup

IRAN

Sherbet-i-Albalu

We live in sour cherry country in upstate New York, but for some reason these cherries, whether grown here, in Michigan, or on the West Coast, are seldom frozen for sale in supermarkets. They are bottled and canned and even dried with added sweeteners but if you want them in their pure state, the season is very short; I have only about 3 weeks in which to make the pies and syrup that my family loves so much.

For this recipe, I used what our local farmer called "3 quarts" of cherries. After weighing, these rather flexible "quarts" came to about 6½ pounds. The fresh cherries need to be pitted (you can use 2 thumbs or a cherry pitter) and then pureed in a blender. The puree is put through a strainer to get rid of all the pulp, leaving just pure sour cherry juice. I started with 4 cups of pure sour cherry juice. If you have more or less, make adjustments to the recipe. You may also need to adjust the amounts of lime juice and sugar depending upon the sourness of the cherries.

I like to pour about ½ inch of syrup into a tall glass, add lots of ice cubes, and then pour in enough club soda to fill the glass. You might prefer water instead. Iranis like to put a sprig of fresh mint and a real sour cherry in the glass as well. *(recipe continues)*

6½ pounds fresh sour cherries

Scant 11 cups sugar

¾ cup fresh lime juice

Wash the cherries, then stem and pit them. Working in batches, put them into a blender and puree. Strain this puree through a mesh strainer, pushing out as much juice as possible; you should have about 4 cups.

Combine the sugar, lime juice, and 5½ cups of water in a large, heavy stainless steel pan and bring to a boil. Turn the heat down to medium and simmer vigorously for 10 minutes, removing all the scummy froth that will rise to the top with a slotted spoon. Now turn the heat to medium-low and cook at a steady, low simmer for an hour, or until the syrup is thick but still flowing (somewhat thinner than a light maple syrup). Strain into clean, sterilized glass jars and allow to cool. Cover with noncorrosive lids.

MAKES ABOUT 3 QUARTS

Shamsi Davis'

Persian Rhubarb Syrup

IRAN

Sherbet-i-Rivas

This sherbet or syrup is made in the spring and is meant to last through the hot summer months when the addition of a little water or seltzer and ice produces an instantaneous quenching and cooling drink.

For this recipe I bought 3½ pounds of rhubarb. After trimming, I had about 3 pounds left.

Limes vary so much in the amount of juice they release. To be on the safe side, buy 16 good, large juicy limes.

3 pounds washed and trimmed rhubarb, cut crosswise into ½-inch pieces

4¾ cups sugar

2 cups fresh lime juice

Fresh mint sprigs (optional)

Put the rhubarb in a large stainless steel pan along with ¾ cup of water. Bring to a boil. Cover, turn the heat down to low, and simmer very gently for 30 minutes. Strain, saving just the juice. Put the rhubarb juice back into a clean stainless steel pan. Add the sugar and lime juice. Stir and bring to a simmer on low heat. Simmer gently for 30 minutes or longer, until the juice turns slightly syrupy. Strain into clean, sterilized glass jars and allow to cool. Cover with noncorrosive lids.

To make a drink, pour ½ inch of syrup into a glass, and add 4 to 5 ice cubes and then enough water or seltzer to make a drink of the strength you like. Stir (you may add a fresh mint sprig to the glass) and serve.

MAKES ABOUT 5 CUPS

Shamsi Davis'
Fresh Lime Syrup
Sherbet-E-Ablimu

IRAN

Like most fruity syrups in Iran, this one is served mixed with ice and water and drunk through much of the year. Syrups, once made, help to preserve the life of the fruit and, in a country where drinking is frowned upon, every household proudly offers guests a choice of sherbets.

I used about 10 large limes here but get a few extra, as not all limes are very juicy.

6 cups sugar

1½ cups fresh lime juice

Fresh mint sprigs (optional)

Put the sugar and 2 cups of water into a large stainless steel pan and bring to a simmer over medium heat, stirring now and then. Turn the heat down to low and simmer very gently for 15 minutes. Add the lime juice, stir, and bring to a simmer again. Simmer gently for another 15 minutes, or until the liquid has turned lightly syrupy. Strain into clean, sterilized glass jars and allow to cool. Cover with noncorrosive lids.

To make a drink, pour about ½ inch of syrup into a glass, and add 4 to 5 ice cubes and then enough water or seltzer to make a drink of the strength you like. Stir (you may add a fresh mint sprig to the glass) and serve.

MAKES ABOUT 3 PINTS

Fresh Lime and Ginger Syrup
Neebu Aur Adrak Ka Sharbat

INDIA

India drinks about as many sherbets *as Iran, only the name, which is of Persian origin, is pronounced somewhat differently—*sharbat. *This is one I love and, instead of mixing it with ice and plain water, I like to mix it with ice and soda water.*

(recipe continues)

647

6 cups sugar

3-inch piece of fresh ginger, peeled and cut
　　into thin slices

1½ cups fresh lime juice

Fresh mint sprigs (optional)

Combine the sugar, 2 cups of water, and the ginger slices in a large stainless steel saucepan and bring to a simmer on medium heat, stirring now and then. Turn the heat down to low and simmer very gently for 15 minutes. Add the lime juice, stir, and bring to a simmer again. Simmer gently for another 15 minutes, or until the liquid has turned slightly syrupy. Strain into clean, sterilized glass jars and allow to cool. Cover with noncorrosive lids.

To make a drink, pour about ½ inch of syrup into a glass, and add 4 to 5 ice cubes and then enough water or seltzer to make a drink of the strength you like. Stir (you may add a fresh mint sprig to the glass) and serve.

MAKES ABOUT 6 CUPS

Irani Minty Lemonade

IRAN

Shikanjebeen

This dish can be served two ways. In a more concentrated form, it serves as a dip for crisp lettuce leaves (so enjoyable in the summer); with the addition of extra water, it turns into a minty lemonade.
Because our mint leaves are often quite coarse, unless you can get young tender ones, it is best to strain the lemonade once the leaves have been allowed to steep for a bit.

About 50 tender mint leaves, very finely
　　chopped

1 cup hot Simple Sugar Syrup (page 735)

¼ cup fresh lemon juice

16 to 20 crisp lettuce leaves, such as romaine,
　　as needed for the dip

10 to 12 ice cubes for the dip and 14 to 16 for
　　the drink

Put the mint leaves in a mixing bowl. Pour the hot syrup over them, stir, and leave to cool. Add the lemon juice and mix.

To serve as a dip, strain the mixture into a small serving bowl. Place the bowl on a large platter and surround with lettuce leaves. Add 10 to 12 ice cubes to the bowl just before serving.

For a drink, add about 1 cup of water to the flavored syrup and mix. Strain into 2 glasses. Add 7 or 8 ice cubes to each glass, stir each glass, and serve.

SERVES 4 AS A DIP, 2 AS A DRINK

Moroccan Milk and Apple Drink

Lait de Pomme

This drink, offered in parfait or wineglasses in the Moroccan hotels where I was first served it, may be sipped or eaten with a spoon. There it is served as a nutritious breakfast drink and given to children in a wineglass in the evening when other diners are drinking wine (that is what I do with my grandson!). It is very refreshing. I often have a glass for lunch.

1 cup whole, low-fat, or fat-free milk

1 to 2 teaspoons honey, according to taste

½ medium Granny Smith or other crisp apple, peeled, cored, and coarsely chopped

Combine all the ingredients in a blender. Blend to a light puree (4 to 6 ice cubes may be added to the blender, if desired). Pour into 2 wineglasses. Serve cold.

SERVES 2 OR MAKES 1½ CUPS

Milk and Yogurt Drink

Charnamrit   INDIA

Charnamrit, which means the "heavenly nectar from the feet of God," is the "holy water" that was served to us after prayers in India. Holy basil (tulsi) grows outside prayer rooms in almost every Hindu home; it is sold by Thai grocers. Ordinary basil leaves may be substituted but reduce the quantity to 5.

Have this drink for breakfast or as a snack.

1½ cups whole milk

4 teaspoons honey

3 tablespoons (1.5 ounces) slivered almonds

½ cup plain yogurt (the fresher, the better)

½ teaspoon crushed cardamom seeds

10 fresh holy basil leaves (or 5 fresh basil leaves), torn by hand

Ice cubes (optional)

Combine the milk, honey, almonds, yogurt, and cardamom in a blender and blend to a fine puree. Pour into a storage container and add the holy basil leaves. Cover and leave in the refrigerator for 1 to 2 hours. Strain, pushing out as much liquid as possible. Pour into wineglasses. Add 2 ice cubes to each glass, if desired, and serve.

SERVES 4 OR MAKES 2 CUPS

Kashmiri Tea

INDIA

Kahva

Known as Kahva, *this is consumed in Kashmiri households from morning until night. It is generally the job of the first person to awaken to get the samovar going. Lit charcoal is thrown down the central chimney of the samovar. Then water goes into the main body. When it begins to boil, green tea, either of the pellet, gunpowder variety, or a crumbled section from an old-fashioned hard cake of tea, is put into the water, together with some cardamom and almonds, if they can be afforded. Kashmiri almonds are exquisite. They grow on local trees in abundance and perfume the tea quite magically. The tea is served in tiny metal cups without handles that can only be held with the help of little towels and handkerchiefs and scarves. The tea is accompanied by wonderful Kashmiri breads.*

4 teaspoons green gunpowder tea

12 cardamom pods, lightly crushed

4 teaspoons blanched slivered almonds

4 teaspoons sugar

Combine the tea, cardamom, almonds, sugar, and 4 cups of water in a medium pot. Bring to a boil over medium-high heat. Cover, turn the heat off, and let sit for 5 minutes. Strain into 4 individual cups. Serve hot.

SERVES 4

Lemongrass Tea

INDIA

Leelee Chai

I have only seen this drunk in the West Indian state of Gujarat. In the city of Ahmedabad we were offered large, handleless bowlfuls of it. It had been made very strong and was served sweetened, with milk. You might like to make it weaker and have it without the milk and sugar.

2 stalks fresh lemongrass, the bottom 6 inches, thinly sliced

5 teaspoons Assam or Darjeeling black tea

Milk and sugar to taste

Combine the lemongrass and 4¼ cups of water in a pan and bring to a boil. Cover, lower the heat, and simmer gently for 20 minutes. Strain the water into a warmed teapot and immediately add the tea. Allow to steep for 5 minutes. Serve with milk and sugar or plain.

SERVES 4

Melle Derko Samira's

Moroccan Mint Tea   MOROCCO

No major shopping trip is complete in Morocco without offers of sweet, minty tea. Small glasses, often with swiggles of gold and red and green on them, sit on a round tray. The enticing smell makes it impossible to refuse. Similar welcomes are proffered in every single home.

I was shown how to make this tea by Melle Derko Samira, a professional chef, who prepared it right in her metal teapot. First, she poured water into the pot as it stood over a medium flame on her stove. Then, she added little pellets of green gunpowder tea, a healthy handful of mint, and some cubes of sugar. She brought the water to a boil, turned off the heat, and left the tea to steep in the covered pot for about 5 minutes. Then began the ritual of stirring and pouring. She poured a small amount of tea out into a glass, then poured this tea back into the teapot. Then she stirred the teapot. Then she decided to adjust the sugar, adding a little bit more. Only then did she pour the tea for us into little glasses. She did this from a height, perhaps because this is the way it has always been done, perhaps because this is the way to insure that the tea will cool enough on its way not to crack the delicate glass.

4 teaspoons green gunpowder tea

8 healthy stalks of fresh mint leaves

8 teaspoons sugar, or to taste

Combine the tea, mint stalks with leaves, sugar, and 4 cups of water in a medium pot. Set the heat on medium-high and bring to a boil. Cover, turn the heat off, and let sit for 5 minutes. Strain into delicate glasses or cups. Serve hot.

SERVES 4 TO 8

Neeru Row Kavi's

Spicy Indian Tea   INDIA

Masala Chai

This spicy Indian tea is drunk all over North India. Generally, a special spice mixture, water, tea leaves, sugar, and milk are all boiled together. If you do not like such strong tea, you might want to boil the water by itself, putting ¼ teaspoon of the spice mixture into it for every cup of tea and then make your tea any way you like using this water. What follows below is the traditional Indian method.

(recipe continues)

For the tea spice mixture

1 tablespoon ground ginger

2 teaspoons cardamom seeds, green and
  peeled

1 teaspoon whole cloves

1 teaspoon whole black peppercorns

3-inch cinnamon stick, broken up into 1-inch
  pieces

To make 4 cups of tea

5 teaspoons loose black tea, such as
  Darjeeling or Assam

1 teaspoon ground tea spice mixture

4 teaspoons sugar, or to taste

½ cup whole milk

Combine the ginger, cardamom, cloves, peppercorns, and cinnamon in a clean coffee grinder. Grind as finely as possible. Sift through a fine sieve and store in a jar.

Combine the tea leaves, spice mixture, 4 cups of water, and sugar in a medium pot set over medium-high heat and bring to a boil. Turn the heat down to low and simmer, uncovered, for 10 minutes. Add the milk. Turn the heat up to medium and bring to a boil. Strain into 4 individual cups. Serve hot.

SERVES 4

Tomato and Cucumber Drink

If you have a juicing machine, you can make your own tomato juice using red-ripe summer tomatoes. You could also blend the tomatoes in a blender and then push the resulting puree through a strainer. Out of season, use a good, preferably organic, canned or bottled tomato juice. Prepared juices are already salted and often have a little sugar in them as well, so add extra amounts with care.

2 (5-inch) cucumbers or 1 long English one
  (do not use waxed cucumbers)

4 cups tomato juice

½ teaspoon salt, or to taste

½ teaspoon sugar, or to taste

¼ cup fresh lemon juice

Ice cubes

Leave the skin on the cucumbers and grate them coarsely. Combine the grated cucumbers, tomato juice, salt, sugar, and lemon juice in a pitcher or jar, tasting as you go. Stir, cover, and refrigerate for at least 3 hours or longer. Strain and serve over ice cubes.

SERVES 4

Variation
Spicy Tomato and Cucumber Drink

Follow the last recipe until the addition of the lemon juice. Now add 1 teaspoon ground roasted cumin seeds (page 724) and a generous pinch of cayenne. Stir well and proceed with the recipe.

Shamsi Davis'
Vinegar Syrup
Shikanjebeen 11

IRAN

This popular syrup is the basis of a beverage that is drunk throughout the year. Even though there is a fair amount of vinegar in it, the final taste is not at all vinegary.

6 cups sugar

1½ cups white wine vinegar

6 to 7 fresh mint sprigs

Put the sugar and 2 cups of water, the vinegar, and mint into a large stainless steel pan and bring to a simmer over medium heat, stirring now and then. Turn the heat down to low and simmer very gently for 30 minutes, or until the liquid has turned slightly syrupy. Strain into clean sterilized glass jars and allow to cool. Cover with noncorrosive lids.

To make a drink, pour about ½ inch of syrup into a glass, and add 4 to 5 ice cubes and then enough water to make a drink of the strength you like. Stir (you may add a fresh mint sprig to the glass) and serve.

MAKES ABOUT 6 CUPS

Watermelon Juice

Watermelon juice is so refreshing in the summer. All you need to do is combine the watermelon and a little sugar in a blender. Sometimes when I want the juice to be like slush, I freeze the chopped pieces of watermelon (no seeds, of course) until they are as hard as ice cubes.

6 cups coarsely chopped watermelon flesh (no seeds)

2 tablespoons extra fine sugar, or to taste

Ice cubes as needed

Purée the watermelon and sugar in a blender until smooth. Serve over ice cubes.

SERVES 3 TO 4

Punjabi Yogurt Drink

Rich, *Sweet Lassi*

The ordinary Punjabi lassi *normally consists of yogurt, thinned out with water and ice and flavored with salt or sugar. In the markets of today's Punjab, it is not uncommon to get a very rich version of the original where the yogurt is thinned out with milk. Here is that rich version, though you could make it less caloric by using skim milk yogurt and skim milk.*

Serve with a meal or as a snack.

2 cups plain yogurt

1 cup rich whole milk

2 tablespoons sugar

About 20 ice cubes

Put the yogurt in a bowl. Beat lightly with a fork or whisk until smooth and creamy. Slowly add the milk, beating continuously with a fork or whisk. Then add the sugar. Mix well. Stir in the ice cubes. Keep stirring until they have partially melted. Pour the *lassi* into 2 tall glasses and serve cold. (You could also put all the ingredients in a blender, blend briefly, and then strain out the ice cubes.)

FILLS 2 TALL GLASSES

Sweet Mango *Lassi*

Aam Ki Lassi

Indians often add about ¼ teaspoon ground cardamom seeds to this mixture. You may do so if you wish or leave it plain. Because most mangoes in the West are fairly fibrous, it is best to strain the lassi.

1 cup plain yogurt

1 cup peeled chopped flesh from a ripe mango

2 tablespoons extra fine sugar

10 ice cubes

Combine all the ingredients in a blender and blend until smooth. (A few pieces of ice may remain.) Strain through a sieve, pushing out as much liquid as possible. Pour into 2 glasses and serve.

SERVES 2

Sweet Banana *Lassi*   INDIA

Kelay ki Lassi

A nourishing lassi, *this could well replace a breakfast or lunch. As with the mango* lassi, *you could add ¼ teaspoon ground cardamom seeds for added aroma.*

1 cup plain yogurt

1 ripe peeled and sliced banana

2 tablespoons extra fine sugar

10 ice cubes

Combine all the ingredients in a blender and blend until smooth. (A few pieces of ice may remain.) Pour into 2 glasses and serve.

SERVES 2

Madras-Style Spicy Yogurt Drink   INDIA

Neer Mor

This may be drunk out of a glass or it can be poured over rice and eaten almost as a soup on a hot day. As a drink, it would serve 2 people, but when eaten over rice, it could easily serve 4. In South India, they might eat some very hot pickles with the rice as well.

2 cups plain yogurt

½ teaspoon salt

2 teaspoons peeled and very finely grated fresh ginger

1 teaspoon very finely chopped fresh hot green chile

2 tablespoons very finely chopped cilantro leaves

6 to 8 fresh curry leaves, if available, lightly bruised

Generous pinch of ground asafetida

Few fresh rose petals, if unsprayed aromatic ones are available, or a drop of rose essence (optional)

About 16 ice cubes

Put the yogurt in a bowl. Beat lightly with a fork or whisk until smooth and creamy. Add the salt and all the remaining ingredients. Stir to mix until the ice cubes have partially melted (the curry leaves are best not eaten and may be removed before serving). Pour into glasses and serve cold.

SERVES 2 TO 4

Sauces and
Added Flavorings

Sauces, Fresh Chutneys, and Condiments   658

Preserved Pickles and Chutneys   685
     Pickling or Preserving Lemons   688
     Mangoes for Pickling and Preserving   693

Spice Mixtures   704

The world has a long, venerable history of pairing specific condiments with cooked foods: hot dogs with mustard, hamburgers with ketchup, asparagus with hollandaise, Indian samosas with chutney, and Chinese dumplings with soy sauce and vinegar. These have become such traditional pairings that we have even stopped examining them.

Sauces, chutneys, and pickles add pep to foods. They titillate the palate. They make it possible to vary one bite from the next when eating from the same plate and they give zest and magic to what might be considered plain, everyday foods.

In the West, I have begun to see a great change in attitudes toward these zesty condiments. As we all travel more and as immigration patterns bring more people from the East to the West and from the South to the North, the trend toward hotter and hotter foods is growing. We have only to look at our supermarket shelves. What started as a slow trickle of influence from Mexico—hottish salsa to go with corn chips—has now become a wide river that is overflowing its banks. At a recent fancy food show in New York, where new gourmet food products are introduced, I saw hot chutneys and hot sauces influenced by the cuisines of Thailand, China, the Caribbean, Mexico, and India: ten different hot peanut sauces, green and red chile sauces, habanero sauces, roasted chile sauces from Sichuan and Mexico, roasted chile and onion sauces, Moroccan chile and garlic sauce, mango chutneys by the dozen, lime pickles from Morocco and India—I could go on forever.

The Western palate has learned to relish hotter and hotter foods, and there is no turning back. Hot foods give our bodies a cheap, harmless high and those who experience it come back eagerly for more.

Of course, not all condiments are hot. Some are piquant, some are sour, some are sweet-and-sour, and some are spicy without being hot. A few are just aromatic, such as an Ethiopian butter flavored with cardamom and oregano, or just plain garlicky, such as a seasoned Spanish olive oil. You will find a mix of these—and more—here, ready to enhance a wide variety of foods.

How do you find anything in this chapter, which has everything from coconut chips to spice mixes. There are three sections. The first has an array of sauces, fresh chutneys, and condiments. The second has preserved foods, which includes preserved chutneys and pickles. The third section has spice mixes. The first two are arranged alphabetically according to major ingredient. Hence, I start with flavored butter, move on to cherry chutneys, then go on to things with coconut (coconut chips and coconut chutneys). Garlicky and gingery items come next, to be followed by oil, peanuts, pecans, pepper sauces, soy-based sauces, tamarind sauces, tomatillos, tomatoes, and walnuts. The preserved foods start with kimchi, which is made with cabbage, and end with a sweet tomato preserve. The spice mixtures are arranged according to complexity, so the simple mixtures come first and those requiring more spices follow. I hope you will be able to find everything with ease!

Sauces, Fresh Chutneys, and Condiments

Adapted from Amanuel at the Massawa

Ethiopian Aromatic Butter

ETHIOPIA

Esme

This is really a clarified butter infused with the aromas of cardamom, oregano, fenugreek, garlic, and onion. Ethiopians like to drizzle it on meats but I love it on plain rice, baked or boiled potatoes, and simple boiled or steamed vegetables like carrots, green beans, and corn. You may also use it for cooking.

You can double the quantity, if you wish; the clarified butter keeps well in the refrigerator for several weeks. Most Ethiopian restaurants have large tubs of it!

The cooking time for the butter may vary according to its water content, so keep an eye on it as it simmers.

½ pound (2 sticks) unsalted butter

5 whole cardamom pods, lightly crushed but left whole

¼ teaspoon whole fenugreek seeds

1 large shallot (about 1½ ounces), peeled and finely chopped

1 large garlic clove, peeled and finely chopped

1 fresh oregano sprig or ½ teaspoon dried

Cut the butter into smaller pieces and put them in a small, heavy pan. Set the pan on lowish heat until the butter has melted. Add all the remaining ingredients and let the butter come to a simmer again. Now turn the heat to very low and let the butter simmer gently for about 20 minutes; do not let it burn. However, little light brown bits will begin to collect on the sides of the pan and at the bottom. This is as it should be.

Strain this clarified butter through a piece of cheesecloth into a jar. Once it has cooled, it may be covered and refrigerated.

MAKES ABOUT 1 CUP

Afghani Sour Cherry Chutney   AFGHANISTAN

Turshi Alubalu

Very simple and very good, sour cherry chutney is commonly eaten in Afghanistan, and it may be served with all meals. All that you need are sour cherries (bottled, canned, or frozen ones work well), some hot red chiles (cayenne may be substituted), vinegar, and salt. The cherries add their own natural sweetness but if they are exceedingly sour, you may add a tiny bit of sugar. If the cherries are fresh, pit and chop them well before measuring them.

1 tablespoon red wine vinegar

1 very well packed cup pitted sour cherries (if
 bottled, canned, or frozen, drain first)

1 long, fresh hot red chile, coarsely chopped
 (with or without seeds, as desired)

1¼ teaspoons salt, or to taste

Put all the ingredients into a blender in the order listed and blend until very smooth. This chutney should last 4 to 5 days in the refrigerator. It may also be frozen.

MAKES ABOUT 1 CUP

Kashmiri Sour Cherry and Walnut Chutney   INDIA

Cherry Aur Akhrote Ki Chutney

Cherries, which most likely originated in East Asia, spread quickly to Kashmir, where they have been growing for several millennia. In season, when fallen cherries carpet the gardens and cherry-stained children are a common sight, they find their way into every conceivable dish. One particularly popular use is a chutney made with sour cherries and walnuts, another Kashmiri product.

This chutney may be served with most Indian and Middle Eastern meals. If you leave out the cayenne, it makes an excellent topping for fresh fruit as well. A few leaves of chopped fresh mint may be added if you like.

I have used bottled, pitted cherries here, but you may use canned or frozen ones as well. All of them will need to be drained first. If you can get fresh sour cherries, pit them and chop them coarsely before measuring them. The salt may need to be adjusted to balance the sourness of the cherries.

½ cup shelled walnut halves

½ cup pitted sour cherries

¼ teaspoon salt, or to taste

¼ teaspoon cayenne, or more, to taste

(recipe continues)

Bring a small pot of water to a rolling boil. Put in the walnuts and boil rapidly for 3 minutes. Drain. (This removes the bitterness from the walnuts.)

Put the cherries, walnuts, salt, and cayenne into a blender and blend until you have a smooth paste.

MAKES 1 CUP

Delhi-Style Cilantro and Mint Chutney   INDIA
Hari Chutney

This is my hometown chutney, a rather specific one found almost exclusively in the storefront restaurants that fill the Lane of Fried Breads (Parathe Wali Gulley) *in the Old City, not far from where my parents were born, raised, and married. Serve it with all meals as a vitamin-rich, spicy relish, or use it as a spicy pesto: smear it on bread when you make a cheese sandwich, dribble it over canned beans (after draining and washing them), and add a few dollops to your lasagna to give it a new twist.*

Generally, when we use cilantro, we use only the leaves. Here you may use the slender stems as well. The same applies to the mint.

This chutney may be kept in the refrigerator for at least 2 days, but it is best the day it is made.

2 well-packed cups fresh cilantro

¾ well-packed cup fresh mint

3 to 4 fresh hot green chiles

1 teaspoon ground cumin

Generous pinch of ground asafetida

2 tablespoons fresh lime juice

½ teaspoon salt, or to taste

Combine all the ingredients as well as ½ cup of water in a blender. Blend, stopping and pushing down with a rubber spatula whenever necessary, until you have a smooth paste.

MAKES ABOUT 1 CUP

Amaral Milbredt's

Coconut Chips   BRAZIL

These chips, when made with salt, are an excellent garnish for all manner of rice dishes and stews that require coconut milk. If made without salt, they serve as a wonderful topping for dessert pancakes and ice cream. They are crunchy, airy, light, and delicious.

Taste your coconut after you have cracked it open and use it only if the flesh is sweet. It is always better to buy an extra coconut just to ensure that you end up with a good one. Extra coconut meat may be pulverized in the blender and frozen for future use.

1 fresh coconut   Kosher salt (optional)

Preheat the oven to 400°F.

Pierce 2 of the coconut's eyes with a sharp instrument and drain all the liquid out; it is not needed. Put the whole coconut in the oven for 15 minutes. When the time is up, the shell will be loose. Crack it with a hammer and pull it off. Cut the coconut in half crosswise and taste the meat to make sure it is good. Now peel off the coconut's brown skin with a potato peeler. Using the same peeler, shave off thin "chips" along the cut edge that are 1 to 1½ inches long. Keep shaving off chips until you have about 2 cups. (The rest of the coconut may be stored as suggested above.)

Spread the coconut chips out in a baking tray in a single layer (slight overlapping does not matter), sprinkle lightly with salt, if desired, and bake for 15 minutes, or until the chips are golden brown and crisp. Store in an airtight container until needed.

MAKES 2 CUPS

Cheryl Rathkopf's

Coconut Milk Sauce   SRI LANKA

Kiri Hodi

In Sri Lanka, this all-purpose sauce is served with soft rice noodles or used as a base for curries. Four hard-boiled eggs (page 514) and 2 medium potatoes, boiled and diced, can also be cooked in it briefly and then served with rice.

To peel tomatoes, drop them in boiling water for 10 seconds.

(recipe continues)

½ teaspoon whole fenugreek seeds

3 tablespoons very finely chopped onion

3 fresh hot green chiles, cut crosswise into
¾-inch chunks

15 fresh curry leaves (use fresh holy basil or
basil leaves as a different but equally
interesting substitute)

2 (3-inch) cinnamon sticks

3 pieces *goraka* (page 724) or 1 tablespoon
tamarind pulp (page 737) (see Note)

1 cup canned coconut milk (shake the can
well before using)

¼ teaspoon turmeric

2 small tomatoes or 1 large tomato (6 ounces
in all), peeled and finely chopped

1¼ teaspoons salt

1½ tablespoons fresh lime juice (see Note)

Soak the fenugreek seeds in 2 tablespoons of warm water to cover for 2 to 3 hours.

Combine the fenugreek seeds, their soaking liquid, the onion, green chiles, curry leaves, cinnamon sticks, *goraka*, coconut milk, ½ cup of water, the turmeric, tomatoes, and salt in a medium pan. Mix well and bring to a boil. Turn the heat down to low and cook, uncovered, stirring very frequently, for 15 minutes. Add the lime juice and stir to mix. Taste for the balance of flavors.

Note: If you cannot find *goraka* or tamarind, increase the lime juice to 2 tablespoons.

SERVES 4

Cheryl Rathkopf's
Coconut Sambol
SRI LANKA
Pol Sambola

Serve this relish with any meal that could do with a little spicing! In Sri Lanka, it is made with freshly grated coconut. If you wish to do the same, you will need about 1¼ cups. In the version below I have used finely grated desiccated unsweetened coconut.

The sambol needs to be the color "of a Buddhist monk's robes." Sri Lanka produces very good chile powder (both lightly roasted and "raw") with a strong orange-red color. This colors the coconut naturally. If you are going to use cayenne with a dull red color, put in some bright red paprika as well.

This relish will last in the refrigerator for 3 to 4 days. If it starts to dry out, add some coconut milk or water to moisten it.

1 cup very finely grated desiccated
    unsweetened coconut

½ cup very finely chopped peeled shallots or
    grated onion

1¼ teaspoons salt

2 teaspoons good-quality chile powder (see
    recipe introduction)

¼ teaspoon freshly ground black pepper

1½ tablespoons fresh lime juice, or to taste

½ cup canned coconut milk, heated

Combine all the ingredients and mix well.

SERVES 8 TO 10

Coconut and Cilantro Chutney   INDIA

Nariyal Aur Haray Dhaniay Ki Chutney

You may use 1 cup unsweetened desiccated coconut soaked in ¾ cup of hot water for 30 minutes instead of fresh coconut, if you prefer. Use the soaking water as you grind.

    I prefer to use a blender here in order to get a fine paste. You will need to make the chutney in at least 2 batches.

1 cup freshly grated coconut (page 718)

1 teaspoon salt

1 teaspoon sugar

2 tablespoons fresh lemon juice

2 fresh hot green chiles, chopped

2 medium shallots, peeled and chopped

3 cups cilantro leaves, chopped

1 (1-inch) piece of fresh ginger, peeled and
    finely chopped

2 teaspoons peanut or canola oil

½ teaspoon whole brown mustard seeds

Combine the coconut, salt, sugar, lemon juice, chiles, shallots, and 4 tablespoons of water in a blender. Blend, pushing down as needed, until you have a fine paste. Add the cilantro and ginger. Grind until you have a fine paste again, adding a little more water if needed. Empty into a bowl and taste for the balance of flavors.

Put the oil in a small pan and set over medium heat. When very hot, put in the mustard seeds. As soon as the mustard seeds begin to pop, a matter of seconds, pour the oil and seeds over the coconut chutney and stir them in. Chill if not serving immediately. This chutney should last for 3 to 4 days in the refrigerator. It may also be frozen. If it becomes too thick, thin it out with a little water.

SERVES 6

Shiu-Min Block's

Crunchy Sichuan Garlic Relish   CHINA

La Jiao Chiang

This hot, garlicky, and crunchy condiment may be served with almost all meals. It will keep unrefrigerated for several months. To make a spicy dip, add it to soy sauce or a mixture of soy sauce and vinegar.

I use a very large 14-inch frying pan or a wok. Under ideal circumstances, one should have very good ventilation when making this, as chiles can give off pungent fumes. I have no window in my city kitchen so I do cough a bit whenever I make the relish, but it does serve to clear the head beautifully!

2 cups peanut or canola oil

24 whole scallions, cut into fine rounds (both white and green sections)

1 (1-inch) piece of ginger, peeled and finely chopped

Cloves from 6 whole heads of garlic, peeled and finely chopped (this may be done in a food processor, using the stop-and-start "pulse" method)

45 dried hot red chiles, 1 to 3 inches long, coarsely crumbled

2 teaspoons salt

1 tablespoon Chinese light soy sauce

3 tablespoons roasted sesame seeds (page 734)

1 teaspoon oriental sesame oil

Put the oil in a very large frying pan or wok and set over medium-high heat. When hot, put in the scallions. Stir and fry, making sure to scrape the bottom and sides, until the scallions just begin to take on some color, 8 to 10 minutes. Now put in the ginger and garlic. Continue to fry and stir for another 10 minutes or so, or until the scallions, ginger, and garlic are golden and crisp. You will need to turn the heat down gradually during this period to prevent the ingredients from getting too dark. Put in the chiles and stir for 30 seconds. Add the salt and soy sauce, stir and mix for a minute, then turn off the heat. Stir in the sesame seeds and sesame oil. Cool completely, then store the condiment—seasonings and oil—in tightly closed jars.

MAKES 3¼ CUPS

From Pinocho in Barcelona

Spanish-Style Garlic and Parsley-Flavored Olive Oil

SPAIN

For lovers of garlic and olive oil—and I am definitely one of them—this is an indispensable flavoring. You can dress slices of summer tomatoes with it, dribble it over all manner of grilled vegetables, such as slices of zucchini and slices of portobello mushrooms or grilled peppers, and even put it on bread.

In Andalusia, I was served Ensalada de Cogollo, a small heart of lettuce accompanied by a hot dish of this garlic-flavored oil for dipping. It turned out to be a superb combination. Use Bibb, Boston, or romaine lettuce hearts, using only the tender inner leaves.

1 cup olive oil

5 garlic cloves, peeled and finely chopped

1 teaspoon salt

1 tablespoon finely chopped fresh parsley

Put the oil and garlic in a small pot and set over medium-low heat. Bring to a simmer and cook for just 5 seconds, then immediately turn off the heat. Let the oil cool for 15 minutes, then stir in the salt and parsley. The oil is ready to use, or it may be transferred to a jar and refrigerated for 3 to 4 days. Bring it to room temperature before using.

MAKES 1 CUP

Fresh Ginger and Green Chile Relish   INDIA

This relish was always on our table, especially when young ginger was in the market. We all loved ginger in its myriad forms. It was thought to be extremely beneficial—it aided digestion, was good for colds, and was even supposed to help those who suffered from travel sickness!

Young ginger has taut, glistening skin that can often be scraped off. The skin is generally lighter in color than that of older ginger. If you can find it, do use it. If you cannot, use the freshest, least wrinkled ginger available.

This relish will last for a week in the refrigerator.

1 (3-inch) piece of fresh ginger

7 to 10 fresh hot green chiles

1½ teaspoons salt

½ teaspoon sugar

⅓ cup fresh lemon juice

(recipe continues)

Peel the ginger and then cut it crosswise into the thinnest slices possible. Cut the green chiles crosswise into fine slices. In a small, clean glass jar, combine the ginger, chiles, salt, and sugar.

Put the lemon juice in a small stainless steel or enameled pot and bring to a boil. Turn off the heat and allow the juice to become lukewarm. Pour the juice over the ginger and cover the jar with a noncorrosive lid. Shake to mix. This relish may be eaten after an hour. Store in the refrigerator.

MAKES ½ CUP

Shamsi Davis'

Crisply Fried Onions or Shallots in the Persian Style

IRAN

Pyaz Doug

Throughout Asia, crisply fried onion or shallot flakes serve both as a garnish and as a seasoning. There are many ways of making them crisp and keeping them that way. As I travel, I am shown an endless variety of tricks. In Indonesia I was told that shallot flakes turn much crisper if they are soaked in lightly salted water before being fried. (This makes sense as salt draws out some of the moisture.) I have also heard that starting the frying at a medium-hot rather than a very hot temperature also helps.

Now I have learned something new from the Persians, who take smallish onions (or shallots) and cut them into very fine half rings, which are spread out overnight to dry off slightly. The next day they are deep-fried very quickly with a light sprinkling of turmeric and salt. (I have amended the Persian recipe somewhat and sprinkle the frying flakes with a solution of turmeric and salt—a very Indian tradition that prevents the turmeric from burning!)

It is a good idea to fry onions or shallots in quantity and keep them in tightly lidded jars to be used as needed. They are wonderful sprinkled over pilafs, into salads, and over all manner of bean dishes. They can be kept for several days.

I actually prefer to use shallots as they make more delicate flakes but smallish onions (not larger than 3 ounces) work well too.

½ pound onions or shallots (see recipe
    introduction)
1¼ teaspoons salt

½ teaspoon ground turmeric
Peanut oil for deep-frying

Peel the onions or shallots. Cut them in half lengthwise and then crosswise into paper-thin slices. Spread the slices out in a single layer on paper towels and leave overnight, uncovered.

Combine the salt, turmeric, and 2 tablespoons of water in a small cup.

Put about 2 inches of oil in a wok or medium frying pan set over medium-high heat. Set a sieve over a bowl and keep it nearby. Put the cup of turmeric mixture nearby as well. When the oil is hot, put in all of the onions or shallots. Quickly dip your fingers into the turmeric solution and sprinkle whatever liquid your fingers pick up over the onions or shallots. Stir for a few seconds. As soon as the onions or shallots are golden and crisp—this happens very fast—empty the contents of the pan into the sieve set over a bowl. Now spread the flakes out on paper towels. When they are cool, store them in a tightly lidded jar and use as needed.

MAKES ENOUGH TO FILL A 12-OUNCE JAR

Indonesian Peanut Sauce   INDONESIA

This is a spicy, sweet, sour, and nutty Indonesian sauce as delicious as it is nutritious. You may pour it as a dressing over lightly boiled, blanched, or steamed vegetables, adding both protein and flavor to the meal. Pour it over boiled or baked potatoes or hard-boiled eggs. Try it also as a dip for vegetable fritters and as a topping for lightly sautéed bean curd.

1¼ cups skinned roasted peanuts

2 tablespoons peanut oil (olive oil may be substituted)

3 medium shallots, peeled and very finely chopped

3 garlic cloves, peeled and very finely chopped

½ to ¾ teaspoon cayenne

½ teaspoon salt, or to taste

1 tablespoon sugar

1½ to 2 tablespoons fresh lemon juice

Put the peanuts into a clean coffee grinder or other spice grinder and grind as finely as possible.

Put the oil in a small pan and set over medium heat. When hot, put in the shallots and garlic. Stir and fry until medium-brown. Now put in 2 cups of water, the ground peanuts, cayenne, salt, and sugar. Stir well and bring to a simmer. Turn the heat down to low and simmer gently for 20 minutes, or until the sauce thickens to the consistency of heavy cream, stirring now and then. Turn off the heat. Let the sauce cool a little and then beat in the lemon juice. Taste to check the balance of flavors. Store for up to 2 to 3 days in the refrigerator and serve at room temperature.

SERVES 4

Juanita Jarillo's
Pecan-Chile Sauce
MEXICO
Salsa Morita

The tall, gracious pecan tree probably spread into Mexico from Texas and in Huseade de Ocampo, a small town near Pachuca in Hidalgo, it seems to have found a very loving home. Here this popular spicy salsa is ground up on the metate *(grinding stone) and then eaten rather simply, with soft corn tortillas. It also makes a wonderful dip for potato chips, corn chips, or raw vegetables. I sometimes pour it over boiled/steamed vegetables and hard-boiled eggs, making a kind of Indonesian* gado gado. *Its texture is that of crepe batter (or slightly thinned-out peanut butter), flowing but creamy.*

The dried Mexican chile used here, about 2 inches long and quite fat in the middle, is called morita. *I have only seen it in Mexican markets (both in the United States and Mexico). If you cannot get it, use the plain, slim, cayenne-type dried hot red chile that is available everywhere. Four* morito *chiles (or the slim cayennes) make a medium-hot sauce. It is best, however, to start with 2 to 3 chiles, taste the sauce, and add more later if you want the sauce hotter.*

Any unused sauce may be stored in the refrigerator.

3 tablespoons peanut or canola oil

3 to 4 dried hot red chiles (preferably *morita* chiles)

2⅔ cups (8 ounces) shelled pecan halves

1 large garlic clove, peeled but left whole

Salt

About 5 tablespoons extra-virgin olive oil

Put the vegetable oil in a medium frying pan and set over medium heat. When hot, put in the chiles, turning them over as soon as they darken at the bottom and swell. (This takes just a few seconds.) When the second side has darkened as well (another second or so), remove the chiles with a slotted spoon and set aside. Put the pecans into the same oil. Stir and fry for 2 minutes, or until the pecans just start to give off a nutty odor. Turn the heat down to low. Keep stirring and frying them until they are just golden, another 5 to 6 minutes. Avoid burning them. Transfer to a bowl with a slotted spoon. Put the clove of garlic into the oil remaining in the frying pan. Stir and fry it until it is golden and then remove it with a slotted spoon.

Examine the pecans. If any part has turned dark brown or black, scrape it off with a sharp knife.

Into a running blender, put 3 of the chiles and blend until they are coarsely powdered. Now add the garlic and a handful of nuts. As soon as they are coarsely ground, empty the contents of the blender into a bowl. Coarsely powder the remaining pecans, a handful at a time, removing each batch as it is pulverized. Add about 1/2 teaspoon salt to the contents of the bowl. Mix and taste for both salt and heat. If you think you will want the sauce hotter (remember, it still has to get thinned out with oil), put the remaining chile into a running blender and blend until powdered. Now put the contents of the bowl back into the blender. Blend, stirring from the bottom frequently and slowly adding 1 tablespoon of the olive oil at a time until all the olive oil is used up and you have a flowing, creamy paste. (If you need a tiny bit more olive oil, do use it.) Taste again for salt, adding a bit more if you need it, and mix well. Store in a covered jar in the refrigerator for up to 2 to 3 days.

MAKES ABOUT 9 OUNCES

From Chef Rosa Gran's at the Florian Restaurant in Barcelona
Classic Romesco Sauce   SPAIN

Here is a sauce that I cannot live without. It is a little trouble to make but I generally make it ahead of time and freeze it. This Romesco sauce may be served with Escalivada, the Spanish mix of grilled vegetables (page 311), or any batter-fried or fried vegetables. You may also serve it as a dressing for cold, poached, or steamed vegetables. I even love to serve it with Tabbouleh, a Salad Made with Bulgur and Arugula (page 424). Leftover sauce may be frozen; beat lightly after defrosting.

2 medium onions (11 ounces total), peeled but left whole

8 to 10 large garlic cloves, unpeeled

3 large very ripe tomatoes (26 ounces)

3 dried ancho chiles

1/2 cup red wine vinegar

5 tablespoons (2 ounces) blanched slivered almonds

6 tablespoons extra-virgin olive oil

1 3/4 teaspoons salt

Turn on the broiler.

Spread the onions, garlic, and tomatoes on a baking tray lined with aluminum foil. Broil 4 to 5 inches from the heat for 5 to 7 minutes, turning the onions, garlic, and tomatoes as the outside skins char. The garlic will get done first. Remove the garlic cloves and continue for another 10 minutes or so until the onions and tomatoes are also browned on all sides. Remove the tomatoes at this stage.

Reduce the oven temperature to 350°F. and bake the onions for 25 to 35 minutes, or until they have softened all the way to the inside.

(recipe continues)

Meanwhile, remove the stems and seeds of the ancho chiles by cutting the tops off and shaking out as many seeds as possible. Put the chiles in a small pot along with the vinegar and ¼ cup of water and bring to a boil. Cover the pot, turn the heat down to low, and simmer for 5 minutes, or until all the chiles are soft. Turn the heat off. Let the ancho mixture sit, covered, for another 5 minutes, or until the peppers are very soft. Cool slightly in the liquid, then remove the peppers from the liquid and peel away the skin. (If the skin does not peel easily, leave it; it will come off later.) Remove any seeds that are still clinging to the flesh. Save any vinegar left in the pot.

Put the tomatoes and ancho chiles into a coarse sieve set over a bowl. Using your fingers or a wooden spoon, push out as much pulp as possible. Make sure you collect all the pulp on the underside of the sieve as well.

Put the almonds in a small cast-iron pan and set over medium heat. Stir the almonds quickly for 2 to 3 minutes, or until golden brown. Set aside to cool, then grind to a fine powder in a clean spice grinder.

When the onions are very tender, remove them from the oven and discard the charred outer layer. Chop them coarsely. Peel the garlic cloves.

Put the ancho-tomato mixture, onions, garlic, ground almonds, oil, leftover vinegar, if any, and salt into a blender. Blend to a puree. Serve at room temperature or chilled.

MAKES ABOUT 3 CUPS

Maricel Presilla's
Simple Romesco Sauce SPAIN

There are many recipes for this delightful red pepper sauce. The simplest—and perhaps the one I love most—is the one Maricel Presilla generously gave me on our trip through Spain. It can be served with Escalivada, the mix of grilled vegetables (page 311), Spanish Egg and Potato Cake (page 536), over an omelet, or with any grilled, fried, poached, or steamed vegetables, or even as a base for stuffed vegetables. I also think it is quite spectacular with plain boiled potatoes.
This sauce may also be frozen.

1 dried ancho chile

3 large red bell peppers

¼ cup extra-virgin olive oil

2 tablespoons red wine vinegar

⅛ teaspoon cayenne

2 garlic cloves, peeled

1 teaspoon salt

Remove the stem and seeds of the ancho chile. Put the chile in a small pot with ¾ cup of water and bring to a boil. Cover the pot, turn the heat down to low, and continue simmering for 5 minutes. Turn the heat off and let it sit, covered, for another 5 minutes, or until the chile is very soft. Cool slightly in the liquid. Remove the chile from the liquid and peel away the skin. Save the liquid and the flesh.

Heat the broiler.

Remove the stems and seeds of the red peppers and cut into quarters lengthwise. Lay the peppers, skin side up, on a baking tray and place under the broiler 4 to 5 inches from the source of heat. Broil for 7 to 10 minutes, moving the pepper quarters as needed, until the outside skins are evenly charred. You will need to turn the tray now and then to help them char evenly. Put the red peppers in a paper bag. Close the bag and set it aside for 10 minutes. (You could also cover the tray with a heavy towel for 10 minutes.) When they have finished resting in the paper bag or tray, peel away the red pepper skins.

Put the flesh of the chile, 2 tablespoons of the ancho chile liquid, peeled red peppers, oil, vinegar, cayenne, garlic, and salt into the container of a blender and puree. Empty into a decorative bowl and serve at room temperature.

MAKES 2 CUPS

From Tiffin's, Port of Spain
Trinidadian Pepper Sauce   TRINIDAD

When Lola gets an order, say, for a curry to go, at the small, coffee shop–style Tiffin's in Port of Spain where she works, she seems programmed to yell back, "Any pepper any ting?" By this she means, do they want some pepper sauce added on? A Trinidadian and his/her pepper sauce are seldom parted. It can be dribbled into soups and stews, on sandwiches and bean dishes—indeed on most savory foods.

Generally, fiery Scotch bonnet chiles (of the habanero family), chiles that are 50 times hotter than a jalapeño, are used; if you can take that amount of heat—and can find habaneros or habanero types—do by all means use the squat, lantern-shaped chiles (just the orange and red ones). These chiles, which are said to have originated in the jungles of the Amazon, do tend to give the body a jolt from head to toe and should be used only by the hardiest!

For the rest of us any fresh red hot chiles that are available will do. I tend to buy red chiles that are a brilliant Chinese red, about 4 to 6 inches long and ¾-inch wide (and habaneros are the only peppers I know of that are too hot even for me). To be on the safe side, wear thin rubber gloves while handling them and refrain from touching your face. I tend not to wear gloves but I am very careful. My fingers still tingle for a few days! (recipe continues)

At Tiffin's, the herb of choice used for flavoring the sauce is culantro, a New World herb, which the locals of Indian descent call bandhania *(Hindi for "coriander-of-the-woods"). This consists of long serrated leaves, which taste and smell a bit like cilantro. (The Thais use it too and call it, interestingly,* pak chee farang, *or foreign coriander.) Cilantro is the best substitute.*

¼ pound fresh hot red chiles

2 medium garlic cloves, peeled and coarsely
    chopped

1½ teaspoons salt

2 tablespoons coarsely chopped cilantro or
    culantro, if available

5 tablespoons white wine vinegar (or any
    white vinegar)

½ teaspoon dried mustard powder

Cut the stem end off the chiles, then slit them in half lengthwise and remove all the seeds. Cut the chiles crosswise into coarse strips.

In the container of a blender, combine the chiles, garlic, salt, cilantro, vinegar, and mustard. Blend until you have a fine paste.

Put the paste into a small pot and bring to a boil over medium heat. When bubbling, turn the heat down to low and cook very gently, stirring now and then, for 3 to 4 minutes. Turn off the heat and allow the sauce to cool. Put in a clean jar, cover tightly, and refrigerate. This pepper paste will last for months.

MAKES ABOUT 1 CUP

Moroccan Chile-Garlic Paste   MOROCCO
Harissa

The traditional way of making harissa *is with a mortar and pestle. The Moroccans crush the salt and garlic together, then add soaked red chiles, one at a time. This process is time consuming but yields a wonderfully fragrant and powerful paste.*

An easier method that also produces successful results is to put the chiles, salt, and garlic into a blender. As some liquid is required, it is best to dribble olive oil into the blender a little at a time until you have a coarse paste. Additional seasonings, such as cumin, coriander, even mint and vinegar, can also be added.

Harissa *can be used as an ingredient in other sauces and other dishes, or served on the side as an incendiary chutney.*

2 cups (1 ounce) dried hot red chiles

1½ teaspoons whole coriander seeds

1½ teaspoons whole cumin seeds

8 garlic cloves, peeled and coarsely chopped

¾ teaspoon salt

¼ cup olive oil, plus additional oil to pour over the top

Soak the red chiles in 2 cups of warm water for 1 to 2 hours, or until softened. Drain.

Meanwhile, put the coriander and cumin in a small dry cast-iron pan and set over medium heat. Roast lightly, stirring frequently. The spices will be done when they turn a couple of shades darker and emit a strong fragrance. Now put the cumin and coriander in a clean spice grinder and grind to a fine powder. Set this mixture aside.

Cut off the tops of the chiles, cut them open lengthwise, and remove the seeds. Chop the chiles coarsely. Wash your hands thoroughly.

Put the chiles, spice mixture, garlic, and salt into a blender. Puree, slowly dribbling the ¼ cup of oil into the container. Continue to puree until you have a coarse pulp, pushing down the mixture with a rubber spatula when necessary. Spoon into a jar and top with enough olive oil to completely cover the puree. Store in the refrigerator for a week to 10 days.

MAKES ABOUT ½ CUP

Red Pepper Paste TURKEY

Red pepper pastes, which can be plain or enhanced with seasonings, are sold by Middle Eastern grocers but they are really not hard to make at home and actually taste much better. Just as Italians make tons of tomato paste in tomato season, Turks dry off their meaty red peppers in the hot sun and transform them into a dark, thick mass that drops off the spoon with the greatest reluctance. Rather like tomato paste in texture, it is then used to perk up a soup, a stew, a sauce, or a salad in the months ahead. Of the dozens of pastes that I saw and tasted in Turkey, this is perhaps my favorite recipe.

If your red chiles are small and not the cherry peppers suggested here, do not bother to roast them. Just seed them, chop them, and put them directly into the blender.

This paste will last for several weeks in the refrigerator. It may also be frozen in tablespoon-sized dollops set side by side in a flat plastic container.

(recipe continues)

2 pounds red bell peppers, halved lengthwise, seeded, and cored

4 hot red cherry peppers (or 1 to 4 of any other fresh hot red chiles), halved lengthwise and seeded

1 large tomato (6 ounces), cored but left whole

2 large or 4 medium garlic cloves, unpeeled

6 tablespoons olive oil

1¼ teaspoons salt

Preheat the oven to 325°F.

Arrange the red bell pepper halves and the red cherry pepper halves, skin side up, as well as the tomato on a large baking tray in a single layer. Tuck the garlic cloves under the bell pepper halves (as if they were hiding in a cave). Bake for 2 hours. Remove from the oven and allow to cool just enough to handle. Peel the peppers, using a spoon, if necessary, to scoop out the flesh. Put the pepper flesh in a blender. Squeeze out the flesh from the garlic cloves and put in the blender. Peel the tomato and cut it in half crosswise. Remove the seeds. Chop the tomato coarsely and put it in the blender as well. Blend to a smooth puree.

Put 4 tablespoons of the oil in a large, heavy, nonstick frying pan and set over medium-high heat. When hot, put in the paste from the blender and the salt. Stir and sauté for about 10 minutes, or until you have a thick dark paste that is rather like tomato paste. Put the paste in an 8-ounce jar and smooth out the top with the back of a spoon. Pour the remaining 2 tablespoons of oil over the top. Once cool, cover and refrigerate or freeze (see recipe introduction).

MAKES ¾ CUP

Ethiopian Hot Sauce

ETHIOPIA

Awaze

This is closely related to the harissa *of Morocco, with one major difference—the addition of mustard seeds! Like* harissa, *it is a condiment that may be used as is or thinned out further with the liquid from a stew.*

Add drops of this sauce to cooked beans, lentils, vegetables, and chunky soups. Add it to yogurt dishes that you want to spice up, even to salad dressings. (How about a potato salad with a bit of this sauce in its dressing?)

The traditional way to make the mixture is in a mortar, first crushing the ingredients, then pounding in liquid. I have simplified the entire procedure, grinding the chiles, salt, and mustard seeds together and keeping them nice and dry in a jar. Whenever I need some sauce, I crush some garlic and add it to the dry spices along with some liquid.

You can use commercial cayenne here, but it is best to find a good-quality pure chile powder.

1 teaspoon good-quality chile powder

2 teaspoons whole brown mustard seeds

½ teaspoon salt

2 large garlic cloves or 4 smaller ones, peeled and crushed to a pulp

2 tablespoons peanut or canola oil (optional)

Put the chile powder, mustard seeds, and salt into a clean electric coffee grinder and grind until fine. (Store in a tightly lidded jar if not using immediately.)

Before eating, empty the seasonings into a bowl. Add the garlic. Now beat in the oil and 2 tablespoons of water or leave out the oil and beat in 4 tablespoons of water.

MAKES ABOUT ¼ CUP OF CONCENTRATED SAUCE

Margaret Arnold's

Caribbean Seasoning Sauce

MOST OF THE CARIBBEAN

An herb-filled base sauce, this is used on many Caribbean islands for marinades and to flavor everything from soup and bean dishes to green vegetables and roots. Make it as hot as you can tolerate pleasurably and use it, as the islanders do, to flavor any dish of your choice. Sauté it in a little oil first and then add, say, boiled diced potatoes, or uncooked okra, or cooked chickpeas, or even a can of drained kidney beans. Keep it in the refrigerator, where it will last for months.

As many people will have trouble weighing the fresh herbs when buying them, I have given the circumference of the herbs at their widest when they are compressed.

1 (1-ounce) bunch fresh oregano (about ¾-inch circumference when compressed), leaves only

1 (1-ounce) bunch fresh thyme (about 1-inch circumference when compressed), leaves only

1 (½-ounce) bunch fresh chives (about ¾-inch circumference when compressed), coarsely chopped

1 to 4 jalapeño chiles or ½ to 1 habanero chile, coarsely chopped (with seeds)

10 ounces fresh basil leaves (about 2 generous handfuls), coarsely chopped

1 large onion (8 ounces), peeled and coarsely chopped

10 to 12 garlic cloves, peeled and coarsely chopped

1 celery stalk, coarsely chopped

½ teaspoon salt

1 teaspoon ground cumin

½ teaspoon ground turmeric

1½ teaspoons paprika

½ teaspoon sugar

½ cup red wine vinegar

(recipe continues)

Combine all the ingredients in a food processor or blender. Blend, pushing down if necessary, until you have a very coarse paste. You should be able to see bits of the seasonings. Put into a clean jar and refrigerate until needed.

MAKES 2½ CUPS

Korean Soy Dipping Sauce

KOREA

¼ cup soy sauce

2½ tablespoons rice vinegar

2 teaspoons oriental sesame oil

Mix all the ingredients in a small bowl.

SERVES 4

Spicy Soy Korean Sauce

KOREA

¼ cup soy sauce

2 tablespoons oriental sesame oil

1 teaspoon sugar

1 tablespoon roasted and lightly ground
    sesame seeds (page 734)

1 scallion (white portion only), cut into fine
    rounds

¼ teaspoon cayenne

Combine all the ingredients in a small bowl and mix well.

SERVES 4 TO 6

Japanese Soy Dipping Sauce

2 tablespoons soy sauce

1 tablespoon mirin

1 teaspoon sugar

1 teaspoon oriental sesame oil

¼ cup very light stock (*Konbu* Stock, page 576,
    may be used here)

Combine all the ingredients in a small bowl and mix well.

SERVES 4

Shiu-Min Block's

Chinese Soy Sauce Salad Dressing CHINA

Chiang Yow Tru Chiang

This is a soy-based salad dressing that can be used for all manner of salads, including those made with lettuce leaves.

3 tablespoons distilled white vinegar

7 tablespoons Chinese light soy sauce

1 tablespoon sugar

1 garlic clove, peeled and lightly crushed

2 teaspoons oriental sesame oil

Put all the ingredients in a jar, cover tightly, and shake well.

MAKES ABOUT ¾ CUP

Plain Tamarind Chutney INDIA

Saadi Imli Ki Chutney

This chutney may be eaten with grilled eggplants; it may be drizzled on yogurt relishes and soups as well as salads of mixed fruit and vegetables. It can, of course, be served as a relish. The variation incorporates raisins and nuts for a chunkier, more substantial chutney used as a condiment.

⅔ cup tamarind paste (page 736)

¾ teaspoon salt, or to taste

Freshly ground black pepper

½ to ⅔ cup sugar

¼ teaspoon cayenne, or to taste

1½ teaspoons ground roasted cumin seeds

(page 724)

Combine all the ingredients and mix well. Taste for the correct balance of seasonings, especially salt and sugar, adding more of what you need. This chutney may be stored in the refrigerator for a week and may also be frozen.

SERVES 6

Variation

Tamarind Chutney with Raisins and Walnuts

Imli Aur Ahkrote Ki Chutney

To the plain chutney, add ¼ cup golden raisins that have been plumped in boiling water for 1 to 2 hours and drained, and 5 tablespoons of chopped walnuts. Mix well.

Tamarind-Yogurt Chutney

Imli Or Dahi Ki Chutney

Here tamarind and yogurt are combined but not thoroughly mixed, leaving swirls of white in the chocolate brown. Serve small dollops over warm boiled potatoes, grilled/fried eggplant, or boiled chickpeas. It's heavenly.

For the tamarind

⅔ cup thick tamarind paste (page 736)

½ teaspoon salt, or to taste

Freshly ground black pepper

½ to ⅔ cup sugar

¼ teaspoon cayenne, or to taste

1½ teaspoons ground roasted cumin seeds
(page 724)

1 teaspoon finely minced fresh ginger

1 tablespoon finely chopped fresh mint

For the yogurt

½ cup plain yogurt

⅛ teaspoon salt

Freshly ground black pepper

1 tablespoon finely chopped fresh cilantro

½ to 1 teaspoon finely chopped fresh hot
green chile

1 teaspoon sugar

For garnish

1 mint sprig

Combine all the ingredients for the tamarind and mix well. Taste for the correct balance of seasonings, especially salt and sugar, adding more of what you need.

Put the yogurt in a bowl. Beat lightly with a fork until light and creamy. Add the salt, pepper, cilantro, chile, and sugar and mix well.

To serve, put half of the tamarind chutney into a clear bowl. Pour half of the yogurt over the top. Pour the remaining tamarind chutney over the yogurt. Now take the rest of the yogurt and arrange it in a large dollop on top of the tamarind. Plunge a table knife straight down in the center of the bowl, then move the knife outward in concentric circles once and remove it. You should have swirls of white and brown. Garnish with the mint sprig and serve. You could also chill before serving.

SERVES 6

Green Tomatillo Salsa

Salsa Verde

Green salsas in Mexico are often based on the tomatillo.

Use this sauce as a dip or dribble it over quesadillas or French fries. You can also spread it over layers of stale tortillas along with cheese [such as the Homemade White Latin American Cheese (Queso Blanco), page 564] and then bake it to make a kind of Mexican lasagna.

½ pound tomatillos, husks removed and washed

¼ cup well-chopped fresh cilantro

1 to 2 fresh hot green chiles (serranos or jalapeños are ideal, but use what you can find)

About ½ teaspoon salt, or to taste

Put the whole tomatillos in a medium pan. Add about 2 cups of water and bring to a boil. Cover, turn the heat down to medium-low, and simmer for 10 minutes. Lift the tomatillos out with a spoon (they will be full of water) and put them into a blender. Add the remaining ingredients and blend until you have a coarse puree. If you need to add more water, use some that has been left over from boiling the tomatillos. Check for the balance of flavors.

MAKES 1 CUP

Simple Tomato Sauce

for Pasta, Vegetables, and Beans

This sauce is made from canned tomatoes and is a favorite. I cook it up at least once a week and serve it with pasta or with stuffed or baked vegetables or beans.

Instead of using a can of chopped tomatoes, I prefer to use whole tomatoes in their own liquid, breaking up the tomatoes myself as they cook. I do not like very thick tomato sauces, as I feel they tend to overwhelm the pasta.

¼ cup olive oil

4 garlic cloves, peeled and very finely chopped

2 whole dried hot red chiles

1 (1-pound, 12-ounce) can whole tomatoes

½ teaspoon dried oregano

1 teaspoon salt, or to taste

Freshly ground black pepper

(recipe continues)

Put the oil, garlic, and chiles in a medium sauté pan and set over medium-high heat. Let the garlic sizzle until it just starts to brown, then put in all the tomatoes with their liquid, oregano, salt, and pepper. Stir, breaking up the tomatoes into smaller pieces, and bring to a simmer. Turn the heat down to low and simmer gently for 12 to 15 minutes, or until the sauce is just a little bit thicker, stirring now and then.

SERVES 4

Moroccan-Style Fresh Tomato Sauce MOROCCO

Serve with fried zucchini, fried eggplant, or fried eggs.

1 medium very ripe tomato (5 ounces)

¼ to ½ teaspoon salt

¼ teaspoon Moroccan Chile-Garlic Paste (*Harissa,* page 672) *or* 1 garlic clove, crushed, and ¼ teaspoon cayenne

Using the coarsest section of a grater, grate the tomato into a bowl. Add the salt and Moroccan Chile-Garlic Paste and mix well. Serve at room temperature or chilled.

MAKES ½ CUP AND SERVES 4

Tomato Sauce with Mushrooms

This is a simple sauce with a bit of bite that can be used over pasta, polenta, or stuffed vegetables.

¼ cup olive oil

4 garlic cloves, peeled and finely chopped

8 medium white mushrooms, wiped with a damp cloth and sliced lengthwise into ⅛-inch-thick slices

1 whole dried hot red chile

1 (1-pound, 12-ounce) can whole tomatoes, tomatoes coarsely chopped

¾ teaspoon salt

Put 2 tablespoons of the oil and half of the garlic into a large frying pan and set over medium-high heat. As soon as the garlic sizzles and turns golden, turn up the heat to high and put in the mushrooms. Stir and fry for 1 to 2 minutes, or until the mushrooms are glossy. Empty the contents of the pan into a bowl and clean out the pan.

Put the remaining 2 tablespoons of oil, the remaining garlic, and the red chile into the same frying pan. As soon as the garlic sizzles and turns golden, put in the tomatoes and all their liquid as well as the salt. Stir to mix and cook, uncovered, on medium-low heat for about 20 minutes. The sauce should not be too pasty. Add the mushrooms and cook another 3 minutes. Remove the chile.

SERVES 4 AND MAKES ABOUT 2¼ CUPS

Sambal with Roasted Tomatoes, Shallots, and Chiles

INDONESIA

Dabu Dabu Lilang

Very similar to the salsas of Mexico, this actually comes from the Indonesian island of Sulawesi. It goes particularly well with thick soups and stews, adding a tart, hot element where it is most needed.

1 pound ripe medium tomatoes, halved

1 to 2 fresh or canned jalapeños (use any hot fresh green or red chiles)

3 large shallots (3 ounces), peeled but left whole

About 3 tablespoons fresh lime juice (a bit less if using canned chiles)

About 1½ teaspoons salt, or to taste

Preheat the broiler.

Spread the tomatoes, jalapeños, and shallots out on a broiling pan and place about 5 inches below the source of heat. Keep watching. The chiles will begin to darken in spots first. Turn them over. When the shallots get brown spots, turn them over as well. When the tomatoes begin to spot, turn them over. Remove the chiles as soon as they have dark spots on all sides. Remove the shallots next and finally the tomatoes. Everything should have black spots. Put the tomatoes, chiles, and shallots in a blender, spotted skin and all, and blend to a puree. Remove to a bowl, add lime juice and salt according to your taste and the general flavor of the tomatoes, and mix well.

SERVES 6 TO 8

South Indian Tomato Relish

This is a small saladlike relish to be served with all Indian meals.

3 medium tomatoes (about 12 ounces), cut into ¼-inch dice

3 thin slices of fresh ginger, peeled and cut into minute dice

1 teaspoon salt

⅛ teaspoon cayenne, or to taste

1 tablespoon fresh lemon juice

1 tablespoon peanut or canola oil

Generous pinch of ground asafetida

¼ teaspoon *urad dal* (or *chana dal* or yellow split peas)

½ teaspoon whole brown mustard seeds

In a stainless steel or nonmetallic bowl, combine the tomatoes, ginger, salt, cayenne, and lemon juice. Toss to mix.

Put the oil in a small frying pan and set over medium-high heat. When hot, put in the asafetida. A second later, put in the *urad dal* and stir for a few seconds, or until the *dal* turns red. Now put in the mustard seeds. As soon as the mustard seeds begin to pop, a matter of seconds, pour the contents of the frying pan over the tomatoes. Stir to mix.

SERVES 4

Tomato and Onion Relish

Timatar Aur Pyaz Ka Salaad

This is an everyday relish served at lunches and dinners in many North Indian homes and known simply as "salaad" or salad.

8 ounces very ripe tomatoes, diced coarsely

½ large onion (3 ounces), diced coarsely

2 Kirby cucumbers or 1 medium cucumber (5 ounces in all), diced coarsely

¾ to 1 teaspoon salt

½ teaspoon cayenne

½ to 1 teaspoon ground roasted cumin seeds (page 720)

2 to 3 tablespoons fresh lemon juice

4 tablespoons chopped fresh cilantro

Put the tomatoes, onion, and cucumbers in a bowl. Sprinkle the salt, cayenne, cumin, lemon juice, and cilantro over the top and toss. Taste and adjust the seasonings as needed. Serve at room temperature.

SERVES 4

Simple Red Salsa

This salsa may be served as a dip with tortilla chips or as a topping for Quesadilla with Cheese (page 352). As a relish, it may be served with all Mexican, South Asian, and Southeast Asian meals. If jalapeño peppers are unavailable, any other fresh or canned hot green chile may be used.

1 good-sized tomato (about 8 ounces), peeled (see page 300 if you need directions)

2 tablespoons very finely chopped onion

½ to 1 fresh or canned jalapeño, finely chopped

½ teaspoon salt

2 tablespoons finely chopped fresh cilantro

1 tablespoon fresh lime juice

Chop the tomato finely and put it in a bowl. Add all the remaining ingredients and mix well. Serve chilled or at room temperature.

SERVES 4 TO 6

Cooked Tomato Salsa

Salsa de Jitomate

Here the salsa is lightly cooked. This is particularly good over fried eggs but you may serve it as a dip or over pasta. I rarely remove chile seeds but if you want a milder flavor, you may do so.

1 tablespoon olive oil

1 garlic clove, peeled and finely chopped

1 (28-ounce) can tomatoes, drained and very finely chopped

2 to 4 very finely chopped fresh hot green chiles (canned serrano chiles may be used)

½ teaspoon salt

Freshly ground black pepper

2 tablespoons very finely chopped fresh cilantro

Put the oil and garlic in a shallow medium pan and set over medium-high heat. When the garlic sizzles and turns golden, add all the remaining ingredients except the cilantro and bring to a boil. Stir and cook for 3 to 4 minutes, or until the sauce has thickened a bit. Stir in the cilantro. Serve hot, at room temperature, or even chilled.

MAKES ABOUT 2 CUPS

Walnut Sauce

CAUCASUS, EAST ASIA

Walnut sauces are found throughout the belt that stretches from the Caucasus mountains all the way to Kashmir in northern India. This version is Caucasian and may be used to dress cooked dried beans or any vegetable, such as broccoli. It is rather thick and needs to be thinned out either with the water used for cooking the beans or vegetables or even stock or plain water.

It is best to blanch the walnuts first in order to get rid of some of the bitterness in the skins.

1/2 cup shelled walnuts

5 tablespoons olive oil

3 tablespoons fresh lemon juice

1/2 teaspoon salt, or to taste

1/4 cup vegetable stock or cooking liquid from
   boiling dried beans or vegetables

Bring 4 cups of water to a boil. Put in the walnuts and let them boil rapidly for 3 minutes; drain.

Combine the olive oil, lemon juice, salt, and stock in a blender. Crumble the walnuts and add them as well. Blend, pushing down with a rubber spatula when needed, until you have a smooth paste.

MAKES ABOUT 1 CUP

From the Çiragan Hotel, Istanbul

Circassian Sauce—A Walnut and Bread Sauce

TURKEY

Also known as Tarator Sauce, this particular walnut sauce seems to have been created by the Ottomans. It is enriched with bread and milk and has the consistency of a crepe batter. You may make it thinner or thicker according to whatever you are serving it with. It goes well with many vegetable dishes such as Green Bean Salad (page202) and eggplants.

1 cup coarsely chopped walnuts

2 thinnish slices of bread, crusts removed and
   broken up into small pieces (about 1 cup)

3/4 cup milk or a bit more, as needed

1 tablespoon extra-virgin olive oil or walnut
   oil

Scant 1/2 teaspoon salt

Freshly ground black pepper

Combine all the ingredients in a blender or food processor and blend until you have a smooth sauce.

MAKES ABOUT 1 1/2 CUPS

Preserved Pickles and Chutneys

L d. Lawrence's

Instant Korean Cabbage Pickle   KOREA

Mok Kimchi

Most kimchis, Korean pickles, take several days to mature. This one, known as mok kimchi, *may be eaten right away. Because of the vinegar and sesame oil, it does not ferment easily, though if it is kept in the refrigerator, some extra souring and fizzing may occur. If that happens it may still be eaten as a relish. It is also excellent as a soup base for bean curd.*

If you like, this salad may be made both hotter and sweeter with the addition of more Korean pepper powder and sugar. Crushed Korean red pepper is sold only by Korean grocers. It has a lovely color, aroma, and taste.

1 small napa cabbage (about 1½ pounds)

4½ tablespoons salt

2 teaspoons rice flour

1 garlic clove, peeled and finely chopped

1-inch piece of ginger, peeled and finely chopped

5-inch length of daikon, about 2 inches in diameter (½ pound), peeled and cut into very fine julienne strips

1 tablespoon crushed Korean red pepper or 1½ teaspoons cayenne

2 tablespoons roasted sesame seeds (page 734)

1 tablespoon sugar

2 tablespoons oriental sesame oil

5 teaspoons rice vinegar

Rinse the cabbage and discard any damaged or bruised leaves. With a knife, trim off any discoloration on the bottom end. Cut a deep (2-inch) cross in the bottom end and then, with your hands, tear the head apart into long quarters. One at a time, hold the cabbage quarters over a large bowl and sprinkle a tablespoon of salt in between the leaves and all over that quarter. Drop the cabbage pieces into the bowl. Invert a plate over the cabbage and put a weight (such as a full can or a pot of water) on top. Set aside for 4 hours.

Meanwhile, put the rice flour into a small saucepan. Slowly add ¾ cup of water, stirring as you do so. Bring the pot to a simmer. The mixture will thicken almost immediately. Cook for 1 minute and turn off the heat. Allow to cool.

(recipe continues)

Combine the garlic, ginger, daikon, red pepper, roasted sesame seeds, sugar, sesame oil, 3 teaspoons of the rice vinegar, and ½ tablespoon salt in a bowl. Toss to mix.

Rinse the cabbage well and squeeze out the excess moisture. Stuff the radish mixture between the cabbage leaves. This is best done by laying a cabbage quarter down in a bowl, with the smaller leaves facing up. Lift the first small leaf and put a little stuffing between it and the next leaf. Now lift the second, slightly larger leaf, and put in some more stuffing. Continue until an entire quarter has been stuffed. Fold the largest leaves over the smaller ones to form a small packet. Place the packet, folded side down, in a plastic container or widemouthed jar. Stuff the remaining quarters of the cabbage the same way and place the remaining 3 packets in the container. Any leftover stuffing or liquid from the stuffing may be poured over the top. Sprinkle the remaining 2 teaspoons of rice vinegar over the packets, cover, and refrigerate.

MAKES ENOUGH TO FILL A 5-CUP CONTAINER

Carrots Pickled with Mustard Seeds   INDIA
Gaajar Ka Achaar

This is a simple pickle that may be eaten with all meals. You could even chop up the carrots and put them in a salad dressing.

I like to use hulled and split mustard seeds for this pickle. Known as mustard seed dal, *these are sold only in Indian shops and are used mainly for pickling. You may use yellow or brown mustard seeds instead. Leave out the cayenne if you prefer a gentler pickle.*

12 ounces carrots (4 to 5 medium)

¼ cup hulled and split mustard seeds

2 teaspoons whole fennel seeds

1 to 2 teaspoons cayenne

½ teaspoon ground turmeric

2 teaspoons salt

6 tablespoons peanut or olive oil

Peel the carrots and cut them into sticks 2 inches long, ¼ inch wide, and ¼ inch thick. Put in a bowl.

Put the mustard and fennel seeds in a clean coffee grinder or other spice grinder and grind for a second to get a coarse mixture. Empty this mixture over the carrots. Add the cayenne, turmeric, and salt to the bowl. Toss to mix. Set aside for 3 to 4 hours.

Put the carrot mixture in a clean 24-ounce jar. Heat the oil until very hot and then allow it to become lukewarm. Pour over the carrots and shake the jar to mix. Close the jar and leave it in a sunny spot for 5 to 7 days, or until the carrots have "pickled"—turned sour. Shake the jar once or twice a day during this period and, if it is outside, bring it in if the nights are cool. Once the pickle is ready, it can be stored in the refrigerator for several months.

MAKES ENOUGH TO FILL A 24-OUNCE JAR

Pickled Garlic Cloves INDIA

Indians firmly believe that garlic cleanses the blood and so it is eaten with great enthusiasm. Here the smaller, more delicate cloves are pickled. Get the small purplish heads of garlic and make sure that they are very young and fresh.

2 small heads garlic (about 4 ounces)

1 to 2 fresh hot green chiles

2 tablespoons hulled and split mustard seeds (mustard seed *dal*) or whole yellow mustard seeds, ground coarsely in a clean coffee grinder

2 teaspoons salt

½ teaspoon ground turmeric

1 teaspoon cayenne

¾ cup peanut, corn, or olive oil

Generous pinch of ground asafetida

1 teaspoon whole brown mustard seeds

8 to 10 fresh curry leaves (or basil leaves or holy basil leaves)

Separate the garlic heads into individual cloves and peel the cloves. Wipe the chiles with a damp cloth and dry them off. Cut them crosswise into coarse rings. In a stainless steel or nonmetallic bowl, combine the garlic cloves, chiles, hulled and split mustard seeds, salt, turmeric, and cayenne. Toss to mix.

Put the oil in a small frying pan and set it over medium-high heat. When hot, put in the asafetida. A second later, put in the mustard seeds. As soon as the mustard seeds begin to pop, a matter of seconds, put in the curry leaves and stir once. Remove the pan from the heat and let it cool off, then pour its contents over the garlic mixture. Stir to mix. Transfer to a 1-cup widemouthed ceramic or glass jar with a noncorrosive lid. Store for 7 to 10 days on a sunny windowsill (or, in the summer, out of doors in the sun, remembering to bring the jar inside in the evenings) or in a warm spot in your home. Shake the jar at least once a day. When the garlic cloves have "pickled"—softened and soured a little—refrigerate the jar. The pickle will keep for several months.

MAKES ENOUGH TO FILL A 1-CUP JAR

Shiu-Min Block's

Daikon Pickle

CHINA

Bai Lowa Baw Liang Tsai

An almost instant, sweet, sour, and salty pickle, this is made with the large, long oriental white radish known as daikon (page 175). The pickle is appropriate for both oriental and Western meals.

1¼ pounds daikon

¼ cup sugar

1 teaspoon salt

3 tablespoons distilled white vinegar

Peel the daikon and then slice it crosswise into very thin, even rounds. (This is best done with a mandoline or other such slicer.)

Combine the sugar, salt, and vinegar in a large bowl and mix. Add the sliced daikon and mix well. Set aside for at least 30 minutes before eating. You may refrigerate this pickle and store it in a closed container for a few weeks.

SERVES 6 TO 8

PICKLING OR PRESERVING LEMONS

While it is somewhat unclear where citrus fruits of the lemon and lime family originated, it is well documented that their use in India dates back to antiquity. The early pickles used salt for preserving and also added locally grown black pepper and cardamom for extra pep and aroma. Today, there must be hundreds of lime, lemon, and other citrus pickles in every Indian state—some sweet-and-sour, some just sour, some hot, and some highly aromatic. Morocco is another nation that has become synonymous with simply preserved lemons that are used most imaginatively in cooking.

The chief aim of all these preserving and pickling techniques is to soften the skin and remove its bitterness and to mellow the eye-crossing sourness of the flesh. There are many methods for achieving this. Salt, all by itself, will do it, given enough time. Lemons and limes are sometimes pricked and then boiled briefly in brine or salted sugar syrup, to hasten the process.

As lemon peels are invariably a part of the pickle—indeed, they hold the fruit together—it is essential to buy unsprayed, preferably organically grown lemons.

Salted Lemons, Moroccan Style   MOROCCO

Salted lemons are one of the glories of Moroccan food. They may be bought in any market, from the same shops that sell preserved olives in every color and every flavor. The lemons are loosely quartered but generally kept whole and preserved just with salt—though spices like cloves and cinnamon are sometimes added, making them fairly similar to Simple Lemon Pickle (page 690), a recipe of very ancient Indian origin.

Once preserved and properly softened, the Moroccan lemons are used in a variety of ways. First, the amount called for is removed from the holding crock with a wooden spoon and rinsed off. This step removes extra salt as well as a whitish accretion that sometimes develops. If only the peel is required, as it often is for salads and stews, the pulp is removed and the skin chopped as needed. (The pulp can go to flavor dried bean dishes or rice dishes, or it can be finely chopped and added to vegetables.) Both the skin and pulp add sourness but it is a special, mellow sourness with echoes of an ancient world.

2 pounds fresh lemons

9 tablespoons salt

Extra lemon juice as needed

Wipe the lemons with damp paper towels and dry them off. Now cut them into quarters, lengthwise in such a way as to leave them attached at the bottoms. Remove the seeds. Rub the lemons with most of the salt, inside and out, closing them up again so they look whole.

Put a little bit of salt at the bottom of a 1-quart widemouthed ceramic or glass jar and start putting the salted lemons inside it, pushing down slightly with the second layer. Some juice will come out of the lemons. Add enough more juice to cover the lemons with juice. Screw a noncorrosive lid on the jar. Store for 7 to 10 days on a sunny windowsill (or in the summer, out of doors in the sun, remembering to bring the jar inside in the evenings) or in a warm spot in your home. Shake the jar at least once a day. This pickle keeps maturing with time. After 21 to 30 days, when the skin has softened completely, you may refrigerate it. It will keep for several months.

MAKES ENOUGH TO FILL A 1-QUART JAR

Simple Lemon Pickle

Many lemons are native to India where this sort of pickling has been favored since ancient times. Salt is the main preservative here, with the added flavors of cardamom, cloves, and black pepper. The pickle may be eaten with all meals as a condiment or chopped and used to give an extra bite to vegetable dishes and bean stews. It may also be used in any dish that calls for Moroccan-style preserved lemon.

2 pounds fresh lemons

1/2 teaspoon cardamom seeds

16 whole cloves

1 1/2 tablespoons sugar

9 tablespoons salt

1 teaspoon cayenne

1 teaspoon freshly ground black pepper

Wipe the lemons with damp paper towels and dry them off. Cut the lemons lengthwise into quarters and remove the seeds. Grind the cardamom seeds and cloves to fine powder in a clean spice or coffee grinder.

In a large bowl, mix together the sugar, salt, cayenne, black pepper as well as the ground cardamom and cloves. Now add the lemons and toss to coat them completely with the spices. Transfer to a 1-quart widemouthed ceramic or glass jar with a noncorrosive lid. Store for 7 to 10 days on a sunny windowsill (or, in the summer, out of doors in the sun, remembering to bring the jar inside in the evenings) or in a warm spot in your home. Shake the jar at least once a day. This pickle keeps maturing with time. After 21 to 30 days, when the skin has softened completely, you may refrigerate it. It will keep for several months.

MAKES ENOUGH TO FILL A 1-QUART JAR

Sweet-and-Sour Lemon Chutney

Because the lemon is boiled, this chutney matures faster than the usual preserved lemon and is ready to eat in 5 days. The cayenne may be omitted if a gentler chutney is desired.

2 large fresh lemons (about 12 ounces)

2 1/2 teaspoons salt

1/2 teaspoon ground turmeric

1 teaspoon cayenne, or to taste

7 tablespoons sugar

2 tablespoons fresh lemon juice

Wipe the lemons with damp paper towels and dry them off. Cut the lemons into 1/8-inch-thick slices and then cut the slices into 1/8-inch-thick dice. Remove the seeds. Put the lemons into a stainless steel or enameled saucepan and add the salt, turmeric, cayenne, sugar, and lemon juice. Bring to a simmer and cook gently for 5 to 6 minutes, or until the chutney has thickened slightly. Remember that it will thicken more as it cools.

Transfer to a 12-ounce widemouthed ceramic or glass jar with a noncorrosive lid. Store for 5 to 7 days before serving. The chutney may now be refrigerated. It will keep for several months.

MAKES ENOUGH TO FILL A 12-OUNCE JAR

Sweet Gujarati Lemon Pickle INDIA

This is a delightful pickle that helps perk up dried bean and split pea dishes as well as grain stews. Try chopping just a little bit finely and putting it on a cheese sandwich!
If you cannot get hulled and split mustard seeds, use whole yellow mustard seeds instead.

2 large fresh lemons (about 12 ounces)

1 teaspoon whole fenugreek seeds

2 tablespoons hulled and split mustard seeds

2 teaspoons salt

½ teaspoon ground turmeric

1 to 1½ teaspoons cayenne

1-inch piece of fresh ginger, peeled, thinly sliced, then cut into minute dice

5 tablespoons sugar

3 tablespoons peanut, corn, or olive oil

1 teaspoon whole brown mustard seeds

Wipe the lemons with damp paper towels and dry them off. Cut the lemons into ⅛-inch-thick slices and then cut the slices into ⅛-inch-thick dice. Remove the seeds. Put the lemons into a stainless steel or nonmetallic bowl.

Combine the fenugreek seeds and mustard seeds in a clean coffee grinder or other spice grinder and grind coarsely. Empty over the lemons. Add the salt, turmeric, cayenne, ginger, and sugar. Toss all to mix.

Put the oil in a small frying pan and set it over medium-high heat. When it is very hot, put in the mustard seeds. As soon as they start to pop, a matter of seconds, pour the contents of the frying pan, oil and seeds, over the lemon mixture. Toss to mix.

Transfer to a 4-cup widemouthed ceramic or glass jar with a noncorrosive lid. Store for 7 to 10 days on a sunny windowsill (or, in the summer, out of doors in the sun, remembering to bring the jar inside in the evenings) or in a warm spot in

(recipe continues)

your home. Shake the jar at least once a day. This pickle keeps maturing with time. After 21 to 30 days, when the skin has softened completely, you may refrigerate it. It will keep for several months.

MAKES 3 CUPS

South Indian Lemon Pickle INDIA
Daxshini Neebu Ka Achaar

This is a much-loved pickle in our family. I often chop it finely and add it to the stuffing for eggplants and other vegetables. Sometimes I add it to stir-fried green beans as they are being tossed for the last time and sometimes I mash a few pieces of this pickled lemon and add them to a cooked dish of dried beans or split peas. It is full of aroma and flavor.

2 large lemons (about 12 ounces)

2 tablespoons salt

1½ teaspoons cayenne

¼ teaspoon ground turmeric

3 tablespoons peanut or canola oil

Pinch of ground asafetida

½ teaspoon *urad dal* (use *chana dal* or yellow split peas as a substitute)

½ teaspoon whole brown mustard seeds

10 to 12 fresh curry leaves (use basil or holy basil as a substitute)

Wipe the lemons with a damp cloth and dry them off. Cut the lemons lengthwise into ¼-inch-thick slices. Stacking a few slices together, cut the lemons into ¼-inch dice. Remove the seeds. Put the lemons in a stainless steel or nonmetallic bowl and add the salt, cayenne, and turmeric. Toss to mix, cover, and set aside for 24 hours.

Put the oil in a small frying pan and set over medium-high heat. When hot, put in the asafetida. A second later, put in the *urad dal* and stir until it turns red; this will happen fairly quickly. Now put in the mustard seeds. As soon as the mustard seeds begin to pop, a matter of seconds, put in the curry leaves. Stir them for 5 seconds, then empty the contents of the pan, oil and seasonings, over the lemons. Stir to mix.

Transfer the pickle to a clean, widemouthed ceramic or glass pint jar with a noncorrosive lid. Close tightly and store for 10 to 15 days on a sunny windowsill (or, in the summer, out of doors in the sun, remembering to bring the jar inside in the evenings) or in a warm spot in your home. Shake the jar at least once a day. When the skin softens a bit, the pickle is ready to eat. You may now refrigerate it. It should keep for several months.

MAKES 2 CUPS

MANGOES FOR PICKLING AND PRESERVING

Seven hundred years ago, an esteemed Turkik poet in the court of Emperor Mohammad Bin Tughlak in Delhi, India, wrote:

> The mango is the pride of the garden,
> The choicest fruit of Hindustan.
> Other fruit we are content to eat when ripe,
> But the mango is good in all stages of growth.

It is not the ripe mango that I am concerned with in this chapter but the fruit in an "earlier stage of growth"—the green mango.

One day, I hope, green mangoes will be found as commonly in Western supermarkets as lemons and limes but until that time, hunt them down in Indian markets—the only places where they seem to be sold—order them by the box and use them in everything from pies and salads to chutneys. (In the nineteenth century, English housewives in India used sliced green mangoes to make their "apple" pies!)

Green mangoes are unripe mangoes. They are not hard mangoes that, if wrapped in newspaper, might soften and ripen in a few days. No, these mangoes have been plucked prematurely when no thought of ripening had ever entered their green heads. They have pale green, crisp flesh and are hard and sour—often very sour, sometimes sweet-and-sour. This sour flesh is sliced and offered with salty dipping sauces in the Philippines; in Thailand it is sold in the streets with generous sprinklings of salt, sugar, and red chile powder; and in Malaysia I have had it mixed into salads. But it is in India that the green mango is truly at home.

The mango has been cultivated in India for more than four thousand years. Its highly auspicious leaves garland doorways at all festivities and the ripe fruit reigns over the hot summers in the form of juices, ice creams, sweetmeats, and best of all, just the way it is, cooled and eaten out of hand.

But mangoes manage to find their way into Indian meals through the entire year, even when the fruit is not in season, in the form of dried powders and dried slices, pickles, preserves, and chutneys, all of which are made with green mangoes. These traditions seem to be almost as old as India itself.

Amchoor is the name for dried green mango, which is used as a seasoning. It can come in the form of a powder or in the form of slices. *Amchoor* is sour with just a hint of sweetness and is used mostly to impart piquancy. In its ground version, it can be sprinkled over fried potatoes or fried cauliflower to add a bit of tartness without destroying the crispness. In its sliced version it may be added to okra pods or eggplants as they cook, giving the dish a sweet-and-sour quality. The sliced version may also be made into sweet chutneys.

It is this world of chutneys, pickles, and preserves that, in India at any rate, the green mango completely dominates. It is true that Indians make pickles and chutneys out of carrots, cauliflower, turnips, eggplants, bitter gourds, radishes, rose petals—even dumplings, herbs, and hundreds of other ingredients. A meal without some pickle or preserve would be unthinkable. But without doubt, it is the mango that dominates. Apart from its firm texture and exquisite flavor, the mango is rich in pectin, making it a natural for all manner of preserves.

Green mangoes come in many sizes. They can be as little as 2 inches long or as long as 8 inches. The weight too can vary considerably. So for all my recipes, I have suggested both the quantity of mangoes and the weight. Buy unblemished, rock-hard green mangoes. Many recipes for mango pickle require that the skin be used as well, so look for unspotted green skin. The ideal green mangoes have flesh with very little fiber, but that is hard to judge from the outside.

If the recipe requires that the mango be peeled, use a peeler or a sharp paring knife and peel it as you would an apple or pear. To cut the mango flesh into dice or strips, it is important to understand the basic anatomy of the fruit. Mangoes generally have a somewhat oval shape. Even if the mango itself is fairly rounded, the seed inside is oval with two flattish sides. It is best to start by cutting two slices from the top of the fruit to the bottom of the fruit, as close to the stone as possible, on both sides of the flat of the stone. You just have to gauge how fat the stone is. These are the big, wide slices. As some flesh will still remain, you will need to cut two more narrow slices along the sides of the oval. These four slices may now be cut as desired. If grated flesh is required, peel the mango but do not cut it. Now just grate the flesh off the stone. The amount of flesh on each mango will vary according to the size of the stone.

Many pickles require that you use part of the stone as well. The stone has two sections: the hard, hairy outer covering or wall and inside it a softer seed. The inside seed is never used in pickles but the outside covering is often left attached to the flesh. The skin, which is often also left attached, and the outer covering of the seed give the flesh something to hang onto as the pickle matures and softens.

How to cut a green mango: The stones of green mangoes have not had a chance to harden completely so you can actually cut right through them. Take a sharp knife, bear down hard, and cut right through the center of the mango, going from top to bottom, imagining that the flat sides of the stones—and of the mango itself —are on either side of the knife. You will find that you have cut through the seed as well. Just discard the inner seed halves and proceed to cut the mango, with the stone wall included, as the recipe suggests.

All mango pickles in India mature in the sun. Crocks and jars are placed on racks outdoors where the summer sun does its work. Even after they have matured, they are given an occasional "sunning" to keep them free of any undesirable mold. Since the sun is not always as obliging in the West, I just keep my pickles in a sunny window until they mature and then transfer them to the refrigerator.

Mango Chutney

Aam Ki Chutney

This is a basic mango chutney that can be made very easily. Just remember that the chutney thickens considerably as it cools so remove it from the heat while the chutney is still more watery than you would like.

The sourness of mangoes varies so add more sugar or salt as needed.

You can make this chutney as hot as you like. Taste it toward the end of the cooking time and add more cayenne if you so desire. Mine is of medium heat.

In India, the mangoes are salted and left in the sun for 3 to 4 days to draw out the water. If you have access to the summer sun, by all means use this method. If not, follow the one given below.

3 small or 2 large sour green mangoes (about 1 pound)

2 to 2½ teaspoons salt

2 to 4 garlic cloves, peeled

1-inch piece of fresh ginger, peeled and coarsely chopped

1½ cups cider vinegar or distilled white vinegar

2 cups plus 2 tablespoons sugar

¼ cup golden raisins

½ teaspoon ground turmeric

1 teaspoon cayenne

Peel the mangoes and cut them into slices (page 694). Now cut the slices into ¾-inch dice. Put in a stainless steel or nonmetallic bowl. Sprinkle with 1 teaspoon of the salt, toss to mix, and set aside for 24 hours. Drain and pat dry, then spread out on paper towels.

Put the garlic and ginger into a food processor or blender. Add just enough of the vinegar to puree to a fine paste.

In a stainless steel or porcelain-lined pan, combine the remaining vinegar, the sugar, raisins, turmeric, cayenne, 1 teaspoon salt, and the ginger-garlic paste. Stir and bring to a simmer. Simmer, uncovered, on medium heat for 15 minutes, or until very slightly thickened. Add the mango pieces and bring the chutney to a simmer again, stirring as you do so. Simmer gently, uncovered, for 20 to 30 minutes, or until the mango pieces look translucent and the chutney has thickened some more. Check for salt and add more if needed. Put into a clean glass or ceramic jar while still hot and allow to cool. Cover tightly with a noncorrosive lid. Keep refrigerated. The chutney may be eaten as soon as it is made, though it mellows as it sits.

MAKES ENOUGH TO FILL A 3½-CUP JAR

(recipe continues)

Variation I

Mango Chutney with Fennel and Fenugreek

Aam Ki Lonji

Follow the master recipe for Mango Chutney (page 695). Make the garlic-ginger paste. Then heat 2 tablespoons peanut oil in a stainless steel or porcelain-lined pan over a medium-high flame. When hot, put in 1 teaspoon whole fennel seeds, ½ teaspoon whole brown mustard seeds, ½ teaspoon cumin seeds, ¼ teaspoon *kalonji* (nigella) seeds, and ¼ teaspoon fenugreek seeds. Stir once and quickly pour in the garlic-ginger paste. Also add the remaining vinegar, the sugar, raisins, turmeric, cayenne, and 1 teaspoon salt. Stir and bring to a simmer. Proceed with the recipe as above.

Variation II

Royal Mango Chutney

Shahi Aam Ki Chutney

Follow the master recipe for Mango Chutney (page 695). Make a ginger paste, leaving out the garlic.

In a stainless steel or porcelain-lined pan, combine the remaining vinegar, the sugar, raisins, turmeric, cayenne, 1 teaspoon salt, the ginger paste, 1 teaspoon whole fennel seeds, 2 tablespoons chopped seedless dates, 2 tablespoons chopped figs, ¼ teaspoon ground cardamom, and a generous pinch of saffron threads. Stir and bring to a simmer. Proceed with the recipe as above.

Simple South Indian Mango Pickle   INDIA

Saada Daxshini Aam Ka Achaar

This is one of the quick pickles that may be eaten within 48 hours of making it, though it continues to mellow with time.

1 large sour green mango (about ½ pound)

1½ teaspoons salt

1 teaspoon cayenne

¼ teaspoon ground turmeric

1 tablespoon peanut or corn oil

Pinch of ground asafetida

¼ teaspoon *urad dal* (use *chana dal* or yellow split peas as a substitute)

½ teaspoon whole brown mustard seeds

6 fresh curry leaves (use basil or holy basil leaves as a substitute)

Scrub the mango under running water and then dry it off thoroughly. Cut the mango into slices (page 694) without peeling it. Now cut the slices into ¼-inch dice. Put in a stainless steel or nonmetallic bowl. Sprinkle with the salt, cayenne, and turmeric, toss to mix, cover, and set aside for 24 hours.

Next day, put the oil in a small frying pan and set over medium-high heat. When hot, put in the asafetida. A second later, put in the *urad dal*. Stir it until it turns red (this does not take long). Now put in the mustard seeds. As soon as the mustard seeds begin to pop, a matter of seconds, put in the curry leaves. Five seconds later, take the pan off the heat and pour its contents over the mango.

Transfer the pickle to a clean, widemouthed 8-ounce ceramic or glass jar with a noncorrosive lid. Close tightly and store on a sunny windowsill (or, in the summer, out of doors in the sun, remembering to bring the jar inside in the evenings) or in a warm spot in your home. Shake the jar at least once a day. It may be eaten after 48 hours if you like, or leave it for 10 to 15 days, allowing the skin to soften a bit. You may refrigerate it now.

MAKES A SCANT CUP

Mango and Ginger Chutney
Aam Aur Adrak Ki Chutney

My grandmother always had monstrous crocks of this chutney in our storeroom. It was eaten with savory biscuits made of short crust pastry (mutthries) *at teatime and was on the table at lunch and dinner. Like most chutneys, this one thickens considerably as it cools so stop the cooking while the chutney is still more watery than you would like. Taste it toward the end of the cooking time and add more salt, sugar, and cayenne as needed.*

3 small or 2 large sour green mangoes (about 1 pound)

2 to 2½ teaspoons salt

¼ pound fresh ginger (7 to 8 inches), peeled and cut crosswise into very thin round slices, the slices then stacked a few at a time and cut into fine slivers

3 garlic cloves, peeled and finely crushed

1½ cups cider vinegar or distilled white vinegar

2 cups plus 2 tablespoons sugar

½ teaspoon ground turmeric

1 teaspoon cayenne

(recipe continues)

Peel the mangoes and grate them coarsely (page 316). Put in a stainless steel or enameled saucepan and add the salt, ginger, garlic, vinegar, sugar, turmeric, and cayenne. Stir and bring to a simmer, then cook, uncovered, on medium heat for 15 minutes, or until very slightly thickened. Lower the heat and simmer very gently, uncovered, for 30 to 40 minutes, or until the chutney has thickened some more. Check for salt and add more if needed. Put into a clean glass or ceramic jar and allow to cool. Cover tightly with a noncorrosive lid. Keep refrigerated. The chutney may be eaten as soon as it is made, though it mellows as it sits.

MAKES ENOUGH TO FILL A 3¹/₂-CUP JAR

Variation
Mango and Ginger Chutney with Bengali Five Spices

Bengali Chutney

Assemble all the ingredients for the chutney in a stainless steel or enameled saucepan as in the previous recipe.

Put 1 tablespoon peanut or corn oil in a small frying pan and set over medium-high heat. When hot, put in 1 teaspoon of *panchphoran* (page 731). The spices should sizzle or pop within seconds. Now empty this mixture, oil and spices, into the pan with the mangoes. Stir to mix and proceed to cook the chutney as above.

Rajasthani Mango Pickle with Fennel Seeds INDIA

A sour, spicy pickle that is easy and quick to prepare, this version may be served with all Indian, Middle Eastern, and North African meals. You may also chop it up and put a thin layer on sandwiches or in pita bread pockets that are filled with spiced chickpeas or spiced potatoes.

 If you cannot get hulled and split mustard seeds, use whole yellow mustard seeds instead. For detailed notes on cutting green mangoes, see page 694.

2 large sour green mangoes (about 1 pound)

2 teaspoons whole fennel seeds

1 teaspoon whole fenugreek seeds

1 tablespoon hulled and split mustard seeds
 (mustard seed *dal*)

4¹/₂ teaspoons salt

1 teaspoon ground turmeric

Generous pinch of ground asafetida

1 to 1¹/₂ teaspoons cayenne

5 tablespoons mustard oil (use peanut, corn,
 or olive oil as a substitute)

Wash the mangoes and then dry them off thoroughly. Take a sharp knife, bear down hard, and split the mango lengthwise, imagining that the flat sides of the stone are on either side of the knife. You will find that you have cut through the inner seed as well. Discard the inner seed halves and proceed to cut the mango, the stone wall and skin included, into ¼-inch dice. Place in a stainless steel or non-metallic bowl.

Set a small, cast-iron frying pan over medium heat. When hot, put in the fennel and fenugreek seeds. Stir and roast the seeds until the fennel is a shade darker and emits a toasted aroma. Cool off the seeds slightly and put into the container of a clean coffee grinder or other spice grinder along with the mustard seeds. Grind coarsely. Empty over the mangoes. Add the salt, turmeric, asafetida, cayenne, and the oil. Toss all to mix.

Transfer the pickle to a clean, 2½-cup widemouthed ceramic or glass jar with a noncorrosive lid. Close tightly and store for 10 to 15 days on a sunny windowsill (or, in the summer, out of doors in the sun, remembering to bring the jar inside in the evenings) or in a warm spot in your home. Shake the jar at least once a day. When the skin softens a bit, the pickle is ready to eat and may now be refrigerated.

MAKES ENOUGH TO FILL A 2½-CUP JAR

Bombay-Style Green Mango Pickle INDIA
Bumbai Vala Aam Ka Achaar

In the Bombay region the poor sometimes have this pickle just with rice, and, if they are fortunate, with a dried bean dish as well; the rich, they eat it with everything!
If you cannot get hulled and split mustard seeds, use whole yellow mustard seeds instead. For detailed notes on cutting green mangoes, see page 694.

1 large sour green mango (about ½ pound)

10 small whole fresh green chiles

20 tender green beans

4 teaspoons plus 1 tablespoon salt

4 tablespoons whole coriander seeds

1 teaspoon whole fenugreek seeds

7 tablespoons hulled and split mustard seeds (mustard seed *dal*)

1½ teaspoons ground turmeric

1 tablespoon cayenne

1 cup peanut, corn, or olive oil

Wash the mango and then dry it off thoroughly. Take a sharp knife, bear down hard, and split the mango lengthwise, imagining that the flat sides of the stone are

(recipe continues)

on either side of the knife. You will find that you have cut through the inner seed as well. Discard the seed halves and proceed to cut the mango, the stone wall and skin included, into ¾-inch dice. Put into a stainless steel or nonmetallic bowl. Wipe the chiles with a damp cloth, dry them off, and add to the mango. Wipe the green beans with a damp cloth and dry them off as well. Cut each bean in half lengthwise and then into thirds. Add the beans to the mango. Sprinkle 4 teaspoons salt over the ingredients in the bowl, toss, and set aside for 24 hours. Drain and pat dry.

Set a small cast-iron frying pan over medium heat. When hot, put in the coriander and fenugreek seeds. Stir and roast the seeds very lightly until the coriander is just a shade darker and emits a toasted aroma. Cool the seeds slightly and put them into the container of a clean coffee grinder or other spice grinder along with the mustard seeds. Grind coarsely, then empty over the mangoes. Add the remaining 1 tablespoon salt, turmeric, and cayenne. Toss all to mix.

Heat the oil in the frying pan until it is very hot, then turn off the heat and let it cool to lukewarm. Add to the mango mixture and toss again.

Transfer the pickle to a clean, 1-quart widemouthed ceramic or glass jar with a noncorrosive lid. Close tightly and store for 15 to 20 days on a sunny windowsill (or, in the summer, out of doors in the sun, remembering to bring the jar inside in the evenings) or in a warm spot in your home. Shake the jar at least once a day. When the mango skin softens a bit, the pickle is ready to eat. You may refrigerate it now.

MAKES ENOUGH TO FILL A QUART JAR

Delhi-Style Peach Chutney INDIA

This is a family recipe. My mother always made it with unripe green mangoes, but I find that peaches, when they are in season, are perfect for this chutney and much more readily available. The fruit can be of any size, but make sure they are ripe, yet quite firm. The chutney should be stored in the refrigerator, where it will last for a week. Serve with all Indian meals.

½ teaspoon whole fenugreek seeds

2 pounds peaches

3 tablespoons fresh lemon juice

3 tablespoons mustard oil or peanut oil

1 teaspoon whole cumin seeds

½ teaspoon whole brown mustard seeds

¼ teaspoon whole fennel seeds

2-inch piece of fresh ginger, peeled and cut into very fine slices, the slices stacked and cut into very fine slivers

¼ teaspoon ground turmeric

5 tablespoons sugar

1 teaspoon salt

¼ teaspoon cayenne

1 to 3 whole fresh green chiles (optional)

Put the fenugreek seeds in a small cup and cover with 2 tablespoons of boiling water. Set aside for 4 hours or overnight.

Peel the peaches and cut each into 8 slices, removing the pit. Cut each slice crosswise into 2 pieces. As you cut the peaches, sprinkle with the lemon juice and toss.

Heat the oil in a medium, heavy-bottomed pan over a medium flame. When hot, put in the cumin and mustard seeds. As soon as the mustard seeds pop, a matter of seconds, put in the fennel seeds. Stir once and quickly put in the ginger. Stir and fry for 1 minute. Quickly add the soaked fenugreek seeds and their soaking liquid. Add 1 cup of water and the turmeric. Stir and bring to a simmer. Cover, lower the heat, and simmer gently for 15 minutes.

Uncover the pan and add the peaches as well as any juice that may have accumulated in the bowl. Add the sugar, salt, cayenne, and the whole green chiles, if you wish. Simmer vigorously, uncovered, on medium heat, for about 20 minutes, or until the peaches are soft and satiny and the sauce has thickened. Stir frequently, especially toward the end of the cooking time.

Once the chutney has cooled, it may be put in jars and refrigerated.

MAKES 18 OUNCES

Sweet Tomato Preserve with Almonds

MOROCCO

Known as tomates sucrées, *this is really a sweet chutney or jam made with tomatoes, sugar, and roasted almonds. It may be served with any meal.*

3 cups peeled fresh or canned peeled
   tomatoes, coarsely chopped
6 tablespoons sugar

¾ teaspoon salt
6 tablespoons slivered almonds

Combine the tomatoes, sugar, and salt in a medium pot and bring to a boil over medium-high heat. Turn the heat to medium and cook for about 45 minutes, stirring now and then, until the tomatoes look jamlike.

Put the almonds in a small cast-iron pan and set over medium heat to roast lightly, stirring frequently. The almonds will be done when they turn a couple of shades darker and emit a strong fragrance. Empty onto a paper towel and let cool. Coarsely chop the almonds into ¼-inch pieces and stir into the tomato mixture. Cool and store in a glass jar with a noncorrosive lid.

MAKES ABOUT 1 CUP

Neeru Row Kavi's

Mixed Sour Pickles Indian Style

INDIA

This is the Indian version of the sour cucumber pickles found in all Jewish delicatessens; only the pungency of the ground mustard seeds makes them somewhat different. In India, we like to drink the liquid from the pickle as well. Almost anything can be pickled this way, from turnips and watermelon rind to carrots. Indians tend to use the tiny cucumber-like vegetable called a tindli *or a* tindora *rather than cucumbers. If you can find them, cut them in half lengthwise first. The pickling process takes 4 to 7 days, depending upon the weather. Once the pickle has soured to your taste, it may be refrigerated. Serve with all Indian, Middle Eastern, and North African meals and on the side with sandwiches and soups.*

2½ teaspoons salt

¼ pound cauliflower, cut into delicate florets

¼ pound small pickling cucumbers, quartered
    lengthwise and cut into 2-inch-long pieces

1 medium carrot, peeled and cut into
    2 × ½-inch sticks

2½ tablespoons whole brown mustard seeds

1½ teaspoons cayenne

¼ teaspoon ground asafetida

2 tablespoons fresh lime juice

Bring 3 cups of water to a boil in a large pan. Add the salt. Drop the cauliflower, cucumbers, and carrot into the pan and bring to a boil again. Drain immediately, saving the cooking liquid. Spread the vegetables out on a clean platter and let them and the cooking liquid cool.

Put the mustard seeds in a clean spice grinder and grind coarsely.

In a large, clean, 8-cup widemouthed ceramic or glass jar with a noncorrosive lid, combine the vegetables, reserved cooking liquid, ground mustard seeds, cayenne, asafetida, and lime juice and mix well. Seal tightly and set aside on a sunny windowsill for 4 to 7 days. When the pickles have soured to your taste, they may be refrigerated and kept several months.

MAKES ENOUGH TO FILL A 2-QUART JAR

Punjabi-Style Sweet-and-Sour Mixed Vegetable Pickle

A sweet-and-sour pickle that can be served with all meals. The vegetables can be removed from their liquid, chopped up, and put into sandwiches as well. You should have approximately 2 pounds of vegetables in all.

1 carrot, peeled and cut into 2 × ¼-inch sticks

1 to 2 turnips, peeled and cut into ¾-inch dice

About ½ head cauliflower, cut into delicate florets

1 cup mustard oil

1 cup brown sugar, packed

⅔ cup distilled white vinegar

6 tablespoons whole brown or yellow mustard seeds

2 tablespoons well-crushed peeled garlic

2½ tablespoons finely grated ginger

2 teaspoons cayenne

3 tablespoons salt

Bring a large pan of water to a boil. Drop the carrot, turnips, and cauliflower into the water and bring to a boil again. Drain immediately. Spread the vegetables out on a clean platter and let them cool. Set aside.

In a separate pan, heat the mustard oil until it begins to smoke. Remove it from the heat and let it cool completely.

Meanwhile, dissolve the brown sugar in the vinegar. Grind the mustard seeds to a fine powder in a clean spice grinder.

In a large ceramic or stainless steel bowl, combine the garlic, ginger, cayenne, salt, ground mustard seeds, and sugar mixture. Add the vegetables and toss to coat completely. Transfer to a 1½-quart widemouthed ceramic or glass jar with a non-corrosive lid. Pour in the mustard oil. Seal the top tightly and shake to distribute the oil. Leave for 10 to 15 days on a sunny windowsill (or out of doors in the sun, remembering to bring it inside in the evenings). Shake the jar at least once a day. Once the pickle has matured, it may be refrigerated. It will keep for several months.

MAKES ENOUGH TO FILL A 1½-QUART JAR

Spice Mixtures

Sesame Salt

Goma Shio

This wonderful seasoning may be sprinkled over salads, bean curd, lightly cooked vegetables, rice, and even some fruit (try it with sour apples!). It's especially attractive made with black sesame seeds.

1 tablespoon coarse sea salt or kosher salt

7 tablespoons black sesame seeds (use the beige seeds if you cannot find the black)

Put the salt in a small cast-iron or other heavy frying pan over medium heat. Stir the salt around until it is very hot. Add the sesame seeds and continue to stir and roast until the sesame seeds are a few shades darker and emit a toasted aroma; some seeds will actually start to pop out of the pan. Empty the contents of the frying pan onto a plate and cool slightly. Now put this mixture into a clean coffee grinder or other spice grinder and grind for a second to get a coarse mix. Cool completely and store in a clean jar with a tight lid.

MAKES ABOUT ½ CUP

Roasted Sichuan Pepper and Salt

Hu Jiao Yen

Sprinkle this aromatic Chinese mixture over all manner of vegetables, nuts, and even bean curd.

3 tablespoons kosher or coarse sea salt

1 tablespoon Sichuan peppercorns

Put the salt and Sichuan peppercorns in a small cast-iron frying pan over medium-low heat. Stir and roast for about 5 minutes, or until the salt turns darker and the peppercorns give off a pronounced aroma. Empty the ingredients onto a clean paper towel and allow to cool somewhat, then transfer to a clean coffee grinder and grind finely. Store in a tightly closed jar away from sunlight.

MAKES ABOUT ¼ CUP

Zahtar

This nutty and sour blend of seasonings is used in Turkey, Syria, and other regions of the Middle East and Eastern Mediterranean. Roll yogurt cheeses in it, use it to season plain yogurt and potato salads, and even sprinkle it on a slice of bread lathered with yogurt cheese (pages 556 to 560) or plain cream cheese.

2 tablespoons roasted sesame seeds, cooled (page 734)

2 tablespoons dried thyme

1 tablespoon ground sumac

Combine all the ingredients and store in a tightly closed jar in a cool spot. This mixture may also be frozen.

MAKES 6 TABLESPOONS

An Indian Salt Mixture

Here is a very pleasing salt mixture to have on the table.

1 teaspoon whole cumin seeds

1 teaspoon whole coriander seeds

1 teaspoon whole black peppercorns

1 tablespoon kosher salt

Put the cumin, coriander, and peppercorns in a small cast-iron frying pan over medium-high heat. Stir and roast for 2 to 3 minutes, or until the cumin seeds turn a shade darker. Turn off the heat and cool off. Grind the seeds finely in a clean coffee grinder or spice grinder. Add the salt and mix. Store in a tightly lidded jar.

MAKES ABOUT 2 TABLESPOONS

Sesame Seed Seasoning

This is wonderful sprinkled over Japanese and Chinese soups and noodle dishes. Regular, beige-colored sesame seeds are fine here.

1 tablespoon sesame seeds

1 tablespoon Sichuan peppercorns

1 small dried hot red chile

¼ teaspoon coarse sea salt

(recipe continues)

Set a small cast-iron pan on medium heat and allow it to get hot. Put in the sesame seeds, Sichuan peppercorns, and chile. Stir these around until the sesame seeds smell toasted and start to pop. Empty onto a piece of paper towel and allow to cool off. Transfer to a clean coffee grinder or other spice grinder, add the salt, and grind coarsely. Store in a clean, closed bottle.

MAKES ABOUT 2½ TABLESPOONS

Trinidadian Mixed Spices TRINIDAD
Amchar Masala

For an Indian from India, it is sometimes hard to understand the Trinidadian names of foods and spices that are of Indian origin. The names resonate of something familiar, yet time and distance have distorted them, though not, at least yet, beyond all recognition. Masala, of course, means "spices," but amchar *is curious. Achar is the word for "pickle," so these could originally have been pickling spices. Indeed, such spices are used for pickling in India. Aam is "mango," so this spice could origi-nally have been used for pickling mangoes and later, the words* aam *and* achar *got put together to become* amchar. *This, however, is just a guess. We may never know how this spice mixture got its name. Today, it is sprinkled on Indian-type dishes toward the end of the cooking period.*

¼ cup whole coriander seeds

1 tablespoon whole cumin seeds

2 teaspoons whole black peppercorns

1 teaspoon whole fennel seeds

1 teaspoon whole brown mustard seeds

1 teaspoon whole fenugreek seeds

Put all the spices in a small, cast-iron frying pan and set over medium heat. Stir and roast for 2 to 3 minutes, or until the spices turn a shade or two darker. Remove from the skillet, allow to cool, and then grind as finely as possible in a clean coffee grinder or other spice grinder. Store in an airtight jar in a dark cupboard.

MAKES ABOUT 8 TABLESPOONS

Shamsi Davis'
Persian Spice Mix IRAN

A very aromatic mixture, this requires highly perfumed dried roses. If you grow such roses yourself and have dried petals, you may use them, providing they have not been sprayed. If not, most Middle Eastern and North African stores sell them. If you cannot find the rose petals, make the mixture with the remaining ingredients.

3 (3-inch) cinnamon sticks, broken up

1 tablespoon cardamom seeds

1½ teaspoons whole cumin seeds

2 tablespoons dried rose petals

Combine all the ingredients in a clean coffee grinder and grind as finely as possible. Store in a tightly closed jar away from sunlight.

MAKES ABOUT 3 TABLESPOONS

Sri Lankan Raw Curry Powder   SRI LANKA

This curry powder is perfect for all vegetable curries, such as Green Bean and Potato Curry (page 208.)

2 tablespoons whole coriander seeds

1 tablespoon whole fennel seeds

1½ tablespoons whole cumin seeds

1 tablespoon whole fenugreek seeds

3 whole sprigs fresh curry leaves (about 60), if available (or a small handful of dried ones)

1 tablespoon desiccated coconut

1½ teaspoons raw rice

½ teaspoon whole brown mustard seeds

Preheat the oven to 150°F. or the lowest temperature setting.

Spread the seasonings out on a tray and put them into the oven for 1 hour. Cool. Transfer to a clean coffee grinder or other spice grinder and grind as finely as possible. Store in a tightly lidded jar away from heat and sunlight.

MAKES ½ CUP

My Curry Powder

Here is a very pleasant spice mix that could be called a basic curry powder and is perfect for vegetarian foods. Use it whenever curry powder is needed. Be careful not to overroast the spices. They need to roast just until they emit a light aroma and have barely turned a shade darker.

2 tablespoons whole coriander seeds

1 tablespoon whole cumin seeds

2 teaspoons whole peppercorns

1½ teaspoons whole brown mustard seeds

1 teaspoon whole fenugreek seeds

5 to 6 whole cloves

3 dried hot red chiles, crumbled

1½ teaspoons ground turmeric

(recipe continues)

Set a small cast-iron frying pan over medium heat. When it is hot, put in the coriander, cumin, peppercorns, mustard seeds, fenugreek seeds, cloves, and chiles. Stir until the spices emit a light, toasted aroma. A few of the spices will turn a shade darker. Add the turmeric and stir for 10 seconds, then empty the spices out onto a clean plate to cool. Transfer the spices to a clean coffee grinder or other spice grinder, in 2 batches if necessary, and grind as finely as possible. Store in a clean jar away from heat and sunlight.

MAKES 5 TO 6 TABLESPOONS

Sambar Powder

Here, split beans and peas are used as spices. Even though this mixture is used mainly to make the South Indian dish called sambar, *it may be added to bean soups and other beans dishes for a spicy, South Indian flavor. Stored in a tightly closed jar, this will last for several months.*

All the dals *(split peas and split beans) may be bought from an Indian grocer.*

1 teaspoon peanut or canola oil

5 tablespoons whole coriander seeds

1 teaspoon whole brown mustard seeds

1 teaspoon *moong dal*

½ tablespoon *chana dal*

½ tablespoon *urad dal*

1 teaspoon whole fenugreek seeds

1 teaspoon whole black peppercorns

¼ teaspoon ground asafetida

1 teaspoon whole cumin seeds

20 fresh curry leaves, if available

12 dried hot red chiles

Heat the oil in a large heavy frying pan or heavy wok over medium heat. Put in the coriander seeds, mustard seeds, *moong dal, chana dal, urad dal*, fenugreek seeds, black peppercorns, asafetida, and cumin seeds. Stir and roast for 3 to 4 minutes. Add the curry leaves and stir and roast for another 5 minutes. Add the dried chiles and continue stirring and roasting for 2 to 3 minutes or until the chiles darken. Empty out onto a plate to cool.

When the spices have cooled, put them into a coffee grinder or other spice grinder in small batches and grind as finely as possible. Store in a tightly closed jar.

MAKES ABOUT 1 CUP

Equipment, Glossary, and Resources

While no special equipment is absolutely essential for cooking the foods in this book, it is useful to have the following:

Wok This all-purpose utensil may be used for steaming, simmering, stir-frying, or deep-frying.

A wok is traditionally a round-bottomed pan. Because of its shape, flames can encircle it and allow it to heat quickly and efficiently. It is most economical for deep-frying as it requires less oil to reach a good depth than a straight-sided pan would. It is ideal for stir-frying, as foods can be vigorously tossed around in it. As they hit nothing but well-heated surfaces, they cook fast and retain their moisture at the same time.

Choosing a wok: What kind of wok should you buy? A traditional Indian wok *(karhai)* is generally made out of cast iron and a Chinese one of carbon steel but any wok will do. Every year seems to bring new woks to the marketplace, including nonstick models. The ideal wok is wide and fairly deep. (Saucer-shaped shallow woks are quite useless.) A round-bottomed wok set on a ring or inverted burner grid works well on a gas burner. A new, somewhat flat-bottomed wok has been invented for people who have electric burners.

Seasoning a wok: Most woks leave the factory coated with oil, which needs to be scrubbed off with a cream cleanser. The wok should then be seasoned. Rinse it in water and set it over low heat. Now brush it all over with about 2 tablespoons of vegetable oil. Let it heat for 10 to 15 minutes. Wipe the oil off with a paper towel. Brush the wok with more oil and repeat the process 3 to 4 times. The wok is now seasoned. Do not scrub it again; just wash it with hot water and then wipe it dry. It will *not* have a scrubbed look. It will, however, become more and more nonstick as it is used.

Wok accessories: For use on a gas burner, a wok needs a stand that not only stabilizes it but allows air to circulate underneath. The perfect stand is made of wire. The collar variety with punched holes seems to kill free circulation of air heat and should not be used on gas burners.

When you buy a wok, it is also a good idea to invest in a curved spatula, a steaming tray, and a lid.

Cast-Iron Frying Pans I find a 5-inch cast-iron frying pan ideal for roasting spices and a large one perfect for pan grilling. All cast-iron frying pans can be heated without any liquid and they retain an even temperature. Once seasoned, they should never be scrubbed with abrasive cleaners.

Nonstick Sauté Pans and Frying Pans I love heavy-duty nonstick pans. They are perfect for browning potatoes, for cooking sweet potatoes, and for browning ginger paste (which can stick). You can make pancakes without a worry in the frying pans as well as all manner of eggs.

Large Pan for Making Noodles and Pasta This pan can also double for making stocks.

Heavy Pan with a Good Lid for Making Rice The size of this pan can depend upon the number of people you like to feed. Be sure it has a tight-fitting lid.

Blender, Coffee Grinder, Mortar and Pestle, and Food Processor In ancient times, pestles and grinding stones of varying shapes, sizes, and materials were used to pulverize everything from garlic to dried hot red chiles. I find it much easier to use an electric blender for wet ingredients and a clean electric coffee grinder for dry ones. For small quantities, you might still want to use a heavy mortar and pestle. I also find that a food processor, while excellent for grating and chopping and even making some pastes and doughs, does not always do an adequate job of making fine purees and blending soups. Blenders seem better at that.

Ginger Grater The Japanese make a special grater for ginger and Japanese horseradish that produces a fine pulp. It has tiny hairlike spikes that are perfect for this purpose. Otherwise use the finest part of an ordinary grater for grating fresh ginger.

Double Boiler This is simply one pan balanced over another. The lower pan holds simmering water and allows the ingredients in the other pan to cook very gently. Double boilers are available from good kitchenware shops, but they can be easily improvised.

Electric Rice Cooker Its main use is to free all burners for other purposes and make the cooking of rice an easy, almost mindless task. I do have one and use it for plain rice.

Deep-Fat Fryer For those who are afraid of deep-frying, this is a godsend. Because it has a lid that closes over all splattering foods, this piece of equipment also helps to make deep-frying a painless, safe, and clean task.

Peelers I cannot live without good sharp peelers. I always peel my asparagus and if a peeler makes a good job of that, it has my vote.

Knives Of course you need good, sharp knives. They are expensive. If you were to invest in just three, get a good bread knife (this will also slice through tomatoes), a good paring knife, and a large chef's knife.

Glossary

For information on vegetables, dried beans, legumes and split peas, grains, and dairy products, look in the chapters with those titles. You will find detailed information there, generally in alphabetical order. A few details on special vegetables used very rarely in this book may be found here.

Ajwain (or *Ajowan*). These small seeds look like celery seeds but taste more like a pungent version of thyme. (A student of mine compared it to a mixture of anise and black pepper!) In India, they are sprinkled sparingly over breads, savory biscuits, and numerous noodlelike snacks made with chickpea flour. Being rich in thymol—as thyme is—they add a thymelike taste to vegetables like green beans and potatoes. They are fairly strong so should be used sparingly.

Aleppo Pepper. See Chile powders.

Amchar Masala. See page 706 for the recipe and details.

Amchoor (Green Mango Powder). Unripe green mangoes are peeled, sliced, and their sour flesh sun-dried and ground to make *amchoor* powder. (The dried slices are also used in Indian cookery.) The beige, slightly fibrous powder, rich in vitamin C, is tart but with a hint of sweetness and is used as lemon juice might be. As the powder can get lumpy, crumble it well before use. If you cannot get *amchoor*, substitute ½ teaspoon of lemon juice for every teaspoon of *amchoor* powder.

Anardana. These dried sour seeds of red pomegranates are used in North Indian cookery, especially as stuffing for *parathas* and in some spice mixtures.

Asafetida. The sap from the roots and stem of a giant fennel-like plant, which is allowed to dry into a hard resin, it is sold in both lump and ground forms. Only the ground form is used here. It has a strong fetid aroma and is used in very small quantities both for its legendary digestive properties and for the much gentler, garliclike aroma it leaves behind after cooking. (James Beard compared it to the smell of truffles.) It is excellent with dried beans and vegetables. Store in a tightly closed container.

Ata. See Chapati flour.

Bamboo Shoots. Unfortunately, we cannot easily get fresh bamboo shoots in the West and must make do with canned ones. A good can should have bamboo shoots that are crisp, creamy white with a clean refreshing taste. (Among the better brands is Companion; their winter bamboo shoots in water are generally of excellent quality, as are those labeled Green Bamboo Shoots.) You can buy bamboo shoots in rather large hunks, which can then be cut up into cubes of the desired

711

size, or you can buy the cone-shaped very tender bamboo shoot tips, which are usually cut into comblike wedges. All bamboo shoots that come out of a can have a faint tinny taste and should be washed in fresh water and drained before use. Any bamboo shoots that are unused may be covered with clean water and stored in a closed jar in the refrigerator for 3 to 4 days; the water should be changed every day.

Basil. I have used two types of basil in this book, regular European basil and holy basil, *ocinum sanctum* (*bai kaprow* in Thailand). Ordinary basil and fresh mint are the best substitutes for the very aromatic Southeast Asian basils. Sometimes I have also suggested basil leaves as a substitute for curry leaves, but remember that their aromas and textures are totally different.

Bean Curd. See pages 92 to 93 for different types and other details.

Bean Curd, Fermented. Sold in bottles by Chinese grocers, this consists of small, salty cubes of bean curd that have been allowed to ferment and turn cheeselike (the best comparison would be to a very ripe Brie). These can be plain or seasoned with hot chiles and other spices. Generally, the cubes are mashed and then added as a flavoring to vegetables, such as spinach, in Chinese cookery. In Thailand the mashed cubes are combined with lime juice and made into sauces.

Bean Sauce, Black. Commercially prepared sauces made out of fermented soybeans are used throughout Malaysia and other parts of East and Southeast Asia. They can be very thick, filled with crumbled beans, or they can be smooth and somewhat thinner. Use any black bean sauce that is available. Once you have opened a bottle you should keep it tightly closed in the refrigerator.

Bean Sauce with Chili or Black Bean Sauce with Chile, Chinese. Sometimes called bean paste with chile, this reddish-brown paste is sold in bottles at Chinese grocers. It is quite hot and goes into spicy Sichuan and Hunan dishes.

Bean Sauce, Yellow. Like the sauce above, this is a commercially prepared sauce of fermented soybeans, only it has a very pale brown, almost yellowish color. It can be smooth but I like to use the kind that has whole or halved beans in it.

Bean Sprouts, Mung. These sprouts are crisp, grown from the same mung beans that are sold in Indian stores as whole *moong*. They can now be bought in supermarkets and health food stores as well as all Eastern groceries. Choose sprouts that are crisp and white. As they are usually kept in water, they tend to get soggier and soggier as they get older. When you buy bean sprouts and bring them home you should rinse them off first and then put them into a bowl of fresh water. The bowl should be covered and then refrigerated. If the beans are not used by the next day, you should change the water again.

It is considered proper to top and tail bean sprouts before using them. This means pinching off the remains of the whole bean at the top as well as the thread-like tail at the bottom. This requires a lot of patience. The sprouts do indeed look better when they have been pinched this way but I have to admit that I very rarely do it. Bean sprouts are also sold in tins. I never use them as they do not have the crunch that makes the sprouts worthwhile in the first place.

For details on making your own sprouts, see page 74.

Beans and Peas, Dried. See the chapter on dried beans, dried peas, lentils, and nuts for details. In India a few of the split peas are also used as spices. Here is a quick glance at them:

Chana dal: The Indian version of yellow split peas but with better texture and very nutty flavor. In the South, it is ground and used as a spice.

Urad dal: A small, pale yellow split pea that is also used as a seasoning. It is South Indians who seem to have discovered that if you throw a few of these dried split peas into hot oil, using the *tarka* method (page 7), the seeds will turn red and nutty. Anything stir-fried in the oil afterward will pick up that nutty flavor and aroma.

Black Beans, Fermented (or Salted). These are salted, spiced, and fermented soybeans. In their dry form they are sold in plastic bags or jars. To temper their aggressively salty flavor they need to be rinsed slightly to remove excess salt and then chopped before being used. They are also available in cans as Black Beans in Salted Sauce. These are whole black beans that tend to float in liquid. Lift them out of their liquid, chop them, and use them as the recipe suggests.

Black Fungus. See Fungus, black, tree ear.

Black Pepper. Native to India, whole peppercorns are added to rice and meat dishes for a mild peppery-lemony flavor. Ground pepper was once used in large amounts, sometimes several tablespoons in a single dish, especially in South India, where it grows. The arrival of chiles from the New World around 1498 changed that usage somewhat, though it still exists. In some South Indian dishes pepper-corns are lightly roasted before use to draw out their lemony taste.

Cardamom Pods and Seeds. Small green pods, the fruit of a gingerlike plant, hold clusters of black, highly aromatic seeds that smell like a combination of camphor, eucalyptus, orange peel, and lemon. Whole pods are put into rice dishes and ground seeds are the main flavor in garam masala (page 723). This versatile spice is the vanilla of India and used in most desserts and sweetmeats. It is also added to spiced tea and sucked as a mouth freshener. Cardamom seeds that have been taken out of their pods are sold separately by Indian grocers. If you cannot get them, buy the whole pods and take the seeds out yourself. The most aromatic pods are green in color. The white ones have been bleached and have less flavor.

Cardamom Seeds, Ground. The seeds of the cardamom pods are sold by themselves in both their whole and ground forms. This powder can be used in rice dishes and desserts.

Cashew Nuts. These nuts traveled from the Americas via Africa and India all the way to China. All so-called raw cashews have been processed to remove the prussic acid in their outer shells, which they contain in their natural state. They are grown widely on India's west coast and are used in pilafs, desserts, and even made into *bhajis* and curries. They are an important part of the Indian vegetarian diet.

Cassia Bark. This is Chinese cinnamon. Sometimes known as "false cinnamon," it is thicker, coarser, and generally cheaper than true cinnamon but with a stronger flavor.

Cayenne. This hot powder is made today by grinding the dried red skins of several types of chiles. It should simply be called chile powder. But since that name can be confused with the Mexican-style chile powder that also contains cumin, garlic, and oregano, the name "cayenne" hangs on. Even though chiles came from the New World, India today is the largest producer and one of the largest exporters *and* consumers. When adding the powder to recipes, use your discretion.

Celery, Chinese. Rather like our celery in taste, this has much thinner stalks and larger, darker leaves. It is sold only in East Asian markets.

Chapati Flour. Very finely ground whole wheat flour used to make chapatis, pooris, and other Indian breads and sometimes called *ata,* it is sold by all Indian grocers.

Charoli Nuts. A tiny nut that tastes a bit like hazelnuts, it is used in rich meat sauces and in sweets and stuffings in India.

Chayote (Sayote). A pale green vegetable of the New World shaped somewhat like a large, slightly flattened pear, it needs to be peeled first and then cut into sections. The seed, which has a slightly different texture from the rest of the vegetable, need not be removed; it is, for some people, their favorite part. The chayote must be cooked before being eaten. This generally takes no more than 20 minutes. Once cooked, the vegetable has the texture of a zucchini, except that it is firmer—and nicer.

Chiles, Whole Dried Hot Red. When I call for a whole dried chile, it is the cayenne-type of dried chile that I want. This is the most commonly used dry chile around the world. Chiles are often added to Indian food through the *tarka* method (page 7). A quick contact with very hot oil enhances and intensifies the flavor of their skins. It is that flavor that Indians want. Sichuan stir-fry dishes use chiles in a similar manner. Then, if actual chile heat is desired, the chiles are allowed to stew with the food being cooked. To remove seeds from dried chiles, break off the stem end and shake the seeds out. Rotating a chile between the fingers can help. Sometimes it is necessary to break the chile in order to get all the seeds out. Some dishes call for a crumbled chile. If so, you may remove the seeds as suggested above if you wish.

Mexicans traditionally intensify the flavor of their chiles by roasting them. Mexico is home to a vast number of chiles, often referred to as peppers, several of which have different names when they are sold fresh than in their dried form. Here are some of the dried ones I have used in this book:

Anchos: These are dried poblanos. They are long (about 4 inches) but fat at the top and can vary in heat. They require soaking or boiling in order to soften up. Once soft, they are peeled and either chopped or pureed. Look for pliable, dark red chiles with thick flesh; these will give the most pulp.

Chipotles: These are dried jalapeños, about 2½ inches in length. Because jalapeños have thick flesh, they are hard to dry in the sun, so they are dried artificially over a low fire that is more smoke than fire, causing them to pick up a lovely smoky aroma. Chipotle chiles are also sold in cans in adobo sauce, which basically tastes of a deliciously hot, slightly sweet smokiness.

Morita: I have referred to this chile from Pueblo but not used it as it was hard to find. Fat and dark red, it is of medium size and has a hot but sweetish flavor.

Chiles, Whole Fresh Green and Red. Chiles originated in the Americas and then traveled via Africa and India all the way to China and Korea. The East has adopted them with a passion. The fresh green chile used in much of Asian cooking is of the cayenne type, generally about 3 inches long and slender. Its heat can vary from mild to fiery. (Stupid bees, it seems, unthinkingly cross-pollinate different varieties that grow in proximity.) The only way to judge the heat is by tasting a tiny piece of skin from the middle section. (Keep some yogurt handy!) The top part of the chile with more seeds is always the hottest, the bottom tip, the mildest. The hot seeds of the chile are rarely removed in Asia but you may do so if you wish. To do this, split the chile in half lengthwise and then remove the seeds with the tip of a knife. Try not to touch the seeds. If you do, wash your hands very carefully before touching any part of your face. In the Mediterranean, a very mild, paler green chile is also very popular.

Red chiles are just ripe green chiles. However, their flavor is slightly different, though their intensity can be exactly the same.

Chiles are a very rich source of iron and vitamins A and C. To store fresh red or green chiles wrap them first in newspaper, then in plastic, and store in the refrigerator. They should last several weeks. Any that begin to soften and rot should be removed as they tend to infect the whole batch.

Other fresh chiles:

Bird's eye: Both red and green (called *prik-khi-nu* in Thailand), these are very hot. They are often thrown in whole or cut into thin rounds over curries, partly as a colorful garnish and partly for flavor.

Cachucha, also called ijo dulce: A highly aromatic, small, very squat, green chile used on the Hispanic Caribbean islands and in Colombia and Venezuela, it has no heat but does have an intense, tropical citrus aroma. The seeds are hard and tasteless and need to be removed. Chop up the flesh and add it to onions and garlic as you sauté them for use in stews and soups. Its aroma is addictive.

Habanero: Rather like the Scotch bonnet but with a little pointed tip, the habanero also comes in many pretty colors and is fiery. It is said to have originated in the Amazon area and then traveled north.

Jalapeño: Commonly used in Mexico and the United States, about 2½ inches long, this squattish chile has a thick skin and tends to be very hot. Use it with discretion.

Poblano: The fresh dark green version of the ancho, this is about 4 inches long and fairly wide at the top. It is nearly always roasted and peeled before it is used in cooking.

Scotch bonnet: These small (1- to 1½-inch) chiles seem as wide as they are long and have a squat, lanternlike shape. They come in orange, yellow, green, and red and are fiery. Generally, they are dropped into stews and soups whole and then removed so their main firepower stays inside. Some people dare to poke a tiny hole or two in them with a needle if they want the heat. These are the darlings of the Caribbean. They are also made into hot pepper sauces.

Serrano: Smaller and paler in color than the jalapeño but still very hot, these can be used when any fresh, hot, green chiles are called for.

Chile Powders. Powders made by grinding dried hot red chiles, not the Mexican-style chili powder that is mixed with cumin. Since people prefer different degrees of hotness, you should add as much or as little of the chile powder as you like. Be warned that chile powders vary in their heat. Cayenne is a chile powder. Others I use in this book include Korean coarse red pepper, made by pounding dried red chile skins. It is hot but not excruciatingly so and has an exquisite carmine color. I tend to stock up on it whenever I visit Korean supermarkets. They are the only ones who seem to sell it. It is this powder that gives many Korean foods their rich red color. There is also a very aromatic *Aleppo pepper* that I love. It is bright red, comes from Turkey and Syria, is very coarsely ground, and is sold by Middle Eastern grocers. Both the Aleppo pepper and Korean coarse red pepper should be stored in the refrigerator.

Chile Oil. This orange-colored oil gets its heat and color from red chiles. Small amounts can be added to dishes as they cook to add a bit of pep. Many Chinese restaurants have small bottles of chile oil on the table for those who wish to season their own foods further. Chile oil can be bought from any oriental grocer.

Chili Paste with Garlic. A reddish sauce made with sautéed red chiles, soybeans, and garlic and sold in jars by Chinese grocers, this is used mostly in West Chinese cooking but it may be used to heat up soups and salad dressings of any nationality.

Chili Paste with Soybean. A reddish-brown, very hot and spicy sauce made of soybeans, red chiles, and other seasonings. It is used in the cooking of Western China and is sold in bottles by oriental grocers.

Chili Paste with Soybean and Garlic. Similar to the two pastes above, this has more soybeans than the first and more garlic than the second.

Chili Sauce. This ready-made, sweet, sour, and hot sauce is sold bottled by Chinese grocers.

Chinese Mushrooms. See Mushrooms.

Chinese Shao Hsing Wine. See Shao Hsing wine, Chinese.

Chives, Chinese. The leaves of Chinese chives are flat and have a pronounced garliclike flavor. During the season in which the plant is budding, buds, still attached to their stalks, are sold as well. They add a wonderful touch to stir-fried dishes. Ordinary chives can be used as a substitute (use their young buds as well).

Cilantro, Fresh, Leaves, Roots, and Stem. This is the parsley of the eastern and southern half of Asia, also known as green coriander. Generally just the delicate, fragrant green leaves are used. In Thai curries, however, the equally fragrant white root is ground or chopped in as well; it should be very well washed first. Some recipes also call for the stems, which are generally cut crosswise into minute dice. The best way to store fresh cilantro is to stand it in a glass of water, cover it with a plastic bag, and refrigerate the whole thing. Break off the leaves, stems, and roots as you need them and keep the rest refrigerated. The water should be changed daily and the dead leaves removed.

Cinnamon. Used mainly for desserts in the West, cinnamon, often in its stick form, is added to many Indian rice dishes for its warm, sweet aroma. This inner bark from a laurel-like tree is also an important ingredient in the aromatic mixture garam masala (page 723). Cinnamon is an important ingredient in Moroccan cookery, where it can be used in lavish quantities.

Cloves. The West calls for cloves when making desserts. Indians rarely use cloves

717

in desserts but do use them in bean and rice dishes and in the spice mixture garam masala (page 723). Small quantities of cloves also go into a few Thai curry mixes and into North African and Middle Eastern foods.

Indians carry the pungently aromatic cloves as well as cardamom pods in tiny silver boxes to use as mouth fresheners when needed. For the same reason cloves are always part of the betel leaf paraphernalia that is offered as a digestive at the end of Indian meals. Indonesians use cloves to flavor their cigarettes! The whole nation smells of cloves, which are native to some of the islands.

Coconut, Fresh. When buying a coconut, look for one that shows no signs of mold and is free of cracks. Shake the coconut. If it has a lot of water in it, it has a better chance of being good. People generally weigh a coconut in each hand and pick the heavier of the two. In the West it is always safer to buy an extra coconut just in case one turns out to be bad.

To break open a coconut, use the blunt edge of a cleaver and hit the coconut hard all around its equator. You can hold the coconut in one hand over a large bowl while you hit with the other or you can rest the coconut on a stone while you hit it and then rush it to a bowl as soon as the first crack appears. The bowl is there to catch the coconut water, which some people like to drink. I do. This coconut water, by the way, is not used in cooking, but it is a good indication of the sweetness and freshness of the coconut.

You should now have two halves. Before proceeding any further, cut off a small bit of the meat and taste it. The dreaded word here is *rancid!* The coconut should taste sweet. If it is lacking in sweetness, it can be endured. But it must never be rancid or moldy inside. Now remove the tough outer shell by slipping a knife between it and the meat and then prizing the meat out. Sometimes it helps to crack the halves into smaller pieces to do this.

This meat now has a thin brown skin. If your recipe calls for fresh grated coconut, peel the skin off with a vegetable peeler or a knife, cut the meat into small cubes, and throw the cubes into a food processor or blender. When you blend you will not get a paste. What you will get is something resembling grated coconut. You can freeze what you don't use. Grated coconut freezes very well and it is a good idea to keep some on hand.

As a substitute for freshly grated coconut, you can use desiccated, unsweetened coconut, which is sold in most health food stores. It should, however, be rehydrated first. Here is how you do this: To get the equivalent of ½ cup of freshly grated coconut, take 5 tablespoons unsweetened desiccated coconut and soak it in 4 tablespoons of water for about an hour. Most of the water will be absorbed.

Coconut Milk. This is best made from fresh coconuts but is also available canned or can be made using powdered coconut milk, unsweetened desiccated coconut, or blocks of creamed coconut. No prepared coconut milk keeps well—this includes canned coconut milk once the can has been opened. Its refrigerated life is no longer than two days.

To use fresh coconut, first prize the flesh off the shell as suggested above. Whether you peel the brown skin or not depends on the dish. If it needs to look pale and pristine, remove the skin. If not, leave it on and grate the meat in a food processor or blender. (See above.) To make about 1½ cups of coconut milk, fill a glass measuring cup to the 2-cup mark with grated coconut. Empty it into a blender or food processor. Add 1¼ cups of very hot water and blend for a few seconds. Line a sieve with a piece of muslin or cheesecloth and place it over a bowl. Empty the contents of the blender into the sieve. Gather the ends of the cloth together and squeeze out all the liquid. For most of my recipes, this is the coconut milk that is needed. It is sometimes referred to as thick coconut milk. If a recipe calls for thin coconut milk, you must repeat the entire process using the squeezed-out coconut and the same amount of water. If you let the thick coconut milk sit for a while, cream will rise to the top. That is why I suggest that you always stir the coconut milk before using it. If just the cream is required, simply spoon it off the top.

Canned Coconut Milk: This is available at most Asian groceries, but the quality varies. I like the Chaokoh brand very much and use it frequently. A product of Thailand, it is white, creamy, and quite delicious. As the cream tends to rise to the top in a can as well, always stir it well before using it. Sometimes, because of the fat in it, canned coconut milk tends to get very grainy. You can either whir it for a second in a blender or else beat it well. I find that whereas you can cook foods in fresh coconut milk for a long time, canned coconut milk behaves differently and is best added toward the end. Canned coconut milk is very thick, partly because it has thickeners in it. As a result, many of my recipes require that canned coconut milk be thinned before use.

Powdered Coconut Milk: You can now buy packets of powdered coconut milk from oriental grocers and supermarkets. Their quality varies from good to poor, the poor ones containing hard-to-dissolve globules of fat. Emma brand from Malaysia is acceptable. Directions for making the milk are always on the packets, but the process usually involves mixing an equal volume of powder and hot water and stirring well. Unwanted lumps should be strained away. This milk is best added to recipes toward the end of the cooking time.

Coconut Milk from Unsweetened Desiccated Coconut: Put 2 cups of unsweetened desiccated coconut into a pan. Add 2½ cups of water and bring to a simmer. Now pour the contents into a blender or food processor and blend for a minute. Strain the resulting mixture through a double thickness of cheesecloth, pushing out as much liquid as you can. You should get about 1½ cups of thick coconut milk. If you repeat the process with the same amount of water using the leftover coconut, you can get another 2 cups of thin coconut milk.

Coconut Milk from Creamed Coconut: Available in block form, it can also be turned into coconut milk. I do not advise that you do this if you need large quantities of milk. However, if just a few tablespoons are required, you can, for example, take 2 tablespoons of creamed coconut and mix them with 2 tablespoons of hot water. The thick coconut milk that will result should be added to dishes only at the last moment.

Coriander Seeds, Whole and Ground. Native to the Middle East and southern Europe, these are the round, beige seeds of the coriander plant. They are sold either whole or ground. You can grind them yourself in a coffee grinder and then put them through a fine sieve. If roasted and ground coriander seeds are called for, put a few tablespoons of seeds in a small cast-iron frying pan over medium-high heat. Stir and roast for a few minutes, or until the seeds are a few shades darker and smell roasted. Then grind them in a clean coffee grinder or other spice grinder. If they are very coarse, put them through a fine sieve. What is not needed immediately may be stored in a tightly lidded jar and saved for later use.

Culantro. The narrow, serrated leaves of this green herb are used in the Caribbean, Central America, and parts of Southeast Asia. It is called *pak chee farang*, or "foreign green coriander" by the Thais, *recao* in Hispanic shops, *shadow beni* or *chadon bené* by the Trinidadians of mixed Mediterranean descent, and *band-hania*, or "green coriander of the woods" by Trinidadians of Indian descent. If you cannot find it, use cilantro, which it resembles in taste.

Cumin Seeds, Black. This rare and therefore more expensive form of cumin has sweeter, smaller, and more delicate seeds. Their mild pungency is perfect for the aromatic mixture of spices known as garam masala (page 723). The seeds can also be lightly dry-roasted and sprinkled whole over rice pilafs.

Cumin Seeds, Whole and Ground. These look like caraway seeds but are slightly larger, plumper, and lighter in color. Their flavor is similar to caraway, only gentler and sweeter. They are used both whole and ground. When whole, they are often subjected to the *tarka* technique (page 7), which intensifies their flavor and makes them slightly nutty. This spice of possible northern Egyptian or Middle Eastern ancestry has now become very central to the cuisines of India (where it must have arrived in ancient times) and Morocco. It is used in Spain and Mexico and in much of the Middle East as well. Sometimes used whole, it can also be ground into various spice mixtures. If roasted and ground cumin seeds are called for, put a few tablespoons of seeds in a small cast-iron frying pan over medium-high heat. Stir and roast for a few minutes, or until the seeds are a few shades darker and smell roasted. Then grind in a clean coffee grinder or other spice grinder. What is not needed immediately may be stored in a tightly lidded jar and saved for later use.

Currants, Persian (Dried Barberries or *Zareshk*). These tart, lemony currants are used in Irani cooking. They are generally soaked or cooked in a little sugar syrup first to plump them up.

Curry Leaves, Fresh and Dried. These highly aromatic leaves are used fresh in much of Indian and some Southeast Asian cookery. In Indonesia they are known as *daun salaam* and are a slightly larger variety. They are now increasingly available in the West. You can use the dried leaf if the fresh is unavailable, though its aroma is very limited. Indian grocers sell both fresh and dried curry leaves. The fresh ones come attached to stalks in sprays which can be pulled off their stalks in one swoop. Store curry leaves flat in a plastic bag. They last for several days in the refrigerator. They may also be frozen, so when you do see them in the market, buy a quantity and store them in the freezer; the frozen leaves seem to have a bit more aroma than the sun-dried leaves.

Curry Powder. This blend of spices generally includes cumin, coriander, red chiles, mustard, and fenugreek. The mixtures vary in their strength and potency and are generally sold mild and hot. You will find a recipe for My Curry Powder on page 707.

Daikon (Radish, White). The oriental radish, the one used in this book, is large, thick, and mild. It can be 3 inches in diameter. It should be peeled with a knife in thick strips before it is used. Peelers tend to remove only one layer of the skin so I find them inadequate. In Japan, it is called daikon. It is sold by all oriental and South Asian grocers.

Dasheen Leaves. These very large colocasia leaves, which look a bit like lotus leaves but are elongated into heart shapes, grow in the Tropics. Their slightly glutinous roots (known in the Caribbean as *eddoes,* in India as *arvi,* and in Cyprus as *colocasi*) are also eaten. The stems can be peeled and added to the greens as well. The leaves are generally shredded and used in soups and stews. They are also dipped in batters and fried to make all manner of fritters.

Daun Salaam. See Curry leaves, fresh and dried.

Dried Mandarin Peel. See Mandarin peel, dried.

Dry-Roasting Spices. Spices are sometimes dry-roasted before use. It is best to do this in a heavy cast-iron frying pan that has first been heated. No oil is used: The spices are just stirred around until they brown lightly. Roasted spices develop a heightened, nutty aroma. They can be stored for several months in an airtight jar, though they are best when freshly roasted.

Epazote. Also known as pigweed or wormseed, the fresh serrated leaves are used in some Mexican dishes. Although it grows wild in many backyards, it is not an easy herb to find, except in Mexican markets. If you have to, use cilantro as a substitute though it is not at all the same.

Fennel Seeds. These look and taste like anise seeds but are larger and plumper. To grind fennel seeds, just put 2 to 3 tablespoons into a clean coffee grinder or other spice grinder and grind as finely as possible. Store in an airtight container.

In North and West India, the whole seeds are used in pickles and chutneys and in snack foods. Using the *tarka* technique (page 737), they are also used in the stir-frying of vegetables, particularly in Bengal (East India), where they are part of the five-spice mixture called *panchphoran* (page 731). Fennel seeds can be dry-roasted and then eaten after a meal as both a digestive and mouth freshener.

Fenugreek Greens. Bunches, which consist of small (¾-inch) leaves on stalks, are sold by Indian grocers. The leaves need to be removed from the stalks, washed well, and chopped before being added to Indian dishes of potatoes, carrots, or spinach. They have an earthy, grassy aroma, which seems to stay in the pores long after meals. (In North Africa, the greens are fed to camels!)

Fenugreek Seeds. Known for their digestive properties, these angular, yellowish seeds give many commercial curry powders their earthy, musky "curry" aroma. In most of North India they are used mainly in pickles, chutneys, and vegetarian dishes. They are a part of the Bengali spice mixture *panchphoran* (page 731). In the Arab world, they are soaked and then whipped up into drinks and sauces. They may also be sprouted. They are thought to have cooling properties.

Five-Spice Powder. A Chinese spice mixture, it contains star anise, fennel, cloves, cinnamon, and Sichuan peppercorns. It is sold already ground by Chinese grocers. To make it yourself, combine 2 whole star anise, 1 teaspoon whole fennel seeds, 1 teaspoon whole cloves, a 2-inch stick of cinnamon or cassia bark, and 1 tablespoon Sichuan peppercorns. Grind as finely in a coffee grinder or other spice grinder as possible and store in a tightly lidded jar.

Fungus, Black, Tree Ear. Also known as *mo-er* mushrooms, tree ear fungus, and cloud ears, this tree fungus is a specialty of the Sichuan province. It is sold in the form of little, dried, curled-up black chips, which enlarge quite a bit once they have been soaked. At this stage, you should feel for the little hard eyes they have with your fingers and snip them off. Rinse them well, as they tend to be very gritty. They have no particular flavor of their own but add a very nice crunchy texture. Of late, it has been rumored that they are very good for the heart as well. Black fungus comes in two sizes, small and large. Unless otherwise stated, use only the smaller, more delicate kind.

Galangal. Known as *laos* and *lengkuas* in Indonesia, *langkuas* in Malaysia, and *kha* in Thailand, this gingerlike rhizome has a very distinct earthy aroma of its own. It is now sold, both fresh and frozen, by Southeast Asian grocers. In the curry-type recipes that require it, you could use the sliced, dried galaingal. To make curry paste, you would have to soak it before you grind it.

Garam Masala. This spice combination varies with each household, though the name seems constant. *Garam* means "hot" and *masala* means "spices" so the spices in this mixture were traditionally those that "heated" the body according to the ancient Ayurvedic system of medicine. They all happened to be highly aromatic as well.

Here is how you make a classic ground mixture: Combine in a clean coffee grinder 1 tablespoon cardamom seeds, 1 teaspoon whole cloves, 1 teaspoon whole black peppercorns, 1 teaspoon whole black cumin seeds, a 2-inch stick of cinnamon, 1/3 of a whole nutmeg, and a curl of mace. Grind to a fine powder. Store in a tightly closed jar and use as needed. Many people add a bay leaf to the mixture. Generally, though not always, garam masala is sprinkled toward the end of the cooking time to retain its aroma. The garam masala spices can also be used whole. If two or more of them are used together, they are still loosely referred to as garam masala.

Recipes where the strong aromas of my cardamom-filled mixture are not required call for store-bought garam masala. This just means that for that particular recipe the milder commercial version, which tends to be heavy on the cheaper coriander and cumin, will do.

Ghee **(Clarified Butter).** Butter that has been so thoroughly clarified that it can even be used for deep-frying. As it no longer contains milk solids, refrigeration is not necessary. *Ghee* has a nutty, buttery taste. All Indian grocers sell it and I find it more convenient to buy it than to make my own. If, however, you need to make it, put 1 pound unsalted butter in a pot over low heat and let it simmer very gently until the milky solids turn brownish and cling to the sides of the pot or fall to the bottom; the time that this takes will depend on the amount of water in the butter. Watch carefully toward the end and do not let it burn. Strain the *ghee* through a triple layer of cheesecloth. Homemade *ghee* is best stored in the refrigerator.

Ginger, Fresh. You almost cannot cook without ginger in South Asia and the Far East. This rhizome has a sharp, pungent, cleansing taste and is a digestive to boot. It is said to help with travel sickness as well. Its brown skin is generally peeled, though in Chinese cookery the skin is often left on.

When *slices of ginger* are called for, just cut a thinnish slice crosswise from a knob of ginger. If peeled slices are needed, peel a section of the knob before you start slicing.

When *slivers or minute dice* are called for, first cut the ginger into very thin slices. The slices should then be stacked and cut into very fine strips to get the slivers. To get the dice, cut the slivers crosswise into very fine dice.

When *finely grated ginger* is required, it should first be peeled and then grated on the finest part of a grater so it turns into pulp. When a recipe requires that 1 inch of ginger be grated, it is best to keep that piece attached to the large knob. The knob acts as a handle and saves you from grating your fingers.

When a little *ginger juice* is called for (excellent for salad dressings), just pick up a teaspoon or two of finely grated ginger and squeeze out as much liquid as you can.

Ginger should be stored in a dry, cool place. Many people like to bury it in dryish, sandy soil. This way they can break off and retrieve small portions as they need them while the rest of the knob generously keeps growing.

Glutinous Rice. See Grains and look under glutinous rice (page 373).

Glutinous Rice Powder. This powder, made from glutinous rice (also called sweet rice), is used mainly for desserts. It is sold by all East Asian grocers. Store as you would any flour.

Goraka. A sour, dried fruit used for souring cooked foods in parts of Sri Lanka, where it is called *goraka,* and southern India, where it is known as *kodampali.* The best substitute for this hard-to-find seasoning *(Garcinia cambozia)* is either tamarind pulp or lemon juice. Follow individual recipes for suggestions.

Hijiki. A black seaweed rich in calcium and iron. When soaked in warm water, the tiny strands elongate to about 2 inches in length.

Hoisin Sauce. This is a thick, slightly sweet, smooth Chinese bean sauce with a light garlic flavor. It may be used in cooking or as a dip. It is sold by Chinese grocers. If you buy it in a can, store the unused portion in a tightly lidded jar, which you should refrigerate.

Holy Basil *(Bai Kaprow).* See Basil.

Jaggery. A form of raw, lump cane sugar, it is sold in pieces that are cut off from larger blocks. Look for the kind that crumbles easily and is not rock-hard. It can be found in Indian groceries.

Japanese Seven-Spice Seasoning *(Shichimi).* Available only in Japanese groceries, where it is also sold as Seven-Spice Red Pepper *(Shichimi Togarashi),* it contains a coarsely crushed mixture of red pepper, a special Japanese pepper called *sansho*, roasted sesame seeds, roasted white poppy or hemp seeds, white pepper, and tiny bits of orange peel and seaweed. Use my easy mixture called Sesame Seed Seasoning (page 705) as a substitute.

Jicama. Shaped like a large beet with a coarse potato-like skin, this root is half fruit and half vegetable. Generally it is eaten raw and needs to be peeled fairly deeply. Possibly of Mexican origin, it is now popular as far away from its origins as China. In the Far East, it is generally sliced into salad-type dishes, where its white flesh (rather like a hard, crisp, somewhat bland pear) happily absorbs all dressings. Look for light-skinned, unblemished, unshriveled jicama. Generally the smaller they are, the less woody the flesh. In the streets of Mexico City, they are sold in slices with just salt, chile powder, and lime juice on them. This is how I ate them for the very first time and I still love them that way.

Kaffir Lime, Leaves and Rind. A dark-green knobbly lime whose peel and leaves are used in Southeast Asian cookery. They are both highly aromatic and their flavors can never quite be substituted. If you are lucky enough to get fresh leaves, tear them in half and pull off their coarse center veins before using them in a dish. If a recipe requires that the leaves be cut into fine, hair-thin shreds, first remove the center vein and then use a pair of kitchen scissors to cut the shreds. Leftover leaves can be made to last by freezing them in a flat plastic packet. Whole limes may be frozen as well. The peel and leaves are sometimes available dried. You should use them in whatever form you can find them. The leaves, dried rind, and lime itself are sold by Far Eastern and some Chinese grocers. The rind is sometimes labeled *piwma grood*. The dried rind needs to be soaked in water first. When soft, discard the soaking water (it is bitter) and then scrape off any pith that may be clinging to the rind.

Kailan (Gailan). This is the Cantonese name for a wonderful green of the cabbage family. Deep green in color, it is close in taste to broccoli but has no head. It is basically all leaves with tasty stems and small flowering heads. It is usually available in Chinese groceries.

Kalonji. See Nigella.

Kenari Nuts. These almondlike nuts grow profusely in the Moluccas, the Spice Islands of Indonesia, on tall trees that provide shade for the more delicate nutmeg trees. The nuts are put into everything from ginger tea and cakes to salad dressings. Almonds make the best substitute.

Ketjap Manis. See Soy sauces.

Kochu Chang. A spicy paste made with fermented soybeans and red chiles, this is a very common seasoning in Korea that can be bought in the West only from Korean grocers and East Asian supermarkets. You can, however, approximate it yourself at home by combining 4 to 5 tablespoons brown or red miso, 1½ tablespoons nicely red paprika, 1 teaspoon cayenne, and 1 tablespoon sugar and then mixing them well together.

Kokum. This is the pliable, semidried, sour, and astringent skin of a mangosteen-like fruit *(Garcinia indica)* that grows along India's coast. It is used for souring, rather like tamarind. It can sometimes be a bit salty as well, so use with care. Store in an airtight container to prevent drying out. When kokum is used in a dish, it is rarely eaten. It is left in the pot or the serving dish.

Konbu. Green, calcium-rich, dried kelp used for making stock *(dashi)* in Japan, it is sometimes sold as *dashi-konbu.* It resembles long, large leaves and comes either folded up or cut into small pieces. *Konbu* (sometimes called *kombu*) should never be washed as its flavor resides near the surface; simply wipe with a damp cloth just before use. *Konbu* may be allowed to simmer gently but should never boil vigorously. Price is generally a good indication of quality.

Korean Coarse Red Pepper. See Chile powders.

Lemongrass, Fresh and Dried. Known as *seré* in Indonesia, *serai* in Malaysia, *takrai* in Thailand, and *tanglad* in the Philippines, lemongrass is a tall, hard grayish-green grass used for its aroma and flavor in much of Southeast Asian cookery. Usually, only the bottom 6 inches are used. The very bottom can be bruised (hitting it with a hammer does the trick) and then thrown into a pot or else the lemongrass can be sliced first.

Lemongrass is fairly hard. To slice, first cut off the hard knot at the very end and then slice crosswise into paper-thin slices. Even when lemongrass is to be ground to a pulp in a blender, it needs to be sliced thinly first or else it will not grind properly. Lemongrass is best stored with its bottom end in a little water. This prevents it from drying out. You can also freeze stalks of lemon grass. To defrost, just run under hot water briefly.

In Southeast Asia, lemongrass is always used fresh. We are beginning to see it more and more in the West. Unfortunately, many of us in the West still have to make do with the dried variety. I buy dried, sliced lemongrass and then soak it before I use it. It generally needs to be strained out as it is very coarse. Lemongrass, as its name suggests, has a citrus flavor and aroma, though it is not at all sour. The best (though nowhere as good) equivalent is lemon peel; substitute the peel of a quarter of a lemon for one stalk of lemongrass.

Limes, Dried, Persian. Persian dried limes are a world unto themselves. They are sold by Middle Eastern grocers and are very hard when you buy them, though they feel quite hollow and are. You need to hit them with a well-aimed mallet so they break into 3 to 4 pieces. The black insides are the gold you are after. To get at them you need to pull or scrape the insides out and collect them in a bowl, making sure you discard the bitter seeds. Now grind this black gold that you have collected in a clean coffee grinder and store it in a jar. Do just 2 to 3 limes at a time. If all this sounds arduous, it isn't. It took me less than 5 minutes to do 2 limes, the smallest quantity you can do to make the grinder run properly. As a substitute, use fresh lime juice.

Mace. See Nutmeg and mace.

Maggi Cubes. These are stock cubes. Any other stock cubes may be substituted.

Mandarin Peel, Dried. This is the dried peel of a mandarin orange, used in cooking. It should not be confused with preserved mandarin peel, which is seasoned and generally eaten out of hand.

Melon Seeds. Shelled melon seeds are sold by Indian grocers for use in drinks and white sauces.

Minari. A Korean herb found in the West only in Korean supermarkets, it is somewhat like a tall, elongated version of parsley but with its own special aroma. Generally only the long stems are used in cooking. I have used the stems of flat-leaf Italian parsley as a substitute.

Mirin. This sweetened sake used in cooking is available at Japanese grocers, where it is sometimes labeled aji-mirin or with some other prefix. If you cannot find it, make an approximation by combining equal parts of sake and sugar and then cooking them gently until the sugar dissolves and the liquid is reduced by half.

Miso. A Japanese paste made from fermented soybeans, also containing other fermented grains. Among the miso readily available in the West is aka-miso, a reddish-brown variety. Miso can always be found in health food shops. Sometimes it is labeled according to its color, such as red miso, brown miso, yellow miso, and white miso. In Japan, miso is available in almost every shade and texture. It can be used for soups and stews, it can be lathered onto vegetables such as eggplants before they are grilled, and it can also be used in the preparation of pickles and dressings. To make soup, miso needs to be dissolved in water and then strained. In Japan, it is never allowed to boil vigorously. However, the Koreans, who use a similar paste called *toen chang*, do allow it to boil, with no disastrous results.

Mushroom Soy Sauce. This soy sauce flavored with mushrooms can be found only in Chinese supermarkets. If you cannot find it, use Chinese light soy sauce as a substitute.

Mushrooms. There are hundreds of different mushrooms, going from tiny pin-heads to large meaty ones. Here are some of the Asian varieties used in this book that you may be less familiar with:

Chinese dried mushrooms: These are available in most oriental shops. The Japanese shiitake is the same mushroom. Price is generally an indication of quality. The thicker the caps, the meatier the texture. They need to be soaked in plenty of warm water before they are used. Once they are soft, lift the mushrooms out of their soaking liquid—this leaves the grit behind. The texture of the stalks remains hard, even after soaking, so they should be cut off. The water in which the mushrooms have soaked can be strained and saved. Add it to stocks or use for cooking vegetables.

Straw mushrooms: There is nothing quite as delicious as a fresh straw mushroom, which is smooth and meaty at the same time. I eagerly await the day when they will be as commonly available in the West as they are in the East. For now, we have to make do with the canned variety. Drain them first, rinse well, then use as the recipe suggests.

Among the fresh oriental mushrooms now increasingly available in specialty shops are *oyster mushrooms* (delicate, excellent in stir-fries) and *shiitake* (the Japanese name for the mushroom commonly used both fresh and dried in China, Korea, and Japan; they have meaty caps but woody stems and can be used in soups, stews, and stir-fries).

Mustard Oil. See Oils.

Mustard Seeds, Brown and Yellow. Of the three varieties of mustard seeds, white (actually yellowish), brown (a reddish-brown), and black (slightly larger, brownish-black seeds), it is the brown and yellow that I use in this book.

All mustard seeds have Jekyll and Hyde characteristics. When crushed, they are nose-tinglingly pungent. However, if they are thrown into hot oil and allowed to pop using the *tarka* method (page 737), they turn quite nutty and sweet. In India, both these techniques are used, sometimes in the same recipe. Whole mustard seeds, popped in oil, are used to season vegetables, legumes, yogurt relishes, salads, and rice dishes. Crushed seeds are used in sauces and in pickles.

Yellow mustard seeds may be substituted for the brown ones.

Mustard Seeds, Hulled and Split. As far as I know, these are only used in India, mainly for pickling and in pungent sauces. It is the brown seeds that are skinned and split, making them look like tiny grains of yellow *dal* (split peas). They are sold only by Indian grocers as mustard *dal*.

Nigella *(Kalonji).* These black, aromatic seeds that may have originated in the southern Caucasus region, are used extensively on flatbreads from Turkey all the way east to India. In India, they are also an important spice for pickling and are a part of the Bengali five-spice mixture *panchphoran* (page 731). Their oregano-like taste is quite strong, so they should be used with some discretion.

Noodles. Here are some of the noodles that you might be less familiar with:

Fresh Chinese egg noodles: Ask for lo mein noodles in a Chinese grocery store and *ramen* in a Japanese one. They are usually sold in the refrigerated section in plastic bags. One pound usually serves 4 to 6 people. If you intend using smaller portions, it is a good idea to divide the noodles as soon as you buy them, wrap the portions separately, and freeze what you are not going to use that day. The rest can be refrigerated until you are ready to cook it. Frozen egg noodles defrost quickly and easily when dropped into boiling water. Just stir them about in the beginning. The best way to cook these noodles is to drop them into a large pot of boiling water. As soon as the water comes to a boil again, throw in a cup of fresh water. Repeat this about 3 times, or until the noodles are just tender. The noodles can now be drained and used as the recipe suggests.

Dried Chinese egg noodles: When fresh noodles are not available, use the dried. Drop them into a large pot of boiling water and cook as you would the fresh. Some varieties tend to cook very fast, so test them frequently.

Fresh rice noodles: These are white, slithery, and absolutely delicious. In Southeast Asia, they are available in all sorts of sizes and shapes. They generally do not remain fresh for more than a day. Many do not need to be cooked at all; others are heated through very briefly. Unfortunately, these noodles are very hard to find in the West except in areas where there are large concentrations of Asians.

Dried rice noodles: We have to make do with dried rice noodles in the West. For most of the recipes in this book, buy *banh pho* or any other flat rice noodle, soak it in warm water for about 30 minutes, or until it is soft (or in tap water for 2 hours), and then cook it very briefly in a large pot of boiling water. Drain it and rinse it in cold water before using it as the recipe suggests. This gets rid of the extra starch. If you wish to hold the noodles for a while, toss with a little oil, cover, and set aside. The noodles may be reheated by dropping them into boiling water for a second or two. You may also use the microwave for this.

Soba: These fine Japanese buckwheat noodles are often eaten cold. They are cooked by dropping into lots of boiling water just like pasta. Once just done, they are removed and rinsed thoroughly in cold water.

Somen: These fine Japanese wheat noodles generally come in 1-pound packages with the noodles bundled with ribbons into 5 portions. Drop them into boiling water and cook for 1 to 2 minutes, or until just done. Drain and rinse under cold water to remove some of the starch. These noodles are often used as a substitute for fresh rice noodles in Southeast Asian recipes.

Udon: Slightly rounded or flat Japanese wheat noodles that can be bought most easily in the West in their dried form. Cook them as you would Chinese fresh egg noodles, but then rinse them under cold water to remove some of their starchiness.

Nori. A special seaweed (often referred to as lava), brimming with vitamins, that is dried and roasted to give it a papery texture. The blacker it is, the better its quality seems to be. It was first cultivated in what is now called Tokyo Bay in the seventeenth century and then processed in the town's Asakusa district. Today's pollution has curtailed this practice, but the seaweed is still referred to frequently as Asakusa nori. It is generally sold in sheets that are about 7×8 inches. In order to bring out its flavor, one side should be passed over a lowish flame several times until it becomes crisp. It may then be eaten as is, crumbled over rice and noodles, or used to make sushi. Store in an airtight container.

Nutmeg and Mace. Nutmegs are the dried seeds of a round pearlike fruit. Mace is the red, lacy covering around the seeds that turns yellowish-orange when dried. Both have similar warm, sweetish, and slightly camphorous flavors, though mace has a slightly bitter edge. Both nutmeg and mace are used in the garam masala mixture (page 723). A nutmeg breaks easily; just hit it lightly with a hammer to get the third needed for the garam masala recipe.

Nutritional Yeast. A yellow powder rich in protein (with all the amino acids) and the B vitamins, sold in all health food shops. A few teaspoons of it may be stirred into foods during the last stages of cooking.

Oils. For most of the recipes in this book, I recommend using peanut or canola oil. If oil is used for deep-frying, it can be reused. Skim off all extraneous matter with a skimmer and then drop a chunk of ginger or potato into it and let it fry. This chunk will absorb a lot of the unwanted flavors. When it is cool enough to handle, strain the oil through a triple thickness of cheesecloth or a large handkerchief. Let it cool completely and then store it in a tightly sealed jar. When reusing, mix half old oil with half fresh oil.

Mustard oil: This oil has the same characteristics as the seeds it comes from. When raw, it smells hot and pungent. When heated, the pungency goes into the air (you can smell it in your kitchen) and the oil turns sweet. It is used in Indian cookery, and in most Indian oil pickles. It is also good for a massage! Because it has more uricic acid than recommended for Western diets, I have suggested extra-virgin olive oil as a substitute in many of the recipes. Extra-virgin olive oil has an equivalent potency and aroma even though of an entirely different nature.

Olive oil: A mild-tasting oil with 4 percent or more oleic acid, this is a good choice when you do not want a pronounced olive flavor. It is generally labeled just "olive oil."

Extra-virgin olive oil: By this I mean a cold-pressed oil made by crushing the olive and its pit without the use of chemical solvents. This oil, with 1 percent or less oleic acid, is usually expensive. I tend to use it in salads and as a final flavoring. Of course, if you can afford it and like its taste, you can use it to cook all the foods of your choice.

Oriental sesame oil: Even though it goes against my very being to use the word *oriental,* I have here succumbed to expediency. Sesame oil, like any other oil, can be and *is* turned into a nondescript, flavorless, colorless oil to be used in general cooking. However, in East Asia, a purer version, made by just crushing sesame seeds, is used as a final flavoring for many dishes. This oil is brown and has a pronounced sesame flavor. It is used in very small quantities.

Oriental Sesame Oil. See Oils.

Palm Sugar. This is a delicious, raw, honey-colored sugar used in much of South and Southeast Asia. It is sold by Southeast Asian grocers both in cans and in plain plastic containers. It comes in lump or more granular forms. The best substitute for it is either Indian jaggery (make sure it is not rock hard) or brown sugar. It keeps well if tightly covered. Refrigeration is not needed.

Panchphoran **(Five-Spice Mixture).** This very Bengali spice mixture consists of fennel seeds, mustard seeds, fenugreek seeds, cumin seeds, and *kalonji* mixed in equal proportions.

Pappadums. Also called *papar,* these are Indian wafers made of dried split peas. Sold either plain or studded with black pepper (or garlic or red pepper) by Indian grocers, they should be deep-fried for a few seconds in hot oil or toasted very quickly. They are served with most Indian vegetarian meals and are also good with drinks.

Paprika. It is important that you use a good-quality paprika that is bright red. It tends to darken as it sits in glass bottles.

Parmigiano-Reggiano/Parmesan Cheese. For all my recipes that call for Parmesan cheese, I suggest you use good-quality Italian Parmigiano-Reggiano cheese. Buy it in a chunk and grate it yourself or buy it already grated from a reputable cheese shop where it is freshly grated. Store it in the freezer as it spoils rapidly.

Peanut Oil. See Oils.

Pecans. One of the finest nuts, with a delicate flavor and texture, it is native to the southern United States and is now also grown extensively in Mexico. Store in the freezer as it has a high fat content and can become rancid.

Pine Nuts. These are sold in Far Eastern, Middle Eastern, and South Asian groceries. To roast them, put them in a heated cast-iron frying pan and stir them around until they turn golden brown.

Plum Paste, Sour *(Umeboshi).* These unripe Japanese plums (actually a variety of apricot that is somehow always referred to as a "plum") are pickled in brine with the aromatic red *shiso* leaf, which both colors and flavors them. Considered to be digestives, they are also very high in vitamin C and are often eaten at breakfast. *Bainiku* is the paste made from seeded *umeboshi*. It is used as a seasoning and souring agent. Bottled paste is sold by Japanese grocers. You can also make it yourself by mashing the plums after removing their seeds. Opened bottles of plums and pastes should be kept in the refrigerator.

Plum Sauce. This sweet-and-sour Chinese sauce is sold by all Chinese grocers in bottles and cans. Once opened, it should be stored in the refrigerator.

Plums, Pickled, Chinese. Known as *suanmei*, this sour fruit is actually a variety of apricot. It is pickled in brine and often crushed before being used. Chinese grocers sell it as pickled plums. Japanese *umeboshi* may be substituted.

Polenta. See page 334.

Poppy Seeds, White. In India only the white seeds are used, mainly to thicken sauces.

Radish, Preserved. Even though these long white radishes are preserved with both salt and sugar, they are not brined and appear quite dry when you buy them. They tend to be yellowish-brown in appearance. Possibly Chinese in origin, they are used throughout East Asia. When chopped up and added to foods, they add a great deal of flavor. They are sold by Chinese and other oriental grocers. There is really no substitute for them, so if you cannot find them, it is best to do without.

Red Bean Paste, Sweet. This is to the Far East what chocolate is to the West. A mixture of red azuki beans and sugar, it is not hard to make, only time-consuming. Luckily, it is sold in cans at Chinese grocers and is used in hundreds of Eastern sweets, especially as a filling for pastries.

Rice, Roasted and Ground. In many parts of Southeast Asia, such as Thailand, Laos, and Vietnam, rice is roasted in a dry wok and then ground to a powder. This nutty powder is then used as both a flavoring and a thickener. Generally, glutinous rice is used for this purpose, though you may use plain long-grain rice as well. To roast and grind rice, put a small, cast-iron frying pan over medium-low heat. Allow it to get very hot. Now put in about 4 tablespoons of rice. Stir and roast it until it turns a medium brown; some of the grains might even pop. Empty the rice onto a plate and let it cool a bit, then put it into the container of a clean coffee grinder or other spice grinder and grind to a powder. Store what is not needed immediately in a tightly lidded jar.

Rice Sticks. This very fine, dried, rice vermicelli may be fried until golden and crisp—it takes but a few seconds—or soaked in warm water for a couple of hours, drained, and then soaked in boiling water for 2 minutes. They are used throughout much of East Asia. (To make matters confusing, wider, flat rice noodles are sometimes labeled "rice sticks," though they tend to say *banh pho* below it.)

Rock Sugar. Lump sugar consisting of big, clear crystals is used both in China and India. (In India, it is called *misri*.) It gives sauces a lovely sheen.

Rose Petals, Dried. Used in many cuisines with a Moorish or Muslim influence (India, Persia, Morocco), these may be bought from Middle Eastern grocers. You could, of course, dry your own roses, provided they are the old-fashioned kind: highly aromatic and unsprayed.

Saffron. I have only used "leaf" saffron (whole saffron threads) in this book. Known in ancient Greece and Rome as well as in ancient Persia and India, this valued spice consists of the whole dried stigma of a special autumn crocus. Look for a reliable source for saffron, as it is very expensive and there can be a great deal of adulteration. Indians often roast the saffron threads lightly before soaking them in a small amount of hot milk to bring out the color. This milk is then poured over rice in dishes such as *biryani* to give it its orange highlights. In Iran, the saffron is pounded with a cube of sugar and allowed to soak in a buttery syrup before it is used. This also brings out its color. In much of European cookery a very light pinch of saffron is thrown directly into broths to make risottos and soups.

Sake. This is the Japanese rice wine used for both cooking and drinking. For drinking, it may be served chilled or it may be heated by putting some into a small bottle (preferably ceramic) and setting the bottle in a pan of water. Heat to 130°F. in small batches and drink each bottle while its contents are still warm.

***Sansho* Pepper.** Also known as "Japan pepper." Like Chinese Sichuan pepper, it is of the prickly ash family but has an entirely different flavor and aroma. It is sold, already ground, by Japanese grocers.

Screw Pine. The leaves of the screw pine *(Pandanus odorus)* are the vanilla of Southeast Asia. Known as *daun paandaan* (in Thailand) and *rampe* (in Sri Lanka), the pandanus leaves are used fresh and lend a sweetish, very tropical aroma to foods. Many Southeast Asian stores sell an essence made from the leaves. In India, it is the spathes of the flowers from a slightly larger tree *(Pandanus odoratissimus)* that are used to make an essence known as *kewra*. This is used in both savory and sweet dishes and drinks. It has an almost overpoweringly sensual, flowery aroma.

Sesame Paste. Chinese and Japanese sesame pastes are made from roasted sesame seeds and have a darker color than Middle Eastern sesame paste, *tahini*, which is made from unroasted seeds. All sesame pastes have oil floating on the top, so you need to mix the contents of the jars or cans thoroughly before using them. This can be very hard initially—you feel as if you are mixing cement—but after a while, the paste softens up. Once a jar or can has been opened, store it in the refrigerator.

Sesame Seeds. Said to be native to India, they certainly can be found in many ancient Indian recipes as well as in recipes from ancient China, ancient Egypt, ancient Persia, and the Roman world.

Hulled sesame seeds are almost white and unhulled ones are beige in color. I much prefer the unhulled beige ones, though you may use either for all the recipes in this book. Black sesame seeds have much more oil in them and are quite delicious. They are used to decorate and flavor breads in the Middle East and for special seasonings in Japan. When one of my recipes calls for sesame seeds, use the beige ones unless I suggest otherwise.

To roast sesame seeds: Put a small, cast-iron frying pan over medium-low heat. When it is hot, put in 1 to 3 tablespoons of sesame seeds. Stir them around until they turn a shade darker and give out a wonderful roasted aroma. Sesame seeds do tend to fly around as they are roasted. You could turn down the heat slightly when they do this or cover the pan loosely. Remove the seeds from the pan as soon as they are done. You may roast sesame seeds ahead of time. Cool them and store them in a tightly lidded jar. They can last several weeks this way, though I must add that they are best when freshly roasted.

To roast and lightly crush sesame seeds: Roast the seeds as suggested above. Now put them into the container of a spice grinder or clean coffee grinder and whir it for just a second or two. The seeds should *not* turn to a powder. You may also crush them lightly in a mortar.

Shallots. For Westerners who tend to use shallots in small quantities, it is always a bit startling to see Southeast Asians and South Asians use them in generous amounts. The shallot is the onion of Southeast Asia, south and southwestern India, and Sri Lanka. It is ground into curry pastes, sliced into salads, and fried into crisp flakes to be used both as a garnish and as a wonderful flavoring. In places like Goa, shallots hang in kitchens in long ropes, to be plucked at will.

Shao Hsing Wine, Chinese. A Chinese, whisky-colored rice wine, it is used in cooking and sold by Chinese grocers or in Chinese liquor shops. A reasonable substitute is dry sherry; I find that La Ina comes the closest in flavor. This sherry has a far better taste than what is labeled "Chinese cooking wine." Japanese sake may be used in its place as well though its flavor is quite different.

Shiso (**Beefsteak Leaves**). Medium-sized, serrated heart-shaped leaves that are aromatic in a very lemony way, these are used fresh in Japanese cookery. In Japan, this popular flavoring is also used in candy! Look for them at Japanese groceries.

Sichuan Peppercorns. These reddish-brown, highly aromatic pods of the prickly ash family are slightly larger than peppercorns. They are ground to make Sichuan pepper and are available in Chinese groceries. They should be stored in a tightly lidded jar. To roast Sichuan peppercorns, set a small cast-iron frying pan over medium-low heat. When hot, put in the peppercorns. Stir and fry until they release their fragrance. They might smoke a bit, but the smoke will be highly aromatic.

Simple Sugar Syrup. When cooked slowly with water, sugar blends more readily into drinks and other dishes that require sweetening without further cooking. To make about 1¼ cups, combine 8 tablespoons of sugar and 1 cup of water in a small pan and bring to a boil. Quickly turn the heat down to low, stir, and simmer for 5 minutes. Use as needed or cool and store in the refrigerator in a tightly covered jar.

Soy Sauces. Many different soy sauces are used in East Asia. Not only do countries have their very own brands of soy sauces but regions, towns, and even villages sometimes proudly boast of producing their very special creations. All soy sauces are made from fermented and salted soybeans. They range from salty to sweet, from light to dark, from thick to thin, and have many different textures. Dark soy sauces tend to be thicker than the light ones and generally add a dark color to the dish they are put in. Light soy sauce tends to be thinner and saltier. Since soy sauces vary so much in their saltiness, it is always advisable to put slightly less than the amount required in the recipe, as more can be added later.

Ketjap manis: A thick, very sweet—indeed syrupy—soy sauce used in Indonesia. If you cannot find it you can make an approximation of it yourself by combining 1 cup of dark soy sauce with 6 tablespoons molasses and 3 tablespoons brown sugar and simmering gently until the sugar has dissolved.

Japanese and Chinese soy sauces: They tend to have very different flavors. Thus, it is best to use Japanese soy sauces for Japanese and Korean dishes and Chinese soy sauces for Chinese dishes. Pearl River, a good brand of Chinese soy sauce, is sold by Chinese grocers. It is most confusingly labeled: "Soy Superior Sauce" is dark and "Superior Soy" is light. The best-known Japanese brand is Kikkoman, though Hi-Maru is also good. The Japanese also make dark and light soy sauces, which are sold by all Japanese grocers.

Tamari: The roots of *tamari* (literally, "that which accumulates") go back to China when the liquid left over from making fermented soybean pastes was used as a sauce. This concept was brought to Japan in the seventh century. The Japanese called the fermented soybean paste miso and the sauce left over as the miso matured tamari. By the eighteenth century, the making of soy sauces had been turned into a commercial industry. To make the miso, half wheat and half soybeans were used and soy sauces reflected the same mixture. Today's tamari, sold by most health food shops, is an attempt to go back to its original source. It is naturally brewed using primarily soybeans with very little wheat and is the result of an enzymatic reaction rather than an alcoholic fermentation (as is the case when there is a lot of wheat). Tamari has a more complex flavor than commercial soy sauces and is blessed with eighteen amino acids.

Sri Lankan Raw Curry Powder. See page 707.

Star Anise. A flower-shaped collection of pods that are brownish-black in color, this spice has a decided anise flavor. It is used in Chinese-style braised dishes and in several dishes from western India (where the China trade was brisk, especially in ancient times). Store in a tightly lidded jar. If a pod of star anise is called for, think of a pod as a petal of the flower and break off one section.

Steaming. Steaming is used for cooking anything from rice cakes to custards. The process cooks gently and preserves flavor.

One of the most satisfactory utensils for steaming is a wok because its width easily accommodates a casserole or a large plate of food. Use a wok with a flat base or set a round-based wok on a metal ring. Put a metal or wooden rack or a perforated tray into the wok. (You could invert a small empty tin can instead.)

Now pour in some water. Bring it to a gentle boil and lower the food so it sits on the rack, tray, or can. The water should stay about ¾ inch below the level of the food that is being steamed. Extra boiling water should be kept on hand just in case it is needed to top up the level.

Cover the whole wok, including the food, with a domed wok lid or a large sheet of aluminum foil. The domed lids are preferable as they cause the condensed steam to roll down the sides instead of dripping on the food itself.

If you like, you can also invest in the many-tiered bamboo or aluminum steamers sold in Chinese markets.

Straw Mushrooms. See Mushrooms.

Sumac. A sour red berry found in the Middle East that is ground and used as a souring agent, sumac is sold by Middle Eastern grocers; store it in the refrigerator or freezer.

Tahini. See Sesame paste.

Tamarind. The fruit of a tall shade tree, tamarinds look like wide beans. As they ripen, their sour green flesh turns a chocolate color. It remains sour but picks up a hint of sweetness. For commercial purposes, tamarinds are peeled, seeded, semi-dried, and their brown flesh compacted into rectangular blocks that must be softened in water.

To make tamarind paste: Break off ½ pound from a brick of tamarind and tear it into small pieces. Put into a small nonmetallic pot, cover with 2 cups of very hot water, and set aside for 3 hours or overnight. (You could achieve the same result by simmering the tamarind with the water for 10 minutes or by putting them in a microwave oven for 3 to 5 minutes.) Set a sieve over a nonmetallic bowl and empty the tamarind and its soaking liquid into it. Push down on the tamarind with your fingers or the back of a wooden spoon to extract as much pulp as you can. Put whatever tamarind remains in the sieve back into the soaking bowl. Add ½ cup of hot water to it and mash a bit more. Return it to the sieve and extract as much more pulp as you can. Don't forget to retrieve the pulp clinging to the underside of the sieve.

Tarka (Popping Spices in Hot Oil). The *tarka* technique, also known as *baghaar, chhownk,* or seasoning in oil, is quite unique to India, though simple versions of it are done in Italy, Spain, Cyprus, and even China. First, oil is heated until very hot. Next, spices such as mustard seeds or cumin seeds—or just dried hot red chiles—are dropped into it. As they pop and sizzle, their whole character changes in an instant. They get much more intense. Their flavors change. Then, this flavored oil with the seasonings in it is poured over cooked foods or is added to the oil and cooked in it. Since four or five spices can go into a *tarka,* they are often added to the hot oil in a certain order so those that burn easily, such as dried chiles, go in last. The flavor of each is imparted to the oil. In the case of the chiles, the flavor comes only from the browned skin of the chile. Any food cooked in this oil picks up the heightened flavor of all the spices.

Doing a *tarka* takes just a few seconds so it is important to have all spices ready and at hand. A *tarka* is sometimes done at the beginning of a recipe, sometimes at the end, and sometimes both. Legumes, for example, are usually just boiled with a little turmeric. When they are tender, a *tarka* is prepared in a small skillet, perhaps with asafetida, whole cumin, and red chiles, and then the entire contents of the skillet, hot oil and spices, are poured over the legumes and the lid shut tight for a few minutes to trap the aromas. These flavorings can be stirred in later. They perk up the boiled legumes and bring them to life.

Tien Jing Preserved Vegetables. Also known as *dung tsai,* this consists of turnip-like roots or stems that are preserved and then packed in ceramic crocks or sometimes in plastic bags. They are used as an added flavoring in many vegetarian dishes. They are sold only by Chinese grocers.

Toen Chang. A medium brown Korean paste made out of fermented soybeans, it is diluted, strained, and used as a base for stews. In the West, it is sold only by Korean supermarkets. The best substitute is Japanese medium brown miso, sold in all health food stores.

Tomatillos. These look like small green tomatoes with a papery, lanternlike covering. Pull off the husk and rinse the sometimes-sticky fruit. For raw salsas, just drop the tomatillos into boiling water and boil for 7 to 8 minutes before chopping up or blending. They may be chopped raw and used to season other foods that require cooking. Their taste is tomato-like but with a tartness not unlike that of lime. They are also sold in cans; a 13-ounce can, once drained, yields about 8 ounces of tomatillos.

Tomatoes, To Peel, Seed, and Chop. Drop tomatoes in boiling water for 15 seconds. Remove and peel. Cut in half crosswise. Gently squeeze out all the seeds. Now chop the skinned shell.

Turmeric. A rhizome like ginger, only with smaller, more delicate "fingers," fresh turmeric is quite orange inside. When dried and ground, it turns bright yellow. It is this musky yellow powder that gives some Indian dishes a yellowish cast. As it is cheap and is also considered to be an antiseptic, it is used freely in the cooking of legumes and vegetables.

Turnip, Green, Chinese. This looks like a squat daikon but is fairly green, especially near the top. Peel it deeply, just like daikon, and then proceed with the recipe.

Udon. See Noodles.

Vinegars. There are just so many types of vinegar, each with its own flavor and strength. You should experiment and see which you like. Vinegars may be made out of rice, grapes, sugar cane juice, and coconut toddy, a liquor from the coconut palm. One of the mildest is Japanese rice vinegar. You can make a version of this yourself by combining 3 parts of distilled white vinegar, 1 part water, and ¼ part sugar.

Wakame Seaweed. A dark, dried seaweed rich in calcium and vitamins, it needs to be broken up and soaked for 10 to 15 minutes after which it turns green and slithery. It is sold by Korean and Japanese grocers as well as in health food shops.

Wasabi. A pungent, green Japanese horseradish that is grated finely and made into wasabi paste, it used as mustard might be in the West. As it is not often available in its fresh form in the West, Japanese grocers here sell wasabi paste, all ready to be used, in tubes. Remember that this nose-tinglingly sharp paste should be used in minute quantities because a little goes a long way. You can also buy dry wasabi powder in tins. Mix small quantities with a little warm water to make a paste in the same way as you would make a paste with powdered mustard. Allow it to stand for about 10 minutes before using.

Water Chestnuts. Dark-skinned and chestnut-sized, these tubers grow in water and are sold fresh only by Chinese grocers. The inside flesh is deliciously crisp and white. Canned water chestnuts do not compare but may be used in cooked dishes.

Watermelon Seeds. A common snack in China, these are sold shelled and dried in India to be ground into sauces and drinks.

Wonton Skins. These very thin sheets of pastry, about 3 inches square, are sold wrapped up in stacks of 30 or 36 or more by Chinese grocers and supermarkets. In cities with large Chinese districts, it is well worth looking for a source that prepares them fresh every day. Such places often make noodles and bean curd products as well. Wonton skins last several days in the refrigerator and may be frozen easily. Defrost thoroughly before using. They dry out easily, so keep them well wrapped, even as you work.

Zahtar. A spice blend containing roasted sesame seeds, sumac, and herbs such as thyme. See page 705 for a recipe.

Resources

Adriana's Caravan
409 Vanderbilt Street
Brooklyn, NY 11218
(718) 436-8565
   or (800) 316-0820
Adricara@aol.com
*Spices and ethnic ingredients,
   grains and seeds*

**The Chile Pepper
Emporium**
528 San Felipe N.W.
Albuquerque, NM 87194
(800) 288-9648
Chiles and chile products

The Cooking Post
The Puebla of Santa Ana
2 Dove Road
Bernalillo, NM 87004
(888) 867-5198
www.cookingpost.com
*Red and blue corn, chiles,
   posoles, wild rice*

Frieda's
4465 Corporate Center Drive
Los Alamitos, CA
   90720-2561
Mail-order address:
P.O. Box 58488
Los Angeles, CA 90058
(714) 826-6100
   or (800) 421-9477
www.frieda.com
Exotic and specialty produce

Kalustyan's
123 Lexington Avenue
New York, NY 10016
(212) 685-3451
fax: (212) 683-8458
www.kalustyans.com
*Rices and grains, spices,
   seasonings, vinegars, and
   more*

Katagiri
224 East 59th Street
New York, NY 10022
(212) 755-3566
fax: (212) 752-4197
www.katagiri.com
*Japanese noodles, seasonings,
   spices, and pickles*

**Oriental Food Market and
Cooking School, Inc.**
2801 West Howard Street
Chicago, IL 60645
(773) 274-2826
Chinese products and spices

Penzeys Spices
W19362 Apollo Drive
Muskego, WI 53150
800-741-7787
fax: (414) 574-0278
www.penzeys.com
Spices and flavorings

The Spanish Table
1427 Western Avenue
Seattle, WA 98101
(206) 682-2827
fax: (206) 682-2814
email: tablespan@aol.com
*Spanish, Portuguese, and
   Moroccan products, grains
   and cheeses*

Sultan's Delight
P.O. Box 090302
Brooklyn, NY 11209
(800) 852-5046
fax: (718) 745-2563
www.sultansdelight.com
*Mediterranean and Middle
   Eastern products*

Whole Foods Market, Inc.
www.wholefoods.com
*Grains, nuts, herbs and spices,
   all cuisines*

Index

Acarajé, 16
Acorn squash. *See* Squashes,
winter
Aduki beans. *See* Azuki beans
Adzuki beans. *See* Azuki beans
Afghanistan, recipes from
Eggplant with Minty Tomato
Sauce and Yogurt, 192–93
Naan, Kandahari, 434
Sour Cherry Chutney, 659
Ajwain
about, 711
Homemade Indian Cheese
Flavored with Black
Pepper, Roasted Cumin
Seeds, and, Roasted, 563
in Spicy Corn Salad, 622
Aleppo pepper, 716
Almond(s)
in Classic Romesco Sauce,
669–70
Milk, 643
Soup, Cold, 578–79
Soup, Indian Cashew Nut
and, 583–84
Soup, Sweet, 610
Tomato Preserve with, Sweet,
701
Amchoor
about, 693, 711
in Carrots with Fresh Fenu-
greek or Fresh Cilantro,
159
in Chickpeas Cooked in a
Moghlai Style, 32–33
in Sour Fennel-Flavored Egg-
plant, 195
in Spicy Corn Salad, 622
in Spicy Punjabi Red Kidney
Bean Stew, 47–48
in Sweet-and-Sour Eggplants,
194
American "French" Toast, 543
Anardana. See Pomegranate seeds
Anatolian Red Lentil Stew with
Wheat Berries and Chick-
peas, 71–72
Ancho chiles, about, 715
An Ancient Drink with Ginger
and Cardamom, 644
Apple(s)
and Milk Drink, Moroccan,
649
and Yogurt, Rice with, 396–
97
Apricots, Carrots with Dried,
Persian-Style, 160
Arepas, 335
Arhar dal. See Pigeon peas
Aromatic Cuban White Beans
and Pumpkin Stew, 54–56
Artichoke(s)
buying and storing, 127
cooking methods for boiled,
127–28
cooking methods for raw,
128–29
Fried, 132–33
Heart and Fresh Fava Bean
Salad, 612

Hearts with a White Sauce,
Poached Eggs over, 522
Hearts with Peas, 131–32
Hearts with Wine and
Coriander Seeds, 130
Jerusalem (*see* Jerusalem
artichokes)
and Peas, Penne with, 484
with Potatoes, Stewed, 129
trimming, 128
Arugula and Bulgur, Tabbouleh
Salad Made with, 424
Asafetida
about, 711
in Carrots with Fresh Fenugreek or Fresh Cilantro,
159
with Collard Greens, 220
and Cumin, Mung Beans
with, 77
in Delhi-Style Cilantro and
Mint Chutney, 660
in "Javanese" Noodles,
477–79
in Mung Beans with Greens,
79–80
in Rajasthani Mango Pickle
with Fennel Seeds, 698–99
in Semolina "Risotto" with
Cabbage and Peas, 489–90
in South Indian Cabbage,
152–53
in South Indian Coconut
Rice, 382
in Split Urad Beans in the
Dehli Style, 113–14
Asparagus
Basic, My Way, 134
buying and storing, 133
Cheese Salad with Tomato
and Basil Topped with,
620–21
Cold, with a Chinese Dressing, 134–35
Cold, with a Korean Dressing, 135
cooking methods for, 133
with French Omelet, 532
with Ginger and Red Pepper,
Stir-Fried, 137–38
Mushrooms, Corn, and, Wild
Rice Sautéed with, 508
and Mushrooms, Bean Curd
with, 96–97
and Mushrooms, Couscous
with, Israeli, 504
with Pine Nuts, 136
in Poached Eggs on Japanese
Noodles, 523–24
with Polenta, 344–45
precooking preparation, 133
with Romesco Sauce,
136–37
Ata (chapati flour), about, 714
Australia, recipes from
Okra Cooked in an Aus-
tralian Manner, 252
Avocado(es)
and Buttermilk Soup, Cold,
579
in Guacamole, 613–14
Azuki beans
cooking methods for, 8

with Green Pepper from
Yunnan, Stir-Fried, 9
and Rice with Sesame Salt,
399
in sweet red bean paste, 732
in Sweet Red Bean Soup, 612
and Whole Mung Beans,
Crushed and Sautéed,
10–11

Baby Bok Choy with Chinese
Mushrooms, 216–17
Bai kaprow (Ocinum sanctum),
about, 712
Bakes, 455–58
Bamboo shoots, about, 711–12
Banana(s)
Lassi, Sweet, 655
Yogurt Cheese with, 557–58
Yogurt with, in the South
Indian Style, 555
Bandhania, about, 720
Banh pho (rice sticks), about,
375, 415
Barberries, dried, about, 721
Barley
cooking methods for pearled,
325
pearled, 325
pressed, 326
Pressed, Sesame Seeds, Nori,
Mushrooms, and, Japanese
Rice with, 327–28
with Spinach and Shallots,
326
Stew, 327
Basic recipes
Asparagus, My Way, 134
Basmati Rice, 375
Brown Rice, 376
Buckwheat, Whole, 329
Chickpea Flour Pancakes, 37
Chickpea Flour Pizza, 39–40
Couscous, Toasted Whole
Wheat, 497
Couscous, Whole Wheat, 497
"Forbidden" Black Rice, 377
Homemade Yogurt, 545
Hulled and Split Mung
Beans, 75–76
Hulled and Split Pigeon Peas,
86
Hulled and Split Urad Beans,
113
Japanese Rice, 378
Lemon Pickle, 690
Long-Grain Rice, 376
Mango Pickle, South Indian,
696–97
Millet, 358
Mushrooms, Stir-Fried, 243
Pumpkin Soup, 589–90
Red Lentils, 60–61
Red Salsa, 683
"Risotto" of Rice and Split
Peas, 401–2
Sugar Syrup, 658
Tamarind Chutney, 677
Tomato-Cucumber Salad,
Palestinian, 638
Tomato Salad, Syrian, 637
Tomato Sauce, 679–80
Wild Rice, 507

Yogurt Cheese, 556–57
Zucchini, "Grilled," 295–96
Basil
about, 712
Cheese Salad with Tomato
and, Topped with Aspara-
gus, 620–21
Okra Cooked with Fresh
Curry or, Fried, 252–53
and Tomatoes, Yogurt with,
551
and Zucchini, Penne with, 482
Basmati rice, about, 372–73
Batatas. See Sweet potato(es)
Batter-Fried Okra, 255
Bean curd
about, 92
with Asparagus and Chinese
Mushrooms, 96–97
with Black Bean Sauce, 102
Cold, Salad, 97–98
fermented, 93, 712
fried, 93
Ginger-Garlic, 99
with Hot Sauce, 100
"Mayonnaise," Green Salad
with a, 631
with Mushrooms, 100–101
Omelet with Sesame Seeds
and, Japanese/Korean-
Style, 533
Portobello Mushrooms
Stuffed with, 245–46
pressed, 93
Pressed, Braised with Five
Flavorings, 105
Pressed, Stir-Fried with Hot
Peppers, 106
Salad, Cold, 97–98
Salad or Spread, 615
Scrambled Eggs with, Japan-
ese/Korean-Style, 529
Scrambled Eggs with Ginger
and, Chinese-Style, 530
Scrambled Eggs with Sesame
Seeds and, Japanese/
Korean-Style, 530
Soup and, Sichuan Vegetable,
593
Soup with Snow Peas and,
Miso, 606
Soup with Spinach and, Miso,
605–6
with Tomatoes and Cilantro,
98–99
and Tomato-Flavored Salad,
616
Vegeburgers, 103
Vegeburgers, Curried, 104
Vegeburgers in Brown Mush-
room Sauce, 104
Beans. *See* Legumes; *specific types
of beans*
Bean sauce with chile, Chinese,
about, 712
Bean sprouts
about black-eyed pea, 16
Fava, Stir-Fried, 46
about fava bean, 44
Lentil, with Ginger, Stir-
Fried, 67
Lentil, with Mustard Seeds
and Chiles, Stir-Fried, 67

Bean sprouts (cont.)
  about lentil, 59
  Mung, Stir-Fried with Ginger, 85
  Mung, Sweet-and-Sour, 83
  about mung, 74–75, 712–13
  about soybean, 91–92
Bean thread vermicelli, 75
Beefsteak leaves, about, 735
Beet greens, about, 211–12
Beet(s)
  and Beet Greens with a Horseradish Dressing, Boiled, 139–40
  boiling, 138
  buying and storing, 138
  with Mint and Yogurt, 141
  and Mushroom Curry, 142
  roasting in foil, 138
  Salad, Pureed, 140
  with Shallots, Grated, 139
Belgian endives
  with Bread Crumbs and Parmesan Cheese, 144
  preparing, 142–43
  in Their Own Juices, Browned, 143
Bengali-Style Green Beans, 207
Besan. See Chickpea flour
Bhagaar. See Tarka
Bhutanese Red Rice, 377
Bird's eye chiles, about, 716
Bitter melons
  buying, 295
  preparing, 295
  Stuffed with Onions and Pomegranate Seeds, 299
Black bean(s)
  "Charros," 13–14
  cooking methods for, 11
  Refried Beans, 12–13
  with Rice or "Spotted Rooster," 14
  Soup, Costa Rican, 595–96
Black beans, fermented
  about, 712, 713
  with Long Beans, 209
Black bean sauce
  with Bean Curd, 102
  about fermented, 712, 713
Black-eyed pea(s)
  cooking methods for, 15
  cooking sprouts of, 16
  with Corn and Dill, 19
  Fritters, 16–17
  frozen, 15–16
  with Herbs, 18
  in Mixed Bean Soup, 601–2
  Pancakes, 23–24
  and Rice with Pumpkin, 403
  Soup, Trinidadian, 594
  sprouting, 16
  Sprouts with Garlic and Thyme, 24
  with Swiss Chard, 20–21
  Trinidadian Seasonings, 21
  in a Walnut Sauce, 18
  with Watercress, 22
Black fungus, about, 722–23
Black pepper, about, 713
Black rice, "forbidden" Chinese
  about, 373–74
  Plain, 377

Black Tuscan Kale (Cavolo Nero)
  with Raisins, 222
Bleached flour, 419
Blenders, about, 710
Bok choy
  about, 212
  with Chinese Mushrooms, Baby, 216–17
Bombay-Style Green Mango Pickle, 699–700
Brazil, recipes from
  Coconut Chips, 661
Breads and flatbreads
  Bake, Fry, 456–58
  Bake, Pepper, 456
  about bakes, 455
  Circassian Sauce—A Walnut and Bread Sauce, 684
  with Coconut, Sri Lankan, 446–47
  Doubles, 458–60
  Dumplings, Vegetable, Boiled, 485–88
  Everyday Moroccan, 460–61
  Float, Fry, 456–58
  "French" Toast, American, 543
  "French" Toast, Indian, 542
  Griddle, Indian, 444–45
  Layered, Moroccan, 442–44
  Naan, 432–33
  Naan, Kandahari, 434
  Pizza, Cheese, 435
  Pizza with Oven-Dried Tomatoes, Cheese, and Rosemary, 435–36
  Potato, Flaky, 441–42
  Puffed, Sweet, 454–55
  Ridged, Turkish, 436–37
  Roti Stuffed with Split Peas, Trinidadian, 449–51
  "Roti," Trinidadian, 448–49
  Semolina, with Coconut and Pistachios, 461–63
  Sindhi, Sweet, 453
  Sindhi, with Black Pepper, 452
  Sindhi Seasoned, 454
  about Sindhi Whole Wheat, 451
  Stuffed with Cauliflower, Flaky, 439–40
  Wheat Tortillas, 445–46
  Whole Wheat, with Sprouted Wheat, Sunflower Seeds, and Rolled Oats, 463–65
  Whole Wheat, with Walnuts and Mint, 465–66
  Whole Wheat Flaky, Punjabi Village-Style Flat, 437–38
  about Whole Wheat Sindhi, 451
  Whole Wheat Tandoori, 430–31
  with Yeast, Moroccan, 429–30
  See also Pancakes
Broccoli
  blanching, 144
  buying, 144
  cutting and washing, 144
  with Ginger and Garlic, Stir-Fried, 146
  with Potatoes, 147

  with Spinach, 145–46
  with Walnut Sauce, 145
Broccoli rabe, 212
  with Fava Beans, 218
  with Garlic, 217
  with Garlic and Chili Flakes, 217
  with Mustard Seeds, Sautéed, 219
  with Polenta, 345
Browned Belgian Endives Cooked in Their Own Juices, 143
Brown Mushroom Sauce, 709
Brown rice
  about, 372
  Basic Recipe for, 376
  with Green Beans and Fresh Herbs, Spicy, 392
  with Sprouted Spelt, Spicy, 379
  Wild Rice with, 507–8
Buckwheat
  about, 328
  Noodles, Cold, 330–31
  Pancakes, 330
  Stir-Fried, 329
  Whole, Plain, 329
Bulgur wheat
  about, 418
  with Lentils, 425
  Pilaf with Peas and Carrots, 427
  with Red Pepper Paste, 426–27
  Risotto with Pumpkin, 428
  Tabbouleh, A Salad Made with Arugula and, 424
  Tabbouleh, A Salad of Parsley and, 423
Buttas, 445
Butternut squashes. See Squashes, winter
Butter(s)
  Ethiopian Aromatic, 658
  Ghee, 723
Buttery Soft Slices of Deep-Fried Eggplant with Garlic, 191–92

Cabbage
  buying, 147
  Celery, with a Gingery Milk Sauce, Stir-Fried, 153–54
  with Garlic and Shallots, 152
  and Peas, Semolina "Risotto" with, 489–90
  Pickle, Instant Korean, 685–86
  Red, with Cranberry Juice, Curried, 151–52
  with Rice and Currants, 149–50
  Salad, Orange and, Moroccan, 620
  Salad with Mustard Seeds, 617
  Salad with Oregano, 616
  South Indian, 152–53
  with Spicy Red Paste, Stir-Fried, 150
  in Sri Lankan Greens, 224–25
  in Stuffed Chinese Pancakes, 468–70

  Sweet-and-Sour, 148
  types of, 148
Cachucha chiles
  about, 716
  in Aromatic Cuban White Beans and Pumpkin Stew, 54–56
Cake(s)
  Oat, 365–66
  Potato, Mexican, 278–79
  Potato, with Herbs, 276–77
  Potato and Egg, Indian, 539
  Potato and Egg, Persian, 538–39
  Potato and Egg, Spanish, 536
  Scallion, 466–67
  See also Patties
Cardamom
  about, 713–14
  in An Ancient Drink with Ginger and Cardamom, 644
  Drink with Lemon and Mint, A Cold Ginger-, 644
  Sweet Potatoes with Chiles and, Sri Lankan, 285
Caribbean Seasoning Sauce, 675–76
Caribbean Style Chickpea and Potato Curry, 33–34
Carrot olives, to make, 155
Carrot(s)
  and Cilantro Salad, 618
  diced, 155
  with Dried Apricots, Persian-Style, 160
  with Fresh Fenugreek or Fresh Cilantro, 159
  with Ginger, Quick Glazed, 155
  and Ginger Relish, South Indian, 618–19
  and Ginger with Mustard Seeds, Stir-Fried, 157
  and Green Beans, Quinoa with, 367
  with Herbs, Sautéed, Lightly Sweetened, 157
  julienned, 155
  Kohlrabi, and Daikon Salad, 627–28
  and Peas, Bulgur Pilaf with, 427
  Pickled, with Mustard Seeds, 686–87
  with Potatoes and Peas, Village-Style, 158
  preparing, 154–55
  Raita, 547
  Salad, Thai "Pickled," 619
  Salad with Orange Juice, Moroccan, 620
  Sesame Seeds, Chard, and, Millet with, 359–60
  and Sliced Shallots, Toovar Dal with, 87–88
  Stew of Chickpeas, Potatoes, and, Middle Eastern, 29
Cashew(s)
  about, 117, 714
  and Almond Soup, Indian, 583–84

in Coconut Rice, South
Indian, 382
cooking methods for, 116, 117
and Green Beans, Semolina
"Risotto" with, 491–92
and Green Pea Bhaji, Indian-
Style, 120
in a Green Spice Paste, 119
in a Mediterranean Tomato
Sauce, 118–19
origins of, 116
storing raw, 117
Zapped in the Microwave,
Quick, 118
Cassia bark, about, 714
Cast-iron skillets, about, 710
Caucasus, recipes from
Walnut Sauce, 684
Cauliflower
blanching, 161–62
buying and storing, 161
with Corn, 173–74
and Cumin, Whole Wheat
Couscous with, 498–99
cutting into florets, 161
Flaky Flatbreads Stuffed
with, 439–40
Fritters, 165–66
with Ginger and Cilantro,
Stir-Fried, 162
with Ginger and Cream,
162–63
and Green Beans in Red
Chile Dressing, 164–65
and Potatoes with Ginger,
Punjabi-Style, 163–64
with Rice Noodles, 415
with Scrambled Eggs, 528–29
in Vegetable Stew with
Chickpea Flour Sauce, 36
Cayenne, about, 714
Celery
buying and storing, 166
and Chickpeas, Yogurt Soup
with, Cold, 581–82
about Chinese, 714
with Fennel and Black
Pepper, Gratin, 167
and Pistachios, Yogurt with,
551–52
preparing, 166
with Snow Peas, Stir-Fried,
168
Celery cabbage
about, 148
with a Gingery Milk Sauce,
Stir-Fried, 153–54
Cellophane noodles, mung bean,
75
Chadon bené, about, 720
Chana dal
about, 26–27, 713
and Chickpeas, Cooked
Together in a Mint Sauce,
34–35
See also Chickpea flour;
Chickpea(s)
Chapatis
flour for, 714
Oat, 362–63
Charoli nuts, about, 714
Chayotes
about, 714

with a South Indian Yogurt
Sauce, 553–54
Cheese
and Corn, Mexican-Style Rice
Casserole with Sour
Cream, 398
Corn Tortillas Stuffed with,
350–51
Corn Tortillas Stuffed with
Refried Beans and, 351
Curds and Vegetables, Deli-
cate Stir-Fry of Soft, 567
Egg Pie with Herbs and,
Persian-Style, 538
Feta, and Zucchini Salad, 640
Feta, Red Peppers Stuffed
with, 266
about homemade, 561
Homemade Indian, 561–62
Homemade Indian, Cooked
in the Style of Scrambled
Eggs, 569–70
Homemade Indian, Crispy
Slices of, 571–72
Homemade Indian, Flavored
with Black Pepper,
Roasted Cumin Seeds, and
Roasted *Ajwain* Seeds, 563
Homemade Indian, Flavored
with Rosemary, Thyme,
and Oregano, 563
Homemade Indian, Served
with a "Salsa," 568
Homemade Indian, with
Spinach, 570–71
Homemade Indian, with
Tomatoes, 568–69
Homemade Italian Mascar-
pone, 565
Homemade Latin American,
564
Homemade Syrian, 566–67
Parmesan, Eggplants with
Tomato and, Stir-Fried,
185
about parmesan, 731
Pizza, 435
Pizza with Oven-Dried Toma-
toes, Rosemary, and, 435–
36
Poblano Peppers with, Mexi-
can, 267
Polenta, and Butter Mixed
with, 344
Polenta Draped over, 346
in Pumpkin Pie, Savory
Greek, 293–94
in Pumpkin Risotto Made in
a Pressure Cooker, Greek,
410–11
Quesadilla with, 352
in Quesadilla with Mush-
rooms, 353
in Risotto with Dried Porcini
Mushrooms, 407–8
in Risotto with Spinach,
Golden Raisins, and Pine
Nuts, 409–10
in Risotto with Tomato,
Roasted Eggplant, and
Mint, 409
in Risotto with Tomato and
Eggplant, 408–9

Salad, Zucchini and Feta, 640
Salad with Tomato and Basil
Topped with Asparagus,
620–21
Syrian, with Olives, 572
Syrian, with Tomatoes, 573
Syrian Cheese with Cucum-
ber and Sesame Seeds, 573
See also Yogurt cheese
Cherries
Chutney, Afghani Sour, 659
Chutney, Kashmiri Walnut
and Sour, 659–60
Syrup, Sour, 645–46
Chickpea flour
batter, 27–28
in Batter-Fried Okra, 255
in Cauliflower Fritters,
165–66
Chickpeas and *Chana Dal*
Cooked Together in a
Mint Sauce, 34–35
cooking methods for, 27–28
"French Fries," 41–42
"French Fries," the Indian
Way, 42–43
Pancakes, Basic Recipe for
Plain, 37
Pancakes with Crushed
Green Peas and Cilantro,
38
Pancakes with Fresh Green
Herbs, 38
Pancakes with Sesame Seeds,
38
Pancakes with Tomato and
Onion, 38–39
Pizza, Basic Recipe for Plain,
39–40
Pizza with Rosemary, Tomato,
and Parmesan Cheese, 40
Pizza with Thyme and Sage,
40
in Pumpkin Fritters, 292
Sauce, Vegetable Stew with, 36
Chickpea(s)
about, 25
canned, 25, 26
and *Chana Dal* Cooked
Together in a Mint Sauce,
34–35
in Doubles, 458–60
Eggplant Stew with Potatoes,
Mushrooms, and, Spicy,
196
in a Moghlai Style, 32–33
and Potato Curry, Caribbean
Style, 33–34
preparing, 26–27
Pumpkins, Raisins, and, with
Couscous, 501–2
Red Lentil Stew with Wheat
Berries and, Anatolian,
71–72
removing skins of, 26
Soup, and Rosemary-Flavored
Spinach, 598
Soup, Mexican-Style, 597
Soup with Escarole, 596–97
Soup with Escarole and Dried
Porcini Mushrooms, 597
Soup with Escarole and
Tomato, 597

Spinach with, Spanish-Style,
228–29
Stew of Potatoes, Carrots,
and, Middle Eastern, 29
Stew with Spinach, Cypriot, 31
Swiss Chard with Tomatoes
and, 231
Whole Grain or "Bead"
Hummus, 28
Yogurt Soup with Celery and,
Cold, 581–82
Yogurt with Onion, Mint,
and, 549
Chile oil, about, 717
Chile powders, about, 716–17
Chiles, dried
about, 714–15
in Pecan-Chile Sauce, 668–69
Tex-Mex Pinto Bean Stew
with Ancho, 89
Chiles, fresh
about, 715–16
buying and storing, 262
Hot Peppers with Ginger and
Garlic, Stir-Fried, 263
in Mexican Potato Cake,
278–79
in Mexican-Style Rice Casse-
role with Corn, Sour
Cream, and Cheese, 398
Pepper Bake, 456
Pressed Bean Curd Stir-Fried
with Hot Peppers, 106
in Red Pepper Paste, 673–74
Relish, Fresh Ginger and
Green, 665–66
roasting, 262–63
Tomatoes, Shallots, and,
Sambal with Roasted, 681
in Trinidadian Pepper Sauce,
671–72
See also Poblano chiles
Chili
Polenta with Tex-Mex, 346
Vegetarian, Tex-Mex, 64–65
Chili pastes, about, 717
Chili sauce, about, 717
China, recipes from
Asparagus with a Chinese
Dressing, Cold, 134–35
Azuki and Whole Mung
Beans, Crushed and
Sautéed, 10–11
Azuki Beans with Green
Pepper from Yunnan, Stir-
Fried, 9
Bean Curd Braised with Five
Flavorings, Pressed, 105
Bean Curd with Hot Peppers,
Pressed Stir-Fried, 106
Bean Curd with Hot Sauce,
100
Bean Curd with Mushrooms,
100–101
Bean Curd with Tomatoes
and Cilantro, 98–99
Broccoli with Ginger and
Garlic, Stir-Fried, 146
Cabbage, Sweet-and-Sour,
148
Celery Cabbage with a Gin-
gery Milk Sauce, Stir-
Fried, 153–54

Chinese Chives, Stir-Fried, 169

Daikon, Stewed or "Red-Cooked," 176

Daikon Pickle, 688

Dry Green Beans with Tien Jing Preserved Vegetable, Stir-Fried, 204

Dumplings, Vegetable, Boiled, 485–88

Eggplants, Hot and Spicy Sichuan-Style, 188–89

Egg Whites with Peas, 530

Fava Bean Sprouts, Stir-Fried, 46

"Foreign Vegetable," i.e., Watercress, Stir-Fried, 233

Garlic Relish, Crunchy Sichuan, 664

Kohlrabi, Stir-Fried, 238–39

Long Beans with Fermented Black Beans, 209

Mixed Vegetable Salad, 642–43

Mung Bean Thread Salad, 84

Mushrooms, Three Kinds of, 244

Noodles, Pan-Fried, 476–77

Noodles Sautéed with Vegetables, 479–80

Pancakes, Stuffed, 468–70

Peanuts, "Pickled," 122–23

Peanuts Boiled with Five Flavorings, 122

Pepper and Salt, Roasted Sichuan, 704

Radish Salad, 634–35

Rice, Emerald Fried, 391–92

Scallion Cakes, 466–67

Scrambled Eggs with Ginger and Bean Curd, 530

Snow Pea Shoots, Stir-Fried, 223–24

Snow Peas with Scallions, Stir-Fried, 261

Soy Sauce Salad Dressing, 677

Sweet-and-Sour Mung Bean Sprouts, 83

Sweet "Green Pea" Soup, 611

Sweet Red Bean Soup, 612

Tea Eggs, 516

Chinese-American recipes

Baby Bok Choy with Chinese Mushrooms, 216–17

Bean Curd and Vegetable Soup, Sichuan, 593

Bean Curd with Black Bean Sauce, 102

Potato Shreds, Stir-Fried Sweet-and-Sour, 271

Chinese broccoli (gailan)

about, 212, 725

in Emerald Fried Rice, 391–92

Chinese celery, about, 714

Chinese chives

about, 717

buying and storing, 168

cleaning, 169

Stir-Fried, 169

Chinese mushrooms. See Mushroom(s)

Chinese parsley. See Cilantro

Chipotle chiles, about, 715

Chironji nuts, in Semolina Bread with Coconut and Pistachios, 461–63

Choka, 186

Tomato, 300

Chowli. See Black-eyed pea(s)

Chutney(s)

Cilantro and Coconut, 663

Cilantro and Mint, Delhi-Style, 660

Lemon, Sweet-and-Sour, 690–91

Mango, 695

Mango, Royal, 696

Mango and Ginger, 697–98

Mango and Ginger, with Five Bengali Spices, 698

Mango with Fennel and Fenugreek, 696

Peach, Delhi-Style, 700–701

Sour Cherry, Afghani, 659

Sour Cherry and Walnut, Kashmiri, 659–60

Tamarind, Plain, 677

Tamarind with Raisins and Walnuts, 677

Tamarind-Yogurt, 678

Tomato Preserve with Almonds, Sweet, 701

See also Pickle(s)

Cilantro

about, 717

and Carrot Salad, 618

Carrots with Fresh, 159

and Coconut, Green Peas with, 259

and Coconut Chutney, 663

and Ginger, Skinned Wheat Berry Soup with, 609

and Mint Chutney, Delhi-Style, 660

and Tomatoes, Bean Curd with, 98–99

Cinnamon, about, 717–18

Circassian Sauce—A Walnut and Bread Sauce, 684

Classical Method of Cooking Polenta, 342

Classic Romesco Sauce, 669–70

Cloves, about, 717

Coconut

in Cashews in a Green Spice Paste, 119

in Cauliflower and Green Beans in Red Chile Dressing, 164–65

and Cilantro, Green Peas with, 259

and Cilantro Chutney, 663

Flatbreads with, Sri Lankan, 446–47

about fresh, 718

in Greens, Sri Lankan, 224–25

and Mango, Yogurt with, 320

and Pistachios, Semolina Bread with, 461–63

Rice, South Indian, 382

Sambol, 662–63

in White Egg Curry, Sri Lankan, 515

in Yogurt with Banana in the South Indian Style, 555

Coconut Chips, 661

Coconut milk

canned, 718

in Coconut Sambol, 662–63

in Egg Curry, Goan Style, 518

in Eggplant Curry, Sri Lankan, 189–90

fresh, 719

in Green Beans and Potato Curry, 208–9

made from creamed, 720

powdered, 719

in Red Kidney Beans for Jamaican "Peas and Rice," 48–49

Sauce, 661–62

Sweet "Green Pea" Soup with, 612

Coconut Sambol, 662–63

Coffee grinders, about, 710

Cold dishes

Almond Soup, 578–79

Asparagus with a Chinese Dressing, 134–35

Asparagus with a Korean Dressing, 135

Avocado and Buttermilk Soup, 579

Bean Curd Salad, 97–98

Buckwheat Noodles, 330–31

Eggplants with a Soy Sauce Dressing, 180

Eggplants with Spicy Chinese Peanut Dressing, 181

Ginger-Cardamom Drink with Lemon and Mint, 644

Pomegranate Soup, 580

Wakame Seaweed Soup, 580–81

Yogurt Soup in the South Indian Style, 582

Yogurt Soup with Chickpeas and Celery, 581–82

Collard greens

about, 212–13

with Asafetida, 220

with Browned Onions, 219

Coo-Coo (Cornmeal and Okra Mold), 336

Cooling Cucumber and Mint Drink, 643–44

Coriander seeds, about, 720

Corn

about, 332–33

buying and storing, 170

with Cauliflower, 173–74

Cheese, Sour Cream, and, Mexican-Style Rice Casserole with, 398

cooking methods for, 169–70

and Dill, Black-Eyed Peas with, 19

dried kernel, 333

frozen and canned, 170

with Ginger, 171–72

Grilled Sweet, 171

grits, hominy, 335

Grits with Mushrooms, 337

Kohlrabi with, Spicy, 239–40

masa, 335

masa harina, 335, 348–49

masa harina "precocida," 335

Mushrooms, Asparagus, and, Wild Rice Sautéed with, 508

popping, 334

Posole, Green, 338–39

posole/hominy, 334–35

and Potatoes, Quinoa with, 369

Quesadilla with Cheese, 352

Quesadilla with Mushrooms, 353

removing kernels from fresh, 170

Salad, Spicy, 622

with Sesame Seeds and Tomatoes, Spicy, 174–75

Soup, Indonesian, 584

Stew, Rice, Vegetable, and, Indonesian, 340–41

in Yogurt, 172–73

See also Corn breads; Cornmeal; Polenta; Tortillas: corn

Corn bread(s)

Ecuador-Style Corn Muffins, 356–57

Flat Indian, 354–55

with Sesame Seeds, 356

Cornmeal

about, 334

in Corn Bread with Sesame Seeds, 356

in Corn Muffins, Ecuador-Style, 356–57

in Flat Indian Corn Breads, 354–55

masa, 335

and Okra Mold, 336

Corn Tortillas. See Tortillas: corn

Costa Rica, recipes from

Black Bean Soup, 595–96

Black Beans with Rice or "Spotted Rooster," 14

Couscous

about, 418–19, 494–95

with Asparagus and Fresh Mushrooms, Israeli, 504

Chickpeas, Pumpkins, and Raisins with, 501–2

Instant (or Quick-Cooking), 496

about instant or quick-cooking, 495

about Israeli, 496

about Lebanese, 496

about Moroccan, 496

with Red Potato Sauce, Speckled Green, 502–3

Traditional Moroccan, 499–500

Whole Wheat, Plain, 497

Whole Wheat, Plain Toasted, 497

Whole Wheat, with Cumin and Cauliflower, 498–99

Whole Wheat, with Sesame Seeds and Raisins, 498

about whole wheat, 495

Cranberry Juice, Curried Red Cabbage with, 151–52

Cream

in Poached Eggs over Artichoke Hearts with a White Sauce, 522

Sauce, Hard-Boiled Eggs in a Tomato-, 517
Creamed Eggplant, 183
Creamy Sweet "Green Pea" Soup, 611
Crisply Fried Onions or Shallots in the Persian Style, 666–67
Crisply Fried Tortillas, 354
Crisp Potato Cake with Herbs, 276–77
Crispy Slices of Homemade Indian Cheese, 571–72
Crumbled Potatoes with Peas, 280
Crunchy Sichuan Garlic Relish, 664
Cuba, recipes from
  Aromatic Cuban White Bean and Pumpkin Stew, 54–56
Cucumber(s)
  in Cold Wakame Seaweed Soup, 580–81
  and Green Pepper Salad, 632
  and Mint Drink, Cooling, 643–44
  "Raita," Gujarati, 550
  and Sesame Seeds, Syrian Cheese with, 573
  and Tomato Drink, 652
  and Tomato Drink, Spicy, 653
  –Tomato Salad, Simple Palestinian, 638
  Yogurt Cheese with, 558
Culantro, about, 720
Cumin seeds
  about black, 720
  about whole and ground, 720–21
Currants
  about, 721
  and Rice, Cabbage with, 149–50
  Rice with, Persian, 389–90
  and Walnuts, Spelt Berries with, 421–22
Curry leaves
  about, 721
  in Black-Eyed Peas with Corn and Dill, 19
  in Cabbage, South Indian, 152–53
  in Cashews in a Green Spice Paste, 119
  in Chayote with a South Indian Yogurt Sauce, 553–54
  in Coconut Milk Sauce, 661–62
  in Coconut Rice, South Indian, 382
  in Corn Cooked in Yogurt, 172–73
  in Egg Curry, Goan Style, 518
  in Eggplant Curry, Sri Lankan, 189–90
  in Eggplant "Pickle," Sri Lankan, 197–98
  Fried Okra Cooked with Fresh Basil or, 252–53
  in Green Beans and Potato Curry, 208–9
  in Green Peas with Coconut

and Cilantro, 259
  in Greens, Sri Lankan, 224–25
  in Grits with Mushrooms, 337
  in Hard-Boiled Eggs in a Tomato-Cream Sauce, 517
  in "Javanese" Noodles, 477–79
  and Mustard Seeds, Figs with, 623–24
  in Potatoes, Gujarati-Style Hot Sweet-and-Sour, 273
  Pumpkin Soup with Fresh, 590
  in Red Lentils Hyderabadi, 69
  Red Lentil Soup with, and Mustard Seeds, 600–601
  in Rice with Yogurt and Apple, 396–97
  in Roasted Red Bell Peppers with Mustard Seeds, 264
  in Semolina "Risotto" with Cabbage and Peas, 489–90
  in Stir-Fried Fresh Shiitake Mushrooms, 249
  in Sweet Potatoes with Cardamom and Chiles, Sri Lankan, 285
  Tomato Sambal, 302
  in Toovar Dal with Sliced Shallots and Carrots, 87–88
  in Vegetable Mulligatawny Soup, 592
  in Vegetable Stew with Chickpea Flour Sauce, 36
  in Yogurt with Green Mango, 553
Curry powder
  about, 721
  My, 707–8
  Raw, Sri Lankan, 707
Cyprus, recipes from
  Artichoke Hearts with Wine and Coriander Seeds, 130
  Black-Eyed Peas with Swiss Chard, 20–21
  Bulgur Risotto with Pumpkin, 428
  Chickpea Stew with Spinach, 31
  Lentils with Rice, 63
  Lima Bean Stew, 56–57
  Mushrooms with Wine and Coriander Seeds, 247

Daikon
  about, 721
  in Buckwheat Noodles, Cold, 330–31
  buying and storing, 175
  Kohlrabi, Carrot, and, Salad, 627–28
  Pickle, 688
  preparing, 175
  in Radish Salad with Orange Juice, 636
  Stewed or "Red-Cooked," 176
Dairy foods, about, 511
  See also specific dairy foods
Dal, definition of, 4
Dasheen leaves
  about, 721

in Greens, Sri Lankan, 224–25
in Kallaloo, 585–86
Daun paandaan, about, 733
Daun salaam. See Curry leaves
Deep-fat fryers, about, 710
Deep-Fried Eggplants with a Soy Sauce Dressing, 180–81
Delhi-Style Cilantro and Mint Chutney, 660
Delhi-Style Peach Chutney, 700–701
Delicate Stir-Fry of Soft Cheese Curds and Vegetables, 567
Dill
  and Corn, Black-Eyed Peas with, 19
  in Greek Pumpkin Risotto Made in a Pressure Cooker, 410–11
  Spinach with Onion and, Sautéed, 225
  in Yogurt Cheese with Cucumber, 558
Dipping sauces, 412, 413
Double boilers, about, 710
Doubles, 458–60
Dried corn kernels, 333
Dried Mushroom Stock, 577–78
Drink(s)
  about, 576
  Almond Milk, 643
  Banana Lassi, Sweet, 655
  Cooling Cucumber and Mint, 643–44
  Fresh Lime and Ginger Syrup, 647–48
  Fresh Lime Syrup, 647
  with Ginger and Cardamom, An Ancient, 644
  Ginger-Cardamom Drink with Lemon and Mint, A Cold, 644
  Ginger Fruit Punch, 645
  Lemongrass Tea, 650
  Mango Lassi, Sweet, 656
  Milk and Apple, Moroccan, 649
  Mint Lemonade, Irani, 648
  Mint Tea, Moroccan, 651
  Rhubarb Syrup, Persian, 646–47
  Simple Sugar Syrup, 739
  Sour Cherry Syrup, 645–46
  Spicy Tomato and Cucumber, 653
  Tea, Kashmiri, 650
  Tea, Mint, Moroccan, 651
  Tea, Spicy Indian, 651–52
  Tomato and Cucumber, 652
  Vinegar Syrup, 653
  Watermelon Juice, 655
  Yogurt, Madras-Style Spicy, 657
  Yogurt, Punjabi, 655
  Yogurt and Milk, 649
"Dry" Hulled and Split Mung Beans with Browned Garlic and Onions, 78
"Dry" Red Lentils, 68
Dry-roasting spices, about, 721
Dumplings
  Mung Bean, in a Spicy Tomato Sauce, 82–83

Vegetable, Boiled, 485–88

Ecuador, recipes from
  Ecuador-Style Corn Muffins, 356–57
Egg noodles, about, 729
Eggplant(s)
  buying and storing, 177
  Creamed, 183
  Curry, Sri Lankan, 189–90
  Deep-Fried, with a Soy Sauce Dressing, 180–81
  with Garlic, Buttery Soft Slices of Deep-Fried, 191–92
  Hot and Spicy Sichuan-Style, 188–89
  with a Korean Hot Sauce, Poached, 182
  with Minty Tomato Sauce and Yogurt, 192–93
  with Peanut Dressing, Cold Spicy Chinese, 181
  "Pickle," Sri Lankan, 197–98
  in Red Lentil Stew with Wheat Berries and Chickpeas, Anatolian, 71–72
  roasting techniques for, 177–79
  roll cutting, 179
  Salad, Greek, 621
  and Shiitake Mushrooms Cooked in a Japanese Sauce, 187–88
  Smoked, 183–84
  Sour Fennel-Flavored, 195
  with a Soy Sauce Dressing, Cold, 180
  with Spicy Shallot-Tomato Sauce, 190–91
  Stew with Potatoes, Mushrooms, and Chickpeas, Spicy, 196
  Stuffed Baby, 184–85
  Sweet-and-Sour, 194
  and Tomato, Risotto with, 408–9
  with Tomato, Mint, and Roasted, 409
  with Tomato and Parmesan Cheese, Stir-Fried, 185
  and Tomato Choka, 186–87
  types of, 177
  and Walnuts, Yogurt with, 552
Egg(s)
  about, 512–13
  Curry, Goan Style, 518
  Curry, Sri Lankan White, 515
  French Omelet, 531–32
  French Omelet with Asparagus, 532
  French Omelet with Cheese and Chives, 532
  French Omelet with Herbs, 532
  in "French" Toast, American, 543
  in "French" Toast, Indian, 542
  Fried, Mexican, 525
  Fried, Western, 524–25
  about fried, 524

Egg(s) *(cont.)*
Frittata with Swiss Chard, 540
Hard-Boiled, 514
Hard-Boiled, in a Tomato-Cream Sauce, 517
in a Mulligatawny Sauce, 519
Omelet with Sesame Seeds and Bean Curd, Japanese/Korean-Style, 533
Pie, Zucchini, Tuscan, 541
Pie with Herbs, Persian, 537
Pie with Herbs and Cheese, Persian-Style, 538
Pie with Tomato and Herbs, Persian-Style, 538
Poached, 519–20
Poached, on Japanese Noodles, 523–24
Poached, over Artichoke Hearts with a White Sauce, 522
Poached, Served in a Korean Manner, 520
Poached in a Tomato Sauce, Persian, 521
and Potato Cake, Indian, 539
and Potato Cake, Persian, 538–39
and Potato Cakes, Spanish, 536
Scrambled, the Western Way, 526
Scrambled, with Bean Curd, Japanese/Korean-Style, 529
Scrambled, with Cauliflower, 528–29
Scrambled, with Fresh Herbs, 526
Scrambled, with Ginger and Bean Curd, Chinese-Style, 530
Scrambled, with Onion and Tomatoes, Indian, 526–27
Scrambled, with Scallions and Mushrooms, 527
Scrambled, with Sesame Seeds and Bean Curd, Japanese/Korean-Style, 530
about scrambled, 525
Soft-Boiled, 513–14
Soy Sauce, with Rosemary, 514–15
Stir-Fried, Indian-Style, 528
Strands and Shiitake Mushrooms, Miso Soup with, 607–8
Tea, 516
Whites with Peas, 530
Electric rice cookers, about, 710
El Salvador, recipes from
Cabbage Salad with Oregano, 616
Corn Tortillas Stuffed with Cheese, 350–51
Corn Tortillas Stuffed with Cheese and Refried Beans, 351
Corn Tortillas Stuffed with Potatoes and Green Pepper, 351
Emerald Fried Rice, 391–92

Epazote
about, 722
in Mexican Potato Soup, 588–89
Equipment, cooking, 709–10
Escarole, 213
and Chickpea Soup, 596–97
and Chickpea Soup with Dried Porcini Mushrooms, 597
and Chickpea Soup with Tomato, 597
Ethiopia, recipes from
Aromatic Butter, 658
Hot Sauce, 674–75
Lentil Salad with Crushed Mustard Seeds, 629–30
Everyday Moroccan Bread, 460–61

Fava bean(s), dried
Broccoli Rabe Served on a Bed of, 218
cooking methods for, 44
origins of, 43
Puree, 45
sprouting, 44
Sprouts, Stir-Fried, 46
types of, 44
Fava bean(s), fresh
with Garlic and Thyme, Sautéed, 199
with Ginger, Stir-Fried, 200
preparing, 198–99
Salad, Artichoke Heart and Fresh, 612–13
Fennel and Orange Salad, 623
Fennel seeds
about, 722
and Cumin, Green Beans with, 202–3
and Fenugreek, Mango Chutney with, 696
Mango Pickle with, Rajasthani, 698–99
Potatoes with, 274
Potatoes with Ginger and, 274
Fenugreek leaves
about, 722
Carrots with Fresh, 159
in Mung Beans with Greens, 79–80
Fenugreek seeds, about, 722
Fermented Black Beans, Long Beans with, 209
Fettucine
with a Mushroom Ragout, 484–85
with Ricotta, Spinach, and Pine Nuts, 483–84
Fiddlehead ferns, 200–201
Figs with Mustard Seeds and Curry Leaves, 623–24
Filo pastry, in Savory Greek Pumpkin Pie, 293–94
Fireman's Soup, 608
Five-Spice Powder, 722
Flaky Flatbreads Stuffed with Cauliflower, 439–40
Flatbreads. *See* Breads and flatbreads
Flat Indian Corn Breads, 354–55

Flour tortillas, 445–46
Food processors, about, 710
"Forbidden" Chinese black rice. *See* Black rice, "forbidden" Chinese
"Foreign Vegetable." *See* Watercress
France, recipes from
Chickpea Flour "French Fries," 41–42
Chickpea Flour Pizza, Basic Recipe for Plain, 39–40
Chickpea Flour Pizza with Rosemary, Tomato, and Parmesan Cheese, 40
Chickpea Flour Pizza with Thyme and Sage, 40
Omelet, 531–32
Omelet with Asparagus, 532
Omelet with Cheese and Chives, 532
Omelet with Herbs, 532
"French Fries," chickpea flour
French, 41–42
the Indian Way, 42–43
French lentils, 59, 64
"French" Toast
American, 543
Indian, 542
Fried rice, Emerald, 391–92
Fritters
Black-Eyed Pea, 16–17
Mung Bean, 81–82
Pumpkin, 292
Zucchini, Crisp, 298
Fruit
Punch, Ginger, 645
"Ratatouille" of Vegetables and, Persian Sweet-and-Sour, 312–13
and Vegetable Salad with Sweet Soy and Peanut Dressing, Malaysian Mixed, 626
See also specific fruits
Fry Bake or Float, 456–58
Frying pans, about, 740

Gailan. See Chinese broccoli (gailan)
Galangal, about, 723
Garam Masala, about, 723
Garbanzos. *See* Chickpea(s)
Garcinia cambozia, about, 724
Garlic
Eggplant with, Buttery Soft Slices of Deep-Fried, 191–92
and Ginger, Broccoli Stir-Fried with, 146
and Ginger, Hot Peppers Stir-Fried with, 263
-Ginger Bean Curd, 99
in *Harissa*, 672–73
Mushrooms, Lentils Topped with, 66
and Onions, "Dry" Hulled and Split Mung Beans with Browned, 78
Paste, Moroccan Chile-, 672–73
Pickled, 687
Potatoes with, Mashed the

New-Fashioned Way, 281
Relish, Crunchy Sichuan, 664
and Thyme, Black-Eyed Pea Sprouts with, 24
and Thyme, Fresh Fava Beans Sautéed with, 199
Ghee (Clarified Butter), about, 723
Ginger
about, 723
and Bean Curd, Scrambled Eggs with, Chinese-Style, 530
Broccoli with Garlic and, Stir-Fried, 146
and Cardamom, An Ancient Drink with, 644
-Cardamom Drink, with Lemon and Mint, Cold, 644
and Carrot Relish, South Indian, 618–19
with Carrots, Quick Glazed, 155
and Carrots with Mustard Seeds, Stir-Fried, 157
with Cauliflower and Cilantro, Stir-Fried, 162
with Cauliflower and Cream, 162–63
and Cauliflower with Potatoes, Punjabi-Style, 163–64
and Cilantro, Skinned Wheat Berry Soup with, 609
with Corn, 171–72
Fava Beans with, Stir-Fried Fresh, 200
and Fennel Seeds, Potatoes with, 274
Fruit Punch, 645
and Garlic, Hot Peppers with, Stir-Fried, 263
-Garlic Bean Curd, 99
and Green Chile Relish, Fresh, 665–66
Lentil Bean Sprouts with, Stir-Fried, 67
Lentils Topped with Yogurt and Spinach, 62
and Lime Syrup, Fresh, 647–48
and Mango Chutney, 697–98
and Mango Chutney with Five Bengali Spices, 698
Mung Bean Sprouts with, Stir-Fried, 85
with Peas and Sesame Oil, 257
with Potatoes and Fennel Seeds, 274
and Potatoes with Cauliflower, Punjabi-Style, 163–64
and Red Pepper, Asparagus with, Stir-Fried, 137–38
Scrambled Eggs with Bean Curd and, Chinese-Style, 530
Wheat Berry Soup with Cilantro and, Skinned, 609
Ginger graters, about, 741
Gluten, wheat
about, 419

Mock Lamb Curry, 505
Mock Minced Chicken, 506
Glutinous or sweet rice
  about, 373
  Steamed Plain, 378
Glutinous rice powder, about, 724
Gobi Bhajjia (Cauliflower Fritters), 165–66
Gobi Ka Paratha (Flaky Flatbreads Stuffed with Cauliflower), 439–40
Goraka, about, 724
Grains. *See specific grains*
Granola, 362
Greece, recipes from
  Artichoke Heart and Fresh Fava Bean Salad, 612–13
  Beet Salad, Pureed, 140
  Beets and Beet Greens with a Horseradish Dressing, Boiled, 139–40
  Eggplant Salad, 621
  Leeks with Rice, 242
  Lentil Salad, Greek-Style, 629–30
  Lima Beans or Large White Beans, Baked, 53
  Mixed Greens, 232
  Pancakes, Semolina, 470–71
  Potatoes, Baked, 277
  Pumpkin Pie, Savory Greek, 293–94
  Pumpkin Risotto Made in a Pressure Cooker, 410–11
  Red Peppers Stuffed with Feta Cheese, 266
  Spinach with Rice, 227
  Tomatoes Stuffed with Wheat Berries, 420–21
  Yogurt Cheese with Cucumber, 558
  Yogurt Cheese with Feta, Soft, 559
  Zucchini Fritters, Crisp, 298
Green beans
  Bengali-Style, 207
  blanching, 202
  with Browned Shallots, 206
  Brown Rice with Fresh Herbs and, Spicy, 392
  and Carrots, Quinoa with, 367
  and Cauliflower in Red Chile Dressing, 164–65
  Cumin, Browned Onions, and, Millet with, 358–59
  with Cumin and Fennel, 202–3
  in Fireman's Soup, 608
  with Garlic and Preserved Lemon, 205
  about long, 201–2
  Long Beans, Soft, 210
  Long Beans with Fermented Black Beans, 209
  with Mushrooms, 206
  Pearl Onions, Lentils, and, Wild Rice Stew with, 509
  Pilaf with Lime and, Persian, 384–85
  and Potato Curry, 208–9
  in Rice with Yogurt and Apple, 396–97

"Risotto" with Cashews and, Semolina, 491–92
  with Roasted Red Pepper and Preserved Lemon, 205
Salad, 202–3
string, 201
  in Tex-Mex Pinto Bean Stew with Ancho Chiles, 89
  with Tien Jing Preserved Vegetable, Stir-Fried Dry, 204
  in Vegetable Stew with Chickpea Flour Sauce, 36
Green Curry Sauce, Peas and Mushrooms in a, 258
Green Lettuce in a Korean Dressing, 631
Green mango powder. *See Amchoor*
Greens
  buying and storing, 211
  types of, 211–15
  washing, 211
  See also specific greens
Green Salad with a Bean Curd "Mayonnaise," 631
Green Spice Paste, Cashews in a, 119
Grilled dishes
  Corn, Sweet, 171
  Mixed Vegetables, Indian Style, 314–15
  Portobello Mushrooms, Spanish-Style, 248–49
  Zucchini, Simple, 295–96
  Zucchini, Spanish-Style, 296–97
Grits
  about, 335
  with Mushrooms, 337
Guacamole, 613–14
Gudangan (Cauliflower and Green Beans in Red Chile Dressing), 164–65
Gujarati Cucumber "Raita," 550
Gujarati-Style Hot Sweet-and-Sour Potatoes, 273
Gun Chow Si Ji Do (Stir-Fried Dry Green Beans with Tien Jing Preserved Vegetable), 204

Habanero chiles, about, 716
Hard-boiled eggs
  about, 514
  in a Tomato-Cream Sauce, 517
Harissa
  in Chickpea Stew with Six Vegetables, 30–31
  Moroccan Chile-Garlic Paste, 672–73
Hash Brown Potatoes, Spicy, 278
Herbs
  Black-Eyed Peas with, 18
  with Bread, Fresh, 627
  Brown Rice with Green Beans and Fresh, Spicy, 392
  in Caribbean Seasoning Sauce, 675–76
  Carrots with, Sautéed, Lightly Sweetened, 157
  Chickpea Flour Pancakes with Fresh Green, 38

Egg Pie with, Persian, 537
Egg Pie with Cheese and, Persian-Style, 538
Egg Pie with Tomato and, Persian-Style, 538
French Omelet with, 532
Potato Cake with, Crisp, 276–77
Scrambled Eggs with Fresh, 526
Yogurt with Herbs, 548
Hijiki
  about, 724
  in Soybeans with Brown Sugar, 94
Hoisin sauce, about, 724
Holy basil *(Ocinum sanctum)*, about, 712
Homemade cheeses. *See entries beginning with "homemade" under "cheese"*
Hominy, about, 334–35
Hominy grits, about, 335
Hong Kong, recipes from
  Asparagus with Ginger and Red Pepper, Stir-Fried, 137–38
  Bean Curd with Asparagus and Chinese Mushrooms, 96–97
  Creamy Sweet "Green Pea" Soup, 611
  Eggplants with a Soy Sauce Dressing, Cold, 180
  Eggplants with Spicy Chinese Peanut Dressing, Cold, 181
  Horseradish Dressing, Boiled, Beets and Beet Greens with a, 139–40
Hot and Spicy Sichuan-Style Eggplants, 188–89
Hubbard Squash Cooked with Bengali Seasonings, 289
Hulled and split mung beans. *See Mung bean(s)*
Hung do. See Azuki beans

Ijo dulce chiles, about, 716
India, recipes from
  Almond and Cashew Nut Soup, 583–84
  Beet and Mushroom Curry, 142
  Beet Greens with Ginger and Green Chiles, Stir-Fried, 215–16
  Beets with Mint and Yogurt, 141
  Bitter Melons Stuffed with Onions and Pomegranate Seeds, 299
  Black-Eyed Pea Pancakes, 23–24
  Black-Eyed Pea Sprouts with Garlic and Thyme, 24
  Black-Eyed Peas with Corn and Dill, 19
  Black-Eyed Peas with Watercress, 22
  Breads, Sweet Puffed, 454–55
  Breads, Whole Wheat Tandoori, 430–31

Bulgur Pilaf with Peas and Carrots, 427
Cabbage, South Indian, 152–53
Carrot and Ginger Relish, South Indian, 618–19
Carrot Raita, 547
Carrots and Ginger with Mustard Seeds, Stir-Fried, 157
Carrots Pickled with Mustard Seeds, 686–87
Carrots with Fresh Fenugreek or Fresh Cilantro, 159
Carrots with Potatoes and Peas, Village-Style, 158
Cashew and Green Pea Bhaji, 120
Cashews in a Green Spice Paste, 119
Cauliflower and Potatoes with Ginger, Punjabi-Style, 163–64
Cauliflower Fritters, 165–66
Chayote with a South Indian Yogurt Sauce, 553–54
Cheese, Crispy Slices of Homemade Indian, 571–72
Chickpea Flour "French Fries," the Indian Way, 42–43
Chickpea Flour Pancakes with Crushed Green Peas and Cilantro, 38
Chickpea Flour Pancakes with Fresh Green Herbs, 38
Chickpea Flour Pancakes with Sesame Seeds, 38
Chickpea Flour Pancakes with Tomato and Onion, 38–39
Chickpeas and *Chana Dal* Cooked Together in a Mint Sauce, 34–35
Chickpeas Cooked in a Moghlai Style, 32–33
Coconut Rice, South Indian, 382
Collard Greens with Asafetida, 220
Collard Greens with Browned Onions, 219
Corn Breads, Flat, 354–55
Corn with Cauliflower, 173–74
Corn with Kohlrabi Spicy, 239–40
Corn with Sesame Seeds and Tomatoes, Spicy, 174–75
Cucumber "Raita," Gujarati, 550
Egg and Potato Cake, 539
Egg Curry, Goan Style, 518
Eggplant, Smoked, 183–84
Eggplants, Sweet-and-Sour, 194
Eggplant Stew with Potatoes, Mushrooms, and Chickpeas, Spicy, 196
Eggs, Stir Fried, 528

India, recipes from *(cont.)*
Flatbreads, Flaky Potato, 441–42
Flatbreads, Seasoned Sindhi, 454
Flatbreads, Sweet Sindhi, 453
Flatbreads Stuffed with Cauliflower, Flaky, 439–40
Flatbreads with Black Pepper, Sindhi, 452
Flat Whole Wheat Flaky Breads, Punjabi Village-Style, 437–38
"French" Toast, 542
Fritters Made with Hulled and Split Mung Beans, 81–82
Garlic Cloves, Pickled, 687
Ginger and Cardamom, An Ancient Drink with, 644
Ginger and Green Chile Relish, Fresh, 665–66
Ginger Fruit Punch, 645
Green Beans, Bengali-Style, 206–7
Green Beans with Cumin and Fennel, 202–3
Green Beans with Mushrooms, 206
Green Peas with Coconut and Cilantro, 259
Griddle Flatbreads, 444–45
Homemade Cheese, 561–62
Homemade Cheese Cooked in the Style of Scrambled Eggs, 569–70
Homemade Cheese Flavored with Black Pepper, Roasted Cumin Seeds, and Roasted *Ajwain* Seeds, 563
Homemade Cheese Flavored with Rosemary, Thyme, and Oregano, 563
homemade cheese patties, 562
Homemade Cheese Served with a "Salsa," 568
Homemade Cheese with Spinach, 570–71
Homemade Cheese with Tomatoes, 568–69
Kohlrabi Stew with Tomatoes, Spicy, 240
Kohlrabi with Corn, Spicy, 239–40
Lemon and Mint, A Cold Ginger-Cardamom Drink with, 644
Lemon Chutney, Sweet-and-Sour, 690–91
Lemon Pickle, Simple, 690
Lemon Pickle, South Indian, 692
Lemon Pickle, Sweet Gujarati, 691–92
Lentil Sprouts with Mustard Seeds and Chiles, Stir-Fried, 67
Lime and Ginger Syrup, Fresh, 647–48
Mango, Yogurt with Green, 553
Mango and Ginger Chutney, 697–98

Mango and Ginger Chutney with Five Bengali Spices, 698
Mango and Plantain, Yogurt with, 318–19
Mango Chutney, 695
Mango Chutney, Royal, 696
Mango Chutney with Fennel and Fenugreek, 696
Mango Lassi, Sweet, 656
Mango Pickle, Bombay-Style Green, 699–700
Mango Pickle, Simple South Indian, 696–97
Mango Pickle with Fennel Seeds, Rajasthani, 698–99
Milk and Yogurt Drink, 649
Millet with Cumin, Browned Onions, and Green Beans, 358–59
Mixed Sour Pickles Indian Style, 702
Mixed Vegetable Pickle, Punjabi-Style Sweet-and-Sour, 703
Mixed Vegetables, A Delicious Puree of, 308–9
Mung Bean Dumplings in a Spicy Tomato Sauce, 82–83
Mung Bean Pancakes, 80–81
Mung Beans, Master Recipe for Cooked Hulled and Split, 75–76
Mung Beans with Browned Garlic and Onions, "Dry," 78
Mung Beans with Browned Onions, 76
Mung Beans with Cumin and Asafetida, 77
Mung Beans with Greens, 79–80
Mung Beans with Spinach, 77–78
Mushrooms, Simple Stir-Fried, 244
Mushrooms with Coriander and Cumin, 246
Naan, 432–33
Okra Cooked with Fresh Curry or Basil Leaves, Fried, 252–53
Okra with Potatoes, 251
Omelet, Masala, 537
Onion and Mint "Raita," 548
Pancakes, Rice Flour, 414
Pancakes with Onion and Tomato, South Indian, 472–73
Pasta in a Split Pea Sauce, 474–76
Peach Chutney, Delhi-Style, 700–701
Plantain and Mango, Yogurt with, 318–19
Pomegranate Soup, Cold, 580
Potato Cooked in a Punjabi Village Style, 275
Potatoes, Gujarati-Style Hot Sweet-and-Sour, 273
Potatoes the Maharashtrian Way from West India, Mashed, 282

Potatoes the North Indian Way, Mashed, 282
Potatoes the South Indian Way, Mashed, 282
Potatoes with Fennel Seeds, 274
Potatoes with Ginger and Fennel Seeds, 274
Potatoes with Mustard Oil and Ground Mustard Seeds from Orissa in East India, Mashed, 281
Potatoes with Peas, Crumbled, 280
Potato Patties, 283
Pumpkin Cooked in the Delhi Style, 290
Pumpkin Fritters, 292
Pumpkin or Hubbard Squash Cooked with Bengali Seasonings, 289
Red Kidney Bean Stew, Spicy Punjabi, 47–48
Red Lentils Hyderabadi, 69
Red Lentil Soup, Curried, 599–600
Red Lentils with Cumin and Scallion, 68
Red Lentils with Zucchini, 70
Red Lentil with Mustard Seeds and Curry Leaves, 600–601
Rice, Lemon, 380
Rice, Plain Basmati, 375
Rice, Saffron Orange, 381
Rice Noodles with Cauliflower, 415
Rice with Cloves and Cinnamon, Parsi, 379–80
Rice with Yogurt and Apple, 396–97
Rice with Yogurt and Fresh Pomegranate Seeds, 397
"Risotto" of Rice and Split Peas, Delicious, 400–401
"Risotto" of Rice and Split Peas, Simple, 401–2
Salt Mixture, 705
Scrambled Eggs with Cauliflower, 528–29
Scrambled Eggs with Onion and Tomatoes, 526–27
Scrambled Eggs with Scallions and Mushrooms, 527
Semolina "Risotto" with Cabbage and Peas, 489–90
Semolina "Risotto" with Cashews and Green Beans, 491–92
Semolina "Risotto" with Peanuts and Cilantro, 492
Semolina "Risotto" with Rosemary and Potatoes, 493
Sour Cherry and Walnut Chutney, Kashmiri, 659–60
Spinach with Browned Onions, 229–30
Spinach with Sorrel, 226
Spinach with Tomato, 228
Split Urad Beans Cooked in the Punjabi Style, 115–16

Split Urad Beans in the Dehli Style, 113–14
Tamarind Chutney, Plain, 677
Tamarind-Yogurt Chutney, 678
Tea, Kashmiri, 650
Tomato and Onion Relish, 682
Tomato Relish, South Indian, 682
Tomato Soup, Madras Curried, 591
Toovar Dal, Sweet-and-Sour, 87
Turnips with Yogurt and Tomato, 307
Urad Beans, Basic Recipe for Hulled and Split, 113
Vegetable Mulligatawny Soup, 592
Vegetable Stew with Chickpea Flour Sauce, 36
Yogurt, "Pickled," 546–47
Yogurt Cheese with Bananas, 557–58
Yogurt Drink, Madras-Style Spicy, 657
Yogurt Drink, Punjabi, 655
Yogurt Soup in the South Indian Style, Cold, 582
Yogurt with Banana in the South Indian Style, 555
Yogurt with Green Mango, 553
Yogurt with Herbs, 548
Yogurt with Mango and Coconut, 320
Yogurt with Mango and Plantain, 318–19
Yogurt with Onion, Mint, and Chickpeas, 549
Yogurt with Spinach and Cloves, 549–50
Yogurt with Walnuts and Raisins, 555–56
Indian-American recipes
Broccoli with Spinach, 145–46
Cauliflower with Ginger and Cream, 162–63
Grilled Mixed Vegetables, Indian Style, 314–15
Semolina Bread with Coconut and Pistachios, 461–63
Wheat Berry Soup with Ginger and Cilantro, Skinned, 609
Indonesia, recipes from
Cabbage with Garlic and Shallots, 152
Cabbage with Spicy Red Paste, Stir-Fried Green, 150
Cauliflower and Green Beans in Red Chile Dressing, 164–65
Corn, Rice, and Vegetable Stew, 340–41
Corn Soup, 584
Eggplants with Spicy Shallot-Tomato Sauce, 190–91
Noodles, "Javanese," 477–79
Peanuts, Boiled, 121
Peanut Sauce, 667

Sambal with Roasted Tomatoes, Shallots, and Chiles, 681
Sweet "Green Pea" Soup with Coconut Milk, 612
Tempeh, Fried Spiced, 107
Tempeh with Peanuts, Sweet-and-Sour, 108
Instant couscous, about, 495
Instant Couscous (or Quick-Cooking), 496
Instant Korean Cabbage Pickle, 685–86
Iran, recipes from
 Carrots with Dried Apricots, 160
 Cucumber and Mint Drink, Cooling, 643–44
 Egg and Potato Cake, 538–39
 Egg Pie with Herbs, 537
 Egg Pie with Herbs and Cheese, 538
 Egg Pie with Tomato and Herbs, 538
 Eggs Poached in a Tomato Sauce, 521
 Herbs with Bread, Fresh, 627
 Lime Syrup, Fresh, 647
 Mint Lemonade, 648
 Onions or Shallots in the Persian Style, Crisply Fried, 666–67
 Pilaf with a Potato Crust, 386–87
 Pilaf with Fresh Green Herbs, 387–88
 Pilaf with Lime and Green Beans, 384–85
 "Ratatouille" of Fruit and Vegetables, Sweet-and-Sour, 312–13
 Red Peppers Stuffed with Herbed Rice in the Persian Manner, 265
 Rhubarb Syrup, 646–47
 Rice with Currants, 389–90
 Sour Cherry Syrup, 645–46
 Spice Mix, 706–7
 Vinegar Syrup, 653
 Yogurt with Celery and Pistachios, 551–52
 Yogurt with Eggplant and Walnuts, 552
 Zucchini Puree, 297
Irani Mint Lemonade, 648
Israel, recipes from
 about couscous, 496
 Israeli Couscous with Asparagus and Fresh Mushrooms, 504
Italian-American recipes
 Penne or Fusili with Fresh Tomatoes, 481
Italian lentils. See Lentil(s)
Italy, recipes from
 Artichoke Hearts with Peas, 131–32
 Broccoli Rabe Served on a Bed of Fava Beans, 218
 Broccoli Rabe with Garlic, 217
 Chickpea and Escarole Soup, 596–97

Chickpea and Spinach Soup, Rosemary-Flavored, 598
Chickpea Flour Pizza, Basic Recipe for Plain, 39–40
Chickpea Flour Pizza with Rosemary, Tomato, and Parmesan Cheese, 40
Chickpea Flour Pizza with Thyme and Sage, 40
Chickpea Soup with Escarole and Dried Porcini Mushrooms, 597
Fettucine (or Tagliatelle) with Ricotta, Spinach, and Pine Nuts, 483–84
Fettucine with a Mushroom Ragout, 484–85
Frittata with Swiss Chard, 540
Mascarpone, Homemade, 565
Penne or Fusili with Fresh Tomatoes, 481
Penne with Artichokes and Peas, 484
Polenta Lasagne, 347–48
Polenta with Broccoli Rabe, 345
Risotto with Dried Porcini Mushrooms, 407–8
Risotto with Peas, 406–7
Spaghetti with Fresh Tomatoes and Lemon Peel, 480
Swiss Chard with Tomatoes and Chickpeas, 231
Tomato Sauce, Simple, 679–80
Zucchini Pie, Tuscan, 541
Itiakiet Stew (Nigerian Red Kidney Bean Stew with a Peanut Sauce), 49–50

Jaggery, about, 724
Jalapeño chiles, about, 716
Jamaica, recipes from
 Red Kidney Beans for Jamaican "Peas and Rice," 48–49
Japan, recipes from
 Azuki Beans and Rice with Sesame Salt, 399
 Buckwheat Noodles, Cold, 330–31
 Eggplants and Shiitake Mushrooms Cooked in a Japanese Sauce, 187–88
 Eggs on Japanese Noodles, Poached, 523–24
 Konbu Dashi, 577
 Miso Soup with Bean Curd and Spinach, 605–6
 Miso Soup with Pumpkin and Onion, 606–7
 Miso Soup with Shiitake Mushrooms and Egg Strands, 607–8
 Omelet with Sesame Seeds and Bean Curd, 533
 Rice, Plain, 378
 Rice with Sesame Seeds, Nori, Mushrooms, and Pressed Barley, 327–28
 Scrambled Eggs with Bean Curd, 529

Scrambled Eggs with Sesame Seeds and Bean Curd, 530
Sesame Salt, 704
Soy Dipping Sauce, 676
Young Swiss Chard with Sesame Seeds, 230
Japanese rice, about, 373
Japanese Seven-Spice seasoning, about, 724
"Japan" pepper, about, 733
Jerusalem artichokes
 buying and storing, 234
 cleaning, 234
 with Cumin and Shallots, 235
 preparing, 234
 Roasted, 234–35
Jicama, about, 725
Julienned vegetables, 155

Kaffir lime, leaves and rind, about, 725
Kailan. See Chinese broccoli (gailan)
Kale, 213
 Black Tuscan (Cavolo Nero), with Raisins, 222
 with Leek, Kale, 221–22
Kallaloo, 585–86
Kalonji
 about, 728–29
 in Naan, 432–33
 in Potatoes Cooked with Fennel Seeds, 274
 in Potatoes Cooked with Ginger and Fennel Seeds, 274
 in Pumpkin Cooked in the Delhi Style, 290
 in Pumpkin or Hubbard Squash Cooked with Bengali Seasonings, 289
 in Turkish Ridged Bread, 436–37
Kandahari Naan, 434
Kasha. See Buckwheat
Kashmiri Sour Cherry and Walnut Chutney, 659–60
Kashmiri Tea, 650
Kenari nuts, about, 725
Ketjap manis, about, 735
Kewra, about, 733
Kha, about, 723
Kidney beans, red large
 about, 46–47
 canned, 47
 Casserole, 50–51
 cooking methods for, 47
 for Jamaican "Peas and Rice," 48–49
 Stew, Spicy Punjabi Red Kidney Bean, 47–48
 Stew with a Peanut Sauce, Nigerian, 49–50
 in Tex-Mex Vegetarian Chili, 64–65
Kidney beans, white. See White beans
Kimchi, 147
Knives, about, 710
Kochu Chang, 726
Kodampali, about, 724

Kohlrabi
 buying and storing, 237
 Carrot, and Daikon Salad, 627–28
 with Corn, Spicy, 239–40
 greens, 213
 Greens Cooked with Garlic, 223
 preparing, 237
 Salad, 628–29
 Sautéed, 238
 Stew with Tomatoes, Spicy, 240
 Stir-Fried, 238–39
Kokum, about, 726
Konbu
 about, 726
 Stock, 577
Korea, recipes from
 Asparagus with a Korean Dressing, Cold, 135
 Azuki Beans and Rice with Sesame Salt, 399
 Cabbage Pickle, Instant, 685–86
 Dipping Sauce, 676
 Eggplants with a Korean Hot Sauce, Poached, 182
 Kohlrabi, Carrot, and Daikon Salad, 627–28
 Mung Bean Sprouts Stir-Fried with Ginger, 85
 Omelet with Sesame Seeds and Bean Curd, 533
 Pancakes with Peppers and Mushrooms, Savory, 411–12
 Poached Eggs Served in a Korean Manner, 520
 Rice with Sesame Seeds, Nori, Mushrooms, and Pressed Barley, Japanese, 327–28
 Scrambled Eggs with Bean Curd, 529
 Scrambled Eggs with Sesame Seeds and Bean Curd, 530
 Soy Korean Sauce, Spicy, 676
 Swiss Chard with Sesame Seeds, 230
 Wakame Seaweed Soup, Cold, 580–81
Korean-American recipes
 Green Lettuce in a Korean Dressing, 631

Langkaus, about, 723
Laos, about, 723
Lasagne, Polenta, 347–48
Lassis. See Drink(s)
Latin America, recipes from
 Homemade Latin American Cheese, 564
 See also specific countries
Lava, about, 730
Lebanese couscous, about, 496
Leek(s)
 buying and storing, 241
 preparing, 241
 with Rice, 242
 with Summer Kale, 221–22
 washing, 241
Legumes
 buying, 5

Legumes *(Cont.)*
  canned, 5
  digestion of, 4
  general cooking methods for, 6
  picking over and washing, 5
  Quick-Soak Method, 6
  seasonings for, 6–7
  soaking, 5–6
  storing, 5
  See also specific legumes
Lemongrass
  about, 726
  in Eggplant "Pickle," Sri
    Lankan, 197–98
  Tea, 650
  with Tomato Soup, 590–91
Lemon Rice, 380
Lemon(s)
  Chutney, Sweet-and-Sour,
    690–91
  Green Beans with Garlic and
    Preserved, 205
  Green Beans with Roasted
    Red Pepper and Preserved,
    205
  Lemonade, Irani Mint, 648
  and Mint, A Cold Ginger-
    Cardamom Drink with,
    644
  in Moroccan Green Pepper
    Salad, 634
  Pickle, Simple, 690
  Pickle, South Indian, 692
  Pickle, Sweet Gujarati,
    691–92
  Salted, Moroccan Style, 689
  in Spaghetti with Fresh
    Tomatoes and Lemon
    Peel, 480
Lengkaus, about, 723
Lentil(s)
  with Bulgur Wheat, 425
  cooking methods for, 59
  with Garlic Mushrooms, 66
  with Onion and Garlic, 61
  origins of, 58
  Pearl Onions, Green Beans,
    and, Wild Rice Stew with,
    509
  and Rice, Tomatoes Stuffed
    with, 303–4
  with Rice, 63
  Rice with Browned Onions
    and, Palestinian, 404
  Salad, Greek-Style, 629–30
  Salad with Crushed Mustard
    Seeds, Ethiopian, 629–30
  in a Sauce, 64
  with Spinach and Yogurt, 62
  sprouting, 59
  Sprouts with Ginger, Stir-
    Fried, 67
  Sprouts with Mustard Seeds
    and Chiles, Stir-Fried, 67
  Tomatoes with Rice and,
    Stuffed, 303–4
  types of, 59–60
  in Vegetarian Chili, Tex-Mex,
    64–65
  See also Red lentil(s)
Lettuce in a Korean Dressing,
  Green, 631
Lima beans, dried

Baked, 53
Stew, Cypriot, 56–57
Limes, dried Persian, about, 726
Lobhia. See Black-eyed pea(s)
Lo mein noodles, about, 729
Long beans
  about, 201–2
  Curried, 210
  with Fermented Black Beans,
    209

Ma. See Pea(s), split
Mace, about, 730
Madras Curried Tomato Soup,
  591
Madras-Style Spicy Yogurt
  Drink, 657
Maggi cubes, about, 727
Malaysia, recipes from
  "Javanese" Noodles, 477–79
  Mixed Fruit and Vegetable
    Salad with Sweet Soy and
    Peanut Dressing, 626
  Pineapple Curried with Cin-
    namon and Star Anise,
    322–23
Mali, recipes from
  Black-Eyed Pea Fritters,
    16–17
Mandarin peel, dried, about, 727
Mango(es)
  buying and storing, 316
  Chutney, 695
  Chutney, and Ginger, 697–98
  Chutney, and Ginger with
    Five Bengali Spices, 698
  Chutney, Royal, 696
  Chutney with Fennel and
    Fenugreek, 696
  Curry, Trinidadian, 321
  fully ripe, 316
  Lassi, Sweet, 656
  peeling and cutting, 316–17
  Pickle, Bombay-Style Green,
    699–700
  Pickle, Simple South Indian,
    696–97
  Pickle with Fennel Seeds,
    Rajasthani, 698–99
  pickling and preserving, 693–
    94
  ripeness signs of, 315–16
  semiripe, 316
  unripe, 316
  Yogurt with, and Coconut,
    320
  Yogurt with, and Plantain,
    318–19
  Yogurt with Green, 553
Masa, about, 335
Masa harina "precocida," 335
Masarepa
  about, 335
  in *arepas,* 335
  in Corn Muffins, Ecuador-
    Style, 356–57
Mascarpone, Homemade Italian,
  565
Mashed Potatoes. *See entries
  beginning with* "Mashed"
  under "potato(es)"
Masoor dal. See Red lentil(s)
Master Recipe for Cooked

Hulled and Split Mung
  Beans, 75–76
Mediterranean, recipes from
  Carrots, Mushrooms, and
    Onions à la Greque, 156
  Fava Beans Sautéed with
    Garlic and Thyme, Fresh,
    199
  Whole Wheat Berries Salad,
    640
  Zucchini, Simple "Grilled,"
    295–96
Melon seeds, about, 727
Mexico, recipes from
  Black Beans "Charros," 13–
    14
  Chickpea Soup, 597
  Eggs, Fried, 525
  Green Tomatillo Salsa, 679
  Poblano Peppers with Cheese,
    267
  Potato Cake, 278–79
  Potato Soup, 588–89
  Quesadilla with Cheese, 352
  Quesadilla with Mushrooms,
    353
  Red Kidney Bean Casserole,
    50–51
  Refried Beans, 12–13
  Rice Casserole with Corn,
    Sour Cream, and Cheese,
    398
  Rice with Stuffed Poblano
    Peppers, Green, 393
  Salsa, Simple Red, 683
  Tomato Salsa, Cooked, 683
  Tortillas, Corn (*see* Tortillas:
    corn)
  Tortillas, Wheat, 445–46
Microwave, Quick Cashews
  Zapped in the, 118
Middle East, recipes from
  Chickpeas, Potatoes, and
    Carrots Stew, 29
  Lentils, "Dry" Red, 68
  Tabbouleh, A Salad of Bulgur
    and Parsley, 423
  See also specific countries
Milk
  Drink, Apple and, Moroccan,
    649
  Sauce, Stir-Fried Celery Cab-
    bage with a Gingery, 153–
    54
  Soup, Avocado and Butter-
    milk, Cold, 579
  See also Yogurt
Millet
  about, 357
  with Cumin, Browned
    Onions, and Green Beans,
    358–59
  Flatbreads, 360–61
  flour, 357
  grains, 357
  Plain, 358
  with Sesame Seeds, Carrot,
    and Chard, 359–60
  storing, 357
Minari, about, 727
Mint
  and Chickpeas, Yogurt with
    Onion, 549

Chickpeas and *Chana Dal*
  Cooked Together in a
  Sauce with, 34–35
  and Cilantro Chutney, Delhi-
    Style, 660
  and Lemon, A Cold Ginger-
    Cardamom Drink with,
    644
  Lemonade, Irani, 648
  and Onion "Raita," 548
  Soybean Patties with, Spicy,
    94–95
  Soybean Patties with, Stuffed
    Spicy, 96
  Sugar Snap Peas with Dried,
    260
  Tea, Moroccan, 651
  and Walnuts, Whole Wheat
    Bread with, 465–66
  and Yogurt, Beets with, 141
Mirin, about, 727
Miso
  about, 603–4, 727
  Soup with Bean Curd and
    Spinach, 605–6
  Soup with Pumpkin, Curried,
    607
  Soup with Pumpkin and
    Onion, 606–7
  Soup with Shiitake Mush-
    rooms and Egg Strands,
    607–8
  Soup with Snow Peas and
    Bean Curd, 606
Mixed Bean Soup, 601–2
Mixed Sour Pickles Indian Style,
  702
Mock Lamb Curry, 505
Mock Minced Chicken, 506
Morita chiles, about, 715
Morocco, recipes from
  Almond Milk, 643
  Artichokes Stewed with Pota-
    toes, 129
  Black-Eyed Peas with Herbs,
    18
  Bread, Everyday, 460–61
  Bread, Layered, 442–44
  Cabbage and Orange Salad,
    617
  Carrot and Cilantro Salad,
    618
  Carrot Salad with Orange
    Juice, 620
  Chickpeas, Pumpkins, and
    Raisins with Couscous,
    501–2
  Chickpea Stew with Six Veg-
    etables, 31
  Chile-Garlic Paste, 672–73
  Couscous, Traditional, 499–
    500
  Fava Bean Puree, 45
  Flatbread with Yeast, 429–30
  Green and Red Pepper Salad,
    633
  Green Pepper Salad, 634
  Lemons, Salted, 688
  Lentils in a Sauce, 64
  Milk and Apple Drink, 649
  Orange and Cabbage Salad,
    617
  Pancakes, Soft Spongy, 473–74

Potato Stew with Turmeric, 276
Radish Salad with Orange Juice, 636
Split Pea Puree, Yellow, 110
Sweet Potatoes with Raisins and Cinnamon, 284
Tea, Mint, 651
Tomato Preserve with Almonds, Sweet, 701
Tomato Salad, 636–37
Tomato Sauce, Fresh, 681
Vegetables, Casserole of, 309–10
Mortar and pestles, about, 710
Mulligatawny Sauce, Eggs in a, 519
Mung bean(s)
  Azuki and Whole, Crushed and Sautéed, 10–11
  with Browned Onions, 76
  cooking methods for, 73–74
  with Cumin and Asafetida, 77
  "dry," 739
  "Dry" Hulled and Split, with Browned Garlic and Onions, 78
  Dumplings in a Spicy Tomato Sauce, 82–83
  in Fireman's Soup, 608
  Fritters Made with, 81–82
  with Greens, 79–80
  Hulled and Split, Master Recipe for Cooked, 75–76
  origins of, 72
  Pancakes, 80–81
  with Spinach, 77–78
  sprouting, 74–75
  Sprouts, Sweet-and-Sour, 83
  Sprouts Stir-Fried with Ginger, 85
  in Sweet "Green Pea" Soup, 611
  in Sweet "Green Pea" Soup, Creamy, 611
  in Sweet "Green Pea" Soup with Coconut Milk, 612
  Thread Salad, 84
  types of, 72–73
Mung bean vermicelli
  about, 75
  Salad, 84
Mushroom(s)
  about, 242, 727
  with Bean Curd, 100–101
  Bean Curd with Asparagus and Chinese, 96–97
  Bok Choy with Chinese, 216–17
  Brown Sauce, Vegeburgers in, 104
  buying and storing, 243
  Carrots, and Onions à la Greque, 156
  Chickpea Soup with Escarole and Dried Porcini, 597
  about Chinese dried, 717
  in Chinese Noodles Sautéed with Vegetables, 479–80
  with Coriander and Cumin, 246
  Corn, Asparagus, and, Wild Rice Sautéed with, 508

Couscous with Asparagus and Fresh, Israeli, 504
Curry, Beet and, 142
Eggplant Stew with Potatoes, Chickpeas, and, Spicy, 196
  with Green Beans, 206
  in Green Posole, 338–39
  with Grits, 337
  Lentils Topped with Garlic, 66
  in Mexican Potato Cake, 278–79
  and Mustard Seeds, Quinoa with, 368
  Pancakes with Peppers and, Savory Korean, 411–12
  and Peas in a Green Curry Sauce, 258
  Portobello, Spanish-Style Grilled, 248–49
  Portobello, Stuffed with Bean Curd, 245–46
  and Potato Stew, 248
  preparing, 243
  Quesadilla with, 353
  Ragout, Fettucine with a, 484–85
  reconstituting dried, 243
  Risotto with Dried Porcini, 407–8
  Sauce, Brown, 709
  Scrambled Eggs with Scallions and, 527
  Sesame Seeds, Nori, Pressed Barley, and, Japanese Rice with, 327–28
  with Sesame Seeds, 243
  Stew, Polenta with a Potato and, 345
  Stir-Fried, Simple, 244
  Stock, Dried, 577–78
  in Stuffed Chinese Pancakes, 468–70
  Three Kinds of, 244
  Tomato Sauce with, 680
  in Vegetable Dumplings, Boiled, 485–88
  with Wine and Coriander Seeds, 247
  See also Shiitake mushroom(s)
Mushroom soy sauce, about, 727
Mustard greens, about, 213–14
Mustard oil, about, 730
Mustard seeds, about, 730
My Curry Powder, 707–8

Naan, 432–33
  Fresh Herbs with Bread, 627
  Kandahari, 434
Napa cabbage, 148
Nigella
  about, 728–29
  in Naan, 432–33
  in Potatoes with Fennel Seeds, 274
  in Potatoes with Ginger and Fennel Seeds, 274
  in Pumpkin Cooked in the Delhi Style, 290
  in Pumpkin or Hubbard Squash Cooked with Bengali Seasonings, 289
  in Turkish Ridged Bread, 436–37

Nigeria, recipes from
  Baked Beans with Nigerian Seasonings, 57–58
  Black-Eyed Pea Fritters, 16–17
  Nigerian Red Kidney Bean Stew with a Peanut Sauce, 49–50
Nonstick sauté pans, about, 710
Noodles and pasta
  Buckwheat, Cold, 330–31
  cooking methods for, 419–20
  Fettucine (or Tagliatelle) with Ricotta, Spinach, and Pine Nuts, 483–84
  Fettucine with a Mushroom Ragout," 484–85
  "Javanese," 477–79
  mung bean cellophane, 75
  Mung Bean Thread Salad, 84
  Pan-Fried, 476–77
  pans for cooking, 740
  Penne or Fusili with Fresh Tomatoes, 481
  Penne with Artichokes and Peas, 484
  Penne with Zucchini and Basil, 482
  Poached Eggs on Japanese, 523–24
  Rice, with Cauliflower, 415
  about rice, 374–75, 729
  Spaghetti with Fresh Tomatoes and Lemon Peel, 480
  in a Split Pea Sauce, 474–76
  types of, 729–30
  with Vegetables, Chinese Sautéed, 479–80
  wheat, 419–20
  about wheat, 419–20
Nori
  about, 730
  Japanese Rice with Sesame Seeds, Mushrooms, Pressed Barley, and, 327–28
  North African Green and Red Pepper Salad, 633
Nutmeg, about, 730
Nuts. See specific nuts

Oat(s)
  about, 361
  Bread with Sesame Seeds, 364
  Cakes, 365–66
  Flatbreads, 362
  Flatbreads, Spicy, 363
  flour, 361
  Granola, 362
  rolled, 361
  Rolled, and Sprouted Wheat, Sunflower Seeds, Whole Wheat Bread with, 463–65
Ocinum sanctum (holy basil, bai kaprow), about, 712
Oils, flavored
  Spanish-Style Garlic and Parsley-Flavored Olive Oil, 665
Okra
  in an Australian Manner, 252
  Batter-Fried, 255

buying, 250
cleaning, 250
and Cornmeal Mold, 336
Fried, with Fresh Curry or Basil Leaves, 252–53
Fried, with Onions, 254–55
frying, 250–51
with Potatoes, 251
preparing, 250
with Tomatoes, 253–54
Olive oil
  about, 730–31
  Garlic and Parsley-Flavored, Spanish-Style, 665
  and Zahtar, Yogurt Cheese with, 557
Olives
  Syrian Cheese with, 572
  Yogurt Cheese with Gherkins and, Spiced, 559–60
Omelets
  French, 531–32
  French, with Asparagus, 532
  French, with Cheese and Chives, 532
  French, with Herbs, 532
  Japanese/Korean-Style, with Sesame Seeds and Bean Curd, 533
Onion(s)
  Collard Greens with Browned, 219
  and Garlic, "Dry" Hulled and Split Mung Beans with Browned, 78
  Lentils, Green Beans, and Pearl, Wild Rice Stew with, 509
  Millet with Cumin, Green Beans, and Browned, 358–59
  and Mint "Raita," 548
  Mushrooms, Carrots, and, à la Greque, 156
  Okra Cooked with, Fried, 254–55
  or Shallots in the Persian Style, Crisply Fried, 666–67
  Pancakes with Tomato and, South Indian, 472–73
  Pomegranate Seeds and, Bitter Melons Stuffed with, 299
  Pumpkin and, Miso Soup with, 606–7
  Rice with Lentils and Browned, Palestinian, 404
  in Romesco Sauce, Classic, 669–70
  Scrambled Eggs with Tomatoes and, Indian, 526–27
  Shallots or, in the Persian Style, Crisply Fried, 666–67
  Spinach with Browned, 229–30
  Spinach with Dill and, Sautéed, 225
  in Sweet Potatoes with Cardamom and Chiles, Sri Lankan, 285

Onions (Cont.)
    Tomato and, Chickpea Flour
        Pancakes with, 38–39
    Tomatoes and, Scrambled
        Eggs with, Indian, 526–27
    and Tomato Relish, 682
    in Tomato Soup with Lemon-
        grass, 590–91
    Wild Rice Stew with Lentils,
        Green Beans, and, 509
    Yogurt with Chickpeas, Mint,
        and, 549
Onion Salad, 632
Orange(s)
    and Cabbage Salad, Moroc-
        can, 617
    Carrot with Orange Juice
        Salad, Moroccan, 620
    and Fennel Salad, 623
    Radish Salad with Orange
        Juice, 636
    Rice, Saffron, 381
Oriental sesame oil, about, 731
Oven-dried tomato(es)
    Cheese, Rosemary, and, Pizza
        with, 435–36
    Plum, 305
    Tomatoes, 304–5
Oyster mushrooms, about, 728

Pakistan, recipes from
    Seasoned Sindhi Flatbreads,
        454
    Spinach with Sorrel, 226
    Sweet Sindhi Flatbreads, 453
Palestine, recipes from
    Eggplant with Garlic, Buttery
        Soft Slices of Deep-Fried,
        191–92
    Rice with Lentils and
        Browned Onions, 404
    Tomato-Cucumber Salad,
        Simple, 638
    Tomatoes in a Tomato Sauce,
        Sliced, 303
Palm sugar, about, 731
Panaji, 117
Pancakes
    Black-Eyed Peas, 23–24
    Buckwheat, 330
    Chickpea Flour, Basic Recipe
        for Plain, 37
    Chickpea Flour, with Crushed
        Green Peas and Cilantro, 38
    Chickpea Flour, with Fresh
        Green Herbs, 38
    Chickpea Flour, with Sesame
        Seeds, 38
    Chickpea Flour, with Tomato
        and Onion, 38–39
    Mung Bean, 80–81
    with Onion and Tomato,
        South Indian, 472–73
    with Peppers and Mush-
        rooms, Savory Korean,
        411–12
    Rice Flour, Indian, 414
    Scallion Cakes, 466–67
    Semolina, Greek, 470–71
    Soft Spongy, 473–74
    Stuffed Chinese, 468–70
    Vietnamese, 413–14
Pan-Fried Noodles, 476–77

Pappadums, about, 731
Paprika, about, 731
Parmesan cheese, about, 731
Parsley
    in Bulgur Wheat with Red
        Pepper Paste, 426–27
    in Tabbouleh, 423, 424
Pasta. See Noodles and pasta
Paste(s)
    Cashews in a Green Spice,
        119
    Chile-Garlic, Moroccan,
        672–73
    about chili, 717
    plum, sour, about, 732
    Red Pepper, 673–74
    tamarind (see Tamarind
        paste)
Patata Psiti (Baked Potatoes, the
    Greek Way), 277
Patatas. See Potato(es)
Patties
    homemade Indian cheese,
        562
    Potato, 283
    Soybean, with Mint, Spicy,
        94–95
    Soybean, with Mint, Stuffed
        Spicy, 96
    See also Cake(s)
Peach Chutney, Delhi-Style,
    700–701
Peanut oil, about, 730
Peanut(s)
    Boiled, Indonesian-Style, 121
    Boiled with Five Flavorings,
        122
    Chinese "Pickled," 122–23
    cooking methods for, 120–21
    Dressing, Eggplants with
        Spicy Chinese, Cold, 181
    Dressing, Mixed Fruit and
        Vegetable Salad with
        Sweet Soy and, Malaysian,
        626
    origins of, 120
    Sauce, Indonesian, 667
    Sauce, Nigerian Red Kidney
        Bean Stew with a, 49–50
    Semolina "Risotto" with
        Cilantro and, 492
    storing fresh, 121
    with Tempeh, Sweet-and-
        Sour, 108
Pea(s), fresh
    and Artichokes, Penne with,
        484
    Bhaji, Cashew and Green,
        Indian-Style, 120
    and Cabbage, Semolina
        "Risotto" with, 489–90
    and Carrots, Bulgur Pilaf
        with, 427
    Chickpea Flour Pancakes
        with Cilantro and Crushed
        Green, 38
    with Coconut and Cilantro,
        259
    Egg Whites with, 530
    with Ginger and Sesame Oil,
        257
    and Mushrooms in a Green
        Curry Sauce, 258

    and Potatoes, Village-Style
        Carrots with, 158
    with Potatoes, Crumbled, 280
    Risotto with, 406–7
    Sugar Snap, with Cumin and
        Thyme, 260–61
    Sugar Snap, with Dried Mint,
        260
    types of, 256–57
    See also Snow pea(s)
Pea(s), split
    about, 713
    Basic Recipe for Hulled and
        Split Urad Beans, 113
    cooking methods for, 109, 112
    in the Dehli Style, 113–14
    in "Javanese" Noodles, 477–79
    in the Lucknow Style, 114–15
    origins of, 109, 112
    in the Punjabi Style, 115–16
    "Risotto" of Rice and, Deli-
        cious, 400–401
    "Risotto" of Rice and, Simple,
        401–2
    Roti Stuffed with, Trinida-
        dian, 449–51
    Sauce, Pasta in a, 474–76
    Soup, Trinidadian, 602–3
    Soup Trinidadian, 602–3
    Yellow, Puree, Moroccan, 110
    Yellow, with Thyme and
        Cumin, Puree, 111
Pecan(s)
    about, 731
    –Chile Sauce, 668–69
Peelers, about, 710
Penne. See Noodles and pasta:
    penne
Pepper and Salt, Roasted
    Sichuan, 704
Pepper Bake, 456
Peppers, bell
    buying and storing, 262
    and Cucumber Salad, 632
    Green Beans with Preserved
        Lemon and Roasted Red,
        205
    and Mushrooms, Pancakes
        with, Savory Korean,
        411–12
    Ped Peppers Stuffed with
        Herbed Rice in the Per-
        sian Manner, 265
    Red, with Mustard Seeds,
        Roasted, 264
    Red Pepper Paste, Bulgur
        Wheat with, 426–27
    Red Pepper Paste, Spelt
        Berry Salad with, 639
    Red Pepper Paste, Yogurt
        Cheese with, 560
    in Red Pepper Paste, 673–74
    Red Pepper Soup, 586–87
    Red Peppers Stuffed with
        Feta Cheese, 266
    Red Peppers Stuffed with
        Herbed Rice in the Per-
        sian Manner, 265
    roasting, 262–63
    Salad, and White Beans, 614
    Salad, Moroccan, 634
    Salad, North African Green
        and Red, 633

    in Simple Romesco Sauce,
        670–71
    and White Beans Salad, 614
Peppers, hot. See Chiles, fresh
Persia, recipes from. See Iran,
    recipes from
Peru, recipes from
    Potatoes in the Huancayo
        Style, 272–73
Pickle(s)
    Cabbage, Instant Korean,
        685–86
    Carrots Pickled with Mustard
        Seeds, 686–87
    Daikon, 688
    Garlic Cloves, 687
    Lemon, Simple, 690
    Lemon, South Indian, 692
    Lemon, Sweet Gujarati,
        691–92
    Lemons, Salted, Moroccan
        Style, 689
    Mango, Bombay-Style Green,
        699–700
    Mango, Simple South Indian,
        696–97
    Mango, with Fennel Seeds,
        Rajasthani, 698–99
    Mixed Sour, Indian Style, 702
    Mixed Vegetable, Punjabi-
        Style Sweet-and-Sour, 703
    Peanuts, Chinese, 122–23
    Yogurt, 546–47
    See also Chutney(s)
Pigeon peas
    cooking methods for, 86
    Hulled and Split, Basic
        Recipe for, 86
    origins of, 85
    with Sliced Shallots and Car-
        rots, 87–88
    Sweet-and-Sour, 87
Pigweed, about, 722
Pineapple(s)
    buying, 318
    Curried with Cinnamon and
        Star Anise, Malaysian,
        322–23
    peeling and preparing, 318
Pine nuts
    about, 731
    Asparagus with, 136
    Ricotta, Spinach, and, Fet-
        tucine (or Tagliatelle)
        with, 483–84
    Risotto with Spinach, Golden
        Raisins, and, 409–10
Pinkish-mauve eggplants, 177
Pinto bean(s)
    Stew with Ancho Chiles, Tex-
        Mex, 89
    as substitute for kidney
        beans, 47, 88
Pistachio(s)
    and Celery Yogurt with,
        551–52
    Coconut and, Semolina Bread
        with, 461–63
    in Persian Rice with Cur-
        rants, 389–90
Piwma grood, about, 725
Pizza
    Cheese, 435

Chickpea Flour, Basic Recipe for Plain, 39–40
Chickpea Flour, with Rosemary, Tomato, and Parmesan Cheese, 40
Chickpea Flour, with Thyme and Sage, 40
with Oven-Dried Tomatoes, Cheese, and Rosemary, 435–36
Plain recipes. *See* Basic recipes
Plantain(s)
  barely ripe, 317
  black, 317–18
  green, 317
  and Mango, Yogurt with, 318–19
  ripeness signs of, 317–18
  Yellow, Sautéed, 323
Plum(s)
  paste, sour *(umeboshi),* about, 732
  pickled, about Chinese, 732
  sauce, about, 732
Poblano chiles
  about, 716
  with Cheese, Mexican, 267
  in Green Posole, 338–39
  Green Rice with Stuffed, 393
  in Mexican Potato Cake, 278–79
  in Mexican-Style Rice Casserole with Corn, Sour Cream, and Cheese, 398
Polenta
  about, 334, 341–42
  with Asparagus, 344–45
  with Broccoli Rabe, 345
  Classical Method of Cooking, 342
  Lasagne, 347–48
  with a Mushroom and Potato Stew, 345
  in the Oven, 343
  Slices, Fried, 343–44
  Slices, Toasted, 343
  Soft, Draped over Cheese, 346
  Soft, Mixed with Cheese and Butter, 344
  with Tex-Mex Chili, 346
Pomegranate seeds
  about, 711
  and Onions, Bitter Melons Stuffed with, 299
  Rice with Yogurt and Fresh, 397
  Soup, Cold, 580
Poppadums, 112
Popping corn, 334
Poppy seeds, white, about, 732
Porcini mushrooms
  Chickpea Soup with Escarole and Dried, 597
  Risotto with Dried, 407–8
Portobello mushrooms
  Grilled, Spanish-Style, 248–49
  Stuffed with Bean Curd, 245–46
Posole
  about, 334–35
  Green, 338–39

Potato(es)
  about, 268–69
  Artichokes Stewed with, 129
  Baked, the Greek Way, 277
  baking, 269–70
  boiling, 269
  Broccoli with, 147
  buying and storing, 269
  Cake, Egg and, Persian, 538–39
  Cake, Egg and, Spanish, 536
  Cake, Mexican, 278–79
  Cakes, Egg and, Indian, 539
  Cake with Herbs, Crisp, 276–77
  and Cauliflower with Ginger, Punjabi-Style, 163–64
  Chickpea and, Curry, Caribbean Style, 33–34
  and Corn, Quinoa with, 369
  Crust, Persian Pilaf with a, 386–87
  Eggplant Stew with Mushrooms, Chickpeas, and, Spicy, 196
  with Fennel Seeds, 274
  with Fennel Seeds and Ginger, 274
  Flatbreads, Flaky, 441–42
  and Green Bean Curry, 208–9
  and Green Pepper, Corn Tortillas Stuffed with, 351
  Hash Brown, Spicy, 278
  Hot Sweet-and-Sour, Gujarati-Style, 273
  in the Huancayo Style, Peruvian, 272–73
  Mashed, Basic, 281–82
  Mashed, My Husband's Old-Fashioned Way, 281
  Mashed, the Maharashtrian Way from West India, 282
  Mashed, the North Indian Way, 282
  Mashed, the South Indian Way, 282
  Mashed, with Garlic the New-Fashioned Way, 281
  Mashed, with Mustard Oil and Ground Mustard Seeds from Orissa in East India, 281
  and Mushroom Stew, 248
  with Okra, 251
  Patties, 283
  with Peas, Crumbled, 280
  Pilaf with a Potato Crust, Persian, 386–87
  preparing, 269
  in a Punjabi Village Style, 275
  Rosemary and, Semolina "Risotto" with, 493
  Sauce, Speckled Green Couscous with Red, 502–3
  Shreds, Stir-Fried Sweet-and-Sour, 271
  Soup, Chard, Bean, and, Spanish, 587–88
  Soup, Mexican, 588–89
  steaming, 269
  Stew of Chickpeas, Carrots, and, Middle Eastern, 29

Stew with Turmeric, Moroccan, 276
Preserved lemon(s)
  about, 688
  and Green Beans with Garlic, 205
  and Green Beans with Roasted Red Pepper, 205
  in Moroccan Green Pepper Salad, 634
Preserved vegetable
  Stir-Fried Dry Green Beans with Tien Jing, 204
Pressure cooker, using for
  azuki beans, 8
  black-eyed peas, 15
  chickpeas, 26
  general instructions for, 6, 8
  kidney beans, 47
  pigeon peas, 86
  pinto beans, 47
  risotto, 406
  soybeans, 91
  white beans, 52
Pulses. *See* Legumes; *specific legumes*
Pumpkin(s)
  about, 286–87
  with Bengali Seasonings, 289
  Black-Eyed Peas and Rice with, 403
  Bulgur Risotto with, 428
  buying and storing, 287, 288
  Chickpeas, Raisins, and, with Couscous, 501–2
  in the Delhi Style, 290
  freezing prepared, 288
  Fritters, 292
  Miso Soup with, Curried, 607
  Miso Soup with Onion and, 606–7
  peeling and cutting, 287
  Pie, Savory Greek, 293–94
  Pumpkin Soup with Tomato, 590
  Risotto Made in a Pressure Cooker, Greek, 410–11
  and Sage, Risotto with, 411
  seeds, 287
  Soup, Simple, 589–90
  Soup with Fresh Curry Leaves, 590
  Stew, White Beans and, Aromatic Cuban, 54–56
  Trinidadian, 291
  See also Squashes, winter
Punjabi-style recipes. *See* India, recipes from
Pureed Beet Salad, 140
Puree of Zucchini, 297
Purple eggplants, 177

Quesadillas
  with Cheese, 352
  with Mushrooms, 353
Quick-cooking couscous, 495
Quick Glazed Carrots with Ginger, 155
Quick-Soak Method, for legumes, 6
Quinoa
  about, 366
  cooking methods for, 366–67

with Corn and Potatoes, 369–70
  with Green Beans and Carrots, 367
  with Mushroom and Mustard Seeds, 368
  with Tomato and Thyme, 368–69
  washing and draining, 366

Radish(es)
  about preserved, 732
  Salad, 634–35
  Salad, Ukranian, 636
  Salad with Orange Juice, 635
  Seasoned, 635
Raisin(s)
  Black Tuscan Kale *(Cavolo Nero)* with, 222
  Chickpeas, Pumpkins, and, with Couscous, 501–2
  and Cinnamon, Sweet Potatoes with, 284
  Risotto with Spinach, Pine Nuts, and Golden, 409–10
  in Semolina Bread with Coconut and Pistachios, 461–63
  and Sesame Seeds, Whole Wheat Couscous with, 498
  and Walnuts, Tamarind Chutney with, 677
  and Walnuts, Yogurt with, 555–56
Rajasthani Mango Pickle with Fennel Seeds, 698–99
Ramen, about, 729
Rampe, about, 733
Rapini, 212
"Ratatouille" of Fruit and Vegetables, Persian Sweet-and-Sour, 312–13
Recao, about, 720
Red beans, sweet. *See* Azuki beans
Red Bhutanese rice, about, 374
Red Chile Dressing, Cauliflower and Green Beans in, 164–65
"Red-Cooked" or Stewed Daikon, 176
Red kidney bean(s)
  Casserole, 50–51
  for Jamaican "Peas and Rice," 48–49
  Stew, Spicy Punjabi, 47–48
  Stew with a Peanut Sauce, Nigerian, 49–50
  in Tex-Mex Vegetarian Chili, 64–65
Red lentil(s)
  about, 59–60
  Basic Red Lentils, 60–61
  with Cumin and Scallion, 68
  "Dry," 68
  Hyderabadi, 69
  Soup, Curried, 599–600
  Soup, Simple, 600
  Soup with Mustard Seeds and Curry Leaves, 600–601
  Stew with Wheat Berries and Chickpeas, Anatolian, 71–72
  with Zucchini, 68, 70

Red peppers, bell. *See* Peppers, bell
Refried beans
 and Cheese, Corn Tortillas Stuffed with, 351
 Refried Beans, 12–13
Relish(es)
 Carrot and Ginger, South Indian, 618–19
 Coconut Sambol, 662–63
 Garlic, Crunchy Sichuan, 664
 Ginger and Green Chile, Fresh, 665–66
 Tomato, South Indian, 682
 Tomato and Onion, 682
Rhizopus, 90
Rhubarb Syrup, Persian, 646–47
Rice
 about, 370–72
 and Azuki Beans with Sesame Salt, 399
 Basmati, Plain, 375
 Bhutanese Red, 377
 about Bhutanese red, 374
 with Black Beans or "Spotted Rooster," 14
 and Black-Eyed Peas with Pumpkin, 403
 Casserole with Corn, Sour Cream, and Cheese, Mexican-Style, 398
 with Cloves and Cinnamon, Parsi, 379–80
 Coconut, South Indian, 382
 cooking methods for, 372, 374
 and Currants, Cabbage with, 149–50
 with Currants, Persian, 389–90
 Emerald Fried, 391–92
 "Forbidden" Black, Plain, 377
 about "forbidden" Chinese black, 373–74
 Glutinous, Steamed Plain, 378
 about glutinous or sweet, 373
 Green, with Stuffed Poblano Peppers, 393
 Japanese, Plain, 378
 Japanese, with Sesame Seeds, Nori, Mushrooms, and Pressed Barley, 327–28
 about Japanese, 373
 Leeks with, 242
 Lemon, 380
 and Lentils, Tomatoes Stuffed with, 303–4
 with Lentils and Browned Onions, Palestinian, 404
 Lentils with, 63
 Long-Grain, Plain, 376
 pans for cooking, 740, 741
 Pilaf with a Potato Crust, Persian, 386–87
 Pilaf with Fresh Green Herbs, Persian, 387–88
 Pilaf with Lime and Green Beans, Persian, 384–85
 Red Peppers Stuffed with Herbed, in the Persian Manner, 265
 about roasted and ground, 732–33

Saffron Orange, 381
 soaking and draining, 374
 with Spinach, 227, 383
 Stew, Corn, Vegetable, and, Indonesian, 340–41
 storing, 374
 about sweet or glutinous, 373
 Swiss Chard Leaves Stuffed with Sweet-and-Sour, 394–95
 washing, 374
 about white basmati, 372–73
 with Yogurt and Apple, 396–97
 with Yogurt and Fresh Pomegranate Seeds, 397
 See also Brown rice; Rice flour; Rice noodles; Risotto; Wild rice
Rice flour
 about, 374
 Pancakes, Indian, 414
 in Pumpkin Fritters, 292
 in Savory Korean Pancakes with Peppers and Mushrooms, 411–12
 in Vietnamese Pancakes, 413–14
Rice noodles
 about, 374–75, 729
 with Cauliflower, 415
Rice sticks, about, 375, 733
Ricotta, Spinach, and Pine Nuts, Fettucine (or Tagliatelle) with, 483–84
Risotto
 about, 373
 Bulgur, with Pumpkin, 428
 cooking methods for, 405–6
 with Dried Porcini Mushrooms, 407–8
 with Peas, 406–7
 pressure cooker for, 406
 Pumpkin, Made in a Pressure Cooker, Greek, 410–11
 with Pumpkin and Sage, 411
 of Rice and Split Peas, Delicious, 400–401
 of Rice and Split Peas, Simple, 401–2
 semolina, 488–89
 Semolina, with Cabbage and Peas, 489–90
 Semolina, with Cashews and Green Beans, 491–92
 Semolina, with Peanuts and Cilantro, 492
 Semolina, with Rosemary and Potatoes, 493
 with Spinach, Golden Raisins, and Pine Nuts, 409–10
 with Tomato, Roasted Eggplant, and Mint, 409
 with Tomato and Eggplant, 408–9
Roasted Sichuan Pepper and Salt, 704
Rock sugar, about, 733
Roll cutting, vegetables, 179
Romesco sauce
 with Asparagus, 136–37
 Classic, 669–70
 Simple, 670–71

Rosemary
 -Flavored Chickpea and Spinach Soup, 598
 White Beans with, 54
Rose petals, dried, about, 733
Royal Mango Chutney, 696

Saffron
 about, 733
 Orange Rice, 381
Sage
 with Butternut Squash, 288
 and Pumpkin, Risotto with, 411
Sake, about, 733
Salad(s)
 about, 575
 Artichoke Heart and Fresh Fava Bean, 612–13
 Bean Curd, Cold, 97–98
 with a Bean Curd "Mayonnaise," Green, 631
 Bean Curd Salad or Spread, 615
 Beet, Pureed, 140
 of Broiled and Roasted Vegetables, 310–11
 Cabbage, with Mustard Seeds, 617
 Cabbage and Orange, Moroccan, 617
 Cabbage with Oregano, 616
 Carrot, Thai "Pickled," 619
 Carrot and Cilantro, 618
 Carrot and Ginger Relish, South Indian, 618–19
 Carrot with Orange Juice, Moroccan, 620
 Cheese with Tomato and Basil Topped with Asparagus, 620–21
 Corn, Spicy, 622
 Eggplant, Greek, 621
 Fennel and Orange, 623
 Figs with Mustard Seeds and Curry Leaves, 623–24
 Fruit and Vegetable, Thai, 624–25
 Green, with a Bean Curd "Mayonnaise," 631
 Green and Red Pepper, North African, 633
 Green Bean, 202–3
 Green Lettuce in a Korean Dressing, 631
 Green Pepper and Cucumber, 632
 Green Pepper Salad, Moroccan, 634
 Guacamole, 613–14
 Herbs with Bread, Fresh, 627
 Kohlrabi, 628–29
 Kohlrabi, Carrot, and Daikon, 627–28
 Lentil, Greek-Style, 629–30
 Lentil Salad with Crushed Mustard Seeds, Ethiopian, 629–30
 Mixed Fruit and Vegetable, with Sweet Soy and Peanut Dressing, Malaysian, 626
 Mixed Vegetable, Chinese, 642–43

Mung Bean Thread, 84
 Onion, 632
 Radish, 634–35
 Radish, Ukranian, 636
 Radishes, Seasoned, 635
 Radish with Orange Juice, 635
 Spelt Berry with Red Pepper Paste, 639
 Tabbouleh, A Salad of Bulgur and Parsley, 423
 Tabbouleh, Made with Bulgur and Arugula, 424
 Tomato, Moroccan, 636–37
 Tomato, Simple Syrian, 637
 Tomato-Cucumber, Simple Palestinian, 638
 Tomato-Flavored Bean Curd Spread or, 616
 Turnip, 639
 Turnip, Green, 638
 Vegetable, with Red Pepper Dressing, Turkish, 641–42
 of White Beans and Peppers, 614
 of Whole Wheat Berries, 640
 Zucchini and Feta Cheese, 640
Salt and Pepper, Roasted Sichuan, 704
Salted Lemons, Moroccan Style. *See* Preserved lemon(s)
Sambal(s)
 with Roasted Tomatoes, Shallots, and Chiles, 681
 Tomato, 302
Sambar Powder, 708
Sambars, 87–88
Sansho pepper, about, 733
Sauce(s)
 Brown Mushroom, 709
 Caribbean Seasoning, 675–76
 Circassian—A Walnut and Bread, 684
 Coconut Milk, 661–62
 dipping, 412, 413
 Dipping, Japanese Soy, 676
 Dipping, Korean, 676
 Eggplants with Spicy Shallot-Tomato, 190–91
 Eggplant with Yogurt and Minty Tomato, 192–93
 Green Tomatillo Salsa, 679
 Hot, Ethiopian, 674–75
 Peanut, Indonesian, 667
 Pecan-Chile, 668–69
 Pepper, Trinidadian, 671–72
 Red Salsa, Simple, 683
 Romesco, Classic, 669–70
 Romesco, Simple, 670–71
 Sambal with Roasted Tomatoes, Shallots, and Chiles, 681
 Soy Dipping, Japanese, 676
 Soy Korean, Spicy, 676
 Soy Sauce Salad Dressing, Chinese, 677
 Tomato, Moroccan-Style Fresh, 681
 Tomato, Simple, 679–80
 Tomatoes in a Tomato, Sliced, 303
 Tomato Salsa, Cooked, 683

Tomato with Mushrooms, 680
Walnut, 684
See also Black bean sauce
Savory Greek Pumpkin Pie, 293–94
Savoy cabbage, 148
Sayote. *See* Chayotes
Scallion(s)
Cakes, 466–67
and Mushrooms, Scrambled Eggs with, 527
Scotch bonnet chiles, about, 716
Scotland, recipes from
Oat Cakes, 365–66
Scrambled eggs. *See* Eggs: scrambled
Screw pine *(Pandanus odorus),* about, 733
Seasoned Radishes, 635
Seasoned Sindhi Flatbreads, 454
Seaweed
about, 724, 730
Japanese Rice with Sesame Seeds, Nori, Mushrooms, and Pressed Barley, 327–28
Seed corn, 333
Seitan
about, 419
Mock Lamb Curry, 505
Mock Minced Chicken, 506
Self-rising flour, 419
Semolina
about, 418–19
Bread with Coconut and Pistachios, 461–63
Pancakes, 470–71
Pancakes, Greek, 470–71
about "Risottos," 488–89
"Risotto" with Cabbage and Peas, 489–90
"Risotto" with Cashews and Green Beans, 491–92
"Risotto" with Peanuts and Cilantro, 492
"Risotto" with Potato and Rosemary, 493
Serai, about, 726
Seré, about, 726
Serrano chiles, about, 716
Sesame oil, oriental, about, 731
Sesame paste, about, 734
Sesame salt
Azuki Beans and Rice with, 399
Sesame Salt, 704
Sesame seed(s)
about, 734
and Bean Curd, Japanese/Korean-Style Scrambled Eggs with, 530
Carrot, Chard, and, Millet with, 359–60
Chickpea Flour Pancakes with, 38
Corn Bread with, 356
and Cucumber, Syrian Cheese with, 573
in Everyday Moroccan Bread, 460–61
in Moroccan Layered Bread, 442–44
Mushrooms with, 243

Nori, Mushrooms, Pressed Barley, and, Japanese Rice with, 327–28
Oat Bread with, 364
Omelet with Bean Curd and, Japanese/Korean-Style, 533
in Peas with Ginger and Sesame Oil, 257
and Raisins, Whole Wheat Couscous with, 498
Scrambled Eggs with Bean Curd and, Japanese/Korean-Style, 530
Seasoning, 705–6
with Swiss Chard, 230
and Tomatoes, Spicy Corn with, 174–75
Seven-Spice seasoning, about, Japanese, 725
Shadow beni, about, 720
Shallot(s)
about, 734
Beets with, Grated, 139
and Chiles, Sambal with Roasted Tomatoes, 681
Fried, in the Persian Style, 666–67
and Garlic, Cabbage with, 152
Green Beans with Browned, 206
in Kohlrabi Salad, 628–29
in Malaysian Pineapple Curried with Cinnamon and Star Anise, 322–23
or Onions in the Persian Style, Crisply Fried, 666–67
in Persian Pilaf with Lime and Green Beans, 384–85
and Spinach, Barley with, 326
-Tomato Sauce, Eggplants with Spicy, 190–91
Shichimi Togarashi, about, 725
Shiitake mushroom(s)
about, 728
in Azuki Beans with Green Pepper from Yunnan, Stir-Fried, 9
and Eggplants Cooked in a Japanese Sauce, 187–88
Fresh, Stir-Fried, 249
Miso Soup with Egg Strands and, 607–8
in Pancakes, Vietnamese, 413–14
Shiso, about, 735
Sichuan peppercorns, about, 735
Simple recipes. *See* Basic recipes
Sindhi flatbreads. *See* Breads and flatbreads
Skinned Wheat Berry Soup with Ginger and Cilantro, 609
Sliced Tomatoes in a Tomato Sauce, 303
Smoked Eggplant, 183–84
Snow pea(s)
about, 257
and Bean Curd, Miso Soup with, 606
with Celery, Stir-Fried, 168
with Scallions, Stir-Fried, 261

Shoots, Stir-Fried, 223–24
about shoots, 214
in Three Kinds of Mushrooms, 244
Soba noodles, about, 729
Sofrito
in Aromatic Cuban White Beans and Pumpkin Stew, 54–56
and legumes, 7
Somen, about, 729
Sorrel
about, 214
with Spinach, 226
Soup(s)
about, 575
Almond, Sweet, 610
Almond and Cashew Nut, Indian, 583–84
Almond Soup, Cold, 578–79
Avocado and Buttermilk, Cold, 579
Black Bean, Costa Rican, 595–96
Black-Eyed Pea, Trinidadian, 594
Chickpea, Mexican-Style, 597
Chickpea and Escarole, 596–97
Chickpea and Spinach, Rosemary-Flavored, 598
Chickpea with Escarole and Dried Porcini Mushrooms, 597
Chickpea with Escarole and Tomato, 597
Corn, Indonesian, 584
Curried Red Lentil, 599–600
Fireman's, 608
Kallaloo, 585–86
Konbu Stock, 577
about miso, 603–5
Miso with Bean Curd and Spinach, 605–6
Miso with Pumpkin, Curried, 607
Miso with Pumpkin and Onion, 606–7
Miso with Shiitake Mushrooms and Egg Strands, 607–8
Miso with Snow Peas and Bean Curd, 606
Mixed Bean Soup, 601–2
Mushroom Stock, Dried, 577–78
Pomegranate, Cold, 580
Potato, Chard, and Bean, Spanish, 587–88
Potato, Mexican, 588–89
Pumpkin, Simple, 589–90
Pumpkin, with Fresh Curry Leaves, 590
Pumpkin, with Tomato, 590
Pumpkin Soup with Fresh Curry Leaves, 590
Red Lentil, Simple, 600
Red Lentil with Mustard Seeds and Curry Leaves, 600–601
Red Pepper, 586–87
Sichuan Vegetable and Bean Curd, 593

Split Pea, Trinidadian, 602–3
stocks for, 576–78, 604
Sweet "Green Pea," 611
Sweet "Green Pea," Creamy, 611
Sweet "Green Pea" with Coconut Milk, 612
Sweet Red Bean, 612
Tomato, Madras Curried, 591
Tomato, with Lemongrass, 590–91
Vegetable Mulligatawny, 592
Vegetable Stock, 576
Wakame Seaweed, Cold, 580–81
Wheat Berry with Ginger and Cilantro, Skinned, 609
Yogurt, Cold, in the South Indian Style, 582
Yogurt, with Chickpeas and Celery, Cold, 581–82
Sour cherry
Chutney, Afghani, 659
Chutney, Walnut and, Kashmiri, 659–60
Syrup, 645–46
Sour Cream, Corn, and Cheese, Mexican-Style Rice Casserole with, 398
Sour Fennel-Flavored Eggplant, 195
South Indian recipes. *See* India, recipes from
Soybean(s)
about, 90
with Brown Sugar, 94
cooking methods for, 91
origins of, 90
Patties with Mint, Spicy, 94–95
Patties with Mint, Stuffed Spicy, 96
soy milk, 92
sprouting, 91–92
See also Bean curd; Tempeh
Soy milk, to make, 92
Soy Sauce Eggs with Rosemary, 514–15
Soy sauces, about, 735–36
Spaghetti with Fresh Tomatoes and Lemon Peel, 480
Spain, recipes from
Almond Soup, Cold, 578–79
Asparagus with Romesco Sauce, 136–37
Garlic and Parsley-Flavored Olive Oil, 665
Portobello Mushrooms, Grilled, 248–49
Potato, Chard, and Bean Soup, 587–88
Potato and Egg Cake, 536
Romesco Sauce, Classic, 669–70
Romesco Sauce, Simple, 670–71
Salad of Broiled and Roasted Vegetables, 310–11
Spinach with Chickpeas, 228–29
Zucchini, Grilled, 296–97
Speckled Green Couscous with Red Potato Sauce, 502–3

Spelt
  about, 417–18
  Berries, Winter Squash
    Stuffed with, 422
  Berries with Walnuts and
    Currants, 421–22
  Berry Salad with Red Pepper
    Paste, 639
  Brown Rice with Sprouted,
    Spicy, 379
Spice mixtures
  Brown Mushroom Sauce, 709
  Curry Powder, My, 707–8
  Curry Powder, Sri Lankan
    Raw, 707
  Five-Spice Powder, 722
  Garam Masala, 723
  Persian Spice Mix, 706–7
  Roasted Sichuan Pepper and
    Salt, 704
  Salt Mixture, An Indian, 705
  Sambar Powder, 708
  Sesame Salt, 704
  Sesame Seed Seasoning,
    705–6
  Trinidadian Mixed Spices,
    706
  Zahtar, 705
  See also Pastes
Spinach
  about, 214
  and Bean Curd, Miso Soup
    with, 605–6
  Broccoli with, 145–46
  with Browned Onions, 229–
    30
  with Chickpeas, Spanish-
    Style, 228–29
  and Chickpea Soup,
    Rosemary-Flavored, 598
  Chickpea Stew with, Cypriot,
    30–31
  and Cloves, Yogurt with, 549–
    50
  with Dill and Onion, Sautéed,
    225
  with Homemade Indian
    Cheese, 570–71
  Lentils Topped with Yogurt
    and Gingery, 62
  with Mung Beans, 77–78
  in Mung Beans with Greens,
    79–80
  Raisins, Pine Nuts, and,
    Risotto with, 409–10
  with Rice, 227
  Ricotta, Pine Nuts and, Fet-
    tucine (or Tagliatelle)
    with, 483–84
  and Shallots, Barley with, 326
  with Sorrel, 226
  with Tomato, 228
Split peas. *See* Pea(s), split
Split urad beans. See Pea(s),
  split
Spread, Tomato-Flavored Bean
  Curd, 616
Spring Deer Restaurant, 122
Sprouted Wheat, Sunflower
    Seeds, Rolled Oats, and,
    Whole Wheat Bread with,
    463–65
Sprouts, bean. *See* Bean sprouts

Squashes, summer. *See* Bitter
  melons; Zucchini
Squashes, winter
  about, 286–87
  Butternut, with Sage, 288
  buying and storing, 287, 288
  freezing prepared, 288
  Hubbard, with Bengali Sea-
    sonings, 289
  peeling and cutting, 287
  seeds, 287
  Stuffed with Spelt Berries,
    422
  See also Pumpkin(s)
Sri Lanka, recipes from
  Coconut Milk Sauce, 661–62
  Coconut Sambol, 662–63
  Curry Powder, Raw, 707
  Eggplant Curry, 189–90
  Eggplant "Pickle," 197–98
  Flatbreads with Coconut,
    446–47
  Green Beans and Potato
    Curry, 208–9
  Greens, 224–25
  Sweet Potatoes with Car-
    damom and Chiles, 285
  Tomato Sambal, 302
  White Egg Curry, 515
Star anise, about, 736
Steamed Plain Glutinous Rice,
  378
Steaming, about, 736
Stew
  Barley, 327
  Chickpea, with Six Vegeta-
    bles, 30–31
  with Chickpea Flour Sauce,
    Vegetable, 36
  of Chickpeas, Potatoes, and
    Carrots, Middle Eastern,
    29
  Corn, Rice, and Vegetable,
    Indonesian, 340–41
  with Eggplant, Potatoes,
    Mushrooms, and Chick-
    peas, Spicy, 196
  Kohlrabi, with Tomatoes,
    Spicy, 240
  Mushroom and Potato, 248
  Mushroom and Potato,
    Polenta with a, 345
  Pinto Bean, with Ancho
    Chiles, Tex-Mex, 89
  Potato, with Turmeric,
    Moroccan, 276
  White Beans and Pumpkin,
    Aromatic Cuban, 54–56
Stewed or "Red-Cooked"
  Daikon, 176
Stir-fried dishes
  Asparagus, with Ginger and
    Red Pepper, 137–38
  Azuki Beans with Green
    Pepper from Yunnan, 9
  Bean Curd, with Hot Pep-
    pers, Pressed, 728
  Beet Greens with Ginger and
    Green Chiles, 215–16
  Broccoli with Ginger and
    Garlic, 146
  Buckwheat, 329
  Carrots and Ginger with

Mustard Seeds, 157
Cauliflower with Ginger and
  Cilantro, 162
Celery Cabbage with a Gin-
  gery Milk Sauce, 153–54
Celery with Snow Peas, 168
Cheese Curds and Vegeta-
  bles, 567
Chinese Chives, 169
Eggplants with Tomato and
  Parmesan Cheese, 185
Eggs, Indian, 528
Fava Bean Sprouts, 46
Fava Beans with Ginger, 200
"Foreign Vegetable," i.e.,
  Watercress, 233
Green Beans with Tien Jing
  Preserved Vegetable, Dry,
  204
Green Cabbage with Spicy
  Red Pepper, 150
Hot Peppers with Ginger and
  Garlic, 263
Kohlrabi, 237–38
Lentil Sprouts with Ginger,
  67
Lentil Sprouts with Mustard
  Seeds and Chiles, 67
Mung Bean Sprouts, with
  Ginger, 85
Mushrooms, Fresh Shiitake,
  249
Mushrooms, Simple, 243
Pressed Bean Curd, with Hot
  Peppers, 106
Snow Pea Shoots, 223–24
Snow Peas with Scallions, 261
Sweet-and-Sour Potato
  Shreds, 271
Straw mushrooms, about, 728
Sugar snap peas
  about, 256–57
  with Cumin and Thyme, 260–
    61
  with Dried Mint, 260
Sumac
  about, 736
  in Turkish Vegetable Salad
    with Red Pepper Dressing,
    641–42
Summer Kale with Leek, 221–22
Sunchokes. *See* Jerusalem
  artichokes
Sunflower Seeds, Sprouted
  Wheat, Rolled Oats, and,
  Whole Wheat Bread with,
  463–65
Sweet-and-sour dishes
  Cabbage, 148
  Lemon Chutney, 690–91
  Mixed Vegetable Pickle,
    Punjabi-Style, 703
  Mung Bean Sprouts, 83
  Potatoes, Gujarati-Style Hot,
    273
  "Ratatouille" of Fruit and
    Vegetables, Persian,
    312–13
  Tempeh with Peanuts, 108
  Toovar Dal, 87
Sweet or glutinous rice
  about, 373
  Steamed Plain, 378

Sweet potato(es)
  baking, 270
  boiling, 270
  buying and storing, 270
  with Cardamom and Chiles,
    Sri Lankan, 285
  preparing, 270
  with Raisins and Cinnamon,
    284
Swiss chard
  about, 214–15
  with Black-Eyed Peas, 20–21
  Frittata with, 540
  Leaves Stuffed with Sweet-
    and-Sour Rice, 394–95
  Potato, and Bean Soup, Span-
    ish, 587–88
  Sesame Seeds, Carrot, and,
    Millet with, 359–60
  with Sesame Seeds, 230
  with Tomatoes and Chick-
    peas, 232
Syria, recipes from
  Black-Eyed Peas with Herbs,
    18
  Bulgur Wheat with Lentils,
    425
  Cheese with Cucumber and
    Sesame Seeds, 573
  Cheese with Olives, 572
  Cheese with Tomatoes, 573
  Homemade Cheese, 566–67
  Rice with Spinach, 383
  Tomato Salad, Simple, 637
  Whole Grain or "Bead"
    Hummus, 28
  Zahtar, 705
Syrup(s)
  Lime, Fresh, 647
  Lime and Ginger, Fresh, 647–
    48
  Persian Rhubarb, 646–47
  Simple Sugar, 739
  Sour Cherry, 645–46
  Vinegar, 653

Tabbouleh
  A Salad Made with Bulgur
    and Arugula, 424
  A Salad of Bulgur and Pars-
    ley, 423
Tagliatelle with Ricotta,
  Spinach, and Pine Nuts,
  483–84
Tahini, about, 736
Takrai, about, 726
Tamari, about, 735
Tamarind paste
  about, 737
  in Cashews in a Green Spice
    Paste, 119
  in Chickpeas and *Chana Dal*
    Cooked Together in a
    Mint Sauce, 34–35
  to make, 737
  in Plain Tamarind Chutney,
    677
  in Potatoes, Gujarati-Style
    Hot Sweet-and-Sour, 273
  in Sweet-and-Sour *Toovar Dal*,
    87
  in Tamarind Chutney with
    Raisins and Walnuts, 677

in Tamarind-Yogurt Chutney, 678
in Toovar Dal with Sliced Shallots and Carrots, 87–88
in Vegetable Stew with Chickpea Flour Sauce, 36
Tanglad, about, 726
Tea
 Kashmiri, 650
 Moroccan Mint, 651
 Spicy Indian, 651–52
Tea Eggs, 516
Tempeh, 90, 93
 Fried Spiced, 107
 with Peanuts, Sweet-and-Sour, 108
Tex-Mex dishes
 Pinto Bean Stew with Ancho Chiles, 89
 Polenta with Chili, 346
 Vegetarian Chili, 64–65
Thailand, recipes from
 Carrot Salad, "Pickled," 619
 Fruit and Vegetable Salad, 624–25
 Kohlrabi Salad, 628–29
Tien Jing preserved vegetables, about, 738
Toasted Polenta Slices, 343
Toen chang, about, 727, 738
Tomatillo(s)
 about, 738
 in Green Posole, 338–39
 in Guacamole, 613–14
 in Quinoa with Corn and Potatoes, 369–70
 Salsa, Green, 679
Tomato(es)
 and Basil, Yogurt with, 551
 Bean Curd with Cilantro and, 98–99
 buying and storing, 300
 Cheese with, Syrian, 573
 Chickpea Flour Pancakes with Onion and, 38–39
 and Chickpeas, Swiss Chard with, 231
 in Chickpeas, Pumpkins, and Raisins with Couscous, 501–2
 Chickpea Soup with Escarole and, 597
 "Choka," 300
 and Cucumber Drink, 652
 and Cucumber Drink, Spicy, 653
 in Doubles, 458–60
 Egg Pie with Herbs and, Persian-Style, 538
 Eggplant, Mint, and, Risotto with Roasted, 409
 and Eggplant, Risotto with, 408–9
 and Eggplant Choka, 186–87
 Eggplants with Parmesan Cheese and, 185
 -Flavored Bean Curd Spread or Salad, 616
 grating, 300
 in Hard-Boiled Eggs in a Tomato-Cream Sauce, 517
 with Homemade Indian Cheese, 568–69

in "Javanese" Noodles, 477–79
Kohlrabi Stew with, Spicy, 240
with Okra, 253–54
in Okra with Potatoes, 251
and Onion Relish, 682
Oven-Dried, 304–5
Oven-Dried Plum, 305
Pancakes with Onion and, South Indian, 472–73
Penne or Fusili with Fresh, 481
preparing, 300, 738
Preserve with Almonds, Sweet, 701
Pumpkin Soup with, 590
Quinoa with Thyme and, 368–69
in Red Kidney Bean Casserole, 50–51
Relish, South Indian, 682
in Romesco Sauce, Classic, 669–70
Salad, Moroccan, 636–37
Salad, Simple Palestinian Cucumber, 638
Salad, Simple Syrian, 637
Sambal, 302
Sambal with Shallots, Chiles, Roasted, 681
Sauce, Cashews in a Mediterranean, 118–19
Sauce, Eggplant with Yogurt and Minty, 192–93
Sauce, Eggs Poached in a, Persian, 521
Sauce, Fresh, Moroccan-Style, 681
Sauce, Mung Bean Dumplings in a Spicy, 82–83
Sauce, Simple, 679–80
Sauce with Mushrooms, 680
Scrambled Eggs with Onion and, Indian, 526–27
and Sesame Seeds, Corn with, 174–75
Sliced, in a Tomato Sauce, 303
Soup, Madras Curried, 591
Soup with Lemongrass, 590–91
in Spicy Punjabi Red Kidney Bean Stew, 47–48
Stuffed with Lentils and Rice, 303–4
Stuffed with Wheat Berries, 420–21
Turnips with Yogurt and, 307
Toovar dal. See Pigeon peas
Tortilla press, 348, 349
Tortillas
 Corn, 348–49
 Corn, Stuffed with Cheese, 350–51
 Corn, Stuffed with Cheese and Refried Beans, 351
 Corn, Stuffed with Potatoes and Green Pepper, 351
 Crisply Fried, 354
 Quesadilla with Cheese, 352
 Quesadilla with Mushrooms, 353

Wheat, 445–46
Traditional Moroccan Couscous, 499–500
Tree ear, about, 722–23
Trinidad, recipes from
 Black-Eyed Peas and Rice with Pumpkin, 403
 Black-Eyed Pea Soup, 594
 Black-Eyed Peas with Trinidadian Seasonings, 21
 Chickpea and Potato Curry, Caribbean Style, 33–34
 Cornmeal and Okra Mold, 336
 Eggplant and Tomato Choka, 186–87
 Fry Bake or Float, 456–58
 Kallaloo, 585–86
 Long Beans, Curried, 210
 Mango Curry, 321
 Mixed Spices, 706
 Pepper Bake, 456
 Pepper Sauce, 671–72
 Pumpkin, 291
 "Roti" or Flatbreads, 448–49
 Roti Stuffed with Split Peas, 449–50
 Split Pea Soup, 602–3
 Split Peas with Thyme and Cumin Puree, Yellow, 111
 Tomato "Choka," 300
Tunisia, recipes from
 Green Pepper and Cucumber Salad, 632
 North African Green and Red Pepper Salad, 633
 Speckled Green Couscous with Red Potato Sauce, 502–3
Turkey, recipes from
 Bread, Ridged, 436–37
 Bulgur Wheat with Red Pepper Paste, 426–27
 Cabbage with Rice and Currants, 149–50
 Circassian Sauce—A Walnut and Bread Sauce, 684
 Eggplant, Creamed, 183
 Eggplants, Stuffed Baby, 184–85
 Green Bean Salad, 202–3
 Onion Salad, 632
 Red Lentil Soup, Simple, 600
 Red Lentil Stew with Wheat Berries and Chickpeas, Anatolian, 71–72
 Spinach with Dill and Onion, Sautéed, 225
 Swiss Chard Leaves Stuffed with Sweet-and-Sour Rice, 394–95
 Vegetable Salad with Red Pepper Dressing, 641–42
 Yogurt Cheese with Olives and Gherkins, Spiced, 559–60
 Yogurt Cheese with Red Pepper Paste, 560
 Zahtar, 705
Turmeric, about, 738
Turnip greens, about, 215
Turnip(s)
 about, 305

Braised with Soy Sauce and Sugar, 306
buying and storing, 306
about green Chinese, 738
preparing, 306
Salad, 639
Salad, Green, 638
with Yogurt and Tomato, 307
Tuscan Zucchini Pie, 541

Udon, about, 729–30
Uganda, recipes from
 Okra with Tomatoes, 253–54
Ukraine, recipes from
 Ukranian Radish Salad, 636
Unbleached flour, 419
Unhulled and uplit mung beans. *See* Mung bean(s)
United States, recipes from
 Bean Curd, Ginger-Garlic, 99
 Black-Eyed Pea Soup, 594
 Broccoli Rabe Served on a Bed of Fava Beans, 218
 Broccoli Rabe with Garlic, 217
 Carrots with Ginger, Quick Glazed, 155
 Corn, Grilled Sweet, 171
 Corn Bread with Sesame Seeds, 356
 "French" Toast, American, 543
 Kohlrabi, Sautéed, 238
 Pinto Bean Stew with Ancho Chiles, Tex-Mex, 89
 Swiss Chard with Sesame Seeds, 230
 Vegetarian Chili, Tex-Mex, 64–65
 Zucchini, Simple "Grilled," 295–96
Uppama. See entries under "risottos: semolina"
Urad dal. See Pea(s), split

Vegeburgers
 Bean Curd, 103
 in Brown Mushroom Sauce, 104
 Curried Bean Curd, 104
Vegetable Mulligatawny Soup, 592
Vegetables, mixed
 about, 125–26
 Casserole of, Moroccan, 309–10
 and Cheese Curds, Delicate Stir-Fry of, 567
 Chickpea Stew with Six, 30–31
 Dressing, Malaysian Mixed Fruit and Vegetable Salad with Sweet Soy and Peanut, 626
 Dumplings, Boiled, 485–88
 Grilled, Indian Style, 314–15
 in Kallaloo, 585–86
 in Mixed Sour Pickles Indian Style, 702
 Noodles Sautéed with, Chinese, 479–80
 Pickle, Punjabi-Style Sweet-and-Sour, 703

Vegetables, mixed (Cont.)
    Puree of, A Delicious, 308–9
    "Ratatouille" of Fruit and,
        Persian Sweet-and-Sour,
        312–13
    Salad, Chinese, 642–43
    Salad of Broiled and Roasted,
        310–11
    Salad with Red Pepper Dress-
        ing, Turkish, 641–42
    Stew, Corn, Rice, and,
        Indonesian, 340–41
    Stew with Chickpea Flour
        Sauce, 36
    See also specific vegetables
Vegetable Stock, 576
Vietnam, recipes from
    Kohlrabi Salad, 628–29
    Pancakes, 413–14
Village-Style Carrots with Pota-
    toes and Peas, 158
Vinegar
    about, 738
    Syrup, 653

Wakame seaweed
    about, 738
    Soup, Cold, 580–81
Walnut(s)
    Chutney, Sour Cherry and,
        Kashmiri, 659–60
    Circassian Sauce—A Walnut
        and Bread Sauce, 684
    and Currants, Spelt Berries
        with, 421–22
    and Eggplant, Yogurt with,
        552
    and Mint, Whole Wheat
        Bread with, 465–66
    and Raisins, Yogurt with,
        555–56
    Sauce, 684
    Sauce, Black-Eyed Peas in a,
        18
    Sauce, Broccoli with, 145
Wasabi, about, 739
Water chestnuts, about, 739
Watercress, 215
    Black-Eyed Peas with, 22
    Stir-Fried "Foreign Veg-
        etable," i.e., 233
Watermelon
    Juice, 655
    seeds, 739
Wheat
    about, 416–20
    nutrient content, 416
    storing, 417

types of flours, 419
about wheat berries, 417
See also specific forms of wheat;
    specific wheat-based products
Wheat berries
    about, 417
    Red Lentil Stew with Chick-
        peas and, Anatolian,
        71–72
    Salad of Whole, 640
    Soup with Ginger and
        Cilantro, Skinned, 609
    Tomatoes Stuffed with,
        420–21
    See also Spelt
Wheat Tortillas, 445–46
White beans
    Baked, 53
    Baked, with Nigerian Season-
        ings, 57–58
    canned, 52
    cooking methods for, 52
    in Green Posole, 338–39
    Lima Bean Stew, Cypriot,
        56–57
    in Mixed Bean Soup, 601–2
    and Peppers, Salad of, 614
    in Potato, Chard, and Bean
        Soup, Spanish, 587–88
    and Pumpkin Stew, Aromatic
        Cuban, 54–56
    with Rosemary, 54
White radish. See Daikon
Whole Grain or "Bead"
    Hummus, 28
Whole wheat
    Breads, Flaky, Punjabi
        Village-Style Flat, 437–38
    Breads, Tandoori, 430–31
    Bread with Sprouted Wheat,
        Sunflower Seeds, and
        Rolled Oats, 463–65
    Bread with Walnuts and
        Mint, 465–66
    couscous, about, 495
    Couscous with Cumin and
        Cauliflower, 498–99
    Couscous with Sesame Seeds
        and Raisins, 498
Wild rice
    about, 506–7
    with Brown Rice, 507–8
    with Corn, Mushrooms, and
        Asparagus, Sautéed, 508
    Plain, 507
    Stew with Pearl Onions,
        Lentils, and Green Beans,
        509

Wine
    and Coriander Seeds, Mush-
        rooms with, 247
    in Mushroom and Potato
        Stew, 248
Woks, about, 709–10
Wonton skins, about, 739
Wormseed, about, 722
Wraps. See Breads and
    flatbreads

Yeast, nutritional, about, 730
Yellow bean sauce, about, 712
Yellow split peas. See Pea(s), split
Yogurt
    about, 544
    and Apple, Rice with, 396–97
    with Banana in the South
        Indian Style, 555
    in Banana Lassi, Sweet,
        655
    in Barley Stew, 327
    Beets with Mint and, 141
    in Carrot Raita, 547
    with Celery and Pistachios,
        551–52
    Chayote, Sauce, with a South
        Indian, 553–54
    Corn Cooked in, 172–73
    Drink, 649
    Drink, Madras-Style Spicy,
        657
    Drink, Milk and, 649
    Drink, Punjabi, 655
    with Eggplant and Walnuts,
        552
    Eggplant with Tomato Sauce
        and, Minty, 192–93
    in Gujarati Cucumber
        "Raita," 550
    with Herbs, 548
    Homemade, Basic Recipe for,
        545
    Made with Thickened Milk,
        545
    with Mango, Green, 553
    with Mango and Coconut,
        320
    with Mango and Plantain,
        318–19
    in Mango Lassi, Sweet, 656
    and Milk Drink, 649
    and Mint, Beets with, 141
    with Onion, Mint, and Chick-
        peas, 549
    in Onion and Mint "Raita,"
        548
    "Pickled," 546–47

with Plantain and Mango,
    318–19
and Pomegranate Seeds, Rice
    with, 397
Soup, Cold, in the South
    Indian Style, 582
Soup, Cold, with Celery and
    Chickpeas, 581–82
and Spinach, Lentils Topped
    with Gingery, 62
with Spinach and Cloves,
    549–50
in Spinach with Dill and
    Onion, 225
–Tamarind Chutney, 678
and Tomatoes, Turnips with,
    307
with Tomatoes and Basil, 551
with Walnuts and Raisins,
    555–56
See also Yogurt cheese
Yogurt cheese
    about, 556
    with Bananas, 557–58
    basic recipe, 556–57
    with Cucumber, 558
    with Feta, 559
    with Olives and Gherkins,
        Spiced, 559–60
    with Red Pepper Paste, 560
    with Zahtar and Olive Oil,
        557
    See also Yogurt
Young Swiss Chard with Sesame
    Seeds, 231

Zahtar, 705
    about, 739
    and Olive Oil, Yogurt Cheese
        with, 557
Zareshk, about, 721
Zucchini
    and Basil, Penne with, 482
    buying and storing, 294
    in Chickpeas, Pumpkins, and
        Raisins with Couscous,
        501–2
    and Feta Cheese Salad, 640
    Fritters, Crisp, 298
    "Grilled," Simple, 295–96
    Grilled, Spanish-Style,
        296–97
    Pie, Tuscan, 541
    in Potato Cake, Mexican,
        278–79
    preparing, 294–95
    Puree of, 297
    with Red Lentils, 70